In a comprehensive and original study of the early history of Islam, Wilferd Madelung describes the conflict that developed after the death of the Prophet Muḥammad, between his family, Hāshim, and his tribe, Quraysh, for the leadership of the Muslim community. He pursues the history of this conflict through the reign of the four 'Rightly Guided' caliphs to its climax in the first Inter-Muslim War. The outcome of the war, which marked the demise of the reign of the Early Companions, led to the establishment of dynastic despotism under the Umayyad caliphate and to the lasting schism between Sunnite and Shi'ite Islam. In contrast to recent scholarly trends, Professor Madelung brings out 'Alī's early claim to legitimate succession, which gained support from the Shi'a, and offers a radical and convincing reinterpretation of early Islamic history after the death of Muḥammad. This important and original study will make a major contribution to the scholarship of the period and rekindle the debate over the succession to Muḥammad.

The succession to Muḥammad

The succession to Muḥammad

A study of the early Caliphate

Wilferd Madelung
University of Oxford

CAMBRIDGE
UNIVERSITY PRESS

PUBLISHED BY THE PRESS SYNDICATE OF THE UNIVERSITY OF CAMBRIDGE
The Pitt Building, Trumpington Street, Cambridge, United Kingdom

CAMBRIDGE UNIVERSITY PRESS
The Edinburgh Building, Cambridge CB2 2RU, UK
40 West 20th Street, New York, NY 10011–4211, USA
477 Williamstown Road, Port Melbourne 3207, Australia
Ruiz de Alarcón 13, 28014 Madrid, Spain
Dock House, The Waterfront, Cape Town 8001, South Africa

http://www.cambridge.org

First published 1997
Reprinted 1997, 2001, 2004

Printed in the United Kingdom at the University Press, Cambridge

A catalogue record for this book is available from the British Library

Library of Congress Cataloguing in Publication data
Madelung, Wilferd.
The succession to Muhammad: a study of the early Caliphate / Wilferd Madelung.
p. cm.
Includes bibliographical references (p. 388) and index.
ISBN 0 521 56181 7
1. Islamic Empire – History – 622–661. I. Title.
DS38.1.M336 1996
909'.097671 – dc20 95-26105 CIP

ISBN 0 521 56181 7 hardback
ISBN 0 521 64696 0 paperback

In memory of my mother
Emma Elisabeth Madelung, née Messerschmitt
(1907–1990)
who opened my eyes to history as it really is

Contents

Preface

This book was at first planned as a monograph on the nature of the caliphate at its foundation and during its earliest phase, before the establishment of Umayyad dynastic rule, with only a minimal discussion of the events and persons determining its evolution. The extreme distrust of most western historians with regard to the Muslim literary sources for the early age of Islam seemed to suggest a restriction of the inquiry to a few salient events whose reality, if not their interpretation, is not seriously disputed. As the research progressed, it became evident that such an approach would not do justice to the subject. The question of the caliphate is too intricately tied to much of the internal history of the early Muslim community to be discussed without a solid understanding of that history based on more than abstract speculation. Work with the narrative sources, both those that have been available to historians for a long time and others which have been published recently, made it plain that their wholesale rejection as late fiction is unjustified and that with a judicious use of them a much more reliable and accurate portrait of the period can be drawn than has so far been realized.

The introduction of large narrative sections into the presentation has, apart from substantially expanding the volume, inevitably changed the character of the book and produced a certain dichotomy which may at times obscure its basic purpose. Especially the detailed description of the *fitna*, the Inter-Muslim War opening with the revolt against the third caliph and outlasting the reign of the fourth, may appear to have marginalized the discussion of the caliphate itself. Narrative history carries its own momentum and dictates its appropriate ways of presentation. Persons, their motivation, action and reaction move to the foreground and confine the interpretation of ideas and documentary texts. The book, especially its latter parts, can now be read as a partial history of the period. The reader should, however, be aware of its selective perspective. The Inter-Muslim War was the climax of the conflict about the caliphate and as such a proper understanding of its nature was vital.

Selective narration from the large pool of narrative source material imposed compromises for the sake of readablity. I have tried to strike a proper balance between abridgement and faithful rendering of reports and texts. Colourful detail which the early reporters thought worth recording, and their personal comments, may convey to the late observer living in a very different environment a sense of the times which the abstract factual data largely fail to convey. In general those reports that seemed most reliable were chosen for presentation. Significant divergent reports are often briefly summarized in the notes without full argumentation for my preference. In narrative reporting there is obviously a wide range of shades of reliability between outright fraudulent fiction and accurate factual testimony. It would have served no good purpose to weigh and assess every statement and expression of the narrators as might be appropriate in more narrowly focused studies.

The book stands in a scholarly tradition on which it builds and to which it reacts. Much of the basic western research on the history of the early succession to Muḥammad was carried out and published by a few scholars in the early decades of this century. Later research has generally accepted the substance of their conclusions while modifying some detail. The revision proposed here is more radical. The discussion naturally puts the differences into sharp relief and brings out aspects passed over or distorted in the earlier studies more prominently than if the book had been written in a vacuum of scholarship. Severe criticism, however, should not obscure its indebtedness to the tradition.

My special thanks are due to my wife who patiently read and reread through an unfamiliar subject and made valuable suggestions to improve the presentation.

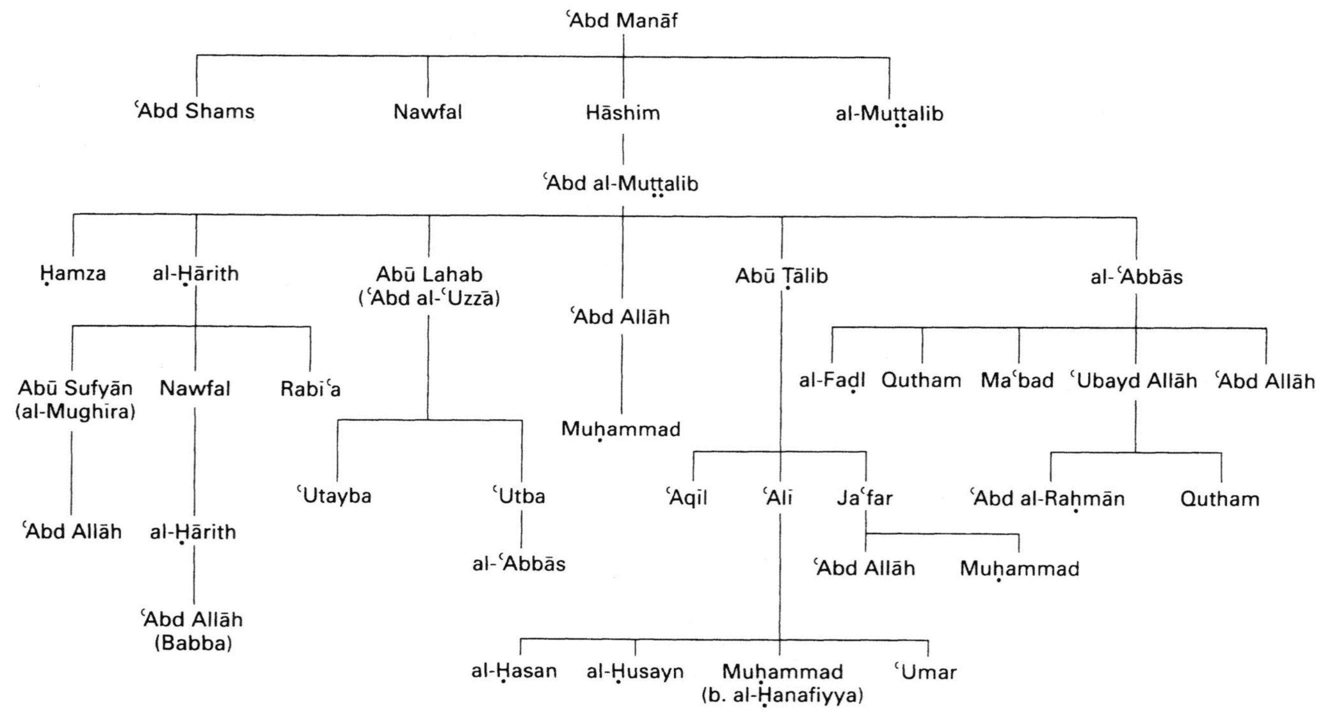

1 Banū Hāshim

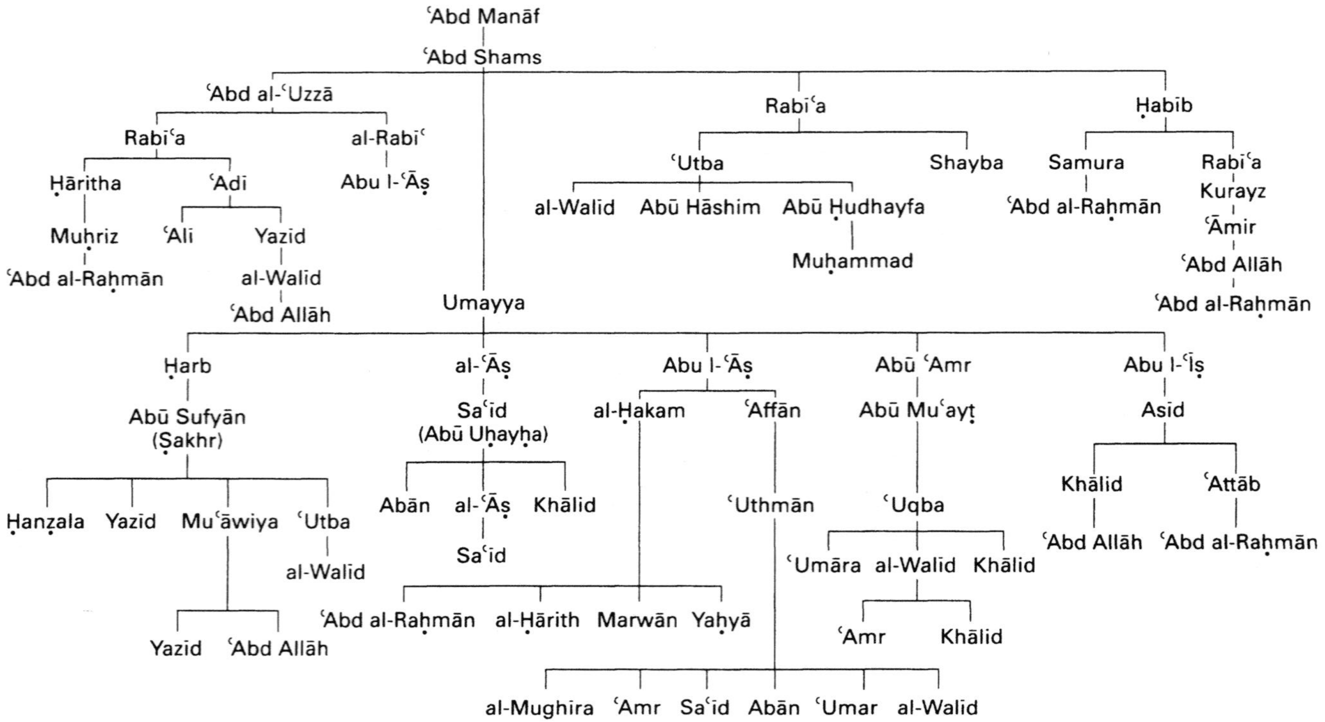

2 Banū ʿAbd Shams

Chronological survey

615	Muslim emigration to Abyssinia
616–19	Boycott of Hāshim by Quraysh
622	*Hijra*: emigration of Muḥammad from Mekka to Medina
2/624	Badr: Muslim victory over Mekkans
3/625	Uḥud: Muslim defeat by Mekkans
6/628	Al-Ḥudaybiyya: truce between Muḥammad and Mekkans. Pledge (of loyalty) under the Tree
7	Muslim conquest of Khaybar
8/629	Expedition to Mu'ta
630	Muslim conquest of Mekka
	Ḥunayn: Muslim victory over Hawāzin. Siege of al-Ṭā'if
11/632	13 Rabī I/8 June Death of Muḥammad
	Election of Abū Bakr as successor at Saqīfat Banī Sā'ida
12/633	Battle of al-Yamāma at al-'Aqrabā'
13/634	Beginning of Muslim invasion of Iraq and Palestine
	22 Jumādā II/23 August Death of Abū Bakr
	Succession of 'Umar
15/636	Battle on the Yarmūk: decisive Muslim victory in Syria
16	Battle of al-Qādisiyya: decisive Muslim victory in Iraq
17/638	Council of al-Jābiya: 'Umar establishes pension register (*dīwān*) and immobilizes conquered land as *fay'*
18/639	Plague of 'Amwās
	Invasion of Egypt
21/642	Battle of Nihāwand: decisive Muslim victory in Iran
23/644	26 Dhu l-Ḥijja/3 November Murder of 'Umar
	Shūrā election of 'Uthmān
25/645–6	Northern Syria and Upper Mesopotamia included in governorship of Mu'āwiya
	'Abd Allāh b. Sa'd b. Abī Sarḥ governor of Egypt
	Al-Walīd b. 'Uqba governor of Kūfa

27/647	Victorious campaign of Ibn Abī Sarḥ to Ifrīqiya
29/649–50	ʿAbd Allāh b. ʿĀmir governor of Baṣra
30/650–1	Saʿīd b. al-ʿĀṣ governor of Kūfa
32/652–3	Death of ʿAbd al-Raḥmān b. ʿAwf
34/654	Revolt in Kūfa. Abū Mūsā al-Ashʿarī appointed governor
35/656	1 Dhu l-Qaʿda/1 May Egyptian rebels at Dhū Khushub. 'First siege'
	1 Dhu l-Ḥijja/31 May Egyptian rebels in Medina. 'Second siege'
	18 Dhu l-Ḥijja/17 June Murder of ʿUthmān
	19 Dhu l-Ḥijja/18 June Pledge of allegiance to ʿAlī
36	Ṣafar/August Qays b. Saʿd governor of Egypt
	29 Rabīʿ II/25 October Departure of ʿAlī from Medina
	15 Jumādā I/8 December Battle of the Camel
657	1 Ramaḍān/21 February Appointment of Muḥammad b. Abī Bakr as governor of Egypt
	Dhu l-Ḥijja/May Departure of ʿAlī from Kūfa for Ṣiffīn
37	8–11 Ṣafar/26–29 July Main battle of Ṣiffīn
	15 Ṣafar/2 August Signing of arbitration agreement
658	10 Shawwāl/21 March Kharijites leave Kūfa for al-Nahrawān
	Shawwāl-Dhu l-Qaʿda/March–April Meeting of arbitrators at Dūmat al-Jandal. Recognition of Muʿāwiya as caliph in Syria
	Dhu l-Ḥijja/May Battle of al-Nahrawān
38	Ṣafar/August Conquest of Egypt by ʿAmr b. al-ʿĀṣ. Murder of Muḥammad b. Abī Bakr
659	Shaʿbān/January Meeting of arbitrators at Adhruḥ
39/660	Dhu l-Ḥijja/April–May Campaign of Yazīd b. Shajara to Mekka
40/661	19 Ramaḍān/28 January Death of ʿAlī Succession of al-Ḥasan
41	Rabīʿ II/August Surrender of al-Ḥasan
49–50/669–70	Death of al-Ḥasan
56/676	Nomination of Yazīd as crown prince
60/680	Death of Muʿāwiya. Succession of Yazīd
61	Death of al-Ḥusayn at Karbalāʾ
61–73/680–92	Revolt and counter-caliphate of ʿAbd Allāh b. al-Zubayr

63/683	Battle of al-Ḥarra. Medina subdued by Syrians
64	Death of Yazīd. Succession and death of Muʿāwiya II
684	Succession of Marwān
	Battle of Marj Rāhiṭ
65/685	Death of Marwān. Succession of ʿAbd al-Malik

Abbreviations

Aghānī	Abu l-Faraj al-Iṣfahānī, *Kitāb al-Aghānī*
Annali	L. Caetani, *Annali dell' Islam*
EI	*Encyclopaedia of Islam*
JSAI	*Jerusalem Studies in Arabic and Islam*
JSS	*Journal of Semitic Studies*
Ṭabarī	al-Ṭabarī, *Ta'rīkh al-rusul wa l-mulūk*

Introduction

No event in history has divided Islam more profoundly and durably than the succession to Muḥammad. The right to occupy the Prophet's place at the head of the Muslim community after his death became a question of great religious weight which has separated Sunnites and Shiʿites until the present. The issue of right and wrong in the matter has long since been settled in their minds. For Sunnites, the first caliph, Abū Bakr, was the only rightful successor since he was the most excellent of men after the Prophet. Although Muḥammad had not explicitly appointed him as his successor, his preference for him was indicated by his order for Abū Bakr to lead the Muslims in the prayers during his final illness. The consensus reached by the Muslims in favour of Abū Bakr merely confirmed what was ultimately God's choice. For Shiʿites it was Muḥammad's cousin and son-in-law ʿAlī who, on account of his early merits in Islam as well as his close kinship, had been appointed by the Prophet as his successor. His rightful position was then usurped by Abū Bakr with the backing of the majority of Muḥammad's Companions.

In spite of the fundamental importance of this conflict for the history of Islam, modern historians have devoted relatively little effort to the study of the background and circumstances surrounding the succession. This general lack of interest is evidently grounded in the view that the conflict between Sunna and Shīʿa, although revolving around the question of the succession, in reality arose only in a later age. Such a view is well supported by early Sunnite tendentious historiography, represented most blatantly by Sayf b. ʿUmar (d. 180/796). According to his account, ʿAlī, on being informed of Abū Bakr's election, was in such a hurry to offer his pledge of allegiance that he arrived dressed merely in his shirt and had to send for his clothes.[1] Perfect concord then prevailed among the Muslims until ʿAbd Allāh b. Sabaʾ, a converted Jew from Ṣanʿāʾ, began to agitate against the third caliph, ʿUthmān, and, after the murder

[1] Al-Ṭabarī, *Taʾrīkh al-rusul wa l-mulūk*, ed. M. J. de Goeje *et al.* (Leiden, 1879–1901; henceforth Ṭabarī), I, 1825.

of the latter, spread extremist views about ʿAlī having been the *waṣī*, the legatee or the executor of the will, of Muḥammad.[2] Ibn Saba' thus became the founder of the Shīʿa who retrospectively turned ʿAlī into the legitimate successor of Muḥammad.

While few if any modern historians would accept Sayf's legend of Ibn Saba', the underlying view that the succession of Abū Bakr to Muḥammad was in itself – aside from the abortive attempt of the Medinan Anṣār to seize the caliphate – unproblematic and that the conflict about it was artificially created by the Shīʿa after the death of ʿAlī and against his own lifelong attitude is widely taken for granted. It is fully reflected in the most recent discussions of the origins of the ʿAlid and the ʿAbbasid, or Hashimite, Shīʿa by M. Sharon. According to Sharon, the very concept of the 'Family of the Prophet', later expressed in the terms of *ahl al-bayt*, Āl Muḥammad, *āl al-nabī* and Banū Hāshim, did not exist in the time of Muḥammad and under the early caliphs. Although the term *bayt* had sometimes been used in pre-Islamic Arabia for the noble families of famous chiefs and prominent men, this was not the case with respect to Muḥammad. In Islam the term *ahl al-bayt* first came to be applied to the families of the caliphs. The Shiʿite supporters of ʿAlī, according to Sharon, then developed the idea of the *ahl al-bayt* of the Prophet and of Āl Muḥammad in order to establish hereditary rights of their man and his descendants to the caliphate. In the later Umayyad age the ʿAbbasids appropriated the idea and still later, from the caliphate of al-Mahdī, propagated the concept of the Banū Hāshim as the Family of the Prophet to bolster their own claim to legitimate succession.[3] Yet ʿAlī himself had still accepted the caliphate on the terms laid down by Abū Bakr and ʿUmar without pretence to any special title based on his personal blood relationship with Muḥammad.[4]

If concord prevailed among the Muslims until the caliphate of ʿUthmān and the controversy between Sunna and Shīʿa arose only after the caliphate of ʿAlī, there is obviously not much incentive to study in depth the circumstances of the succession and the establishment of the caliphate. Abū Bakr's and ʿUmar's success during their reigns was decisive and spectacular, and recent historical research has tended to concentrate mostly on their activity in suppressing the dangerous movement of the Apostasy (*ridda*) of the Arab tribes and initiating the great Muslim conquests outside Arabia.

[2] *Ibid.*, 2941–2.

[3] M. Sharon, *Black Banners from the East* (Jerusalem, 1983), 75–85; M. Sharon, 'Ahl al-Bayt – People of the House', *Jerusalem Studies in Arabic and Islam*, 8 (1986), 169–84; M. Sharon, 'The Umayyads as Ahl al-Bayt', *JSAI*, 14 (1992), 115–52, esp. 134–49.

[4] M. Sharon, 'Notes on the Question of Legitimacy of Government in Islam', *Israel Oriental Studies*, 10 (1980), 116–23, at 121.

The few earlier studies dealing specifically with the succession as such, however, suggest that it was certainly not as unproblematic as implied in the prevalent view of the origins of the schism between Sunna and Shī'a. In 1910 H. Lammens published his article on the 'Triumvirate of Abū Bakr, 'Umar, and Abū 'Ubayda' in which he argued that it was the common purpose and close co-operation of these three men, initiated in the lifetime of Muḥammad, that enabled them to found the successive caliphates of Abū Bakr and 'Umar. The latter would have appointed Abū 'Ubayda as his successor if Abū 'Ubayda had not died during his caliphate.[5] Although Lammens did not speak of a conspiracy to seize the succession, his presentation of the activity of the triumvirate suggests this term. In particular through Abū Bakr's and 'Umar's daughters 'Ā'isha and Ḥafṣa, who kept their fathers informed about every move and secret thought of their husband Muḥammad, these two men came to exert great influence on the Prophet's actions and thus prepared the stage for their seizure of power. This conspirational aspect of Lammens' theory has probably provoked the common warnings of more recent western scholars that his study is unreliable.[6] Lammens noted that the purpose of the triumvirate was to exclude the Hashimites, in particular 'Alī, as the kin of Muḥammad from the succession, although 'Alī, in Lammens' view, was hardly a serious rival for them. Dull-witted, incapable, and married to the pitiful figure of the Prophet's daughter Fāṭima, who was easily outmanoeuvred by the clever and headstrong daughter of Abū Bakr in their competition for Muḥammad's favour, 'Alī could not have been an attractive choice for Muḥammad as his successor. Having experienced mostly disappointment in respect of his blood relations, the Prophet naturally turned away from them. His *ahl al-bayt*, Lammens affirmed with reference to Qur'ān XXXIII 33, consisted exclusively of his wives.[7]

The only comprehensive and thorough investigation of the establishment, nature and development of the caliphate until 'Alī's reign has been offered by L. Caetani in his monumental *Annali dell' Islam*. In his initial discussion, Caetani noted the gravity of the conflict between Abū Bakr and the Banū Hāshim following his surprise claim to the succession during the assembly of the Anṣār in the Hall (*saqīfa*) of the Banū Sā'ida

[5] H. Lammens, 'Le triumvirat Abou Bakr, 'Omar et Abou 'Obaida', *Mélanges de la Faculté Orientale de l'Université St Joseph de Beyrouth*, 4 (1910), 113–44.

[6] See, for instance, J. Sauvaget and C. Cahen, *Introduction to the History of the Muslim East: A Bibliographical Guide* (Berkeley, CA and London, 1965), 126.

[7] H. Lammens, *Fāṭima et les Filles de Mahomet* (Rome, 1912), 99. Lammens' portrayal of Fāṭima was taken up by L. Caetani, who suggested that Muḥammad married off Fāṭima to 'Alī because she, of suspect legitimacy and lacking any physical and moral attractions, was not desired by anyone, and the union was for him a means to liberate himself from the annoyance of a daughter for whom he did not feel any sympathy (*Annali dell'Islam* (Milan, 1905–25; henceforth *Annali*), X, 470).

just hours after the death of Muḥammad. The Banū Hāshim refused to recognize Abū Bakr and buried their illustrious kinsman privately, depriving the new caliph and 'Ā'isha of the honour of attendance. Caetani indirectly acknowledged the potential seriousness of 'Alī's claim to the succession by rejecting the common accounts that Abū Bakr based his claim before the assembly of Anṣār on the prior rights of Quraysh as Muḥammad's tribe, since this argument would have strengthened the case of 'Alī as the closest relative of the Prophet.[8] Rather, Caetani suggested, Abū Bakr argued the need to elect a successor to Muḥammad who would most closely follow in his footsteps, propagate his teachings and maintain the unity of the Muslim Community. He was chosen solely for his superior qualities as a statesman and his personal merits.[9] In view of these merits, Caetani judged the opposition of the Hashimites and other Companions to Abū Bakr to be motivated merely by personal ambition and rancour.[10] If Muḥammad had been able to choose his successor, he would presumably have preferred Abū Bakr to anyone else.[11]

In a later volume of the *Annali*, however, Caetani opted for Lammens' theory of the triumvirate of Abū Bakr, 'Umar and Abū 'Ubayda[12] as the most likely explanation for the origins of the caliphate. The inspirer of their joint action had been 'Umar, 'the greatest statesman after the Prophet and in some respects even greater than the master himself'.[13] 'Umar had the practical and political intelligence to foresee the demise of Muḥammad and to prepare the agreements for resolving the problem of the succession with energy and in the best way possible, thus saving the Muslim Community from disaster.[14] The true founder of the caliphate thus was 'Umar who merely put forward Abū Bakr as the first caliph in recognition of his righteousness and his high standing with the Prophet.

As a result of the reaction of later scholars against the conspiracy theory, Caetani's earlier view that Muḥammad, had he made a choice, would most likely have preferred Abū Bakr as his successor and that, in any case, Abū Bakr was the natural choice for the Muslims on account of his merits in Islam has become the prevalent opinion among non-Muslim

[8] *Annali*, II/1, 516. It is to be noted here that in Caetani's view Muḥammad was not in fact a Hashimite or even a Qurayshite, but rather an orphan of unknown origin who had been taken into the family of Abū Ṭālib b. 'Abd al-Muṭṭalib. The fake genealogy making him a descendant of Hāshim and Quṣayy (Hāshim's grandfather) was invented by 'Abd Allāh b. al-'Abbās and Hishām b. al-Kalbī. (See in particular *Annali*, I, 58–75). On this basis Caetani referred to 'Alī as 'the (alleged) nephew of Muḥammad' (*Annali*, VII, 15) and to al-'Abbās as 'the alleged uncle of the Prophet' (*Annali*, II/1, 407).

[9] *Annali*, II/1, 523, 528. [10] *Ibid.*, 542. [11] *Ibid.*, 523.

[12] The third volume of Caetani's work in which he discussed the theory of Lammens was published in 1910, the same year as Lammens' monograph. Caetani was, however, informed by personal letters from Lammens about the latter's views.

[13] *Ibid.*, III, 123. [14] *Ibid.*; *ibid.*, V, 477–81.

historians of Islam. It is expressed, for instance, by W. M. Watt in his standard biography of Muḥammad in the words: 'Certainly before Muḥammad left Mecca for Medina Abū Bakr had established himself as his chief lieutenant and adviser; and this position he maintained to Muḥammad's death, so that he was the obvious choice for successor.'[15] Yet the critical observer may well question here whether the choice was really so obvious. It is true that in modern life the choice of a chief lieutenant and adviser to succeed, for instance, the head of a corporation or the leader of a political party must seem reasonable enough. But the succession to a ruler or king in traditional society was normally based on dynastic kinship and inheritance, and the succession of a lieutenant and adviser, however close to the ruler, would have been considered highly irregular. It has, of course, often been argued that the succession to tribal leadership among the Arabs was not based on heredity, and Lammens went so far as to assert that hereditary power and the dynastic principle were among the concepts most repugnant to the Arab mind.[16] This assertion has, however, rightly been challenged by E. Tyan, who pointed out that hereditary succession was not unknown among the Arab tribes, as was consistent with the importance of noble lineage, *nasab*, among them and that among the Quraysh in particular hereditary succession was the rule.[17] It may be countered that the succession to Muḥammad cannot be compared to that of a ruler or king and that the classical Sunnite theory of the caliphate indeed sharply distinguishes between it and kingship, *mulk*, which it condemns in part for its principle of hereditary succession. But the classical theory is obviously posterior to the succession and its opposition to *mulk* and the principle of heredity presumably reflects in part its essential purpose of justifying the early historical caliphate.

There is thus *prima facie* good reason to suspect that the common view of western scholars of Islam about the succession to Muḥammad may not be entirely sound and to propose a fresh look at the sources for a proper reassessment. The starting point for establishing what Muḥammad may have thought in general about his succession and what his contemporary

[15] W. M. Watt, *Muhammad: Prophet and Statesman* (Oxford, 1961), 35–6.

[16] H. Lammens, *Le Berceau de l'Islam: l'Arabie occidentale à la veille de l'Hégire* (Rome, 1914), 314.

[17] E. Tyan, *Institutions du droit public Musulman* (Paris, 1954–6), I, 97–9, 114–16. In his *Islamic Political Thought* (Edinburgh, 1968), W. M. Watt likewise affirms that it was Arab practice to select the chief of a tribe from a certain family. He suggests that, had Muḥammad's adoptive son Zayd b. Ḥāritha been alive at the time of the Prophet's death, he might have succeeded without difficulty (although Qur'ān XXXIII 40 had expressly denied that Muḥammad was a father in relation to Zayd). 'Alī, though extolled by the Shi'ites, must have been unacceptable to many Muslims (p. 31). Watt praises the restoration of dynastic rule by the Umayyads as an achievement in accordance with Arab tribal practice (p. 39).

followers could have seen as basic guidelines after his death must certainly be a study of the Qur'ān. The Qur'ān, as is well known, does not make any provisions for, or even allude to, the succession of Muḥammad, and for this reason non-Muslim historians have virtually ignored it in this regard. It contains, however, specific instructions about the maintenance of kinship ties and inheritance as well as stories and statements about the succession of the past prophets and their families, matters which could not be irrelevant to the succession to Muḥammad.

The obligations of kinship and the families of the prophets in the Qur'ān

The Qur'ān places great emphasis on the duty of all Muslims to maintain the bonds of blood relationship. In numerous passages the faithful are enjoined to act kindly (*iḥsān*) towards their close kin, to assist them, and to provide for their sustenance: 'Surely, God commands justice, doing of good, and providing for the close kin (*ītā' dhi l-qurbā*), and forbids the abominable, the reprehensible, and transgression' (XVI 90). Most often the relatives are mentioned in this context together with the orphans, the poor and the wayfarer (*ibn al-sabīl*) as those entitled to the generosity of the faithful. The fact, however, that they are regularly enumerated in the first place seems to indicate their primary right before any other beneficiaries: 'And give to the close kin his due, to the indigent, and the wayfarer. That is best for those who seek the Countenance of God and they will be the prosperous' (XVII 26). Righteousness (*birr*) consists, among other things, in giving money for the love of God to the kin (*dhawi l-qurbā*), the orphans, the poor, the wayfarer, those begging, and for the manumission of slaves (II 177). When the faithful ask Muḥammad what they should spend (in charity), he is charged to tell them: 'Whatever good you spend, it is for the parents (*wālidayn*) and for the close relatives (*aqrabīn*), the orphans, the poor, and the wayfarer. Whatever good you do, God has knowledge of it' (II 215).

In a wider sense, it is obligatory to treat relatives kindly: 'And remember, We took the covenant of the Banū Isrā'īl: Do not worship anyone but God, treat with kindness (*iḥsān*) parents, kin, orphans, and the poor, speak gently to the people, perform the prayer, and give alms' (II 83). The Muslims are likewise ordered: 'Worship God and do not join partners with Him, treat with kindness parents, kin, orphans, the needy, the client who is a relative (*jār dhi l-qurbā*), the client who is a stranger, the companion by your side, the wayfarer, and your slaves' (IV 36). Relatives, orphans and the poor are also entitled to be provided for and to be received with kindness when they present themselves at the time of the division of the inheritance of a deceased person (IV 7–8). It is evidently relatives without a right to a share of the inheritance who are meant here.

Kindness to relatives and material support of them are thus recognized as a cardinal religious obligation in the Qur'ān. This obligation, however, is not unconditional. It applies only to kin who have become Muslims. In the Sūra of Repentance the faithful are warned: 'O you who believe, do not take your fathers and your brothers as friends (*awliyā'*) if they prefer infidelity to the faith. Those of you who take them as friends, they are the wrongdoers. If your fathers, your sons, your spouses, your clan (*'ashīra*), [if] riches you have acquired, or a trade whose decline you fear, and dwellings which please you, are dearer to you than God, His Messenger, and striving in His path, then wait until God will bring about His order. God does not guide the people who offend' (IX 23–4). It is not even permitted to pray for forgiveness for relatives who have failed to join Islam: 'It is not proper for the Prophet and for those who believe to pray for forgiveness for those who set up partners with God, even though they be of close kin, after it has become clear to them that they are inmates of the hell-fire. And Abraham prayed for his father's forgiveness only because of a promise he had made to him. But when it became clear to him that he was an enemy of God, he dissociated himself from him' (IX 113–14). Furthermore, the faithful must not deviate from honesty and fairness even if it were for the benefit of parents or close kin: 'O you who believe, stand firmly for justice, as witnesses to God, even though it be against yourselves, your parents, or close kin, whether rich or poor, for God is closest to them both. Do not follow passion in place of justice' (IV 135). Quite in general the faithful are admonished: 'And whenever you speak, be just, even though it concern a close relative' (VI 152).

Within these limitations, however, the right of the kindred to kindness, care and material support is absolute and clearly takes precedence over any voluntary ties of friendship and alliance: 'Blood relations (*ulu l-arḥām*) have closer ties (*awlā*) to each other in the Book of God than believers and Emigrants (*muhājirūn*). You may, however, do kindness to your [unrelated] friends (*awliyā'ikum*). That is recorded in the Book' (XXXIII 6). It is known that after their emigration to Medina many Muslims, in the 'brothering' (*mu'ākhāt*) arranged by Muḥammad, established formal alliances with Medinan and other foreign Muslims in order to compensate for the absence of their blood relations who still remained polytheists. The Qur'ān states in that regard: 'Surely, those who believed and have emigrated and have fought with their property and their persons in the path of God, and those who sheltered and aided [them], they are the allies (*awliyā'*) of each other. As for those who believed but did not emigrate, you have no ties of alliance whatsoever with them until they emigrate; but if they ask for your aid in religion, it is your duty to aid them, except against a people with whom you have a compact. And God sees whatever you do. The infidels are allies of each other. Unless you do this [aid other Muslims], there would be temptation [to apostatize] on earth and much corruption. Those who believed and have emigrated and fought in the path of God and those who sheltered and aided [them], they are the faithful truly. For them, there will be forgiveness and generous sustenance' (VIII 72–4). These verses established a close solidarity among the Muslims, Mekkan Emigrants and Medinan Helpers (*anṣār*) assembled in the Community at Medina. Yet verse 75, which follows the passage and was evidently added later, modified the meaning in favour of the blood relations even if they joined the Medinan Community at a later date: 'Those who believed afterwards and emigrated and fought together with you, they are of you. And blood relations have closer ties with each other in the Book of God.' The latter sentence, according to the commentators of the Qur'ān, specifically restored the right of inheritance of the relatives in disregard of the alliances earlier concluded with strangers.[18]

The obligation to provide for the needy kin must not be suspended because of personal grudges: 'Let not those among you who are [materially] favoured and have ample means commit themselves by oath not to help their kin (*uli l-qurbā*) and the needy and the Emigrants in the path of God. Let them forgive and overlook. Do you not desire that God shall forgive you? And God is forgiving, merciful' (XXIV 22). According to the commentators, this verse referred to Abū Bakr and his nephew Misṭaḥ. The latter had been among those who cast doubt on the fidelity of 'Ā'isha during the affair of her absence from the camp of the Muslims. Abū Bakr, deeply offended by the conduct of his nephew, vowed that he would no longer provide for him as he had done in the past, even after Misṭaḥ formally repented of his mistake. The Qur'ān, however, commanded him not to neglect his duty towards his needy nephew and to pardon him.[19]

In the story of the past prophets, as it is related in the Qur'ān, their families play a prominent role. The families generally provide vital

[18] Al-Ṭabarī, *Jāmi' al-bayān fī tafsī*r al-Qur'*ān*, ed. Maḥmūd Muḥammad Shākir and Aḥmad Muḥammad Shākir (Cairo, 1373–88/1955–69), XIV, 89.

[19] Al-Ṭabarī, *Jāmi' al-bayān fī tafsīr al-Qur'ān* (Cairo, 1321/1903), XVIII, 72–3. Misṭaḥ is 'Awf b. Uthātha b. 'Abbād b. al-Muṭṭalib (Ibn Ḥajar al-'Asqalānī, *al-Iṣāba fi tamyīz al-Ṣaḥāba* (Cairo, 1323–5/[1905–7]), VI, 88; al-Zubayrī, *Kitāb Nasab Quraysh*, ed. E. Lévi-Provençal (Cairo, 1953), 95). As a Muttalibid he was also entitled to support from the Prophet's fifth of booty and *fay*'. He is mentioned among the recipients of the produce from Muḥammad's share of Khaybar (see W. Madelung, 'The Hāshimiyyāt of al-Kumayt and Hāshimī Shi'ism', *Studia Islamica*, 70 (1989), 5–26, at 12 and n. 36).

assistance to the prophets against the adversaries among their people. After the death of the prophets, their descendants become their spiritual and material heirs. The prophets ask God to grant them the help of members of their family and they pray for divine favour for their kin and their offspring. The prophets of the Banū Isrā'īl were in fact all descendants of a single family from Adam and Noah down to Jesus: 'Truly, God chose Adam, Noah, the family of Abraham, and the family of 'Imrān above all the worlds, as off-spring one of the other' (III 33–4). After narrating the story of Moses, Ishmael and Idrīs, the Qur'ān adds: 'Those were the prophets on whom God bestowed his blessings of the off-spring of Adam and of those whom We carried [in the ark] with Noah, and of the off-spring of Abraham and Israel, of those whom We guided and chose' (XIX 58).

The chain of the prophets and their families is described with more detail in the following verses: 'And We gave him [Abraham] Isaac and Jacob, all of whom We guided. And before him We guided Noah, and of his off-spring, David, Solomon, Job, Joseph, Moses, and Aaron. Thus We recompense those who do good. And Zachariah, and John, and Jesus, and Elias, all of them among the righteous, and Ishmael, and Elisha, Jonah, and Lot: Each of them We preferred above the worlds, and [some] of their fathers, their descendants, and their brothers: We chose them and We guided them to the straight path. That is the guidance of God with which He guides whomever He wishes of His worshippers. But if they had set up partners [with Him], whatever they have been doing would have been in vain for them. They are the ones to whom We have given the Book, the rule (*ḥukm*) and prophethood' (VI 84–9).

Noah was saved together with his family while the rest, or the great majority, of his people were drowned in the Flood because of their sins: 'And [remember] Noah when he implored [Us] in former time, and We responded to him and rescued him and his family from the great disaster. We aided him against the people who treated Our signs as lies. They were an evil people, so We drowned them all together' (XXI 76–7). 'We rescued him and his family from the great disaster and made his descendants the survivors' (XXXVII 76–7). God commanded Noah: 'Place in it [the ark] pairs of every [species] and your family (*ahl*) except for those of them against whom the sentence has already gone forth. Do not address Me concerning those who were unjust. They shall be drowned' (XXIII 27; see also XI 40). The wife and one of the sons of Noah were in fact excluded from the rescue, even though Noah pleaded for his son: 'And Noah called to his Lord and said: O my Lord, surely my son is of my family, and Your promise is the truth, and You are the justest of judges. [God] said: O Noah, he is not of your family. Surely, it is not righteous action. Do not ask of Me that of which you have no knowledge' (XI 45–6).

Likewise, the family of the prophet Lot was saved together with him while the remainder of the people of his town were annihilated: 'The people of Lot treated the warnings as lies. We sent against them a shower of stones, except for the family of Lot. We rescued them at dawn, as a favour from Us. Thus We recompense those who give thanks' (LIV 33–5). The family of Lot had acquired a state of purity which distinguished them from the ordinary people. When Lot reproached his people for having surrendered to turpitude, 'the only answer of his people was to say: Expel the family of Lot from your town. They are indeed people who purify themselves (*yataṭahharūn*). But We saved him and his family, except his wife. We desired that she be of those who stayed behind' (XXVII 56–7). Lot's wife, like Noah's, was punished because of her betrayal of her husband. 'God has set as an example for the unbelievers the wife of Noah and the wife of Lot. They were married to two of Our righteous servants but betrayed them. Thus they were of no avail at all for them before God, and they were told: Enter the fire together with those who will enter it' (LXVI 10).

Abraham was the patriarch of the prophets of the Banū Isrā'īl. All later prophets and transmitters of the scripture among them were of his descendants: 'And We sent Noah and Abraham and placed among their off-spring prophethood and the Book' (LVII 26). The father of Abraham, however, was an obstinate idolater and a persecutor of the confessors of the unity of God. As mentioned above, Abraham at first prayed for him, on account of a promise made to him, but later dissociated himself from him. When God chose Abraham as imam for his people, Abraham prayed to his Lord that He grant this honour also to his descendants: 'And remember when Abraham was tried by his Lord with certain commandments which he fulfilled, [God] said: I shall make you an imam for the people. He said: And also of my off-spring? [God] said: My compact will not comprise the evil-doers' (II 124). God's compact thus covered the just among the descendants of Abraham. God gave him his son Isaac and his grandson Jacob who became prophets: 'When [Abraham] had turned away from them [the idolaters of his people] and from what they worshipped besides God, We granted him Isaac and Jacob, and each one We made a prophet. We bestowed of Our mercy on them, and We accorded them a high truthful repute' (XIX 49–50). 'And We gave him Isaac and Jacob and placed among his progeny prophethood and the Book. We gave him his reward in this world and surely he will be of the righteous in the hereafter' (XXIX 27).

When the angels announced to Abraham the imminence of the birth of his son Isaac and, after him, of his grandson Jacob, his wife Sarah doubted the good news in view of their advanced age, but the angels reminded her of her elevated rank as the spouse of Abraham: 'And his [Abraham's] wife was standing, and she laughed. Then We gave her good tidings of Isaac and, after Isaac, Jacob. She said: Alas for me, shall I bear child, as I am an old woman and this my husband is an old man? This is indeed a wonderful thing. They said: Do you wonder at God's order? The mercy and the blessings of God are upon you [m. pl.], o people of the house (*ahl al-bayt*). He is indeed worthy of praise and full of glory' (XI 71–3). The 'people of the house' are here certainly the family of the prophet Abraham to whom Sarah belonged through marriage, not the adherents of the cult of the House, i.e. the Kaʿba, as has been suggested by R. Paret.[20] The miraculous birth of Isaac is justified by God's supreme favour for the family of his chosen prophet. Those distinguished by such favour of God must not be envied their elevated rank: 'Or do they envy the people for what God has given them of His favour? We had already given the family of Abraham the Book and wisdom (*ḥikma*), and bestowed upon them a mighty kingship (*mulk*)' (IV 54).

Isaac and Jacob are also described as imams who direct the people by the order of God: 'And We gave him Isaac and Jacob as an additional gift, and We made all of them righteous men. We made them imams who guide by Our command, and We inspired them to do good things, to perform the prayer, and to give alms. They constantly served Us' (XXI 72–3). But there were also renegades among the descendants of Abraham and Isaac: 'We blessed him [Abraham] and Isaac, but of their progeny there are some who do good and some who manifestly wrong themselves' (XXXVII 113; see also LVII 26).

In the face of the opposition of the Banū Isrāʾīl, Moses implored his Lord to grant him the help of his brother Aaron: 'Give me an assistant from my family, Aaron, my brother, increase my strength through him and make him share my task' (XX 29–32). God responded to his prayer: 'We indeed gave Moses the Book and appointed his brother Aaron with him as an assistant' (XXV 35; see also XX 36). Aaron thus was chosen as the associate of Moses in the revelation: 'Certainly We gave Moses and Aaron the salvation (*furqān*) and a light and a reminder for the pious who fear their Lord in the unseen and are frightened of the hour [of the Judgment]' (XXI 48–9). A mysterious relic (*baqiyya*) of the family of Moses and the family of Aaron became one of the signs of the divine investiture with the royalty of the Banū Isrāʾīl: 'Their prophet [Samuel]

[20] R. Paret, 'Der Plan einer neuen, leicht kommentierten Koranübersetzung', in *Orientalistische Studien Enno Littmann zu seinem 60. Geburtstag*, ed. R. Paret (Leiden, 1935), 121–30, at 127–30.

said to them: The sign of his [Saul's] rule is that the Ark of the Covenant shall come to you, carried by angels, containing a divine immanence (*sakīna*) from your Lord and a relic of what the family of Moses and the family of Aaron left. Truly, in that is a sign for you if you have faith' (II 248).

To David, prophet and vicegerent (*khalīfa*) on earth, God gave his son Solomon as his assistant and successor: 'We gave to David Solomon, how excellent a servant' (XXXVIII 30). Solomon inherited from David both his kingship and his prophetic wisdom and judgement: 'And Solomon became David's heir (*wa-waritha Sulaymānu Dāwūda*) and said: O people, we have been taught the speech of the birds and have been given of every thing' (XXVII 16). Jointly David and Solomon gave judgment, witnessed by God, in a case of damage to the fields (XXI 78).

Zachariah, the father of John the Baptist, said in his prayer: 'Indeed, I fear the *mawālī* after my death. My wife is barren, so grant me a descendant (*waliyyan*) from you who will inherit from me and inherit from the family of Jacob, and make him, o my Lord, pleasing [to You]' (XIX 5–6). The commentators generally take the term *mawālī* to mean relatives.[21] As R. Blachère has observed, however, it seems that there is here rather an allusion to the hostility of the other priests towards Zachariah, who had no offspring, as narrated in the Gospel of Thomas.[22] In any case, John became the heir of the family of Jacob.

In the story of the non-Israelite prophets, their families likewise play a vital part as their disciples and protectors. The sinful people of Madyan answered their prophet Shu'ayb: 'O Shu'ayb, we do not understand much of what you say, and surely we see you weak among us. If it were not for your clan (*rahṭ*) we would certainly have stoned you, for you are not powerful over us' (XI 91). A group of Thamūd, the people of the prophet Ṣāliḥ, said to each other: 'Swear a mutual oath by God that we attack him and his family by night. Then we shall say to the one entitled to his vengeance: We did not witness the destruction of his family, and we are surely telling the truth' (XXVII 49). God prevented their plot and annihilated the guilty and all the people of Thamūd.

The eminent position of the families and the descendants of the past prophets and the parallelism often observed between the history of the former prophets in the Qur'ān and that of Muḥammad must raise expectations of a distinguished place reserved for his family. The kin of Muḥammad are mentioned in various contexts, sometimes probably in a wider sense than that of his family. This order is addressed to the Prophet: 'Warn your nearest clan (*'ashīrataka l-aqrabīn*), and lower your wing to the faithful who follow you' (XXVI 214–15). The 'nearest clan'

[21] Ṭabarī, *Jāmi'*, XVI 32. [22] R. Blachère, *Le Coran* (Paris, 1957), 329, n. 5.

refers most likely to the Quraysh, although a narrower interpretation does not seem impossible.

Shiʿites frequently quote as evidence verse XLII 23 where Muḥammad is commanded to address the faithful: 'Say: I do not ask you for any recompense for this [the communication of the revelation] except the love for near kinship (*al-mawadda fi l-qurbā*).' They interpret it as asking the Muslims to love the *ahl al-bayt*, the family of the Prophet. This interpretation, however, does not agree with the wording of the text. Al-Ṭabarī in his commentary on the verse[23] offers three interpretations and prefers the first one, according to which the demand is for love of the faithful for the Prophet to whom they are related by blood ties. This explanation would be the most plausible if the verse were Mekkan and addressed to the Quraysh. The verse is, however, usually considered Medinan, pronounced at a time when many Muslims were not related to Muḥammad by blood ties. Preference might thus be given to the third interpretation of al-Ṭabarī (the second is rather improbable), that love towards relatives in general is meant. However, an interpretation close to that preferred by al-Ṭabarī seems to suggest itself by reference to another verse which affirms that Muḥammad is nearer to all Muslims than they are to each other: 'The Prophet has closer ties (*awlā*) to the faithful than they themselves have to each other, and his wives are their mothers' (XXXIII 6).

There are, in any case, other references to the kin of the Prophet which certainly refer to his family and blood relations. The Qur'ān reserves a part of the fifth (*khums*) of booty (*ghanīma*) and a part of the *fay'*, that is property of the infidels taken by the Muslims without combat, to the kin of Muḥammad in association with himself: 'Know that whatever you capture as booty, the fifth of it belongs to God, to the Messenger, to the near kin (*dhi l-qurbā*), the orphans, the poor, and the wayfarer, if you believe in God and in what He has sent down on His servant on the day of salvation, the day of the meeting of the two groups' (VIII 41). 'What God has granted as *fay'* to His Messenger from the people of the towns belongs to God, the Messenger, the close kin, and the orphans, the poor, and the wayfarer, in order that it may not circulate among the rich among you' (LIX 7). The Sunnite and Shiʿite sources agree that by the 'near kin' in these verses were meant the descendants of Hāshim b. ʿAbd Manāf, the great-grandfather of Muḥammad, and of Hāshim's brother al-Muṭṭalib,[24]

[23] Ṭabarī, *Jāmiʿ*, XXV, 13–15.

[24] According to a report of the ʿAlid ʿĪsā b. ʿAbd Allāh, Muḥammad also gave portions of the *khums* to the the Banū ʿAbd Yaghūth (Ibn Shabba, *Taʾrīkh al-Madīna al-munawwara*, ed. Fahīm Muḥammad Shaltūt (Qumm, 1410/[1989/90]), 645). The descendants of Muḥammad's maternal uncle ʿAbd Yaghūth b. Wahb b. ʿAbd Manāf of the clan of Zuhra are meant.

to the exclusion of the descendants of the other two brothers of Hāshim, ʿAbd Shams (the ancestor of the Umayyads) and Nawfal. The association of the Banu l-Muṭṭalib with the Banū Hāshim dated from the pre-Islamic *ḥilf al-fuḍūl*, a pact grouping these two families and some other clans of Quraysh in an alliance opposed to the other two and their allies.[25] This alliance was confirmed at the time of the boycott of Muḥammad by the Quraysh when the Banu l-Muṭṭalib joined the Hāshim in extending protection to him.[26] Because of their association with the Banū Hāshim, a number of the Banu l-Muṭṭalib received portions of the produce of Khaybar belonging to the Prophet.

The portion of the booty and *fay*ʾ reserved to the kin of the Prophet was, according to numerous reports in the sources, a recompense for them for their exclusion from the alms (*ṣadaqa*, *zakāt*). The relatives of Muḥammad were, like himself, forbidden to receive any part of the alms. The reason usually given for this exclusion was that the alms accrued from the defilements (*awsākh*) of the people, alms-giving being considered an act of purification. On account of their state of purity, it was improper for the close kin of the Prophet to receive or to handle the alms. The schools of religious law, Sunnite and Shiʿite alike, have preserved this prohibition for the Banū Hāshim to partake of the alms of the ordinary Muslims.[27]

This state of purity, which distinguished the family of Muḥammad from the common Muslims, agreed with the elevated rank of the families of the earlier prophets. As mentioned above, the Qurʾān described the family of Lot as people who kept themselves pure (*yataṭahharūn*). The same state of purity is evidently referred to in the verse addressed to the wives of the Prophet: 'Stay in your houses, and do not show yourselves in spectacular fashion like that of the former time of ignorance. Perform the prayer, give alms, and obey God and His Messenger. God desires only to remove defilement from you, o people of the house (*ahl al-bayt*), and to purify you (*yuṭahhirakum*) completely' (XXXIII 33). Who are the 'people of the house' here? The pronoun referring to them is in the masculine plural, while the preceding part of the verse is in the feminine plural. This change of gender has evidently contributed to the birth of

[25] W. M. Watt, *Muhammad at Mecca* (Oxford, 1953), 6–8.

[26] *Ibid.*, 8, 120–1. In his *Muhammedanische Studien* (Halle, 1889–90), I. Goldziher suggested that the hadith of Jubayr b. Muṭʿim about the Prophet's preference of Hāshim and al-Muṭṭalib over ʿAbd Shams and Nawfal was an ʿAbbasid anti-Umayyad partisan invention. This judgement rests on a complete disregard of the facts of Muḥammad's career and his conflict with his Mekkan opponents.

[27] See Madelung, 'The Hāshimiyyāt', 24–6. Caetani mistranslated the phrase (*ahl baytih*) *man ḥurrima l-ṣadaqa baʿdah* in the hadith about Ghadīr Khumm attributed to Zayd b. Arqam as 'people of his house are those who are excluded from the obligation of paying the legal alms after the death of the Prophet' (*Annali*, X, 455). There was no such exclusion.

various accounts of a legendary character, attaching the latter part of the verse to the five People of the Mantle (*ahl al-kisāʾ*): Muḥammad, ʿAlī, Fāṭima, Ḥasan and Ḥusayn. In spite of the obvious Shiʿite significance, the great majority of the reports quoted by al-Ṭabarī in his commentary on this verse support this interpretation.[28]

It seems quite unlikely, however, that this part of the verse could have been in effect a separate revelation which was later attached to the rest, as these reports imply. Just as in respect to the similar verse addressed to the wife of Abraham, R. Paret has argued that *ahl al-bayt* may here rather refer to the adherents of the cult of the Kaʿba.[29] This interpretation, however, is incompatible with the clear aim of the verse to elevate the rank of the wives of the Prophet above all other Muslim women. The previous verse begins with the declaration: 'O women of the Prophet, you are not like any other women' (XXXIII 32). The women are addressed here as members of the purified family of the Prophet through marriage. It is known that Muḥammad on other occasions addressed his wives individually as *ahl al-bayt*, evidently with the intention of honouring them.[30] Here they are admonished in clearly critical terms to conform to their elevated state in their conduct. The *ahl al-bayt* of Muḥammad meant, as was consistent with the general usage of the term at the time, primarily his blood relations, the same Banū Hāshim who were forbidden to receive alms in order that their state of purity not be soiled and, in second place, the wives.

There is still the verse of the 'mutual imprecation (*mubāhala*)' whose religious significance is, in view of the uncertainty about the circumstances surrounding its revelation, difficult to evaluate.[31] Muḥammad is addressed:

[28] Ṭabarī, *Jāmiʿ*, XXII, 5–7. [29] Paret, 'Der Plan', 127–30.

[30] Ibn Ḥanbal, *Musnad* ([Cairo] 1313/1895), III, 246. In his *Fāṭima et les filles de Mahomet*, 99, Lammens asserted that *ahl al-bayt*, as understood in Arabic, basically means a man's wives assembled under the same roof. Yet the references given by him in n. 4 as evidence for the use of the term with respect to families other than Muḥammad's clearly show that the primary meaning was close kin, blood relations.

[31] The significance of the verse of the *mubāhala* has been barely discussed in western studies and biographies of Muḥammad. L. Massignon's monograph *La Mubâhala de Médine et l'hyperdulie de Fatima* (Paris, 1955) and W. Schmucker's articles 'Die christliche Minderheit von Nağrān und die Problematik ihrer Beziehungen zum frühen Islam', in *Studien zum Minderheitenproblem im Islam*, Bonner Orientalistische Studien, Neue Serie, ed. O. Spies (Bonn, 1973), vol. XXVII/1, 183–281 and 'Mubāhala' in the *Encyclopaedia of Islam* (2nd edn, Leiden, 1954–) deal largely with later doctrine and legend. Schmucker argues that the part ascribed to the Christians of Najrān is wholly fictitious and that the verse, which he describes as obscure, does not relate to any historical event. The wording of the verse would seem, however, to refer to a historical occasion. Yet even if the verse were merely intended to extol Muḥammad's religious rank in abstract terms, the question would remain why his 'wives and sons' were included in it and who was meant by them. The contemporaries could hardly avoid understanding it as referring to his *ahl al-bayt*.

'If anyone dispute with you in this matter [concerning Jesus] after the knowledge which has come to you, say: Come let us call our sons and your sons, our women and your women, ourselves and yourselves, then let us swear an oath and place the curse of God on those who lie' (III 61). The commentators are agreed that the verse was occasioned by the visit of a delegation of Christians from Najrān in the year 10/631–2 who did not accept the Islamic doctrine about Jesus. Modern scholars have critically noted a certain tendency of the commentators to relate many Qur'anic passages concerning Christians to this visit.[32] Who is meant by 'our sons' and 'our women' on the part of Muḥammad? The *mubāhala*, according to the reports, did not take place, since the Christians excused themselves from it, and the majority of the Sunnite reports quoted by al-Ṭabarī do not identify the members of the family of Muḥammad who were expected to participate. Other Sunnite reports mention Fāṭima, Ḥasan and Ḥusayn, and some agree with the Shi'ite tradition that the *ahl al-kisā'*, including 'Alī, were assembled for the occasion. Irrespective of the circumstances, there does not seem to be a plausible alternative to the identification of the 'sons' in the verse with the two grandsons of Muḥammad and, in that case, the inclusion of their parents, 'Alī and Fāṭima, would be reasonable. The term 'our women', in place of 'our wives', does not exclude the daughter of the Prophet. The participation of the family was perhaps traditional in the ritual of the *mubāhala*. Yet the proposal itself of this ritual by the Prophet under circumstances of an intense religious significance and its sanction by the Qur'ān could not have failed to raise the religious rank of his family.

The Qur'ān thus accorded the *ahl al-bayt* of Muḥammad an elevated position above the rest of the faithful, similar to the position of the families of the earlier prophets. God desired to purify them from all defilement. Certainly the renegades of the Prophet's family who opposed his mission were excluded from the divine grace, just like the renegades among the families of the past prophets. Abū Lahab, the uncle of Muḥammad, and his wife were even singled out for divine curse in a Sūra of the Qur'ān. But such exceptions did not affect the divine favour for the *ahl al-bayt* in general.

Insofar as the Qur'ān expresses the thoughts of Muḥammad, it is evident that he could not have considered Abū Bakr his natural successor or have been pleased by his succession. The Qur'ān certainly does not fully reflect Muḥammad's views about the men and women surrounding him and his attitude towards them. Yet he could not have seen his succession essentially other than in the light of the narrations of the

[32] T. Nöldeke and F. Schwally, *Geschichte des Qorāns* (Leipzig, 1909–38), I, 177, n. 2.

Qur'ān about the succession of the earlier prophets, just as he saw his own mission as a prophet, the resistance of his people with which he met, and his ultimate success by divine grace in the light of the experience of the former prophets as related in the Qur'ān. These earlier prophets considered it a supreme divine favour to be succeeded by their offspring or close kin for which they implored their Lord. Modern Sunnite apologists argue against this on the basis of Qur'ān XXXIII 40 which describes Muḥammad as the Seal of the Prophets. They maintain that, as the last of the prophets, Muḥammad was not to be succeeded by any of his family according to God's design. In order to reveal this design, God also let all of Muḥammad's sons die in infancy.[33] For the same reason Muḥammad did not appoint a successor, since he wished to leave the succession to be settled by the Muslim Community on the basis of the Qur'anic principle of consultation (*shūrā*).

The argument rests, however, on a fancifully wide interpretation of the term 'Seal of the Prophets'. For even if its meaning in the Qur'ān is accepted to be the 'last of the prophets', which is itself not entirely certain,[34] there is no reason why it should imply that Muḥammad as the spiritual and worldly leader of the Muslim Community, aside from his prophethood, should not be succeeded by his family. In the Qur'ān, the descendants and close kin of the prophets are their heirs also in respect to kingship (*mulk*), rule (*ḥukm*), wisdom (*ḥikma*), the book and the imamate. The Sunnite concept of the true caliphate itself defines it as a succession of the Prophet in every respect except his prophethood. Why should Muḥammad not be succeeded in it by any of his family like the earlier prophets? If God really wanted to indicate that he should not be succeeded by any of them, why did He not let his grandsons and other kin die like his sons? There is thus good reason to doubt that Muḥammad failed to appoint a successor because he realized that the divine design excluded hereditary succession of his family and that he wanted the Muslims to choose their head by *shūrā*. The Qur'ān advises the faithful to settle some matters by consultation, but not the succession to prophets. That, according to the Qur'ān, is settled by divine election, and God usually chooses their successors, whether they become prophets or not, from their own kin.

[33] The argument has a basis in hadith. According to statements ascribed to several Companions, Muḥammad's son Ibrāhīm did not survive because he would have become a prophet. See Goldziher, *Muhammedanische Studien*, II, 105–6; Y. Friedmann, 'Finality of Prophethood in Sunni Islam', *JSAI*, 7 (1986), 177–215, at 187–9.

[34] Friedmann, 'Finality of Prophethood'; G. G. Stroumsa, 'Seal of the Prophets: The Nature of a Manichaean Metaphor', *JSAI*, 7 (1986), 61–74; C. Colpe, 'Das Siegel der Propheten', *Orientalia Suecana*, 33–5 (1984–6), 71–83, revised version in C. Colpe, *Das Siegel der Propheten*, (Berlin, 1990), 227–43.

Why then did Muḥammad fail to make proper arrangements for his succession, even though he presumably hoped for a successor from his family? Any answer must remain speculative. A simple Islamic explanation would be that in an important decision of this nature he expected a Qur'anic revelation, but did not receive one. Non-Muslim historians may be more inclined to speculate that Muḥammad hesitated because he was aware of the difficulties a Hashimite succession might face given the intense rivalry for leadership among the clans of Quraysh and the relative weakness of the Banū Hāshim. In the year 10/631 Muḥammad sent 'Alī as his representative to the Yemen, where his conduct seems to have provoked some criticism. Upon his return, just three months before the Prophet's death, Muḥammad found it necessary to make a strong public statement in support of his cousin.[35] It was evidently not a suitable occasion to appoint him successor. Muḥammad might also have delayed a decision hoping to live long enough to be able to appoint one of his grandsons. His death was generally unexpected among his followers even during his mortal illness. He himself may also have been unaware of the approaching end until it was too late.

Two witnesses: 'Ā'isha and 'Abd Allāh b. al-'Abbās

Among the extant reports about the succession and the early caliphate those attributed to Abū Bakr's daughter 'Ā'isha and to 'Abd Allāh b. al-'Abbās, cousin of Muḥammad and of 'Alī, are of primary importance. Both were in a position to observe closely the events in which they were emotionally deeply involved and in some of which they played a direct part, although in opposite camps. 'Ā'isha, as is well known, championed her father's right to the succession of Muḥammad and backed the caliphate of his appointed successor, 'Umar. In the election of the *shūrā* after the murder of 'Umar, she clearly preferred 'Uthmān to her personal enemy 'Alī. She soon became, however, a vocal critic of 'Uthmān's conduct as caliph and her agitation against him contributed to the outbreak of open rebellion. When 'Uthmān was murdered by the rebels and they raised 'Alī to the caliphate, she immediately turned against the latter, claiming revenge for the dead caliph. After the defeat of her alliance in the battle of the Camel, she withdrew from active politics. Her relations with the Umayyad Mu'āwiya, under whose reign she died in 58/678, were cool.[36]

'Abd Allāh b. al-'Abbās, born in 619, three years before the *hijra*,

[35] L. Veccia Vaglieri, 'Ghadīr Khumm', *EI* (2nd edn) and below, 253.

[36] On the life of 'Ā'isha see especially N. Abbott, *Aishah the Beloved of Mohammad* (Chicago, 1942).

appeared first in public life under the caliph ʿUmar. The latter seems to have tried to draw him into his company as a representative of the Banū Hāshim, who mostly avoided him. During the siege of ʿUthmān's residence in Medina by the rebels from Egypt and Kūfa, he was among the group of sons of prominent Companions who protected the palace of the caliph. ʿUthmān then appointed him leader of the pilgrimage to Mekka and entrusted him with an open letter to the pilgrims, from whom he hoped for relief. ʿAlī initially relied extensively on his advice and appointed him governor of Baṣra. Ibn al-ʿAbbās, however, later defected temporarily and was evidently critical of some aspects of his cousin's reign. After ʿAlī's murder he wrote a letter to his son al-Ḥasan encouraging him to continue his father's war against Muʿāwiya and to fight for his rights. He did not back the revolt of al-Ḥasan's brother al-Ḥusayn under the caliph Yazīd. Together with ʿAlī's other son Muḥammad b. al-Ḥanafiyya, he refused to recognize the caliphate of ʿAbd Allāh b. al-Zubayr, who imprisoned both of them. They were freed by Kufan horsemen sent by the Shiʿite rebel leader al-Mukhtār. Ibn al-ʿAbbās died soon afterwards in 68/687–8.[37]

Caetani considered the attribution of historical reports to these two Companions as mostly fictitious. He argued that the use of the chain of transmitters (*isnād*) became customary only long after their time and it was then often traced back to Companions in order to raise the authority of anonymous traditions.[38] ʿĀ'isha in particular was chosen because it was assumed that she must have had first-hand knowledge of the events.[39] Reports thus could be old and reliable except for their attribution. In practice, however, Caetani tended to reject these reports as apocryphal or to express serious reservations about them while preferring, wherever possible, accounts reported without *isnād* by the early compilers of history such as Ibn Isḥāq. Somewhat inconsistently, he described Ibn al-ʿAbbās as an arch liar and fabricator on account of the fictitious biblical stories and cosmological myths which he spread in his exegesis of the Qur'ān.[40] Yet if this exegesis can reliably be attributed to Ibn al-ʿAbbās, why should the attribution of historical reports to him be regularly fictitious? A further problem regarding Caetani's view is that many of the reports ascribed to ʿĀ'isha and Ibn al-ʿAbbās quote them speaking in the first person. It is evident that these can never have been anonymous traditions and that only the formal *isnād* could be a later addition. If the attribution is rejected the reports themselves must be presumed to be later fabrications.

[37] For a short summary of the career of ʿAbd Allāh b. al-ʿAbbās see L. Veccia Vaglieri, "ʿAbd Allāh b. al-ʿAbbās', *EI* (2nd edn).

[38] See in general his discussion in *Annali*, I, 38ff.

[39] *Ibid.*, II/1, 691–2.

[40] *Ibid.*, I, 47–51.

The date of the introduction of the formal *isnād* is thus of little relevance to the question of correct attribution. This must be judged largely on the basis of the mutual consistency of the reports attributed to the same witness and their consistency with what is known of his or her life and political attitudes. 'Ā'isha and Ibn al-'Abbās were, as noted, deeply involved in the events, though in opposite camps. Their testimony can be expected to be partisan in both what they reported and how they presented it, rather than neutral and disinterested. Since the tendentious aspect of the reports often agrees with later Sunnite or Shi'ite partisan positions, there has been a common tendency among western scholars to regard them as later fabrications, in particular those favouring Shi'ite views. Yet tendentiousness alone is no evidence for late origin. If some reports, because of particular circumstances, can be seen to be almost certainly correctly attributed, the burden of the proof with regard to similar ones, where matters are more ambiguous, is on those who wish to consider them as late forgeries.

The historical reports attributed to 'Ā'isha and Ibn al-'Abbās in the major sources such as Ibn Hishām, al-Ṭabarī, Ibn Sa'd and al-Balādhurī fulfil this condition of consistency to a high degree. They reflect sharply defined personal views and political attitudes. There are variant versions in which some of their outspoken statements, which must have seemed objectionable to the later transmitters, appear toned down or are omitted. Only a few reports must be definitely rejected as at variance with their political attitudes.

'Ā'isha's reports are highly laudatory and apologetic for Abū Bakr, whom she presents as a kindly father figure full of the *ḥilm*, gentleness and prudence, valued so highly among the Arabs as a leadership quality, quite in contrast to the coarse and rude 'Umar who was feared by everybody in spite of his undeniable righteousness. At the beginning of his mortal illness, Muḥammad told the assembled Muslims that he knew no man more excellent in his actions *(afḍal yadan)* among the Companions than Abū Bakr and ordered that all (private) doors leading to the mosque (and his living quarters) be blocked except for Abū Bakr's.[41] He insisted, in

[41] Ṭabarī, I, 1808. As against the numerous reports of 'Ā'isha and others about the last public prayer led by Muḥammad, according to which he primarily manifested his preference for Abū Bakr, 'Abd Allāh b. al-'Abbās is quoted as having given a completely different account on the authority of his elder brother al-Faḍl. According to this account, the Prophet did not mention, or allude to, Abū Bakr at all. He confessed his repentance for any offences he had committed against others and asked those present to confess their wrongdoings so that he could pray for them. When one of them acknowledged being a liar, hypocrite and guilty of every offence, 'Umar self-righteously told him: 'You have disgraced yourself.' But the Prophet said: 'The disgrace of this world is lighter than the disgrace of the hereafter. O God, grant him truthfulness and faith and bring his matters to a good end.' 'Umar insisted: 'Speak to him.' The Prophet laughed and said (to the man): "Umar is with me and I am with 'Umar. After me, stick to 'Umar, wherever he shall be' (Ṭabarī, I, 1801–3).

spite of ʻĀ'isha's protests, that Abū Bakr, and no one else, should take his place in leading the prayers. It is evident that in ʻĀ'isha's view her father was the rightful successor of Muḥammad on the basis of the latter's implicit choice of him, not the events at the Saqīfat Banī Sāʻida. Abū Bakr's greatest concern was to treat the family of his deceased friend kindly and fairly, a duty which he placed even higher than his obligation towards his own kin. ʻĀ'isha spared no effort to portray her husband's kin in general, and ʻAlī in particular, in the most negative light; their incompetence was matched only by their arrogance. Muḥammad's uncle al-ʻAbbās greatly upset the ill Prophet when he, in the company of several pro-Hashimite women, infused medicine through the side of his mouth (*laddahū*) without his permission and then explained that they thought he had pleurisy (*dhāt al-janb*), a suggestion angrily rejected by Muḥammad, for God would not have afflicted him with 'this devil's disease'.[42] Not even to the dead body of the Prophet would his kin have shown due respect had it not been for divine intervention. ʻAlī, encouraged by his wife Fāṭima and al-ʻAbbās, who falsely pretended to the inheritance of Muḥammad's worldly possessions, imagined that he was entitled to the caliphate as Muḥammad's cousin and son-in-law. But as everybody deserted him after the death of Fāṭima, he was forced to offer Abū Bakr his allegiance. His condition for meeting him was that the rude ʻUmar should not be present. After he recognized that Abū Bakr had been right all along, people began to speak to him again.

ʻAbd Allāh b. al-ʻAbbās presented the views of the Banū Hāshim about their own right much more cautiously. He recognized that 'the people (*qawm*)', meaning Quraysh, had decided against what the former firmly considered as their legitimate claim as the Prophet's kin. His attitude to ʻAlī was not without reservations. He mentioned having repeatedly

[42] Ibn Hishām, *Sīrat sayyidinā Muḥammad rasūl Allāh*, ed. F. Wüstenfeld as *Das Leben Muhammeds nach Muhammed Ibn Ishâk* (Göttingen, 1859–60), 1007; Ṭabarī, I, 1809. The women named as present by ʻĀ'isha were Umm Salama and Maymūna, wives of Muḥammad, and Asmā' bt ʻUmays. All three were pro-Hashimite and therefore odious to ʻĀ'isha. On Asmā' see Abbott, *Aishah*, 113–15. ʻĀ'isha added with satisfaction that Maymūna was given an infusion of medicine through her mouth while she was fasting because of the curse of the Prophet and as a punishment for what they did. In other versions ʻĀ'isha is quoted as saying that she was also present (Ṭabarī, I, 1808–9). In one of them, transmitted by her nephew al-Qāsim b. Muḥammad, she tells the assembled women not to give the medicine to the Prophet, but she is nevertheless also affected by his curse and forced to swallow medicine (Balādhurī, *Ansāb al-ashrāf*, vol. I, ed. Muḥammad Ḥamīd Allāh (Cairo, 1959), 546). Other versions, not attributed to ʻĀ'isha, mostly blame Asmā', rather than al-ʻAbbās, for giving Muḥammad the medicine (Ṭabarī, I, 1810; Ibn Saʻd, *Kitāb al-Ṭabaqāt al-Kabīr*, ed. E. Sachau *et al.* (Leiden, 1905–40), II/2, 31–2, where one version is attributed to ʻAbd Allāh b. al-ʻAbbās). Caetani misunderstood the tendency of ʻĀ'isha's account as implying that Muḥammad distrusted everybody except his uncle al-ʻAbbās (*Annali*, II/1, 499). The impression conveyed is rather that Muḥammad was strict with the women but unduly lenient with his kinsman al-ʻAbbās, who was the main culprit.

criticized his cousin's actions and warned him of their consequences. He rejected the belief of some of ʿAlī's partisans that the Prophet actually made a will (*awṣā*) in his favour. Yet this, he suggested, was probably only because ʿĀ'isha and Ḥafṣa prevented Muḥammad from seeing him alone when he asked for him during his illness and they insisted on calling their fathers. When the ill Muḥammad proposed to write a letter of guidance for his Companions, ʿUmar intervened, asserting that he was raving. ʿAbd Allāh's father al-ʿAbbās recognized the approaching death in the face of Muḥammad and tried to persuade ʿAlī to approach him concerning the succession. He told ʿAlī that the Prophet would either give the rule to them or, if not, would at least commend (*awṣā*) them to the good care of 'the people'. ʿAlī refused, however, expressing fear that if the Prophet denied them the succession, 'the people' would never give it to them.

The presentation of Ibn al-ʿAbbās, however, leaves no doubt that he considered ʿAlī as entitled to the succession, although not formally appointed, and held that he was arbitrarily deprived by Abū Bakr with the connivance of 'the people'. The Banū Hāshim expressed their distrust and then their disapproval of their conduct by excluding virtually all outsiders from the preparation of the funeral and the burial of the Prophet, thus depriving the new caliph of the honour of paying his final tribute to his predecessor. Abū Bakr denied them illegally their inheritance and the share of the *fay'* to which they were entitled according to the Qur'ān. ʿUmar later tried to meet their grievance by offering them partial restitution, but this was rejected by the Banū Hāshim as insufficient. ʿUmar's views evidently interested Ibn al-ʿAbbās in particular. ʿUmar admitted in public that the decision taken at the Saqīfat Banī Sāʿida constituted a *falta*, a precipitate and ill-considered deal. He nevertheless insisted that Abū Bakr's caliphate, in view of its manifest success, was determined by God's choice and legitimate. He expressed his regret to Ibn al-ʿAbbās that ʿAlī continued to shun him and would not join him in a journey. Yet while he sought to treat ʿAlī as a distinguished early Companion, he was greatly worried about the possibility of ʿAlī's succession to the caliphate since he and his clan would turn it into a hereditary reign depriving 'the people' of their right to it. Privately he explained to Ibn al-ʿAbbās that 'the people' would not countenance the rule of the Banū Hāshim out of jealousy, since these would then enjoy the monopoly of both prophethood and caliphate.

The authenticity of the reports attributed to ʿĀ'isha and Ibn al-ʿAbbās is no guarantee of their reliability. It will be seen that both of them were prepared to invent stories to bolster their claims and to discredit their opponents. The temptation was obviously great. Their authority as the Prophet's favourite wife and as his cousin was beyond challenge and no one would question their veracity openly. They could say what others could not, but what many wanted to hear. For their partisan distortions merely reflected the passions that were tearing the Muslim Community apart. Yet they were also generally better informed than others, and even distorted and dressed up reports may be expected to reflect their knowledge of the facts, in particular for events they personally witnessed. The later narrators relied heavily on their accounts in their own summaries of events. For the historian, their conflicting points of view and bias must be of as much interest as the facts they report.

Some of the narrations either of 'Ā'isha or of Ibn al-'Abbās were clearly intended to counter the stories of the other. 'Ubayd Allāh b. 'Abd Allāh b. 'Utba b. Mas'ūd heard 'Ā'isha tell that the ill Prophet asked leave from his wives to be nursed in 'Ā'isha's apartment and that he walked there supported by two men of his family, one of them al-Faḍl b. al-'Abbās and 'another man'. Later he presented the report to Ibn al-'Abbās, who asked him if he knew who the other man was and, on his reply in the negative, told him: "Alī b. Abī Ṭālib, but she could not bring herself to mention anything good of him even if she would have been in a position to do so.'[43] Ibn al-'Abbās could not have had first-hand knowledge of the event. Given 'Ā'isha's well-known hostility towards 'Alī, however, the assumption that he was the man whom she would not name was reasonable enough. Ibn al-'Abbās disputed 'Ā'isha's account that the Prophet died in her arms.[44] When Abū Ghaṭafān told him that he had heard 'Urwa b. al-Zubayr transmitting 'Ā'isha's claim, he countered: 'Are you in your right mind (*a-ta'qilu*)? By God, the Messenger of God died reclining on the chest of 'Alī. He was the one who washed him together with my brother al-Faḍl b. al-'Abbās. My father refused to attend saying: The Messenger of God used to order us to stay behind a curtain [when he washed himself]. Thus he remained behind the curtain.'[45]

Ibn al-'Abbās narrated that the Prophet before his death expressed the

[43] Ṭabarī, I, 1800–1, quoting Ibn Isḥāq; Ibn Hishām, *Sīrat sayyidinā*, 1005; 'Abd al-Razzāq al-Ṣan'ānī, *al-Muṣannaf*, ed. Ḥabīb al-Raḥmān al-A'ẓamī [Beirut, 1390–2/1970–2], V, 429–30 and Ibn Ḥanbal, *Musnad*, VI, 34 (Ma'mar *'an* al-Zuhrī). Ibn Hishām suppressed the comment of Ibn al-'Abbās on 'Ā'isha's unwillingness to mention anything positive about 'Alī.

[44] For 'Ā'isha's account see Ibn Hishām, *Sīrat sayyidinā*, 1011; Ibn Sa'd, *Ṭabaqāt*, II/2, 50. There 'Ā'isha is quoted as stating that it happened during her turn for Muḥammad's company and that she did not wrong anyone in relation to him. She apologizes that it was only due to her foolishness and extreme youth that the Prophet died in her arms. This is in conflict with her other reports that Muḥammad had ceased to circulate among his wives, having taken leave to stay with her during his illness.

[45] Ibn Sa'd, *Ṭabaqāt*, II/2, 51. The latter part of the report about the washing of Muḥammad's body by 'Alī in the absence of al-'Abbās is paralleled by a report of 'Ubayd Allāh b. 'Abd Allāh b. 'Utba from Ibn al-'Abbās (*ibid.*, 62). That Muḥammad died with his head in the lap of 'Alī and that his body was washed by 'Alī singly is also affirmed in a speech that the latter is reported to have addressed to his followers at Ṣiffīn. Naṣr b. Muzāḥim al-Minqarī, *Waq'at Ṣiffīn*, ed. 'Abd al-Salām Muḥammad Hārūn (Cairo, 1382/[1962]), 224).

wish to write a letter for those present 'after which you will not go astray'. 'Umar said: 'The Messenger of God is overcome by pain. You have the Qur'ān, the Book of God is sufficient for us.' The people present started to quarrel, some demanding that the Prophet should be given the chance to write, others siding with 'Umar. As their noise pained Muḥammad, he told them to leave him. Ibn al-'Abbās, according to the report, used to comment that the greatest calamity was thus caused by their disagreement and noise which prevented the Prophet from writing his will.[46] Although Ibn al-'Abbās refrained from suggesting what the Prophet wanted to write, it was assumed that he hinted at Muḥammad's intention to name 'Alī his successor, and Shi'ites have always interpreted the report in this sense. 'Ā'isha countered the story with one of her own: 'The Messenger of God told me during his illness: Call your father Abū Bakr and your brother ['Abd al-Raḥmān] to me so that I may write a letter. For I fear that someone will have wishful fancies (*yatamannā mutamannin*) and someone will say: I am more worthy, but God and the faithful refuse anyone but Abū Bakr.'[47] No one could doubt that the wishful man was 'Alī.

As further illustration of the reporting of 'Ā'isha and Ibn al-'Abbās and their opposite bias, two examples relating to Muḥammad's actions during his last illness and to his funeral may be briefly analysed here. The Kufan al-Arqam b. Shuraḥbīl al-Awdī, a companion of 'Abd Allāh b. Mas'ūd,[48] asked Ibn al-'Abbās whether the Prophet had made a will (*awṣā*). Ibn al-'Abbās denied this and explained that (during his last illness) Muḥammad had demanded: 'Send for 'Alī.' 'Ā'isha, however, suggested: 'Would you send for Abū Bakr?', and Ḥafṣa joined her, proposing: 'Would you send for 'Umar?' When all three men assembled, Muḥammad dismissed them, saying that he would ask for them when he had a need. As the time of prayer came he said: 'Give order to Abū Bakr to pray with the people', but 'Ā'isha replied: 'Abū Bakr is frail (*raqīq*), so order 'Umar.' Muḥammad gave order for 'Umar to lead the prayer, but 'Umar refused, saying: 'I would not precede when Abū Bakr is present.' Then Abū Bakr went forward. The Prophet, feeling a temporary recovery, went out after him, and when Abū Bakr heard his movement, he drew back. Muḥammad dragged him forward by his clothes and stood him in his place. Then he himself sat down and recited the Qur'ān from where Abū Bakr had left off.[49]

Caetani considered this report to be apocryphal and invented by the Muslim traditionists in order to explain why Muḥammad had not left a

[46] 'Abd al-Razzāq, *Muṣannaf*, V, 438–9; al-Bukhārī, *Ṣaḥīḥ* (Cairo, 1312/[1894]), *Marḍā*, 17; Ibn Sa'd, *Ṭabaqāt*, II/2, 37–8; *Annali*, II/1, 508.

[47] Muslim, *Ṣaḥīḥ* (Būlāq, 1290/[1873]), *Faḍā'il al-ṣaḥāba*, 11.

[48] Ibn Ḥajar, *Tahdhīb al-tahdhīb* (Hyderabad, 1325–7/[1907–9]), I, 198–9.

[49] Ṭabarī, I, 1810–11.

testament.[50] The attribution to Ibn al-ʿAbbās is, however, entirely reasonable. The Kufan Shiʿites had been claiming since the time of ʿAlī's caliphate that the Prophet had made ʿAlī the executor of his will. The question of the Kufan al-Arqam b. Shuraḥbīl thus had a motive. The position of Ibn al-ʿAbbās on the question is the same as in other reports attributed to him. Muḥammad did not actually make a will in favour of ʿAlī, but would probably have done so if he had not been prevented. The first part of the story was presumably invented by Ibn al-ʿAbbās who, in any case, could not have had first-hand knowledge. The second part is based on the account of ʿĀ'isha quoted below. Muḥammad gave the order for Abū Bakr to lead the prayer of the Muslims but ʿĀ'isha objected that her father was too frail. Then Ibn al-ʿAbbās deviates. Muḥammad gave order that ʿUmar lead the prayer, and only when ʿUmar refused to precede Abū Bakr, the latter went ahead. The message is clear: in the eyes of Muḥammad the leadership of the prayer had no significance for the succession. He did not care whether Abū Bakr or ʿUmar performed the task. When Abū Bakr still hesitated, the Prophet rudely grasped him by his clothes, pushing him into his place and then, apparently not quite satisfied with his performance, continued Abū Bakr's recitation of the Qur'ān.

ʿĀ'isha reported the event as follows: when the prayer was called, the Prophet said: 'Order Abū Bakr to pray with the people.' ʿĀ'isha countered: 'Abū Bakr is a frail man, and if he were to take your place, he could not bear it.' Muḥammad repeated: 'Order Abū Bakr to pray with the people', and ʿĀ'isha made the same objection. Now the Prophet grew angry and said: 'You [women] are consorts of Joseph (*ṣawāḥib Yūsuf*).' A third time he commanded: 'Order Abū Bakr to pray with the people.' As he was led out into the mosque, Abū Bakr stood back. Muḥammad made a sign to him to stand in his place. ʿĀ'isha added: 'Abū Bakr thus followed the prayer of the Prophet, and the people followed the prayer of Abū Bakr.'[51] Three times the Prophet had thus insisted that Abū Bakr, and only he, should lead the prayer of the Muslims in his place. This was shortly after he, according to ʿĀ'isha, had told them that Abū Bakr was in his view the most excellent of his Companions and had ordered all private doors of the mosque to be closed except for Abū Bakr's. The message was equally clear: Muḥammad wished to indicate that Abū Bakr was his choice for the succession.

[50] *Annali*, II/1, 506.

[51] Ṭabarī, I, 1811–12. According to the version related by al-Zuhrī, ʿĀ'isha explained that her objection to Muḥammad's order was motivated by her fear that the people would not like anyone occupying the place of Muḥammad and would blame him for any misfortune that occurred: Ibn Hishām, *Sīrat sayyidinā*, 1008; Ibn Saʿd, *Ṭabaqāt*, II/2, 18; Balādhurī, *Ansāb*, I, 559.

There is, however, a second account by 'Ā'isha which may have induced Ibn al-'Abbās to mention 'Umar. According to it, Muḥammad, while ill in the apartment of his wife Maymūna, asked her nephew 'Abd Allāh b. Zam'a to order the people to pray. 'Abd Allāh met 'Umar and told him to lead the prayer. The Prophet recognized 'Umar's stentorian voice and asked: 'Is this not the voice of 'Umar?' Upon receiving confirmatory answer, he said: 'God refuses this as do the faithful. Order Abū Bakr, let him pray with the people.' It was now that 'Ā'isha entreated Muḥammad twice to excuse Abū Bakr until he put an end to the argument by calling her and the women 'consorts of Joseph'.[52] This may well be 'Ā'isha's initial version[53] which she then revised because of the unflattering part given in it to 'Umar. It would thus appear that 'Umar did lead the prayer at first during Muḥammad's illness and that 'Ā'isha, in order to maintain that the appointment to the leadership of the prayer by Muḥammad was meant to signify appointment to the succession, had to create the impression that 'Umar's leadership occurred against the will of Muḥammad and was disapproved of by him.[54]

About the washing of Muḥammad's body for the funeral, al-Ṭabarī relates, on the authority of Ibn Isḥāq, an account that differs from the one quoted above.[55] Both Ibn Hishām and al-Balādhurī quote Ibn Isḥāq's account without the attribution to Ibn al-'Abbās.[56] There could thus be some doubt about the correctness of the attribution. The reliability of al-Ṭabarī in his quotations is generally high, however, and the attribution of the account to Ibn al-'Abbās is confirmed by Aḥmad b. Ḥanbal.[57] Thus it seems likely that Ibn al-'Abbās gave two different accounts about the same event on different occasions. The account related by Ibn Isḥāq is, in any case, distinctly pro-Hashimite and provoked 'Ā'isha to give a

52 Ibn Ḥanbal, *Musnad*, VI, 24.

53 The report continues the narration of 'Ubayd Allāh b. 'Abd Allāh, al-Zuhrī's main source for the events, about the beginning of Muḥammad's illness. Ibn Isḥāq and most later sources preferred the toned down version which al-Zuhrī related on the authority of Ḥamza b. 'Abd Allāh, grandson of the caliph 'Umar. 'Ā'isha may have hesitated to tell him the unflattering story about his grandfather. Al-Ṭabarī's *isnād* is independent of al-Zuhrī.

54 'Abd Allāh b. Zam'a is himself quoted as narrating the story. According to his account, Abū Bakr was absent at the time and 'Umar led the complete prayer. 'Umar afterwards reproached him and insisted that he, 'Umar, had thought that the Prophet had actually named him and that otherwise he would not have led the prayer. 'Abd Allāh b. Zam'a excused himself saying that, in the absence of Abū Bakr, he had considered 'Umar the most worthy of leading it: Ibn Hishām, *Sīrat sayyidinā*, 1008–9; Ibn Ḥanbal, *Musnad*, IV, 322.

55 Ṭabarī, I, 1830–1.

56 Ibn Hishām, *Sīrat sayyidinā*, 1818–9; Balādhurī, *Ansāb*, I, 569.

57 Ibn Kathīr, *al-Bidāya wa l-nihāya* (Cairo, 1351/1932), V, 260–1. The *isnād* is Ibn Isḥāq – Ḥusayn b. 'Abd Allāh – 'Ikrima – Ibn al-'Abbās. Caetani strangely asserted that this report of Ibn Isḥāq was without *isnād* and thus was a genuine and authentic tradition of Ibn Isḥāq. He considered it therefore as particularly authoritative (*Annali*, II/1, 519).

counter-report. Ibn al-ʿAbbās related that ʿAlī, al-ʿAbbās and his sons al-Faḍl and Qutham, Usāma b. Zayd and Shuqrān, both clients of Muḥammad, undertook to wash his body. Aws b. Khawalī, a Medinan veteran of the battle of Badr, implored ʿAlī to let him join for the sake of the stake of the Anṣār in the Prophet and was let in by him. ʿAlī drew the body to his chest, and al-ʿAbbās, al-Faḍl and Qutham helped him to turn it. Usāma and Shuqrān proceeded to pour water on the dead body without removing his shirt. ʿAlī washed him, rubbing the shirt from the outside without his hand touching the body. He said: 'You are dearer to me than my father and mother, how sweet you are alive and dead.' Nothing of the body of the Prophet thus was seen, contrary to the case with ordinary men.

The report stresses that only Muḥammad's close kin and two of his clients were present. The women, including ʿĀ'isha, in whose apartment Muḥammad had died and was buried, were excluded. Only one of the Anṣār, but none of the Mekkan Emigrants, was exceptionally admitted. Out of reverence for the Prophet, great care was taken, against the common practice, not to uncover his body.

ʿĀ'isha did not take her exclusion with good grace. She reported that when the men wanted to wash the Prophet, they disagreed, saying: 'By God, we do not know whether we should bare the Prophet of his clothes as we bare our dead or whether we should wash him with his clothes on.' As they were thus quarrelling, a slumber was cast upon them and every one of them fell asleep with his chin on his chest. Then a speaker, known to no one, addressed them from the direction of the house: 'Wash the Prophet with his clothes on.' Muḥammad's kinsmen obeyed the command. The transmitter of the report added: ʿĀ'isha used to say that with hindsight (*law istaqbaltu min amrī mā istadbartu*) she thought that only his wives should have washed him.[58] The listeners were thus left in no doubt that the wives, under ʿĀ'isha's guidance, would not have needed a divine reprimand to stop them from committing an act of disrespect to the Prophet's body, unlike Muḥammad's insensitive and quarrelsome kin.

[58] Ṭabarī, I, 1831. Ibn Hishām, *Sīrat sayyidinā*, (1019) omitted the venomous comment of ʿĀ'isha.

1 Abū Bakr: the Successor of the Messenger of God and the caliphate of Quraysh

The fundamental account about the assembly at the Saqīfat Banī Sā'ida, in which the succession of Abū Bakr to Muḥammad was decided, goes back to 'Abd Allāh b. al-'Abbās. All other reports make use of information drawn from it or are later elaborations of it.[1] Slightly variant versions with different chains of transmission are provided by Ibn Hishām, al-Ṭabarī, 'Abd al-Razzāq b. Hammām, al-Bukhārī and Ibn Ḥanbal. The *isnād*s meet in al-Zuhrī, who related the report of Ibn al-'Abbās on the authority of 'Ubayd Allāh b. 'Abd Allāh b. 'Utba b. Mas'ūd.[2] The account clearly reflects the characteristic point of view of Ibn al-'Abbās, and there is no reason to doubt the reliability of the chain of transmitters.[3]

Ibn al-'Abbās narrated that on the occasion of the last pilgrimage led by the caliph 'Umar, that is in Dhu l-Ḥijja 23/October 644, he, Ibn al-'Abbās, was visited at his campsite (*manzil*) at Minā by 'Abd al-Raḥmān b. 'Awf,[4] whom he used to assist in the recitation of the Qur'ān (*uqri'uhu l-Qur'ān*). 'Abd al-Raḥmān reported that he had witnessed the caliph on that day being approached by a man who addressed him: 'What are you going to do about a man who says: By God, if 'Umar b. al-Khaṭṭāb were to die, I would swear allegiance to so-and-so (*fulān*). By God, the oath of

[1] The account that Abū Mikhnaf received from the Khazrajite 'Abd Allāh b. 'Abd al-Raḥmān b. Abī 'Amra, quoted at length by al-Ṭabarī (I, 1837–44), has been briefly analysed by M. Muranyi ('Ein neuer Bericht über die Wahl des ersten Kalifen Abū Bakr', *Arabica*, 25 (1978),233–60, at 233–4). It was composed in the late Umayyad age and reflects clear awareness of the account of 'Abd Allāh b. al-'Abbās. The lengthy account discussed and partly edited by Muranyi (*ibid.*, 234–60) is later and filled with fictitious speeches and poetry.

[2] Ibn Hishām, *Sīrat sayyidina*, 1013–16; Ṭabarī, I, 1820–3; 'Abd al-Razzāq, *Muṣannaf*, V, 439–45; Bukhārī, *Ṣaḥīḥ*, *ḥudūd*, 31; Ibn Ḥanbal, *Musnad*, I, 55–6. The transmitters from al-Zuhrī are respectively: Ibn Isḥāq, Ma'mar, Ma'mar, Ṣāliḥ b. Kaysān, Mālik b. Anas.

[3] Caetani recognized the basic importance of the report. He ignored, however, the vital introductory section and considered the fact that the caliph 'Umar is quoted in direct speech to be 'suspicious' (*Annali*, II/1, 511–14).

[4] That 'Abd al-Raḥmān b. 'Awf accompanied 'Umar during the pilgrimage in 23/644 is independently confirmed (Ibn Sa'd, *Ṭabaqāt*, III/1, 95; *Annali*, VII, 549).

allegiance for Abū Bakr was merely a precipitate deal which then was carried out (*mā kānat bay'at Abī Bakr illā falta fa-tammat*).' 'Umar grew angry and said: 'God willing, I shall stand up tonight among the people and shall warn them about this clan who want to usurp the rule from the people (*fa-muḥadhdhiruhum hā'ulā'i l-rahṭa lladhīna yurīdūna an yaghṣubū l-nāsa amrahum*).' 'Umar's answer referring to the ambitions of 'this clan' leaves no room for doubt that the unidentified candidate for the caliphate was 'Alī. It was Ibn al-'Abbās' consistent contention that 'Umar was greatly worried about the Banū Hāshim arrogating the reign to themselves and depriving 'the people', Quraysh, of their collective right to it.[5]

'Abd al-Raḥmān b. 'Awf advised the caliph against speaking out immediately, since the pilgrimage season brought together the riff-raff and the rabble of the people who might misinterpret his words and cause serious trouble. 'Umar should wait until his return to Medina where he would be among the Companions of the Prophet, Muhājirūn and Anṣār, who could be trusted to understand his speech properly and to act accordingly. The caliph took the advice.

On the Friday after 'Umar's return to Medina, Ibn al-'Abbās hastened to the mosque and sat down next to the pulpit, eager to hear what the caliph would have to say. He confided to 'Umar's brother-in-law, Sa'īd b. Zayd b. 'Amr b. Nufayl,[6] who sat there already before him, that today the Commander of the Faithful would make a revelation he had never made before, a suggestion angrily brushed aside by the other. After stressing the special importance of his speech, the caliph first reminded the community that the punishment of stoning for adultery had been part of the Qur'ān and was practised by the Prophet; let no one go astray therefore by neglecting a religious duty (*farīḍa*) and saying: 'We do not find stoning in the Book of God!' 'Umar went on: 'We also used to recite in the Book of God: Do not desire fathers other than your own, for it is

[5] That 'Alī was alluded to in the report of Ibn al-'Abbās was generally assumed. In a version quoted by al-Balādhurī (*Ansāb*, I, 583) he is expressly named. According to Ibn Abi l-Ḥadīd (*Sharḥ nahj al-balāgha*, ed. Muḥammad Abu l-Faḍl Ibrāhīm ([Cairo] 1959–64), II, 25), al-Jāḥiẓ identified the person making the statement as 'Ammār b. Yāsir and the man intended as 'Alī. In another version quoted by al-Balādhurī (*Ansāb*, I, 581), al-Zubayr is identified as the one who said: 'If 'Umar were to die, we would pledge allegiance to 'Alī.' According to Ibn Abi l-Ḥadīd (*Sharḥ*, II, 25) some of the *ahl al-ḥadīth* rather asserted that Ṭalḥa was the unnamed candidate for the succession. If that were the case, however, Ibn al-'Abbās would hardly have suppressed his name, and Ṭalḥa was not backed by a clan trying to deprive Quraysh of their collective right. 'Alī is also correctly identified by E. Shoufani, *Al-Riddah and the Muslim Conquest of Arabia* (Toronto, 1972), 57.

[6] Sa'īd b. Zayd, of the Qurayshite clan of 'Adī, is counted among the ten of whom Muḥammad had testified that they would enter paradise. He was converted to Islam before 'Umar, whose grandfather, Nufayl, was his great-grandfather and to whose sister Fāṭima he was married. 'Umar's conversion took place in his house (Ibn Ḥajar, *Iṣāba*, III, 96–7).

infidelity for you.[7] Surely the Messenger of God also said: Do not extol me [excessively] as Jesus, son of Mary, has been extolled, but say: the servant of God and His messenger.'

Then 'Umar turned to the main subject. 'It has reached me that one of you has said: By God, if 'Umar b. al-Khaṭṭāb were to die, I would swear allegiance to so-and-so. Let no one be seduced to saying: The oath of allegiance for Abū Bakr was a *falta*, yet it succeeded. It was indeed so, but God has warded off its evil (*waqā sharrahā*).[8] Towards no one among you have necks been stretched out as for Abū Bakr. Whoever were to swear allegiance to any man without consultation (*mashwara*) among the Muslims, his oath of allegiance would be invalid and both of them would be subject to being killed.'

'Umar then gave an account of the events after the death of Muḥammad. While the Anṣār with their noble men (*ashrāf*) assembled in the Saqīfat Banī Sā'ida, 'Alī, al-Zubayr and 'those with them' gathered in Fāṭima's house. 'The Muhājirūn' joined Abū Bakr, and 'Umar suggested that they go to 'our brethren' the Anṣār. On the way there they met two 'upright' men of them who told them about the plotting of the Anṣār and advised them to turn back and settle their own affairs, but 'Umar insisted on proceeding.[9] They found the Anṣār and in their midst Sa'd b. 'Ubāda, distinguished Companion and chief of the Banū Sā'ida and of all of Khazraj, a sick man wrapped in a mantle. One of the Anṣār stood up and addressed the Muhājirūn: 'We are the Helpers and the legion (*katība*) of Islam, and you, company of Quraysh, are the clan of our Prophet, and a group (*dāffa*) of your people have made their way to us.' 'Umar realized that they intended 'to cut us off from our root [i.e. the Quraysh of Mekka] and to usurp the rule from us'. He wanted to give a speech which he had prepared in his mind, but Abū Bakr stopped him and spoke himself. He said what 'Umar had ready in his mind, only better than he could have done. Abū Bakr stated: 'O group of Anṣār, every virtue you mention of yourselves you are worthy of, yet the Arabs will not recognize the rule of

[7] See Nöldeke and Schwally, *Geschichte des Qorāns*, I, 248.

[8] 'Umar's admission that the election of Abū Bakr at the Saqīfat Banī Sā'ida had been a *falta* was obviously hard to accept for Sunnite supporters of the caliphate. In the version of Ibn al-'Abbās' account reported by al-Balādhurī (*Ansāb*, I, 584), 'Umar is quoted as saying: 'By God, the oath of allegiance for Abū Bakr was no *falta*. Rather, the Messenger of God set him up in his own place and chose him for his religion over anyone else stating: God and the believers refuse anyone but Abū Bakr.' This is quite remote from 'Umar's real views. Likewise in a report quoted by al-Balādhurī (*ibid.*, 581), the statement that the election of Abū Bakr was a *falta* is ascribed to al-Zubayr and is rejected by 'Umar as a lie.

[9] The later tradition rather suggests that the two men, 'Uwaym b. Sā'ida and Ma'n b. 'Adī, were opponents of Sa'd b. 'Ubāda and friends of Abū Bakr. They went to urge Abū Bakr and 'Umar to take action, and Ma'n b. 'Adī led them to the Saqīfa. See Ibn Abi l-Ḥadīd, *Sharḥ*, VI, 19.

anyone but this tribe of Quraysh. They are the most central [=noble] of the Arabs in lineage and abode. I am satisfied with either of these two men for you, so swear allegiance to whichever you want', and he took both 'Umar and Abū 'Ubayda b. al-Jarrāḥ by the hand. 'Umar commented that this was the only matter in his speech that he found loathsome, since it was inconceivable for himself to command a people that included Abū Bakr.

Al-Ḥubāb b. al-Mundhir of the Anṣār, a veteran of Badr, now proposed to settle the dispute fairly by agreeing that the Anṣār and the Quraysh should each choose an amir. As tempers flared and voices were raised, 'Umar told Abū Bakr: 'Stretch out your hand', and gave him the handshake of the pledge of allegiance (*bay'a*). The Muhājirūn and the Anṣār followed suit. 'Then we jumped upon Sa'd until one of them called out: 'You have killed Sa'd b. 'Ubāda.' I said: 'May God kill Sa'd!'' 'Umar concluded: 'By God, we did not find any case stronger than for the oath of allegiance to Abū Bakr. We feared that if we left the people without a pledge of allegiance they might after our departure suddenly make a pledge. We would then have had either to follow them in [a choice] with which we were not pleased, or to oppose them, and evil (*fasād*) would have resulted.'

Several aspects of the report deserve closer attention. 'Umar accused the Anṣār of plotting to seize the reign in succession to Muḥammad and to deprive the Muhājirūn of their right. Modern historians generally understand the initiative of the Anṣār in the same sense. This interpretation must, however, be questioned. The idea of the caliphate, the succession of Muḥammad in all but his prophetic mission, had not yet been born. It is difficult to see how the Anṣār, meeting alone among themselves, could have aspired to it. Like so many of the Arab tribes involved in the *ridda*, the Anṣār, while firm in their Muslim faith, no doubt considered their allegiance to Muḥammad as lapsing on his death. Expecting the political community founded by Muḥammad to fall apart, they met to restore their control over their own city. This is why they met without consulting the Muhājirūn. They assumed that these, having no longer any good reason to remain in Medina, would return home to Mekka. Those who might wish to remain in Medina would presumably accept the rule of the Anṣār. The suggestion that the Anṣār and the Muhājirūn should each choose a leader for themselves was evidently meant as a fair compromise proposal rather than a devious ploy to split the Muslim community, as it was seen by later Muslim tradition. It was only Abū Bakr and 'Umar, if his claim of having intended to give much the same speech as the former can be trusted, who were thinking in terms of a succession to Muḥammad entailing rule over all the Arabs. Such a succession, Abū Bakr argued, could be provided only by Quraysh since the Arab tribes would not submit to anyone else.

By those who assembled together with ʿAlī and al-Zubayr in the house of Fāṭima, ʿUmar evidently meant al-ʿAbbās and the Banū Hāshim. Of other prominent Companions, only Ṭalḥa is mentioned, probably erroneously, by Ibn Isḥāq as having joined the Hashimites.[10] That 'the Muhājirūn' at that time joined Abū Bakr was, on the other hand, an apologetic obscuration on ʿUmar's part. Aside from Abū Bakr, ʿUmar and his friend Abū ʿUbayda certainly none of the prominent Mekkan Companions was present at the Saqīfa meeting. It is reasonable to assume that the three men were accompanied by a few personal attendants, family members and clients. Yet not even a middle-ranking or lowly Mekkan Companion is recorded as having later claimed the honour of participating in this so crucial event for the future of Islam. Various later sources report the presence of Sālim, the client (*mawlā*) of Abū Ḥudhayfa, among the first who pledged allegiance to Abū Bakr at the Saqīfa.[11] Although his attendance is not confirmed by any of the early standard sources, the reports may well be reliable. Sālim, a Persian client first of a Medinan woman and then of her husband, the Mekkan Companion Abū Ḥudhayfa, who later adopted him, became himself a Companion at an early date. He was counted among both the Anṣār and the Muhājirūn and had close relations to both Abū ʿUbayda, with whom he was associated as a brother by the Prophet during the *mu'ākhāt*, and to ʿUmar.[12] ʿUmar is known to have held him in high esteem. Thus he could either have been present at the meeting as a member of the Anṣār or have come along with Abū ʿUbayda and ʿUmar as a close associate. The absence of the great majority of the Muhājirūn, in any case, explains the lack of reports independent of ʿUmar's own about the meeting and Ibn al-ʿAbbās' excited eagerness to hear it first hand. The Anṣār present were evidently reluctant to report about an ignominious defeat in a cause that soon came to be considered as anti-Islamic even by most of them. After the early deaths of Abū Bakr,

[10] Ibn Hishām, *Sīrat sayyidinā*, 1013. Ibn Isḥāq's mention of Ṭalḥa among those joining ʿAlī is not corroborated by other sources. It may well be a case of mistaken association of Ṭalḥa with al-Zubayr which is common in later sources because of their joint action in the Mekkan revolt against ʿAlī.

[11] Al-Mufīd, *al-Jamal wa l-nuṣra li-sayyid al-ʿitra fī ḥarb al-Baṣra*, ed. ʿAlī Mīr Sharīfī (Qumm, 1413/[1993]), p.91; al-Mawardī, *al-Aḥkām al-sulṭāniyya*, ed. R. Enger (Bonn, 1853), 6–7; Ibn Abi l-Ḥadīd, *Sharḥ*, VI, 18. According to al-Mufīd, the Muʿtazilite Abū ʿAlī al-Jubbāʾī held that Sālim was among the five men whose initial pledge of allegiance to Abū Bakr was binding for the rest of the Community. Ibn Abi l-Ḥadīd expresses his conviction (*thabata ʿindī*) that Sālim was the third man after ʿUmar and Abū ʿUbayda to swear allegiance to Abū Bakr before any of the leaders of the Anṣār. In this case, his master Abū Ḥudhayfa was presumably not present, for as a *mawlā* and adoptive son Sālim would hardly have preceded him.

[12] On Sālim see especially Ibn Saʿd, *Ṭabaqāt*, III/1, 60–2.

Abū 'Ubayda and Sālim, who was killed at al-'Aqrabā' during the *ridda* war, there was only 'Umar left to tell the true story.

'Umar judged the outcome of the Saqīfa assembly to be a *falta* because of the absence of most of the prominent Muhājirūn, including the Prophet's own family and clan, whose participation he considered vital for any legitimate consultation (*shūrā*, *mashwara*). It was, he warned the community, to be no precedent for the future. Yet he also defended the outcome, claiming that the Muslims were longing for Abū Bakr as for no one else. He apologized, moreover, that the Muhājirūn present were forced to press for an immediate oath of allegiance since the Anṣār could not have been trusted to wait for a legitimate consultation and might have proceeded to elect one of their own after the departure of the Mekkans.

Another reason for 'Umar to censure the Saqīfa meeting as a *falta* was no doubt its turbulent and undignified end, as he and his followers jumped upon the sick Khazrajī leader Sa'd b. 'Ubāda in order to teach him a lesson, if not to kill him, for daring to challenge the sole right of Quraysh to rule. This violent break-up of the meeting indicates, moreover, that the Anṣār cannot all have been swayed by the wisdom and eloquence of Abū Bakr's speech and have accepted him as the best choice for the succession, as suggested by Caetani.[13] There would have been no sense in beating up the Khazrajī chief if everybody had come around to swearing allegiance to 'Umar's candidate. A substantial number of the Anṣār, presumably of Khazraj in particular, must have refused to follow the lead of the Muhājirūn.

The question must arise as to the identity of the supporters of Abū Bakr and 'Umar who enabled them to impose their will on the assembly by force, given that there was only a handful of Mekkan Muhājirūn present and the Khazraj presumably made up the majority of the Anṣār. Caetani accepted the statement of Ibn Isḥāq that the Anṣārī Usayd b. Ḥuḍayr and his clan, the 'Abd al-Ashhal of Aws, had already joined Abū Bakr together with the Muhājirūn before the meeting and suggested that in fact all of the Aws opposed the initiative of the Khazraj from the beginning.[14] This is clearly at variance with 'Umar's account and quite unlikely. It would obviously not have been reasonable for the Khazraj, whatever their majority, to meet alone to decide the future government of the town. Usayd, however, appears to have decided soon after the arrival of the Muhājirūn to back Abū Bakr, carrying with him the 'Abd al-Ashhal and perhaps the majority of the Aws. Among the Khazraj, Bashīr b. Sa'd, rival of Sa'd b. 'Ubāda for the chieftainship, is said to have

[13] *Annali*, II/1, 528. [14] *Ibid.*, 510–11.

been the first to break ranks with him and to support Abū Bakr.[15] It is, however, most unlikely that he or the Aws, whatever their lack of enthusiasm for Saʿd, would have followed ʿUmar in physically attacking him.

Decisive for the developments probably was, as duly noted by Caetani, the arrival, during the meeting, of the Banū Aslam. They came forward, according to a report, 'in full number such that the streets became narrow through them. They then swore allegiance to Abū Bakr, and ʿUmar used to say: It was only when I saw the Aslam that I was certain of victory.'[16] The Banū Aslam, a branch of Khuzāʿa, were known as enthusiastic supporters of Muḥammad who had rewarded them for their loyalty by granting them the status of Muhājirūn irrespective of whether they had performed the *hijra* to Medina or stayed in their own territory. A sizeable number of them had come to dwell near Medina, ever ready to back the Prophet. They were known to be enemies of the Anṣār and thus could be counted upon to oppose Saʿd's aspiration to power.[17] It was evidently they who, by their large number, provided momentum to the *bayʿa* of Abū Bakr and who readily responded to the signal of ʿUmar to give the recalcitrant Saʿd b. ʿUbāda a mauling.

After the general pledge of allegiance, Abū Bakr sent to Saʿd b. ʿUbāda demanding that he do homage. Saʿd answered defiantly: 'No, by God, I shall not pledge allegiance until I have shot every arrow in my quiver at you [pl.] and fought you with those of my people and tribe who will follow me.' Bashīr b. Saʿd advised Abū Bakr not to press him since all of Khazraj and Aws would stand in solidarity with him before he be killed. When ʿUmar succeeded to the caliphate, he met Saʿd by chance and asked him whether he still held on to his position. His answer was: 'Yes, I do so, since 'this matter' [the reign][18] has devolved on you. Your companion, by God, was preferable in our eyes to you, and I have come to loathe your

[15] Ṭabarī, I, 1842–3. According to al-Zubayr b. Bakkār (quoted by Ibn Abi l-Ḥadīd, *Sharḥ*, VI, 18), Ibn Isḥāq reported that the Aws asserted that Bashīr b. Saʿd was the first of the Anṣār to swear allegiance to Abū Bakr while the Khazraj claimed that it was Usayd b. Ḥuḍayr. Each side thus blamed the other for breaking ranks first. The later standard view was that Bashīr b. Saʿd was the first of the Anṣār to back the supremacy of Quraysh and that he pledged allegiance to Abū Bakr even before ʿUmar. See the account in the *Kitāb al-Saqīfa* of Abū Bakr al-Jawharī, a pupil of ʿUmar b. Shabba (Sezgin, *Geschichte des arabischen Schrifttums* (Leiden, 1967–84), I, 322), in Ibn Abi l-Ḥadīd, *Sharḥ*, VI, 9–10, 40; see also Mufīd, *Jamal*, 91, 115.

[16] Ṭabarī, I, 1843; *Annali*, II/1, 514. Did the Aslam appear on the scene entirely by chance or were they warned of the threatening conduct of the Anṣār by Abū Bakr or ʿUmar? There is no information to answer the question.

[17] On the Banū Aslam see J. Wellhausen, *Muhammed in Medina: Das ist Vakidis Kitab alMaghazi in verkürzter deutscher Wiedergabe* (Berlin, 1882), 373–4; al-Wāqidī, *Kitāb al-Maghāzī*, ed. M. Jones (London, 1966), 939–40; *Annali*, II/1, 94–5, 180; M. J. Kister, 'Khuzāʿa', *EI* (2nd edn).

[18] The expression *hādha l-amr*, this matter, was often used in early texts in the meaning of the reign or the caliphate. When used in this sense, it will be placed in quotation marks.

neighbourhood.' 'Umar suggested that he leave, and Sa'd went to Syria, where he died in Ḥawrān, probably in the year 15/636. His grandson 'Abd al-'Azīz b. Sa'īd reported that the jinn were heard chanting from a well that they had killed the lord of Khazraj.[19] 'Abd al-'Azīz did not speculate whether the jinn were acting at the behest of God or of 'Umar. Sa'd b. 'Ubāda's son Qays was to become one of the most loyal supporters of 'Alī.

That many of the Anṣār failed to pledge allegiance to Abū Bakr at the Saqīfa meeting is affirmed at the end of an account of it by the Kufan Ibrāhīm al-Nakha'ī (d. 96/714–15). After mentioning that, following 'Umar's example, the people swore allegiance to Abū Bakr, he added: 'But the Anṣār, or some of them, said: We will not swear allegiance to anyone but 'Alī.'[20] Caetani dismissed this notice as 'of tendentious Shi'ite character'.[21] Ibrāhīm al-Nakha'ī is, however, not known for Shi'ite sympathies, and the tenor of the whole account is distinctly Sunnite. Whether the Anṣār raised the name of 'Alī during the Saqīfa meeting in response to Abū Bakr's bid for power must remain uncertain, though it is not unlikely.[22] That they did so soon after Abū Bakr's succession is proven by some of the elegiac poetry of the Khazrajī Anṣārī Ḥassān b. Thābit on the Prophet's death preserved by Ibn Isḥāq.

In one of his elegies Ḥassān bitterly complained about the fate of the Anṣār and of the Prophet's kin after his death:

> Woe to the Helpers (*anṣār*) of the Prophet and his kin (*rahṭ*) after his absence in the midst of the grave.
> The land has become narrow for the Anṣār and their faces have turned black like the colour of antimony.
> We have given birth to him and among us is his tomb, we have not denied the overflow of his bounty to us.
> God has honoured us through him and through him has guided his Anṣār at every moment of witness.[23]

19 Ibn Sa'd, *Ṭabaqāt*, III/2, 144–5; *Annali*, III, 623–4.

20 Ṭabarī, I, 1817–18.

21 *Annali*, II/1, 513.

22 Al-Zubayr b. Bakkār in his *al-Akhbār al-Muwaffaqiyyāt* (ed. Sāmī Makkī al-'Ānī (Baghdad, 1972)) quoted Ibrāhīm b. Sa'd b. Ibrāhīm (d. 183/799), great-grandson of 'Abd al-Raḥmān b. 'Awf, as stating that many of the Anṣār after the *bay'a* for Abū Bakr regretted their oath of allegiance. They blamed each other, mentioned 'Alī, and called out his name. This led to a renewed dispute with the Quraysh (Ibn Abi l-Ḥadīd, *Sharḥ*, VI, 18). Al-Zubayr b. Bakkār's detailed story about the conflict between the Anṣār and Muhājirūn (*ibid.*, 17–38) does not inspire confidence, however, and the poetry quoted in the context generally gives the impression of late fabrication. See further the discussion of the attitude of the Anṣār during and after the meeting at the *saqīfa* by I. Hasson, 'Contributions à l'étude des Aws et des Ḫazraǧ', *Arabica*, 36 (1989), 1–35, at 29–32. Hasson takes a more positive view with respect to the reliability of sources such as the *Muwaffaqiyyāt* of al-Zubayr b. Bakkār and the *Kitāb al-Saqīfa* of al-Jawharī than is taken here.

23 Ibn Hishām, *Sīrat sayyidinā*, 1025; A. Guillaume, *The Life of Muhammad: A Translation of Ibn Isḥāq's Sīrat Rasūl Allāh* (London, 1955), 797–8.

The claim of the Anṣār to have given birth to Muḥammad was based on the fact that the wife of Hāshim, mother of ʿAbd al-Muṭṭalib, was Salmā bt ʿAmr of the Banu l-Najjār of Khazraj. They viewed the Prophet and his kin, the Banū ʿAbd al-Muṭṭalib, as belonging to them as much as to Quraysh. They had provided shelter to Muḥammad on that basis at a time when few of them had become Muslims and when they could not be considered under any other obligation to protect him. The other Qurayshite Muhājirūn, who had no blood ties with them, were given shelter merely as followers of Muḥammad. Yet now they claimed the right to rule their former protectors while pushing aside the Prophet's kin. It was only natural that the Anṣār, in particular the Khazraj, should turn to ʿAlī as soon as a succession to Muḥammad was proposed. The faces of the Anṣār and of the Prophet's kin were thus, in Ḥassān's view, blackened by the usurpation of their title to the succession.

In another elegy for Muḥammad, Ḥassān attacked Abū Bakr and the Quraysh more openly:

> Would that on the day they covered him in the grave, removed him and cast earth on him
> God had not left a single one of us, and neither man nor woman had survived him.
> The Banu l-Najjār altogether have been humiliated, but it was a matter ordained by God:
> The booty (*fay'*) has been divided up to the exclusion of all the people and they have openly and wantonly squandered it among themselves.[24]

The last line clearly alludes to Abū Bakr's deprival of the Banū Hāshim of the Prophet's inheritance and of the Prophet's and their Qur'anic shares of the *fay'*.[25] Yet there was resignation in Ḥassān's caustic charge. The usurpation had been decreed by God. The resistance of the Anṣār did not last long.

The Banū Hāshim themselves did not remain silent. According to Ibn Isḥāq, one of the descendants of Abū Lahab responded to the boasting of Abū Bakr's clan Taym b. Murra about the success of their kinsman with the following lines of poetry:

> I did not think that 'this matter' would turn away from Hāshim, and then among them from Abū Ḥasan [ʿAlī].
> Is he not the first who prayed towards your *qibla* and the most learned of men about the Qur'ān and the norms (*sunan*)?
> The last of men in touch with the Prophet and the one whose helper was Gabriel in washing and shrouding him. Whatever is in them is in him, they have no doubts about him, but what there is of good in him is not in the people.

[24] Ibn Hishām, *Sīrat sayyidinā*, 1025; Guillaume, *Life of Muhammad*, 690.

[25] Guillaume, *Life of Muhammad*, (690 n.1) evidently did not understand the significance of the line when suggesting that its connection with the preceding was obscure.

What is it that has turned them away from him? Let us know! Surely, we
have been cheated in the most monstrous way.

The poem is probably by al-ʿAbbās b. ʿUtba b. Abī Lahab, who was married to Āmina, daughter of al-ʿAbbās b. ʿAbd al-Muṭṭalib,[26] and seems to have been a poet of no mean talent. Because of his close relationship to Muḥammad's uncle cursed in the Qurʾān, however, most of his poetry was forgotten, and what is left is attributed to others, in particular his son al-Faḍl.[27] ʿAlī sent to him and forbade him to recite this and similar poetry, commenting that the welfare of the faith was dearer to him than anything else.[28]

ʿUmar's justification of the quick election of Abū Bakr, in what amounted to a *falta*, because of the danger that the Anṣār might otherwise have sworn allegiance to someone with whom the Muhājirūn would not have been pleased, thus raises another question. Was it perhaps not only the possibility that the Medinans would have elected one of their own, but also that they might have put forward ʿAlī, that worried the Muhājirūn present and induced them to act without proposing a broad *shūrā* of all concerned? If ʿUmar's summary account can be trusted on this point, Abū Bakr in his speech did everything to avoid the case of ʿAlī being raised. He based the right of Quraysh to rule solely on the claim that only they would be obeyed by all the Arabs, not on their relationship to Muḥammad. In the later elaborations of the events at the Saqīfa, Abū Bakr is, in contrast, described as basing the case of Quraysh primarily on their being Muḥammad's kin. Such an argument, however, would have been an invitation to raise the question of the right of the Banū Hāshim as the closest kin of Muḥammad, a line ever pursued by Shiʿite polemicists

26 Zubayrī, *Nasab*, 28; Balādhurī, *Ansāb al-ashrāf*, ed. Muḥammad Bāqir al-Maḥmūdī (Beirut, 1974), III, 22.

27 The present lines were attributed by al-Yaʿqūbī (*Taʾrīkh*, ed. M. T. Houtsma (Leiden, 1883), II, 138) to ʿUtba b. Abī Lahab; by the Muʿtazilite Abū Jaʿfar al-Iskāfī in his *Kitāb al-ʿUthmāniyya* to the Umayyad Abū Sufyān b. Ḥarb (Ibn Abi l-Ḥadīd, *Sharḥ*, XIII, 232); by the Shaykh al-Mufīd in his *al-Irshād* (ed. Kāẓim al-Mūsawī al-Miyāmawī (Tehran, 1377/[1957–8])), 14–15, on the authority of the Basran Ibn ʿĀʾisha, d. 228/843 to Khuzayma b. Thābit al-Anṣārī; in his *al-Jamal* (p. 118) to ʿAbd Allāh b. Abī Sufyān b. al-Ḥārith b. ʿAbd al-Muṭṭalib; and in his *al-ʿUyūn wa l-maḥāsin* (see al-Murtaḍā, *al-Fuṣūl al-mukhtāra min al-ʿUyūn wa l-maḥāsin* (Najaf, 1365/[1964]), II, 61) to Rabīʿa b. al-Ḥārith b. ʿAbd al-Muṭṭalib; in the *Kitāb al-Saqīfa* (Dār al-Kutub al-Islāmiyya, n.d.) ascribed to Sulaym b. Qays al-Hilālī (p. 78) to al-ʿAbbās b. ʿAbd al-Muṭṭalib; and by Ibn al-Athīr (*Usd al-ghāba fī maʿrifat al-ṣaḥāba* [Cairo, 1285–7/1869–71], IV, 40) to al-Faḍl b. al-ʿAbbās b. ʿUtba b. Abī Lahab (who can hardly have been born at this time). I am obliged to Prof. H. Modarressi for providing some of these references. Ibn Ḥajar's note on al-ʿAbbās b. ʿUtba b. Abī Lahab (*Iṣāba*, IV, 30–1) is ambiguous as to whether he attributed the poetry to al-ʿAbbās b. ʿUtba or to his son al-Faḍl. For other examples of al-ʿAbbās b. ʿUtba's poetry being attributed to his son al-Faḍl see below, pp. 186, 221 with n.312.

28 Ibn Abi l-Ḥadīd, *Sharḥ*, VI, 21, quoting the *Muwaffaqiyyāt* of al-Zubayr b. Bakkār. See al-Zubayr, *Muwaffaqiyyāt*, 581.

against the Sunnite doctrine that the caliphs must be of Quraysh, the Prophet's broader kin. It is thus likely that Abū Bakr avoided the argument of blood relationship.[29]

Did the three Muhājirūn at the Saqīfa meeting act spontaneously or according to a concerted plan? More specifically, had they discussed the question of the succession among themselves even before Muḥammad's death and perhaps even agreed on putting forward Abū Bakr as the most reasonable choice, as Lammens' thesis of the 'triumvirate' seems to imply? Good arguments can be raised against such an assumption. An immediate one is provided by 'Umar's stand right after Muḥammad's death in which he vigorously denied it and harangued the assembled Muslims with warnings against accepting the false rumours spread by some hypocrites. According to Abū Hurayra, 'Umar asserted that Muḥammad had gone to his Lord as Moses had done, leaving his people for forty days and returning after he had been pronounced dead. Muḥammad would do likewise and would cut off the hands and feet of those who claimed that he was dead.[30] If there had been previous agreement, it would have to be assumed that 'Umar's action was calculated and planned in order to gain time. Abū Bakr's immediate repudiation of 'Umar's position shows that this was not the case. It rather seems that 'Umar was partly sincere in his apology on the next day to the Muslims assembled for the general *bay'a* that he had believed the Prophet would 'manage our affairs until he would be the last one of us (*sa-yudabbiru amranā ḥattā yakūna ākhiranā*)'.[31] Even later, during his caliphate, he confided to 'Abd Allāh b. al-'Abbās that he had been misled by Sūra II 143: 'Thus we have made them a community in the middle that you may be a witness about the people and the Messenger may be a witness about you' into thinking that the Prophet would remain among his community so that he would be the witness about their last acts.[32] 'Umar, to be sure, can hardly have not thought at all of the possibility that Muḥammad would die. It was a thought, however, that he, an impetuous and ardent champion of the cause of Islam, strove to keep off his mind. His reaction denying the Prophet's death was certainly spontaneous; he did not want to believe it.[33] 'Umar thus had scarcely envisaged the consequences of

[29] Caetani went further to deny that Abū Bakr argued for the right of Quraysh at all. He held that Abū Bakr was not elected for his kinship, but solely for his moral qualities (*Annali*, II/1, 540). That the exclusive right of Quraysh to the caliphate was instituted by Abū Bakr is, however, hardly questionable. [30] Ṭabarī, I, 1815–16. [31] *Ibid.*, 1828.

[32] *Ibid.*, 1829–30; Balādhurī, *Ansāb*, I, 568.

[33] Ibn Abi l-Ḥadīd (*Sharḥ*, II, 42–3) found it incredible that a man of 'Umar's rank could have failed to realize that the Prophet was dead and suggests that he tried to conceal it on his own initiative, fearing anarchy and rebellion and trying to calm the people. That 'Umar's public action was motivated by such fear and concern is obvious, but this does not mean that he personally must have been convinced that Muḥammad was dead. If that

Muḥammad's death, not to mention having agreed on plans for the succession.

Quite different was the case of Abū Bakr. Although he did not expect the death of Muḥammad when it happened, as is evident from his being away in his family home in al-Sunḥ,[34] he cannot have had any doubts that Muḥammad would some time die. As a consummate, coolly calculating Mekkan businessman and politician, closely involved in managing and planning the affairs of the Muslim community as the Prophet's trusted adviser, he must have carefully contemplated what would happen if the latter should die before him. Deeply committed to the commonwealth founded by Muḥammad in the name of Islam, he was most eager to see it continue to grow and expand its authority over all the Arabs and, as far as possible, beyond. If it was not to fall apart, the Prophet must have a political successor, a *khalīfa*. But who should he be? Abū Bakr had decided, no doubt well before Muḥammad's death, that he was the man. He also recognized that, without a nomination by the Prophet, he would have to neutralize potentially strong opposition in order to realize his ambition. Most obviously Muḥammad's own *ahl al-bayt*, who had been accorded a rank above the rest of the Muslims by the Qur'ān, would have to be prevented from putting forward their claim.

The initiative of the Anṣār gave Abū Bakr the opportunity for which he was looking. It was he who provoked the *falta* by proposing two candidates for election in a manoeuvre to have himself proposed. That his own proposal was not meant seriously was plain enough from his offering two nominations for the assembly to quarrel about. Abū Bakr was well aware that neither of the two candidates stood a chance of being accepted. Abū 'Ubayda, although a respected early Companion, did not have the prominence and stature to be seriously considered. He was present primarily as a close friend of 'Umar. 'Umar, although most closely associated with the Prophet, prominent in the community, and used to command, had just discredited himself by publicly denying the death of Muḥammad. Abū Bakr was sure that 'Umar, shattered by the loss of the Prophet and having since twice allowed himself to be pushed around by

had been the case, there would have been no reason for him to conceal it afterwards and to admit that he had been mistaken. It is evident that his honest admission damaged his political standing, at least temporarily, whereas a claim that he had in fact been acting in the interest of the community would have raised it. For later Muslims, no longer aware of the intense religious feeling of the approaching end of the world and of the closeness of the Hour created by the Prophet's message, it was naturally difficult to believe that 'Umar had been so 'naive'.

[34] Abū Bakr's home in al-Sunḥ was located among the houses of the Banu l-Ḥārith of Khazraj (Ibn Shabba, *Ta'rīkh al-Madīna*, 243; M. Lecker, *Muslims, Jews and Pagans: Studies in early Islamic Medina* (Leiden, 1995), 6). He had also an apartment opening into the Prophet's mosque where he could have stayed if he had expected Muḥammad's death.

Abū Bakr, would again defer to him. 'Umar took the hint and offered Abū Bakr the handshake of allegiance. Abū Bakr did not hesitate a moment to accept. He had what he wanted.

The precipitate move of the Anṣār to choose a leader among themselves was thus a true stroke of luck for Abū Bakr. It gave him the chance to make himself the spokesman for the continued unity of the Muslim community under a single leader which was threatened by the action of the Anṣār. Equally important from his point of view, it gave him the chance to secure an oath of allegiance to himself before there could be a general discussion about candidates for the succession. Abū Bakr was well aware that a *shūrā* of those most directly involved, Quraysh and the Anṣār, would not have been in his interest. It would have almost inevitably led either to failure or to the choice of 'Alī as the closest relative of Muḥammad. The great majority of the Anṣār would have backed 'Alī, if he had been proposed as a candidate for the succession, since they considered him, like Muḥammad, as partly belonging to them. Among Quraysh, the situation was evidently less clear cut. 'Umar's later assessment of it, as reported by Ibn al-'Abbās, that the Quraysh were not willing to countenance the hereditary reign of one clan which had already been privileged by having been divinely chosen for prophethood, carries some weight. There were certainly many who would not have liked the prospect of dynastic rule of the Prophet's family and who were flattered by Abū Bakr's initial claim that Quraysh was collectively entitled to the rule and that he was acting in their name. Once this claim had been made and Abū Bakr had secured the backing of a few dedicated men, it was apt to swing the majority support among Quraysh quickly behind him. But in a *shūrā* on the succession, the purely negative principle of avoiding dynastic rule and therefore excluding Muḥammad's kin from consideration would have been difficult to promote. Once the name of 'Alī had come up, the 'Abd Shams, one of the two most powerful clans of Quraysh, would have been honour bound by the tribal code of ethics to back him. For although the conflict between the Banū Hāshim and the Banū 'Abd Shams was older than Islam and the majority of the latter under Abū Sufyān had played a leading part in the opposition to Muḥammad, the two clans were nevertheless closely related. So long as the 'Abd Shams could not hope to put forward a candidate of their own, it would have been shameful for Abū Sufyān, the chief of 'Abd Shams, not to back 'Alī, especially since the Prophet had treated him and his clan most generously after the conquest of Mekka.

There is indeed good evidence that Abū Sufyān, immediately after the election of Abū Bakr, offered 'Alī his support in order to counter the decision. In a letter 'Alī later reminded Mu'āwiya of his father's offer, explaining that he, ʿAlī, had not accepted it because Abū Sufyān and his people had only recently been infidels and their involvement might have provoked division among the Muslims.[35] Western scholars have usually treated reports that Abū Sufyān in fact offered ʿAlī support against Abū Bakr, but was dismissed by him as a mere troublemaker, as sheer anti-Umayyad fiction.[36] Yet even if such reports reflect a bias against the father of the founder of the Umayyad dynasty and regardless of whether he actually made such an offer under the circumstances of Abū Bakr's *fait accompli*, they clearly show what was generally considered as reasonable on Abū Sufyān's part. The refusal of the Umayyad Khālid b. Saʿīd b. al-ʿĀṣ, one of the earliest converts to Islam and a prominent Companion, to swear allegiance to Abū Bakr when he returned from the Yemen to Medina a month after the latter's succession and his insistence on the rights of the Banū ʿAbd Manāf (including both Hāshim and ʿAbd Shams) are significant.[37] Khālid's brother Abān b. Saʿīd is also reported to have refused to swear allegiance to Abū Bakr in solidarity with the Banū Hāshim and to have done so only when these decided to swear allegiance.[38] The joint backing of the Anṣār and ʿAbd Shams for ʿAlī would no doubt have persuaded otherwise uncommitted clans and individuals to support his candidacy. The other powerful clan of Quraysh, Makhzūm, although certainly opposed to hereditary rule by the Banū Hāshim, would have found it extremely difficult to unite the opposition behind a counter-candidate.

The plain logic of dynastic succession would thus almost certainly have asserted itself in a general consultation. For the principle of heredity clearly provides the most natural, simple and uncontentious basis for

[35] Naṣr b. Mūzaḥim al-Minqarī, *Waqʿat Ṣiffīn*, ed. ʿAbd al-Salām Muḥammad Hārūn (Cairo, 1382/[1962]), 91; Balādhurī, *Ansāb al-ashrāf*, ed. Muḥammad Bāqir al-Maḥmūdī (Beirut, 1974), II, 281. Concerning the question of the authenticity of the letter see below, p. 210 n. 280.

[36] So *Annali*, II/1, 518. Caetani's contention that Abū Sufyān in fact contributed vitally to the election of Abū Bakr (*ibid.*, VII, 479) lacks any foundation.

[37] Ṭabarī, I, 2079–80; H. Loucel, 'Khālid b. Saʿīd', *EI* (2nd edn) In the case of Khālid b. Saʿīd, too, Sunnite tradition presents ʿAlī as a loyal supporter of Abū Bakr unable to understand how Khālid could have considered him as overpowered by Abū Bakr. He is quoted as stating: 'This is the order of God which He places wherever He wants' (Balādhurī, *Ansāb*, I, 588). Yet this was at a time when ʿAlī himself still refused to swear allegiance to Abū Bakr. Another prominent member of ʿAbd Shams who refused to swear allegiance to Abū Bakr and sided with ʿAlī was Abu l-ʿĀṣ b. al-Rabīʿ b. ʿAbd al-ʿUzzā b. ʿAbd Shams. He was married to Muḥammad's eldest daughter Zaynab before Islam, but became a Muslim only after having been captured by the Muslims first at Badr and again during a commercial trip to Syria. When he finally accepted Islam, Muḥammad allowed him to remarry Zaynab, who had come earlier to Medina. He accompanied ʿAlī during his expedition to the Yemen. After Fāṭima's death he gave ʿAlī his daughter Umāma, granddaughter of Muḥammad, in marriage. See Ibn Ḥajar, *Iṣāba*, VII, 118–20; *Annali*, II/2, 1239–40.

[38] See *Annali*, VIII, 345.

succession to power. It is because of this that it has been so widely accepted throughout human history. The common argument of Sunnite Muslims and western scholars that ʿAlī could not have been a serious candidate because of his youth and lack of experience compared to Companions such as Abū Bakr and ʿUmar is quite beside the point. It would be valid only after an initial agreement to exclude the principle of hereditary succession. But such an agreement, as Abū Bakr well realized, would have been virtually impossible to reach in a *shūrā*.

Abū Bakr's clear determination to seek the succession and to prevent the election of ʿAlī requires further explanation. Abū Bakr was at the time an old man who could not expect to enjoy his reign for long. He had apparently no sons or close relatives suited to succeed him.[39] Would it not have been more reasonable for him to back the succession of the Prophet's cousin and father of his grandsons in the expectation that ʿAlī, lacking political experience, would have continued to rely on Abū Bakr's counsel as Muḥammad had done? It was evidently the poor relationship, distrust and hostility between the two men that stood in the way of such a course. ʿAlī's stand in the affair of ʿĀ'isha's lost necklace and her unnoticed absence from the Muslim campsite, his advice to Muḥammad to divorce her and his attempt to press a confession of guilt out of ʿĀ'isha's maid had brought upon him the life-long hatred of the Prophet's favourite wife which she never made an effort to conceal. Abū Bakr must have shared much of her ill feeling, although he was too refined a politician ever to vent it in public. The disgrace of ʿĀ'isha would not only have stained the honour of his family but would also most likely have affected his own position of trusted friend of the Prophet. Rightly or wrongly, he no doubt assumed that ʿAlī was motivated by jealousy of his influence on Muḥammad and was trying to undermine it by accusing his daughter. Abū Bakr thenceforth saw in him a rival and an enemy. He could expect nothing

[39] Neither of Abū Bakr's two grown-up sons joined him at the time of his *hijra* to Medina. ʿAbd al-Raḥmān, the eldest son and full brother of ʿĀ'isha, was present at the battle of Badr on the side of the Mekkan enemies of Islam. He is said to have become a Muslim shortly before the conquest of Mekka. It is possible that he stood by Abū Bakr's father Abū Quḥāfa, who did not accept Islam until after the conquest. ʿAbd al-Raḥmān's relations with his father appear to have been strained, but he had later good relations with his sister. ʿAbd Allāh b. Abī Bakr, borne by a different mother, is said to have supplied his father and the Prophet with provisions and news while they were hiding in a cave before their *hijra*. Still later he used to visit Medina secretly bringing information about the Mekkans and was concealed by ʿĀ'isha. It is unknown when he definitely joined the Muslims. While fighting on the Muslim side at the siege of al-Ṭā'if, he was seriously wounded by an arrow. He died of the wound two years later at the beginning of his father's reign. Abū Bakr's third son, Muḥammad, was borne by Asmā' bt ʿUmays, the widow of ʿAlī's brother Jaʿfar, less than a year before Abū Bakr's accession. After Abū Bakr's death, Asmā' married ʿAlī. Muḥammad b. Abī Bakr thus grew up in ʿAlī's household and became an ardent partisan of his step-father.

good for himself or for 'Ā'isha if the succession fell to 'Alī. 'Alī would presumably have relied rather on his uncle al-'Abbās for political advice and would have reduced the station of 'Ā'isha. Abū Bakr thus had sound reason for seeking to prevent 'Alī's succession, aside from his personal ambition. Whatever 'Alī's motivation, his youthful folly in trying to interfere in the Prophet's marital relations thus cost him dearly. Aided by the precipitate move of the Anṣār, Abū Bakr could realize the designs which he must have been harbouring ever since the unfortunate affair.

In spite of 'Umar's claim that 'the necks of all Muslims were stretched out for Abū Bakr', the situation of the caliph was at first highly precarious, and not only because of the *ridda* of numerous tribes. In Medina 'Umar took charge of securing the pledge of allegiance of all residents. He dominated the streets with the help first of the Aslam and then the 'Abd al-Ashhal of Aws who, in contrast to the majority of Khazraj, quickly became vigorous champions of the new regime. The sources mention the actual use of force only with respect to the Companion al-Zubayr who had been together with some others of the Muhājirūn in the house of Fāṭima. 'Umar threatened to set the house on fire unless they came out and swore allegiance to Abū Bakr. Al-Zubayr came out with his sword drawn, but stumbled and lost it, whereupon 'Umar's men jumped upon him and carried him off.[40] There is some evidence that the house of Fāṭima was searched (*futtisha*). 'Alī is reported to have later repeatedly said that had there been forty men with him he would have resisted.[41] To what extent force was used in other cases must remain uncertain. In general the threat of it was probably sufficient to induce the reluctant to conform. Isolated reports about the use of force against 'Alī and the Banū Hāshim[42] who, according to al-Zuhrī, unanimously refused to swear allegiance for six months,[43] are probably to be discounted. Abū Bakr no doubt was wise enough to restrain 'Umar from any violence against them, well realizing that this would inevitably provoke the sense of solidarity of the majority of 'Abd Manāf whose acquiescence he needed. His policy was rather to isolate the Banū Hāshim as far as possible. 'Ā'isha's comment that the prominent people ceased to

[40] Or: seized his sword. See Ṭabarī, I, 1818.

[41] Minqarī, *Waq'at Ṣiffīn*, 163. According to the *Kitāb al-Safīna* of Abū Bakr al-Jawharī, 'Alī was led by 'Umar before Abū Bakr. He refused to pledge allegiance to him, arguing that he had a better title to the rule. Abū 'Ubayda tried to persuade him to change his mind on the basis that Abū Bakr was older and more experienced than he and that, if 'Alī survived him, he would certainly be most worthy to succeed because of his close kinship with the Prophet and his early merits. 'Alī insisted, however, that the authority of Muḥammad should not be removed from his house and did not pledge allegiance until after the death of Fāṭima (Ibn Abi l-Ḥadīd, *Sharḥ* ,VI, 11–12).

[42] See, for instance, Ṭabarī, I, 1819–20 where it is claimed that al-Zubayr and 'Alī were both forced by 'Umar to pledge allegiance. [43] *Ibid.*, 1825.

speak to ʿAlī until he acknowledged his mistake and pledged allegiance to Abū Bakr is significant. The Banū Hāshim thus found themselves in a situation strangely reminiscent of the boycott that the pagan Mekkans organized against them in order to force them to withdraw their protection from Muḥammad. This time, however, it was the Muslims putting pressure on them to abandon their support of ʿAlī who, in contrast to Muḥammad, gave in, surrendering his claim after the death of Fāṭima.

Crucial for Abū Bakr, however, was gaining the allegiance of the Mekkan Quraysh. With the loyalty of the Anṣār in doubt and many of the Arab tribes deserting, only Mekka, the former enemy city which had submitted to Muḥammad just two years before, could now save the Islamic commonwealth. In Mekka Abū Bakr could not rely on the use or threat of force. It was solely his diplomatic skills that counted. The Mekkans had since their surrender done very well under the rule of Islam. Muḥammad had treated them most generously and had appointed a number of their leading men, even though they had been among his most vigorous opponents, to powerful and lucrative positions as army leaders, governors and alms-tax collectors. The Mekkans had thus little reason to question the continuation of Islamic government in principle or to long for their former state of independence.[44] But Abū Bakr had more to offer them than Muḥammad could, or would, ever have done. The Islamic state was henceforth to be based on the rule of Quraysh over all Arabs. Their right to rule in the name of Islam derived from the claim that the Arabs would not obey anyone else. Abū Bakr had safeguarded their innate right by thwarting the ambitions of the Anṣār. The Anṣār, with whose backing Muḥammad had been able to humiliate them, would be put in their proper place and become, like the rest of the Arabs, subjects of Quraysh. Without a family or clan who could seriously aspire

[44] Not much is known about the events in Mekka at this time. According to Muṣʿab al-Zubayrī, the Mekkans, when learning of the death of Muḥammad, became agitated and were ready to apostatize from Islam. Then Suhayl b. ʿAmr of the Banū ʿĀmir stood up and delivered among them 'the like of Abū Bakr al-Ṣiddīq's speech in Medina, as if he had heard it'. The people calmed down and accepted his guidance. Their governor at the time was, according to al-Zubayrī, ʿAttāb b. Asīd of ʿAbd Shams (Zubayrī, *Nasab*, 418). Suhayl b. ʿAmr, well known as an orator, had been one of the most vigorous enemies of Muḥammad and Islam until the Muslim conquest of Mekka. He may have persuaded the Mekkans that now, after Muḥammad's death, Quraysh was destined to rule the Arabs in the name of Islam, just as Abū Bakr persuaded the Muslims in Medina. Suhayl and his family then joined the conquest of Syria where he and all of his sons were killed. The Banū ʿĀmir (b. Lu'ayy) of Quraysh were, it may be noted, traditionally closely allied to ʿAbd Shams and opposed to Hāshim. See further M. J. Kister, '. . . *illā bi-ḥaqqihi*, A Study of an Early *Ḥadīth*', *JSAI*, 5 (1984), 33–52, at 34–5. Kister quotes reports to the effect that Suhayl urged the Mekkans to pay their *zakāt* to their governor and promised to compensate them for any *zakāt* payment if Abū Bakr's government were to collapse.

to hereditary rule, Abū Bakr was truly their man, the caliph of Quraysh.

Abū Bakr's heavy reliance on the old Mekkan aristocracy for the leadership of the Muslim armies in the suppression of the *ridda* and the beginning of the conquests outside Arabia has been duly noted by E. Shoufani[45] and F. Donner.[46] In particular the two most powerful clans of Quraysh, Makhzūm and 'Abd Shams, were given preference. Among Abū Bakr's commanders in the *ridda* wars were 'Ikrima b. Abī Jahl of Makhzūm and Yazīd b. Abī Sufyān of Umayya, sons of the two former leaders of the Mekkan opposition to Muḥammad. Of Makhzūm were also Khālid b. al-Walīd and al-Muhājir b. Abī Umayya; of 'Abd Shams, Khālid b. Asīd b. Abi l-'Īs, Khālid b. Sa'īd b. al-'Āṣ and, by clientage, al-'Alā' b. al-Ḥaḍramī. Most of these Mekkan leaders had, to be sure, already been employed by Muḥammad in various functions. Yet their dominant position under Abū Bakr is put into proper relief by the complete exclusion of the Anṣār from leadership and the greatly reduced role of the early Muhājirūn. Among the Muslim army leaders during the *ridda* there was only one early Companion of Muḥammad, Shuraḥbīl b. Ḥasana, a confederate of the Banū Zuhra of Quraysh of South Arabian (Kinda) origin.

When Abū Bakr later laid the plans for the conquest of Syria, he appointed as the first commander Khālid b. Sa'īd b. al-'Āṣ, who had previously refused to swear allegiance for some time. The reason for this choice was certainly not that he was one of the earliest Companions, but rather that he was an Umayyad. When he was dismissed because of strong representations by 'Umar against him, Abū Bakr replaced him by the Umayyad Yazīd b. Abī Sufyān. It is evident that the caliph intended to give the 'Abd Shams a stake in the conquest of Syria. Abū Sufyān is known to have owned some land near Damascus before Islam.[47] The aim of gratifying the powerful Mekkan clan evidently outweighed in Abū Bakr's eyes the slight he had been dealt by Khālid b. Sa'īd. On the other hand, the role given to Abū 'Ubayda b. al-Jarrāḥ, who, as one of the two prominent Companions backing Abū Bakr at the Saqīfa assembly, could have expected a leading part, was quite limited. He was evidently not among the leaders of the three armies initially dispatched and in some accounts is not mentioned at all before the caliphate of 'Umar.[48] Most likely he was sent secondarily with some auxiliary troops to aid the first invading armies.[49] 'Umar later appointed him general commander in

[45] Shoufani, *al-Riddah*, 58–64.

[46] F. Donner, *The Early Islamic Conquests* (Princeton, 1981), 86–8.

[47] Al-Balādhurī, *Futūḥ al-buldān*, ed. M J. de Goeje as *Liber expugnationis regionum* (Leiden, 1866), 129; Donner, 96.

[48] Shoufani, *al-Riddah*, 140–3; Donner, *Conquests*, 114–15.

[49] M. J. de Goeje, *Mémoire sur la conquète de la Syrie* (Leiden, 1900), 25.

Syria. In initially sending Khālid b. al-Walīd to invade Iraq, Abū Bakr may have similarly had it in mind to give Makhzūm a stake in the conquest of that country.

With the Muslim armies mostly under the command of members of the old Mekkan aristocracy, Medina was virtually at the mercy of Muḥammad's recent enemies, especially during the *ridda*. If the leaders of Quraysh had chosen to conspire, they could have done away with the caliphate at a stroke. Abū Bakr's resolute rejection of 'Umar's demands for the dismissal, or at least censure, of Khālid b. al-Walīd for his un-Islamic conduct may have been motivated by more than just the recognition of his superior qualities as a military leader. Yet Abū Bakr could also be generally confident that the Mekkan leaders would co-operate, realizing that they would profit more than anyone else from the Qurayshite caliphate in the name of Islam.

It was the declared intention of Abū Bakr to follow as caliph the policies and practices of Muḥammad in every respect. He adopted the official title *khalīfat rasūl Allāh*, Successor or Vicegerent of the Messenger of God.[50] In order to comply with the Prophet's wishes, he immediately ordered the planned campaign towards the Syrian border area to go ahead, although the absence of the army would expose the caliphate, before it had been firmly established, to considerable danger. He insisted on retaining Usāma b. Zayd, son of Muḥammad's freedman, as the commander despite the unpopularity of this choice because of Usāma's youth and lack of experience. Breaking ranks with the Banū Hāshim, Usāma had evidently pledged allegiance to the caliph. Abū Bakr must have appreciated his stand at this time.

Abū Bakr also justified his immediate demand that all Arab tribes pay the Islamic alms-tax to him by his duty as Muḥammad's successor to follow the Prophet's path. The obligation of Muslims to pay a regular annual tax, rather than giving voluntary alms, seems to have been initiated in the year 9/630.[51] Ibn Sa'd gives a list of the first tax collectors sent out by Muḥammad in Muḥarram (April–May) to some tribes in the Ḥijāz and north-east of Medina. The impression is created that initially only a few loyal tribes were asked to pay the tax. A number of the tax

[50] The Muslim sources may be trusted in this respect; Abū Bakr wished to be seen as acting in the name of the Prophet. The assumption of P. Crone and M. Hinds (*God's Caliph: Religious authority in the First Centuries of Islam* (Cambridge, 1986), 19–22) that the title of *khalīfa* meant from the beginning *khalīfat Allāh*, vicegerent of God, takes no account of the historical situation and the different circumstances that induced 'Uthmān to adopt the title *khalīfat Allāh*.

[51] See for the following especially Shoufani, *al-Riddah*, 44–7. Shoufani's assumption that the first tax collectors were not sent out before the beginning of the year 10 H. and that no taxes were returned to Medina before Muḥammad's death seems untenable.

collectors were members of the tribes to whom they were sent, and it is unclear to what extent the rates of taxation were fixed.[52] During the pilgrimage season at the end of the year (February 631) the proclamation of the Sūra of Renunciation (*al-Barā'a*) was made that polytheists in general would no longer be granted protection and would be subject to Muslim attack unless they repented. Excepted were, however, those who had concluded pacts with Muḥammad and had kept them. These pacts were to be fulfilled until their expiration. While the pressure on the Arab pagans to submit to Islam and the Prophet was thus increased, the exception for treaty allies shows that Muḥammad was not yet prepared simply to impose Islam on all of them. The enforcement of the alms-tax was probably also handled with caution and discretion on the part of Muḥammad during the following, last, year of his life. There are no reports of any force used against tribes failing to pay, of which there must have been more than a few.

The significance of the alms-tax for the Arab tribes was indeed different from that of any other obligation previously imposed by Islam. Unlike the duty to pray, to fast, to join collectively in the *jihād* and to give voluntary alms as the Qur'ān and Muḥammad had demanded in the early days of Islam, the alms-tax potentially meant the surrender of tribal autonomy, the acceptance of tax officials with the right to inspect and assess private property, of governors with the right to force recalcitrant subjects. It meant the subjection of the tribes to a ruler or government, something the tribes had ever most vigorously resisted. Their fear of subjection no doubt contributed to the spread of opposition movements to Islam in the last year of Muḥammad's life.

At the beginning of Muḥarram 11/end of March 632, two months before his death, Muḥammad again sent out tax collectors to the tribes for the new year. The tribes named in the report were mostly the same as in the year 9/630, those relatively close to Medina and to Mekka.[53] In the outlying regions, it was evidently the Muslim governors who were generally responsible for the collection of the tax, but payment was probably largely voluntary and patchy.[54] The latent resentment against the levy came out into the open on the Prophet's death, as many of the loyal tribes offered to recognize Abū Bakr as his successor but refused payment of the alms-tax. Despite his precarious position, Abū Bakr immediately took a hard line in the matter. 'Umar, Abū 'Ubayda and

[52] There is evidence that the detailed rates of *zakāt* stipulated by Islamic law were not introduced before Abū Bakr. See J. Schacht, 'Zakāt' in *Encyclopaedia of Islam* (Leiden, 1913–38). [53] *Annali*, II/1, 575–6.

[54] For a list of the governors at the time of Muḥammad's death according to Sayf b. 'Umar see *ibid.*, 569–70, where a separate tax official is mentioned for Najrān. The alms-tax in these outlying regions may have been spent locally rather than being delivered to Medina.

Sālim, the client of Abū Ḥudhayfa, urged him to rescind the tax for the year and to treat the tribes loyal to Islam leniently in order to enlist their support for fighting those who had abandoned Islam.[55] Abū Bakr rejected any compromise on the tax, making it the yardstick for the loyalty of the tribes to Islam itself. Going well beyond any precedent set by Muḥammad, he insisted that those refusing payment of the tax were to be treated and fought as apostates, just like those who had abandoned Islam and those who had never accepted it. Abū Bakr's attitude was well summarized in the statement widely attributed to him in the sources: 'If they withheld only a hobbling-cord of what they gave the Prophet, I would fight them for it.'

Later Muslim scholars found it difficult to explain and justify Abū Bakr's conduct. 'Umar was quoted questioning the caliph as to his right to fight the tribes since the Prophet had said: 'I was ordered to fight people until they say that there is no god but God. If they say this, they safeguard themselves and their property from me.'[56] Some speculated that Abū Bakr must have been acting on the basis of a hadith quoting Muḥammad as telling a tax collector who had been sent back empty-handed to him by a bedouin: 'Return to him, and if he does not give you the tax, cut his head off!'[57] Others argued that the Companions were calling the withholders of the tax apostates merely metaphorically. In reality they were Muslim rebels and as such deserved to be fought. Yet while later lawyers such as al-Shāfiʿī might be prepared to consider peaceable Muslims refusing to fulfil a previously accepted religious obligation as rebels whose blood could legitimately be shed, such a notion of 'rebellion' had in reality no basis in the Qur'ān[58] or the practice of the Prophet but arose out of the caliphate as conceived by Abū Bakr. Although the impact of Muḥammad's authority on the lives of the Muslims had steadily widened, it had remained essentially a moral authority. The Qur'ān frequently admonished them to obey God, the Prophet and those in command among them, and threatened the disobedient with severe divine punishment. The problem of nominal or lukewarm Muslims who resisted and contravened many of his orders and decisions was a serious one for Muḥammad, as is evident from the numerous denunciations of hypocrites (*munāfiqūn*) in the Qur'ān. Yet the Qur'ān did not sanction the

55 *Ibid.*, 572–3.

56 Shoufani, *al-Riddah*, 102. See further the detailed study of the dispute about Abū Bakr's conduct by Kister, '. . . *illā bi-ḥaqqihi*'.

57 *Annali*, II/1, 572.

58 The Qur'anic proof text for the treatment of Muslim rebels (*bughāt*) was Sūra XLIX 9: 'If two groups of the believers fight, conciliate (*aṣliḥū*) between them, but if one of them transgresses (*baghā*) upon the other, fight the one which transgresses until it returns to the order of God. Then if it returns, conciliate between them with justice and act fairly.' It is evident that the verse could not be applied to the 'rebel' tribes.

shedding of their blood or physical coercion of them. By Qur'anic standards, Abū Bakr might at most have castigated the tribes withholding the alms-tax as hypocrites. He could not make war on them either as apostates or as rebels.

Behind the front of merely claiming his due as the vicegerent of the Prophet, Abū Bakr thus brought about a radical change of policy. The full significance of his affirmation that the caliph must be of Quraysh because the Arabs would obey none but them now became apparent. The caliph was to be not so much the religious leader of the *umma*, the community of Islam, as Muḥammad had been, but the ruler of all Arabs, commanding their obedience in the name of Islam. For this reason peaceable Muslims withholding the alms-tax from the caliph, genuine renegades and other Arabs who had never become Muslims were all to be classed as apostates and to be fought until they would submit to both Islam and the rule of the caliph of Quraysh.

Among the official titles of the later caliphs, *amīr al-mu'minīn*, Commander of the Faithful, was the preferred and most commonly employed one.[59] According to historical tradition, it was 'Umar who first adopted it. It reflected most closely the concept of the caliphate established by Abū Bakr. The caliph was primarily the ruler of the faithful. Quraysh provided the ruling class, his aides, and the other Arab tribes were to be his subjects. Abū Bakr set out with unbending determination to subdue them.

The early Companions including even 'Umar, a man deeply committed to the expansion of the authority of Islam by force, initially had misgivings, especially about the flagrant aggression against fellow Muslims. Had not the Qur'ān admonished the Muslims that they were brothers and should strive to settle their conflicts by conciliation? Abū Bakr could again count on the backing of the Quraysh, who readily saw the benefits that the subjugation of the Arabs would bring for them. In order to secure their caravan trade, Quraysh had long relied on alliances with some Arab tribes. Yet such alliances with autonomous tribes were by nature unstable and often meant sharing of material benefits and the enmity of other tribes. The subjugation of all Arabs proposed by the caliph offered them safe and unimpeded trade relations and opened up new sources of material gain as leaders of Muslim armies and future governors and tax officials in the subjugated lands. Quraysh pursued the war against the 'apostates' with enthusiasm. The spirit with which it was waged is clearly reflected in the cold-blooded execution of Mālik b. Nuwayra and others of the Banū Yarbū' after their surrender and confession of Islam and in

[59] Crone and Hinds, *God's Caliph*, 11.

the appropriation of his wife by Khālid b. al-Walīd. Earlier in the year Mālik had been entrusted by Muḥammad with the collection of the alms-tax among his tribe. When he learned of the Prophet's death he returned the camels gathered by him to his fellow tribesmen or, according to another report, raided and drove off the camels collected from various tribes as alms. According to both major accounts, Abū Bakr himself, infuriated by Mālik's evident refusal to recognize him as the legitimate successor of Muḥammad, instructed Khālid to kill him if he could lay his hands on him.[60]

Abū Bakr's front of meticulously following the practice and precedents set by the Prophet in every respect was most difficult to maintain in his treatment of his predecessor's kin, the Banū Hāshim. It was evident that the primary purpose of establishing caliphal rule on a sound basis was inconsistent with maintaining the privileged status of Muḥammad's *ahl al-bayt*, of applying the Qur'anic rules of inheritance to them, and of continuing to pay their Qur'anic shares of the war booty and the *fay'*. Abū Bakr's solution was both radical and ingenious. According to 'Ā'isha's account, he told Fāṭima and al-'Abbās when they came to claim their inheritance from Muḥammad, and in particular his land in Fadak and his share of the land of Khaybar: 'As for me, I have heard the Messenger of God say: "We [the prophets] do not have heirs (*lā nūrith*). Whatever we leave is alms (ṣadaqa). The family of Muḥammad (*āl Muḥammad*) can eat from that property." Surely, by God, I would not leave any matter undone which I have seen the Messenger of God do.'[61] Abū Bakr's reply solved the problem of the *ahl al-bayt* in one stroke without his losing face. Not only had Muḥammad disinherited his family, he had also specifically affirmed that after his death his family should, if in need, accept alms which he had strictly forbidden them during his life because of their status of purity. As recipients of alms like ordinary Muslims, there was also no longer any justification for paying them their Qur'anic share of booty and *fay'*. All this the Prophet had confided to Abū Bakr, and no one else, thus confirming that he was his chosen successor charged with implementing his instructions. The daughter of the Prophet must have

[60] See E. Landau-Tasseron, 'Mālik b. Nuwayra' *EI* (2nd edn). The account of the fiction writer Sayf b. 'Umar, according to which Mālik backed the prophetess Sajāḥ, can be discounted, in spite of Caetani's acceptance of it (*Annali*, II/1, 654). 'Umar and other Muslims would hardly have protested against Khālid's treatment of someone 'who had become a true apostate'.

[61] Ṭabarī, I, 1825; Ibn Shabba, *Ta'rīkh al-Madīna*, 196–7. The report transmitted by Ibn Lahī'a claiming that Abū Bakr granted Fāṭima the palm grove of al-A'wāf out of the property of the Prophet in Medina (Ibn Shabba, *Ta'rīkh al-Madīna*, 211) is certainly unreliable.

been dumbfounded. Not even she could openly question the word of her father's chosen successor. According to 'Ā'isha, she henceforth kept away (*hājarat*) from Abū Bakr and did not speak to him again about the matter until she died six months later. 'Alī buried her at night and did not inform the caliph of her death.[62]

While the Prophet's daughter and kin were thus disinherited and demoted from their rank of religious purity, his widows were treated comparatively better. They obviously also could not be given an inheritance from Muḥammad's land in Fadak and Khaybar, which Abū Bakr claimed as public property. 'Urwa b. al-Zubayr reported, on the authority of 'Ā'isha, that the widows intended to send 'Uthmān to Abū Bakr to ask for their share of inheritance from Fadak and Khaybar, but 'Ā'isha reproached them: 'Don't you fear God? Have you not heard the Messenger of God say: "We do not have heirs; whatever we leave is alms. This money is for the Family of Muḥammad, [to provide] for them [in case of] misfortune and for their hospitality (*li-nā'ibatihim wa-ḍayfihim*). When I die it will belong to the ruler (*walī l-amr*) after me." ' The women desisted.[63] They no doubt understood that they would fare better if they admitted having heard the Prophet say so. Abū Bakr decided that they could keep their dwellings. In order to protect him against a possible charge that he acted arbitrarily with what Muḥammad had left for the public treasury, later tradition asserted that the Prophet had made a bequest of the houses to his wives.[64] Unlike the status of purity of the Prophet's kin, that of his wives was not to lapse after his death. No man was allowed to marry them. The highest respect was due to the 'Mothers of the Faithful'. They were now truly the only *ahl al-bayt* of Muḥammad whose purification from all filth was guaranteed by Sūra XXXIII 33. Abū Bakr recognized his obligation to provide generously for the widows.[65] To 'Ā'isha, as Muḥammad's favourite wife and daughter of his chosen successor, belonged the first place. Abū Bakr granted her some lands in the 'Āliya quarters of Medina and in al-Baḥrayn. The property in Medina was said to have been part of the land of the Banu l-Naḍīr which Abū Bakr had been given by Muḥammad.[66]

62 Ṭabarī, I, 1825; Ibn Shabba, *Ta'rīkh al-Madīna*, 197.

63 Balādhurī, *Futūḥ*, 30; Ibn Ḥanbal, *Musnad*, VI, 262.

64 Ibn Sa'd, *Ṭabaqāt*, III, 87, VIII, 120; *Annali*, II/1, 521.

65 Abū Hurayra remembered that Muḥammad, while leaving all his property as alms, had not completely forgotten his wives. He reported hearing the Prophet say: 'My heirs (*warathatī*) shall not divide up a single dinar or dirham among themselves. Whatever I leave, after sustenance (*nafaqa*) for my wives and provision for my agent [executor of my will, *mu'nat 'āmilī*], shall be alms' (Ibn Sa'd, *Ṭabaqāt*, II/2, 86).

66 *Ibid.*, III/1, 138; Abbott, *Aishah*, 85.

From a political point of view, the confiscation of the Prophet's extensive land holdings, from which he himself had partly financed the Muslim military efforts, was certainly a necessity. The diplomatic skill with which Abū Bakr carried out the measure, asserting that the Prophet himself had left all his property to the public treasury, matched his clever political manoeuvre at the Saqīfa assembly. Ḥassān b. Thābit's protest against the usurpation of the Prophet's *fay'* quickly ceased and was forgotten. The prominent Companions would soon be vying with each other in attesting that they, too, had heard Muḥammad say that prophets have no heirs and that, on their death, their belongings become alms. Abū Bakr's policy of isolating the Banū Hāshim without the use of force proved a full success. After six months, by the time of Fāṭima's death, Abū Bakr's victory seemed complete. Yet the news of it and of her clandestine burial at night, in order to prevent the caliph's attendance, must have shocked him. Whatever his satisfaction about the humiliation of his personal enemy 'Alī, the realization of the deep offence that his political machinations and treachery had caused the daughter of the man whose best and most sincere friend he was acclaimed to be by the public, the awareness of her death in a state of embitterment, perhaps hastened by his conduct, could not easily be brushed off his conscience.[67]

'Ā'isha reported: after Fāṭima's death, the few prominent men who had continued to see 'Alī while she was alive turned away from him. 'Alī humbly sued (*ḍara'a*) for reconciliation with Abū Bakr, sending him word: 'Come to us, but let no one be with you.' Knowing 'Umar's toughness (*shidda*), 'Alī did not want him to come along. 'Umar advised Abū Bakr not to go alone, but the latter insisted: 'By God, I shall go to them alone, what could they do to me?' The caliph thus came alone to 'Alī, who had assembled the Banū Hāshim in his house. 'Alī rose and,

[67] The Kufan loyalist 'Āmir al-Sha'bī, evidently stung by the Shi'ite contentions that the Prophet's daughter died in anger at Abū Bakr, countered with the following story: when Fāṭima fell ill Abū Bakr came to visit her and asked for permission to enter. 'Alī told Fāṭima: 'There is Abū Bakr at the door, will you not permit him to enter?' She answered: 'And you prefer this?' He said: 'Yes.' Abū Bakr entered, apologized to her, and talked with her. She was satisfied with him (Ibn Sa'd, *Ṭabaqāt*, VIII, 17). Yet what was there to apologize for if he had simply said the truth? The same tendency is also apparent in another report of al-Sha'bī transmitted by 'Umar b. Shabba. Al-Sha'bī narrated that 'Umar and Khālid b. al-Walīd, on Abū Bakr's order, went to Fāṭima's house in order to get al-Zubayr and 'Alī to pledge allegiance to Abū Bakr. 'Umar used force against both men, who were then led before Abū Bakr. Fāṭima loudly protested against the violence committed on the Family of the Messenger of God. After al-Zubayr and 'Alī pledged allegiance, Abū Bakr visited her and interceded on behalf of 'Umar. She accepted his apologies and expressed her satisfaction with 'Umar (Ibn Abi l-Ḥadīd, *Sharḥ*, II, 57, VI, 48–9).

after giving due praise to God, said: 'What has prevented us from pledging allegiance to you, Abū Bakr, was neither denial of your excellence, nor consideration of you as unworthy of any bounty which God has conveyed to you. Rather we held that we had a right in "this matter" which you [pl.] have arbitrarily seized (*istabdadtum*) from us.' 'Alī then mentioned his kinship (*qarāba*) with the Messenger of God and the right of kin and continued until Abū Bakr wept. When he finished, the caliph pronounced the confession of faith (*shahāda*) and in turn gave due praise to God. Then he said: 'By God, my link to the kinship of the Messenger of God is dearer to me than my own kinship. Surely, I have not sought in these chattels which have come between me and you anything but the good. But I have heard the Messenger of God say: We have no heirs, whatever we leave is alms. The family of Muḥammad may only eat from this money. I seek refuge with God lest I remember anything which Muḥammad, the Messenger of God, did in respect to it, yet fail to do it.' 'Alī promised his public pledge of allegiance for the evening. When the afternoon prayer was over, Abū Bakr turned to the assembled people and offered some excuses for 'Alī. Then 'Alī rose and extolled the right of Abū Bakr, mentioning his excellence and prior merit (*sābiqa*). He went forward to the caliph and pledged allegiance to him. The people hastened towards 'Alī, congratulating him: 'You have hit the mark, well done.' 'Ā'isha added: 'The people thus drew near to 'Alī when he drew near to the truth and what is proper.'[68]

'Alī's public act of submission put an end to the isolation of the Banū Hāshim and, on the surface, closed the ranks of the Muslims in support of Abū Bakr. Yet reconciliation there was none and could not be. Each of the two men looked through the other's motives and thoughts all too well to believe his reassuring words and gestures. Under the circumstances, 'Alī could see nothing but hypocrisy in Abū Bakr's tears and protestations of his love for the Prophet's kin. He knew that the caliph would continue doing all he could to keep the Banū Hāshim away from power and influence and above all to prevent him, 'Alī, from ever succeeding to the caliphate. Abū Bakr likewise understood the insincerity of the younger man's recognition of his prior title to the succession of Muḥammad and knew that 'Alī, if ever given the opportunity, would disavow the legitimacy of his caliphate of Quraysh and establish his own based on the rights of Muḥammad's *ahl al-bayt*. There could be no relationship of trust between them. 'Alī continued to keep away from

[68] Ṭabarī, I, 1826–7.

the caliph, and the latter was hardly eager to draw him into his company.[69]

While predominant Sunnite doctrine has come to affirm that the Prophet died without having named a successor and that Abū Bakr was elected by the Muslim community at the Saqīfa, a minority of prominent scholars, among them al-Ḥasan al-Baṣrī, Ibn Ḥazm and Ibn Taymiyya, have always held that Abū Bakr was chosen as successor by Muḥammad. There is strong evidence that the latter view was officially backed during Abū Bakr's caliphate and that it was 'Umar who insisted that the Prophet had died without naming a successor. This is clearly implied in a comment of Abū Bakr's grandson al-Qāsim b. Muḥammad on the hadith of his aunt 'Ā'isha, according to which the Prophet just before his death, when hearing 'Umar pronounce the *takbīr* in the public prayer, had said: 'Where is Abū Bakr? God refuses this as do the Muslims.' Al-Qāsim commented: 'If it were not for something 'Umar said at the time of his death, the Muslims would not doubt that the Messenger of God appointed Abū Bakr as his successor (*istakhlafa*). But he ['Umar] said at his death: If I appoint a successor, someone better than myself [Abū Bakr] has appointed a successor. And if I leave them [i.e. the Muslims to choose the successor], someone better than myself left them [to choose]. Thus the people knew that the Messenger of God did not appoint anyone his successor, and 'Umar cannot be accused [of bias] against Abū Bakr.'[70] Abū Rāfi' al-Ṭā'ī, who had been converted to Islam by Abū Bakr and accompanied him during the raid of Dhāt al-Salāsil in the year 8/629, is quoted as reporting that he asked Abū Bakr later about the *bay'a* for him at the Saqīfa. Abū Bakr told him that it was 'Umar's reminder to the people that the Prophet had ordered Abū Bakr to lead the prayer during his illness that swayed them to swear allegiance to him.[71] The oath of allegiance thus merely confirmed Muḥammed's previous choice. 'Ā'isha,

[69] Later Sunnite sources on Abū Bakr's caliphate, especially Sayf b. 'Umar, mention 'Alī on various occasions as giving advice to the caliph (see *Annali*, II/1, 584, 594–5, 597, II/2, 1116, 1150, 1197). The unreliability of these reports is evident especially since most of the occasions mentioned were during the six months before 'Alī's pledge of allegiance. 'Alī is thus described as, together with 'Umar, urging the caliph not to lead the Muslim army in person at Dhu l-Qaṣṣa (*ibid.*, II/1, 594–5) and as being put in charge, together with al-Zubayr, Ṭalḥa and 'Abd Allāh b. Mas'ūd, of the the defences of Medina (*ibid.*, 597). The traditionalist Sunnite historian Ibn Kathīr insisted on the basis of such reports that 'Alī swore allegiance to Abū Bakr immediately after the Saqīfa assembly and that his pledge of allegiance after Fāṭima's death was merely an act of confirmation (*bay'a mu'akkida*), necessitated by the disloyalty of Fāṭima whose anger at Abū Bakr Ibn Kathīr found incomprehensible and inexcusable (*al-Bidāya*, V, 249–50, 286–7). But then, Ibn Kathīr commented with an anti-Shi'ite edge, Fāṭima was merely a woman who could not hope for infallibility (*hiya imra'a min al-bashar laysat bi-rājiyat al-'iṣma*, V, 249). 'Ā'isha's account, however, is incompatible with such an interpretation.

[70] Ibn Hishām, *Sīrat sayyidinā*, 1010.

[71] Ibn Ḥanbal, *Musnad*, I, 8. Abū Bakr added that he accepted out of fear that there might be discord (*fitna*) leading to apostasy.

as has been seen, consistently maintained that Abū Bakr was chosen by Muḥammad for the succession and apparently never mentioned the events at the Saqīfa. Only when asked pointedly whom the Prophet would have appointed if he had made an appointment she replied: 'Abū Bakr'; adding, upon further questioning: 'After him 'Umar and then Abū 'Ubayda b. al-Jarrāḥ.' There she stopped.[72]

Since Abū Bakr did not view the caliphate as an elective office, it was only natural that he appointed, without prior consultation, his successor, 'Umar b. al-Khaṭṭāb. Only after he had made up his mind is he reported to have confidentially asked 'Abd al-Raḥmān b. 'Awf and 'Uthmān for their opinions. The former expressed some reservations on account of 'Umar's well-known harshness (*ghilẓa*). 'Uthmān answered more diplomatically that 'Umar's inside was better than his outside and that, in any case, 'there is no one like him among us'.[73] Ṭalḥa is reported, after the official announcement, to have protested at the ill caliph's bedside against the choice of 'Umar because of the latter's ill treatment of the people even during Abū Bakr's reign. Abū Bakr, however, angrily rejected this criticism, declaring 'Umar the best of God's people.[74]

While some of the details may be unreliable, the tenor of these reports probably reflects the situation correctly, and the fact that Abū Bakr appointed his successor rather than leaving the choice to the Muslim community cannot seriously be doubted. In spite of the prominent part played by 'Umar in Abū Bakr's reign, he could not have simply taken over and been universally recognized as *de facto* caliph as suggested by Caetani and Levi della Vida.[75] For while the choice of 'Umar certainly must have appealed to many strict Muslims who appreciated his uncompromising loyalty to Islam and his vigorous insistence on enforcing its norms on everybody, he was far from popular. It was not only some of the early Companions, whom Caetani accused of petty jealousy, incompetence and unjustifiable personal ambition, who had misgivings about 'Umar. More importantly, the Qurayshite aristocracy, on whose support Abū Bakr had built the caliphate and who were now firmly in control of the Muslim armies, would hardly have accepted their old opponent 'Umar without formal appointment by Abū Bakr, whom they had come to respect. Khālid b. al-Walīd, in particular, must have been aware that his days in powerful leadership would now be numbered.

Abū Bakr, on the other hand, realized that he could not afford to leave the succession open at a time when the Muslim armies were engaged in the decisive battles for the conquest of Syria. Despite the stunning

[72] Muslim, *Ṣaḥīḥ*, *Faḍā'il al-ṣaḥāba*, 9. [73] Ṭabarī, I, 2137; *Annali*, III, 88.
[74] Ṭabarī, I, 2143–4; *Annali* III, 85.
[75] *Annali*, III, 128; G. Levi della Vida, "Omar b. al-Khaṭṭāb', *EI*.

success of his policies, the caliphate was, only two years after its foundation, far from being safely established and a divisive election for a successor might have been fatal. He recognized that above all he must prevent any discussion of the rights of the family of the Prophet just as he had done before. For while now, given the vested interest of all of Quraysh in the caliphate, an easy election of ʿAlī was much less likely, his name could still have served as the rallying point of the opposition in the absence of an obvious candidate.

From Abū Bakr's point of view, the choice of ʿUmar almost imposed itself, despite their substantial differences of opinion in political questions. Among the early Companions, only ʿUmar was really closely associated with him and involved in the daily running of the government. Abū Bakr owed him a considerable debt. ʿUmar had made the coup at the Saqīfa in his favour possible and had brought Medina firmly under control for him. Having backed Abū Bakr's concept of the caliphate of Quraysh from the outset with enthusiasm, he could be trusted not to jolt its foundations, whatever change of direction he might introduce. ʿUmar continued to be in effective control of Medina and was presumably not the man to cede his power to any of the other early Companions. The only serious alternative would perhaps have been Khālid b. al-Walīd, now at the peak of his popularity after his recent victories. Khālid would have clearly been preferred by the Mekkan aristocracy and would have had the backing of the Muslim armies. ʿUmar, his personal enemy, would have been unable to put up any resistance to him. Whether Abū Bakr ever seriously considered the alternative must remain a speculative question. When the time for the decision came, Khālid was in command in Syria and apparently indispensable for the war effort. The choice of ʿUmar was the most reasonable.

2 ʿUmar: Commander of the Faithful, Islamic meritocracy, consultation, and Arab empire

The privileged position of ruling the Islamic state which Abū Bakr had allotted Quraysh had no foundation in the Qur'ān. In the early Mekkan Sūra (CVI) addressed to them, the Quraysh were pointedly admonished to serve the Lord of the Kaʿba in gratitude for the prosperity and safety He had granted them. During most of Muḥammad's mission, the majority of Quraysh in Mekka were his staunchest opponents, the unbelievers (*kuffār*) and polytheists (*mushrikūn*) unequivocally condemned by the Holy Book. The Muhājirūn, those who left their homes to join Muḥammad in Medina in support of the cause of Islam, were greatly praised in the Qur'ān, given hope for God's mercy (II 218), and promised reward on earth and in the hereafter (XVI 41). By Muhājirūn the Qur'ān, however, meant not only the Mekkan, Qurayshite emigrants, but equally bedouin tribesmen and others who joined the Prophet from all over Arabia. Although more often mentioned in the Qur'ān than the Anṣār, the Muhājirūn were put strictly on a par with them (VIII 72–4, IX 100, 117) and nowhere were they given a preferred rank above them. The poor of the Muhājirūn were granted a share of the estates of the Banu l-Naḍīr on the grounds that they had been expelled from their homes and property, not because they stood higher in merit than the Anṣār (LIX 8-9). The Qur'ān, however, clearly accorded a higher religious merit on the basis of early conversion to Islam, a principle favouring the early Mekkan, mostly Qurayshite, Companions of Muḥammad. The Muslims joining Islam after the early Muhājirūn and the Anṣār, who had sheltered them, were lower in religious rank (VIII 74–5, LIX 8–10). 'Those who preceded [in faith] are the ones who precede (*wa l-sābiqūna l-sābiqūn*). They are the ones brought close [to God] in the Gardens of Bliss' (LVI 10–12).[1] Specifically were those who joined Islam only after the conquest of Mekka sharply reminded that they were not equal to those who had earlier spent of their property and fought for Islam, and who were thus

[1] The precedence was here widely understood in a temporal sense, although verses 13–14 could to some extent contradict this interpretation.

greater in rank (*aʿẓam darajatan*, LVII 10). It was generally held that the duty of *hijra* ended with the conquest of Mekka, so that even those Muslims who still came to join Muḥammad in Medina did not acquire the title and merit of Muhājirūn.

ʿUmar b. al-Khaṭṭāb, Abū Bakr's successor, had always stood for a rigorous, unconditional backing of the cause and principles of Islam. In the time of Muḥammad, he had repeatedly, but unsuccessfully, opposed diplomatic overtures to the Mekkan enemies of the Muslims. Thus he had demanded that the Mekkan captives in the battle of Badr should be killed rather than freed for ransom. He had protested against the compromise agreement of al-Ḥudaybiyya and, at the time of the conquest of Mekka, objected to the amnesty granted to the Umayyad chief Abū Sufyān whom he wanted to have executed for his leading part in the opposition to Islam.[2] Under Abū Bakr he had objected to the war against the Muslim tribes withholding the *zakāt* tax and to the leading position given to some members of the Mekkan aristocracy such as Khālid b. al-Walīd, whose conduct he considered to be inconsistent with the ethics of Islam, and Khālid b. Saʿīd, whose loyalty to Abū Bakr seemed doubtful. As caliph, ʿUmar, while not questioning the exclusive right of Quraysh to rule established by his predecessor, undertook to strengthen the Islamic character of the state by implementing Qur'anic principles and to curb the excessive power of the pre-Islamic Mekkan aristocracy. He relied in particular on two Qur'anic principles, that of *sābiqa*, early merit in Islam, which, given the established prerogative of Quraysh, benefited primarily the early Qurayshite Companions of Muḥammad, and that of *shūrā*, consultation in the government of the Muslim community.

ʿUmar's concept of *sābiqa* was reflected in his institution of the *dīwān*, the army register, for the distribution of the revenue from the conquered territories among the Muslims. Abū Bakr is reported to have given all Muslims equal shares of any sums of money delivered to Medina which, in any case, cannot have been very substantial. Against this practice, ʿUmar is said to have insisted that he could not put those who had fought together with the Prophet on the same level as those who had fought against him.[3] The highest stipends were thus awarded to the Muslims who had fought in the battle of Badr, and those who had joined, and fought for, Islam at later stages were given progressively smaller amounts. Exceptions were made for the Family of the Prophet. His widows received pensions more than double those of the veterans of Badr, and al-ʿAbbās, as the surviving heir of Muḥammad, was granted the same amount as the widows. The share of Muḥammad's grandsons al-Ḥasan

[2] Shoufani, *al-Riddah*, 55. [3] *Annali*, IV, 385–6, 391.

and al-Ḥusayn was also raised, evidently in recognition of the rights of Fāṭima. They were allotted the same stipend as their father 'Alī, whose award was that of the other veterans of Badr.[4]

'Umar's reliance on consultation is well illustrated by a report of 'Abd Allāh b. al-'Abbās on the caliph's voyage to Syria in the year 18/639.[5] As the caliph and his escort reached Sargh, they were met by the commanders of the Muslim armies in Syria who informed him of the seriousness of the plague there. 'Umar ordered Ibn al-'Abbās to assemble the early Emigrants (*al-muhājirīn al-awwalīn*) for consultation. When they disagreed among themselves as to whether to continue the voyage or to return to Medina, 'Umar ordered the Anṣār to be assembled for consultation. They, too, were divided in their opinion, and the caliph finally had Ibn al-'Abbās gather the leaders of Quraysh converted after the conquest of Mekka. They unanimously recommended retreat to Medina, and the caliph followed their advice.[6]

Usually 'Umar confined himself to consulting with the prominent early Mekkan Companions. Numerous reports describe him as seeking their opinion on important political and legal questions. Caetani was evidently right in suggesting that 'Umar retained them generally in Medina to assist and counsel him while he sent others of less standing in Islam to lead the military campaigns abroad.[7] His resolve to leave the election of his successor to an electoral conclave of early Companions after his death was an extension of his general procedure in reaching important decisions. It differed only insofar as the final word during his caliphate had always remained his.

Various reports suggest that 'Umar, immediately on his accession, moved to reduce the power of the old Mekkan aristocracy and to rectify some of the wrongs that, in his view, had been done to Muslims in the

[4] *Ibid.*, 388–427; G. Puin, *Der Dīwān von 'Umar ibn al-Ḫaṭṭāb: Ein Beitrag zur frühislamischen Verwaltungsgeschichte* (Bonn, 1970). Caetani's rejection of the reports about the preference given on the basis of kinship to the Prophet as Shi'ite and 'Abbasid fabrications (pp. 376, 379–82, 388, 393) is baseless.

[5] Ṭabarī I 2511–3. Al-Ṭabarī, relying on Ibn Isḥāq and al-Wāqidī, erroneously places the expedition under the year 17/638. See *Annali*, IV, 18.

[6] See also the similar procedure of 'Umar with regard to the introduction of the pension ('*aṭā*') system as described by al-Zubayr b. Bakkār (*Jamharat nasab Quraysh wa-akhbārihā*, ed. Maḥmūd Muḥammad Shākir (Cairo, 1381/1961), I, 373).

[7] *Annali*, IV, 140, V, 43–4, 503. Caetani (*ibid.*, IV, 139) stresses that 'Umar kept the Companions in Medina for this reason, 'not so much out of suspicion and jealousy'. He contradicts this assessment, however, in other passages where he suggests that 'Umar suspected the prominent Companions of disloyalty and treachery and kept them under close surveillance while denying them any share in the government (V, 42–5). See also IV, 453 where he maintains that 'Umar consistently excluded the early Muhājirūn from any share in the power, considering them his personal enemies and perhaps as men dangerous to the integrity of the Islamic state.

ridda. They mention as the first act of the second caliph the dismissal of Khālid b. al-Walīd and the appointment of Abū 'Ubayda as supreme commander of the Muslim armies in Syria. Khālid was certainly not deposed until much later, and there is uncertainty about the date of the appointment of Abū 'Ubayda to the high command. According to al-Zuhrī, 'Umar's order giving Abū 'Ubayda the supreme command in place of Khālid arrived at the time of the battle on the Yarmūk. Abū 'Ubayda, however, did not inform Khālid for two months out of a feeling of shame towards him.[8] Yet it seems likely that 'Umar from the beginning relied more on his personal friend Abū 'Ubayda. According to further reports he also ordered the immediate release of Arab prisoners made during the *ridda* wars and lifted the restriction on the participants in the *ridda* to join the Muslim armies of conquest.[9]

In the long run, 'Umar's efforts to curb the power of the Mekkan aristocracy in favour of the early Companions were only partially successful. Khālid b. al-Walīd was reduced to insignificance in Syria and was not allowed to return to Iraq. There 'Umar first commissioned Abū 'Ubayd b. Mas'ūd, a Thaqafite who could not aspire to build a personal power base in the territories he might conquer, with the general command. A year after Abū 'Ubayd was killed in battle, the caliph, planning a major offensive in Iraq, appointed the early Mekkan Companion Sa'd b. Abī Waqqāṣ supreme commander. Under Sa'd, the decisive battle of al-Qādisiyya was won, Mesopotamia was completely subdued, Kūfa was founded and Iran invaded. When Sa'd was recalled to Medina after six years, Muslim rule in Iraq was already solidly established. 'Umar's other governors of Kūfa, Baṣra and al-Baḥrayn and the leaders of the conquests in Iran were mostly of relatively humble, non-Qurayshite origin, such as 'Utba b. Ghazwān of Qays 'Aylān, early Companion and confederate (*ḥalīf*) of the Banū Nawfal of Quraysh, the Thaqafites al-Mughīra b. Shu'ba, 'Uthmān b. Abi l-'Āṣ and his brother al-Ḥakam, the Yamanite Abū Mūsā al-Ash'arī, 'Ammār b. Yāsir, son of a *mawlā* of the Makhzumite Abū Ḥudhayfa, the Muzanite al-Nu'mān b. 'Amr b. Muqarrin. The members of the Qurayshite aristocracy, so prominent in the leadership of the Muslim armies under Abū Bakr, were conspicuously absent.

In Syria 'Umar promoted the early Companion Abū 'Ubayda b. al-Jarrāḥ to the high command chiefly with the aim of reducing the power of Khālid b. al-Walīd, but also in the hope of keeping the Sufyanids under control. When Abū 'Ubayda, who resided in Ḥimṣ, died in the plague of the year 18/639, the caliph appointed Yazīd b. Abī Sufyān, who had been

[8] 'Abd al-Razzāq, *Muṣannaf*, V, 483. [9] *Annali*, III, 131–3.

in control of Damascus as deputy of Abū 'Ubayda since 16/637, governor of Damascus, al-Urdunn and Palestine and 'Iyāḍ b. Ghanm governor of Ḥimṣ, Qinnasrīn and Upper Mesopotamia (al-Jazīra).[10] Shortly afterwards Yazīd, too, fell victim to the plague, and 'Umar appointed his brother Mu'āwiya b. Abī Sufyān successor and governor of Damascus. Caetani saw this appointment as proof for 'Umar's high esteem of the Umayyads, to whom he particularly wanted to give a leading part in the government of Islam.[11] This interpretation is, however, hardly reasonable in the light of 'Umar's deep-seated aversion towards the Mekkan aristocracy and former opponents of Muḥammad. 'Umar probably did not have much of a choice at the time. The only serious rival to Mu'āwiya for the leadership in Syria after the death of so many other commanders was probably, as noted by Caetani,[12] 'Amr b. al-'Āṣ. 'Amr, however, had probably already received 'Umar's approval for the invasion of Egypt. It was obviously not the time to send a Companion of high standing from Medina before it was certain that the plague had run its course.

Another consideration in 'Umar's choice of the Sufyanid Mu'āwiya may have been the strength and high ambitions of the Yamanite, especially Himyarite, element among the Arab conquerors. These Yamanites had joined the Muslim army making no secret of their aspiration to establish a Himyarite kingdom under their leader Dhu l-Kalā' Samayfa' b. Nākūr, whom they called 'king of Ḥimyar', in defiance of the claim of Quraysh to rule the empire of Islam. Dhu l-Kalā' had hoped to gain control of Damascus, where he acquired much property, but he was instead forced to settle together with his followers in Ḥimṣ, while the Umayyads entrenched themselves in Damascus.[13] 'Umar probably realized that the Sufyanids, who in opposition to Ḥimyar formed an alliance with the tribe of Kalb, were in the best position to thwart such Himyarite designs, which he must have viewed as a threat to Abū Bakr's and his own concept of the caliphate.

The invasion of Egypt was undertaken by 'Amr b. al-'Āṣ, who had old

[10] According to al-Zuhrī, Abū 'Ubayda had appointed Khālid b. al-Walīd and his own cousin 'Iyāḍ b. Ghanm as his successors. 'Umar confirmed only 'Iyāḍ b. Ghanm. See 'Abd al-Razzāq, *Muṣannaf*, V, 455.

[11] *Annali*, IV, 30–1; V, 496. Caetani suggested that the plebeian Mekkan 'Umar might have favoured the Umayyads, Qurayshite aristocrats, out of snobbishness, but that he certainly recognized in them qualities that others did not have and found them useful for fortifying the Muslim community (*ibid.*, VII, 5). Less convinced of 'Umar's farsightedness, Lammens commented on this interpretation that 'Umar was probably forced to give the Umayyads some positions in order to secure the internal peace and to disarm the opposition. There might indeed have been a secret accord between 'Umar and Abū Sufyān which would explain why 'Umar never tried to depose Mu'āwiya from his governorship (*Annali*, VII, *Corregioni ed aggiunte*, liii).

[12] *Annali*, V, 496.

[13] See Madelung, 'Apocalyptic Prophecies in Ḥimṣ in the Umayyad Age', *Journal of Semitic Studies*, 30 (1986), 141–85, at 141–2, 183–4.

trading interests there, perhaps primarily on his own initiative. It is hardly conceivable, however, that he could have proceeded without permission from the caliph, as some sources suggest. Informed of ʿAmr's successful advance, ʿUmar expedited a strong auxiliary force under the early Companion al-Zubayr. His choice of a man of such high standing clearly reflected his intention to curb the independence of ʿAmr.[14] Later ʿUmar confiscated part of the riches that ʿAmr had amassed in the conquest in a manner humiliating to the conqueror of Egypt.[15] He left him, however, as governor until the end of his caliphate. It was to be Muʿāwiya, aided by ʿAmr b. al-ʿĀṣ, who put a definite end to the reign of the early Companions, as conceived by ʿUmar, and who established the dynastic rule of the old Mekkan aristocracy in its place.

Vital for ʿUmar's design of a collective authority of the early Companions was at least a token participation by ʿAlī. ʿUmar made every effort to bring about a reconciliation with the Banū Hāshim without compromising the essential right of all Quraysh to the caliphate. He thus treated ʿAlī basically like the other early Companions. He displayed his favour for the Prophet's kin rather in courting al-ʿAbbās who now, after the death of Fāṭima, was the closest relative of Muḥammad but posed no political threat since he did not belong to the early Companions and had no personal ambitions. ʿUmar also drew ʿAbd Allāh b. al-ʿAbbās, who was too young to pose a political threat, near to himself. Ibn al-ʿAbbās was closely associated with ʿUmar from the beginning to the end of his caliphate and has left the most revealing reports about the caliph's private thoughts.

With regard to the inheritance of Muḥammad, ʿUmar made a cautious concession to the Banū Hāshim. According to ʿĀ'isha, he turned Muḥammad's estates in Medina over to al-ʿAbbās and ʿAlī as endowment to be administered by them, while withholding the Prophet's portion of Khaybar and Fadak. He maintained that the latter two properties, evidently in contrast to the former, were merely assigned to the use of the Prophet for his personal needs and for emergencies and that they were after him at the disposal of the ruler of the time.[16] ʿAlī, according to ʿĀ'isha, soon usurped the rights of al-ʿAbbās with regard to Muḥammad's estates in Medina.[17]

Mālik b. Aws b. Ḥadathān of the Banū Naṣr of Hawāzin reported about a session attended by himself in which the quarrel between al-ʿAbbās and ʿAlī was brought before the caliph. At first the early Companions

[14] *Annali*, IV, 105. [15] *Ibid.*, 618–23.
[16] Bukhārī, *Ṣaḥīḥ, Khums* 2; Ibn Ḥanbal, *Musnad*, I, 6–7. See also this volume, excursus 2.
[17] Ibn Ḥanbal, *Musnad*, I, 6.

'Uthmān, 'Abd al-Raḥmān b. 'Awf, al-Zubayr and Sa'd b. Abī Waqqāṣ[18] were admitted, then al-'Abbās and 'Alī. Al-'Abbās asked the caliph to judge between him and his nephew in the dispute about the Prophet's property from the Banu l-Naḍīr, and the two began to curse each other.[19] Egged on by the group of early Companions to render judgment, 'Umar turned first to them asking whether they all knew that the Prophet had said: 'We do not have heirs, whatever we leave is alms', meaning by 'we' himself. Acknowledgement of Muḥammad's statement denying his family the right of inheritance had evidently become a kind of loyalty oath to the caliphate, and all answered affirmatively. 'Umar now asked 'Alī and al-'Abbās the same question, and they also confessed that the Prophet had said so.

'Umar then quoted Sūra LIX 6, pointing out that God had given the *fay'* of the Banu l-Naḍīr to the Messenger alone, who had distributed its revenue at his discretion. He had provided his family with their annual expenditure and had used the remainder in the cause of God. Abū Bakr after his succession had retained the property and faithfully followed the conduct of the Prophet, and 'Umar had done likewise during the first two years of his reign. Then al-'Abbās and 'Alī had come to him, the former asking for his share of the inheritance of his nephew and the latter asking for his wife's share of the inheritance of her father. 'Umar had reminded them of the Prophet's word: 'We do not have heirs, whatever we leave is alms.'[20] Then, however, he consented to hand the estates over to them on the condition that they would manage them in exactly the same way as the Prophet, Abū Bakr and he himself had done. Now they were asking him for a different decision concerning them, but he would never agree to anything else. If they were unable to carry it out, they should return them to him.[21]

The report, portraying al-'Abbās and 'Alī in the most negative light, distinctly reflects the anti-Hashimite sentiments of Umayyad Sunnism and may not be entirely reliable in detail. In substance, however, it probably describes 'Umar's attitude correctly. The caliph recognized the danger of even partly disavowing the decision of Abū Bakr concerning Muḥammad's inheritance and made sure that everybody 'knew' the

[18] According to another version, Ṭalḥa was also present. See Ibn Ḥajar, *Fatḥ al-bārī* (Cairo, 1319–29/[1901–11]), VI, 125.

[19] *Ibid.* According to one version al-'Abbās called 'Alī 'this liar, sinner, traitor, and cheat (*hādha l-kadhib al-āthim al-ghādir al-khā'in*)'.

[20] In the version quoted by Muslim, 'Umar accused 'Alī and al-'Abbās of holding both Abū Bakr and 'Umar for their actions to be 'a liar, sinner, traitor, and cheat'. 'Umar insisted that Abū Bakr was in every respect the opposite of this description.

[21] Bukhārī, *Ṣaḥīḥ, Khums* 1; Muslim, *Ṣaḥīḥ, Jihād* 49; 'Abd al-Razzāq, *Muṣannaf*, V, 469–71. For further references see A. J. Wensinck, *Concordance et indices de la tradition musulmane* (Leiden, 1936–88), index s.v. Mālik b. Aws.

Prophet's word. His own decision about Muḥammad's estates in Medina did not mean that he surrendered them to al-ʿAbbās and ʿAlī as private property. Rather, they were to administer them for the benefit of the Muslim Community as Muḥammad had done. In support of his position he quoted Sūra LIX 6 which mentioned the Prophet as the sole recipient of the *fay'* from the Banu l-Naḍīr. He did not quote the later verse LIX 7 concerning the *fay'* of the 'people of the towns (*ahl al-qurā*)' which specified a portion for the kin of the Prophet. That portion, he evidently held, referred only to the yield of the *fay'* of Khaybar and Fadak while the land itself became state property after Muḥammad's death.

About the *fay'* land of Khaybar, Jubayr b. Muṭʿim is quoted as reporting that Muḥammad had distributed a portion of it (meaning of its yield) to the Banū Hāshim and the Banu l-Muṭṭalib to the exclusion of the Banū ʿAbd Shams and the Banū Nawfal, to whom Jubayr himself belonged. Abū Bakr used to distribute the yield[22] as the Prophet had done but did not give the kin of the Prophet a share. ʿUmar and those after him, however, allotted them a portion.[23] Jubayr b. Muṭʿim evidently meant here the preference given to the Banū Hāshim in the stipends of the army register (*dīwān*). ʿUmar constituted much of the land conquered during his reign as *fay'*, now in the meaning of communal property, and used the revenue for paying the stipends and pensions of the Muslim warriors. Since the Banū Hāshim were placed first in the *dīwān*, they could be seen as being restored to their proper rank as kin of the Prophet entitled to a special portion of the *fay'*. In fact, however, only Muḥammad's wives, al-ʿAbbās, the two grandsons of the Prophet and Usāma, son of Muḥammad's client and adoptive son Zayd b. Ḥāritha,[24] were granted larger shares than they otherwise deserved. The *fay'* stipends were thus used to make up for the loss of the right of inheritance. ʿAlī, not being considered a primary heir, received only the stipend to which he was entitled as a veteran of Badr, and the other Banū Hāshim and Banu l-Muṭṭalib were, no doubt, dealt with in the same way. While the supporters of the caliphate could thus feel, as suggested by the report of Jubayr b. Muṭʿim, that the kin of the Prophet had been fairly treated in accordance with their Qur'anic title to a portion of the *fay'*, most of these still saw themselves deprived of the benefits they had enjoyed under Muḥammad.

In respect to the fifth of movable war booty, ʿAbd Allāh b. al-ʿAbbās reported that the Qur'anic portion of the Prophet's kin was no longer

[22] The term used throughout the report is *khums*. From the context it is evident that the yield of the *fay'* land is meant.

[23] Abū Dāwūd, *Sunan* (Cairo, 1292/[1875]), XIX, 20; al-Maqrīzī, *al-Nizāʿ wa l-takhāṣum fīmā bayn Banī Umayya wa-Banī Hāshim*, ed. G. Vos, *Die Kämpfe und Streitigkeiten zwischen den Banū Umajja und den Banū Hāšim* (Leiden, 1888), 22.

[24] See Abū Yūsuf, *Kitāb al-Kharāj* (Cairo, 1352/[1933]), 25.

distributed to them after the death of Muḥammad. 'Umar then proposed to the Banū Hāshim to pay for their marriages, debts and servants from the fifth. The Banū Hāshim, however, rejected this proposal unless the full amount of their share was turned over to them. To this the caliph would not agree. In reply to a letter of the Kharijite leader Najda b. 'Āmir, Ibn al-'Abbās left no doubt that he still held the Banū Hāshim to be entitled to this portion of the fifth of booty.[25]

By his overtures to the Banū Hāshim 'Umar evidently hoped to reconcile them with the Muslim community and its new caliphal order without giving them excessive economic and political power. Courting the favour of al-'Abbās and his son 'Abd Allāh, neither of whom could pose a serious political threat because of their relatively low standing in regard to *sābiqa*, seemed to serve this purpose well. Al-'Abbās was thus granted the largest pension aside from the wives of Muḥammad. During the drought of the year 18/639 'Umar honoured him by putting him forward in the ritual prayer for rain (*istisqā'*), thus seeking God's favour through the blessing of the Prophet's uncle.[26] Al-'Abbās seems to have had the ear of the caliph as a counsellor, not among the early Companions, but among the leaders of Quraysh.[27] Sayf b. 'Umar's assessment that under 'Umar people wishing to discover the intentions of the caliph would first turn to 'Abd al-Raḥmān b. 'Awf or 'Uthmān and after them to al-'Abbās[28] may be correct. Al-'Abbās was in a position to protest against 'Umar's order to demolish several houses, including his own, against the will of their owners for the enlargement of the sanctuary of Mekka.[29] In Medina, he successfully resisted 'Umar's wish to include his house in the enlargement of the mosque, but then surrendered it voluntarily to the Muslim community.[30]

Al-Mas'ūdī relates a report attributed to 'Abd Allāh b. al-'Abbās according to which 'Umar once offered the latter the governorship of Ḥimṣ after the death of the previous governor. The caliph expressed at the same time some uncertainty and apprehension as to the propriety of this appointment and asked Ibn al-'Abbās about his own views regarding such an office. As the latter demanded to be first informed about the nature of the caliph's reservations, 'Umar explained that he was afraid that people might protest to him that the office should be given to others than the kin of Muḥammad since the latter had regularly chosen his officials among others and had avoided appointing his kin. 'Umar continued that he did not know whether Muḥammad had done so because

[25] *Ibid.*, 11–12. [26] *Annali*, IV, 14–17, V, 123. [27] See *ibid.*, III, 250, 253.
[28] Ṭabarī, II, 2212–13; *Annali*, III, 279.
[29] Ya'qūbī, *Ta'rīkh*, II, 170; *Annali*, III, 961–2.
[30] Ibn Sa'd, *Ṭabaqāt*, IV/1, 13–14; *Annali*, III, 966–7.

he held them to be above holding office (*ḍanna bi-kum ʿan al-ʿamal*) – and they, ʿUmar added, were worthy of that esteem – or whether the Prophet feared that they might abuse their rank so that they would be subject to reproach, since reproach was inevitable (in public office). Upon this reply Ibn al-ʿAbbās declined to hold any office for ʿUmar and advised him to employ someone 'who can trust you and whom you can trust (*tastaʿmil ṣaḥīḥan minka ṣaḥīḥan laka*)'.[31]

Despite the literary formulation of the report, the substance may well be reliable and reflect ʿUmar's ambiguous position correctly. ʿUmar would have liked to integrate the Banū Hāshim fully in the Muslim community, more particularly among Quraysh, the ruling class. In view of the continued reluctance of ʿAlī, the appointment of ʿAbd Allāh b. al-ʿAbbās to a governorship could, in one respect, have been seen by ʿUmar as a political success. For the same reason Ibn al-ʿAbbās may basically have been hesitant to accept in order to avoid breaking ranks with ʿAlī and the Banū Hāshim. Yet ʿUmar's fear that there might be objections to the appointment of a Hashimite to high office may have been well founded. His mention of Muḥammad's failure to appoint his kin to offices and his questioning the motives behind it may indicate that he in fact was hoping that Ibn al-ʿAbbās would decline.[32]

ʿUmar's relations with ʿAlī were more difficult. Ibn Abī Ṭāhir Ṭayfūr quoted in his *Taʾrīkh Baghdād* a report of ʿAbd Allāh b. al-ʿAbbās about a conversation he had with the caliph early in his reign. ʿUmar asked him about his cousin and whether he was still harbouring ambitions for the caliphate. On Ibn al-ʿAbbās' affirmative answer, he asked whether he claimed that the Prophet had designated him (*naṣṣa ʿalayh*). Ibn al-ʿAbbās replied yes, adding that he had asked his father about the truth of this claim, and al-ʿAbbās had confirmed it. ʿUmar commented that there had been some words of the Prophet in respect to ʿAlī which were not decisive evidence. The Prophet had deliberated (*yarbaʿu*) about this matter for some time, and during his illness he intended to name him expressly, but he, ʿUmar, had restrained him out of concern for, and in order to protect, the cause of Islam. Quraysh would never have agreed to this arrangement. If ʿAlī were to assume the caliphate, the Arabs everywhere would revolt against him. The Prophet, ʿUmar added, had understood what his

[31] Al-Masʿūdī, *Murūj al-dhahab*, ed. C. Pellat (Beirut, 1968–79), III, 65–6; *Annali*, V, 158.

[32] Caetani considered the report to be largely apocryphal and as expressing criticism of the ʿAbbasid practice of appointing members of the ruling family to the highest and most lucrative positions. He held that ʿUmar, like Muḥammad, failed to entrust the latter's kin with public positions because both considered them incompetent. Al-Masʿūdī, a noted pro-ʿAbbasid historian, had tendentiously tried to prove that it was not ʿUmar who excluded the ʿAbbasids from public office, but rather the ʿAbbasids who would not accept it out of a sense of the delicacy of the matter (*Annali*, V, 149).

motives were and had therefore kept silent. God had refused everything but His decree.[33]

Although aware that 'Alī had not entirely renounced his ambitions to rule as the chief of Muḥammad's kin, thus threatening the caliphate of Quraysh, 'Umar sought to draw the Prophet's cousin closer to himself within the council of early Companions. He regularly consulted him together with the other early Companions and insisted on marrying 'Alī's daughter Umm Kulthūm, granddaughter of the Prophet. The latter, a mere child at the time, resisted, presumably aware of 'Umar's harsh treatment of women. 'Alī himself was reluctant, but eventually gave in after the caliph enlisted public support of the Emigrants and Helpers for his demand.[34] 'Alī did, however, turn to 'Umar to ask for a land concession at Yanbu' near Jabal Raḍwā. The caliph granted it to him,[35] and it later remained in the hands of the descendants of al-Ḥasan.[36]

In spite of 'Umar's overtures, there remained a distance between the two men. 'Abd Allāh b. al-'Abbās reported that 'Umar questioned him on one of his journeys as to why 'Alī would not join them.[37] When Ibn al-'Abbās pretended not to know, the caliph pursued: 'O Ibn al-'Abbās, your father is the paternal uncle of the Messenger of God, and you are his cousin. What has turned your people [*qawmakum*, i.e. Quraysh] away from you [pl.)?' Ibn al-'Abbās again denied knowing the answer. 'Umar then explained that Quraysh did not want Muḥammad's kin to rule, since they were loath to see prophethood and caliphate combined in a single family, lest they become overbearing. 'Perhaps you [pl.] say that Abū Bakr fixed that. No, by God, Abū Bakr rather did the most prudent that was possible for him. If he had rendered the caliphate to you, it would have been of no avail to you in view of your closeness [to the Prophet].'[38]

[33] Ibn Abi l-Ḥadīd, *Sharḥ*, XII, 20–1. Ibn Abi l-Ḥadīd does not quote the full *isnād* which, according to him, was provided by Ibn Abī Ṭāhir.

[34] Ibn Sa'd, *Ṭabaqāt*, VIII, 339–40; *Annali*, III, 968–9.

[35] Yaḥyā b. Ādam, *al-Kharāj*, ed. T. W. Juynboll, *Le livre de l'impôt foncier de Yaḥyā Ibn Ādam* (Leiden, 1895), 57; Balādhurī, *Futūḥ*, 14.

[36] Yāqūt, *Mu'jam al-buldān*, ed. F. Wüstenfeld (Leipzig, 1866–73), s.v. Yanbu'; Abu l-Faraj al-Iṣfahānī, *Kitāb al-Aghānī* [Būlāq, 1285/1868] (henceforth *Aghānī*), XIX, 161. According to Ja'far al-Ṣādiq, 'Alī had previously been granted land concessions by Muḥammad at the two Fuqayrs, at Bi'r Qays and at al-Shajara. See Balādhurī, *Futūḥ*, 14. Yaḥyā b. Ādam, *Kharāj*, 57, mentions only Bi'r Qays and al-Shajara.

[37] See also *Aghānī*, IX, 146 (*Annali*, V, 142–3) where 'Umar is quoted as complaining to 'Abd Allāh b. al-'Abbās about 'Alī's absence when he set out for al-Jābiya. Ibn al-'Abbās assured the caliph that the excuses offered by 'Alī were real.

[38] Ṭabarī, I, 2768–9. The second account quoted by al-Ṭabarī (*ibid.*, 2769–71), which is transmitted by Ibn Isḥāq and describes Ibn al-'Abbās as a bold and boastful defender of the rights of his family in front of 'Umar, is probably based on the first. It hardly goes back to either Ibn al-'Abbās or 'Ikrima, who is named as the transmitter from him. (See also the report of Ibn al-'Abbās quoted by al-Jawharī, *Kitāb al-Saqīfa*, on the authority of 'Umar b. Shabba in Ibn Abi l-Ḥadīd, *Sharḥ*, II, 57–8.)

'Umar's words were obviously meant as a lesson for 'Alī as much as for Ibn al-'Abbās. 'Alī could not hope to gain the caliphate on the basis of his kinship with Muḥammad since Quraysh would not countenance the accumulation of prophethood and caliphate in the same clan. It was not Abū Bakr's and 'Umar's coup at the Saqīfat Banī Sā'ida that had prevented 'Alī's succession, but the deep jealousy of Quraysh. The only chance for 'Alī to share in the rule of the Muslim community was to co-operate fully in the consultative assembly of early Qurayshite Companions which 'Umar had set up. On another occasion, Ibn al-'Abbās narrated, 'Umar remarked to him that his companion (*ṣāḥibuka*), 'Alī, was indeed the most worthy (*awlā*) of the people to rule after the Messenger of God, 'but we feared him for two reasons'. When Ibn al-'Abbās asked him eagerly what the reasons were, he mentioned his youth and his love for the Banū 'Abd al-Muṭṭalib.[39]

'Umar's hopes of being able to contain the aspirations of 'Alī and his supporters were, towards the end of his reign, rudely disappointed by the incident reported by Ibn al-'Abbās which led to the caliph's address about the events at the Saqīfat Banī Sā'ida. In the address he reaffirmed his faith in the principle of consultation as the basis for the succession to the caliphate and denounced any future attempt to settle it without *mashwara* among the Muslims. The caliphate belonged to all of Quraysh and could not be monopolized by any particular family. 'Umar was struck by his assassin less than two weeks later.

The caliph's resolve to leave the choice of his successor to a *shūrā* among the most eminent early Companions was no doubt firm long before he was mortally wounded by Abū Lu'lu'a, the Persian slave of al-Mughīra b. Shu'ba, even if he, as commonly affirmed by the historical tradition, chose its members and defined their task only on his deathbed.[40] Various reports quoting 'Umar as affirming that he would have appointed Abū 'Ubayda b. al-Jarrāḥ, or Sālim, the client of Abū Ḥudhayfa, or the Medinan Companion Mu'ādh b. Jabal of Khazraj if one of them had been alive,[41] must be taken with caution. Even if he ever made statements to that effect, they were presumably no more than a hyperbolic homage to his dead friends. Abū 'Ubayda would certainly have been included in any *shūrā*. Sālim, as noted by Caetani,[42] would not have been accepted by Quraysh since he was their client and was clearly excluded from the

[39] Al-Jawharī, *Kitāb al-Saqīfa*, quoting 'Umar b. Shabba (Ibn Abi l-Ḥadīd, *Sharḥ*, II, 57, VI, 50–1).

[40] There are reports, however, that 'Umar named the electoral committee of six in a Friday sermon. See Ibn Sa'd, *Ṭabaqāt*, III/1, 242–3; Ibn Shabba, *Ta'rīkh al-Madīna*, 889; *Annali*, V, 38; al-Balādhurī, *Ansāb al-ashrāf*, V, ed. S. D. F. Goitein (Jerusalem, 1936), 15–16, 18.

[41] *Annali*, IV, 134, V, 64, 80; Ibn Shabba, *Ta'rīkh al-Madīna*, 881, 886–7.

[42] *Annali*, V, 86.

caliphate as conceived by Abū Bakr. Mu'ādh b. Jabal would likewise have been unacceptable as a non-Qurayshite. 'Umar never considered any of his own kin for the succession. There are reports that he angrily rejected suggestions that he appoint his eldest son, 'Abd Allāh, commenting that the latter was not even capable of divorcing his wife.[43]

Caetani maintained that 'Umar did not appoint the famous *shūrā* at all, but that the electoral council rather constituted itself after the caliph's death, presumably on the basis of their earlier activity in advising him. Holding that several of its members, in particular 'Alī, al-Zubayr and Ṭalḥa, were in fact the instigators of 'Umar's murder and that 'Umar most likely was aware of their complicity, he argued that the caliph could not have chosen them.[44] The fact that the assassination occurred so soon after 'Umar's warning against 'the clan who want to usurp the rule from the people' may strengthen the impression of a conspiracy in which 'Alī was involved.

Yet Caetani's hypothesis of a conspiracy among the early Companions to murder 'Umar has no sound basis in the sources. The blind acts of vengeance perpetrated by 'Umar's son 'Ubayd Allāh, which were taken as evidence by Caetani, resembled those of a lunatic, not of someone with inside knowledge. That 'Ubayd Allāh is said to have been encouraged by 'Umar's daughter Ḥafṣa[45] does not lend credibility to the soundness of his motives. Abū Lu'lu'a having been killed, or committed suicide, immediately after his crime, 'Ubayd Allāh murdered not only al-Hurmuzān, the Persian army leader who had converted to Islam and become a counsellor of 'Umar on Persian affairs, but also the Christian Jufayna[46] and the assassin's young daughter. The murder of Jufayna and al-Hurmuzān was provoked solely by a claim by either 'Abd al-Raḥmān b. 'Awf or 'Abd al-Raḥmān b. Abī Bakr of having seen them together with the murder weapon in their possession. When 'Ubayd Allāh was apprehended, he threatened to kill all foreign captives in Medina and some unnamed Emigrants and Helpers. That he had in mind 'Alī in particular is not unlikely, given 'Umar's recent warning against his and his clan's ambitions. In spite of the report about Abū Lu'lu'a's knife, however, 'Ubayd Allāh's action was generally recognized as murder and was not defended as an act of legitimate revenge. He was granted clemency by the

[43] Ibn Sa'd, *Ṭabaqāt*, III/1, 248; Balādhurī, *Ansāb*, V, 17; Ibn Shabba, *Ta'rīkh al-Madīna*, 923; Ṭabarī, I, 2777.

[44] *Annali*, V, 40–51. G. Levi della Vida, who in his *EI* article on 'Umar generally followed Caetani's interpretations closely, rejected his theory of a plot of the Muhājirūn to murder the caliph. He inclined, however, to the belief that 'Umar did not appoint the electoral council for his succession and that he would have made his own choice if he had lived.

[45] *Annali*, V, 70.

[46] Jufayna was a Christian from al-Ḥīra who had been brought to Medina by Sa'd b. Abī Waqqāṣ to teach his children and others reading and arithmetic (Balādhurī, *Ansāb*, II, 294).

caliph 'Uthmān on the basis that it would be undue harshness to spill his blood just after his father had been murdered. 'Alī, among others, strongly protested against this act of clemency and threatened that he would carry out the legal punishment of 'Ubayd Allāh for murder if he were ever in a position to do so.

There is no evidence for any ties between Abū Lu'lu'a and the Companions suspected by Caetani of having conspired to murder 'Umar. If there had been serious suspicions of any complicity on the part of 'Alī, later Umayyad propaganda would certainly have made use of them, just as it accused him of the murder of 'Uthmān.[47] In addition to 'Alī, Ṭalḥa and al-Zubayr, Caetani named Muḥammad, the son of Abū Bakr, among the plotters and suggested that perhaps al-'Abbās and his son 'Abd Allāh were also involved.[48] They were, he suggested, probably the same clique that was later behind the murder of 'Uthmān.[49] The theory of a conspiracy of early Companions to murder both 'Umar and 'Uthmān is in accord with Caetani's basic view that 'Umar, as the effective ruler ever since the death of Muḥammad, had given free rein to the old Mekkan aristocracy and, as caliph, favoured the rise to power of the Umayyads whose political acumen he admired in contrast to the petty jealousy and sinister ambitions of most of the early Companions.

The accounts of the meetings and proceedings of the electoral council that elected 'Uthmān are partly contradictory and legendary.[50] Some

[47] In one of his letters, al-Jāḥiẓ answered a man who had asked him about the accusations of some people that 'Alī had poisoned Abū Bakr, instigated the murder of 'Umar by Abū Lu'lu'a and openly spoken out against 'Uthmān until he was killed. Al-Jāḥiẓ characteristically claimed that this was what the radical Shi'ites (*rawāfiḍ*) who praised 'Alī for this had reported and counted as one of his virtues (Ibn Bakr, Muḥammad b. Yaḥyā, *al-Tamhīd wa l-bayān fi maqtal al-shahīd 'Uthmān*, ed. Maḥmūd Yūsuf Zāyid (Beirut, 1963), 179–81). This claim is probably mere anti-Shi'ite slander. The accusation against 'Alī must, however, have come from obscure pro-Umayyad circles and did not reflect the official Umayyad propaganda line. [48] *Annali*, V, 44. [49] *Ibid.*, 42.

[50] The main eyewitness report was that of al-Miswar b. Makhrama al-Zuhrī, maternal nephew of 'Abd al-Raḥmān b. 'Awf, who was involved in the proceedings through his uncle. His original report is not extant. Al-Ṭabarī (I, 2722–6, 2788–97) quotes the version of it transmitted by 'Abd al-'Azīz b. Abī Thābit (d. 179/795), a descendant of 'Abd al-Raḥmān, who is described as a specialist in genealogy and poetry, unreliable in hadith. According to 'Umar b. Shabba his books were burned, and he transmitted from memory (Ibn Ḥajar, *Tahdhīb*, VI, 350–1). This may account for some legendary elements and the literary air of the report. In substance, however, it seems sound.

The Kufan reports quoted by Ibn Isḥāq which were edited by N. Abbott from a papyrus and described by her as unbiased (*Studies in Arabic Literary Papyri*, (Chicago, 1957), I, 80–99) have for good reason been judged to be anti-Umayyad fiction by H. A. R. Gibb (review, *Journal of Near Eastern Studies*, 17 (1958), 214) and M. J. Kister ('Notes on an Account of the Shura appointed by 'Umar b. al-Khattab', *JSS*, 9 (1964), 320–6). According to these and related reports, 'Umar before his death expressed regret that he had appointed Mu'āwiya governor and accused 'Amr b. al-'Āṣ of encouraging Mu'āwiya's hopes to gain the caliphate to which he, as a freed captive at the time of the Muslim conquest of Mekka (*ṭalīq*), could not aspire. While such reports were clearly invented with hindsight in the light of the later developments, the claim expressed in them that aspects, however, can be established with reasonable certainty. The council consisted in fact of five members, 'Abd al-Raḥmān b. 'Awf, Sa'd b. Abī Waqqāṣ, 'Uthmān, 'Alī and al-Zubayr. The sixth, Ṭalḥa, returned to Medina only after the election of 'Uthmān. Sa'd formally acted as his proxy. An important part in the decision in favour of 'Uthmān fell to the latter's brother-in-law 'Abd al-Raḥmān b. 'Awf.[51] 'Abd al-Raḥmān had been the Companion closest to 'Umar after the death of Abū 'Ubayda, and the caliph often relied on his views.[52] If a report of 'Umar's grandson Sālim b. 'Abd Allāh is reliable, 'Umar considered 'Abd al-Raḥmān, 'Uthmān and 'Alī as serious candidates for the caliphate and warned each one of them in turn not to give free rein to his kin if elected.[53] By mentioning 'Abd al-Raḥmān as the one addressed first by 'Umar, the report may be meant to indicate that the caliph would have preferred him as his successor. It is indeed not unlikely that 'Umar trusted 'Abd al-Raḥmān the most among the three, and 'Alī the least. 'Abd al-Raḥmān, however, did not aspire to supreme power and took himself out of the competition in return for being recognized as the arbitrator between the candidates. Since al-Zubayr and Sa'd equally did not press their own or Ṭalḥa's claim,[54] only 'Uthmān and 'Alī were left. 'Alī pleaded his own case as the closest kin of the Prophet with consistent vigour, while 'Uthmān maintained his candidacy passively. Besides interviewing each of the electors separately, 'Abd al-Raḥmān consulted with the leaders of Quraysh at night and received strong support for 'Uthmān. With the latter a candidate, the Banū 'Abd Shams could no longer feel any obligation to back their more remote relative, 'Alī. Makhzūm also backed 'Uthmān against the Prophet's cousin. The Makhzumite leader 'Abd Allāh b. Abī Rabī'a, governor of al-Janad, warned 'Abd al-Rahmān b. 'Awf: 'If you pledge allegiance to 'Alī, we shall hear and disobey, but if you pledge allegiance to 'Uthmān we shall hear and obey. So fear God, Ibn 'Awf.'[55]

'Umar considered all former enemies of Islam including Mu'āwiya and 'Amr b. al-'Āṣ as ineligible for the caliphate was nonetheless well founded in view of their complete exclusion from his electoral council.

[51] 'Abd al-Raḥmān was married to 'Uthmān's half-sister Umm Kulthūm bt 'Uqba b. Abī Mu'ayṭ (Balādhurī, *Ansāb*, V, 19).

[52] Caetani's assertion, on the basis of the report in al-Ṭabarī, I, 2746 ll. 8–13, that 'Abd al-Raḥmān b. 'Awf was one of the most bitter adversaries of 'Umar (*Annali*, V, 486; see also III, 702) is incomprehensible. The report rather indicates that the people sought 'Abd al-Raḥmān's intercession with the caliph because they knew that he had considerable influence on him.

[53] Ibn Sa'd, *Ṭabaqāt*, III/1, 249–50; *Annali*, V, 65; 'Abd al-Razzāq, *Muṣannaf*, V, 480–1.

[54] Al-Zubayr does not seem to have withdrawn immediately, unlike Sa'd who followed the lead of 'Abd al-Raḥmān b. 'Awf (Ṭabarī, I, 2792).

[55] Balādhurī, *Ansāb*, V, 19; Ṭabarī, I, 2785; Abbott, *Arabic Literary Papyri*, I, 81, 85. 'Abd Allāh b. Abī Rabī'a was governor of al-Janad under 'Umar and was reappointed by 'Uthmān (*Aghānī*, I, 32).

In the electoral council 'Alī had virtually no support. 'Uthmān and 'Alī are each said to have indicated a preference for the other if not elected. According to some reports 'Alī succeeded in persuading Sa'd to switch his backing from 'Uthmān to himself. This was, however, soft support at best. More indicative of the strength of sentiment for 'Uthmān was that al-Zubayr, maternal cousin of 'Alī, who had backed him after the death of Muḥammad, now opted for 'Uthmān. 'Abd al-Raḥmān thus had a convincing mandate for deciding in favour of the latter. He announced his decision, however, only during the public meeting in the mosque in the presence of the two candidates, thus putting heavy pressure on the loser, 'Alī, to pledge allegiance immediately. 'Alī complied reluctantly.

Although 'Umar must have been worried about the possibility of 'Alī becoming caliph, there is no evidence that he tried directly to influence the electoral process against him. His recent warning, in the presence of 'Abd al-Raḥmān b. 'Awf, against the ambitions of the Banū Hāshim to assert their sole right to the caliphate certainly contributed to 'Alī's overwhelming defeat. Although apparently not repeated in his public address, the warning no doubt became common knowledge and, together with the assassination of the caliph shortly afterwards, ruled out any compromise between the supporters of the caliphate of Quraysh and 'Alī, which might otherwise have been possible. 'Abd al-Raḥmān b. 'Awf was fully aware of 'Umar's feelings. He may have withdrawn his own name in order to gain the decisive vote and thus be in a position to block 'Alī's ambitions. But this seems to have been his own spontaneous initiative, not a prearranged manoeuvre suggested by the caliph.[56]

'Abd Allāh b. al-'Abbās narrated the story of a conversation he had with 'Umar in which the latter expressed his concern about a suitable succession. Ibn al-'Abbās questioned him about his views on each of the six men who were to become members of the electoral council, but the caliph expressed grave reservation with regard to each of them. The story is certainly a literary fiction and the answers ascribed to 'Umar reflect to some extent the hindsight of a later age. They nevertheless may not be far

[56] A substantially different account of the *shūrā* was provided by the early Kufan authority al-Sha'bī. According to him, 'Umar had no doubts that the election would be between 'Alī and 'Uthmān. Before he died, he in fact excluded Sa'd b. Abī Waqqāṣ, recommending that he be reappointed governor of Kūfa. Ṭalḥa was absent in Syria. Concerning the remaining four he ordered that if three of them agreed against one, their choice should be decisive. If the vote was hung, 'Abd al-Raḥmān b. 'Awf's choice should prevail. 'Alī recognized this as a stratagem to keep him from the succession, since 'Abd al-Raḥmān would inevitably prefer his brother-in-law, 'Uthmān (Ibn Abi l-Ḥadīd, *Sharḥ*, IX, 29–54, quoting 'Awāna's *Kitāb al-shūrā wa-maqtal 'Uthmān* and al-Jawharī's *Kitāb al-Saqīfa*). Al-Sha'bī's account gives the distinct impression of a secondary reconstruction based on little first-hand information.

from 'Umar's personal views.[57] About 'Alī 'Umar said that he was worthy (*ahl*) of the caliphate but that there was some foolishness (*du'āba*) in him and that he, in 'Umar's opinion, 'would lead you on a path, in respect to what is right, which you know', an allusion perhaps to the likelihood that 'Alī would restrict the title to the caliphate to the Prophet's Family.[58] About 'Uthmān he said that he would give the Banū Abī Mu'ayṭ[59] power over the people; the Arabs would certainly disobey him then and 'strike his neck' (i.e. cut off his head). The formulation reflects hindsight, yet may also express some of 'Umar's real worries with respect to the possible succession of 'Uthmān. Ṭalḥa, the caliph stated, was a vainglorious (*zahw*) man, and God would not allow him to rule the Muslim community in view of his well-known arrogance. Al-Zubayr was a battle hero, but occupied himself with haggling in the markets in Medina. How could he take charge of the affairs of the Muslims? Sa'd, too, was a valiant fighter on horseback, but inapt to command. 'Abd al-Raḥmān was an excellent man, but unsuitable because of his weakness. For this office, 'Umar continued, only someone strong without roughness was suited, someone flexible without weakness, thrifty without miserliness, generous without extravagance.

During the ten years of 'Umar's reign, the nature of the caliphate, the Muslim state, had been transformed. The great conquests outside Arabia had turned the mass of the Arabs, deprived of their former freedom and reduced to tax-paying subjects by Quraysh during the *ridda*, into a military caste sustained by a numerically much larger non-Arab and non-Muslim subject population. It may be questioned whether the caliphate of Quraysh would have lasted very long without this imperial expansion. The memory of a free, though economically meagre and harsh, life was too recent not to have aroused widespread resentment and rebellion against the subjection to Quraysh. The successful diversion of all energy into vast military conquests, in the name of Islam, kept any longing for a restoration of the past at bay. Soon there remained only the sentimental literary attachment to the pre-Islamic poetry and tales of the Arab battle-days (*ayyām al-'Arab*). Quraysh remained, to be sure, the

57 Al-Māwardī, *al-Aḥkām*, 15–16, with the *isnād* Ibn Isḥāq *'an* al-Zuhrī *'an* 'Abd Allāh b. al-'Abbās. A different version given by al-Ya'qūbī, *Ta'rīkh*, II, 181–3, without *isnād* appears to be revised with a Shi'ite bias. Some of the characterizations mentioned by Ibn al-'Abbās were ascribed to 'Umar also in other reports.

58 . . . *ḥamalakum 'alā ṭarīqa min al-ḥaqq ta'rifūnahā*. The phrase may be understood in a negative sense in contrast with the initial affirmation that 'Alī was worthy of the caliphate. In other versions of the statement the end appears unambiguously as *'alā (ṭarīqat) al-ḥaqq*, he would lead you on (the path of) what is right (see Ṭabarī, I, 2777).

59 Abū Mu'ayṭ b. Abī 'Amr b. Umayya was the grandfather of 'Uthmān's uterine brother al-Walīd b. 'Uqba. 'Uqba b. Abī Mu'ayṭ, a stubborn enemy of Muḥammad, was killed by the latter after the battle of Badr.

ruling class. The Arab warriors (*muqātila*) were subjected to strict, sometimes brutal, military discipline. But in return they were provided with generous stipends and pensions apart from their share in the booty gained in battle. They thus had a stake in the imperial policies of Quraysh. The caliphate, still in a precarious state throughout Abū Bakr's reign, was now firmly established.

The task of organizing the government and administration of the conquered territories fell to ʿUmar. He did this on the basis of largely identifying Islam and the Arabs. At this time Islam came close to becoming a national religion for the Arabs. Most of the remaining non-Muslim Arabs, also outside Arabia, quickly followed the summons to Islam, while the number of non-Arab converts was initially insignificant. The tolerance that the Qur'ān offered to the 'People of the Book', mostly Christians and Jews, was extended to all other religious communities in the conquered territories. The Arabs of the tribe of Taghlib in northern Mesopotamia, who refused to give up their Christian faith, were nevertheless incorporated into the Muslim army and were given a special tax status under which they paid double the tithe (*ʿushr*) imposed on Muslims as *zakāt* but not the humiliating head tax (*jizya*) and land tax (*kharāj*) levied on other non-Muslim subjects.[60] ʿUmar no doubt expected that they would soon become Muslims. When the Christian Arab tribe of Iyād sought refuge in Byzantine territory, ʿUmar wrote to the emperor demanding that he expel them and threatened to drive non-Arab Christians into Byzantine lands. Under Byzantine pressure some 4,000 of the tribesmen returned to Muslim territory.[61] It is evident that the caliph regarded all Arabs, whether Muslims or Christians, as his primary subjects.

In contrast to the conquered territories, Arabia was to be, as far as feasible, purely Muslim and Arab. The relatively large Christian and Jewish communities in Najrān and Khaybar were summarily expelled by ʿUmar to the conquered territories.[62] Non-Muslims were generally not to be allowed to settle in the Ḥijāz or to stay in any place there for more than three days.[63] ʿUmar was also anxious to keep most non-Arab Muslims out of Arabia, in particular Medina. There was a general restriction on

[60] *Annali*, IV, 226–32. [61] Ṭabarī, I, 2508–9; *Annali*, IV, 58.

[62] Caetani tried to shift the blame for the expulsion of both groups to the early Companions opposed to ʿUmar whose economic interests, Caetani asserted, were at stake (*Annali*, IV, 350–60). 'In order to dampen the opposition and mute hostility of these powerful intriguers, he saw himself sometimes constrained to acts of weakness of which the expulsion of the Jews of Khaybar is the most dolorous and reprehensible example (*ibid.*, IV, 353).' Caetani had to admit, however, that these measures ultimately agreed with the 'exclusivist' political aims of ʿUmar (*ibid.*, IV, 353–4, V, 506).

[63] Māwardī, *al-Aḥkām*, 291; *Annali*, V, 506.

bringing captives (*saby*) to the capital.[64] This restriction was certainly not confined to non-Muslims, since captives in particular tended to convert to Islam. It was obviously more difficult, however, to keep Arabic-speaking Muslims out of Arabia. After having been struck by Abū Lu'lu'a, 'Umar is reported to have addressed the accusation to Ibn al-'Abbas that he and his father were eager to multiply the non-Arabs (*'ulūj*) in Medina. Ibn al-'Abbās answered, assuring the caliph that al-'Abbās and he would do with them whatever the caliph wished. 'Umar then questioned how anything could be done now that these non-Arabs had learned to speak the language of their masters, prayed their prayers with them, and shared their acts of devotion.[65] In contrast, 'Umar ordered before his death that all Arab slaves held by the state be freed.[66] The strong bias against non-Arabs in 'Umar's policies evidently contributed to creating the atmosphere in which the Persian captive Abū Lu'lu'a Fayrūz,[67] outraged by a perceived slight on the part of the caliph, was prepared to assassinate him in a suicidal attack and in which the caliph's son 'Ubayd Allāh was equally prepared to murder any non-Arabs whom he could reach.

'Umar's deep commitment to Qurayshite and Arab solidarity was balanced by an even deeper commitment to Islam. He was fully aware that it was only Islam that had raised him to the top and was turning the Arabs into the masters of a vast empire. Like other men of great power he saw in his stupendous success a clear sign of divine favour which he could only attribute to Islam. He might be inclined at times to bend the rules of

64 *Annali*, V, 57, 103. According to al-Zuhrī, 'Umar did not allow any non-Arabs (*'ajam*) to enter Medina. Al-Mughīra b. Shu'ba therefore had to seek special permission for his Persian slave Abū Lu'lu'a to live and work in the town ('Abd al-Razzāq, *Muṣannaf*, V, 494). Al-Zuhrī's report of the story of Abū Lu'lu'a and the assassination of 'Umar is the source of al-Mas'ūdī's account (*Murūj*, III, paras. 1559–60).

65 Ibn Sa'd, *Ṭabaqāt*, III/1, 244; *Annali*, V, 55, 178.

66 *Annali*, V, 63, 68.

67 According to al-Zuhrī, Abū Lu'lu'a was originally a Zoroastrian (*kāna majūsiyyan fī aṣlih*, 'Abd al-Razzāq, *Muṣannaf*, V, 474). He may well have been nominally converted to Islam. The narrators evidently did not want to admit this. His daughter, a young girl (*jāriya ṣaghīra*), who was murdered by 'Ubayd Allāh b. 'Umar, is described as 'having pretended to being Muslim' (*tadda'i l-islām*: *ibid.*, V, 479; Ibn Sa'd, *Ṭabaqāt*, III/1, 258, V, 8). According to 'Abd Allāh b. al-'Abbās, 'Umar, on being informed of the identity of his assassin, expressed satisfaction that he was not killed by an Arab ('Abd al-Razzāq, *Muṣannaf*, V, 476; Ibn Sa'd, *Ṭabaqāt*, III/1, 251). The assertions in other sources that Abū Lu'lu'a was a Christian are hardly reliable. They seem to go back to a report of al-Miswar b. Makhrama who did not mention Abū Lu'lu'a's Persian origin (Ṭabarī, I, 2722). The legendary story reported by Sayf b. 'Umar on the authority of al-Sha'bī (Ṭabarī, I, 2632; *Annali*, IV, 500) according to which Abū Lu'lu'a, originally from Nihāwand, had been captured by the Greeks, converted to Christianity, and then was seized from them by the Muslims, is obviously invented to explain why he would have been a Christian convert. His master, al-Mughīra b. Shu'ba, was a prominent leader of the Arab army in the battle of Nihāwand, and there can be little doubt that Abū Lu'lu'a became his slave then as part of the booty. This is expressly affirmed in a report quoted by Ibn Sa'd (*Ṭabaqāt*, III/1, 252).

Islam, as in the case of the Christian Arabs of Taghlib; yet when he perceived a conflict between his Arab bias and his loyalty to Islamic principles, he did not hesitate to obey the latter. This is well illustrated by an anecdotal, but perhaps true, story reported by al-Azraqī. When Nāfiʿ b. ʿAbd al-Ḥārith al-Khuzāʿī, ʿUmar's governor of Mekka, left the town to meet him, the caliph asked him whom he had appointed his deputy there. On being informed that it was his client ʿAbd al-Raḥmān b. Abzā, ʿUmar flew into a rage and reproached Nāfiʿ: 'You have appointed one of the clients over the people of God.' Nāfiʿ told him, however, that he had found Ibn Abzā the one who knew best how to recite the Book of God and the one most informed about the Law of God. ʿUmar calmed down and remembered a saying of the Prophet that God raises some in this religion and abases others.[68]

Modern historians, both Muslim and western, have not been sparing in their admiration for the second successor of Muḥammad. His caliphate is seen as embodying most perfectly the ideal of that institution. Modern Sunnite Muslims in particular have often viewed his application of the Qur'anic principle of *shūrā* and his efforts to base leadership in the community on religious merit and priority in serving the cause of Islam as an exemplary basis for restoring a proper democratic form of the caliphate or other Islamic government. Western scholars have commonly stressed the sheer power of his personality by which he succeeded in imposing his will on the Muslim community and in directing the Arab armies in their extensive conquests without the means of coercion and repression available to later despotic rulers. His great impact on the formation of Islam, seen as second only to that of Muḥammmad, has also been appreciated.[69]

It is probably true that only a man such as ʿUmar, with both a sincere and deep devotion to Islam and a strong sense of group solidarity, *ʿaṣabiyya* in Ibn Khaldūn's terminology, with Quraysh and the Arabs, could safeguard the long-term unity of the Arab and Muslim commonwealth at this stage. The conquests, initiated under Abū Bakr, could certainly have been continued, and perhaps been better co-ordinated, under the leadership of a Khālid b. al-Walīd. It may, however, be doubted that the unity of the conquered empire would have lasted. Most likely powerful factions within Quraysh would soon have established their reign in various regions on an independent basis. Credit for having established

[68] Al-Azraqī, *Akhbār Makka*, ed. F. Wüstenfeld, in *Chroniken der Stadt Mekka*, I (Leipzig, 1858), 380; *Annali*, V, 162. ʿAbd al-Raḥmān b. Abzā, client of Nāfiʿ b. ʿAbd al-Ḥārith, was considered a reliable transmitter from Muḥammad and the early caliphs. He was later appointed governor of Khurāsān by ʿAlī (Ibn Ḥajar, *Tahdhīb*, VI, 132–3).

[69] See H. Lazarus-Yafeh, "Umar b. al-Khaṭṭāb – Paul of Islam?' in *Some Religious Aspects of Islam* (Leiden, 1981), 1–16.

the caliphate firmly as the sole and undivided leadership of the Muslims must go to 'Umar.

Yet it was in reality the caliphate of Quraysh conceived and founded by Abū Bakr that, in spite of its lack of Qur'anic legitimization, now became an essential institution of Islam upheld by the Sunnite creed. 'Umar's attempt to Islamicize this institution by basing it on the Qur'anic principles of *shūrā* and *sābiqa* was doomed to failure almost immediately after his death. Not much later, dynastic succession came to prevail, a development dreaded by 'Umar. Whereas the condition that the caliphs must be descended from Quraysh became a firm legal requirement and retained wide support even after the actual disappearance of the Qurayshite caliphate, *shūrā* and *sābiqa* had at most sentimental appeal for those who looked back from the later caliphate of mere kingship to the ideal caliphate of the Rightly Guided patriarchs of Islam. Not until modern times have suggestions been made to institutionalize *shūrā*.

The reason for the failure of 'Umar's reform is easily discernible. The principle of merit in Islam was in latent conflict with the privileged status of Quraysh. This was concealed at the time when *sābiqa* could be identified with early conversion and backing of Muḥammad in Mekka. The early Companions were now growing old. In order to institutionalize the principles of merit and *shūrā*, 'Umar would have had to repeal the supreme status of Quraysh, a step he was hardly in a position to take, even if he had ever contemplated it, and to open the ranks of the ruling elite to other Muslims. He would have had to set a clear precedent of choosing a non-Qurayshite for his consultative council or to encourage the council to co-opt non-Qurayshites.

The Arab empire that 'Umar established was to last longer, though modified since Mu'āwiya's reign by Syrian Arab hegemony. The domination of Arabs over non-Arabs on an ethnic basis was also in essential conflict with the universal call of Islam. This, however, became patent only in the later Umayyad age when masses of non-Arabs converted to Islam and loudly demanded equality in its name. The caliphate of Quraysh was by that time so deeply rooted in Islam that it survived the decline and disappearance of the Arab military ruling class in the course of the 'Abbasid age.

3 ʿUthmān: the Vicegerent of God and the reign of ʿAbd Shams

ʿUthmān's rule ended after twelve years amid rebellion and with the violent death of the caliph. The grievances against his arbitrary acts were substantial by the standards of the time and widely felt. The historical sources contain lengthy accounts of the wrongdoings (*aḥdāth*) of which he was accused. Towards the end of his reign dissatisfaction and opposition to his conduct appear to have been almost universal except among his kin and close associates. It was only his violent death that, having been turned into a political tool, came to absolve him in Sunnite ideology from any *aḥdāth* and make him a martyr and the third Rightly Guided Caliph.

ʿUthmān's wrongdoings, it should be emphasized, must seem trivial from the perspective of later generations. Not a single Muslim was killed on his orders, except in punishment for murder or adultery. The arbitrary acts of violence of which he was accused were confined to beatings, imprisonment and deportations.[1] The sanctity of Muslim life enjoined by Muḥammad was still respected. Abū Bakr had been forced to declare those refusing to pay the alms-tax to him apostates in order to make war on them. ʿUmar had to call on God and rely on the help of the jinn to get rid of his political enemy Saʿd b. ʿUbāda. ʿUthmān, by nature averse to bloodshed, found it easy to comply with the Prophet's injunction.

As a wealthy member of the Qurayshite aristocracy, son of the Mekkan merchant ʿAffān and grandson of Muḥammad's aunt Umm Ḥakīm bt ʿAbd al-Muṭṭalib,[2] ʿUthmān had occupied a special place among the early

[1] Only Ḍābiʾ b. al-Ḥārith al-Tamīmī al-Burjumī is reported to have died in ʿUthmān's prison. He was first imprisoned for lampooning the Banū Jarwal b. Nahshal, who had taken away from him a hunting dog which they had previously given him at his request. They complained to ʿUthmān. When Ḍābiʾ was released he planned to attack and hurt the caliph in revenge, but was apprehended. This time he was left to die in prison. His son ʿUmayr is said to have jumped upon ʿUthmān's body in revenge when he was carried to his burial. Much later, in 85/704, the Umayyad governor al-Ḥajjāj killed ʿUmayr in retaliation (Balādhurī, *Ansāb*, V, 84–5; Ibn Shabba, *Taʾrīkh al-Madīna* , 1024–7; Ṭabarī, II, 869–72).

[2] Umm Ḥakīm al-Bayḍāʾ was the twin sister of Muḥammad's father ʿAbd Allāh and mother of ʿUthmān's mother Arwā bt Kurayz (Balādhurī, *Ansāb*, V, 1).

Companions of the Prophet. Muḥammad deeply appreciated his adherence to, and loyal support of, Islam at a time when the great majority of 'Abd Shams vigorously strove to eradicate the new religion, and treated him with a kind of politeness and deference not shown to any of the other Companions. He is decribed as covering his bare legs as soon as 'Uthmān entered the room, which he did not do in the presence of Abū Bakr and 'Umar.[3] At the time of 'Uthmān's conversion to Islam Muḥammad gave him his daughter Ruqayya in marriage, and she emigrated to Abyssinia with her husband. When she died in Medina after the battle of Badr, the Prophet married his other daughter, Umm Kulthūm, to him. In terms of the prevailing standards of social equality (*kafā'a*), this placed 'Uthmān distinctly above Abū Bakr and 'Umar, whose daughters Muḥammad married but to whom he would not give any of his own daughters in marriage. 'Umar's demand, during his caliphate, to marry Muḥammad's granddaughter Umm Kulthūm, 'Alī's daughter, was an assertion of his having reached a social status he had not enjoyed during Muḥammad's lifetime.[4]

Muḥammad also humoured 'Uthmān's glaring lack of military prowess. He excused him from participating in the battle of Badr in order to take care of Ruqayya in her illness, yet granted him a share in the booty. 'Uthmān's flight at the battle of Uḥud was said to be forgiven by a Qur'anic revelation. Whenever justifiable, the Prophet exempted him from fighting in battle and assigned other tasks to him. Prominent among the virtues (*faḍā'il*) credited to him were rather his acts of generous support of Muḥammad and the Muslim community from his personal fortune.[5] This liberality, however, hardly dented his great wealth, as is evident from his grand lifestyle in Medina and the royal dowries he was ready to pay for his marriages throughout his career.[6] He carried on his caravan trade in Medina as he had done in Mekka and Abyssinia. For Muḥammad he was also most useful as a diplomatic negotiator accepted by the Mekkan aristocracy, especially in the critical situation of al-Ḥudaybiyya.

[3] *Annali*, VIII, 296; Ibn 'Asākir, *Ta'rīkh Madīnat Dimashq: 'Uthmān b. 'Affān*, ed. Sukayna al-Shihābī (Damascus, 1984), 76–88; see also Abbott, *Aishah*, 103–4.

[4] 'Umar had previously proposed to 'Ā'isha that he marry Abū Bakr's still minor daughter Umm Kulthūm. In spite of 'Ā'isha's pleading on behalf of the Commander of the Faithful, Umm Kulthūm resisted because of 'Umar's reputation for rudeness towards his wives. 'Ā'isha then enlisted the help of 'Amr b. al-'Āṣ, who pointed out to 'Umar that Umm Kulthūm had been brought up under the mild regime of the Mother of the Faithful 'Ā'isha and that 'Umar might offend her by his harshness and thus fail in his duty of rendering due respect to his deceased predecessor. 'Amr then suggested that 'Umar marry 'Alī's daughter Umm Kulthūm and thus establish ties with the Messenger of God (Ṭabarī, I, 2732).

[5] Ibn 'Asākir, *'Uthmān*, 46–70.

[6] It is certainly not the case that 'Uthmān 'had given his whole fortune for Islam' as suggested by H. Djaït, *La Grande Discorde: religion et politique dans l'Islam des origines* (Paris, 1989), 227.

While 'Uthmān was a distinguished, highly successful merchant, he had at no time before his election displayed any qualities of public leadership. Among the six members of the electoral council, he was the only one who had never been entrusted by Muḥammad or the first two caliphs with leading a raid or an army. Before the election he had no political ambitions and can hardly even have thought of himself as a potential candidate for the supreme reign. Yet he was not chosen by the electors for his weakness and insignificance which they hoped to manipulate, as Wellhausen suggested.[7] Rather, he was put forward as the only strong counter-candidate to 'Alī. As an intimate and favourite of Muḥammad, twice the Prophet's son-in-law, he could better rival 'Ali's close kinship ties with the latter than could the rest. More importantly, he could count on the solid backing of the Mekkan aristocracy. Against any of the other council members, none of whom belonged to 'Abd Manāf, 'Abd Shams would still have been honour bound to offer 'Alī their support. The opinion of the Anṣār, excluded by Abū Bakr from the ruling class, no longer had any weight. 'Uthmān was no doubt aware of the situation and of the massive backing of Quraysh for him. He remained entirely passive and made no plea on his own behalf. Quite unprepared for his office, he ascended the pulpit after his election and apologized: 'O people, we have not been orators (*khuṭabā'*). If we live, the oration will come to you in proper shape (*'alā wajhihā*), God willing.'[8]

Muḥammad's exceptional favour towards him and the overwhelming endorsement of his election by Quraysh fostered in 'Uthmān a sense that his personal title to the reign in succession to Muḥammad was more firmly grounded than that of either of his predecessors. Having been raised to the supreme position without any effort on his own part evidently strengthened his belief that he had been chosen and invested by God. Doing away with the cumbersome tradition that had made 'Umar the 'Vicegerent of the Vicegerent of the Messenger of God', he adopted the official title of 'Vicegerent of God' (*khalīfat Allāh*).[9] The new title

[7] J. Wellhausen, *Das arabische Reich und sein Sturz* (Berlin, 1902), 26.

[8] Balādhurī, *Ansāb*, V, 24; Ibn Sa'd, *Ṭabaqāt*, III/1, 43; Ibn Shabba, *Ta'rīkh al-Madīna*, 957–8; *Annali*, VII, 14. Al-Ṭabarī preferred to suppress the reports about this embarrassing occasion and quoted only the pious sermon ascribed to 'Uthmān in Sayf b. 'Umar's account (Ṭabarī, I, 2800–1). An equally fictitious inaugural sermon by 'Uthmān which Sayf evidently reported elsewhere with a different *isnād* is quoted by al-Ṭabarī, I, 3058–9.

[9] See the documentation in Crone and Hinds, *God's Caliph*, 6, to which Ṭabarī, I, 3044: . . . *an atabarra' min 'amal Allāh wa-khilāfatih* may be added. The change of titulature is reflected in the letters exchanged between Mu'āwiya and 'Alī (Balādhurī, *Ansāb*, II, 277–82; Minqarī, *Waq'at Ṣiffīn*, 86–91, where Abū Bakr appears as *al-khalīfa min ba'd (rasūl Allāh)* and 'Umar as *khalīfat khalīfatih* (Minqarī, *Waq'at Ṣiffīn*, 87, in 'Alī's letter *al-khalīfa* and *khalīfat al-khalīfa*). 'Uthmān then is simply named *al-khalīfa al-maẓlūm* by Mu'āwiya while 'Alī abstains from giving him the title *khalīfa*. Following the practice under 'Umar, 'Uthmān was commonly addressed as Commander of the Faithful, a title hardly suitable for him.

became standard under the Umayyads.[10] The caliph reigned now by the grace of God and as His representative on earth, no longer as a deputy of the Messenger of God. On this basis, there could be no question of 'Uthmān resigning when he lost the trust of those who had backed his election.[11]

The grievances against the caliph

'Uthmān thus deemed it within his right to dispose freely of the powers and riches of the caliphate at his own discretion and deeply resented any criticism or interference in his conduct by anyone.[12] During the election, he had twice pledged without hesitation that he would follow the Book of God, the Sunna of His Prophet, and the practice *(fi'l)* of Abū Bakr and 'Umar, while 'Alī had cautiously stated that he would do so to the limit of his ability *('alā juhdī min dhālik)*.[13] The unabashed favouritism towards his close kin that he showed from the beginning of his reign stood in marked contrast to this commitment. The impression of self-assured highhandedness on his part among the public is well reflected in the following anecdote. When the people criticized 'Uthmān for making a gift of 100,000 dirhams to his nephew Sa'īd b. al-'Āṣ, the members of the *shūrā*, 'Alī, al-Zubayr, Ṭalḥa, Sa'd and 'Abd al-Raḥmān, came to make representations to him. He told them that he had kin and maternal relations to take care of. When they asked: 'Did not Abū Bakr and 'Umar have kin and maternal relations?' he answered: 'Abū Bakr and 'Umar sought reward in the hereafter *(yaḥtasibān)* by withholding from their kin, and I seek reward by giving to my kin.' They said: 'By God, their guidance then is preferable to us to your guidance.' He merely replied: 'There is no power and strength but in God.'[14] 'Uthmān could perhaps appear motivated mostly by an almost childlike pleasure to be in a position to gratify his family and to rehabilitate those of them disgraced by Muḥammad for their opposition to Islam. In fact, however, he acted, backed by his close kin, with great determination and the conviction that the house of Umayya, as the core clan of Quraysh, was uniquely qualified to rule in the name of Islam.

Al-Zuhrī explained that 'Uthmān, in granting his cousin Marwān b. al-Ḥakam the *khums* (of the war booty) of Ifrīqiya and giving his close relatives money (from the treasury), was interpreting the Qur'anic

[10] Crone and Hinds, *God's Caliph*, 6–11. [11] See Ṭabarī, I, 3043–4.

[12] Caetani suggested that 'Uthmān rightly considered himself the first caliph elected according to all the proper rules and with popular assent, in contrast to the quasi-coup *(falta)* by which Abū Bakr and 'Umar had attained power. 'Uthmān's attitude to the powers of government differed therefore from that of his predecessors, and he acted arbitrarily in administering the public treasury, which he considered to be entirely at his disposal (*Annali*, VIII, 9). [13] Ṭabarī, I, 2793–4. [14] Balādhurī, *Ansāb*, V, 28.

injunctions to provide for relatives (*ta'awwala fī dhālika l-ṣilata llatī amara llāhu bih*). 'He took the sums of money and borrowed (*istaslafa*) money from the treasury saying: Abū Bakr and 'Umar left what belonged to them of this money, but I take it and distribute to my kin from it. The people criticized him for that.'[15] This implies that 'Uthmān based his generosity to his family on the Qur'anic passages assigning a portion of the fifth of the booty and *fay'* to the kin of the Prophet. While Abū Bakr and 'Umar had denied the Banū Hāshim their Qur'anic share after Muḥammad's death, they had not used it for the benefit of their own kin but left it to the public treasury. Arrogating the integral rights of the Prophet to himself as his legitimate successor, 'Uthmān held that he was entitled and obligated to give the Qur'anic shares to his own close kin. He also seems to have granted the oasis of Fadak and an estate in the Mahzūr valley of Medina, which had belonged to Muḥammad and had been treated by Abū Bakr and 'Umar as a *ṣadaqa*, an endowment for the benefit of the Muslim community, as land concessions to Marwān b. al-Ḥakam and Marwān's brother al-Ḥārith respectively.[16]

Even graver were the implications of 'Uthmān's policy concerning the *ṣawāfī*, the extensive former crown lands and domanial estates in the conquered territories. This land, left ownerless by the Muslim conquest and the death or flight of the Persian king and fief-holders, was, according to the rulings and practice of Muḥammad, unquestionably subject to division among the conquering Muslim warriors with one-fifth to be retained for the imam. Under the caliph 'Umar, however, it had been decided, after some hesitation, to keep the land undivided and to constitute it, together with the conquered land whose owners or fief-holders had stayed, as permanent *fay'*, communal property for the benefit of the garrison towns in whose territories they were located. 'Uthmān viewed this land in the old royal tradition as crown property to be used at the discretion of the Vicegerent of God. According to al-Awzā'ī, Mu'āwiya asked 'Uthmān for control over the *ṣawāfī* in Syria, complaining that he was unable to pay his soldiers adequately, and 'Uthmān acceded to his request.[17]

[15] *Ibid.*, 25; Ibn Sa'd, *Ṭabaqāt*, III/1, 44; *Annali*, VII, 420.

[16] Ibn Qutayba, *al-Ma'ārif*, ed. Tharwat 'Ukāsha (Cairo, 1960), 195. On Mahzūr see Yāqūt, *Buldān*, IV, 701, and M. Lecker, 'Muḥammad at Medina: A Geographical Approach', *JSAI*, VI, (1985), 29–62, at 32 n. 32, 36–7. The sources generally state that it was Mu'āwiya who gave Fadak as a fief to Marwān (Balādhurī, *Futūḥ*, 29–33; Veccia-Vaglieri, 'Fadak', *EI* (2nd edn)). There was, however, not much love lost between Mu'āwiya and Marwān. It seems unlikely that Mu'āwiya would have given Marwān Fadak without the precedent set by 'Uthmān.

[17] See A. Von Kremer, *Geschichte der herrschenden Ideen im Islam*, (Leipzig 1886), 336–7, quoting Ibn 'Asākir's *Ta'rīkh Madīnat Dimashq*. The *isnād* is (Muḥammad) b. 'Ā'idh – al-Walīd (b. Muslim) – Abū 'Amr (al-Awzā'ī).

In Iraq 'Uthmān began to grant land concessions (*iqṭā'*) from the former domanial land of the Persian kings to prominent Companions of Muḥammad. Most of the reports about these grants go back to Mūsā, son of the Companion Ṭalḥa who was a major beneficiary of this policy. Mūsā emphasized that 'Uthmān was the first to make such grants. Among the recipients named by him were 'Abd Allāh b. Mas'ūd, Sa'd b. Abī Waqqāṣ, Khabbāb b. al-Aratt, Usāma b. Zayd, who sold his land, al-Zubayr, Ṭalḥa, and perhaps 'Ammār b. Yāsir, besides tribal leaders who had distinguished themselves during the conquests.[18]

When this alienation of *fay'* land provoked protests in Kūfa, 'Uthmān sought to justify his policy, if a report of Sayf b. 'Umar[19] can be trusted, by allowing the exchange of privately owned land in Arabia for domanial land in Iraq. This manoeuvre allowed him to turn land in Arabia into crown property of which he could freely dispose without interference by the enraged tribal warriors in the garrison towns. Thus Ṭalḥa is reported to have acquired his estate of al-Nashtāstaj near Kūfa for his land at Khaybar and elsewhere in Arabia,[20] while the Kufan chief of Kinda al-Ash'ath b. Qays bought his estate of Ṭīzanābādh from 'Uthmān for his land in Ḥaḍramawt. Marwān b. al-Ḥakam bought his estate, later known as Nahr Marwān, from 'Uthmān with money or property (*māl*, var. *mulk*) which the caliph had previously given him. Some of the land in Arabia was then, according to Sayf's report, granted to residents of Medina who had participated in the battles of al-Qādisiyya and al-Madā'in. By recognizing their claim as a claim to land rather than a share of revenue from the *fay'* 'Uthmān thus undid 'Umar's immobilization of

[18] Balādhurī, *Futūḥ*, 273–4. 'Ammār b. Yāsir is mentioned in one report (*ibid.*, 273) as the recipient of Istīniyā. In another report (*ibid.*, 274), however, Istīniyā is mentioned as an *iqṭā'* of Khabbāb b. al-Aratt. The latter is also named as the recipient of Istīniyā in a report by al-Madā'inī (Yāqūt, *Buldān*, I, 244–5).

[19] Ṭabarī, I, 2854–5. A detailed analysis of this text has recently been presented by A. Noth ('Eine Standortbestimmung der Expansion (*Futūḥ*) unter den ersten Kalifen (Analyse von Tabari I, 2854–2846)', *Asiatische Studien*, 63 (1989), 120–35). Noth is inclined to accept this report as early and reliable on the grounds that it stands apart from the main tradition which he considers to be transformed by secondary distortion. Evidently failing to notice its pervasive 'Uthmanid bias, he states that he did not discover any motive for partisan forgery. Noth does not comment on the *isnāds* which attribute the basic report to 'Ubayd Allāh b. 'Umar b. Ḥafṣ al-'Umarī, one of the 'seven jurists of Medina', who died in 147/764 (Ibn Ḥajar, *Tahdhīb*, VII, 38–40). If this attribution is reliable, the report was composed in the late Umayyad age and is unlikely to reflect views of the contemporaries around the year 650, as Noth suggests. As a jurist, rather than a mere transmitter, 'Ubayd Allāh b. 'Umar would seem to be a prime suspect for that kind of secondary distortion that in Noth's view characterizes the main tradition.

[20] Yāqūt (*Buldān*, IV, 783) quotes a report that Ṭalḥa acquired al-Nashtāstaj in exchange for land in Ḥaḍramawt.

the *fay'* land and justified his own seizure of immobilized land as part of the legal share of the imam.[21]

'Uthmān's alienation of the communal *fay'* and its reconversion into crown land aroused discontent in the garrison towns and provoked accusations that the caliph and his governors were misappropriating *māl al-muslimīn*, money belonging to the Muslims collectively, as *māl Allāh*, money at the discretionary disposal of the Vicegerent of God. In Syria the Early Companion Abū Dharr al-Ghifārī made himself the mouthpiece of the discontent[22] and criticized Mu'āwiya's extravagant spending on his palace, al-Khaḍrā', in Damascus.[23] At Mu'āwiya's request 'Uthmān ordered him to be sent back to Medina. As he continued his agitation, he was exiled to al-Rabadha in the desert, where he died in 31/652.[24]

In Kūfa the unguarded boast of 'Uthmān's governor Sa'īd b. al-'Āṣ that the *sawād*, the fertile cultivated land of Iraq, was the garden of Quraysh provoked a riot among a group of Qur'ān readers led by Mālik al-Ashtar al-Nakha'ī. The governor complained to 'Uthmān, who ordered the group to be deported first to Mu'āwiya in Damascus and later to 'Abd al-Raḥmān b. Khālid b. al-Walīd, governor of Ḥimṣ. The discontent in the town did not subside, however, and open rebellion erupted in 34/654–5, when Sa'īd was away in Medina. As the rebels, led by

[21] Sayf b. 'Umar is obviously trying in his account to obfuscate the facts and to show 'Uthmān acting quite legitimately in the face of the arrogance and rebelliousness of the Kufans. Caetani thus describes the account as 'singularly obscure' (*Annali*, VII, 361) and Noth stresses that he is far from certain to have understood and interpreted the text correctly in all its detail ('Eine Standortsbestimmung', 120). Yet the fraud underlying 'Uthmān's procedure is plain enough in Sayf's affirmation that Ṭalḥa, Marwān and al-Ash'ath b. Qays were buying their estates from 'Uthmān and from land that 'Uthmān owned in Iraq. 'Uthmān could not have owned any private land in Iraq nor could he even have claimed a personal share of the conquered domanial estates since he had not participated in the conquests. He was in fact giving away or selling communal land as crown property.

[22] Sayf b. 'Umar describes him as being duped by the Shi'ite heretic 'Abd Allāh b. Saba' with the argument about *māl al-muslimīn* and *māl Allāh* (Ṭabarī, I, 2858–9). Abū Dharr had begun his agitation in Medina after 'Uthmān had given 500,000 dirhams to Marwān b. al-Ḥakam, 300,000 to al-Ḥārith b. al-Ḥakam and 100,000 to the Medinan Zayd b. Thābit from the *khums* of the booty seized in Ifrīqiya in 27/647. He then quoted relevant Qur'anic passages threatening the horders of riches with hell-fire. Marwān complained to 'Uthmān, who sent his servant Nātil to warn Abū Dharr, but to no avail. 'Uthmān displayed patience for some time until, in the presence of the caliph, Abū Dharr launched an angry verbal attack on Ka'b al-Aḥbār, who had backed 'Uthmān's free use of public money. 'Uthmān now chided Abū Dharr and sent him to Damascus, where he had previously been registered on the public payroll (Balādhurī, *Ansāb*, V, 52).

[23] Balādhurī, *Ansāb*, V, 53.

[24] *Ibid.*, 52–6; Ibn Shabba, *Ta'rīkh al-Madīna*, 1033–41. Whereas the Kufan and Basran tradition mostly affirmed that Abū Dharr was exiled by 'Uthmān against his will, the Medinan tradition was divided, orthodox Sunnite scholars such as Sa'īd b. al-Musayyab insisting that Abū Dharr went voluntarily into exile. The Shi'ite Sharīf al-Murtaḍā quoted in his *Kitāb al-Shāfī* traditions of al-Wāqidī proving that Abū Dharr was exiled by 'Uthmān against his will (Ibn Abi l-Ḥadīd, *Sharḥ*, III, 55–8; further traditions of al-Wāqidī concerning Abū Dharr are quoted in *ibid.*, VIII, 359–61).

al-Ashtar, prevented Sa'īd from re-entering Kūfa, 'Uthmān was forced to agree to their choice of Abū Mūsā al-Ash'arī as their governor.

Modern historians have often maintained that 'Uthmān's policy with respect to the conquered land was essentially the same as 'Umar's. Wellhausen first argued that it was 'Umar who had provoked the conflict with the warriors of the conquests by withholding the seized land from division among them against the traditional Arab right of booty sanctioned by the Qur'ān with little modification. The revolt erupted under 'Uthmān merely because of his weakness in contrast to 'Umar's overpowering authority.[25] Caetani developed this interpretation further, suggesting that 'Uthmān became the victim of 'Umar's administrative mistakes. 'Umar had not prohibited the acquisition of land by Muslims outside Arabia and had himself made grants from domanial land in Iraq.[26] This view was endorsed by G. Levi della Vida in his article on 'Uthmān in the *Encyclopaedia of Islam* and is upheld also in some recent studies.[27] In reality, there is no sound evidence that 'Umar granted concessions from domanial land under cultivation which would have been in breach of his declared policy of keeping such land undivided for the benefit of future generations.[28] 'Uthmān's attempt to reconvert the communal land into crown property was a major step towards turning the caliphate into a traditional kingship. His aim was fully realized by Mu'āwiya during his caliphate as he brought all *ṣawāfī* land throughout the empire under his direct control and discretionary disposal in granting and withdrawing fiefs.[29]

The narrators critical of 'Uthmān's conduct commonly divide his reign into two distinct periods. During the first six years his rule was said to have been unexceptionable, while in the latter six his offences mounted. Al-Zuhrī elaborates that in the former period the people had nothing to hold against him, and he was better liked than 'Umar because of the latter's sternness and 'Uthmān's mildness towards them. In the second period he began to neglect their affairs; he employed his kin and family and heaped money on them. The people now censured him for that.[30] Al-Zuhrī further quotes al-Miswar b. Makhrama al-Zuhrī, 'Abd al-Raḥmān b. 'Awf's nephew and initially a friend of 'Uthmān, as stating that 'Uthmān followed the conduct of his two predecessors for six years

[25] J. Wellhausen, *Skizzen und Vorarbeiten* (Berlin, 1889) VI, 118 n. 3; Wellhausen, *Das arabische Reich*, 28–9, where he adds that Muḥammad had already set certain precedents for 'Umar's fiscal practice. [26] See excursus 4: Domanial land in Iraq under 'Umar.

[27] E.g. W. Schmucker, *Untersuchungen zu einigen wichtigen bodenrechtlichen Konsequenzen der islamischen Eroberungsbewegung* (Bonn, 1972), esp. 134–51; Djaït, *La Grande Discorde*, 84.

[28] *Annali*, V, 304, VII, 376.

[29] Mu'āwiya thus confiscated the estate called Zurāra near Kūfa from Zurāra b. Yazīd of the Banū Bakkār and claimed it as crown property (*uṣfiyat*). Zurāra b. Yazīd had been chief of the police (*shurṭa*) under 'Uthmān's governor Sa'īd b. al-'Āṣ (Yāqūt, *Buldān*, II, 921) and as such had presumably been granted the estate. The older *iqṭā*'s had generally been treated as permanent personal property. [30] Balādhurī, *Ansāb*, V, 25.

without infraction, but then 'the old man grew soft and feeble, and came to be dominated [by his kin]'.[31]

In reality 'Uthmān's policy of establishing members of his clan as governors throughout the empire was fully evident even during the early years of his reign. In 24/644–5, shortly after his accession, he appointed 'Alī b. 'Adī b. Rabī'a of 'Abd Shams governor of Mekka.[32] In the following year he deposed the sick 'Umayr b. Sa'd al-Anṣārī, governor of Ḥimṣ, Qinnasrīn and Upper Mesopotamia, at his request,[33] and turned these provinces, which since the death of Abū 'Ubayda had been kept by 'Umar under separate governors independent of the Umayyad governors of Damascus, over to Mu'āwiya. Given the great strength of the garrison of Ḥimṣ at that time, this meant a substantial increase in Mu'āwiya's power which enabled him later to challenge and defy the caliph 'Alī.[34]

In the same year 'Uthmān dismissed 'Amr b. al-'Āṣ as governor of Egypt and appointed his own foster-brother 'Abd Allāh b. Sa'd b. Abī Sarḥ of 'Āmir Quraysh in his place. Most likely also in 25/645–6[35] he replaced Sa'd b. Abī Waqqāṣ, whom he had appointed the previous year, as governor of Kūfa with the Umayyad al-Walīd b. 'Uqba b. Abī Mu'ayṭ,

31 'Abd al-Razzāq, *Muṣannaf*, V, 478. 32 *Annali*, VII, 45.

33 Trying to prove that all governors deposed by 'Uthmān except his Umayyad kin were dishonest or incapable, Caetani mistranslated in Sayf b. 'Umar's account the expression *ṭu'ina fa-adnā* (he was smitten and came close to death) as 'he was [the] object of severe criticism [on the part of his subjects]'. He went on to assert that the parallel report then quoted by Sayf (Ṭabarī, I, 2867) tries to conceal 'Umayr's dishonesty by describing him as ill (*Annali*, VII, 67).

34 Ḥimṣ still had a separate governor during the later part of 'Uthmān's reign. The Kufans exiled as troublemakers under Sa'īd b. al-'Āṣ were sent first to Mu'āwiya in Damascus and then to 'Abd al-Raḥmān b. Khālid b. al-Walīd, governor of Ḥimṣ (Ṭabarī, I, 2913–14, 2921). 'Abd al-Raḥmān was, however, appointed by Mu'āwiya (*ibid.*, 2913) and evidently his subordinate.

35 This date seems preferable to the year 26/646–7 accepted by Wellhausen (*Skizzen*, VI, 115). Caetani left the question of the correct date open (*Annali*, VII, 64). Al-Ṭabarī reports the appointment of al-Walīd under the year 26, following the account of al-Wāqidī, while mentioning that Sayf b. 'Umar's account places it in the year 25 (Ṭabarī, I, 2811 and 2801). Al-Balādhurī, however, quotes both Abū Mikhnaf and al-Wāqidī, the latter on the authority of Ibn Sa'd, as stating that 'Uthmān, in accordance with a recommendation of 'Umar, after his accession confirmed all governors for a year except for al-Mughīra b. Shu'ba whom he, following 'Umar's wish, replaced with Sa'd b. Abī Waqqāṣ. After a year he dismissed Sa'd and appointed al-Walīd in his place (*Ansāb*, V, 29). Sayf's account (Ṭabarī, I, 2901–2) agrees with this. The Kufan campaign to Armenia and Ādharbayjān (*Annali*, VII, 98–103, 159–63), which took place at the beginning of al-Walīd's governorship, is more likely to date from the year 25 than 26. The governorship of al-Walīd moreover lasted, according to Kufan tradition (Balādhurī, *Ansāb*, V, 31; Ṭabarī, I, 2813), five years. According to the more reliable reports he was deposed in the year 30 (*Annali*, VII, 256, 310–60). Caetani's argument that 'Umar could not have ordered his successor to nominate Sa'd governor of Kūfa since he included him in the electoral council (*ibid.*, 26) is tenuous. The composition of the council had been established some time before 'Umar's murder. The recommendation would obviously not have excluded Sa'd from being elected. In this case he could have appointed some other governor.

his uterine brother.[36] In 29/649-50 he removed Abū Mūsā al-Ash'arī[37] from the governorship of Baṣra and gave it to his maternal cousin 'Abd Allāh b. 'Āmir b. Kurayz of 'Abd Shams, who was only twenty-five years old. He added substantially to Ibn 'Āmir's power by joining the governorship of 'Umān and al-Baḥrayn to that of Baṣra and putting their garrison (*jund*) under his command.[38] Five years after his accession, all major governorships were thus solidly in the hands of the caliph's relatives. When al-Walīd b.'Uqba had to be deposed because of misconduct in the year 30/650–1, 'Uthmān replaced him with another Umayyad, Sa'īd b. al-'Āṣ b. Abī Uḥayḥa. He systematically strengthened his ties with these favourites by giving them his daughters in marriage.[39]

There is thus no evidence for a fundamental break in 'Uthmān's policies at mid-term in his caliphate. His nepotism was apparent from the beginning. It did not, however, provoke serious opposition during the first half of his reign. He was able to keep the prominent Companions and Quraysh well disposed by his general leniency, which contrasted sharply with 'Umar's roughness, and through his extravagant presents. He also permitted the Qurayshites to move freely in the conquered provinces, whereas 'Umar had forbidden them to leave the Ḥijāz except by special permission.[40] Some of them grew immensely wealthy under him.[41] It was from the year 30/650–1 on that dissatisfaction and resistance openly manifested themselves throughout most of the empire. 'Uthmān's generosity was now restricted to his kin, who seemed to dominate him. The prominent Companions of the *shūrā* more and more lost their influence over him. At the same time his arrogant mistreatment of several of the earliest Companions of lowly origin, Abū Dharr al-Ghifārī, 'Abd Allāh b. Mas'ūd and 'Ammār b. Yāsir, provoked outrage among the

[36] Arguing that the nomination of al-Walīd b. 'Uqba by 'Uthmān was not an act of personal favouritism, Caetani interpreted the statement by Sayf b. 'Umar that al-Walīd had been *'āmil* of 'Umar over the Rabī'a in al-Jazīra (Ṭabarī, I, 2812) as meaning that 'Uthmān merely transferred him from one governorship to another (*Annali*, VII, 154). In fact al-Walīd had been appointed by 'Umar alms-tax collector among the Banū Taghlib (Balādhurī, *Ansāb*, V, 31) and then had been deposed by him because of a line of poetry threatening Taghlib (*Aghānī*, IV, 183).

[37] Caetani argued, on the basis of a report of al-Madā'inī (Ṭabarī, I, 2831–2) about a Basran delegation to 'Uthmān asking for Abū Mūsā's replacement, that the latter was deposed because of administrative abuses and the accusation that he enriched himself at the expense of the treasury (*Annali*, VII, 238–9). The words of Ghaylān b. Kharasha al-Ḍabbī reported by al-Madā'inī do not imply, however, that Abū Mūsā improperly enriched himself. Ghaylān rather is described as successfully appealing to the caliph's Umayyad greed by suggesting that he give a dashing young Qurayshite the chance to enrich himself instead of the old man of lowly origin. Ghaylān b. Kharasha was a prominent supporter of the prophetess Sajāḥ during the *ridda* (Ṭabarī, I, 1919). He was thus probably one of the disadvantaged latecomers to Baṣra.

[38] Ṭabarī, I, 2833.

[39] See excursus 3: The marriages of 'Uthmān.

[40] Ṭabarī, I, 3025–6; M. Hinds, 'The Murder of the Caliph 'Uthmān', *International Journal of Middle East Studies*, 3 (1972), 450–69, at 466.

[41] See *Annali*, VIII, 69–71.

pious, as well as among their tribes and the clans of Quraysh to whom they were affiliated and who were liable for their protection.

Driven by his unbounded family pride, ʿUthmān must early on have sought a way to secure a hereditary succession to his caliphate. The principle of *shūrā* among the Early Companions, so vigorously upheld by ʿUmar, stood in his way. There is evidence that ʿUthmān attempted to get around it as early as the first year of his reign. According to a tradition quoted by al-Bukhārī, Marwān b. al-Ḥakam, ʿUthmān's first cousin and later caliph, reported that in the 'year of the nosebleed (*sanat al-ruʿāf*)', that is in 24/644–5,[42] Uthmān was afflicted by violent nosebleeding so that he was unable to perform the pilgrimage, and made his testament. An unidentified Qurayshite and Marwān's brother al-Ḥārith[43] came successively to him, suggesting that he appoint a successor. ʿUthmān asked each one of them whether the people had someone in mind, but both remained silent. Then he suggested that the people were mentioning al-Zubayr, and al-Ḥārith confirmed this. ʿUthmān commented that al-Zubayr was indeed the best man and the one dearest to the Prophet.[44]

In his report, Marwān did not mention whether ʿUthmān actually made a testament in favour of al-Zubayr, a matter which he could hardly have been interested in publicizing. The family of al-Zubayr, however, preserved a claim that ʿUthmān had appointed their ancestor as his successor. Muṣʿab al-Zubayrī (d. 236/851) reported: "Uthmān made a testament in favour of al-Zubayr until his son ʿAmr would grow up (*awṣā ʿUthmān . . . ila l-Zubayr b. al-ʿAwwām ḥattā yakbur ibnuh ʿAmr*).'[45] Although no further information about the circumstances is provided, it seems most likely that the report refers to the same occasion. ʿAmr b. ʿUthmān, the caliph's eldest surviving son,[46] had been born during the caliphate of ʿUmar.[47] At the beginning of ʿUthmān's reign he thus had not

[42] That the year 24/644–5 was known as *sanat* (or *ʿām*) *al-ruʿāf* is confirmed by al-Ṭabarī (I, 2799) and other sources. In his commentary on the Bukhārī text, Ibn Ḥajar (*Fatḥ al-bārī*, VII, 58) identifies it as the year 31/651-2, referring to the *Kitāb al-Madīna* of ʿUmar b. Shabba. The account of the latter seems entirely unreliable (see below, pp. 89–90). The year 24 was the only one before the siege of ʿUthmān's residence in which he did not lead the pilgrimage in person during his reign but deputed ʿAbd al-Raḥmān b. ʿAwf to lead it (Balādhurī, *Ansāb*, V, 23–4; *Annali*, VII, 41).

[43] The al-Ḥārith named in the tradition is certainly correctly identified as Marwān's brother by Ibn Ḥajar, *Fatḥ al-bārī*, VII, 58.

[44] Bukhārī, *Ṣaḥīḥ*, *Faḍā'il al-ṣaḥāba* 13; Ibn Shabba, *Ta'rīkh al-Madīna*, 1055; *Annali*, VII, 42. In another version of the tradition an unidentified man names al-Zubayr as the one mentioned by the people, and ʿUthmān confirms that al-Zubayr was 'by three times the best of you' (*Annali*, VII, 42).

[45] Al-Zubayrī, *Nasab*, 106, quoted by al-Balādhurī, *Ansāb*, V, 103.

[46] Al-Balādhurī (*Ansāb*, V, 106) calls ʿAmr the eldest (*akbar*) of the sons of ʿUthmān, presumably meaning the eldest surviving one. Muṣʿab al-Zubayrī describes him as the eldest son of ʿUthmān having offspring (*Nasab*, 105).

[47] Ibn Ḥajar, *Iṣāba*, I, 261, quoting al-Zubayr b. Bakkār's *Kitāb al-Nasab*. See further excursus 3.

yet reached maturity. It is unlikely that 'Uthmān would have appointed al-Zubayr as his successor at any later stage. At the beginning of his reign he evidently felt particularly grateful to al-Zubayr for having backed him in the recent election against 'Alī in spite of his close blood relationship with the latter and was thus prepared to testify that he had been the Companion dearest to the Prophet.

'Uthmān's testament appointing al-Zubayr as his successor to be followed by his son 'Amr was probably not published at the time. It would no doubt have been challenged and opposed by some of the other early Companions. Since 'Uthmān soon recovered his health, it was best to forget the matter. Later during his caliphate, he and his kin viewed 'Amr as his heir apparent[48] although no formal appointment was made. Marwān still later, evidently before his own election as caliph, invited 'Amr to come to Syria in order that 'he be given the oath of allegiance'. This was at the time when Marwān needed to challenge the prerogative of the Sufyanids, the descendants of Mu'āwiya, which was widely backed in Syria, and when he wanted to remind the Syrians that 'Uthmān, not Mu'āwiya, was the real founder of the Umayyad caliphate. 'Amr, no doubt wisely, declined, and died in Minā.[49]

Reports that 'Uthmān at some stage of his caliphate appointed 'Abd al-Raḥmān b. 'Awf as his successor are unreliable. Ibn Shabba quoted an account transmitted by 'Abd Allāh b. Lahī'a that 'Uthmān, afflicted by nosebleeding, ordered his client Ḥumrān b. Abān to write a testament for the succession of 'Abd al-Raḥmān, but the latter prayed that God would let him die before 'Uthmān. He died six months later.[50] From this story

[48] According to a report of the Umayyad Sa'īd b. 'Amr b. Sa'īd b. al-'Āṣ related by 'Umar b. Shabba, al-Walīd b. 'Uqba before his nomination as governor of Kūfa expressed in a poem his hope that 'Uthmān's sons 'Amr and Khālid would grow up quickly so that they could honour him as their uncle. Clearly implied is the expectation that they would succeed 'Uthmān who, according to the poetry, was showing preference for his uncle al-Ḥakam over his half-brother al-Walīd. 'Uthmān was moved by al-Walīd's complaint and appointed him governor (*Aghānī*, IV, 177; *Annali*, VII, 156). If the occasion is reliably reported, al-Walīd expected 'Uthmān to be succeeded by one of his sons as early as the second year of his reign. According to Sayf b. 'Umar, there was persistent enmity between the houses of al-Walīd b. 'Uqba and Sa'īd b. al-'Āṣ (Ṭabarī, I, 2849).

[49] Balādhurī, *Ansāb*, V, 106. According to al-Balādhurī, 'Amr had fought on the side of the Medinans against the Umayyad army at al-Ḥarra and was therefore insulted and flogged by the Syrian commander Muslim b. 'Uqba. That he did not leave Medina before the battle together with the other Umayyads and was insulted and punished is also reported by 'Awāna (Ṭabarī, II, 421). According to Abū Mikhnaf, he did leave Medina with the Umayyads, but refused to give Muslim b. 'Uqba information about the situation in the town (*ibid.*, 410). In an anecdote quoted by Muṣ'ab al-Zubayrī (*Nasab*, 109–10), Marwān is described as encouraging 'Amr b. 'Uthmān to claim the caliphate during the reign of Mu'āwiya.

[50] Ibn Shabba, *Ta'rīkh al-Madīna*, 1028–9; al-Dhahabī, *Ta'rīkh al-islām* (Cairo, 1367–9/[1948–50]), I, 107. 'Uthmān expelled Ḥumrān for his breach of trust. Another version of the story, going back to Ibn Lahī'a's pupil al-Layth b. Sa'd, specified that 'Uthmān banished Ḥumrān to Iraq (Ibn Shabba, *Ta'rīkh al-Madīna*, 1029–30).

Ibn Ḥajar al-ʿAsqalānī derived the date of the 'year of the nosebleed' as being in 31/651–2, since ʿAbd al-Raḥmān b. ʿAwf died in 32/652–3.[51] Freely embellishing the tale, al-Yaʿqūbī narrated that ʿUthmān had Ḥumrān write the letter of appointment but added the name of ʿAbd al-Raḥmān with his own hand. When he sent Ḥumrān to take the letter to Umm Ḥabība bt Abī Sufyān, Ḥumrān read it and informed ʿAbd al-Raḥmān. The latter complained that he had sought ʿUthmān's government openly, while the caliph now nominated him secretly. As the matter became public in Medina, the Umayyads were infuriated. ʿUthmān punished Ḥumrān and sent him off to Baṣra.[52] In reality ʿUthmān had banished Ḥumrān b. Abān to Baṣra at an earlier date and for a different reason.[53]

The dissatisfaction with ʿUthmān's high-handed regime and with the governors appointed by him was not confined to the provinces outside Arabia. In Medina his cousin al-Ḥārith b. al-Ḥakam, whom he put in charge of the market, provoked outrage and protest when he used his office to buy up imported goods and to sell them at a large profit, imposed fees on the stalls of small traders (*yajbī maqāʿid al-mutasawwiqīn*), and committed other reprehensible acts. ʿUthmān refused popular demands for his dismissal[54] and further inflamed the feelings of the people by making al-Ḥārith a gift of camels which had been collected as part of the alms-tax and brought to Medina.[55] The great majority of the Anṣār turned openly against ʿUthmān.

Among the Quraysh ʿAmr b. al-ʿĀṣ of the clan of Sahm seems to have been the first to agitate in Medina against the caliph after his removal from the governorship of Egypt. He vented his anger and resentment by divorcing his wife Umm Kulthūm, ʿUthmān's uterine sister.[56] As he began to criticize the caliph openly, ʿUthmān confronted him with insults, which he returned. Rivalry between their fathers, both leading

[51] Ibn Ḥajar, *Fatḥ al-bārī*, VII, 58. [52] Yaʿqūbī, *Taʾrīkh*, II, 195–6; *Annali*, VII, 42–3.

[53] According to al-Balādhurī (*Ansāb*, V, 57–8), ʿUthmān had sent Ḥumrān to Kūfa to investigate the truth about the complaints against al-Walīd b. ʿUqba. Al-Walīd bribed Ḥumrān, and when he returned to the caliph he lied about his conduct and praised him. Then he met Marwān who asked him about al-Walīd, and he confessed to him that the matter was serious. Marwān informed ʿUthmān, who was furious about Ḥumrān lying to him. He exiled him to Baṣra, assigning a house there in fief to him. A different version is given by Sayf b. ʿUmar (Ṭabarī, I, 2923).

[54] Balādhurī, *Ansāb*, V, 47; Kister, Additional Notes to his article (IX) 'The Market of the Prophet', in *Studies in Jāhiliyya and Early Islam* (Variorum Reprints; London, 1980). The policy of taxing the markets in Medina was later resumed by Muʿāwiya (Kister, 'Market of the Prophet', 275). [55] Balādhurī, *Ansāb* , V, 28.

[56] Ṭabarī, I, 2968. Umm Kulthūm was the full sister of al-Walīd b. ʿUqba whom ʿUthmān at the same time appointed governor of Kūfa. If the report is reliable, she must have been divorced by ʿAbd al-Raḥmān b. ʿAwf. This is not confirmed, however, by al-Zubayrī (*Nasab*, 145). She had first been married to Zayd b. Ḥāritha, who was killed at Mu'ta, then to al-Zubayr, who divorced her, and then to ʿAbd al-Raḥmān b. ʿAwf. Her marriage to ʿAmr b. al-ʿĀṣ was presumably brief.

merchants in Mekka before Islam, was involved in the exchange. 'Amr left, incensed, and began to incite 'Alī, al-Zubayr and Ṭalḥa against 'Uthmān, and stirred up trouble among the Mekka pilgrims, accusing the caliph of 'innovations'.[57] His agitation may well have contributed more to the rebellion in Egypt against 'Abd Allāh b. Sa'd b. Abī Sarḥ than is explicitly stated in the sources.[58] When the Egyptian rebels were encamped at Dhū Khushub outside Medina before the siege of the caliph's palace and 'Uthmān visited 'Ā'isha to seek her advice, she demanded that he reappoint 'Amr governor of Egypt since his soldiers (*jund*) there were satisfied with him. This was mentioned by 'Uthmān in a letter to the Syrians (*ahl al-Shām*) written on 1 Dhu l-Ḥijja 35/31 May 656 at the beginning of the final siege of his palace and in his largely identical message to the Mekka pilgrims read to them by 'Abd Allāh b. al-'Abbās on 7 Dhu l-Ḥijja/6 June. 'Uthmān stated that he had agreed to the demand, but then 'Amr had offended him and had gone beyond what was right.[59] 'Amr's offensive act, to which 'Uthmān probably referred, occurred shortly after the Egyptian rebels left Dhū Khushub, having been promised that the caliph would redress all their grievances.

[57] Ṭabarī, I, 2966–7. The report goes back to information from al-Miswar b. Makhrama transmitted by his client Abū 'Awn.

[58] This has been suspected by Wellhausen (*Skizzen*, VI, 127). Al-Walīd b. 'Uqba in a poem accused 'Amr, together with 'Dulaym' ('Ammār b. Yāsir) and the Egyptian rebel Sūdān b. Ḥumrān al-Murādī, of causing trouble and encouraging others to revile 'Uthmān (Ibn 'Asākir, '*Uthmān*, 306). This was at the time when 'Ammār was sent to Egypt by 'Uthmān to investigate the complaints of the people and to pacify them, shortly before the Egyptian rebel group set out for Medina (see below, p. 117).

[59] Ṭabarī, I, 3043; Ibn 'Asākir, '*Uthmān*, 377. In the letter to the Syrians it is not mentioned that the warriors in Egypt were satisfied with 'Amr. 'Uthmān did not name 'Ā'isha personally in his letters but spoke of his visit to the Mothers of the Faithful (*ummahāt al-mu'minīn*). This was partly out of politeness, partly because the letters inciting the Muslims in the provinces against 'Uthmān were, as will be seen, sent in the name of the Mothers of the Faithful collectively. It is clear, however, that 'Ā'isha played the active part and this was generally recognized by the public. Of the other widows of Muḥammad only Umm Salama is known to have been involved on a minor scale.

The two letters of 'Uthmān are certainly authentic and were independently preserved. The letter to the Syrians, written by 'Uthmān's secretary Unays b. Abī Fāṭima, was transmitted by Ismā'īl b. 'Ubayd Allāh b. Abi l-Muhājir, client of Makhzūm, who was a tutor of the sons of the caliph 'Abd al-Malik and governor of the Maghrib in the time of 'Umar II. He was born during the reign of Mu'āwiya (Ibn Ḥajar, *Tahdhīb*, I, 317–18) and must have had access to the letter either from a copy kept in his family or from the palace archives. The message to the Mekka pilgrims was evidently preserved by Ibn al-'Abbās, who read it to them, and was transmitted by his disciple 'Ikrima (Ṭabarī, I, 3040). It was also transmitted by Muḥammad b. Isḥāq from the 'Alid 'Alī b. al-Ḥusayn who presumably obtained the text from Ibn al-'Abbās (Ibn Shabba, *Ta'rīkh al-Madīna*, 1162–6).

Unays b. Abī Fāṭima was most likely a brother of Mu'ayqīb b. Abī Fāṭima al-Dawsī of Azd, confederate among the Banū 'Abd Shams (Ibn Sa'd, *Ṭabaqāt*, IV/1, 86–7). Mu'ayqīb was in charge of the treasury (*bayt al-māl*) for some time under 'Umar and keeper of the seal of 'Uthmān, during whose caliphate he died (Ibn Ḥajar, *Iṣāba*, VI, 130). Unays presumably succeeded him in that position.

When ʿUthmān, pressed by Marwān, announced in the mosque of Medina that the Egyptians were returning to their country satisfied that all they had heard about the wrong-doings of their imam was untrue, ʿAmr called out from a side of the mosque: 'Fear God, ʿUthmān, for you have ridden over abysses (*rakibta nahābīr*) and we have ridden over them with you. So repent to God, that we may repent.' ʿUthmān at first reacted with scorn: 'So you are here, son of al-Nābigha![60] By God, your jubbah has become lice-infested since I relieved you of your office.' When another voice, however, was raised warning the caliph to repent, he lifted his hands facing the *qibla* and proclaimed his repentance. ʿAmr left for his estate in Palestine, where he anxiously awaited ʿUthmān's end.[61]

As ʿUthmān's kin, in particular Marwān, gained more and more control over his political conduct, the Early Companions of the electoral council, seeing their influence eroded, turned against him. They were still widely recognized as the guardians of the principles of Islam, the informal leaders of the Muslim community collectively responsible for its right guidance. Now each one of them, in varying degrees, withdrew his support from the caliph whom they had elected. Most significant was the defection of ʿAbd al-Raḥmān b. ʿAwf, the king-maker and former brother-in-law of ʿUthmān. Since he died in 32/652–3, three years before the murder of ʿUthmān, it is evident that the deep disaffection had reached dangerous levels long before the actual crisis. ʿAbd al-Raḥmān's nephew al-Miswar b. Makhrama reported that when ʿUthmān had made a present of camels from the alms-tax arriving in Medina to one of the sons of al-Ḥakam,[62] his uncle had sent for him and ʿAbd al-Raḥmān b. al-Aswad b. ʿAbd Yaghūth, grandson of Muḥammad's maternal uncle and a man of rank among the Banū Zuhra. They had seized the camels,

[60] 'Al-Nābigha' refers to ʿAmr's mother who was a slave girl of the tribe of ʿAnaza bought on the market of ʿUkāẓ by the Qurayshite ʿAbd Allāh b. Judʿān al-Taymī, who kept her as a prostitute and later manumitted her (Ibn Abi l-Ḥadīd, *Sharḥ*, II, 100).

[61] Ṭabarī, I, 2972. The account goes back to ʿAlī's grandson Muḥammad b. ʿUmar who died at the beginning of the ʿAbbasid age. That ʿAmr left for his land in Palestine is confirmed by the report of Abū ʿAwn *mawlā* al-Miswar (*ibid.*, 2967). For the location of ʿAmr's estate, called ʿAjlān, in Palestine see M. Lecker, 'The Estates of ʿAmr b. al-ʿĀṣ in Palestine: Notes on a New Negev Arabic Inscription', *Bulletin of the School of Oriental and African Studies*, 52 (1989), 24–37, at 31–7.

In a piece of poetry attributed to ʿAmr, the latter expressed the expectation that the Egyptians, in the face of ʿUthmān's intransigence, would inevitably rise in revolt. If they killed him there would be strife (*fitna*) bearing hard upon Yathrib (Medina). If they left him alive there would be affliction (*ghumma*) and pernicious repression for them. The safe course thus was to escape to Syria and await the decision of fate which never lies (Ibn ʿAsākir, *ʿUthmān*, 307–8). Whether authentic or not, the piece probably expresses ʿAmr's expectations correctly.

[62] *Baʿḍ bani l-Ḥakam*, Ṭabarī, I, 2980. Most likely al-Ḥārith is meant and the report refers to the previously mentioned incident.

and 'Abd al-Raḥmān (b. al-Aswad, or b. 'Awf?) had distributed them among the people.[63]

When 'Uthmān during the pilgrimage of 29/650 performed four *rak'as* (bowings from the waist) in the ritual prayer at Minā instead of the traditional two, 'Abd al-Raḥmān performed only two with his companions and afterwards reproached 'Uthmān privately. 'Abd Allāh b. Mas'ūd, however, suggested to him that contravening the practice of the imam was worse than following him in an unsound one, and 'Abd al-Raḥmān decided to pray four *rak'as* in the future.[64] According to a report by his grandson Sa'd b. Ibrāhīm, 'Abd al-Raḥmān was deeply upset about the death of Abū Dharr in exile at al-Rabadha, which occurred not long before his own death. He defended himself against a charge by 'Alī that he bore responsibility for 'Uthmān's conduct, stating that the latter had broken his commitments (made at the time of his election) to him, and offered to wield his own sword in solidarity with 'Alī.[65] Before his death he expressed a wish that 'Uthmān should not pray over him, and al-Zubayr or Sa'd b. Abī Waqqāṣ led the funeral prayer.[66]

Another prominent Zuhrite who fell out with 'Uthmān much earlier was 'Abd Allāh b. Arqam b. 'Abd Yaghūth, a further grandson of Muḥammad's uncle, and former secretary of the Prophet. 'Umar had put him in charge of the public treasury (*bayt al-māl*) and thought highly of him. According to Ḥafṣa, her father had even thought of appointing him his successor.[67] Under 'Uthmān he continued in his office until 'Abd Allāh b. Khālid b. Asīd, the caliph's nephew and brother-in-law,[68] arrived from Mekka with a group of men volunteering to fight for the faith (*ghuzātan*). 'Uthmān ordered that 'Abd Allāh be given 300,000 dirhams and each of the other men 100,000 and sent a draft on the public treasury to Ibn Arqam. The latter found the amount excessive and returned the draft. When the caliph reprimanded him, calling him 'treasurer for us', he answered that he had considered himself treasurer for the Muslims and resigned, suspending the treasury

63 *Ibid.* 64 *Ibid.*, 2834–5.
65 Balādhurī, *Ansāb*, V, 57.
66 *Ibid.* Caetani dismissed a report that 'Abd al-Raḥmān refused to see 'Uthmān before his death as 'naturally untrustworthy' (*Annali*, VII, 556–7). He argued that the orthodox traditionists because of their pro-'Alid bias could not countenance the fact that 'Abd al-Raḥmān b. 'Awf preferred 'Uthmān. Yet the reports coming from his own family and the Banū Zuhra cannot leave any doubt that 'Abd al-Raḥmān broke with 'Uthmān before his death. 67 Ibn Ḥajar, *Iṣāba*, IV, 32–3.
68 See excursus 3 on the marriages of 'Uthmān, pp. 365–6. This was presumably before 'Uthmān gave 'Abd Allāh b. Khālid his daughter Umm Sa'īd in marriage (see there pp. 366–7).

keys on the pulpit.[69] 'Uthmān sent Zayd b. Thābit to him with a present of 300,000 dirhams, but he refused to accept it.[70]

A further incident involving a Zuhrite occurred late during Sa'īd b. al-'Āṣ' governorship of Kūfa, probably after 'Abd al-Raḥmān b. 'Awf's death. At the end of the fasting month of Ramaḍān, Sa'īd asked the Kufans if anybody had seen the new moon. All denied seeing it except Hāshim b. 'Utba b. Abī Waqqāṣ, nephew of Sa'd b. Abī Waqqāṣ. The governor ridiculed him and referred to his being one-eyed. Hāshim answered that he had lost his eye in the cause of God (he had been hit in the battle on the Yarmūk) and went on to break his fast. In punishment for his insubordination the governor ordered him to be beaten and his house burned. His sister Umm al-Ḥakam, one of the Muhājirāt women, and his brother Nāfi'[71] left for Medina and informed Sa'd b. Abī Waqqāṣ of the incident. When Sa'd complained to 'Uthmān, the caliph conceded the right of retaliation, telling him: 'Sa'īd belongs to you [pl.] for Hāshim, beat him in return, and the house of Sa'īd belongs to you, burn it as he burned his.' Sa'd's son 'Umar, still a boy, went to Sa'īd's house in Medina and attempted to set fire to it. When the news reached 'Ā'isha[72] she intervened with Sa'd, who stopped his son.[73] Sa'īd b. al-'Āṣ, overthrown shortly afterwards by the Kufans, was evidently also spared the humiliation of a beating. Hāshim b. 'Utba became an active supporter of 'Alī in Kūfa.

Sa'd b. Abī Waqqāṣ, the second Zuhrite[74] among the electors, maintained

[69] This happened before the dismissal of Abū Mūsā al-Ash'arī from the governorship of Baṣra. For 'Uthmān gave 'Abd Allāh b. Khālid b. Asīd the money despite Ibn Arqam's protest, and he was later accused of having made the gift from *fay'* money sent by al-Ash'arī (see the line of poetry of 'Abd al-Raḥmān b. Ḥanbal b. Mulayl quoted in *Aghānī*, VI, 60). According to Ibn 'Abd al-Barr (*al-Istī'āb fī mārifat al-aṣḥāb* (Hyderabad, 1336/[1918]), I, 336), 'Abd Allāh b. Arqam was treasurer for only two years under 'Uthmān. Al-Zubayrī (*Nasab*, 262) is evidently mistaken in claiming that he remained treasurer until the end (*ākhir*) of 'Uthmān's caliphate. According to most sources he died during 'Uthmān's reign. 'Uthmān now appointed Zayd b. Thābit treasurer (Balādhurī, *Ansāb*, V, 58, 88; Ibn Abi l-Ḥadīd, *Sharḥ*, III, 36, quoting al-Wāqidī), on whom he bestowed a gift of 100,000 dirhams in 27/648 from the *khums* of the campaign to Ifrīqiya. The variant report (Balādhurī, *Ansāb*, V, 58) that 'Uthmān appointed Mu'ayqīb b. Abī Fāṭima treasurer is probably unreliable.

[70] Balādhurī, *Ansāb*, V, 58–9, 88; Ibn Abi l-Ḥadīd, *Sharḥ*, III, 36.

[71] Nāfi' b. Abī Waqqāṣ can probably be identified as Nāfi' b. 'Utba b. Abī Waqqāṣ (see the annotation to the text in Ibn Sa'd, *Ṭabaqāt*, V, 21).

[72] Sa'īd b. al-'Āṣ' house in Medina seems to have been close to the Prophet's mosque and 'Ā'isha's apartment. He had asked the caliph 'Umar for permission to enlarge it, and 'Umar had, somewhat grudgingly, agreed to a small extension which was considered insufficient by Sa'īd. 'Uthmān had then satisfied his wishes (Ibn Sa'd, *Kitāb*, V, 20–1).

[73] *Ibid.*, 21.

[74] There were claims that the sons of Abū Waqqāṣ were false pretenders to Qurayshite lineage and belonged rather to 'Udhra (Quḍā'a). Ḥassān b. Thābit is quoted as calling Sa'd's pagan brother 'Utba a slave of 'Udhra in a poem after he had broken one of Muḥammad's teeth and wounded him in the face in the battle of Uḥud (Ibn Abi l-Ḥadīd, *Sharḥ*, VI, 55–6). According to a gloss in one of the MSS of Ḥassān's *Dīwān* (ed. W. N. 'Arafat (London, 1971), II, 137), the mother of Abū Waqqāṣ was a woman of 'Udhra.

a certain distance towards 'Uthmān after he had deposed him from the governorship of Kūfa. He does not seem to have joined or actively encouraged the opposition movement, but he also did little to back the embattled caliph. He severely rebuked 'Ammār b. Yāsir, however, when the latter returned from Egypt after having incited the people there to rebellion against the caliph.[75] Sa'd was not among the delegates of Quraysh led by 'Alī who met the Egyptian rebels at Dhū Khushub to persuade them to return home.[76] At 'Uthmān's request, however, he urged 'Ammār b. Yāsir to join the delegation. 'Ammār was influential among the Egyptians, and the caliph probably hoped that his presence would help to calm down the hostility of the rebels. 'Ammār, however, categorically refused to join after discovering that 'Uthmān had secretly sent one of his henchmen, Kathīr b. al-Ṣalt al-Kindī, to spy on him.[77] When a handful of the rebels came to Medina, Sa'd and 'Ammār co-operated with them in the presentation of their grievances to the caliph. 'Uthmān initially did not receive them, and it is uncertain whether Sa'd was still among them when the caliph did speak to them a few days later.[78]

When the main body of the rebels eventually entered Medina and approached Sa'd, asking that he speak for them to 'Uthmān, he declined to intervene, as did Sa'īd b. Zayd b. 'Amr b. Nufayl.[79] After seeing the leaders of the rebel groups from Kūfa, Baṣra and Egypt, he is said to have commented that any cause led by these men could only be evil.[80] Abū

[75] Ibn Shabba, *Ta'rīkh al-Madīna*, 1122–4. [76] Ṭabarī, I, 2971.

[77] *Ibid.*, 2969–70; Ibn Shabba, *Ta'rīkh al-Madīna*, 1125. Kathīr b. al-Ṣalt, a descendant of the kings of Kinda, was captured as a child during the *ridda* and became a confederate (*ḥalīf*) of the Banū Jumaḥ of Quraysh. 'Uthmān employed him as an arbiter in tribal conflicts (M. Lecker, 'Kinda on the Eve of Islam and during the *Ridda*', *Journal of the Royal Asiatic Society* (1994), 333–56, at 354–5). He appears as a close attendant of 'Uthmān during the siege of the palace (Ibn Shabba, *Ta'rīkh al-Madīna*, 1178, 1227) and was suspected by many of being the killer of Niyār b. 'Iyāḍ al-Aslamī and thus to have provoked the attack on the palace (Ṭabarī, I, 3004). He is also known as a transmitter of hadith and became a secretary of the caliph 'Abd al-Malik (Ibn Ḥajar, *Tahdhīb*,VIII, 419–20; Ibn Manẓūr, *Mukhtaṣar Ta'rīkh Madīnat Dimashq li-Ibn 'Asākir*, ed. Rūḥiyya al-Naḥḥās et al. (Damascus, 1984–90), XXI, 140–1).

[78] Balādhurī, *Ansāb*, V, 51–2, 95; Ibn Shabba, *Ta'rīkh al-Madīna*, 1101. The tenor of the report is 'Uthmanid and anti-'Alid. The transmitter, Ḥuṣayn b. Numayr al-Wāsiṭī, of Kufan origin, was known as a harsh critic of 'Alī (*yaḥmilu 'alā 'Alī*: Ibn Ḥajar, *Tahdhīb*, II, 291–2). His source, Juhaym al-Fihrī, is otherwise unknown.

[79] Ṭabarī, I, 2963. Sa'īd b. Zayd had been a member of the delegation meeting the rebels at Dhū Khushub.

[80] Balādhurī, *Ansāb*, V, 97; Ibn Sa'd, *Ṭabaqāt*, III/1, 50. The report goes back to Mālik's staunchly 'Uthmanid grandfather Mālik b. Abī 'Āmir al-Aṣbaḥī, who is omitted in al-Balādhurī's *isnād*. 'Uthmān gave him a pension (*faraḍa lah*: Ibn Ḥajar, *Tahdhīb*, X, 19) and he was, or claimed to be, among the men who carried 'Uthmān's corpse to his burial (Ṭabarī, I, 1348–9; Balādhurī, *Ansāb*, V, 96). Sa'd's visit to 'Uthmān mentioned in Ibn Sa'd's version of the report may well be the same as the one described in Abū Ḥabība's account quoted below.

Ḥabība, a client of al-Zubayr, reported that he saw Sa'd b. Abī Waqqāṣ visiting the caliph on the day that 'Uthmān was killed. As he left the besieged palace, he expressed anxiety at the sight of the enemies in front of the gate. Marwān reprimanded him: 'Now you regret, before you denigrated him (*ash'artahū*).' Sa'd apologized that he had not thought the people would go so far in their boldness or would seek his blood. 'Uthmān, he said, had just renewed his repentance. Marwān urged him to seek 'Alī who was hiding and was the one whose word would not be contravened (by the rebels). Sa'd found 'Alī in the mosque and pleaded with him that he help his kinsman 'Uthmān once more. Then Muḥammad b. Abī Bakr arrived and confided to 'Alī that 'Uthmān had been killed.[81]

Caetani saw the revolt against 'Uthmān as essentially driven by tribal resentment at the hegemony of Quraysh. The Early Companions 'Alī, Ṭalḥa and al-Zubayr, although themselves of Quraysh, had insidiously encouraged these anti-Quraysh sentiments in the provinces out of their personal ambition. The interest of Quraysh, Caetani held, was virtually identical with the interest of the Banū Umayya.[82] Yet while there was certainly some tribal resentment against the domination of Quraysh in general, the defection of the Banū Zuhra, a major clan of Quraysh, clearly shows that anti-Umayyad sentiment was spreading among the Quraysh themselves. None of the Zuhrite leaders was motivated by personal ambition. It was the conduct of 'Uthmān that eventually cost him the support of the majority of Quraysh who had so solidly backed his election.

Ismā'īl b. Yaḥyā al-Taymī, a descendant of the caliph Abū Bakr who after 158/775 composed an account of the murder of 'Uthmān,[83] explained the widespread disaffection by pointing to 'Uthmān's offences against Ibn Mas'ūd, Abū Dharr and 'Ammār b. Yāsir. Ibn Mas'ūd's mistreatment provoked his tribe, Hudhayl, and the Banū Zuhra, whose client he was; Abū Dharr's grievance was shared by his tribe, Ghifār, and the Makhzūm were incensed by the case of 'Ammār, their confederate (*ḥalīf*).[84]

'Ammār had joined a public protest by 'Alī in the mosque against 'Uthmān's assertion of his right arbitrarily to appropriate *fay'* property. The caliph, unable to punish 'Alī, reviled 'Ammār and had him beaten until he lost consciousness. He was carried to Umm Salama, Makhzumite

[81] Ṭabarī, I, 2998–9. Reports that Sa'd made 'Uthmān an offer to fight for him and that he left Medina for Mekka before the murder in order to guard his faith (Ibn Shabba, *Ta'rīkh al-Madīna*, 1130–1, 1274–5) are 'Uthmanid legend.

[82] See in particular *Annali*, VIII, 27–31. H. Djaït is certainly correct in rejecting the view of 'A. Duri, H. A. R. Gibb, and others that the motivation of the rebellion against 'Uthmān was basically 'bedouin, Arab, nomadic', and in stressing its Islamic nature (*La Grande Discorde*, 88).

[83] See excursus 5 on the sources for the crisis of the caliphate of 'Uthmān, pp. 377–8.

[84] Balādhurī, *Ansāb*, V, 26; Ibn 'Asākir, *'Uthmān*, 421.

widow of Muḥammad. Her cousin Hishām b. al-Walīd, brother of Khālid b. al-Walīd, protested to 'Uthmān about the mistreatment of 'our brother' and threatened to kill an Umayyad in retaliation if 'Ammār should die, but 'Uthmān insulted him too, and ordered his removal. 'Ā'isha took up their case and made a scene in the mosque, infuriating 'Uthmān.[85] Makhzūm thus also withdrew their support from him.

'Uthmān's brother al-Walīd b. 'Uqba later inflamed the ill feelings of Makhzūm further when he, in addition to attacking 'Dulaym' ('Ammār) for his disloyal activity in Egypt, lampooned, apparently slanderously, the Makhzumite 'Umar b. Sufyān b. 'Abd al-Asad, asserting that he, encouraged by Dulaym, was faulting 'Uthmān 'like a goat's fart in the desert plains of Iḍam'. The vulgar language was not out of character for a former governor remembered in history chiefly for having vomited in his drunkenness on the pulpit of Kūfa. The Makhzumite answered in a more dignified manner, warning 'Abd Shams that al-Walīd was sapping their rock with his slander.[86]

While under siege in his palace, 'Uthmān called 'Abd Allāh b. al-'Abbās and gave him a message to be read to the pilgrims in Mekka. He told him that he had just appointed Khālid b. al-'Āṣ b. Hishām governor of Mekka. Khālid was a chief of Makhzūm in Mekka and had been governor under 'Umar.[87] The previous governor, still in power, was 'Abd Allāh b. 'Āmir al-Ḥaḍramī, an Umayyad confederate[88] whose father had been killed as a pagan at Badr after having slain Mihja' al-'Akkī, a client of 'Umar and one of the earliest Companions.[89] 'Uthmān evidently hoped to prop up his authority in Mekka by replacing the Umayyad confederate by a distinguished Makhzumite. He told Ibn al-'Abbās, however, that he was afraid that the people of Mekka, having learned of the rebellion in Medina, might resist Khālid, who might thus be impelled to fight them in the Sanctuary of God. Khālid, he suggested, would probably not agree to lead the pilgrimage. 'Uthmān therefore appointed Ibn al-'Abbās as leader of the pilgrimage.[90] When Ibn al-'Abbās conveyed 'Uthmān's instructions to Khālid, the latter, as expected, declined to act as leader of the pilgrimage and to read 'Uthmān's message to the pilgrims. Pointing to the ominous hostility of the crowd towards the caliph, he urged Ibn

[85] Balādhurī, *Ansāb*, V, 48–9. See further below p. 101.

[86] Ibn 'Asākir, '*Uthmān*, 306–7. The text there has 'Amr instead of 'Umar. Sufyān b. 'Abd al-Asad, however, is not known to have had a son 'Amr. 'Umar b. Sufyān was an early Muslim who emigrated to Abyssinia (Zubayrī, *Nasab*, 338).

[87] Ibn Ḥajar, *Iṣāba*, II, 92–3.

[88] His grandfather 'Abd Allāh al-Ḥaḍramī had been a confederate of Ḥarb b. Umayya (*ibid.*, IV, 259).

[89] *Annali*, I, 510, 512.

[90] Ṭabarī, I, 3039–40. The two reports of Ibn al-'Abbās quoted here differ slightly about 'Uthmān's instructions to him but can be properly reconciled.

al-ʿAbbās, as cousin of the man to whom the reign would probably fall, to act as the leader.[91] The account throws light on the total erosion of ʿUthmān's authority among the Mekkan Quraysh. Discontent and unrest were not confined to a few of the conquered provinces, but pervaded the holy cities in Arabia.

Among the electors, the most active and outspoken in the opposition movement was Ṭalḥa of the clan of Taym. A man of strong personal ambition, Ṭalḥa, although formally a member of the electoral council, had not been present at the election of ʿUthmān. When he arrived in Medina after the election, he made clear his displeasure. He is reported to have stayed in his house at first, stating that he was not someone whose opinion could legitimately be ignored (*mithlī lā yuftātu ʿalayh*). ʿAbd al-Raḥmān b. ʿAwf went to see him and implored him for the sake of Islam not to break ranks.[92] When he went to see ʿUthmān, he asked the caliph whether he would agree to have another election if he, Ṭalḥa, rejected the result of the first one. ʿUthmān assured him that he would agree, and Ṭalḥa offered his pledge of allegiance.[93]

ʿUthmān thenceforth made special efforts to secure Ṭalḥa's backing by honouring him and making him extravagant presents. According to Ṭalḥa's son Mūsā, ʿUthmān during his caliphate bestowed gifts upon Ṭalḥa to the amount of 200,000 dinars.[94] Yet Ṭalḥa soon became a sharp critic of ʿUthmān's conduct and is described as personally reproaching the caliph on various occasions.[95] According to Khālid, client of ʿUthmān's son Abān, he intervened when Marwān used the name of the caliph to gain personal advantage on the market in buying date pits as fodder for his camels. When ʿUthmān apologized that he had not ordered this, Ṭalḥa blamed him even more, pointing to the stern scrupulosity of ʿUmar on a similar occasion.[96]

Ṭalḥa wrote letters to the provinces inciting revolt and made common cause with the Egyptian rebels during the siege of ʿUthmān's palace. When he later came to Baṣra calling for revenge for the blood of ʿUthmān, ʿAbd Allāh b. Ḥakīm al-Tamīmī of Mujāshiʿ showed him his earlier letters to them, and he acknowledged having written them.[97] ʿAbd Allāh b. Saʿd b. Abī Sarḥ commented that, in spite of the caliph's generosity towards him, Ṭalḥa was the one toughest against him during the siege.[98] This was equally the impression of later historians such as

[91] *Ibid.*, 3039.
[92] Balādhurī, *Ansāb*, V, 19–20. Ṭalḥa and ʿUthmān are reported to have quarrelled and exchanged insults even during ʿUmar's reign (Ibn Shabba, *Taʾrīkh al-Madīna*, 33–4.)
[93] Balādhurī, *Ansāb*, V, 19, 20. [94] *Ibid.*, 7. [95] *Ibid.*, 42, 44. [96] *Ibid.*, 29.
[97] *Ibid.*, II, 229–30. [98] *Ibid.*, V, 20.

Abū Mikhnaf as well as Ibn Sīrīn (d. 110/728) and 'Awf al-A'rābī, representing Kufan Shi'ite and Basran 'Uthmanid tradition respectively.[99] Abū Mikhnaf reported that it was Ṭalḥa who prevented the delivery of drinking water to the besieged caliph.[100] Looking down from his balcony 'Uthmān greeted a group of the rebels among whom he saw Ṭalḥa. As they failed to return the greeting, he addressed him: 'Ṭalḥa, I did not think I would live to see the day when I should greet you and you do not return the greeting.'[101] According to a report by the Kufan 'Uthmanid Qays b. Abī Ḥāzim al-Bajalī, a man who visited Ṭalḥa during the siege in order to ask him to prevent the death of 'Uthmān was told by him: 'No, by God, not until the Banū Umayya surrender the right on their own accord.'[102]

The Medinan Companion and Qur'ān collector Mujammi' b. Jāriya al-Awsī, evidently one of the few Medinan supporters of 'Uthmān, narrated that he passed by Ṭalḥa, who asked him mockingly what his master was doing. When Mujammi' replied: 'I suspect that you [pl.] shall kill him', Ṭalḥa commented: 'If he should be killed, he is neither an angel brought close [to God] nor a prophet sent [by Him].'[103] The Makhzumite Companion 'Abd Allāh b. 'Ayyāsh b. Abī Rabī'a reported that he visited 'Uthmān during the siege and the caliph let him listen to the talk of those outside the door. He heard them debating whether they should attack or wait for the caliph to retract. Then Ṭalḥa arrived and asked for Ibn 'Udays, the chief of the Egyptian rebels. He whispered something to Ibn 'Udays, who then ordered his companions not to let anyone enter or leave the palace. 'Uthmān told Ibn 'Ayyāsh that it was Ṭalḥa who gave this order and he prayed that God protect him from Ṭalḥa and grant that Ṭalḥa's blood be spilled. Ṭalḥa, he affirmed, had committed illicit offence against him, and he quoted the Prophet's hadith that the shedding of a Muslim's blood was illicit except for apostasy, adultery and manslaughter. Ibn 'Ayyāsh wanted to depart, but was prevented by the rebels until Muḥammad b. Abī Bakr passed by and ordered that he be allowed to leave.[104] 'Abd al-Raḥmān b. Abzā later remembered seeing the Egyptian rebel leader Sūdān b. Ḥumrān coming out of 'Uthmān's palace on the day of the murder and hearing him say:

[99] *Ibid.*, 71, 81; Ibn Shabba, *Ta'rīkh al-Madīna*, 1169. Ibn Sīrīn said specifically that no one among the Companions of the Prophet was more severe against 'Uthmān than Ṭalḥa.

[100] Balādhurī, *Ansāb*, V, 71. This is indirectly confirmed by the report of 'Abd al-Raḥmān b. al-Aswad b. 'Abd Yaghūth (Ṭabarī, I, 2979).

[101] Balādhurī, *Ansāb*, V, 76.

[102] Ibn 'Asākir, *'Uthmān*, 407. Qays b. Abī Ḥāzim al-Bajalī al-Aḥmasī (d. 84/703) was known to put 'Uthmān above 'Alī. Kufan traditionists inclined to Shi'ism therefore shunned him (Ibn Ḥajar, *Tahdhīb*, VIII, 386–7).

[103] Balādhurī, *Ansāb*, V, 74.

[104] Ṭabarī, I, 3000.

'Where is Ṭalḥa b. 'Ubayd Allāh? We have killed the son of 'Affān.'[105]

Ṭalḥa had no motive for hating 'Uthmān, by whom he was treated with particular generosity, and acted out of personal ambition. He must have been confident that he would become his successor. 'Uthmān presumably alluded to him in his message to the Mekka pilgrims conveyed by Ibn al-'Abbās in stating that 'some were seeking to take their right by unrightful means for whom my life has lasted excessively. Their hope for the reign (*imra*) has been delayed too long for them, so they have sought to hasten fate.'[106] It was Abū Bakr's daughter 'Ā'isha who stood behind the ambitions of her kinsman Ṭalḥa.

'Ā'isha apparently held a grudge against 'Uthmān from the beginning of his reign because, if a report of al-Ya'qūbī may be trusted, he had reduced her pension to the level of that of the other widows of the Prophet.[107] She was probably the first one to speak out against 'Uthmān at the mosque of Medina. As a widow of Muḥammad and daughter of the founder of the caliphate she was in the best position to do so. When the Early Companion 'Abd Allāh b. Mas'ūd, accused by al-Walīd b. 'Uqba of fomenting trouble in Kūfa, was deported to Medina and 'Uthmān abused him from the pulpit, 'Ā'isha shouted: "Uthmān, do you say this to the Companion of the Messenger of God?'[108] Shortly afterwards four witnesses arrived from Kūfa to charge al-Walīd with drunkenness. When 'Uthmān threatened them, they complained to 'Ā'isha, who exclaimed: "Uthmān has obstructed the Qur'anic legal punishments (*ḥudūd*) and threatened witnesses.'[109] According to the account of al-Zuhrī, 'Uthmān heard the commotion in 'Ā'isha's room and angrily commented: 'Can the rebels and scoundrels of the people of Iraq find no other refuge than the home of 'Ā'isha?' Hearing this, 'Ā'isha raised one of Muḥammad's sandals and shouted at him: 'You have forsaken the Sunna of the

[105] *Ibid.*, 3000–1. If the report is accepted as going back to him, it should be noted that 'Abd al-Raḥmān b. Abzā is a pro-'Alid source. Al-Balādhurī quotes another report by him, with the same Kufan and Qumman *isnād*, in which he describes 'Alī as being prevented by his son Muḥammad b. al-Ḥanafiyya from going to protect 'Uthmān (Balādhurī, *Ansāb*, V, 94). Both reports must be viewed with reserve.

[106] Ṭabarī, I, 3042. The 'Uthmanid 'Abd al-Raḥmān b. Abī Laylā reported that Ṭalḥa took over the command of the Egyptians during the siege of the palace. Muḥammad b. Abī Bakr was with them, but when he left them in the evenings he, 'Alī and 'Ammār assured the people that the Egyptian rebels were acting under the order of 'Alī (Ibn Shabba, *Ta'rīkh al-Madīna*, 1171). 'Alī is described in other 'Uthmanid accounts as greatly concerned that Ṭalḥa was seizing control (see, for instance, *ibid.*, 1197–9).

[107] See Abbott, *Aishah*, 105. The report of al-Ya'qūbī, generally not a reliable source for early Islamic history, was accepted by Wellhausen (*Skizzen*, VI, 126 n. 2). For 'Ā'isha's relations with 'Uthmān see in general Abbott, *Aishah*, 100–31.

[108] Balādhurī, *Ansāb*, V, 36. Ordering Ibn Mas'ūd's deportation from Kūfa, 'Uthmān also deprived him of his pension for three years (Ibn Shabba, *Ta'rīkh al-Madīna*, 1049), presumably until his death.

[109] Balādhurī, *Ansāb*, V, 34.

Messenger of God, the owner of this sandal.' The people heard of the incident and filled the mosque, where they quarrelled about the propriety of the interference of 'Ā'isha, as a woman, in the dispute. A group of Companions went to see 'Uthmān, and he was forced to depose his brother.[110]

In the case of 'Ammār b. Yāsir, 'Ā'isha, in solidarity with Umm Salama, created a similar scene in the mosque. She brought out a hair, a garment and a sandal of the Prophet and called out: 'How quickly have you [pl.] abandoned the Sunna of your Prophet when his hair, his dress, and his sandal have not yet decayed.' 'Uthmān was left speechless with rage, while the crowd, egged on by 'Amr b. al-'Āṣ, burst into turmoil and exclamations of bewilderment.[111]

'Ā'isha most likely also wrote letters to the provinces stirring up rebellion, although, after the murder of 'Uthmān, she denied it. The letters were written in the name of the Mothers of the Faithful collectively, but it was generally assumed at the time that she was behind them. When she, at the time of the siege, told the Kufan rebel leader al-Ashtar with raised voice: 'God forbid that I would order the spilling of the blood of Muslims, the murder of their imam, the violating of their inviolability', he could point out to her: 'You [f. pl.] have written to us, but now when the war has been set ablaze by your action you forbid us.'[112] Masrūq b. al-Ajda' al-Hamdānī, a prominent disciple of Ibn Mas'ūd, narrated that 'Ā'isha chided the people for slaughtering 'Uthmān like a ram. Masrūq told her: 'This is your work. You [sg.] wrote to the people ordering them to march against him.' She denied that she had ever written them a line. The Kufan traditionist al-A'mash commented that the letters were therefore generally held to have been written in her name.[113] Letters of the Mothers of the Faithful were used by Muḥammad b. Abī Ḥudhayfa to incite the revolt in Egypt. The 'Uthmanid Egyptian 'Abd al-Karīm b. al-Ḥārith al-Ḥaḍramī (d. 136/753–4)[114] asserted that these letters were

110 *Aghānī*, IV, 180–1.

111 Balādhurī, *Ansāb*, V, 48–9, 88–9. The report goes back to al-Zuhrī. The incident concerning 'Ammār cannot be definitely dated. Abbott placed it before the incident concerning Ibn Mas'ūd. It seems more likely, however, that it occurred somewhat later.

112 *Ibid.*, 102; Ibn Shabba, *Ta'rīkh al-Madīna*, 1224–5.

113 Balādhurī, *Ansāb*, V, 103; Khalīfa, *Ta'rīkh*, ed. Akram Ḍiyā' al-'Umarī (Damascus, 1977), 176. Masrūq was among the Kufans who brought 'Uthmān al-Ashtar's letter in which he demanded the dismissal of Sa'īd b. al-'Āṣ and the appointment of Abū Mūsā al-Ash'arī and Ḥudhayfa b. al-Yamān as governors of Kūfa (Balādhurī, *Ansāb*, V, 46). After the murder of 'Uthmān, Masrūq reproached al-Ashtar and 'Ammār for having killed a man who fasted and prayed constantly (*qataltumūhu ṣawwāman qawwāman*). The 'Uthmanid Kufan al-Sha'bī praised him, saying that the women of Hamdān had not given birth to the like of Masrūq (Ibn 'Asākir, *'Uthmān*, 502–3). Masrūq was known to have access to 'Ā'isha and transmitted hadith from her.

114 Ibn Ḥajar, *Tahdhīb*, VI, 371–2.

forged by the rebel leader.[115] His testimony carries little weight, since such letters were also known in Kūfa, and reflects the later Sunnite consensus that ʿĀʾisha could not have written letters against the third Rightly Guided Caliph.

ʿĀʾisha's increasing hostility towards ʿUthmān was certainly not solely personally motivated. As the revered Mother of the Faithful and daughter of the first caliph she also felt a responsibility for guarding the basic principles of the caliphate founded by her father. She could see that under ʿUthmān the caliphate of Quraysh was quickly being turned into a hereditary kingship for the benefit of the Umayyad house. When ʿUthmān came to see her and sought the advice of 'the Mothers of the Faithful' in the crisis, he was told, according to his letters to the Syrians and the Mekka pilgrims, that he must give governorships to ʿAmr b. al-ʿĀṣ and ʿAbd Allāh b. Qays (Abū Mūsā al-Ashʿarī) and retain Muʿāwiya and (ʿAbd Allāh b. ʿĀmir) b. Kurayz. Muʿāwiya had been appointed by a ruler before ʿUthmān, he was governing his territory well, and his soldiers were satisfied with him. ʿUthmān should restore ʿAmr to his governorship, for his soldiers were also satisfied with him, and he would govern his country well.[116]

The mention of Muʿāwiya here may seem surprising. It could indicate that there were suspicions, most likely unjustified, that ʿUthmān might replace even Muʿāwiya, with whom his relations were relatively cool, by one of his favourites. ʿUthmān certainly also mentioned him and ʿAbd Allāh b. ʿĀmir in order to demonstrate that he was faithfully complying with ʿĀʾisha's wishes as well as he could. Abū Mūsā al-Ashʿarī, too, had been reappointed governor by him under pressure from the Kufans before his visit to ʿĀʾisha. The thrust of her demands, however, was to break the Umayyad monopoly in the government of the conquered provinces, which could clearly be seen as ensuring and safeguarding an Umayyad succession to the caliphate. In particular the reappointment of a tenacious critic and formidable opponent of ʿUthmān such as ʿAmr b. al-ʿĀṣ would have acted as a powerful check to Umayyad aspirations.

During the final siege ʿĀʾisha decided to leave, together with Umm Salama, for the pilgrimage. In the hope that her presence in Medina might hold back the rebels from violence, ʿUthmān sent Marwān and

[115] Al-Kindī, *Kitāb al-Wulāt wa-Kitāb al-Quḍāt*, ed. R. Guest (London, 1912), 14. On the basis of this report Abbott inclined to the opinion that the letters attributed to ʿĀʾisha were all forged (*Aishah*, 124). Ibn Lahīʿa also transmitted a highly fictitious Egyptian report in which Ibn Abī Ḥudhayfa is accused of forging letters of the Mothers of the Faithful (Ibn Shabba, *Taʾrīkh al-Madīna*, 1153–4).

[116] Ibn ʿAsākir, *ʿUthmān*, 377; Ṭabarī, I, 3043. ʿAbd Allāh b. ʿĀmir is mentioned only in the letter to the Syrians where it is he, rather than Muʿāwiya, who is described as governing well and being popular among his soldiers.

another cousin, 'Abd al-Raḥmān b. 'Attāb b. Asīd,[117] to persuade her to stay for the sake of his safety. Having completed her preparations for the trip, she rejected all entreaties. When Marwān finally suggested, with a sarcastic poetical quote, that she was running away after having set the country ablaze, she told him angrily that she wished his man were in one of her travel sacks so she could take it along and cast him into the sea.[118]

As she reached al-Sulsul, 'Abd Allāh b. al-'Abbās, sent by the caliph to deliver his message in Mekka, caught up with her. Worried about the impact it might make on the assembled pilgrims, she told him, according to 'Abd Allāh's own report: 'Ibn 'Abbās, I beseech you by God, for you are endowed with an agile tongue, that you turn [the people] away from this man and stir up their misgivings. For their sights have become clear and acute, the light signals have been raised for them, and they have streamed together from all countries for a momentous matter. I have seen Ṭalḥa b. 'Ubayd Allāh take possession of the keys of the treasure houses and storerooms. If he takes over the rule, he will follow the conduct of his cousin Abū Bakr.' 'Abd Allāh suggested: 'My Mother, if anything should happen to the man, the people would seek refuge only with our fellow.' 'Ā'isha drew back: 'Leave this, I do not wish to engage with you in a boasting match or dispute.'[119] When the news of 'Uthmān's miserable end, but not yet of 'Alī's succession, arrived in Mekka, she ordered her pavilion to be pitched in the Sanctuary and announced: 'I believe that 'Uthmān will bring ill luck upon his people [the Umayyads] just as Abū Sufyān brought ill luck on his people on the day of Badr.'[120] Ṭalḥa, she fancied, would now put the clock back to the time of the Prophet.

The animosity of Ṭalḥa and 'Ā'isha towards 'Uthmān was not shared by al-Zubayr of the clan of Asad.[121] Later sources tended to associate

[117] According to the version of Ibn Sa'd (*Ṭabaqāt*, V, 25), Zayd b. Thābit, treasurer and loyalist supporter of 'Uthmān, was sent along with them. Ibn Abi l-Ḥadīd (*Sharḥ*, III, 7) quotes a report from al-Wāqidī's *Kitāb al-Dār* according to which Marwān asked Zayd b. Thābit to accompany him. 'Ā'isha discredited Zayd by enumerating all the gifts of land and money he had received from 'Uthmān, and he said no word in return.

[118] Balādhurī, *Ansāb*, V, 75. For the various versions of the incident and 'Ā'isha's words see Abbott, *Aishah*, 124. According to one of them she included Marwān himself together with 'Uthmān in her wish. Caetani expressed doubts about the authenticity of the story since he knew only the version of the Shi'ite al-Ya'qūbī, but commented that 'with its cynical crudeness it is well invented, worthy of a woman of the Jāhiliyya, which the terrible widow of the Prophet, implacable in her hatred, inflexible in her ambitious designs, had remained to a large extent' (*Annali*, VIII, 197).

[119] Ṭabarī, I, 3040. [120] Balādhurī, *Ansāb*, V, 91 (Wahb b. Jarīr).

[121] With respect to al-Zubayr, too, there were claims that his lineage among Asad was false. Al-Haytham b. 'Adī stated in his *Kitāb Mathālib al-'Arab* that al-Zubayr's grandfather Khuwaylid had visited Egypt and had come back with al-Zubayr's father, al-'Awwām, a Copt whom he adopted. As evidence he referred to a lampoon of the Āl Khuwaylid by Ḥassān b. Thābit who mentioned their longing for the Copts and the adoption of al-'Awwām (Ibn Abi l-Ḥadīd, *Sharḥ* XI 68; Ḥassān, *Dīwān*, I, 374).

al-Zubayr closely with Ṭalḥa because of their joint stand, together with 'Ā'isha, in opposition to 'Alī and in the battle of the Camel. The Basran historian Wahb b. Jarīr even mentioned al-Zubayr together with Ṭalḥa as having been in control of matters during the siege of the palace.[122] This is, however, far from the facts. During the election al-Zubayr had, as noted, broken his earlier alliance with 'Alī to back 'Uthmān. The latter soon afterwards had shown his appreciation and gratitude by proposing al-Zubayr as regent until his son 'Amr should reach maturity. Although this arrangement soon became irrelevant as 'Amr grew up, al-Zubayr never broke completely with the caliph. He also had, however, close ties to 'Ā'isha whose elder sister, Asmā', was his wife. 'Amr b. al-'Āṣ may to some extent have succeeded in inciting him against 'Uthmān.[123] Al-Zubayr certainly joined the other Early Companions in collective action in putting pressure on the caliph to mend his ways and reduce the influence of his assertive kin. He refrained, however, from personal confrontation with the caliph,[124] and it is unlikely that he wrote letters to the provinces encouraging rebellion. 'Abd Allāh b. Mas'ūd, disgraced by 'Uthmān, appointed al-Zubayr executor of his will, recommending that the caliph should not lead his funeral prayer. After his death al-Zubayr was able to persuade 'Uthmān to restore Ibn Mas'ūd's pension rights, of which he had been deprived, to his children.[125] When Ṭalḥa and al-Zubayr later came to Baṣra to seek revenge for the murder of 'Uthmān, the Basrans reminded Ṭalḥa that his letters had come to them with other contents. Al-Zubayr then asked them whether they had received from him any letter concerning 'Uthmān.[126]

It was probably early during the siege that al-Zubayr went to see 'Uthmān and told him there was a group of men assembled in the Prophet's mosque who were ready to prevent violence against him and were seeking a just settlement. He urged him to go out and together with them submit the dispute to the widows of Muḥammad. When 'Uthmān

[122] Balādhurī, *Ansāb*, V, 90: *kāna l-Zubayr wa-Ṭalḥa qad istawlayā 'ala l-amr*. The lengthy narration of Wahb b. Jarīr about the murder of 'Uthmān (*ibid.*, 88–92) was attributed by him to al-Zuhrī. While it does contain some material from al-Zuhrī, it is largely Wahb's own composition. [123] Ṭabarī, I, 2967, see above, p. 91.

[124] The unreliable Abū Sa'īd *mawlā* Abī Usayd mentions an incident in which al-Zubayr beat some Umayyad clients who were breaking 'Uthmān's prohibition on hoarding goods (*ḥukra*). 'Uthmān scolded al-Zubayr, who apologized to the caliph and was forgiven (Ibn Shabba, *Ta'rīkh al-Madīna*, 1005–6).

[125] *Ibid.*, 1050; Balādhurī, *Ansāb*, V, 37. Al-Zubayr's quotation of the line by 'Abīd b. al-Abraṣ mentioned in this report as referring to 'Abd Allāh b. Mas'ūd is mentioned in another report as referring to al-Miqdād b. al-Aswad ('Amr). 'Uthmān is said to have led the funeral prayer and praised al-Miqdād after his death in 33/653–4 (Ibn Sa'd, *Ṭabaqāt*, III/1, 115–16). The report may imply that al-Miqdād's pension, too, was cancelled by 'Uthmān because of his strong stand on behalf of 'Alī.

[126] Ṭabarī, I, 3127; *Annali*, IX, 57.

went out with him the people rushed towards him with their arms. 'Uthmān turned back and told al-Zubayr that he did not see anyone seeking justice or preventing violence.[127] Al-Zubayr's attempt to mediate was thus thwarted.

Later during the siege, al-Zubayr sent his client Abū Ḥabība to 'Uthmān in order to inform him that the Banū 'Amr b. 'Awf, a major clan of Aws, had offered him their backing in whatever he would order them. It was a hot summer day, and Abū Ḥabība found the caliph with leather vessels (*marākin*) filled with water and napkins (*riyāṭ*) spread out in front of him. Abū Ḥabība told him of the Banū 'Amr and that al-Zubayr's obedience to the caliph had not changed. If the latter wished, he would come immediately to join the defenders of the palace or he would wait for the Banū 'Amr to arrive and would protect him with their help. 'Uthmān praised al-Zubayr for his loyalty and indicated that he would prefer him to wait for the Banū 'Amr to protect him, God willing, more effectively. The caliph was killed before the Banū 'Amr arrived.[128]

Al-Zubayr's son 'Abd Allāh had been honoured by 'Uthmān for his outstanding part in the campaign of 'Abd Allāh b. Sa'd to Ifrīqiya in 27/647, where he had observed a weak spot in the array of the enemy army and killed the Greek prefect Gregory (Jarjīr). The caliph exceptionally let him report his battle account from the pulpit in Medina.[129] Later 'Uthmān made him a member of the commission entrusted with establishing the official recension of the Qur'ān.[130] Probably influenced by his aunt 'Ā'isha, he harboured an intense dislike of 'Alī and tried to incite his father against him. According to his own report, he and his father met 'Alī at the time of the advance of the Egyptian rebels on Medina. 'Alī asked al-Zubayr for his opinion as to how he should react. Al-Zubayr suggested

[127] Balādhurī, *Ansāb*, V, 76, quoting Abū Mikhnaf; Ibn Shabba, *Ta'rīkh al-Madīna*, 1193.

[128] See the two slightly variant versions of the report in Ibn 'Asākir, '*Uthmān*, 374–5. After 'Uthmān's murder the poet Ḥanẓala b. al-Rabī' al-Tamīmī, himself 'Uthmanid, praised the 'Amr b. 'Awf for keeping their commitment while lampooning the Banu l-Najjār for soiling themselves with treason (*ibid.*, 553–4). Muḥammad b. al-Munkadir named two clans of Aws, the Banū 'Amr b. 'Awf and the Banū Ḥāritha, as backing 'Uthmān (Ibn Shabba, *Ta'rīkh al-Madīna*, 1280).

[129] 'Abd Allāh b. al-Zubayr's battle account, preserved by Zubayrid family tradition, is quoted in *Aghānī*, VI, 59–60. Ibn al-Zubayr was asked by 'Abd Allāh b. Sa'd to take the victory message to Medina with the words that no one merited more to convey them than he. Ibn al-Zubayr added that Marwān arrived later and laid claim to 500,000 dirhams which 'Uthmān took out of the *khums* of the booty. The honour thus went to 'Abd Allāh b. al-Zubayr and the spoils to Marwān, who does not seem to have distinguished himself in the campaign. That 'Uthmān asked 'Abd Allāh b. al-Zubayr to narrate his battle account from the pulpit was reported by 'Abd Allāh's nephew Hishām b. 'Urwa (Ibn 'Abd al-Ḥakam, *Futūḥ Miṣr wa-akhbāruhā*, ed. C. C. Torrey (New Haven, 1922), 185–6). There is no reason to suspect tendentious fiction by pro-Zubayrid Egyptian tradition, as suggested by Caetani (*Annali*, VII, 189–90).

[130] Nöldeke and Schwally, *Geschichte des Qorāns*, II, 48.

that he confine himself to his house, neither trying to stop them nor guiding them. ʿAlī commended this view and left. ʿAbd Allāh then commented to his father: 'By God, he surely will aid and guide them, and seek support against the Commander of the Faithful.'[131]

At the time of the siege Ibn al-Zubayr was, according to Zubayrid family tradition, given by ʿUthmān the general command of the defenders of the palace.[132] He is said to have been wounded in the fighting[133] and always remained an admirer of ʿUthmān and a defender of his conduct.[134] At a late stage in the siege ʿUthmān ordered him to read a letter to the besiegers in which the caliph promised full redress of all their grievances. ʿUthmān would, the letter continued, obey whatever the wives of the Prophet and those of sound opinion among his critics agreed upon, but he would not 'take off a dress in which God had dressed him'. The besiegers tried to prevent Ibn al-Zubayr from reading the letter and shot arrows at him, but he read it in his strongest voice. Abū Mikhnaf added that according to some it was rather al-Zubayr himself who read the letter, but that the former account was sounder.[135] According to Ṣāliḥ b. Kaysān, al-Zubayr was among twelve men who buried ʿUthmān.[136] This is not confirmed, however, by the other, more reliable reports quoted by al-Wāqidī.[137]

Caetani was firmly convinced that the main instigator of the revolt and chief culprit in the murder of the caliph was ʿAlī. Since the Islamic historical tradition generally does not bear out this thesis, he accused the orthodox Sunnite sources of inveterate ʿAlid, if not Shiʿite, bias and systematical anti-Umayyad distortion. ʿAlī, he argued, could clearly be expected to be the prime beneficiary of the overthrow of ʿUthmān. In fact, ʿAlī, much younger than the caliph, would almost certainly have succeeded him on a legitimate basis if he had patiently awaited ʿUthmān's natural death. Yet he was driven by his inordinate ambition, which was quite incommensurate with his actual lack of political responsibility and acumen. Thus he conspired for the quick removal of ʿUthmān as he had conspired before for the murder of ʿUmar. ʿAlī, Caetani conceded, probably did not incite the masses to murder ʿUthmān, but he secretly created numerous difficulties for him in order to make him unpopular and

[131] Ibn Shabba, *Ta'rīkh al-Madīna*, 1126–7. According to other versions ʿAbd Allāh, intervening before his father could answer, sternly told ʿAlī that he ought to obey his imam. Al-Zubayr rebuked him for lack of respect towards his maternal uncle (ʿAlī) (*ibid.*, 1197). [132] Balādhurī, *Ansāb*, V, 74.

[133] *Ibid.*, 79, quoting Abū Mikhnaf; Ṭabarī, I, 3005. [134] See Balādhurī, *Ansāb*, V, 9.

[135] *Ibid.*, 66, quoting Abū Mikhnaf, and *ibid.*, 90, quoting Wahb b. Jarīr; Ibn Shabba, *Ta'rīkh al-Madīna*, 1193–4. [136] Ṭabarī, I, 3047.

[137] The anecdote quoted by al-Madā'inī on the authority of Ibn Juʿduba according to which ʿAlī heard a Sufyanid woman recite a poem accusing al-Zubayr and Ṭalḥa in the murder of ʿUthmān (Balādhurī, *Ansāb*, V, 105) obviously lacks historical foundation.

to put himself in a favourable light, ultimately in order to force 'Uthmān's abdication.[138]

The premise of Caetani's argument was mistaken. The election of 'Uthmān had demonstrated that Quraysh, as 'Umar had told Ibn al-'Abbās, would not consent to a caliphate of the Prophet's cousin. 'Alī had strongly pleaded his case and had been decisively rejected. Neither he nor his opponents could be under any illusion that the result might be different in another election. It was confidence that 'Alī was no longer a valid candidate that encouraged 'Ā'isha and Ṭalḥa to undermine 'Uthmān's reign. If 'Alī had been the prime mover in the rebellion and its prospective beneficiary, 'Ā'isha would have had no part in it. For whatever her dislike of 'Uthmān's Umayyad arrogance, her hatred of 'Alī was seated more deeply. The same 'Ā'isha who just before the murder of 'Uthmān told Marwān she would like to toss the caliph into the sea only weeks later was to assure the assembled Quraysh in Mekka that 'Alī had killed 'Uthmān, and that a mere fingertip of 'Uthmān was better than the whole of 'Alī.[139]

'Alī, however, had not entirely given up his aspirations. Rejected by the ruling class of Quraysh, he became the natural focal point of tribal discontent in the provinces. In Kūfa, in particular, anti-'Uthmān agitation during the governorship of al-Walīd b. 'Uqba was leaning in favour of 'Alī. As early as the beginning of 'Uthmān's reign, Jundab b. 'Abd Allāh b. Ḍabb al-Azdī, who had been present in Medina during the election and had met 'Alī, began to extol his virtues in his home town Kūfa, but at first met mostly opposition. According to his own account, he was denounced to the governor, al-Walīd, and imprisoned, but soon released upon the intercession of friends.[140] According to Abū Mikhnaf, 'Amr b. Zurāra al-Nakha'ī and Kumayl b. Ziyād al-Nakha'ī were the first to call in public for the removal of 'Uthmān and for homage to 'Alī. Informed of 'Amr b. Zurāra's activity, al-Walīd wanted to ride forth against him and his supporters, but he was warned that the people were assembled around 'Amr in strength. Mālik al-Ashtar, also of the Banu l-Nakha' of Madhḥij, offered to intervene and to vouch for the good conduct of his tribesmen. When al-Walīd reported the situation to 'Uthmān, the latter ordered that 'Amr, whom he described as a boorish bedouin (*a'rābī jilf*), be exiled to Damascus. Al-Ashtar, al-Aswad b. Yazīd b. Qays and his uncle 'Alqama b. Qays

138 *Annali*, VIII, 160.

139 Balādhurī, *Ansāb*, V, 91, variant: a single night of 'Uthmān was better than 'Alī the whole of eternity.

140 Ibn Abi l-Ḥadīd, *Sharḥ*, IX, 56–8. In Medina Jundab made 'Alī an offer to invite the Kufans to his support, but 'Alī declined, stating that it was not the time for that.

al-Nakhaʿī accompanied him and then returned to Kūfa.[141]

Under the governorship of Saʿīd b. al-ʿĀṣ, al-Ashtar and several others were exiled from Kūfa to Damascus. There they stayed initially in the house of ʿAmr b. Zurāra. These men, known as Kufan Qur'ān readers (*qurrā'*), clearly inclined to ʿAlī. Al-Ashtar led the uprising of the Kufans against the governor Saʿīd b. al-ʿĀṣ and the Kufan rebel force entering Medina at the time of the siege. During ʿAlī's caliphate they were among his most steadfast supporters and some of those surviving, such as Kumayl b. Ziyād, remained important figures in the early Shīʿa. This Kufan backing for ʿAlī was probably spontaneous initially and remained loose until the murder of ʿUthmān. There is no evidence that ʿAlī entertained close relations with them at this time or directed their actions. But he was certainly aware of them.

ʿAlī clashed with ʿUthmān in particular on questions of the religious law. As Muḥammad's paternal cousin and foster-son, he evidently saw himself as responsible for the preservation and execution of the norms of the Qur'ān and the Prophet's practice. At the beginning of ʿUthmān's reign he protested against the pardon of ʿUbayd Allāh b. ʿUmar for the murder of al-Hurmuzān and threatened to carry out the legal punishment (*ḥadd*) when he could lay his hands on him.[142] He insisted that the *ḥadd* punishment for wine-drinking be applied to al-Walīd b. ʿUqba, and when others hesitated to flog the caliph's half-brother, he either did so himself or had his nephew ʿAbd Allāh b. Jaʿfar carry out the flogging.[143] His stand in these two cases brought down upon him the lasting hatred of ʿUbayd Allāh and al-Walīd. During the pilgrimage of 29/650 he, like ʿAbd al-Raḥmān b. ʿAwf, confronted ʿUthmān with reproaches for his change of the prayer ritual, which had provoked murmuring among the public.[144] He pointedly contravened ʿUthmān's prohibition of performing the extra-seasonal pilgrimage (*ʿumra*) during the season of the regular pilgrimage (*ḥajj*) or combining the two, insisting that he would not deviate from the Sunna of the Prophet.[145] When ʿUthmān defiantly declared in the mosque of Medina that he would take whatever he needed from the *fay'* in spite of the grumbling of some people, ʿAlī exclaimed that in that case the caliph would be prevented by force.[146] ʿAlī expressed his disapproval of Umayyad largesse from *fay'* money to the elite when Saʿīd b. al-ʿĀṣ sent him gifts

141 Balādhurī, *Ansāb*, V, 30. Al-Aswad b. Yazīd al-Nakhaʿī was a disciple of Ibn Masʿūd and eventually turned against ʿAlī in contrast to his (younger) uncle ʿAlqama b. Qays (al-Thaqafī, Abū Isḥāq Ibrāhīm, *al-Ghārāt*, ed. Jalāl al-Dīn al-Muḥaddith (Tehran, 1395/[1975]), 559–65).

142 Balādhurī, *Ansāb*, V, 24; Ṭabarī, I, 2796; *Annali*, V, 93, VII, 21.

143 Balādhurī, *Ansāb*, V, 33–5; *Annali*, VII, 335–55. Al-Ḥasan is said to have refused to carry out the punishment.

144 Ṭabarī, I, 2833–4.

145 Ibn Shabba, *Ta'rīkh al-Madīna*, 1043–4.

146 Balādhurī, *Ansāb*, V, 48.

from Kūfa and vowed that he, if he were ever in a position to rule, would freely hand out 'the inheritance of Muḥammad' to the people.[147] It was one of the grievances of the Kufans against Saʿīd b. al-ʿĀṣ that he had reduced the pensions of their women from 200 to 100 dirhams.[148]

'Alī also endeavoured to protect men whom he considered meritorious Muslims from maltreatment by the caliph. Thus he intervened on behalf of the Companion Jundab b. Kaʿb al-Azdī, who had killed a non-Muslim sorcerer protected by al-Walīd b. 'Uqba. The governor, whom the sorcerer had been entertaining with his tricks, wanted to execute Jundab for murder, but his tribe, Azd, protected him. He escaped from prison and sought refuge in Medina. On 'Alī's intercession 'Uthmān sent al-Walīd an order to refrain from action against Jundab, who returned to Kūfa.[149] 'Alī also protested against 'Uthmān's brutal treatment of Ibn Masʿūd, reminding the caliph of his early merits as a Companion of the Prophet, and took him to his own house for protection.[150] He stopped 'Uthmān from punishing a Kufan messenger who refused to reveal the names of those who had written a letter severely criticizing the caliph.[151] When 'Uthmān exiled Abū Dharr, 'Alī made a show of solidarity with the deportee by accompanying him with several members of his family and 'Ammār, although Marwān, on the order of 'Uthmān, tried to prevent him. This led to an angry exchange with 'Uthmān.[152] After the death of Abū Dharr, he intervened to forestall the banishment of 'Ammār.[153]

The relationship between 'Alī and 'Uthmān was, however, not entirely antagonistic. Among the members of the electoral council, 'Alī was 'Uthmān's closest kin. Common descent from 'Abd Manāf, the father of both 'Abd Shams and Hāshim, still was seen as an effective bond *vis-à-vis* the rest of Quraysh. 'Uthmān is reported to have honoured al-'Abbās b. 'Abd al-Muṭṭalib on a par with the Umayyads Abū Sufyān b. Ḥarb, al-Ḥakam b. Abi l-'Āṣ and al-Walīd b. 'Uqba by allowing each one to sit with him on his throne.[154] 'Abd Allāh b. al-'Abbās narrated that 'Uthmān had complained to his father not long before the latter's death in 32/652-3

[147] *Aghānī*, XI, 31; *Annali*, VIII, 88–9. Saʿīd b. al-ʿĀṣ is said to have written to 'Alī that he was sending no one such generous gifts as to him. Saʿīd's grandson Saʿīd b. 'Amr described 'Alī rather as driven by personal greed. According to his account 'Alī accepted Saʿīd's gifts, charging that the Banū Umayya were merely giving him bits of the inheritance of Muḥammad and affirming that if he lived he would surely stop them from that (Ibn Saʿd, *Ṭabaqāt*, V, 21). In view of 'Alī's later conduct, this must be viewed as Umayyad misrepresentation. [148] *Aghānī*, XI, 31. [149] Balādhurī, *Ansāb*, V, 21–2.

[150] *Ibid.*, 36–7. According to al-Wāqidī, 'Alī was also said to have protested against the flogging of the Kufan witnesses against al-Walīd on 'Uthmān's order (*ibid.*, 34).

[151] *Ibid.*, 41–2.

[152] *Ibid.*, 54. A detailed account of the incident by Ibn al-'Abbās was quoted by al-Jawharī in his *Kitāb al-Saqīfa* (Ibn Abi l-Ḥadīd, *Sharḥ*, VIII, 352–5).

[153] Balādhurī, *Ansāb*, V, 54–5. [154] *Aghānī*, IV, 177.

about ʿAlī, charging that he, ʿAlī, had cut his kinship ties to him and was stirring up the people against him. When al-ʿAbbās suggested that mutual accommodation was required, ʿUthmān requested him to act as a conciliator. After the meeting, however, ʿUthmān, under the influence of Marwān, changed his mind and sent for al-ʿAbbās to ask him to defer any action. Al-ʿAbbās remarked to his son that ʿUthmān was not master of his own affairs.[155] Perhaps referring to the same occasion, Ṣuhayb, the client of al-ʿAbbās, reported that the latter had addressed ʿUthmān, beseeching him to treat his kinsman ʿAlī with consideration, for he had heard that ʿUthmān intended to act against ʿAlī and his associates (*aṣḥāb*). ʿUthmān answered that he was ready to accept his intercession, and that if ʿAlī only wished it, no one would be above him in the caliph's consideration. Yet ʿAlī had rejected all overtures and stuck to his own point of view. When al-ʿAbbās talked to ʿAlī, the latter commented that if ʿUthmān ordered him to leave his own house, he would do so, but he would not be coaxed into disregarding the injunctions of the Book of God.[156]

According to a report of al-Shaʿbī, ʿUthmān's displeasure with ʿAlī reached such a point that he complained about him to every Companion of the Prophet visiting him. Zayd b. Thābit then offered to see ʿAlī and inform him of the caliph's anger. ʿUthmān consented, and Zayd went together with ʿUthmān's cousin al-Mughīra b. al-Akhnas[157] and several others to visit ʿAlī. Zayd told him that ʿUthmān had two rightful claims on him, that of close kin and that of caliph, and that his complaint was that ʿAlī was turning away from him and was throwing his orders back at him. ʿAlī assured him that he did not wish to object or answer back to the caliph, but he could not keep silent when ʿUthmān overturned a right that was God's due. He would, he promised, refrain from whatever he could. Al-Mughīra now intervened, warning him: 'By God, you shall refrain

[155] Balādhurī, *Ansāb*, V, 13; in the *isnād* read Ḥusayn b. ʿAbd Allāh b. ʿUbayd Allāh b. ʿAbbās for Ḥusayn b. ʿAbd Allāh b. ʿAbd Allāh b. ʿAbbās; l. 19 *ibnuka* must be read *ʿalayya* as in the edition of I. ʿAbbas (al-Balādhurī, *Ansāb al-ashrāf*, 4/1, ed. Iḥsān ʿAbbās (Wiesbaden, 1979)), 498; Ibn Shabba, *Taʾrīkh al-Madīna*, 1045–7. For another report about an exchange of accusations between ʿUthmān and ʿAlī attributed to Ibn al-ʿAbbās and quoted by al-Wāqidī in his *Kitāb al-Shūrā* see Ibn Abi l-Ḥadīd, *Sharḥ*, IX, 15–17. Here ʿAlī is described as telling ʿUthmān, after defending his own conduct, that he must prevent 'the insolent (*sufahāʾ*) of the Banū Umayya' from harming the Muslims and dismiss corrupt officials. ʿUthmān promised to follow his advice, but Marwān persuaded him to ignore it.

[156] Balādhurī, *Ansāb*, V, 14; Ibn ʿAsākir, *ʿUthmān*, 262–3. The *isnād* is from the third transmitter on Kufan. In the Sunnite version of al-Balādhurī and al-Bukhārī the latter part of ʿAlī's answer, suggesting that ʿUthmān was not carrying out the orders of the Qurʾān, is omitted.

[157] Al-Mughīra was the son of al-Akhnas (Ubayy) b. Sharīq al-Thaqafī, confederate of the Banū Zuhra and one of the most vigorous opponents of Muḥammad. His mother was ʿUthmān's paternal aunt Khalda bt Abi l-ʿĀṣ (Zubayrī, *Nasab*, 101).

from troubling him or you shall be made to refrain. Surely he has more power over you than you have over him. He sent these Muslim men only as a show of strength and in order to get their evidence against you.' 'Alī angrily cursed him and alluded to his family's base origin and record of hostility to Islam. Zayd b. Thābit calmed him down, assuring him that they had not come as witnesses or to seek evidence against him, but to reconcile him and the caliph. Then he invoked God's blessings on him and 'Uthmān, and left together with his companions.[158]

His kinship ties made 'Alī a natural mediator between the opposition and 'Uthmān. When the general discontent reached dangerous levels in the year 34/654–5, a group of Mekkan and other Companions asked 'Alī to speak to, and admonish, 'Uthmān. 'Alī thus addressed him as spokesman of the people, but 'Uthmān was not yet prepared to heed his warnings.[159] A year later, when the Egyptian rebels camped at Dhū Khushub, 'Uthmān asked 'Alī to meet them at the head of a delegation of Muhājirūn while also sending the Medinan Companion Muḥammad b. Maslama at the head of a group of Anṣār. 'Alī and Muḥammad b. Maslama persuaded the rebels to turn back by promising them, in the name of the caliph, redress for all their grievances and agreeing to act as guarantors.[160]

In his first sermon after their return, 'Uthmān, pressed by Marwān, announced that the Egyptians had returned to their country realizing that the charges raised against their imam had been false. As this provoked a public outburst in the mosque, 'Alī impressed upon the caliph the need to own up in public to his past misdeeds and to show remorse. 'Uthmān did so in a sermon in which he invited advice from the spokesmen of the people regarding his future conduct. The speech was well received, but Marwān soon succeeded in persuading the caliph that his show of humility was a political mistake. 'Uthmān allowed him to insult and threaten the men assembled in front of the palace ready to offer their advice. 'Alī in a rage warned 'Uthmān that Marwān was out to ruin him and that he, 'Alī, would not visit him henceforth. 'Uthmān now visited him in person but failed to placate him. He left, charging that 'Alī had cut his kinship ties to him and deserted him, thus emboldening the people against him.[161] Shortly afterwards, during 'Uthmān's Friday sermon, public discontent vented itself in a volley of pebbles. 'Uthmān fell from the pulpit and was carried unconscious to his palace. When 'Alī visited him and inquired about his condition, 'Uthmān's kin blamed him for what had happened and defiantly warned

[158] Ibn Abi l-Ḥadīd, *Sharḥ*, VIII, 302–3.
[159] Ṭabarī, I, 2937–8; Balādhurī, *Ansāb*, V, 60–1.
[160] Ṭabarī, I, 2969–71; Balādhurī, *Ansāb*, V, 62.
[161] Ṭabarī, I, 2971–9.

him of dire consequences if he should realize his ambitions; 'Alī left in anger.[162]

He was to see 'Uthmān once more as the Egyptian rebels returned to Medina, outraged by the official letter ordering the punishment of their leaders, which they had intercepted. 'Alī and Muḥammad b. Maslama as guarantors of 'Uthmān's promises to the Egyptians evidently felt obliged to intervene and came jointly to see 'Uthmān. When 'Alī informed the caliph of the rebels' new grievance, 'Uthmān swore that he had no knowledge of the letter. While Muḥammad b. Maslama accepted his word, adding that this was the work of Marwān, 'Alī insisted that 'Uthmān receive the Egyptians himself and put his excuse to them. Reminding him of his kinship ties, the caliph pleaded with him to go out to speak to them, but 'Alī declined. The Egyptians were admitted and stated their grievances. 'Uthmān again denied any knowledge of the letter and both 'Alī and Muḥammad b. Maslama attested that he was speaking the truth. The Egyptians now demanded that he resign if an official letter with his seal could be sent without his knowledge, but the caliph affirmed that he would not take off a garment with which God had clad him. As turmoil broke out, 'Alī stood up and left, followed by Muḥammad b. Maslama. The Egyptians also left and continued their siege of the palace until they killed him.[163] 'Alī intervened only when informed by Jubayr b. Muṭ'im that the rebels were preventing the delivery of water to the besieged caliph. He talked to Ṭalḥa and saw to it that water was delivered.[164] As

162 *Ibid.*, 2979. According to the report of Abū Ḥudhayfa al-Qurashī, 'Uthmān's Umayyad kin sent al-'Abbās b. al-Zibriqān b. Zayd, brother-in-law of al-Ḥārith b. al-Ḥakam, after 'Alī as he left in anger to question him about his attitude towards his cousin. 'Alī reacted angrily, protesting that 'Uthmān committed the offences he did, and that now he, 'Alī, was being questioned and accused with regard to him. Were it not for his, 'Alī's, position, 'Uthmān's eye sockets would have been pulled out (Mufīd, *Jamal*, 143–4, reading *la'jtarra* for *la-ajtazzu*).

163 Ṭabarī, I, 2992–5. Muḥammad b. Maslama was of the Banu l-Ḥārith of Aws and a confederate of the Banū ('Abd) al-Ashhal. An early convert to Islam, he was highly trusted by Muḥammad. 'Umar employed him to investigate 'sensitive matters' (*umūr mu'ḍila*) in the provinces. He was thus commissioned by the caliph to confiscate part of the riches amassed by 'Amr b. al-'Āṣ in his governorship of Egypt and to destroy the gate of the palace built by Sa'd b. Abī Waqqāṣ in Kūfa by means of which the governor hoped to keep the public away. Wellhausen characterized him as 'the old brave and honest Anṣārī' (*Skizzen*, VI, 128). Caetani, in order to discredit his account, called him 'a friend of 'Alī' (*Annali*, VIII, 158). Yet Ibn Maslama was among the few Anṣār who either refused to pledge allegiance to 'Alī or failed to back him in his campaign against 'Ā'isha, Ṭalḥa and al-Zubayr; see below, pp. 145–6. He went to live in voluntary exile in al-Rabadha after the murder of 'Uthmān, evidently in order to avoid harassment from the strongly pro-'Alid Anṣār in Medina. The Umayyads, however, did not forgive him his withdrawal of support from 'Uthmān caused by his despair over the caliph's refusal to remove Marwān, who had made his position as guarantor to the Egyptians impossible. Under Mu'āwiya, in 45/666, a Syrian (*min ahl al-Shām*) from al-Urdunn broke into his house in Medina and murdered him (Ibn Ḥajar, *Iṣāba*, VI, 63–4). There can be little doubt that this was a political revenge killing instigated by the Umayyads.

164 Ṭabarī, I, 2979; Balādhurī, *Ansāb*, V, 77.

noted, Sa'd b. Abī Waqqāṣ on the final day of the siege urged 'Alī once more to intervene to protect his beleaguered kin, but it was too late.[165]

'Alī, so much is evident, was torn for a long time between two loyalties, his traditional obligation to a close kinsman and his commitment to his Islamic principles. Towards the end he seems to have broken with 'Uthmān in despair over his own inability to break the disastrous influence of Marwān on the caliph. It can, of course, be argued that he would have been spared the painful decision and the lasting enmity of the Umayyads had he abandoned his political ambitions completely after the humiliating rejection by Quraysh he had suffered in the election. This would, however, hardly have saved 'Uthmān from his calamitous end. Caetani's portrait of an incompetent and unscrupulous schemer who, driven by inordinate ambition and rancour, plotted to overthrow, if not to murder, a well-meaning but weak caliph is utterly incongruous.

Crisis and revolt

The chronological development of the crisis may be retraced approximately as follows. In the year 34/654–5 agitation against 'Uthmān reached a peak as Companions wrote to each other calling for *jihād* against the caliph. The people in Medina openly reviled him while the Companions listened without defending him except for a few Medinans such as Zayd b. Thābit, Abū Usayd al-Sā'idī, Ka'b b. Mālik and Ḥassān b. Thābit.[166] 'Alī was asked to speak to 'Uthmān in the name of the people. He admonished the caliph, mainly criticizing the appointment of his kin as governors and his lack of control over their actions. 'Uthmān rejected the criticism and told 'Alī that if he, 'Alī, were in his position he would not indulge in such reproaches. In his speech to the people in the mosque he chided his denigrators and faultfinders. He suggested that they blamed him for what they had accepted from 'Umar because of the toughness of the latter and his own gentleness; they should restrain their tongues from defaming him and their governors and appreciate that he had in fact shielded them from men against whom they would not dare speak out; he was materially providing for them as well as his predecessors had done; if there remained

[165] Ṭabarī, I, 2998–9. There are other reports, some of them Kufan, that 'Alī was prevented by his son Muḥammad b. al-Ḥanafiyya or others from going to the palace to protect 'Uthmān in the final stage of the siege. According to one of them Ibn al-Ḥanafiyya told 'Alī that Marwān and his kin wanted to use him as a hostage (Balādhurī, *Ansāb*, V, 94).

[166] Ṭabarī, I, 2936–7. The Medinan Jabala b. 'Amr al-Sā'idī is variously described as the first one to use offensive language towards 'Uthmān and to castigate him in public. The scenes described by al-Balādhurī, *Ansāb*, V, 47, ll. 7–17 and al-Ṭabarī, I, 2980, ll. 13–2981, l. 14 may have occurred about this time. The informant 'Uthmān b. al-Sharīd is perhaps the Makhzumite 'Uthmān b. 'Abd al-Raḥmān b. al-Ḥārith b. Hishām. 'Abd al-Raḥmān b. al-Ḥārith was known as al-Sharīd (Zubayrī, *Nasab*, 303). He had a son 'Uthmān (*ibid.*, 304).

some surplus money, why should not he, as their imam, do with it whatever he wished? Marwān then stood up and challenged the troublemakers: 'If you want we shall, by God, make the sword judge between us', but 'Uthmān silenced him.[167]

The revolt in Kūfa against the governor Saʿīd b. al-ʿĀṣ is placed by the sources in the year 34/654–5. There is no circumstantial evidence that would allow a closer dating. Most likely, however, it took place late in the year, presumably after 'Alī's futile intervention. Wellhausen assumed that the meeting of the provincial governors in Medina with 'Uthmān, during which the revolt occurred, was connected with the annual pilgrimage.[168] This is not confirmed by the account of al-Balādhurī which states only that 'Uthmān summoned his governors Muʿāwiya, 'Abd Allāh b. Saʿd, 'Abd Allāh b. 'Āmir and Saʿīd b. al-ʿĀṣ because of the clamour and complaints of the people.[169] The assumption, however, is attractive since it would explain why Saʿīd b. al-ʿĀṣ stayed so long before setting out on his return. For the Kufans decided to revolt only when informed by one of their men, 'Ilbā' b. al-Haytham al-Sadūsī, that 'Uthmān was sending Saʿīd back in spite of their complaints about him.[170]

The revolt, as described by al-Balādhurī most likely on the basis of Abū Mikhnaf's account, was a major explosion. Al-Ashtar was called from Ḥimṣ; he took control, had the deputy governor Thābit b. Qays b. al-Khaṭīm al-Anṣārī[171] expelled, and sent out troops in several directions in order to secure all access routes to the town. All this must obviously have taken a few weeks.[172] Only then did the governor, Saʿīd b. al-ʿĀṣ, appear, and he was prevented from reaching the Euphrates by Mālik b. Saʿīd al-Arḥabī. Al-Ashtar had the governor's palace looted and asked Abū Mūsā al-Ashʿarī to lead the prayers in the town and Ḥudhayfa b. al-Yamān to take charge of the *sawād* and the land tax. 'Uthmān then sent Abū Bakr's son 'Abd al-Raḥmān and al-Miswar b. Makhrama to summon the rebels back to obedience.

[167] Ṭabarī, I, 2937–9.

[168] Wellhausen, *Skizzen*, VI, 126; Wellhausen, *Das arabische Reich*, 29.

[169] Balādhurī, *Ansāb*, V, 43–4.

[170] *Ibid.*, 44. In the account of al-Zuhrī (*Aghānī*, XI, 30–1) the name 'Ilbā' is erroneously given as 'Alī. 'Ilbā' b. al-Haytham of the Banū Thaʿlaba b. Sadūs of Rabīʿa is described by Ibn al-Kalbī as a lord (*sayyid*) in Kūfa and as the first one there to summon to the allegiance of 'Alī (Ibn Ḥazm, *Jamharat ansāb al-ʿArab*, ed. E. Lévi-Provençal (Cairo, 1948), 299).

[171] Sayf b. 'Umar erroneously speaks of 'Amr b. Ḥurayth as the deputy governor (Ṭabarī, I, 2928).

[172] This account stands in sharp contrast to the farcical report of Sayf b. 'Umar quoted by al-Ṭabarī (*ibid.*, 2927–31; *Annali*, VIII, 81–4) which portrays the revolt as a coup by a handful of villains taking advantage of the absence of all responsible leaders in the Kufan provinces. Al-Zuhrī's summary account (*Aghānī*, XI, 30–1) also conceals the magnitude of the outburst.

Al-Ashtar's reply was couched in insolent language. He demanded that the deviant caliph recant, repent, and appoint Abū Mūsā and Ḥudhayfa. The letter was conveyed to Medina by several distinguished Kufan Qur'ān readers (*qurrā'*) and legal experts. 'Uthmān immediately declared his repentance and confirmed Abū Mūsā and Ḥudhayfa.[173] Al-Ashtar was evidently in firm control, and the caliph gave way under duress.[174]

The governors of the other three provinces at the same governors' meeting counselled tough repression. 'Abd Allāh b. 'Āmir sincerely advised 'Uthmān in verse to 'put a grip on the people with exile which will divide their gathering and to meet them with the sword'. This was, he asserted, plainly right and what they deserved. Mu'āwiya proudly promised 'Uthmān to take care of his province for him and asked him to tell Ibn 'Āmir and 'the lord of Egypt' to take care of theirs. The caliph's perdition at the hands of the rebels, he realized, would mean his own perdition. 'Abd Allāh b. Sa'd admitted that he foresaw only worsening of the situation, but then he addressed the opponents, threatening to match them with the lances and swords of his clan, the Banū 'Āmir of Quraysh, and to trample them in their country (Egypt).[175]

According to Abū Mikhnaf, representatives of the discontent in Kūfa, Baṣra and Egypt met in the mosque of Mekka during the pilgrimage season of 34/655 and decided to return, evidently in larger numbers, the following year to press their demands on 'Uthmān. Whether this detail, given in an account that otherwise reflects a poor knowledge of the events

[173] Balādhurī, *Ansāb*, V, 44–7.

[174] 'Uthmanid historical tradition rather portrayed the caliph as pleased and eager to satisfy public opinion. Sayf thus describes Sa'īd b. al-'Āṣ as ridiculing al-Ashtar and the Kufan rebels who met him in force and as telling them that it would have been sufficient for them to send a single man to the Commander of the Faithful or to him to achieve their purpose rather than bringing out a thousand men (Ṭabarī, I, 2950). The 'Uthmanid Juhaym al-Fihrī claimed that he was present when 'Uthmān made the provincial delegates the offer of choosing their own governors. Only the Kufans stood up and asked that he depose Sa'īd b. al-'Āṣ and appoint Abū Mūsā. 'Uthmān complied immediately (*Aghānī*, XI, 31). In another version of his report, the Egyptians, too, asked that he depose their governor, 'Abd Allāh b. Sa'd, and appoint 'Amr b. al-'Āṣ. 'Uthmān did so, but the Egyptian rebels Abū 'Amr b. Budayl, [al-Bajawī] and al-Tanūkhī (*sic*, perhaps for [Ibn 'Udays] al-Balawī and [Kināna b. Bishr] al-Tujībī) came and murdered him nonetheless (Ibn 'Asākir, *'Uthmān*, 403–4).

[175] Ibn 'Asākir, *'Uthmān*, 308–9. Later, when the Egyptian rebels set out for Medina, 'Abd Allāh b. Sa'd's prognosis was much more gloomy. See the lines of poetry relating to that time quoted by Ibn Bakr, *Tamhīd*, 195, evidently a revised version of his earlier lines. The details of the governors' meeting with 'Uthmān given by Abū Mikhnaf (?, Balādhurī, *Ansāb*, V, 43–4), Sayf b. 'Umar (Ṭabarī, I, 2944–6; Ibn 'Asākir, *'Uthmān*, 303–5; *Annali*, VIII, 11–12), and Ja'far al-Muḥammadī (Ṭabarī, I, 2932–4; *Annali*, VIII, 105–7) are legendary, especially the part ascribed to 'Amr b. al-'Āṣ.

in Medina, is reliable, must be left open.[176] The Egyptians, in any case, were the first to move. In Egypt two Qurayshites, Muḥammad b. Abī Ḥudhayfa and Muḥammad b. Abī Bakr, had been agitating against ʿUthmān and the governor ʿAbd Allāh b. Saʿd b. Abī Sarḥ for some time. The former was born a Muslim, son of the distinguished Early Companion Abū Ḥudhayfa b. ʿUtba of ʿAbd Shams. After his father was killed in the battle of al-ʿAqrabāʾ, he was brought up by ʿUthmān.[177] His grudge against his foster-father was most likely motivated by resentment of ʿUthmān's preference over him, son of an Early Companion and martyr of Islam, for kinsmen who were either sons of enemies of the Prophet such as al-Ḥakam and ʿUqba b. Abī Muʿayṭ or outlaws such as ʿAbd Allāh b. Saʿd.[178] Muḥammad b. Abī Bakr, for unknown reasons, shared his sister's intense dislike of ʿUthmān,[179] but not her hatred of ʿAlī. He had been brought up in the household of ʿAlī since his mother, Asmāʾ bt ʿUmays, married him after Abū Bakr's death.[180]

[176] Balādhurī, *Ansāb*, V, 59. The leaders of the Kufans and Basrans in 34/955 named by Abū Mikhnaf, Kaʿb b. ʿAbda (Dhi l-Ḥabaka) al-Nahdī and al-Muthannā (b. Bashīr) b. Maḥraba al-ʿAbdī, were not identical with their leaders in 35/956. This may speak for the accuracy of the report. Al-Ashtar, the leader of the Kufans in 35/956, was evidently occupied in Kūfa in 34/955.

[177] Born in Abyssinia, Ibn Abī Ḥudhayfa must have been above ten years old when he joined ʿUthmān's household.

[178] ʿAbd Allāh b. Saʿd had been a scribe of Muḥammad at an early stage of his preaching. He changed the wording of some passages in the Qurʾān and, when Muḥammad failed to notice the changes immediately, apostatized and mockingly assured the Prophet's Qurayshite opponents that he himself was a recipient of divine revelation as much as was Muḥammad. At the time of the conquest of Mekka, he was among those whom the Prophet would not pardon. ʿUthmān, however, then persuaded Muḥammad to forgive Ibn Saʿd, his foster brother. Muḥammad b. Abī Ḥudhayfa in Egypt criticized ʿUthmān for appointing a man whose blood the Prophet had declared licit and concerning whom Qurʾān VI 93 had been revealed: 'And who is a greater wrongdoer than he who forges lies about God, or says: "I have received a [divine] revelation" when nothing has been revealed to him, and who says: "I shall send down the like of what God has sent down?"' (Balādhurī, *Ansāb*, II, 387). The verse was held by some early Sunnite commentators to have referred to ʿAbd Allāh b. Saʿd. Others maintained that it referred to the false prophet Musaylima (Ṭabarī, *Jāmiʿ*, VII, 165–7).

Vague charges that Ibn Abī Ḥudhayfa had a grudge against ʿUthmān because he had been flogged for drinking wine (Balādhurī, *Ansāb*, II, 387, V, 50; Ibn al-Athīr, *al-Kāmil fi l-taʾrīkh*, ed. C. J. Tornberg (Leiden, 1851–76), III, 219) are presumably ʿUthmanid. Ibn al-Athīr adds that Ibn Abī Ḥudhayfa now became an ascetic engaging in worship and asked ʿUthmān to appoint him to a governorship. ʿUthmān answered that he would do so if Ibn Abī Ḥudhayfa were worthy of it. Ibn Abī Ḥudhayfa then asked to be sent on a sea raid, and was sent to Egypt.

[179] Just as in the case of Ibn Abī Ḥudhayfa, ʿUthmanid tradition represented by Sayf b. ʿUmar tried to explain his hatred of ʿUthmān by a legal punishment which ʿUthmān inflicted on him without mercy (Ibn ʿAsākir, *ʿUthmān*, 302). The story is certainly fiction.

[180] Muḥammad was only three years of age then. See further the article by G. Hawting on him in *EI* (2nd edn).

'Abd Allāh b. Sa'd had complained to 'Uthmān about the two men, but the caliph wrote that he was not to touch them since Muḥammad b. Abī Bakr was the brother of 'Ā'isha, Mother of the Faithful, and Muḥammad b. Abī Ḥudhayfa was his kin and foster-son, the 'fledgling of Quraysh'.[181] 'Uthmān tried to appease Ibn Abī Ḥudhayfa with a present of 30,000 dirhams and a litter covered with a precious cloth. Ibn Abī Ḥudhayfa exhibited the gift in the mosque of al-Fusṭāṭ, inviting the people to see for themselves how 'Uthmān tried to bribe him and to coax him to betray his religion. 'Uthmān now called 'Ammār b. Yāsir, apologized to him for what he had done before, and sent him to Egypt to investigate the activity of Ibn Abī Ḥudhayfa and to defend the conduct of the caliph while guaranteeing redress of grievances to those who would come to him. Once in Egypt, however, 'Ammār backed Ibn Abī Ḥudhayfa, calling for the removal of 'Uthmān and a march to Medina. From a poem by al-Walīd b. 'Uqba[182] it appears that 'Uthmān at the same time sent agents to the other provincial towns to investigate the activity of 'the traitors'. All of them, according to al-Walīd, carried out their task with fear of God and nobility except for Dulaym ('Ammār). 'Abd Allāh b. Sa'd reported to 'Uthmān asking for permission to punish 'Ammār, but the caliph rejected his advice and ordered him to send 'Ammār generously equipped back to Medina. Others, according to al-Balādhurī, reported that 'Ammār was deported by force (*suyyira*) and that Ibn Abī Ḥudhayfa now succeeded in persuading his followers to march to Medina.[183]

In Shawwāl 35/April 656, between 400 and 700 Egyptians set out for Medina,[184] ostensibly to perform an extra-seasonal pilgrimage (*'umra*). They were led by four men, 'Abd al-Raḥmān b. 'Udays al-Balawī,[185] who had the overall command, Sūdān (Sīdān) b. Ḥumrān al-Murādī, 'Amr b.

[181] Balādhurī, *Ansāb*, V, 50, II, 388. [182] Ibn 'Asākir, *'Uthmān*, 306.

[183] Balādhurī, *Ansāb*, V, 51; Ibn Shabba, *Ta'rīkh al-Madīna*, 1122–3.

[184] The date given by Muḥammad b. 'Umar b. 'Alī, Rajab 35/Jan. 656 (Ṭabarī, I, 2968; the *isnād* was misinterpreted by Caetani, (*Annali*, VIII, 147 and 152) as Ṭabarī – 'Abd Allāh b. Muḥammad – his father al-Wāqidī, making al-Wāqidī the author of the report) is untenable, as pointed out by Wellhausen (*Skizzen*, VI, 127 n. 3).

[185] 'Abd al-Raḥmān b. 'Udays was a Companion of rank, one of those who had given the Pledge under the Tree at al-Ḥudaybiyya, and was among the first conquerors of Egypt (Ibn Ḥajar, *Iṣāba*, IV, 171–2). He is said to have occupied the land (*ikhtaṭṭa*) of the White Palace (*al-dār al-bayḍā'*), located in front of the mosque and the palace of 'Amr b. al-'Āṣ, after the conquest. Others claimed, according to Ibn 'Abd al-Ḥakam, that the space of the White Palace was empty and used as a place for the horses of the Muslims before Marwān b. al-Ḥakam built it when he visited al-Fusṭāṭ as caliph in 65/684–5. Marwān said at the time that it was not proper for the caliph to be in a town where he did not have a palace. The White Palace was then built for him in two months (Ibn 'Abd al-Ḥakam, *Futūḥ Miṣr*, 107). Most likely he confiscated the property of his old enemy.

al-Ḥamiq al-Khuzāʿī and ʿUrwa b. Shiyaym b. al-Nibāʿ al-Kinānī al-Laythī.[186] The presence of ʿAmr b. al-Ḥamiq among the leaders of the Egyptians deserves special attention. He had been one of the Kufan *qurrā'* who wrote the letter to ʿUthmān protesting against the oppressive government of Saʿīd b. al-ʿĀṣ.[187] Perhaps for this reason he was exiled by ʿUthmān to Damascus.[188] Then he went to Egypt, and after the murder of ʿUthmān became a close associate of ʿAlī in Kūfa. He must have played a major part in spreading Kufan revolutionary sentiment in Egypt.[189]

Muḥammad b. Abī Bakr had gone to Medina before the rebels, and Ibn Abī Ḥudhayfa accompanied them as far as ʿAjrūd before returning to al-Fusṭāṭ.[190] The rebels arrived at Dhū Khushub, a night's journey north of Medina, the night before 1 Dhu l-Qaʿda/1 May.[191] In the sources that count the beginning of 'the siege' from that day, it lasted forty-nine days, until the murder of ʿUthmān.[192] Other sources speak of two sieges, or two 'arrivals (*qadma*)', interrupted by the temporary departure of the rebels. Only during the second stay was the palace of ʿUthmān under siege. The first 'siege', the stay at Dhū Khushub, lasted, according to Ibn al-ʿAbbās, twelve days.[193]

After their arrival at Dhū Khushub, the rebels sent a few men to Medina in order to size up the situation and to consult the prominent Companions on how to proceed. One of them, ʿAmr b. (ʿAbd Allāh) al-Aṣamm, reported later that the Companions urged them to enter

186 These are the four leaders named in the account of Muḥammad b. Maslama (Ṭabarī, I, 2991). Abū Mikhnaf named, instead of Sūdān and ʿAmr b. al-Ḥamiq, Abū ʿAmr b. Budayl b. Warqā' al-Khuzāʿī and Kināna b. Bishr al-Tujībī. The latter was, according to Abū Mikhnaf, also the leader of the Egyptians in 23/655 (Balādhurī, *Ansāb*, V, 59). Bishr b. Kināna is often mentioned as the murderer of ʿUthmān. Abū ʿAmr b. Budayl was a Companion and son of a Companion of rank. He is also said to have struck ʿUthmān (*ibid.*, 98). Their prominence in the final act may be the reason why they are sometimes included among the leaders of the Egyptians. It is possible that they joined the rebels in a second group. 187 *Ibid.*, 41. 188 Ibn Manẓūr, *Mukhtaṣar*, XIX, 201.

189 On ʿAmr b. al-Ḥamiq see Ibn Ḥajar, *Iṣāba*, IV, 294. He performed the *hijra* after al-Ḥudaybiyya and was counted among the Companions of Muḥammad. After the conquests he stayed first in Syria and then in Kūfa. In Egypt he related a hadith in which the Prophet had mentioned a time of tribulation (*fitna*) when the soundest or best people would be the western garrison (*al-jund al-gharbī*). For this reason, Ibn al-Ḥamiq said, he had come to Egypt (Ibn ʿAbd al-Ḥakam, *Futūḥ Miṣr*, 305). 190 Ṭabarī, I, 2968.

191 Khalīfa, *Ta'rīkh*, 168. The weekday given there, Wednesday, is incorrect.

192 So the early Egyptian report of Abu l-Khayr (= Marthad b. ʿAbd Allāh al-Yazanī, *muftī* of Egypt, d. 90/708–9; Ibn Ḥajar, *Tahdhīb*, X, 83) in Ṭabarī, I, 2999–3000.

193 Ṭabarī, I, 3088. Wellhausen erroneously assumed that the Medinans besieged ʿUthmān's palace for some time before the second arrival of the Egyptians and that the first siege of twelve days referred to this (*Skizzen*, VI, 128–9). The report in al-Ṭabarī, I, 2975 quoted by him as evidence does not say that the crowds assembled in front of the palace 'would not listen to any demands that they disperse', but rather that they left after being threatened and intimidated by Marwān.

Medina, except for 'Alī, whom they asked last. He warned them of evil consequences if they should advance; they should rather send a delegation to 'Uthmān to ask him to mend his ways.[194] This tallies with the account of 'Alī's grandson Muḥammad b. 'Umar according to whom a messenger from the rebels came at night to see 'Alī, Ṭalḥa and 'Ammār b. Yāsir. The latter two may safely be assumed to have encouraged the rebels to proceed to Medina. To 'Alī the messenger delivered a letter from Muḥammad b. Abī Ḥudhayfa, but 'Alī refused to take cognizance of its contents.[195]

'Uthmān, who had been informed of the intentions of the rebels by a speedy courier sent by 'Abd Allāh b. Sa'd and had first reacted with forebodings of doom,[196] now went to see 'Alī and asked him to meet the rebels and to induce them to turn back since he, 'Uthmān, did not want to receive them as this might encourage others to similar boldness. He gave 'Alī a free hand to negotiate, committing himself to act henceforth in accordance with 'Alī's advice. When 'Alī reminded him that he had previously talked to him but 'Uthmān had preferred to obey Marwān and his Umayyad kin, the caliph affirmed that he would now disobey them and obey him. 'Uthmān then ordered other Muhājirūn and Anṣār to ride out with 'Alī.[197] He wanted 'Ammār in particular to join the delegation, but 'Ammār declined.[198]

According to the contemporary Medinan Maḥmūd b. Labīd b. 'Uqba al-Awsī,[199] the group of Muhājirūn included – aside from 'Alī – Sa'īd b. Zayd, Abū Jahm al-'Adawī, Jubayr b. Muṭ'im, Ḥakīm b. Ḥizām and the Umayyads Marwān b. al-Ḥakam, Sa'īd b. al-'Āṣ and 'Abd al-Raḥmān b. 'Attāb b. Asīd. The Anṣār, led by Muḥammad b. Maslama, included Abū Usayd al-Sā'idī, Abū Ḥumayd al-Sā'idī, Zayd b. Thābit and Ka'b b. Mālik. With them were the Arabs Niyār b. Mikraz (or Mukram) of Aslam and others, in all some thirty men.[200]

The composition of this high-powered delegation reveals the dire straits in which 'Uthmān found himself. The four non-Umayyad Muhājirūn named, Sa'īd b. Zayd b. 'Amr b. Nufayl, Abū Jahm b. Ḥudhayfa (or Ḥudhāfa) al-'Adawī, both of 'Adī and closely associated with 'Umar,

[194] Ibn Shabba, *Ta'rīkh al-Madīna*, 1126: The 'Amr b. 'Abd Allāh named in the second report is evidently the same as 'Amr b. al-Aṣamm in the first; Balādhurī, *Ansāb*, V, 71; Ibn Sa'd, *Ṭabaqāt*, III/1, 45. [195] Ṭabarī, I, 2969.

[196] *Ibid.*, 2968–9. According to the Egyptian Abu l-Khayr, 'Uthmān, after receiving 'Abd Allāh b. Sa'd's warning, spoke (in public) and sent warnings to Mekka about the rebels who were claiming to perform the '*umra* but had been denigrating their imam (*ibid.*, 2999).

[197] *Ibid.*, 2968–9. [198] *Ibid.*, 2969–70. For the circumstances see above p. 95.

[199] He died in 96/714-15 or 99/717-18 and is considered a highly reliable transmitter from 'Umar and 'Uthmān (Ibn Ḥajar, *Tahdhīb*, X, 65–6). [200] Ṭabarī, I, 2970.

Jubayr b. Muṭʿim of Nawfal b. ʿAbd Manāf, the clan traditionally associated with ʿAbd Shams as were the Muṭṭalib with Hāshim, and Ḥakīm b. Ḥizām of Asad, were firm supporters of ʿUthmān, although Saʿīd b. Zayd deserted him in the end.[201] The latter three were among the few who buried ʿUthmān, as was Niyār b. Mikraz al-Aslamī. The four Anṣār, aside from Muḥammad b. Maslama, were among the few Medinan loyalist supporters of the caliph.[202] All these men, closely associated with ʿUthmān and his regime, could not have cut much ice with the rebels. In the absence of any other surviving member of the electoral council, ʿUthmān needed ʿAlī to speak to the rebels and needed ʿAmmār, if he could persuade him to go along. He needed Muḥammad b. Maslama, a highly respected Companion with a politically independent stance, as spokesman for the Anṣār. The double delegation clearly reflected the political situation. The Muhājirūn, Quraysh, were the ruling class, but the Anṣār, as the majority in Medina, were for the moment militarily more important for the fate of the caliph.[203]

[201] On Saʿīd b. Zayd see above, p. 29 n. 6 and below, p. 125. Abu l-Jahm b. Ḥudhayfa converted to Islam at the time of the conquest of Mekka (Ibn Ḥajar, *Iṣāba*, VII, 345). He had married, before Islam, the mother of ʿUbayd Allāh b. ʿUmar when ʿUmar divorced her (Ṭabarī, I, 1554; Ibn Hishām, *Sīrat sayyidinā*, 755). Ḥakīm b. Ḥizām, nephew of Muḥammad's first wife Khadīja, was an early friend of Muḥammad but did not convert to Islam before the conquest of Mekka. At that time the Prophet promised safety to all those seeking refuge in Ḥakīm's house.

[202] Concerning Abū Usayd, Zayd b. Thābit and Kaʿb b. Mālik see above, p. 113. Zayd b. Thābit is in various reports described as urging the Anṣār to defend ʿUthmān against the rebels. He was chided, however, that he did so merely because of ʿUthmān's munificence to him. Abū Ḥumayd al-Sāʿidī is quoted as stating after ʿUthmān's murder: 'By God, we did not think that he would be killed', and as vowing to abstain from some unspecified act and from laughing until his own death (Balādhurī, *Ansāb*, V, 100; Ibn Saʿd, *Ṭabaqāt*, III/1, 56).

[203] Wellhausen suggested that it was Muḥammad b. Maslama whom ʿUthmān sent to negotiate with the rebels and that ʿAlī was tendentiously associated with him, or was substituted in his place, by the historical tradition with the evident aim of demonstrating that he had done everything he could to avert the disaster (*Skizzen*, VI, 128 n. 2). Caetani further developed this thesis, turning it finally upside down with the argument that ʿAlī was not mentioned in some accounts in order to remove him even further from any suspicion of responsibility (*Annali*, VIII, 158 n. 1). In reality there is no inconsistency in the accounts assembled by al-Wāqidī. The ʿAlid Muḥammad b. ʿUmar was naturally interested primarily in the part played by his grandfather ʿAlī, while the Medinan Jābir b. ʿAbd Allāh, who was personally among the delegation of Anṣār (Balādhurī, *Ansāb*, V, 62, 66; Ibn Saʿd, *Ṭabaqāt*, III/1, 44; Jābir was evidently not yet prominent enough to be named by Maḥmūd b. Labīd) and the Ḥijāzī Arab Sufyān b. Abi l-ʿAwjāʾ al-Sulamī (Ibn Ḥajar, *Tahdhīb*, IV, 117) describe the part of Muḥammad b. Maslama, giving the number of Anṣār riding out with him as fifty (Ṭabarī, I, 2995; Ibn Shabba, *Taʾrīkh al-Madīna*, 1134). From the accounts of Maḥmūd b. Labīd and Muḥammad b. Maslama himself it is evident, however, that the two, ʿAlī and Ibn Maslama, met the rebels separately as leaders of the Muhājirūn and Anṣār respectively.

Muḥammad b. Maslama, who is now quoted directly by Maḥmūd b. Labīd, was thus probably right in describing his own words to Ibn 'Udays that the imam 'has promised us to turn back and retract (*yarji' wa-yanzi'*)' as decisive in inducing the Egyptian rebel leader to order his men to retreat.[204] This happened, if Ibn al-'Abbās' dating of the 'first siege' is correct, about 12 Dhu l-Qa'da/12 May. The negotiations presumably lasted some days. In Medina 'Uthmān had in the meantime, against his own wishes, agreed to speak to a few of the rebels after first deferring their visit.[205] 'Ammār, who put pressure on the caliph to see them by staying in front of the palace gate although told to leave, was once more manhandled by a servant, but 'Uthmān was able to satisfy the rebels that he had not ordered this.[206] Most likely 'Uthmān's visit to the Mothers of the Faithful, when 'Ā'isha told him that he must restore 'Amr b. al-'Āṣ to the governorship of Egypt because the army there was satisfied with him, also took place at this time.

The 'second siege' began, after the return of the rebels, on 1 Dhu l-Ḥijja/31 May.[207] There was thus a span of about eighteen days when the immediate threat to 'Uthmān seemed lifted. The sources report about three appearances and sermons by 'Uthmān in the mosque during this period, under very different circumstances. After 'Alī and Muḥammad b. Maslama returned from their mission, each of them warned 'Uthmān of the seriousness of the situation,[208] no doubt impressing on him the need to redress the grievances of the Egyptians in particular. Marwān, worried that any concession would be understood as a sign of weakness and would encourage further mutiny in the provinces, advised the caliph to state in his sermon that the Egyptians had left convinced that the accusations against him were baseless. According to al-Zuhrī he insinuated that 'Alī was behind the rebellion, was controlling the actions of the Egyptians and others and, finding their number insufficient, had sent them back, telling them to prepare while he would send for an army from Iraq to put an end to the oppressive regime of Marwān and his kin. 'Uthmān was persuaded by

[204] Ṭabarī, I, 2971. [205] See above p. 95. [206] Balādhurī, *Ansāb*, V, 51–2, 95.

[207] Ṭabarī, I, 3060. Caetani preferred another report according to which the siege had begun before the return of the Egyptians who arrived on a Friday and killed 'Uthmān on the next Friday (*Annali*, VIII, 141). The report, although going back to the grandson of al-Mughīra b. al-Akhnas who was killed together with 'Uthmān, is certainly unreliable. 'Uthmān was under siege by the Egyptian rebels when 'Ā'isha and 'Abd Allāh b. al-'Abbās left for the pilgrimage early in Dhu l-Ḥijja. It is possible, however, that some more radical Egyptian elements joined the main body a week before the murder. Kināna b. Bishr, the murderer of 'Uthmān, may have been among them.

[208] Ṭabarī, I, 2971–2, 2991.

him[209] and, after some delay, followed his advice in his sermon. This was the occasion when 'Amr b. al-'Āṣ, frustrated in his hope that 'Uthmān would reappoint him governor of Egypt as demanded by 'Ā'isha, made his memorable call for repentance from 'the ride over abysses'. The caliph mocked him, but after another call made a first gesture of repentance.[210]

While 'Amr left Medina in anger, 'Alī now urged 'Uthmān to make a clear public statement of retraction and repentance which would convince the people of his change of heart. In his next sermon 'Uthmān confessed his wrong-doing, declared his repentance to God, and invited the noble (*ashrāf*) among the people to visit him and present their views. Swallowing his arrogance, he stated that if God were to turn him back into a slave, he would humbly follow the path of a slave who is patient when owned and gives thanks when freed. According to the report of 'Abd al-Raḥmān b. al-Aswad, he specifically promised to remove Marwān and his kin.[211] The people were touched and wept, and Sa'īd b. Zayd went up to the caliph, assuring him that everyone was with him and encouraging him to carry out what he had promised.[212]

Caetani introduced his rendering of the report about 'Uthmān's public speech of repentance with this comment:

[209] Balādhurī, *Ansāb*, V, 62, 89. While al-Zuhrī recognized Marwān's accusation of 'Alī as malicious slander, other representatives of the Medinan orthodox Sunnite establishment accepted it as fact. Muḥammad b. al-Munkadir of Taym Quraysh, a leading Medinan scholar of the later Umayyad age, reported that 'Uthmān sent a 'man of the Muhājirūn' – he preferred not to name 'Alī – to meet the Egyptians at Dhū Khushub and to concede to them whatever they demanded. Then a man of Makhzūm asked the caliph to allow him to follow his envoy, since he did not trust him. 'Uthmān gave him permission, and the spy heard the envoy tell the rebels that they had come in a poor state and would not be a match for 'Uthmān's men. The spy informed 'Uthmān, who commented that this man ('Alī), 'may God not bless him', was driven by greed in pursuit of his hopes, but that he, 'Uthmān, had heard the Prophet say that he would never obtain it (the caliphate). 'Abd Allāh b. al-Faḍl al-Hāshimī, a Medinan contemporary of al-Zuhrī (Ibn Ḥajar, *Tahdhīb*, V, 357–8), similarly narrated that 'Alī told the Egyptians that they had come to him insufficiently prepared to meet 'Uthmān's defenders. They should turn back, seek additional strength, and then return (Ibn Shabba, *Ta'rīkh al-Madīna*, 1128).

[210] The account of Muḥammad b. 'Umar b. 'Alī (Ṭabarī, I, 2972) is substantially confirmed by that of Abū Ḥabība, the client of al-Zubayr (*ibid.*, 2982).

[211] *Ibid.*, 2977.

[212] *Ibid.*, 2972–4. Al-Wāqidī gives here a new *isnād*, 'Alī b. 'Umar *'an abīh*. 'Alī b. 'Umar is certainly the brother of Muḥammad b. 'Umar b. 'Alī, previously quoted by him. All this material presumably goes back to 'Alī's son 'Umar. 'Uthmān's sermon of repentance is also described in the report of the Zuhrite 'Abd al-Raḥmān b. al-Aswad (*ibid.*, 2982). Abū Ḥabība mentions the weeping of the public after his summary account of the earlier sermon and gesture of repentance (*ibid*)., creating the false impression that there was only one occasion of public repentance.

There is no need to insist on the absurd tenor of 'Uthmān's speech, an inconceivable speech, equivalent to the basest renunciation of the duties of a caliph, and in open contrast with the stern and almost intractable attitude with which 'Uthmān resisted all demands for his abdication. Al-Wāqidī wants to make the caliph appear as a dotard in the vest of an ascetic, a hater of the world. The picture is entirely false. False is the portrait of 'Uthmān, a man of refined tastes, zestful, and a lover of young women although above seventy years of age. False is, moreover, that he had no will of his own, no firmness. His dignified death is an indication of a proud character which has nothing to do with the Waqidian literary fiction of the following speech.[213]

Did he think the penance of Henry IV, emperor of the Holy Roman Empire, before Pope Gregory VII at Canossa was fiction?

Marwān, Sa'īd b. al-'Āṣ and other Umayyads boycotted the sermon and waited for the caliph as he returned to the palace. When allowed to speak, Marwān told him that his speech would have been agreeable, and he, Marwān, would be the first to be pleased with it, if 'Uthmān were in a safe and impregnable position; yet at this time, as the flood water was overflowing the hilltops, a humble speech was nothing but a sign of weakness: 'By God, to persist in wrongdoing for which you can ask God's forgiveness is preferable to penitence to which you are compelled by fear. If you so wished, you could curry favour with repentance without confessing to any wrongdoing, when crowds like mountains are gathered in front of your gate.'[214]

According to 'Abd al-Raḥmān b. al-Aswad, 'Uthmān for three days was too ashamed to go out and meet the people[215] who were coming to offer their advice. Finally he asked Marwān to go out and talk to them, since he was ashamed to do so. Marwān went out and shouted: 'What is the matter with you that you assemble as if you came for plunder? May your faces be disfigured! . . . You have come coveting to wrest our property (*mulk*) from our hands. Be off from us. By God, if that is what you want, something from us will fall upon you which will not please you, and you will not praise the outcome of your fancy. Go back to your houses, for, by God, we shall not be overwhelmed and deprived of what we have in our hands.' The people left.[216] 'Alī now broke with 'Uthmān, telling him that he would not visit him again.[217]

'Uthmān's third sermon mentioned in the sources, his last, was interrupted, according to the report of Sa'd b. Abī Waqqāṣ' grandson Ismā'īl b. Muḥammad, three times by angry shouts of 'Act in accordance with the Book of God', and ended with the caliph being carried

[213] *Annali*, VIII, 155. [214] Ṭabarī, I, 2985. [215] *Ibid.*, 2977. [216] *Ibid.*, 2975.
[217] See above, p. 111.

unconscious to his palace.[218] In other accounts the chief troublemaker is identified as Jahjāh b. Saʿīd al-Ghifārī, a veteran warrior of Islam and one of those who had given the Pledge under the Tree.[219] The Ghifār had evidently not forgiven ʿUthmān for his deportation of their kinsman Abū Dharr. Jahjāh is described by the eyewitness Abū Ḥabība as shouting: 'Look, we have brought this decrepit she-camel (*shārif*) with a striped woollen cloak and an iron collar on it. Get down [from the pulpit], so that we can wrap you with the cloak, throw the collar on you, carry you on the camel, and then dump you on the Mount of Smoke (*jabal al-dukhān*).'[220]

Muḥammad b. Maslama, according to his own account, had been upset by ʿUthmān's public declaration that the Egyptians had left satisfied that their charges against ʿUthmān were mistaken and had intended to reproach him, but then had kept silent. Next he learned that the Egyptians were back at al-Suwaydā', two night journeys north of Medina.[221] ʿUthmān sent for him as the rebels reached Dhū Khushub and asked him what he thought about their intentions. Ibn Maslama answered that he did not know them, but he did not think they were returning for anything good. ʿUthmān asked him to meet them again and turn them back. Ibn Maslama refused, however, stating that he had guaranteed to them ʿUthmān's retraction in a number of matters, but the caliph had failed to retract a single letter of them. The Egyptians now alighted in al-Aswāf in the sacred district (*ḥaram*) of Medina[222] and laid siege to ʿUthmān's palace.[223]

ʿAbd al-Raḥmān b. ʿUdays and the other three leaders of the rebels

[218] Ṭabarī, I, 2979. This occasion and the volley of pebbles thrown by the crowd were also mentioned by al-Ḥasan al-Baṣrī, who evidently was present. His age at the time was, as stated by him, fourteen or fifteen years. As an ʿUthmanid, al-Ḥasan called the men asking ʿUthmān for the rule of the Book of God 'reprobates (*fasaqa*)' (Balādhurī, *Ansāb*, V, 71, 92; Ibn Abi l-Ḥadīd, *Sharḥ*, IX, 17–18). [219] Ibn Ḥajar, *Iṣāba*, I, 265.

[220] Ṭabarī, I, 2982; Balādhurī, *Ansāb*, V, 47; Ibn Shabba, *Ta'rīkh al-Madīna*, 1110–12, 1218–19. Jabal al-Dukhān was said to have been the place to which another deportee, Kaʿb b. ʿAbda al-Nahdī, was exiled by ʿUthmān (Balādhurī, *Ansāb*, V, 42). It is mentioned by al-Hamdānī (*Ṣifat Jazīrat al-ʿArab*, ed. D. H. Müller (Leiden, 1884–91), 52) as a mountain near ʿAdan in the Yemen, but may here be simply an allusion to hell. Similar threats to fetter and deport ʿUthmān, this time to hell-fire, are ascribed to Jabala b. ʿAmr al-Sāʿidī. [221] Yāqūt, *Buldān*, III, 197. [222] *Ibid.*, 269.

[223] Wellhausen accepted a report that the prominent Medinan ʿAmr b. Ḥazm of the Banu l-Najjār of Khazraj went to meet the rebels at Dhū Khushub and led them to Medina (*Skizzen*, VI, 129; Ṭabarī, I, 2989). This is not unreasonable. The whole account from which this detail is taken, however, is highly unreliable. It is ascribed to Muḥammad b. Isḥāq and related by Jaʿfar al-Muḥammadī. The family of ʿAmr b. Ḥazm, neighbours of ʿUthmān, were evidently strongly opposed to ʿUthmān. Muḥammad b. ʿAmr b. Ḥazm is described as opening a passage-way (*khawkha*) from their house to the side of ʿUthmān's palace for the rebels on the battle day and is named, together with Ibn Abī Bakr and Ibn Abī Ḥudhayfa, as one of the three Muḥammads who were particularly tough against ʿUthmān (Ibn Shabba, *Ta'rīkh al-Madīna*, 1278, 1307). In pro-ʿUthmān poetry of al-Aḥwaṣ the 'Ḥazmī' is mentioned as doing great harm (*ibid.*, 1279).

next went to see Ibn Maslama, reminding him of his guarantee. They then produced a small sheet which they said they had found with a slave (*ghulām*) of 'Uthmān riding on a camel from the alms-tax.[224] The sheet contained instructions to the governor of Egypt to punish the four rebel leaders immediately upon their arrival with a hundred lashes, shaving their heads and beards, and imprisoning them until further instruction.[225]

When Ibn Maslama put their presumption in doubt that 'Uthmān had written this letter, the rebel leaders answered: 'Then Marwān is able to decide this for 'Uthmān without consulting him. This is worse, he excludes himself from "this matter."' They asked Ibn Maslama to accompany them to the caliph, informing him that 'Alī had already promised to come, while Sa'd b. Abī Waqqāṣ and Sa'īd b. Zayd had declined. The latter was evidently appalled by 'Uthmān's apparent turn-about after his public penance. Ibn Maslama and 'Alī, as related above, then came to 'Uthmān and asked him to admit the Egyptians waiting at the gate. Marwān was sitting with the caliph and asked leave to speak to them. This time 'Uthmān brushed him off and sent him away. Eventually allowed to enter, the Egyptians omitted the caliph's title in their greeting, and Ibn Maslama recognized that evil was in the offing. They put forward Ibn 'Udays as their spokesman, who mentioned first the conduct of 'Abd Allāh b. Sa'd in Egypt, his maltreatment (*taḥāmul*) of Muslims and protected people (*ahl al-dhimma*) and his arbitrary arrogation in regard to the war booty of the Muslims. Whenever his actions were questioned, he would say: 'Here is the letter of the Commander of the Faithful to me.' Then he mentioned[226] reprehensible innovations which the caliph had made in Medina, contravening the acts of his two predecessors. He continued: 'Thus we travelled from Egypt to seek either your blood or that you recant. Then 'Alī and Muḥammad b. Maslama turned us back, and Muḥammad guaranteed to us your retraction in everything about which we complained.' They turned to Ibn Maslama,

[224] The camel had the brand mark (*mīsam*) with which camels gathered as alms-tax were marked (Balādhurī, *Ansāb*, V, 67).

[225] Ṭabarī, I, 2991–2. The general reliability of Ibn Maslama's account is underlined by this description of the contents of the letter. In most other accounts 'Abd Allāh b. Sa'd is ordered to put the rebel leaders to death. The execution of rebels was not yet accepted practice of government.

Attempting to discredit Ibn Maslama's account, Caetani asserted that al-Wāqidī, in composing it, put together two mutually contradictory versions. While the former presented the return of the Egyptians as the result of 'Uthmān's reneging on his concessions to them, the latter contained 'the old story' about the false letter (*Annali*, VIII, 177). In reality Ibn Maslama's account nowhere suggested that the Egyptians returned because 'Uthmān reneged on his promises. Ibn Maslama rather told the caliph that he did not know why they were returning. He himself blamed 'Uthmān for reneging and thus undermining his position as the guarantor.

[226] Reading *dhakara* for *dhakarū*: Ṭabarī, I, 2994.

and he confirmed what they had said. Now they recounted their interception of the official letter ordering their punishment as they had described it to Ibn Maslama.[227]

The story of the official letter intercepted by the Egyptian rebels has intrigued and puzzled modern historians. Wellhausen cautiously wrote: 'They claimed to have intercepted a letter of the caliph', without noting the accusations against Marwān in the sources.[228] This non-committal attitude to the question has generally prevailed among modern authors. H. Djaït describes the whole episode as highly doubtful and questions whether the letter itself existed. If it did exist, it could have been produced by the most virulent of the Egyptians in order to create a pretext for their attack on the caliph. Alternatively 'Uthmān and his Umayyad entourage might have had a change of heart in relation to the rebels. 'Uthmān, in any case, was not a mere plaything in the hands of Marwān.[229] Caetani argued at length that the whole story of the letter must be late fiction since 'Abd Allāh b. Sa'd, to whom it was addressed, was not in Egypt at the time. In the end, however, he was convinced that he had found the solution: 'The deception was not by the Umayyads to the detriment of the Egyptians, but rather by the friends of 'Alī to the detriment of the caliph!'[230] G. Levi della Vida,[231] although less sure about the facts, thought that he had found evidence supporting Caetani's intuition in a report of the 'Uthmānid Juhaym al-Fihrī quoted by al-Balādhurī. According to Juhaym, 'Uthmān, in Juhaym's presence, told 'Alī when the latter questioned him about whom he suspected in regard to the letter: 'I suspect my secretary, and I suspect you, 'Alī, because you are obeyed among the people [the Egyptian rebels] and you do not turn them back from me.'[232]

Whether 'Uthmān really made such a sarcastic remark to 'Alī at this time when he must have been aware of his dependence on 'Alī's good will may be open to doubt. He could, however, have been carried away momentarily by anger at being pressed about the part of Marwān who, as he well knew, was suspected by 'Alī and everybody else. The report is obviously no evidence for any actual involvement of 'Alī. The theory that 'Alī could have conspired with the personal secretary of the caliph right under the nose of a suspicious Marwān stretches the imagination.

[227] *Ibid.*, 2993–4; see further above, p. 112.
[228] *Skizzen*, VI, 129; slightly different *Das arabische Reich*, 31.
[229] *La Grande Discorde*, 147. [230] *Annali*, VIII, 159. [231] "Othmān b. 'Affān', *EI*.
[232] Balādhurī, *Ansāb*, V, 95; Ibn Shabba, *Ta'rīkh al-Madīna*, 1154. Ibn Shabba quotes some secondary versions containing 'Uthmān's accusation of 'Alī (1154–5, 1168, 1206). An account attributed to Jābir b. 'Abd Allāh explains that 'Alī's partisans accused 'Uthmān of responsibility for the letter and 'Uthmān's partisans accused 'Alī and his companions (Ibn Shabba, *Ta'rīkh al-Madina*, 1149).

In reality it is plain that Marwān, as suspected by the tradition, was behind the letter. Marwān believed all along that the rebellion must be met head on. After the agreement with the rebels at Dhū Khushub, he put about the rumour that 'Alī had conspired with them, advising them to go back to Egypt in order to gather reinforcements. It was, from his point of view, entirely logical to order 'Abd Allāh b. Sa'd to prevent this by punishing and imprisoning the leaders. Whether he believed his own conspiracy theory is immaterial. He had at least to play the game and sent the letter as soon as he had returned from Dhū Khushub to Medina.

'Abd Allāh b. Sa'd, it is true, probably had just left Egypt or was about to depart. According to the early Egyptian authority Abu l-Khayr, he had been given leave to go to Medina at his own request.[233] Marwān need not have known whether he was still in Egypt. The courier would, in any case, have met him, and 'Abd Allāh could have passed the order on to his deputy. As it happened, 'Abd Allāh on reaching Ayla learned that the rebels were moving back to Medina. He now turned back to Egypt in order, no doubt, to forestall trouble there, but it was too late. Muḥammad b. Abī Ḥudhayfa, also having learned that his men were returning to Medina, had taken control of Egypt.[234] 'Abd Allāh b. Sa'd sought refuge in Palestine.[235]

One may perhaps question, with Djaït, whether 'Uthmān was in fact unaware of the letter being sent in his name. It has ever been a much-cherished privilege of rulers to plead ignorance of the actions of their underlings when matters go awry. 'Uthmān's failure to punish his young cousin may be seen to point to his own complicity. Yet 'Alī and Muḥammad b. Maslama seem to have been sincerely convinced of his innocence. His wavering between public penance and arrogant intractability seems to reveal a deeply troubled man no longer in command of his proper judgement.

The siege of the palace was maintained by the Egyptians, who had the

[233] Ṭabarī, I, 2999. Caetani's argument that 'Abd Allāh b. Sa'd had left Egypt much earlier, because the testimony of al-Kindī as an Egyptian must be considered more authoritative than al-Wāqidī's (*Annali*, VIII, 159), is mistaken. Al-Wāqidī preserved the earlier Egyptian tradition with the excellent *isnād* Shuraḥbīl b. Abī 'Awn – Yazīd b. Abī Ḥabīb – Abu l-Khayr. It is quite out of the question that 'Abd Allāh b. Sa'd could have been absent from Egypt before the rebels left.

[234] Ibn Abī Ḥudhayfa was, no doubt, quickly informed, and perhaps consulted, by the rebels about the interception while they were still in Buwayb. This explains the relatively long span of time before they were back in Medina. According to a report of the Syrian Makḥūl, the rebels, after seizing the courier, wrote to the Egyptians, presumably Muḥammad b. Abī Ḥudhayfa, informing them of what had happened and that they intended to return to Medina. At their suggestion the Egyptians expelled Ibn Abī Sarḥ to Palestine (Ibn Shabba, *Ta'rīkh al-Madīna*, 1152–3.)

[235] Ṭabarī, I, 2999.

most serious grievance against 'Uthmān, although a few Medinan locals joined it at times. The exact date of the arrival of the Kufan and Basran rebel forces is uncertain. They were led by al-Ashtar and Ḥukaym b. Jabala al-'Abdī,[236] and are said to have numbered about two hundred and one hundred men respectively.[237] Their arrival was definitely later than the return of the delegations from Dhū Khushub, most likely about the same time as the second arrival of the Egyptians.[238] They may have left their towns under the guise of Mekka pilgrims and then have stayed in Medina. In any case, they did not join the siege.[239] Al-Ashtar evidently heeded 'Ā'isha's and 'Alī's opposition to the use of violence. According to his own report, he went to see Muḥammad's Umayyad widow Umm Ḥabība bt Abī Sufyān and offered to carry 'Uthmān safely out of the besieged palace in her litter (*hawdaj*). The Umayyads, however, rejected the offer, insisting that they would have nothing to do with him.[240]

[236] The only local grievance in Baṣra mentioned by al-Balādhurī, quoting Abū Mikhnaf 'and others', was the deportation of 'Āmir b. 'Abd Qays al-'Anbarī of Tamīm, a worshipper and ascetic who had criticized 'Uthmān's conduct. On the caliph's order, he was sent to Medina by 'Abd Allāh b. 'Āmir. As this provoked an outcry among the people, 'Uthmān treated him kindly and sent him back to Baṣra (Balādhurī, *Ansāb*, V, 57). Ibn Shabba quotes an early Basran report mentioning a clash between Ḥukaym b. Jabala and 'Abd Allāh b. 'Āmir, after which the governor seized some horses belonging to Ḥukaym in Fārs. Ḥukaym vented his anger, blaming 'Uthmān. The Basrans also complained to 'Uthmān that 'Abd Allāh b. 'Āmir distributed grain spoiled by rain among them. When the caliph ignored their complaint, their attitude towards him changed and they reproached him for replacing Abū Mūsā al-Ash'arī with Ibn 'Āmir (Ibn Shabba, *Ta'rīkh al-Madīna*, 1147–8).

[237] Balādhurī, *Ansāb*, V, 97. Abū Mikhnaf speaks of another fifty Basrans joining them later (*ibid.*, 59). In a piece of poetry evidently composed in the last stage of the crisis, al-Walīd b. 'Uqba names as the leaders of treason Ḥukaym, (al-)Ashtar, ('Amr) b. al-Ḥamiq and Ḥāritha (Ibn 'Asākir, *'Uthmān*, 307). Ḥāritha, most likely one of the Anṣār making common cause with the rebels, cannot be identified with certainty. The name may refer to the Banū Ḥāritha of Aws, to whom Muḥammad b. Maslama belonged, even though they were described by the 'Uthmanid Muḥammad b. al-Munkadir as backing 'Uthmān (Ibn Shabba, *Ta'rīkh al-Madīna*, 1280). The meaning of 'Ḥāritha today peddles the complaint (*yashri l-shakāta*)' could well apply to Muḥammad b. Maslama, who now sided with the rebels in their complaint against 'Uthmān. Less likely to be meant is Ḥāritha b. al-Nu'mān b. Nufay' of the Banu l-Najjār, a prominent Companion and veteran of Badr (Ibn Ḥajar, *Iṣāba*, I, 312–13). The Banu l-Najjār, as noted, were accused of having betrayed 'Uthmān. The Medinan 'Abd Allāh b. Rabāḥ al-Anṣārī reported in 'Uthmanid Baṣra that Ḥāritha b. al-Nu'mān offered 'Uthmān 'our' support. This could be an attempt to clear him of accusations.

[238] The account of Sufyān b. Abi l-'Awjā' (Ṭabarī, I, 2995) seems to imply that they were in Medina during the absence of the Egyptians. The details of this account, however, inspire no confidence in its reliability.

[239] This is categorically stated by the Egyptian Abu l-Khayr (*ibid.*, 2999).

[240] Al-Qāḍī al-Nu'mān, *Sharḥ al-akhbār fī faḍā'il al-a'imma al-aṭhār*, ed. Muḥammad al-Ḥusaynī al-Jalālī (Qumm, n. d.), I, 297; Ibn Shabba, *Ta'rīkh al-Madīna*, 1313. 'Uthmanid tradition, trying to incriminate al-Ashtar in the murder of 'Uthmān, reported that he hit the mule of Muḥammad's widow Ṣafiyya bt Ḥuyayy in the face with his whip in order to stop her when she wanted to persuade the rebels to raise the siege (Ibn Shabba, *Ta'rīkh al-Madīna*, 1311–12).

The 'siege' was initially peaceful. Visitors, official and unofficial, were allowed to enter and leave the palace freely. Even Marwān and 'Abd al-Raḥmān b. 'Attāb were able to go about their business in town and in the palace (perhaps by the use of a side door?). In his letters to the Syrians and the Mekka pilgrims written at the beginning of the siege, 'Uthmān complained that his enemies[241] were preventing him from leading the prayer and from entering the mosque; they also had taken possession of whatever they could put their hands on.[242] The latter statement probably refers to the seizure of the treasury keys by Ṭalḥa. The communal prayers were first led, on 'Alī's instructions, by the Medinan Abū Ayyūb al-Anṣārī, and then, from Friday and the Feast of Immolation on, by 'Alī himself.[243] 'Ubayd Allāh b. 'Adī b. al-Khiyār of Nawfal b. 'Abd Manāf visited 'Uthmān and told him he had scruples about praying behind an 'imam of sedition' (*imām fitna*). The caliph advised him to pray with the people since prayer was their best action, and to abstain from their evil acts.[244] The rebels were evidently still hoping that 'Uthmān would capitulate. According to 'Uthmān's letters, they had written to the Muslims that they were satisfied with the commitments the caliph had made to them.[245] 'Uthmān obviously had no interest in revealing the real cause of their sudden return to Medina, the intercepted letter, and implied that they had returned to seek fulfilment of the caliph's promises.

'Uthmān continued that he did not know of anything he had promised them which he had failed to keep. They had demanded the application of the Qur'ān and the Qur'anic punishments and he had told them: 'Carry them out on anyone, close or remote, who has incurred one of them; apply them to anyone who has wronged you.' They had asked that the Book of God be recited and he had replied: 'Let any reciter recite it without adding anything which God has not sent down in it.' They had demanded that the exiled be returned to their homes, the deprived be provided sustenance, money be spent abundantly so that good practice (*sunna ḥasana*) be followed in it, that (the rules) regarding the *khums* and the alms-tax not be transgressed, that men of strength and integrity be appointed as governors, that grievances of the people be redressed. He

241 'Uthmān speaks of 'my companions who pretend to leadership in this matter and are trying to hasten fate'. The major Early Companions, in particular Ṭalḥa and 'Alī, are presumably meant.

242 Ṭabarī, I, 3043; Ibn 'Asākir, '*Uthmān*, 377.

243 Ṭabarī, I, 3059–60. Reports that the Anṣārī Sahl b. Ḥunayf or his son Abū Umāma, rather than Abū Ayyūb, led the prayer before 'Alī (see also Ibn Shabba, *Ta'rīkh al-Madīna*, 1217–19) seem less reliable. Sahl b. Ḥunayf later led the prayer as 'Alī's governor of Medina.

244 Ibn Shabba, *Ta'rīkh al-Madīna*, 1216–17.

245 The text in Ibn 'Asākir, '*Uthmān*, 376, has *annahum qad raḍū bi 'lladhī a'ṭaytuhum*. This seems preferable to the text in al-Ṭabarī, I, 3042: *annahum raja'ū bi 'lladhī a'ṭaytuhum*. Minor textual differences between the two letters will not be noted in the following rendering of the contents.

had been satisfied with all this and accepted it patiently (*iṣṭabartu lah*). 'Uthmān then mentioned his visit to the 'Mothers of the Faithful', asserting that he had fulfilled all their wishes, but that 'Amr b. al-'Āṣ then had transgressed.[246]

As he was writing, 'Uthmān went on, his enemies were giving him three choices: either they would apply the *lex talionis* to the caliph for every man he had punished, rightly or wrongly, executing it to the letter without any remission;[247] or he must ransom himself by surrendering his reign so that they would appoint someone else; or they would send to those who obeyed them in the provincial garrisons (*ajnād*) and in Medina and they would renounce their duty of 'hearing and obeying' imposed upon them by God. 'Uthmān answered that the caliphs before him had punished rightly and wrongly, but no one had demanded retaliation against them; his enemies, he knew, were out to get him in person; as for abdication, that they would beat him[248] was preferable to his renouncing the reign, the office (*'amal*) and vicegerency of God.[249] Their threat of calling on the garrisons and the people of Medina to renounce their obedience he dismissed haughtily. They had at first offered him their obedience voluntarily, seeking the pleasure of God and concord among themselves; he had not forced them. Those who were merely seeking worldly benefit would not obtain more of it than God had decreed; those, however, who sought only the face of God, the hereafter, the well-being of the community, the pleasure of God, the good Sunna which had been laid down by the Messenger of God and the two caliphs after him, would be rewarded by God for it. Their reward was not in 'Uthmān's hands; even if he were to give them the whole world, it would be of no benefit to their religion and would avail them nothing.

'Uthmān then warned the Muslims against a breach of their covenant,

[246] Ṭabarī, I, 2943; Ibn 'Asākir, *'Uthmān*, 377. The letters attempt to create the impression that 'Uthmān had in fact reappointed 'Amr before his transgression. This is obviously quite out of the question. 'Amr would hardly have attacked 'Uthmān in public if his hopes for the governorship had not been thwarted. Marwān, who wanted to see the Egyptian rebel leaders punished, must have blocked the appointment if 'Uthmān seriously considered it.

[247] This is evidently a misrepresentation of the demands of the rebels. They were not demanding retaliation for those rightfully punished, but they insisted that they, not the caliph, should decide who was rightly or wrongfully punished.

[248] Ṭabarī, I, 3044, reading *yalka'ūnī* for *yaklubūnī* as suggested in the footnote. The text in Ibn 'Asākir, *'Uthmān*, 377 has *yaqtulūnī*, 'that they would kill me'.

[249] The sources describe 'Abd Allāh b. 'Umar in particular as advising 'Uthmān not to abdicate. The caliph's enemies, he told him, could not do more than kill him, and it would be wrong to establish a sunna in Islam that whenever some people were angry at their commander they could depose him. 'Uthmān's cousin al-Mughīra b. al-Akhnas al-Thaqafī, who was killed together with him, is said to have advised him to resign since the rebels were threatening to kill him otherwise (Ibn Sa'd, *Ṭabaqāt*, III/1, 45; Balādhurī, *Ansāb*, V, 76; Ibn 'Asākir, *'Uthmān*, 259).

affirming that neither he nor God would condone it; the choices offered by the rebels amounted to nothing but abdication (*naz'*) and choosing another commander (*ta'mīr*); in the face of this affront, he controlled himself and those with him for the sake of averting discord and bloodshed. The letters concluded with an appeal to justice and mutual support, a confession of repentance for everything the caliph had done, and a request for God's forgiveness for himself and the faithful.[250]

The letters, surely approved by Marwān, made no mention of the rebels' grievance against him, the message he had sent in the caliph's name ordering their punishment. They were firm in tone, excluding the possibility of any further concessions, all reasonable demands already having been met. But they also stressed the caliph's commitment to peace and concord in the community. There was no call to arms to help subdue the troublemakers.[251] The crisis was to be resolved without violence. Any threat that the caliph and 'those with him' might perhaps lose their self-control in the face of the provocation was muted.

The numerous reports stressing 'Uthmān's opposition to armed initiative and violence even in defence against the besiegers are basically reliable. Fully conscious and respectful of the still-recognized sanctity of the life of Muslims, he wished that no blood be shed in the resistance to the rebels, and that these should not be provoked to violence. Later Muslim tradition after the civil war, used to bloody government repression and violence among Muslims, offered stories that 'Uthmān wrote to Mu'āwiya and 'Abd Allāh b. 'Āmir requesting them to send troops to Medina and that they responded to his requests. Mu'āwiya's great-grandson Ḥarb b. Khālid b. Yazīd was perhaps the first one to spread the claim that Mu'āwiya sent Ḥabīb b. Maslama al-Fihrī with 4,000 Syrians to aid 'Uthmān. The vanguard, 1,000 men under Yazīd b. Asad al-Bajalī, had reached Wādi l-Qurā or Dhū Khushub when they learned of the murder of 'Uthmān and turned back. The story was taken up by the pro-Umayyad

[250] Ṭabarī, I, 3043–5; Ibn 'Asākir, *'Uthmān*, 377–9. According to Ṣāliḥ b. Kaysān (quoted by the unreliable Ibn Da'b), 'Uthmān also sent a brief note to the pilgrims which was read to them by Nāfi' b. Zurayb of Nawfal Quraysh on the day of 'Arafa, presumably after Ibn al-'Abbās had read the main message. In it the caliph complained that, as he was writing, he was under siege and was eating only the minimum to sustain himself in fear that his provisions would run out. He was neither being asked to repent nor was any argument on his part listened to. He appealed to those hearing the letter to come to him and establish justice and prevent wrong-doing. Ibn al-'Abbās did not pay attention to Nāfi''s action (Ibn Shabba, *Ta'rīkh al-Madīna*, 1166).

[251] The letter to the Syrians, however, contained an appeal to turn back transgression (*baghy*) of anyone depriving the caliph of his right with a quotation of Qur'ān XLIX 9: 'If two parties of the faithful fight, conciliate between them; but if one transgresses on the other, fight the one that transgresses until it returns to the order of God . . .' The message to the Mekka pilgrims was perhaps intentionally somewhat more conciliatory.

Maslama b. Muḥārib in Baṣra and by al-Shaʿbī in Kūfa.[252] There were similar stories about ʿAbd Allāh b. ʿĀmir sending Mujāshiʿ b. Masʿūd al-Sulamī and Zufar b. al-Ḥārith al-Kilābī with a Basran army.[253] The ʿUthmanid, but anti-Umayyad, Basran Juwayriya b. Asmāʾ (d. 173/789–90) reported that Muʿāwiya dispatched Yazīd b. Asad with firm instructions not to move beyond Dhū Khushub. When asked why Muʿāwiya would give this order, Juwayriya explained that he wanted ʿUthmān to be killed in order to claim the caliphate for himself.[254] All such tales are fictitious. Even a report of the generally reliable contemporary Abū ʿAwn, client of al-Miswar, that troops moving from the provinces provoked the rebels to attack, reflects at best rumours in Medina.[255]

The primary responsibility to defend ʿUthmān and the palace fell, under tribal norms, on his Umayyad kin, their clients and confederates.

[252] Ibn Shabba, *Taʾrīkh al-Madīna*, 1289. Yazīd b. Asad was the grandfather of Khālid b. ʿAbd Allāh al-Qasrī, governor of Iraq in the late Umayyad age.

Maslama b. Muḥārib, an informant of al-Madāʾinī, was closely associated with the Umayyad regime, as is evident from his reports. E. L. Petersen has suggested that he may have been an Umayyad, specifically of the Sufyānid branch (*ʿAlī and Muʿāwiya in Early Arabic Tradition* (Copenhagen, 1964), 112, 128). It seems more likely that he was a client or confederate of the Umayyad house.

[253] Ṭabarī, I, 2985–6 (Muḥammad al-Kalbī) and Balādhurī, *Ansāb*, V, 71–2. The detailed account in the latter (71, l. 19 to 72, l. 8) is most likely taken from Abū Mikhnaf (see Balādhurī, *Ansāb*, V, 87). Jubayr b. Muṭʿim, who is named there as ʿUthmān's messenger to ʿAbd Allāh b. ʿĀmir, is known to have been in Medina during the siege and at the burial of ʿUthmān.

[254] Ibn Shabba, *Taʾrīkh al-Madīna*, 1288–9. The same anti-Muʿāwiya bias is reflected in an Egyptian report transmitted by the unreliable Ibn Lahīʿa according to which ʿAbd Allāh b. Saʿd b. Abī Sarḥ after his escape to ʿAsqalān refused to pledge allegiance to the Umayyad, affirming that he would not do homage to someone who desired the murder of ʿUthmān (*ibid.*, 1152). The report is also in other respects highly fictitious.

There is also a late fake report which tries to explain why Muʿāwiya, in spite of ʿUthmān's appeals, did not send troops. According to it, ʿUthmān sent al-Miswar b. Makhrama during the first ʻsiege' to Muʿāwiya, ordering him to dispatch an army speedily. Muʿāwiya immediately rode in person, together with Muʿāwiya b. Ḥudayj and Muslim b. ʿUqba, to Medina, where he arrived in the middle of the night. ʿUthmān severely reprimanded him for failing to send an army, but Muʿāwiya pointed out that had he done so and the rebels had heard about it they would have killed the caliph before its arrival. He invited ʿUthmān to ride with him to Syria but the caliph declined. During the second siege ʿUthmān again sent al-Miswar with the same order. This time Muʿāwiya blamed first ʿUthmān himself for his troubles and then al-Miswar and his friends for forsaking him. He confined al-Miswar in a room and released him only after the murder of ʿUthmān (Ibn ʿAsākir, *ʿUthmān*, 379–80). The report is ascribed to Muḥammmad b. Saʿd on the authority of al-Wāqidī with four good Waqidian *isnād*s going back to contemporaries. It was not al-Wāqidī's practice, however, to bundle his *isnād*s, and none of the early works quoting al-Wāqidī offer any parallel. The report is a forgery presumably posterior to Ibn Saʿd.

[255] Ṭabarī, I, 3023. According to the report, supporters of the Egyptian rebels arrived from Baṣra, Kūfa and Syria and encouraged the besiegers to action with information about troops coming from Iraq and from ʿAbd Allāh b. Saʿd in Egypt. As the narrator notes, ʿAbd Allāh b. Saʿd had previously fled to Syria. The newcomers would thus have spread false rumours that he had regained control of Egypt.

The caliph, however, trying to avert bloodshed, was reluctant at this stage to rely heavily on them and thus to turn the conflict into a battle between Umayyads and their opponents. Rather, he sought the moral support of the Islamic elite and the widows of the Prophet whose prestige, he hoped, would restrain the rebels from attack. For this reason he did everything to persuade 'Ā'isha to cancel her pilgrimage. During the early stages of the siege, al-Mughīra b. Shu'ba is said to have advised him to make a show of strength by ordering his clients and his kin to arm so as to intimidate the besiegers. 'Uthmān did so, but then ordered them to depart without fighting. As they went away, the Egyptian rebel leader Sūdān b. Ḥumrān followed them. Marwān turned around, and they exchanged blows with their swords without hurting each other. 'Uthmān immediately sent his servant Nātil to order Marwān to retreat with his companions into the palace.[256]

Qaṭan b. 'Abd Allāh b. Ḥuṣayn Dhi l-Ghuṣṣa, chief of the Banu l-Ḥārith b. Ka'b in Kūfa, is said to have made 'Uthmān an offer to come with his men to the defence of the caliph. If the report is reliable, he would presumably have come to Medina in connection with the pilgrimage. 'Uthmān sent him away, affirming that he did not wish to fight the rebels.[257] 'Uthmān b. Abi l-'Āṣ al-Thaqafī, former governor of al-Baḥrayn, is also reported to have offered to fight for 'Uthmān during the siege. Thaqīf had pre-Islamic ties with the Umayyad house. 'Uthmān declined his offer and permitted him, at his request, to leave for Baṣra.[258]

At the same time 'Uthmān surrounded himself with members of the Islamic elite. He delegated command over the defenders gathered in the palace to 'Abd Allāh b. al-Zubayr rather than to an Umayyad. Abū Ḥabība, visiting the besieged 'Uthmān, found him with al-Ḥasan b. 'Alī, Abū Hurayra, 'Abd Allāh b. 'Umar and 'Abd Allāh b. al-Zubayr, besides the Umayyads Sa'īd b. al-'Āṣ and Marwān. Abū Hurayra boosted the morale of the besieged by narrating a hadith. The Prophet had predicted: 'There shall be trials and calamities after us.' Abū Hurayra had asked him: 'Where will be the escape from them?' He answered: 'To the Amīn [the Trustworthy] and his party', and Abū Hurayra pointed at 'Uthmān.[259]

That 'Alī's son al-Ḥasan was among the defenders is too well attested to

[256] Balādhurī, *Ansāb*, V, 72–3. The poetry attributed there to al-Walīd b. 'Uqba is quoted widely and attributed also to al-Mughīra b. al-Akhnas (Ibn Bakr, *Tamhīd*, 215; Ibn 'Asākir, '*Uthmān*, 548 (Sayf b. 'Umar)), to Ḥassān b. Thābit (*Dīwān*, I, 511), to Ka'b b. Mālik (*Aghānī*, XV, 30; Ibn 'Asākir, '*Uthmān*, 547 (al-Sha'bī)), or to an anonymous man of the Anṣār (Ibn 'Asākir, '*Uthmān*, 547). Either of the last two attributions would seem to be the most reliable. Al-Walīd b. 'Uqba was hardly the man to praise his brother for his pacifist stand. [257] Balādhurī, *Ansāb*, V, 73. [258] *Ibid.*, 74.

[259] Ibn 'Asākir, '*Uthmān*, 374–5; Zubayrī, *Nasab*, 103.

be doubtful.[260] He is described, in contrast to his brother Muḥammad b. al-Ḥanafiyya, as fond of ʿUthmān and as later critical of his father for failing to defend him.[261] Al-Ḥusayn b. ʿAlī, according to the pro-ʿAlid Ibn Abzā, also came to offer his backing to ʿUthmān at the beginning of the siege. He was sent by ʿAlī, for whom ʿUthmān had asked. The caliph asked him if he thought he would be able to defend him against the rebels. When al-Ḥusayn denied this, ʿUthmān told him that he was absolved from his pledge of allegiance and that he should tell his father to come. Al-Ḥusayn reported to ʿAlī, but Ibn al-Ḥanafiyya stopped ʿAlī from going to the palace.[262] Among the defenders of the palace was also ʿAbd Allāh b. ʿĀmir b. Rabīʿa al-ʿAnazī, a confederate of ʿUmar's clan, ʿAdī,[263] probably as an associate of ʿAbd Allāh b. ʿUmar. Even Ṭalḥa's son Muḥammad is mentioned in some late accounts,[264] but these are untrustworthy.

The rebels on their part were, as ʿUthmān's letters also indicated, not eager to shed blood. It is true that their demands now amounted simply to abdication and the appointment of another ruler. The alternative of strict retaliation for all the beatings, deportations and imprisonment for which they blamed ʿUthmān was not a realistic one. They were not talking, it seems, about a possible compromise of removing the real source of the ill, Marwān, who held no formal office. Nor was the caliph, still protecting his cousin unconditionally, prepared to offer such compromise. He was equally adamant that he would not abdicate. Yet the last alternative proposed by the rebel leaders was merely a call for general renunciation of obedience. Their private talk about seeking the caliph's blood did not match their real intention, to force him out of office. Their number, moreover, for the time being, hardly exceeded the number of the defenders in the palace, given by Ibn Sīrīn, perhaps with some exaggeration, as 700.[265]

With no compromise in sight, time was running out quickly. The

[260] Caetani dismissed a relevant report of the later Basran Ibn Sīrīn as invented to demonstrate the innocence of ʿAlī 'who defended the caliph with a proper son of his'. He suggested that al-Ḥasan according to another report was not in Medina (*Annali*, VIII, 190–1). The al-Ḥasan mentioned in this other report (*ibid.*, 193) is al-Ḥasan al-Baṣrī.

[261] See the report of the Basran ʿUthmanid Qatāda, where al-Ḥasan is quoted as telling ʿAlī: 'You have killed a man who used to perform the ablution fully for every prayer.' ʿAlī is said to have answered: 'Your grief for ʿUthmān is lasting long' (Balādhurī, *Ansāb*, V, 81).

[262] *Ibid.*, 94. Abū Mikhnaf narrated that Marwān, seeing al-Ḥusayn, said to him: 'Leave us, your father incites the people against us, and you are here with us.' ʿUthmān then said: 'Leave, I do not want fighting and do not order it' (*ibid.*, 73).

[263] Ibn ʿAsākir, *ʿUthmān*, 402–3; Balādhurī, *Ansāb*, V, 73.

[264] See Balādhurī, *Ansāb*, V, 69–70 (Ismāʿīl b. Yaḥyā) where Ṭalḥa is said to have reluctantly sent him to ʿUthmān; Ṭabarī, I, 3013 (Sayf b. ʿUmar); Masʿūdī, *Murūj*, III, paras. 1603, 1605. Al-Masʿūdī's account is based on Ismāʿīl b. Yaḥyā's concoction.

[265] Balādhurī, *Ansāb*, V, 74.

behaviour of the frustrated rebels, perhaps incited by the arrival of more radical elements and rumours of loyalist armies closing in from the provinces, became nastier. They tried at times to cut the water supply to the palace and to hinder the free access of visitors. Even Umm Ḥabība, daughter of Abū Sufyān and one of the Mothers of the Faithful, had some difficulty in getting access to 'Uthmān when she came bringing a leather bag with water (*idāwa*).[266] The rebels shot arrows at 'Abd Allāh b. al-Zubayr as he read 'Uthmān's message which they thought would contain nothing new. Had they listened carefully they might have recognized a basis for genuine compromise. 'Uthmān was offering to govern henceforth only on the basis of the advice of the Mothers of the Faithful and the men of sound opinion among them. This would have meant the end of Marwān's pernicious influence.

On Thursday, 17 Dhu l-Ḥijja/16 June, the peace was broken. The act of aggression, opening the civil war, came from the palace.[267] Among the rebels on that day was Niyār b. 'Iyāḍ of the Banū Aslam, an aged Companion of Muḥammad, who called for 'Uthmān and, when the caliph looked down from his balcony, lectured him, demanding his abdication.[268] Abū Ḥafṣa al-Yamānī, an Arab freedman of Marwān,[269] dropped a rock on him, killing him instantly. In his own account he boasted: 'I, by God, ignited the fighting between the people.' The rebels sent to 'Uthmān demanding the surrender of the murderer. The caliph once more protected Marwān, asserting that he did not know the killer. The next day, Friday 18 Dhu l-Ḥijja/17 June, was the 'battle-day of the Palace (*yawm al-dār*)', and 'Uthmān was slain.

Marwān had his way; it was he who wanted the war. The safety of his old cousin, to whom he owed everything, did not seriously concern him. He could see 'our property', the Umayyad reign, slip away from him if 'Uthmān was to govern according to the advice of the Mothers of the Faithful and the 'people of sound opinion', 'Umar's Islamic meritocracy. He loathed and despised them, these Early Companions who stood in the way of his own ambitions. 'Uthmān's hope that he might hold on to the caliphate while keeping his hands clean of Muslim blood was nothing but pious delusion. Marwān understood well that domination throughout human history could be established and maintained only by

[266] Ṭabarī, I, 3010; Balādhurī, *Ansāb*, V, 77; Ibn Shabba, *Ta'rīkh al-Madīna*, 1312–13.

[267] This was properly recognized by Wellhausen (*Skizzen*, VI, 130, *Das arabische Reich*, 31), who failed to note, however, the vital fact that the murderer, Abū Ḥafṣa, was a client of Marwān. Caetani judged the relevant reports to be unsafe (*Annali*, VIII, 140).

[268] So the account of Ja'far al-Muḥammadī (Ṭabarī, I, 3004).

[269] According to Abū Ḥafṣa's own report, Marwān had bought him, his wife and offspring from a bedouin Arab and had manumitted them (*ibid.*, 3001; Ibn Shabba, *Ta'rīkh al-Madīna*, 1281).

terror, intimidation, violence, or the threat of it. Why should it be different in Islam?

While the murderer under the Umayyad reign would openly boast of his crime, his victim was nicknamed by ʿUthmanid tradition Niyār the Evil (Niyār al-sharr), in order to distinguish him from the other Niyār of Aslam, Niyār b. Mikraz, the loyalist who participated in the burial of ʿUthmān and was therefore named Niyār the Good (Niyār al-khayr). In order to substantiate the charge of evil, Niyār b. ʿIyāḍ was then accused of having been the first to cause ʿUthmān to bleed by striking him in the face with a blade.[270] For the moment, however, the rebels, outraged by the caliph's latest refusal to take responsibility for the offences of his servants, held the moral edge. During the night they assembled in strength, lighting fires around the palace. In the morning the attack began. Some came over the roof of the house of the Āl ʿAmr b. Ḥazm next to the palace. According to Abū Ḥafṣa, Kināna b. Bishr was the first to arrive with a torch in his hand. Naphtha was poured on the flames, and the wood ceiling as well as the outside doors were quickly set on fire in spite of some resistance by the defenders on the roof.

ʿUthmān gave orders to everyone obeying him not to fight but to look after their own houses. He assured them that the rebels wanted only him and would leave them alone once they had laid hands on him.[271] Most of the defenders, including ʿAbd Allāh b. al-Zubayr,[272] respected his wish and laid down their arms. Abū Hurayra later narrated that he threw away his sword and did not know who took it.[273] Marwān, Saʿīd b. al-ʿĀṣ and a handful of men disobeyed ʿUthmān's order. They pushed the intruders out of the one gate that was not burning and attacked the rebels outside the palace. The first to be killed was, according to Abū Mikhnaf's account, al-Mughīra b. al-

[270] Ibn Shabba, *Ta'rīkh al-Madīna*, 1308; Balādhurī, *Ansāb*, V, 83. The accusation against Niyār was transmitted by the pro-Umayyad ʿAwāna on the authority of al-Shaʿbī. The Banū Aslam, who had played such a vital part in the foundation of the caliphate of Quraysh, had evidently become divided over ʿUthmān's reign. Muḥammad b. al-Munkadir described Khuzāʿa and Aslam as hostile towards ʿUthmān (Ibn Shabba, *Ta'rīkh al-Madīna*, 1280–1). When Muʿāwiya later came to Medina on a pilgrimage and saw the houses of the quarter of Aslam leading to the market, he ordered: 'Darken their houses on them, may God darken their graves on them, for they are the killers of ʿUthmān.' Niyār b. Mikraz (the Good) said to him: 'Are you going to darken my house on me when I am one out of four who carried and buried ʿUthmān?' Muʿāwiya recognized him and gave order not to wall up the front of his house (Balādhurī, *Ansāb*, V, 86; Ibn ʿAsākir, *ʿUthmān*, 540). [271] Ṭabarī, I, 3001–3.

[272] In a line of poetry ascribed to al-Mughīra b. al-Akhnas, ʿAbd Allāh b. al-Zubayr is criticized for not fighting (Ibn Bakr, *Tamhīd*, 195).

[273] Balādhurī, *Ansāb*, V, 73; Ibn Shabba, *Ta'rīkh al-Madīna*, 1110.

Akhnas, slain by Rifā'a b. Rāfi' al-Anṣārī of the Banū Zurayq of Khazraj, a veteran of Badr.[274]

Marwān went out, followed by his client Abū Ḥafṣa, and shouted a challenge for anyone to duel with him. When he lifted the loose pendant of his helmet (*rafraf*) to fasten it in his belt, the rebel leader Ibn al-Nibā' ('Urwa b. Shiyaym), sent forward by 'Abd al-Raḥmān b. 'Udays to deal with him, struck him on the neck, felling him. As he turned around on the ground, 'Ubayd, Rifā'a b. Rāfi''s son, went up to him to finish him off. But Fāṭima bt Aws, Marwān's wet-nurse, threw herself on him and told 'Ubayd: 'If you want to kill this man, he is dead, but if you want to play with his flesh, that would be abominable.' He left off, and Fāṭima, with the help of Abū Ḥafṣa, carried the wounded Marwān to her house. 'Abd al-Malik b. Marwān was to reward her son Ibrāhīm b. 'Arabī al-Kinānī with the governorship of al-Yamāma.[275] Sa'īd b. al-'Āṣ also went out, and fought until he received a severe head wound.[276] According to Abū Mikhnaf's account, he was struck by 'Āmir b. Bukayr al-Kinānī, a veteran of Badr, and was rescued by 'Uthmān's wife Nā'ila.[277]

Three other Qurayshites were killed defending 'Uthmān: 'Abd Allāh b. Wahb b. Zam'a and al-Zubayr's nephew 'Abd Allāh b. 'Abd al-Raḥmān b. al-'Awwām, both of Asad, and 'Abd Allāh b. Abī Maysara b. 'Awf b. al-Sabbāq of 'Abd al-Dār. 'Abd Allāh b. 'Abd al-Raḥmān, al-Zubayr's nephew, proposed to the opponents that they settle the conflict on the basis of the Book of God, but was nevertheless attacked and killed by 'Abd al-Raḥmān b. 'Abd Allāh al-Jumaḥī, a Qurayshite. The other two were attacked and killed by a group of men near the palace.[278] Also killed

[274] Balādhurī, *Ansāb*, V, 78–9. On Rifā'a b. Rāfi' see Ibn Ḥajar, *Iṣāba*, II, 209. According to another report, Abū Mikhnaf added, al-Mughīra was killed by one of the common people (*'urḍ al-nās*). Probably unreliable is the report of Ja'far al-Muḥammadī that 'Abd Allāh b. Budayl al-Khuzā'ī killed al-Mughīra (Ṭabarī, I, 3005). The Banū Zurayq collectively are accused of having shared in the murder of 'Uthmān in a line of poetry by Marwān's brother 'Abd al-Raḥmān b. al-Ḥakam (Balādhurī, *Ansāb*, V, 105).

[275] Ṭabarī, I, 3003–4; Ibn Shabba, *Ta'rīkh al-Madīna*, 1281; Balādhurī, *Ansāb*, V, 79. For the correct family names of Fāṭima and Ibrāhīm see the notes to the Balādhurī text.

[276] Ibn Sa'd, *Ṭabaqāt*, V, 23. [277] Balādhurī, *Ansāb*, V, 79–80.

[278] *Ibid.*, 80; Ibn 'Asākir, '*Uthmān*, 532. In al-Balādhurī's report b. Abī Maysara is missing in the genealogy of the last-named. Al-Zubayrī (*Nasab*, 256) gives b. Abī Masarra, but most other sources have b. Abī Maysara. 'Abd al-Raḥmān b. 'Abd Allāh al-Jumaḥī does not seem to be otherwise known. Ibn 'Asākir ('*Uthmān*, 554) quotes a few lines of poetry by 'Abd Allāh b. Wahb b. Zam'a in which he vows that he will not swear allegiance to any other imam after 'Uthmān and, defending him, will not leave 'the two gates'. Ibn al-Munkadir enumerates the three Qurayshites killed as supporters of 'Uthmān. He names also 'Abd al-Raḥmān b. Ḥāṭib b. Abī Balta'a of Lakhm (Ibn Shabba, *Ta'rīkh al-Madīna*, 1280), whose father was a confederate of the family of al-Zubayr (on 'Abd al-Raḥmān b. Ḥāṭib see Ibn Ḥajar, *Tahdhīb*, VI, 158–9).

was 'Uthmān's client Nātil.[279] 'Abd Allāh b. al-Zubayr, al-Ḥasan b. 'Alī and 'Abd Allāh b. Ḥāṭib al-Jumaḥī are said to have been wounded. If the relevant reports are reliable these wounds were most likely not received in fighting.[280]

'Uthmān thus was deserted by his Qurayshite defenders, including his Umayyad kin, at his own wish. His personal servants and guards presumably still protected the gates. But at the time of the afternoon prayer,[281] when the fate he expected struck, he was alone with his wife Nā'ila in her room, reading the Qur'ān. Had his cousin Marwān, after wantonly bringing down the catastrophy on him, been serious about preventing the enemy from reaching the old man, as he claimed in two lines of poetry,[282] he would have been sitting with him, as 'Uthmān had asked him to do,[283] instead of engaging in vainglorious bragging outside the palace. 'Uthmān's brother al-Walīd b. 'Uqba was not even in Medina, but received the news of the caliph's death in the safety of nearby al-Mirāḍ, where he now sanctimoniously professed to the world that he wished he had perished before it arrived.[284] Nothing is known about the whereabouts of 'Uthmān's grown-up sons.

According to the family tradition of the Āl 'Amr b. Ḥazm, Muḥammad b. Abī Bakr scaled the roof of 'Uthmān's palace from that of their house together with Kināna b. Bishr, Sūdān b. Ḥumrān and 'Amr b. al-Ḥamiq and burst into Nā'ila's room. Muḥammad grabbed the caliph by his beard and said: 'May God disgrace you, Na'thal.'[285] 'Uthmān answered: 'I am not Na'thal, but the Servant of God ['Abd Allāh] and Commander of the Faithful.' Muḥammad: 'Mu'āwiya, so-and-so, and so-and-so are of no avail to you now.' 'Uthmān: 'Son of my brother, leave my beard. Your father would not have held what you are holding.' Muḥammad: 'If

[279] Ibn Shabba, *Ta'rīkh al-Madīna*, 1280, where the name of Nātil is omitted.

[280] Balādhurī, *Ansāb*, V, 79, 80, 95. In these reports the three men are vaguely described as fighting for 'Uthmān. Against this stands the unambiguous testimony of other reports that they laid down their arms, obeying the order of 'Uthmān. On 'Abd Allāh b. Ḥāṭib, a Qurayshite of Jumaḥ borne by a slave mother (*umm walad*), see Zubayrī, *Nasab*, 395.

[281] For the time see al-Balādhurī, *Ansāb*, V, 85–6, 98.

[282] Ṭabarī, I, 3022; Balādhurī, *Ansāb*, V, 81.

[283] Ṭabarī, I, 3002.

[284] Balādhurī, *Ansāb*, V, 102–3. Al-Walīd's brother Khālid b. 'Uqba was also absent at the time. According to Sayf b. 'Umar (?) he had the audacity to reproach in verse Azhar b. Sīḥān al-Muḥāribī, one of the defenders of the palace, for not fighting. Azhar answered him, appropriately pointing out that 'Khālid fled from him ['Uthmān] in his armour' (Ibn Bakr, *Tamhīd*, 214). According to Muṣ'ab al-Zubayrī, however, the exchange of this poetry was rather between Khālid b. 'Uqba and 'Abd al-Raḥmān b. Arṭāh b. Sīḥān al-Muḥāribī, confederate of the Banū Ḥarb b. Umayya, on the occasion of the murder of 'Uthmān's son Sa'īd by his Soghdian hostages (Zubayrī, *Nasab*, 111, 141; Balādhurī, *Ansāb*, V, 117–19). The latter version is no doubt more reliable.

[285] Na'thal, besotted old man, was the nickname of 'Uthmān.

my father had seen you do these acts he would have censured you for them. I want stronger medicine for you than holding your beard.' 'Uthmān: 'I seek God's support and help against you.' Muḥammad b. Abī Bakr now pierced his forehead with a blade. Kināna joined in with other blades, striking him behind the ear so that the points entered his throat. Then he killed him with his sword.[286] A variant report by Abū 'Awn, the client of al-Miswar, has it that Kināna hit 'Uthmān on the forehead with an iron rod, causing him to fall to the ground and that Sūdān b. Ḥumrān killed him. In any case, 'Amr b. al-Ḥamiq is then described as sitting on the caliph's chest and piercing his body nine times.[287]

The palace was now pillaged. Nā'ila protected 'Uthmān's body, but it was not possible to bury him before the following evening.[288] The rebels prevented his burial in the cemetery of Baqīʿ al-Gharqad, and he was interred nearby at Ḥashsh Kawkab, which was later incorporated into the cemetery. Present at his funeral were, according to Niyār al-Aslamī (the Good), Ḥakīm b. Ḥizām, Jubayr b. Muṭʿim, Abū Jahm b. Ḥudhayfa and himself. Jubayr led the prayer.[289] From other reports it is certain that his wives Nā'ila and Umm al-Banīn bt 'Uyayna were with them.[290] Others

[286] That Kināna was generally held to be 'Uthmān's killer is well attested in contemporary poetry, especially by al-Walīd b. 'Uqba, where he is called by his tribal affiliation al-Tujībī (Ṭabarī, I, 3064; Balādhurī, *Ansāb*, V, 98).

[287] Ṭabarī, I, 3021–2; Balādhurī, *Ansāb*, V, 82–3; Ibn 'Asākir, *'Uthmān*, 413–14. An eyewitness account is transmitted from Rayṭa, client of Usāma b. Zayd. She claimed to have been sent by her master to see 'Uthmān and to have been present at his murder. In her account Muḥammad b. Abī Bakr is described as pulling back from violence after seizing 'Uthmān's beard, and trying vainly to stop the others (Ibn 'Asākir, *'Uthmān*, 411–12). The authenticity of the report is doubtful. The well-known story about Nā'ila's finger being cut off while she defended 'Uthmān is probably legend. It appears only in the Kufan accounts. Al-Shaʿbī may have been the first to report it (*ibid.*, 412).

[288] This is suggested by most accounts. A report of 'Abd Allāh b. Farrūkh, a client of 'Ā'isha (Ibn Ḥajar, *Tahdhīb*, V, 356), seems to suggest that he was buried in the night after his death, since Ṭalḥa is described as still being in control. According to it, 'Abd Allāh b. Farrūkh was in the presence of Ṭalḥa in Medina at Ḥashsh Ṭalḥa when the latter asked him and Ṭalḥa's nephew 'Abd al-Raḥmān b. 'Uthmān to see what had become of 'Uthmān. They found his body in the palace covered with a white cloth. When they informed Ṭalḥa he instructed them to bury him. They dressed him in his clothes and took the body out of the palace. The Egyptian rebels tried to prevent the holding of funeral prayers for him, but Abu l-Jahm b. Ḥudhayfa rebuked them. 'Uthmān had asked 'Ā'isha for a burial place next to the Prophet's tomb, and she had conceded it to him. The Egyptians, however, would not allow his burial there, protesting that he had not followed the conduct of the Prophet and the first two caliphs buried with him. 'Uthmān was therefore buried at Ḥashsh Kawkab which he had bought as an extension to the cemetery of Baqīʿ al-Gharqad (Ibn Shabba, *Ta'rīkh al-Madīna*, 114–15, 1306–7).

[289] Balādhurī, *Ansāb*, V, 86; Ibn 'Asākir, *'Uthmān*, 540.

[290] See in particular the report of Muḥammad b. Yūsuf in Ibn Saʿd, *Ṭabaqāt*, III/1, 54–5; Ibn 'Asākir, *'Uthmān*, 541; Zubayrī, *Nasab*, 102.

are mentioned elsewhere, but their presence is doubtful or unlikely.[291] None of ʿUthmān's Umayyad kin were there. They had sought refuge with Umm Ḥabība bt Abī Sufyān, widow of Muḥammad, who put most of them in a granary (*kandūj*) and the rest in another place. Muʿāwiya later seems to have joked about their indecorous shelter.[292]

Sunnite tradition and modern western textbooks remember ʿUthmān chiefly as the pious old caliph who was killed while quietly reading the Qur'ān. The picture does not entirely misrepresent him. To the very end he remained faithful to his religious commitment not to spill Muslim blood. In the morning of the Day of the Palace he once more affirmed to Saʿd b. Abī Waqqāṣ his repentance of all his wrongdoings and ordered his defenders to lay down their weapons. Deserted by all but his wife, he faced the inevitable end at peace with himself. Yet he must have felt that he himself had to bear a large share of the blame for the disaster. The cancer in the body of the caliphate which he had nurtured and proved unable to excise because of his doting love for a corrupt and rapacious kin destroyed him. It was to continue to grow and to sweep away ʿUmar's caliphate of the Islamic meritocracy. ʿUthmān's successor, Muʿāwiya, turned it, as predicted by a well-known prophecy ascribed to Muḥammad, into traditional despotic kingship.

[291] The family tradition transmitted by Mālik b. Anas, whose grandfather Mālik b. Abī ʿĀmir claimed to have carried ʿUthmān's body on a door, is definitely faulty in several points and must be considered generally unreliable. Mālik speaks of twelve men taking part in the funeral, among them Ḥuwayṭib b. ʿAbd al-ʿUzzā, ʿAbd Allāh b. al-Zubayr and ʿUthmān's daughter ʿĀ'isha (Ibn ʿAsākir, *ʿUthmān*, 542–3).

[292] Balādhurī, *Ansāb*, V, 80.

4 ʿAlī: the counter-caliphate of Hāshim

Succession dispute and the battle of the Camel

The reign of ʿAlī bore the marks of a counter-caliphate. By the norms of the early caliphate it lacked legitimacy. ʿAlī was not chosen by a *shūrā* of the most eminent Early Companions which ʿUmar had stipulated as a condition for valid succession. Nor had he the backing of the majority of Quraysh who under Abū Bakr's constitution had been recognized as the ruling class solely entitled to decide on the caliphate.

Yet ʿAlī himself was firmly convinced of the legitimacy of his own claim based on his close kinship with the Prophet, his intimate association with, and knowledge of, Islam from the outset, and his merits in serving its cause. The criteria for legitimate rule laid down by Abū Bakr and ʿUmar were irrelevant from his perspective. He had told Abū Bakr that his delay in pledging allegiance to him as successor to Muḥammad was based on his belief in his own prior title. He had not changed his mind when he finally gave his pledge to Abū Bakr and then to ʿUmar and to ʿUthmān. He had done so for the sake of the unity of Islam when it was clear that the Muslims had turned away from him, the rightful successor of Muḥammad. Whenever the Muslim community, or a substantial part of it, would turn to him, it was not only his legitimate right, but his duty, to take upon himself its leadership.

The murder of ʿUthmān left the rebels and their Medinan allies in control of the capital with Ṭalḥa and ʿAlī as potential candidates for the succession. There seems to have been some support among the Egyptians for Ṭalḥa, who had acted as their adviser and had the treasury keys in his possession. The Kufans and Basrans, however, who had heeded ʿAlī's opposition to the use of violence, and most of the Anṣār evidently inclined to the Prophet's cousin. They soon gained the upper hand, and the Kufan leader al-Ashtar in particular seems to have played a major part in securing the election for ʿAlī.

The reports about the events and ʿAlī's movements leading up to his public recognition as successor are partly confused and contradictory.

The developments can thus be retraced only with a substantial margin of uncertainty. A report of ʿAlqama b. Waqqāṣ al-Laythī of Kināna,[1] a close adviser of Ṭalḥa,[2] implies that there was an initial abortive attempt to convene a *shūrā* of prominent Qurayshites to discuss the succession. ʿAlqama described a meeting in the house of Makhrama b. Nawfal, al-Miswar's father. Abū Jahm b. Ḥudhayfa demanded: 'Whoever we pledge allegiance to among you must not interfere with retaliation (*lā yaḥūlu bayna qiṣāṣ*).' ʿAmmār b. Yāsir objected: 'In regard to the blood of ʿUthmān, no.' Abū Jahm answered: 'Ibn Sumayya, do you ask for retaliation for some lashes you were given and deny retaliation for the blood of ʿUthmān?' The meeting then broke up.[3] None of the other participants are named. The presence of ʿAlqama b. Waqqāṣ may indicate that Ṭalḥa was there, but it is unlikely that ʿAlī was present. ʿAmmār probably wanted to block the election of Ṭalḥa, who now was evidently willing to allow retaliation for the death of ʿUthmān in order to gain the caliphate after he had been the most active in inciting the rebels to action.

ʿAlī was, together with his son Muḥammad (Ibn al-Ḥanafiyya), in the mosque when he received the news of ʿUthmān's murder. He soon left for home where he was, according to Muḥammad's report, pressed by Companions visiting him to accept the pledge of allegiance. At first he refused, and then insisted that any pledge should be made in public in the mosque.[4] The next morning, Saturday, ʿAlī went to the mosque. ʿAṭiyya b. Sufyān al-Thaqafī,[5] who went with him, reported that he found a group of people gathered who were united in support of Ṭalḥa. Abū Jahm b. Ḥudhayfa came up to ʿAlī and said to him: 'The people have agreed on Ṭalḥa while you were heedless.' ʿAlī answered: 'Does my cousin get killed and I get deprived of his reign?' He went to the treasury and opened it. When the people heard this, they left Ṭalḥa and turned to ʿAlī.[6]

The latter part of the report is probably unreliable. It is unlikely that

[1] Ibn Saʿd, *Ṭabaqāt*, V, 43; Ibn Ḥajar, *Tahdhīb*, VII, 280.

[2] See Ṭabarī, I, 3104 where Ṭalḥa is described as preferring his advice to that of his own son Muḥammad.

[3] Ibn ʿAsākir, *Taʾrīkh Madīnat Dimashq: Tarjamat al-imām ʿAlī b. Abī Ṭālib*, ed. Muḥammad Bāqir al-Maḥmūdī (Beirut, 1975), III, 96.

[4] Ṭabarī, I, 3066, 3069; Balādhurī, *Ansāb*, II, 209–10.

[5] Regarding him see Ibn Ḥajar, *Tahdhīb*, VII, 226–7.

[6] Balādhurī, *Ansāb*, II, 214–15. Chronologically flawed and less reliable is the parallel report of al-Miswar b. Makhrama (*ibid.*, 210). According to this account ʿAlī left the mosque after the arrival of the news of ʿUthmān's murder because the people seemed to be leaning towards Ṭalḥa. On his way home he met a man of Quraysh who mocked him: 'Look at a man whose cousin has been killed and who is being robbed of his reign.' ʿAlī turned back and ascended the pulpit. The people immediately left Ṭalḥa in order to join ʿAlī and then pledged allegiance to him.

Abū Jahm b. Ḥudhayfa clearly favoured Ṭalḥa and certainly did not wish ʿAlī to stand against him.

'Alī opened the treasury at this time. Rather, he went to the market followed by his supporters who again urged him to accept the pledge of allegiance. Then he visited the house of 'Amr b. Miḥṣan al-Anṣārī of the Banū 'Amr b. Madhbūl of al-Najjār where he received the first pledges. Kufan tradition maintained that al-Ashtar was the first one to give his.[7]

It is likely that Ṭalḥa and al-Zubayr also gave their first reluctant pledges of allegiance at this stage as al-Madā'inī narrated on the authority of the Basran Abu l-Malīḥ b. Usāma al-Hudhalī.[8] This is implied in a statement by al-Ḥasan al-Baṣrī that he remembered seeing al-Zubayr as he gave his pledge to 'Alī in a walled garden (*ḥashsh*) in Medina.[9] Ṭalḥa, too, is quoted as telling the Banū Rabī'a in Basra that he gave his pledge in an enclosed garden with the sword raised over his head.[10] 'Alī, according to the report of Zayd b. Aslam, then insisted again that the pledge should be given in public in the mosque.[11] There, in any case, the official ceremony took place on Saturday, 19 Dhu l-Ḥijja 35/18 June 656.

According to the main general account of the *bay'a* going back to the Kufan moderate 'Uthmanid al-Sha'bī and transmitted by Abū Mikhnaf, Ṭalḥa was the first of the prominent Companions to give his pledge. The homage of 'Alī's main rival was evidently crucial to lend his election credibility and to get it started. Ṭalḥa did not come voluntarily. Al-Ashtar, according to al-Sha'bī, dragged him along roughly while he demanded: 'Leave me until I see what the people do.'[12] Later, as noted, Ṭalḥa claimed that he had given his pledge with the sword over his head. Sa'd b. Abī Waqqāṣ commented on the claim stating that he did not know about the sword, but that Ṭalḥa certainly pledged allegiance against his

[7] Ṭabarī, I, 3075. Abū 'Amra (Bashīr) b. 'Amr b. Miḥṣan, a veteran of Badr, became a major supporter of 'Alī and was killed at Ṣiffīn (Ibn Ḥajar, *Tahdhīb*, XII, 186). Abū 'Amra's grandson 'Abd Allāh b. 'Abd al-Raḥmān b. Abī 'Amra was an important informant of Abū Mikhnaf (U. Sezgin, *Abū Miḥnaf: ein Beitrag zur Historiographie der umaiyadischen Zeit* (Leiden, 1971), 190). Some reports suggest that 'Alī's visit to the home of 'Amr b. Miḥṣan had taken place on Friday (see Ibn 'Asākir, *'Alī*, III, 97). This could also be implied by 'Umar b. Shabba's statement (Ṭabarī, I, 3068) that it was on Saturday, 18 Dhu l-Ḥijja, which would mean Friday night. Since 'Uthmān was killed on Friday afternoon, this would leave very little time for developments. The public pledge of allegiance took place, in any case, on Saturday. The report of the Medinan Ṣāliḥ b. Kaysān according to which 'Alī visited the mosque of the Banū 'Amr b. Madhbūl after the pledge of allegiance in the mosque of the Prophet and received the homage of the Anṣār there is probably unreliable (Balādhurī, *Ansāb*, II, 205).

[8] Ṭabarī, I, 3068. See also the report of Ṣuhbān *mawlā* al-Aslamiyyīn in Balādhurī, *Ansāb*, II, 215–16.

[9] Ṭabarī, I, 3068. The statement may not be reliable, however, since al-Ḥasan was only fourteen years of age at the time, and there is the question of how he could have returned to Medina so quickly, as he was said to have been abroad when he heard of 'Uthmān's death (Ibn Sa'd, *Ṭabaqāt*, III/1, 58; see above, p. 134 n. 260).

[10] Ibn Abī Shayba, *al-Muṣannaf*, ed. Sa'īd Muḥammad al-Laḥḥām (Beirut, 1409/1989), VIII, 709. [11] Mufīd, *Jamal*, 130. [12] Balādhurī, *Ansāb*, II, 206.

will (*kārihan*).[13] The mood of the public in the mosque was, no doubt, sufficiently intimidating for Ṭalḥa to give his pledge without being openly threatened. ʿAlī and his supporters could claim that he had done so voluntarily. ʿAlī now sent someone to take the keys of the treasury from Ṭalḥa. Al-Zubayr was brought by the leader of the Basran rebels, Ḥukaym b. Jabala al-ʿAbdī, and pledged allegiance. He later complained that he had been driven by 'one of the thieves (*liṣṣ min luṣūṣ*) of ʿAbd al-Qays' and had given his pledge under duress.[14] Al-Zubayr cannot have been pleased to do homage to ʿAlī. The two men had become deeply estranged since their common stand after the Prophet's death, and al-Zubayr could see himself with some justification as the Early Companion most entitled to claim the legacy of the murdered caliph. The Zubayrid family tradition transmitted a report by al-Zubayr's client Abū Ḥabība which asserted that al-Zubayr did not pledge allegiance at all. The story, however, has a legendary air and cannot invalidate the widespread reports about al-Zubayr's pledge.[15]

With Medina dominated by the rebels from the provinces and those Anṣār who were still smarting from their humiliation by Abū Bakr and ʿUmar, the Qurayshites present felt under severe pressure to accept their choice of ʿAlī. ʿAbd Allāh b. Thaʿlaba b. Ṣuʿayr al-ʿUdhrī, a confederate of the Banū Zuhra present in Medina, claimed that the chief of the *bayʿa* was al-Ashtar, who said: 'Whoever does not pledge allegiance, I will strike his neck', and that he was aided by Ḥukaym b. Jabala and his followers. What constraint, he commented, could be greater?[16] This was no doubt a distortion. There is less evidence for actual use of violence than in Abū Bakr's *bayʿa*. Yet there were evidently quite a few aside from Ṭalḥa and al-Zubayr who later claimed that they had pledged allegiance

[13] Ṭabarī, I, 2082.

[14] Balādhurī, *Ansāb*, II, 207. Out of al-Zubayr's arrogant Qurayshite gibe Sayf b. ʿUmar, or his source, spun a tale about the thief Ḥukaym b. Jabala (*wa-kāna . . . rajulan liṣṣan*) who regularly absented himself from the Muslim army in Fārs, attacking the *ahl al-dhimma* and stealing whatever he could carry off, and then acted as host to the Shiʿite agitator ʿAbd Allāh b. Saba' in Baṣra (Ṭabarī, I, 2922). In reality Ḥukaym was a highly respected chief of ʿAbd al-Qays in Baṣra. He was sent by ʿUthmān to Sind to investigate the country for its suitability for conquest and returned with a negative report. Later he complained about the conduct of ʿAbd Allāh b. ʿĀmir (Khalīfa, *Ta'rīkh*, 180; Ibn ʿAbd al-Barr, *Istīʿāb*, I, 121–2). There is no sound evidence that ʿUthmān ordered his imprisonment as narrated by Sayf.

[15] Ṭabarī, I, 3072–3. Abū Ḥabība reported that ʿAlī came to see al-Zubayr after the people had sworn allegiance. When informed of his arrival, al-Zubayr hid his sword under his bed in such a way that it could be seen by his visitor. ʿAlī entered and left without asking al-Zubayr to pledge allegiance. He then told the people that everything had been well between the two of them so that it was thought that al-Zubayr had pledged allegiance. If there was any visit of ʿAlī to al-Zubayr it was presumably before the public ceremony when ʿAlī would not have asked him for his pledge.

[16] Mufīd, *Jamal*, 111.

under duress. When Sa'īd b. al-Musayyab asked Sa'īd b. Zayd b. 'Amr b. Nufayl whether he gave his pledge to 'Alī, he answered: 'What could I have done? If I had not done so, al-Ashtar and his partisans would have killed me.'[17] Ḥakīm b. Ḥizām, another close associate of 'Uthmān, also swore allegiance but apparently soon left for Mekka where he gave moral support to those seeking revenge for 'Uthmān against 'Alī.

'Alī personally seems to have abstained from putting pressure upon anyone to do homage. When Sa'd b. Abī Waqqāṣ was brought and asked to pledge allegiance, he answered that he would not do so before the people had given their pledge, but assured 'Alī that he had nothing to fear from him (*lā 'alayka minnī ba's*). 'Alī gave orders to let him go.[18] Then 'Abd Allāh b. 'Umar was brought. He also said that he would pledge allegiance to 'Alī only after the people were united behind him. 'Alī asked him to provide a guarantor that he would not abscond; Ibn 'Umar refused. Now al-Ashtar said to 'Alī: 'This man is safe from your whip and sword. Let me deal with him.' 'Alī answered: 'Leave him, I will be his guarantor. By God, I have never known him other than ill-natured, as a child and as an adult.' Ibn 'Umar's stand was, in contrast to Sa'd's, hostile towards 'Alī. After the election he came to him and told him: "'Alī, fear God and do not jump upon the rule of the Community without a consultation (*mushāwara*).' Then he left for Mekka to join the opposition.[19]

Al-Sha'bī added in his account that 'Alī sent for Muḥammad b. Maslama to pledge allegiance, but the latter excused himself, stating that the Prophet had ordered him, if there was conflict among the people, to break his sword and stay at home. 'Alī let him go. He did the same with an otherwise unknown Wahb b. Ṣayfī al-Anṣārī, who gave a similar answer. 'Alī further invited Usāma b. Zayd to pledge allegiance, but Usāma, while assuring 'Alī that he was the dearest person to him, excused himself on grounds of the commitment he had made to the Prophet never to fight anyone confessing: 'There is no god but God.'[20]

The arguments ascribed by al-Sha'bī to these men can hardly have been made at the time of the initial pledge of allegiance before it was evident that 'Alī would face armed opposition. They must have been put

[17] *Ibid.*, 111–12.

[18] Ṭabarī, I, 3068. Al-Sha'bī mentioned the refusal of 'Abd Allāh b. 'Umar before that of Sa'd (Balādhurī, *Ansāb*, II, 207). His account is here evidently based on Sa'd's own report transmitted by his son Muḥammad and grandson Ismā'īl b. Muḥammad (Mufīd, *Jamal*, 131).

[19] Balādhurī, *Ansāb*, II, 208. Certainly unreliable is the report of Khālid b. Shumayr al-Sadūsī, a Basran transmitter from 'Abd Allāh b. 'Umar, according to whom 'Alī came to Ibn 'Umar the morning after 'Uthmān's murder and asked him to go to Syria as governor to replace Mu'āwiya; when Ibn 'Umar declined the offer, 'Alī threatened him; Ibn 'Umar therefore left for Mekka (*ibid.*, II, 208–9). The report reflects the general hostility of Ibn 'Umar and his followers to 'Alī.

[20] *Ibid.*, 207–8.

forward when 'Alī mobilized for the war against 'Ā'isha and the Mekkan rebels. According to another report transmitted by Abū Mikhnaf and others, 'Alī at that time questioned Sa'd b. Abī Waqqāṣ, Muḥammad b. Maslama, Usāma b. Zayd and 'Abd Allāh b. 'Umar about their attitude. He told them that he would not force them to join his campaign, but asked whether they stood by their pledge of allegiance. They all answered him that they did so, but did not wish to fight against Muslims. Usāma b. Zayd's answer on that occasion is quoted in the same terms as in al-Sha'bī's account of the *bay'a*.[21] It is thus not unlikely that at least Usāma and Ibn Maslama had initially pledged allegiance to 'Alī. Al-Wāqidī's pupil Ibn Sa'd indeed counted Sa'd b. Abī Waqqāṣ, Usama, Ibn Maslama and Zayd b. Thābit among those pledging allegiance.[22] That 'Abd Allāh b. 'Umar also gave his pledge, as the report implies, may be discounted.[23]

'Abd Allāh b. al-Ḥasan b. al-Ḥasan, 'Alī's great-grandson, enumerated several more prominent Anṣār, describing them as 'Uthmāniyya who did not pledge allegiance: the poets Ḥassān b. Thābit and Ka'b b. Mālik, 'Uthmān's treasurer Zayd b. Thābit, Maslama b. Mukhallad of Khazraj, later governor of Egypt under Mu'āwiya and Yazīd,[24] the close Companions Abū Sa'īd al-Khudrī[25] and al-Nu'mān b. Bashīr, both of Khazraj, Rāfi' b. Khadīj of the Banū Ḥāritha of Aws, Faḍāla b. 'Ubayd al-Awsī, probably *qāḍī* of Damascus at the time,[26] and Ka'b b. 'Ujra al-Balawī, confederate of the Anṣār.[27] The great majority of the Anṣār, however, eagerly pledged allegiance.[28]

The irregular election of 'Alī, supported by the rebels from the provinces and the Anṣār disfranchised by Abū Bakr, left the Community deeply divided into three factions. Besides the party supporting the

[21] Mufīd, *Jamal*, 95–6. [22] Ibn Sa'd, *Ṭabaqāt*, III/1, 20; *Annali*, IX, 50.

[23] The Shi'ite al-Mufīd maintained that all of these Companions, including Ibn 'Umar, initially pledged allegiance (*Jamal*, 94–6). The gist of the tradition quoted by al-Mufīd is also contained in the account of 'Alī's *bay'a* taken by 'Abd al-Jabbār, *al-Mughnī*, XX/2, ed. 'Abd al-Ḥalīm Maḥmūd and Sulaymān Dunyā (Cairo, n.d.), 65–8, from the *Kitāb al-Maqāmāt* of Abū Ja'far al-Iskāfī. That account clearly implied that Ibn 'Umar, Sa'd and Ibn Maslama (Usāma is not mentioned) did not initially pledge allegiance. 'Alī is, however, described as asking them whether they were 'departing from my *bay'a*.' They denied this, but affirmed that they would not fight Muslims. According to Ibn Abi l-Ḥadīd, the (later) Mu'tazila also affirmed in their books that the neutralist Companions at first all pledged allegiance to 'Alī and put forward their excuses only when he set out for the battle of the Camel (*Sharḥ*, IV, 9–10). The same view is expressed by the orthodox Sunnite traditionist Abū Bakr b. al-'Arabī (d. 543/1148) in his *al-'Awāṣim min al-qawāṣim fī taḥqīq mawqif al-ṣaḥāba ba'd wafāt al-nabī*, ed. Muḥibb al-Dīn al-Khaṭīb (Cairo, 1387/1968), 147.

[24] Ibn Ḥajar, *Iṣāba*, VI, 97–8. He was probably in Egypt at the time, not in Medina.

[25] Abū Sa'īd al-Khudrī, it should be noted, later supported 'Alī.

[26] *Ibid.*, 210. Mu'āwiya appointed him *qāḍī* of Damascus after Abu l-Dardā', who died around 32/652. It is thus unlikely that he was present in Medina.

[27] *Ibid.*, V, 304–5. [28] Ṭabarī, I, 3069–70.

caliphate of 'Alī, there were the Umayyads and their partisans who believed that the caliphate had through 'Uthmān become 'their property', and the party of the majority of Quraysh who hoped to restore the caliphate of Quraysh on the principles laid down by Abū Bakr and 'Umar. As each party was prepared to fight for its presumed right, Islam became engulfed in a brutal internal war outlasting 'Alī's caliphate. The evil of the *falta* which, 'Umar thought, had been averted by God now erupted with a vengeance.

Mekka became the natural centre of the Qurayshite opposition. Here 'Ā'isha raised the flag of revenge for 'Uthmān. According to the Medinans, she had left Mekka after her pilgrimage happy in the belief that Ṭalḥa had succeeded 'Uthmān. When she reached Sarif, six or twelve miles north of Mekka,[29] she met 'Ubayd b. Maslama al-Laythī, known as Ibn Umm Kilāb, a supporter of 'Alī, who informed her of the succession of her cousin-in-law. She immediately turned back, curtained herself in the Sanctuary, and declared: 'We have reproached 'Uthmān for some matters which we stated and pointed out to him. He recanted and asked his Lord for forgiveness. The Muslims accepted his repentance, as they had no other choice.' Then she accused 'Alī of jumping upon and murdering 'Uthmān, a single finger of whom was better than the whole of 'Alī.[30]

There was now an exodus of prominent Qurayshites from Medina to Mekka. Ṭalḥa and al-Zubayr, seeing that others had successfully resisted pledging allegiance to 'Alī, quickly broke their own oaths and left without leave. 'Abd Allāh b. al-'Abbās, who returned from Mekka to Medina and arrived five days after the murder, saw them on the way at al-Nawāṣif in the company of the Makhzumite Abū Sa'īd (b. 'Abd al-Raḥmān) b. al-Ḥārith b. Hishām[31] and a group of other Qurayshites.[32] The Umayyads must also have quickly come out of their shelter in the granary of Umm

[29] Yāqūt, *Buldān*, III, 77–8.

[30] Balādhurī, *Ansāb*, II, 217–18, V, 91. Abū Yūsuf al-Anṣārī, Abū Mikhnaf's source for the story, is Muḥammad b. Thābit al-Anṣārī al-Khazrajī, a major, otherwise unknown, informant of his (see Sezgin, *Abū Miḥnaf*, 212–13). Abū Yūsuf Muḥammad b. Thābit is the same as Muḥammad b. Yūsuf (b. Thābit). In the indices of al-Ṭabarī, Abū Yūsuf al-Anṣārī is misidentified as Ya'qūb b. Ibrāhīm al-Anṣārī al-Qāḍī.

[31] Abū Sa'īd is enumerated among the sons of 'Abd al-Raḥmān b. al-Ḥārith b. Hishām by al-Zubayrī (*Nasab*, 306). The father, 'Abd al-Raḥmān, participated in the battle of the Camel on 'Ā'isha's side. See below, n. 153.

[32] Ṭabarī, I, 3080. Al-Zuhrī's statements that Ṭalḥa and al-Zubayr left Medina after four months and that they asked 'Alī for the governorships of Kūfa and Baṣra but were disappointed (*ibid.*, 3068–9; Balādhurī, *Ansāb*, II, 218–19) are unreliable. The two men certainly participated in the planning of the Mekkan campaign against 'Alī from the beginning rather than joining at the last moment. This is confirmed by a report of the Mother of the Faithful Umm Salama that Ṭalḥa and al-Zubayr sent a messenger to her, while she was still in Mekka at the beginning of Muḥ. 36/July 656, urging her to participate together with 'Ā'isha in their campaign against 'Alī (Mufīd, *Jamal*, 232–3, quoting al-Wāqidī).

Ḥabība, and soon Marwān and many others of them were assembled in Mekka. Al-Walīd b. ʿUqba, however, made his way to Syria to join Muʿāwiya. The ʿUthmanid Anṣār, Ḥassān b. Thābit, Kaʿb b. Mālik and al-Nuʿmān b. Bashīr also preferred to go to Damascus.[33] Zayd b. Thābit and Saʿd b. Abī Waqqāṣ stayed in Medina, while Muḥammad b. Maslama went into voluntary exile in al-Rabadha. Whereas ʿĀʾisha remained in Mekka, Umm Salama, Muḥammad's Makhzumite widow who had performed the pilgrimage with her, after vainly warning her against joining the rebel campaign returned to Medina and gave ʿAlī her backing.[34]

When ʿAbd Allāh b. al-ʿAbbās arrived in Medina four days after ʿAlī's accession and went to see him, he found, according to his own account, the Thaqafite al-Mughīra b. Shuʿba,[35] renowned for his political cleverness, with ʿAlī. After al-Mughīra had left, he asked ʿAlī what he had said. ʿAlī told him that al-Mughīra had visited him before and at that time had advised him to confirm ʿAbd Allāh b. ʿĀmir, Muʿāwiya and other governors appointed by ʿUthmān in their offices and to entrust them with receiving the pledge of allegiance for him in their provinces so as to calm the people. ʿAlī had rejected that, maintaining that the likes of those men should not be appointed to any office. Now al-Mughīra had come back and told him that he had changed his opinion and thought that ʿAlī should depose these men who were no longer as powerful as before and should employ those whom he trusted. Ibn al-ʿAbbās commented that the first time al-Mughīra had given him sincere advice, whereas now he was deceiving him. 'You know that Muʿāwiya and his companions are people of this world. If you confirm them they will not care who is reigning, but if you depose them they will say: He has seized the rule without consultation (*shūrā*) and has killed our companion, and they will stir up opposition against you. The people of Syria and Iraq will then mutiny against you, while I am not sure that Ṭalḥa and al-Zubayr will not turn around to attack you.' ʿAlī admitted that confirming ʿUthmān's governors would without doubt be better in the short-term, worldly interest so as to restore

[33] The story about their discussion with ʿAlī and reception by Muʿāwiya in *Aghānī*, XV, 29 is poorly attested and legendary. Al-Nuʿmān b. Bashīr, in any case, was not appointed governor of Ḥimṣ by Muʿāwiya at that time, as asserted in the story. The two ʿUthmanid poets Ḥassān and Kaʿb returned to Medina before the battle of the Camel but maintained their hostile attitude to ʿAlī. Kaʿb's daughter Kabsha reported of her father that he was deeply grieved about the murder of ʿUthmān and was prevented from joining the revolt against ʿAlī only by the loss of his eyesight. He did not pledge allegiance to ʿAlī and kept away from him because of his loathing and disgust for him (Mufīd, *Jamal*, 378).

[34] Balādhurī, *Ansāb*, V, 91; Ṭabarī, I, 3101; Mufīd, *Jamal*, 232–3.

[35] According to al-Zuhrī, al-Mughīra b. Shuʿba was among those who did not pledge allegiance to ʿAlī (Ṭabarī, I, 3070). He seems to have left Medina soon after his second visit to ʿAlī, presumably expecting the failure of ʿAlī's caliphate.

order; he, 'Alī, was obliged, however, to act according to what was right and what he knew of these people; he would never appoint any of them; if they turned away, he would meet them with the sword.

Ibn al-'Abbās now urged him to leave for his estate in Yanbu' and lock his door. The Arabs would, he predicted, after much turbulence find no one to turn to but him; if he were to make a stand today with his present supporters, the people would certainly tomorrow saddle him with the guilt for the blood of 'Uthmān. 'Alī refused and suggested that Ibn al-'Abbās go to Syria as governor. Ibn al-'Abbās objected that this was not sound judgement. 'Mu'āwiya is a man of the Banū Umayya, the cousin of 'Uthmān, and his governor of Syria. I am not sure that he would not strike my neck in retaliation for 'Uthmān. The least he would do would be to imprison me so as to rule arbitrarily over me.' In reply to 'Alī's question as to why he would do so, Ibn al-'Abbās said: 'Because of the kinship between me and you. Everything imputed to you will be imputed to me. Rather, write to Mu'āwiya, appeal to his greed, and make promises to him.' 'Alī declared and swore: 'By God, this will never be.'[36]

The account seems on the whole reliable. There may be some suspicion that it is influenced by hindsight with respect to Ibn al-'Abbās' claim to have counselled 'Alī to leave Medina and withdraw to Yanbu' in order to escape the accusation of having connived in the murder of 'Uthmān. In a tradition presumably going back to Usāma b. Zayd, the latter is reported to have given this very advice to 'Alī before the murder, and Ibn al-'Abbās is described as having rebuked Usāma for suggesting that 'Alī withdraw after having been pushed aside by three men of Quraysh.[37] The account, in any case, brings out well the different character of the two cousins: Ibn al-'Abbās, a keen observer of the political scene, experienced since his close association with 'Umar, looking through the motivations and opportunism of the powerful and ambitious, with no unrealistic aspirations of his own; 'Alī, deeply convinced of his right and his religious mission, unwilling to compromise his principles for the sake of political expediency, ready to fight against overwhelming odds.[38] 'Alī's political naïveté, his lack of prudence and calculation, gave rise to the charge of 'foolishness (*du'āba*)' with which 'Umar is said to have characterized him. These qualities became patent at the beginning of his reign in acts such as

[36] *Ibid.*, 3083–5. The parallel account, *ibid.*, 3085–6, displays more literary dressing.

[37] Balādhurī, *Ansāb*, V, 77; the *isnād* is omitted. In the version quoted by Ibn Shabba (*Ta'rīk h al-Madīna*, 1211–12) on the authority of the Basran 'Awf al-A'rābī, the intervention of Ibn al-'Abbās is not mentioned. Usāma is then described as visiting 'Uthmān and offering him the support of his people of Kalb to convey him safely to Syria. 'Uthmān refused, however, to leave Medina.

[38] Djaït rightly characterizes 'Alī as essentially a fighter (*La Grande Discorde*, 397). Caetani's description of him as passive and indolent is entirely mistaken.

his opening the treasury and handing out the money to the common people, as he had promised and as he was to continue doing throughout his caliphate, and in his insistence on deposing all of ʿUthmān's governors except Abū Mūsā al-Ashʿarī, who had been chosen by the Kufan rebels.

In his first sermon, as related by the Basran Abū ʿUbayda Maʿmar b. al-Muthannā, ʿAlī bluntly rebuked the faithful, hinting at instances in which they had inclined against him since the Prophet's death. He said that God had laid down two cures for this community, the sword and the whip, and it was not for the imam to display clemency regarding them; he might, if he saw fit, ask God to forgive their past acts; two men had gone before, then a third one had stood up like a raven whose only care was his belly; it would have been better for him if his wings had been clipped and his head cut off; if after their failures matters were to revert for them (to their state during the Prophet's life), they would be fortunate, yet he feared that they were now in a time of religious slackness (*fatra*); all he and they could do was to strive together.

Abū ʿUbayda reported further that, according to ʿAlī's descendant Jaʿfar (al-Ṣādiq) b. Muḥammad, he had reminded the faithful in this sermon of the elevated rank of the virtuous of his kin who belonged to a family which partook of the knowledge of God and rendered judgment according to His judgment; if the faithful were to follow them, they would be rightly guided by their insight; but if they failed to do so, God would ruin them through their hands.[39]

The exact wording and date of this sermon are open to question. The tenor and contents, however, clearly reflect the style of ʿAlī's speeches and public statements throughout his reign. It is likely that he set the tone right from the beginning. Blunt rebukes and harsh charges of disloyalty, lack of sincere devotion, failure to respond to the summons to the evident just cause, and occasional warm praise for acts of loyalty, were characteristic of his pronouncements. They tended to alienate many of his lukewarm supporters, but also to arouse the enthusiastic backing and fervour of a minority of pious followers. He left them in no doubt that they could find true religious guidance only through him and the Family of the Prophet and reproached them for having turned away from them. While blaming the Community collectively, he refrained from criticizing the first two caliphs whose general conduct he at times

[39] Al-Jāḥiẓ, *al-Bayān wa l-tabyīn*, ed. ʿAbd al-Salām Muḥammad Hārūn (Cairo, 1367/1948), II, 50–2. According to al-Mufīd, the sermon was quoted, aside from Abū ʿUbayda, also by al-Madāʾinī in his books (*Jamal*, 125). A longer version of the sermon is quoted by Qāḍī al-Nuʿmān (*Sharḥ al-akhbār*, I, 369–73) who states that it was delivered two days after the oath of allegiance. According to this version ʿAlī declared all land concessions made by ʿUthmān null and void. This is not confirmed by other sources.

praised highly. In particular he seems to have admired the austere and stern rule of 'Umar and sought generally not to contravene the precedents set by him. He adopted 'Umar's official designation, Commander of the Faithful, but spurned the title caliph which in his eyes had evidently been depreciated by 'Uthmān's pretentious claim to be the Vicegerent of God rather than the deputy of the Prophet. Only under 'Uthmān had it become patent that the Community had gone astray. 'Alī severely censured 'Uthmān's deviation from the straight path of Islam. Generally he neither justified his violent death nor condemned his killers. 'Uthmān had provoked the uprising of the people by his unjust acts and was killed in an act of war. Only when Ṭalḥa and 'Ā'isha and their followers accused him directly of having been behind the murder did he turn the accusation back against them.

'Alī's desire for a radical break with 'Uthmān's nepotist regime was reflected in his determination to replace all of his governors. Only in Kūfa did he reappoint Abū Mūsā al-Ash'arī, apparently on al-Ashtar's recommendation, even though Abū Mūsā's attitude towards the new caliph appears to have been reserved.[40] When the news of 'Alī's accession first spread in Kūfa, the governor counselled the people to wait for further developments. Sa'd b. Abī Waqqāṣ' nephew Hāshim b. 'Utba, who at the time eagerly proclaimed his allegiance to 'Alī in verse, stated defiantly that he did so without fearing his Ash'arite amir.[41] Only when Yazīd b. 'Āṣim al-Muḥāribī[42] arrived with the order to receive the pledge of allegiance of the Kufans on behalf of 'Alī did Abū Mūsā, too, give his. 'Ammār b. Yāsir is said to have predicted that he would certainly break it.[43]

For the government of Baṣra 'Alī appointed 'Uthmān b. Ḥunayf al-Anṣārī of the Banū Aws, a prominent Companion whom 'Umar had entrusted with the land survey of the *sawād*. When he arrived in the town, 'Uthmān's governor 'Abd Allāh b. 'Āmir b. Kurayz had already departed for Mekka leaving 'Abd Allāh b. 'Āmir al-Ḥaḍramī, confederate of the

[40] Ṣāliḥ b. Kaysān's statement to this effect (Balādhurī, *Ansāb*, II, 230) seems reliable. Al-Ashtar had forced Abū Mūsā's appointment on 'Uthmān and was generally pro-Yemenite. See also the report of Ibn Abī Laylā (Ṭabarī, I, 3172) according to which 'Alī told Hāshim b. 'Utba that he had intended to depose Abū Mūsā but had been asked by al-Ashtar to confirm him.

[41] Hāshim b. 'Utba probably left soon afterwards for Medina to join 'Alī. He was with 'Alī when the latter set out to fight Ṭalḥa and al-Zubayr in Baṣra.

[42] Yazīd b. 'Āṣim later became a leader of the Kharijites and was struck down with three of his brothers at al-Nahrawān (Ṭabarī, I, 3361–2).

[43] Balādhurī, *Ansāb*, II, 213. Sayf b. 'Umar's story about 'Alī appointing 'Umar b. Shihāb governor of Kūfa, who then was prevented from entering the town (Ṭabarī, I, 3087–8), is fiction.

Banū ʿAbd Shams, as his deputy. ʿUthmān b. Ḥunayf arrested Ibn al-Ḥaḍramī without difficulty and took control of the town.[44]

For Egypt ʿAlī chose Qays b. Saʿd b. ʿUbāda, son of the unfortunate Khazrajī leader with whom ʿUmar had dealt so roughly at the Saqīfa and whom he had later driven out of his home town of Medina. It was an act of reparation towards the Anṣār and must have been seen by the Qurayshite opposition in Mekka as confirmation of their fear that ʿAlī intended to abolish their privileged status as the ruling class in Islam. ʿAlī ignored Muḥammad b. Abī Ḥudhayfa, to whom the Egyptian rebels looked as their leader and who was now in control of al-Fusṭāṭ. He evidently did not feel indebted to the Egyptian rebels, who had returned home, as he did to al-Ashtar and the Kufans, and wished to keep at a distance from them. He also ignored ʿAmr b. al-ʿĀṣ, whose restoration had been demanded by ʿĀʾisha on the grounds of his popularity among the army in Egypt. ʿAmr's leading role in the agitation against ʿUthmān, based on motives of self-interest rather than Islamic principles, could hardly have appealed to ʿAlī. In general ʿAmr represented the type of unscrupulous opportunist with whom ʿAlī did not want to burden his reign.

According to Sahl b. Saʿd al-Sāʿidī of Khazraj,[45] ʿAlī proposed to Qays b. Saʿd that he choose a military guard in Medina to accompany him, but Qays declined, stating that if he could enter Egypt only with a military escort he would rather never enter the country. He departed with only seven companions and reached al-Fusṭāṭ without trouble.[46] He had ʿAlī's letter informing the Egyptian Muslims of his appointment read in the mosque. As in his sermon in Medina, the caliph mentioned that the Prophet had first been succeeded by two righteous amirs who had acted in accordance with the Book and the Sunna. After them a ruler had taken charge who introduced innovations (*aḥdāth*) such that the community had found occasion to protest and reproach him. Now the faithful had turned to him, ʿAlī, and had pledged allegiance to him. There was no mention of ʿUthmān's violent death and of the part played by the Egyptian rebels. ʿAlī evidently did not wish to touch the divisive matter. The letter was written in Ṣafar 36/August

[44] Balādhurī, *Ansāb*, II, 222. ʿAbd Allāh b. ʿĀmir (b.) al-Ḥaḍramī was a maternal cousin of ʿAbd Allāh b. ʿĀmir b. Kurayz. His mother was Umm Ṭalḥa Amal bt Kurayz (Zubayrī, *Nasab*, 147).

[45] On Sahl b. Saʿd see Ibn Ḥajar, *Tahdhīb*, IV, 252. He died in 88/707 or 91/710 and was fifteen years old when Muḥammad died. He may well have accompanied Qays to Egypt, where he is known to have lived for some time and to have transmitted hadith (see Ibn ʿAbd al-Ḥakam, *Futūḥ Miṣr*, 275–6).

[46] Ṭabarī, I, 3235–6. Sayf's story about Qays' deceiving a Syrian horse troop at Ayla by posing as a refugee from Medina (*ibid.*, 3087) is probably fiction.

656, about two months after 'Alī's accession, by his secretary 'Ubayd Allāh b. Abī Rāfi', son of a client of Muḥammad.[47] Qays then praised 'Alī as the best man after Muḥammad and received the pledge of allegiance for him.

A group of partisans of 'Uthmān who had seceded to the village of Kharbitā near Alexandria after the revolt of Ibn Abī Ḥudhayfa held out against Qays b. Sa'd under their leader Yazīd b. al-Ḥārith al-Mudlijī of Kināna.[48] They informed Qays that they did not want to fight against him and would not interfere with his tax collectors, but they wished to wait and see how matters would develop. The governor agreed not to force them to pledge allegiance. Qays b. Sa'd's kinsman Maslama b. Mukhallad al-Sā'idī also rose, calling for retaliation for the blood of 'Uthmān. Qays assured him that he would not wish to kill him under any circumstances, and Maslama committed himself not to oppose him so long as he remained governor of Egypt. With these agreements Qays was able to collect the land tax throughout Egypt.[49]

Muḥammad b. Abī Ḥudhayfa and the Egyptian rebels against 'Uthmān are not mentioned in the account of Sahl b. Sa'd. According to the Egyptian al-Layth b. Sa'd, Ibn Abī Ḥudhayfa left Egypt for Medina in order to join 'Alī when Qays b. Sa'd was appointed governor. Mu'āwiya, however, was informed of his departure and set up watches. He was apprehended and brought to Mu'āwiya, who imprisoned him. Later he escaped from prison but was pursued and killed by a Yemenite.[50] Also according to al-Layth, he and 'Abd al-Raḥmān b. 'Udays were killed in Dhu l-Ḥijja 36/May–June 657.[51]

These are the most reasonable reports about the end of Ibn Abī Ḥudhayfa. He was accompanied by a group of rebels, among them certainly 'Abd al-Raḥmān b. 'Udays, Abū Shamir b. Abraha b. al-Ṣabbāḥ, and probably Abū 'Amr b. Budayl al-Khuzā'ī. They were kept by

[47] *Ibid.*, 3237. The date of the appointment proves that the anecdote narrated by Muḥammad b. Yūsuf al-Anṣārī on the authority of 'Abbās, the son of Sahl b. Sa'd al-Sā'idī (on him see Ibn Ḥajar, *Tahdhīb*, V, 118–19), about 'Abd Allāh b. Sa'd b. Abī Sarḥ's reaction to the appointment of Qays (Ṭabarī, I, 3233–5) is anachronistic fiction.

[48] Nothing else is known about Yazīd b. al-Ḥārith. In the Egyptian sources Mu'āwiya b. Ḥudayj, Busr b. Abī Arṭāh and Maslama b. Mukhallad appear as the leaders of the seceders.

[49] Ṭabarī, I, 3237–8. Maslama b. Mukhallad appears in the account as rising independently of the seceders at Kharbitā. He may have joined them later.

[50] Balādhurī, *Ansāb*, II, 408. Naṣr b. Muzāḥim identifies the killer of Muḥammad b. Abī Ḥudhayfa as Mālik b. Hubayra al-Kindī (al-Sakūnī) (Minqarī, *Waq'at Ṣiffīn*, 44). He was a chief of Kinda in Ḥimṣ under Mu'āwiya and a prominent military leader during his caliphate (see the references in Ṭabarī, indices s.v. Mālik b. Hubayra al-Sakūnī; Ibn Manẓūr, *Mukhtaṣar*, XXIV, 74–6).

[51] Kindī, *Wulāt*, 20. Al-Layth's mention here of Kināna b. Bishr among those killed at that time is erroneous.

Mu'āwiya at Jabal al-Jalīl near Ḥimṣ, escaped, and were killed.[52] Only Abū Shamir, proud scion of the Himyarite royal house of Dhū Aṣbaḥ, disdained breaking out of prison. Mu'āwiya released him, and he went along with the Syrians to Ṣiffīn, where he soon joined 'Alī's army and was killed in the battle.[53] Egyptian 'Uthmanid tradition narrated on the authority of Ibn 'Udays this hadith of the Prophet: 'Some people will revolt straying from the faith as the arrow strays from the game animal. God will kill them in Mount Lebanon and al-Jalīl.'[54] Ibn 'Udays was thus made the transmitter of his own condemnation by the Prophet.

[52] Yāqūt, *Buldān*, II, 110; Kindī, *Wulāt*, 18–20. In al-Kindī's otherwise highly unreliable report Ibn 'Udays, Kināna b. Bishr and Abū Shamir b. Abraha b. (Shuraḥbīl b. Abraha b.) al-Ṣabbāḥ 'and others' are named together with Ibn Abī Ḥudhayfa. Kināna b. Bishr was certainly not with them since he was killed later together with Muḥammad b. Abī Bakr. On Abū Shamir see Ibn Ḥajar, *Iṣāba*, VII, 99; al-Hamdānī, *al-Iklīl*, ed. Muḥammad b. 'Alī al-Akwa' al-Ḥiwālī (Baghdad, 1980), II, 153–4; Ibn Manẓūr, *Mukhtaṣar*, XXIX, 12. Yāqūt erroneously names Abū Shamir's brother Kurayb b. Abraha. Kurayb later made courtesy visits to Mu'āwiya and 'Abd al-Malik, and died in 75/694-5 or 78/697-8 (Ibn Manẓūr, *Mukhtaṣar*, XXI, 166–8).

The Banū Abraha were, according to Ibn 'Abd al-Ḥakam (*Futūḥ Miṣr*, 113) four brothers: Kurayb, Abū Rishdīn, Abū Shamir, and Ma'dī Karib, who settled in al-Gīza under 'Umar. A sister, Kurayba, was married to Dhul-Kalā' Samayfa' b. Nākūr, the chief of Ḥimyar in Ḥimṣ (Hamdānī, *Iklīl*, II, 158). There is no mention whether Abū Shamir personally participated in the expedition of the Egyptian rebels to Medina. It is, however, not unlikely. His house was next to that of Shiyaym al-Laythī, father of one of the four leaders of the rebels.

The presence of Abū 'Amr b. Budayl among those captured and killed is strongly suggested by the fact that his brother 'Abd Allāh was calling for revenge for his brother 'Uthmān (the *kunya* Abū 'Amr was frequently associated with the name 'Uthmān) in the battle of Ṣiffīn (Minqarī, *Waq'at Ṣiffīn*, 245). Ibn Ḥajar (*Iṣāba*, IV, 40) quotes a report according to which 'Abd Allāh b. Budayl went to see 'Ubayd Allāh b. 'Umar when the latter came to Kūfa and warned him not to shed his blood in this *fitna*. 'Ubayd Allāh returned the warning, and Ibn Budayl answered: 'I seek revenge for the blood of my brother who was unjustly killed.' 'Ubayd Allāh countered: 'And I seek revenge for the blood of the wronged caliph.' If this meeting indeed took place in Kūfa, it would mean that Abū 'Amr b. Budayl was killed earlier than the others. It may, however, have rather occurred on the occasion of 'Ubayd Allāh's visit to the camp of 'Alī before the battle of Ṣiffīn (Minqarī, *Waq'at Ṣiffīn*, 186). The mention of Abū 'Amr by al-Kindī (*Wulāt* , 27) as destroying the houses of the seceders on the order of Muḥammad b. Abī Bakr is, in any case, anachronistic.

[53] See below, p. 232. According to a report of the Egyptian Ḥarmala b. 'Imrān quoted by al-Ṭabarī (II, 210–11), it was Abraha b. al-Ṣabbāḥ who did not break out of Mu'āwiya's prison. Abraha b. al-Ṣabbāḥ b. Abraha seems to have been the cousin of Abū Shamir's father Abraha b. Shuraḥbīl b. Abraha and the senior member of the Himyarite royal family emigrating from the Yemen (Hamdānī, *Iklīl*, II, 158–60). Abraha b. Shuraḥbīl stayed in the Yemen in Wādī Ḍahr (*ibid.*, 154). The mother of their grandfather Abraha b. al-Ṣabbāḥ was Rayḥāna, daughter of the Abyssinian ruler of the Yemen Abraha (al-Ashram), and he, Abraha b. al-Ṣabbāḥ, ruled over Tihāma, the coastal land of the Yemen. His grandson Abraha b. al-Ṣabbāḥ is mentioned in connection with the conquest of al-Faramā in Egypt (Ṭabarī, I, 2586–7), but is otherwise not known to have settled in Egypt. It is thus unlikely, though not impossible, that he was imprisoned by Mu'āwiya. He was in his army at Ṣiffīn (see below, p. 235).

[54] Ibn 'Abd al-Ḥakam, *Futūḥ Miṣr*, 304; Ibn Manẓūr, *Mukhtaṣar*, XIV, 305–6.

In the Yemen 'Alī appointed the Hashimite 'Ubayd Allāh b. al-'Abbās governor of Ṣan'ā' and Sa'īd b. Sa'd b. 'Ubāda, the brother of Qays, governor of al-Janad.[55] 'Uthmān's governors, Ya'lā b. Umayya (Munya) al-Ḥanẓalī al-Tamīmī, confederate of the Banū Nawfal of Quraysh,[56] in Ṣan'ā', and the Makhzumite 'Abd Allāh b. Abī Rabī'a in al-Janad, had already left, some reports suggest, during the siege of 'Uthmān's palace, with the intention of aiding the caliph. 'Abd Allāh b. Abī Rabī'a fell from his mount and broke his thigh before reaching Mekka.[57] Both men arrived there with much money, and Ya'lā brought a large number of camels which he had gathered in the Yemen.[58] When Ibn Abī Rabī'a arrived in Mekka he found 'Ā'isha summoning the people to revolt in order to seek revenge for the blood of 'Uthmān. He ordered a seat to be placed for him in the mosque and proclaimed that he would equip whoever came forth to avenge the caliph's murder. Hearing of his call, Ya'lā b. Munya, who had arrived earlier for the pilgrimage, joined him in the offer.[59]

'Alī's attempt to gain control of Mekka failed. According to Ṣāliḥ b. Kaysān, he wrote to the Makhzumite Khālid b. al-'Āṣ, whom 'Uthmān during the siege had vainly tried to appoint governor as a popular candidate, naming him governor and asking him to receive the pledge of allegiance for him. The Mekkans refused, however, to swear allegiance to 'Alī; a young Qurayshite, 'Abd Allāh b. al-Walīd of 'Abd Shams, seized 'Alī's letter, chewed it up and threw it away. 'Abd Allāh b. al-Walīd would be among the Qurayshites killed while fighting for 'Ā'isha in the battle of the Camel.[60]

The town was now in open rebellion against Medina. 'Ā'isha having given the lead, the Mekkan Quraysh pinned the guilt for the murder of 'Uthmān on 'Alī and called for revenge in fiery war poetry. Ṣafwān b.

[55] Ibn Samura, *Ṭabaqāt fuqahā' al-Yaman*, ed. Fu'ād Sayyid (Cairo, 1957), 42–3. For further references see A. M. M. al-Mad'aj, *The Yemen in Early Islam 9–233/630–847: A Political History* (London, 1988), 150 n. 2.

[56] He was also known as Ya'lā b. Munya after his mother (Ibn Ḥajar, *Iṣāba*, VI, 353).

[57] Mufīd, *Jamal*, 231–2, quoting reports of al-Wāqidī. It is to be noted that 'Abd Allāh b. Abī Rabī'a is here described as governor of Ṣan'ā' and Ya'lā b. Munya as governor of al-Janad. Ibn Abī Rabī'a was riding on a mule outside Mekka when he met Ṣafwān b. Umayya al-Jumaḥī on a horse. The mule bolted, throwing Ibn Abī Rabī'a off. Reports that Ibn Abī Rabī'a died before reaching Mekka (Ibn Ḥajar, *Iṣāba*, IV, 64–5) seem to be mistaken.

[58] Ṭabarī, I, 3102.

[59] Mufīd, *Jamal*, 231–3. Ibn Abī Rabī'a was prevented by his broken thigh from joining the campaign to Baṣra. Ya'lā b. Munya participated, and fled when the battle was lost.

[60] Balādhurī, *Ansāb*, II, 210–11. Ṣāliḥ b. Kaysān's further statement that 'Alī b. 'Adī of 'Abd Shams was at the time of 'Uthmān's murder governor of Mekka is mistaken. 'Uthmān's last governor of Mekka was 'Abd Allāh b. 'Āmir al-Ḥaḍramī who, according to Sayf b. 'Umar, was still in control of the town (Ṭabarī, I, 3098). He was, however, at this time called to Baṣra by his cousin 'Abd Allāh b. 'Āmir b. Kurayz to govern that town in his absence.

Umayya b. Khalaf al-Jumaḥī, one of the grand old aristocrats of Quraysh and a leading enemy of Muḥammad who had fled at the time of the conquest of Mekka rather than accept Islam and eventually had been given permission by Muḥammad to stay in Mekka rather than move to Medina,[61] addressed ʿAlī:

> Surely your kinsmen, the ʿAbd al-Muṭṭalib, are the ones who killed ʿUthmān in incontrovertible truth,
> Out of wrongdoing and aggression, without a claim of blood revenge, and you are the most worthy of the people to be jumped upon, so jump.[62]

Accusing all of Hāshim, he evidently saw a chance of getting back at the old enemy allied with the Medinans who had humiliated Mekka in the time of Muḥammad.

Marwān b. al-Ḥakam, the man who had intentionally provoked the calamity in Medina, accused ʿAlī:

> If you, ʿAlī, have not struck the murdered man openly, you surely struck him in secret.

He went on to assert that ʿAmmār, who had killed the old man, and Muḥammad (b. Abī Bakr) had both confessed to the crime, which made retaliation incumbent upon the people.[63] ʿAlī had therefore cut off his own nose and left behind great evil; they had killed the man closest to goodness in Medina and furthest from evil; if he himself, so Marwān threatened, or Muʿāwiya were to live out the year, ʿAlī would get to taste the bitterness of the crime they had committed.[64]

Ḥakīm b. Ḥizām asked who could give him an excuse for ʿAli, who had turned his face away as ʿUthmān lay dead, struck by numerous swords in turn while but few supported him from among all the tribes.[65] Ḥakīm had, however, pledged allegiance to ʿAlī in Medina and decided not to go to war against him. His son ʿAbd Allāh joined the rebel campaign and was killed in the battle of the Camel. When ʿAlī found his body among the dead on the battlefield, he commented that he had deviated from his father's conduct. Ḥakīm, who failed to support ʿAlī but stayed at home after pledging allegiance, was not blameworthy.[66] Less convinced of

[61] Ibn Ḥajar, *Iṣāba*, III, 246–7. ʿAlī is reported to have been particularly hurt by the hostility of some of Jumaḥ and to have, after the battle of the Camel, expressed regret that they escaped just revenge (Balādhurī, *Ansāb*, II, 261). One of the few non-Hashimite Qurayshites backing ʿAlī, however, was Muḥammad b. Ḥāṭib al-Jumaḥī (Ibn Abī Shayba, *Muṣannaf*, VIII, 705; Balādhurī, *Ansāb*, II, 250), born in Abyssinia as the son of an Early Companion.

[62] Ibn Bakr, *Tamhīd*, 181. Ṣafwān b. Umayya b. Ṣafwān is to be corrected to Ṣafwān b. Umayya b. Khalaf; for *yuṭlab* read *ṭulib*.

[63] ʿAmmār is not known to have participated in the killing of ʿUthmān or in the fighting. His ʿconfession' may refer to his rejection of any claim of retaliation for ʿUthmān.

[64] *Ibid.*, 180–1. [65] *Ibid.*, 179. [66] Mufīd, *Jamal*, 393.

'Alī's complicity than the others was Sa'īd b. al-'Āṣ who spoke in his poetry only of three gangs (*rahṭ*), evidently the Egyptians, Kufans and Basrans, who would get to drink the cup of colocynth for killing an imam in Medina in the state of ritual consecration (*muḥrim*).[67]

To place the full responsibility for the murder of 'Uthmān squarely on 'Alī, although he, in the words of Marwān, had 'not struck him openly', served the political ends of the Mekkan rebels best. For the real aim was not to avenge the death of the wronged caliph but to remove his successor from office and to exclude him from the *shūrā* to be convened for the choice of the next caliph. Moreover, if 'Alī was the chief culprit, anyone backing him could, and should, be fought and punished as an accomplice in the offence which Caetani characteristically defined as 'the terrible crime of regicide'.

In the war council which was, according to al-Zuhrī, held in 'Ā'isha's home, it was first suggested that they attack 'Alī in Medina. The proposal was quickly abandoned as it was realized that the Medinans were militarily more than their match. The idea of joining Mu'āwiya in Syria was also discarded, mostly, no doubt, because Mu'āwiya might have been able to impose his own will upon the projected *shūrā*. The decision to move to Baṣra and to mobilize Basran support for the claim of revenge was influenced by the argument of 'Abd Allāh b. 'Āmir that he could count on strong support there and by the material means he was willing to provide.[68] Ya'lā b. Munya contributed from the funds he had carried off from the Yemen. He is said to have given 400,000 dirhams and provided riding animals for seventy men of Quraysh. He paid eighty dinars for 'Ā'isha's famous camel after which the battle was to be called.[69]

Ṭalḥa and al-Zubayr now appealed to 'Ā'isha to join the campaign. When she asked them whether they were ordering her to fight, they said: 'No, but you will inform the people that 'Uthmān has been wrongfully killed and summon them to restore a *shūrā* among the Muslims so that they will be in the same state as 'Umar left them, and you will conciliate between them.'[70] 'Ā'isha's presence was needed both because of her immense prestige as Mother of the Faithful and as a mediator between the two men who were rivals for the caliphate. 'Ā'isha had clearly favoured Ṭalḥa before 'Uthmān's death, but now she was presumably prepared to

67 Ibn Bakr, *Tamhīd*, 180.

68 Balādhurī, *Ansāb*, II, 219, 221–2; Ṭabarī, I, 3102.

69 Ṭabarī, I, 3102. According to Ṣāliḥ b. Kaysān, Ya'lā provided 400 camels for the campaign (Balādhurī, *Ansāb*, II, 222). The lengthy story attributed to a man of the Banū 'Urayna, who narrated how he sold the camel to a follower of 'Ā'isha and accompanied first 'Ā'isha to al-Ḥaw'ab and then 'Alī to Dhū Qār (Ṭabarī, I, 3108–11), is entirely fictitious.

70 Balādhurī, *Ansāb*, II, 223. Al-Ashtar held that it was 'Abd Allāh b. al-Zubayr who forced (*akraha*) 'Ā'isha to go along to Baṣra (Ṭabarī, I, 3200).

back al-Zubayr if Ṭalḥa, because of his involvement with the murderers, were to be excluded.

Probably late in Rabīʿ II 36/October 656 the Mekkan rebels set out, between six hundred[71] and nine hundred men according to differing reports. On the way to Baṣra they were joined by others, increasing their number to three thousand. At Bi'r Maymūn, Marwān, who was chosen to make the call to prayer, approached al-Zubayr and Ṭalḥa and asked whom he should greet as amir. 'Abd Allāh b. al-Zubayr and Muḥammad b. Ṭalḥa each named his own father. 'Ā'isha sent to Marwān: 'Are you trying to split our cause? Let my sister's son lead the prayer.' 'Abd Allāh b. al-Zubayr led the prayers until their arrival in Baṣra.[72]

While they were staying at Dhāt 'Irq, serious discord occurred among the Umayyads present. According to 'Utba b. al-Mughīra b. al-Akhnas,[73] Saʿīd b. al-'Āṣ went to see Marwān and his companions and questioned them as to where they were going. This had presumably been kept secret in order to keep 'Alī in the dark about their intentions. The ones subject to their revenge, Saʿīd said, were right here on the camels' backs. They ought to kill them and return home. Marwān and his companions suggested that they were going in the hope of killing all the murderers of 'Uthmān. Saʿīd now questioned Ṭalḥa and al-Zubayr as to whom they intended to give the rule if they were victorious. When they answered: 'To one of us, whoever will be chosen by the people', he objected: 'Rather give it to the sons of 'Uthmān since you are going out to seek revenge for his blood.' But they answered: 'Shall we pass over the chiefs of the Emigrants and hand it to their sons?' Saʿīd declared that he would not

[71] This number is given by 'Abd Allāh b. al-'Abbās (Ṭabarī, I, 3105), who mentions among them 'Abd al-Raḥmān, son of Abū Bakr (read thus for Abū Bakra) and 'Abd Allāh, son of Ṣafwān b. Umayya al-Jumaḥī. Ṣafwān himself was evidently too old to join, and died shortly afterwards. His son 'Abd Allāh later became a staunch supporter of 'Abd Allāh b. al-Zubayr. Ibn Abi l-Ḥadīd enumerates of the Banū Jumaḥ participating in the battle of the Camel and surviving, aside from 'Abd Allāh b. Ṣafwān: his nephew Yaḥyā b. Ḥakīm b. Ṣafwān, 'Āmir b. Mas'ūd b. Umayya b. Khalaf and Ayyūb b. Ḥabīb b. 'Alqama b. Rabī'a (*Sharḥ*, XI, 125). 'Ā'isha's brother 'Abd al-Raḥmān evidently went along for her sake, but did not play a prominent part. 'Abd Allāh b. 'Umar did not participate. According to Abū Mikhnaf (*ibid.*, VI, 225) and Sayf b. 'Umar (Ṭabarī, I, 3101) he also persuaded his sister Ḥafṣa not to join 'Ā'isha as she had at first intended. Although politically opposed to 'Alī, Ibn 'Umar consistently defended him against accusations that he was behind the murder of 'Uthmān (see e.g. Balādhurī, *Ansāb*, II, 99).

[72] Ṭabarī, I, 3105–6, according to Ibn al-'Abbās. According to Ṣāliḥ b. Kaysān and Abū Mikhnaf, 'Ā'isha rather decided that al-Zubayr as the older man should lead the prayer (Balādhurī, *Ansāb*, II, 225).

[73] 'Utba and his brother 'Abd Allāh were present no doubt in order to avenge their father. 'Abd Allāh was killed in the battle of the Camel (Mufīd, *Jamal*, 393–4). Also killed was their nephew 'Abd Allāh b. Abī 'Uthmān (so the name in Mufīd, *Irshād*, 122) b. al-Akhnas b. Sharīq. 'Alī is said to have commented on his death that he had tried to save him as he saw him running away, but his order not to harm him was not heard (*ibid.*; Mufīd, *Jamal*, 394).

strive to take the reign away from the Banū ʿAbd Manāf and turned back.[74] He had, as noted, not joined the chorus condemning ʿAlī and evidently saw no good in depriving him of the caliphate in favour of either Ṭalḥa or al-Zubayr. Together with Saʿīd b. al-ʿĀṣ there left ʿAbd Allāh b. Khālid b. Asīd; al-Mughīra b. Shuʿba, approving his view, invited the members of Thaqīf present to turn back with him. The other Umayyads, among them ʿUthmān's sons Abān and al-Walīd,[75] continued on together with Marwān, who was evidently concealing sinister intentions.[76]

If ʿUtba b. al-Mughīra's report is reliable, there was after this setback a disagreement on where to turn and whose support they should seek. Al-Zubayr consulted his son ʿAbd Allāh who favoured going to Syria, while Ṭalḥa consulted his intimate ʿAlqama b. Waqqāṣ al-Laythī who preferred Baṣra. They agreed, however, on Baṣra.[77]

That al-Zubayr and his son would have liked to make common cause with Muʿāwiya is not unlikely. Ṭalḥa and ʿĀ'isha were, no doubt, opposed to any such thought. Muʿāwiya in fact seems to have made overtures to al-Zubayr. According to Abū Mikhnaf's father, Yaḥyā b. Saʿīd b. Mikhnaf, he wrote to al-Zubayr, probably when the Mekkan rebels were already in Baṣra, inviting him to join him in Syria and promising him recognition as caliph by himself and his supporters. Al-Zubayr tried to keep the invitation secret, but Ṭalḥa and ʿĀ'isha learned about it and were seriously dismayed. ʿĀ'isha talked to ʿAbd Allāh b. al-Zubayr, who then asked his father if he intended to go to Muʿāwiya. Al-Zubayr at first confirmed that he wanted to do so since Ṭalḥa was opposed to him. Then he changed his mind; but, having sworn an oath that he would defect, he liberated a slave as atonement for breaking it and summoned the army to battle.[78]

When the rebel army approached Baṣra, ʿAlī's governor ʿUthmān b. Ḥunayf sent Abū Nujayd ʿImrān b. Ḥuṣayn al-Khuzāʿī[79] and Abu l-Aswad al-Du'alī as envoys to enquire about their intentions. They met

[74] Ṭabarī, I, 3103.

[75] ʿAmr, ʿUthmān's eldest son, is not mentioned. He does not seem to have participated in the battle of the Camel. Saʿīd b. ʿUthmān, however, is known to have also been present (Mufīd, *Jamal*, 382).

[76] In the parallel report of Ibn Saʿd (*Ṭabaqāt* V, 23–4) Saʿīd b. al-ʿĀṣ is described as addressing the assembled men in public and then returning to Mekka, where he remained during the battles of the Camel and Ṣiffīn. ʿAbd Allāh b. Khālid's cousin ʿAbd al-Raḥmān b. ʿAttāb b. Asīd was among those who proceeded to Baṣra.

[77] Ṭabarī, I, 3104.

[78] Balādhurī, *Ansāb*, II, 257–8. Al-Zubayr is said to have been greatly upset when his son, backed by Ṭalḥa, opposed his proposal to distribute the money in the treasury of Baṣra to the Basrans in order to gain their support and ʿĀ'isha took their side reproaching him. He then threatened to join Muʿāwiya (Mufīd, *Jamal*, 287).

[79] A Companion joining Islam early or in the year of Khaybar, ʿImrān b. Ḥuṣayn had carried the banner of Khuzāʿa at the conquest of Mekka. ʿUmar sent him to Baṣra to teach the people Islam (Ibn Ḥajar, *Iṣāba*, V, 26).

'Ā'isha and her companions at Ḥafar Abī Mūsā, a watering station on the road from Mekka to Baṣra,[80] and were told that they had come to claim revenge for the blood of 'Uthmān and to see that an electoral council was set up to decide on the succession.[81] Abu l-Aswad, known for his devotion to 'Alī, reported that he asked 'Ā'isha whether she had come on an instruction left by the Prophet or on her own opinion. She answered that she had made up her mind when 'Uthmān was killed. 'We were angry at him for his beatings with the whip, his setting aside rain land enclosures (*mawqi' al-saḥāba al-muḥmāt*), and appointing Sa'īd and al-Walīd governors. But you assaulted him and desecrated three sacred rights, the sanctity of the town [Medina], the sanctity of the caliphate, and the sanctity of the holy month, after we had washed him as a vessel is washed and he had come clean.[82] Thus you perpetrated this offence on him wrongfully. Should we get angry on your behalf at the whip of 'Uthmān and not get angry on behalf of 'Uthmān at your sword?' Abu l-Aswad rejoined: 'Why should you care about our sword and the whip of 'Uthmān when you have been confined for protection (*ḥabīs*) by the Messenger of God? He ordered you to stay in your house, and now you come knocking the people against each other.' She said: 'Is there anyone then who would fight me or say anything different from this?' Abu l-Aswad and 'Imrān answered: 'Yes.' 'Ā'isha: 'And who would do that, perhaps the bastard of the Banū 'Āmir (*zanīm Banī 'Āmir*)?' She meant 'Ammār,[83] who had gone on record opposing retaliation for 'Uthmān. Evidently worried that she had perhaps gone too far, she asked: 'Will you inform on me, 'Imrān?' 'Imrān reassured her: 'No, I would not inform on you in either good or bad.' Abu l-Aswad challenged her: 'But I will inform about you, so let us hear whatever you wish.' She hit back with the curse: 'O God, kill Mudhammam [her brother Muḥammad] in retaliation for 'Uthmān, hit al-Ashtar with one of Your arrows which do

[80] Yāqūt, *Buldān*, II, 294.

[81] Balādhurī, *Ansāb*, II, 225. According to the account of Abū Mikhnaf (quoting al-Kalbī), Ṭalḥa and al-Zubayr wrote to 'Uthmān b. Ḥunayf from Ḥafar Abī Mūsā demanding that he relinquish the governor's palace to them. Ibn Ḥunayf consulted al-Aḥnaf b. Qays and Ḥukaym b. Jabala, who both advised him to call the Basrans to arms and to move against the rebels before they reached the town. The governor, however, wanted to avoid war and decided to send Abu l-Aswad and 'Imrān b. Ḥuṣayn to ascertain their motives. That Ibn Ḥunayf at this time received a letter from 'Alī warning him of the rebels, as the account claims, is unlikely (Ibn Abi l-Ḥadīd, *Sharḥ*, IX, 311–13).

[82] The three charges against 'Uthmān and the three offences of his opponents mentioned here seem to have been 'Ā'isha's standard arguments. Mūsā b. Ṭalḥa, according to al-Wāqidī, reported that he witnessed her making the same argument 'in most eloquent language' just before the battle of the Camel when asked by the people about 'Uthmān (Mufīd, *Jamal*, 309–10; Balādhurī, *Ansāb*, II, 239–40).

[83] 'Ammār was a grandson of 'Āmir b. Mālik of the Banū 'Āmir al-Akbar b. Yām b. 'Ans and client of the Banū Abī Rabī'a of Makhzūm.

not miss, and confine 'Ammār in his pit for the sake of 'Uthmān.'[84]

'Ā'isha's curse of al-Ashtar revealed most strikingly the fraudulence of her call to revenge for 'Uthmān. For al-Ashtar, as noted, had heeded her and 'Alī's warning against violence and was on public record for having been opposed to the murder.[85] He was now anathema to 'Ā'isha because he had vigorously promoted 'Alī's election and had dragged her favourite against his will to swear allegiance to him. 'Ā'isha's fraudulent claim was next used to justify a flagrant aggression shattering the internal peace of Baṣra.

On returning to the town Abu l-Aswad advised 'Uthmān b. Ḥunayf to resist the rebel army, and the governor agreed and called on the people to arm. 'Imrān b. Ḥuṣayn was evidently in favour of accommodating the Mother of the Faithful and stayed neutral in the battle of the Camel.[86] As the rebel army arrived at the Mirbad, the market place outside Baṣra, and stopped next to the quarter of the Banū Sulaym, the governor and the Basrans moved out to face them. Ṭalḥa first addressed them, repeating the case made by 'Ā'isha that 'Uthmān had committed some reprehensible acts, had been asked to recant, and had done so. 'Then a man assaulted him who has robbed this Community of its self-determination without any agreement or consultation and killed him.' Some men who were neither pious nor God-fearing had aided him. 'Therefore we summon you to seek revenge for his blood, for he is the wronged caliph.' Al-Zubayr spoke in a similar vein, and then 'Ā'isha joined in with a forceful voice, stressing the need for a *shūrā*.

The Basrans were left divided by this rhetoric, some saying that they were speaking the truth, others calling them liars. They began hitting each other with their sandals and then separated, one group joining 'Ā'isha. Ḥukaym b. Jabala, in charge of Ibn Ḥunayf's cavalry, gave the call to fight Quraysh, who would perish by their indulgence in comfort and frivolity. They were preparing to fight, but the night separated them.

[84] Jāḥiẓ, *Bayān*, II, 295–6. Mudhammam, blameworhy, was a pun on the name Muḥammad, praiseworthy. Al-Sha'bī gave a toned-down version of Abu l-Aswad's report, suppressing 'Ā'isha's curses. According to him she asked Abu l-Aswad to tell 'Uthmān b. Ḥunayf, whom she called the freedman (*ṭalīq*) of Ibn Abī 'Āmir, that she had heard he wanted to fight her (Mufīd, *Jamal*, 273–4). Why 'Uthmān b. Ḥunayf would be called *ṭalīq* of Ibn Abī 'Āmir is not evident.

[85] See Ṭabarī, I, 3200, where 'Alqama is quoted as telling al-Ashtar: 'You disapproved of the killing of 'Uthmān, what then made you go out to Baṣra [fighting for 'Alī]?' Similarly Ibn Shabba, *Ta'rīkh al-Madīna*, 1313 and al-Nu'mān, *Sharḥ al-akhbār*, I, 397.

[86] 'Imrān visited 'Ā'isha in Baṣra and criticized her for having left her home against the order of Qur'ān XXXIII 33. 'Ā'isha apologized, suggesting that what had happened could not be undone, and asked him either to assist her or to hold his tongue. He affirmed that he would abstain from backing either her or 'Alī. She answered that she was satisfied with that from him (Mufīd, *Jamal*, 310–11). 'Imrān was, probably later, appointed *qāḍī* of Baṣra under 'Abd Allāh b. 'Āmir or Ziyād b. Abīh (Ibn Ḥajar, *Iṣāba*, V, 26–7).

The intruders used the opportunity to move to a better location at al-Zābūqa, near the store-house for provisions (*dār al-rizq*).

Next morning the governor moved to attack them, and there was fierce, but inconclusive, fighting in which many were killed.[87] Then a truce was agreed until ʿAlī should arrive. ʿUthmān b. Ḥunayf was to retain the governor's palace, the treasury and control of the mosque, while the intruders were allowed to stay wherever they wished in the town and were to have free access to the markets and watering places.[88] ʿĀʾisha, Ṭalḥa and al-Zubayr now decided to stay among the Banū Ṭāḥiya of Azd.[89]

The agreement to wait for ʿAlī's arrival was clearly unfavourable to the rebels, and Ṭalḥa persuaded al-Zubayr to break it and take Ibn Ḥunayf by surprise. On a windy and dark night they attacked and seized him as he was leading the evening prayer in the mosque.[90] According to the Khazrajite Sahl b. Saʿd, they then sent Abān b. ʿUthmān to ʿĀʾisha to consult her on what to do. She first advised them to kill Ibn Ḥunayf, but a woman interceded, reminding her of Ibn Ḥunayf's companionship with the Prophet. She recalled Abān and told him: 'Imprison him, do not kill him.' Abān answered that had he known why she had recalled him, he would not have come back. Mujāshiʿ b. Masʿūd, a Basran of the Banū Sulaym,[91] now advised the captors: 'Beat him and pluck his beard.' So they gave him forty lashes, plucked out the hair on his head, his eyebrows and eyelashes, and put him in prison.[92]

On the next morning there was disagreement between Ṭalḥa and al-Zubayr about who should now lead the prayer. Al-Zubayr as the older man was then given precedence, and thereafter the leadership was alternated between them day by day.[93] At dawn on this morning, ʿAbd

87 According to Abu l-Yaqẓān, the two armies merely faced each other (Khalīfa, *Taʾrīkh*, 183).

88 Sayf's story about Kaʿb b. Sūr being sent to Medina at this time in order to enquire whether Ṭalḥa and al-Zubayr were forced to pledge allegiance to ʿAlī and his return confirming their claim (Ṭabarī, I, 3124–5) is fiction designed to cover up the treacherous breach of the accord by Ṭalḥa and al-Zubayr. There was, as noted by Caetani (*Annali*, IX, 85), hardly enough time for such a mission.

89 Khalīfa, *Taʾrīkh*, 183; Ibn Abī Shayba, *Muṣannaf*, VIII, 719.

90 Balādhurī, *Ansāb*, II, 22–8. According to Abū Mikhnaf's account, it was rather the dawn prayer (Ibn Abi l-Ḥadīd, *Sharḥ*, IX, 330).

91 Ibn Ḥajar, *Iṣāba*, VI, 42; M. Lecker, *The Banū Sulaym: A Contribution to the Study of Early Islam* (Jerusalem, 1989), index s.v. Mujāshiʿ was a Companion of the Prophet and played a prominent part in the early conquests in Iraq and Iran. The report quoted by Ibn Ḥajar, however, that he took part in a raid of Kabul and plucked a gem from the eye of an idol there is legend. Under ʿUmar he was briefly deputy governor of Baṣra. In the accounts of Jaʿfar al-Muḥammadī and Sayf b. ʿUmar, he is described as leader of the Basran volunteer force moving as far as al-Rabadha to bring relief to the besieged caliph ʿUthmān (Ṭabarī, I, 2986, 3009).

92 Ṭabarī, I, 3126.

93 Balādhurī, *Ansāb*, II, 228. According to the report of Abu l-Malīḥ (Ṭabarī, I, 3134–5), ʿĀʾisha ordered ʿAbd Allāh b. al-Zubayr to lead the prayer. Al-Zubayr b. Bakkār reported in his *Ansāb Quraysh* that ʿAbd Allāh b. al-Zubayr led the prayers on the order of Ṭalḥa and al-Zubayr (Ibn Abi l-Ḥadīd, *Sharḥ*, XX, 114).

Allāh b. al-Zubayr with a group of men went to the treasury which was guarded by forty[94] Sayābija, former slaves from Sind converted to Islam. Since these resisted, they cut them all down, including their leader, Abū Salama al-Zuṭṭī, a pious man.[95] 'Abd Allāh b. al-Zubayr now wanted to provide for his men from the grain which was ready for distribution to the people in the square of the storage quarter (*madīnat al-rizq*).[96] Ḥukaym b. Jabala, having heard of the ill treatment of Ibn Ḥunayf, also went there with a troop of 'Abd al-Qays and Bakr b. Wā'il.[97] 'Abd Allāh b. al-Zubayr asked Ḥukaym: 'What do you want, Ḥukaym?' Ḥukaym answered: 'We want provisions from this grain and that you set free 'Uthmān [b. Ḥunayf] so that he can reside in the governor's palace as was agreed between [us and] you until 'Alī arrives. By God, if I found helpers against you with whom I could strike you, I would not be satisfied with this until I killed you for those you have killed. Your blood has become licit for us because of our brothers whom you have killed. Don't you fear God? What for do you consider the shedding of blood lawful?' Ibn al-Zubayr: 'For the blood of 'Uthmān b. 'Affān.' Ḥukaym: 'Have then those killed by you killed 'Uthmān? Don't you fear God's loathing?' Ibn al-Zubayr then told him: 'We will not let you take provisions from this grain and will not free 'Uthmān b. Ḥunayf until he deposes 'Alī.' Ḥukaym: 'O my God, You are the just arbitrator, so be witness.' Then he told his companions: 'I am in no doubt about fighting these people. Whoever is in doubt, let him leave.' Fierce fighting ensued, and Ḥukaym's leg was cut off. He picked it up and hit his opponent fatally with it before being himself overcome. Seventy men of 'Abd al-Qays were killed, among them Ḥukaym's son al-Ashraf and his brother al-Ri'l.[98] On the side of Ibn al-Zubayr, Mujāshi' b. Mas'ūd al-Sulamī and his brother Mujālid were killed.[99]

The Mekkan rebels were now in full control of the town. But the people were deeply divided, and Ṭalḥa and al-Zubayr could not count on their loyal support. Al-Zubayr is reported to have appealed for a thousand horsemen to join him in ambushing or attacking 'Alī, evidently before he

[94] The sources speak of 40 or 400 Sayābija. The latter number is no doubt greatly inflated.

[95] Balādhurī, *Ansāb*, II, 228; Balādhurī, *Futūḥ*, 376.

[96] According to al-Balādhurī's main account (*Ansāb*, II, 228), this happened in the morning. According to the account of al-Jārūd b. Abī Sabra quoted here, it could appear that it had happened on the previous evening. It seems unlikely, however, that the ensuing fight would have taken place at night.

[97] According to the general account of al-Balādhurī (*ibid.*) the battle was in al-Zābūqa, and Ṭalḥa and al-Zubayr participated. Ḥukaym's men were about three hundred, among them seventy of 'Abd al-Qays. According to Khalīfa (*Ta'rīkh*, 183), they were 700. According to Ibn Abī Sabra, the majority were 'Abd al-Qays. Abū Mikhnaf narrated that the rebels brought out 'Ā'isha on a camel and that the battle was known as 'the minor day of the Camel', distinguishing it from the battle with 'Alī (Ibn Abi l-Ḥadīd, *Sharḥ*, IX, 322).

[98] Ṭabarī, I, 3135–6; Khalīfa, *Ta'rīkh*, 183. Al-Balādhurī's main account (*Ansāb*, II, 228–9) describes al-Ashraf as a brother of Ḥukaym and speaks of three of his brothers being killed.

[99] Ibn Ḥajar, *Iṣāba*, VI, 42.

could get Kufan support, but no one responded.[100] According to Abu l-Malīḥ, the rebels wanted at first, after the death of Ḥukaym b. Jabala, to kill ʿUthmān b. Ḥunayf as well. He warned them, however, that his brother Sahl was governor of Medina and would avenge his death on their families. They released him, and he joined ʿAlī in al-Rabadha.[101] Al-Zubayr proposed that they give the people of Baṣra their provisions and distribute the money in the treasury, but his son ʿAbd Allāh objected, arguing that the Basrans would then disperse (and fail to fight ʿAlī). Agreement was reached to put ʿAbd al-Raḥmān b. Abī Bakr in charge of the treasury.[102] ʿĀʾisha then wrote letters to Kūfa seeking support there, but apparently with little success. Zayd b. Ṣūḥān al-ʿAbdī, one of the early Shiʿite *qurrāʾ*, whom she asked either to join her cause or to keep the people away from ʿAlī, addressing him as her devoted son, answered that he would be her devoted son if she returned to her home.[103]

ʿAlī had known of ʿĀʾisha's revolt in Mekka from the beginning and must have observed the developments carefully. Yet he probably learned of the planned campaign to Iraq only at a late stage. Umm al-Faḍl bt al-Ḥārith, the widow of al-ʿAbbās, is said to have informed him from Mekka.[104] He now summoned his supporters in Medina to arms. Al-Ḥajjāj (b. ʿAmr) b. Ghaziyya, poet of the Banu l-Najjār,[105] called for speedy action to catch up with Ṭalḥa and al-Zubayr.[106] Abū Qatāda al-Nuʿmān (or al-Ḥārith) b. Ribʿī al-Khazrajī, a prominent Companion,[107]

[100] Ṭabarī, I, 3136; Mufīd, *Jamal*, 288. The reporter is Abū ʿAmra, client of al-Zubayr. Strategically this was the most sensible plan. The Basrans were evidently unwilling to become the aggressors.

[101] The report of Ṣāliḥ b. Kaysān that Ṭalḥa and al-Zubayr released ʿUthmān after receiving a threatening letter from Sahl b. Ḥunayf (Balādhurī, *Ansāb*, II, 230) is probably unreliable. It seems that ʿUthmān was quickly released after the takeover.

[102] Ṭabarī, I, 3135; Mufīd, *Jamal*, 287. Sayf b. ʿUmar describes the partisans of ʿĀʾisha after they had taken control of Baṣra as seeking out in the quarters of the town all the participants in the rebel campaign to Medina and killing every one of them except for Ḥurqūṣ b. Zuhayr, who was concealed by the Saʿd Tamīm (Ṭabarī, I, 3131). All this is not corroborated by other sources and is no doubt fiction. ʿĀʾisha, Ṭalḥa and al-Zubayr were now seeking to gain Basran support against ʿAlī. Killing the raiders of Medina would have antagonized their tribes whose backing they needed. The claim of revenge for ʿUthmān had never been anything for them but a pretext justifying their war against ʿAlī. To punish and kill all those connected with the rebellion against ʿUthmān was later Umayyad policy down to al-Ḥajjāj.

[103] Ṭabarī, I, 3138. Zayd b. Ṣūḥān had belonged to the delegation of ʿAbd al-Qays making their submission to the Prophet (Ibn Ḥajar, *Iṣāba*, III, 36). ʿĀʾisha wrote to him presumably on that basis.

[104] Balādhurī, *Ansāb*, II, 222. The contention of Caetani that the report is tendentious (*Annali*, IX, 32) is baseless. The co-operation of the ʿAbbasids with ʿAlī was certainly close at this time. Umm al-Faḍl is, however, reported to have died before al-ʿAbbās during the reign of ʿUthmān (Ibn Ḥajar, *Iṣāba*, VIII, 266–7).

[105] Ibn Ḥajar, *Iṣāba*, I, 328. [106] Balādhurī, *Ansāb*, II, 233.

[107] Ibn Ḥajar, *Iṣāba*, VII, 155–6.

volunteered to fight against 'those wrongdoers who have never failed to deceive this Community' and offered to take a leading position. 'Alī gave him the command of foot-soldiers in the battle of the Camel.[108] Umm Salama assured 'Alī that she would join his campaign if it were not an act of disobedience to God, and commended her son 'Umar b. Abī Salama al-Makhzūmī[109] to him. 'Umar fought for 'Alī in the battle of the Camel and was then appointed governor of al-Baḥrayn.[110] 'Alī left Medina with 700 men of the Anṣār, according to 'Abd al-Raḥmān b. Abī Laylā, on 29 Rabī' II 36/25 October 656.[111] He had appointed Sahl b. Ḥunayf governor in his absence.

'Alī stopped first at al-Rabadha, on the route from Mekka to Iraq. Most likely he knew that the Mekkans had already passed by there and chose al-Rabadha for its convenience. From al-Rabadha he sent Hāshim b. 'Utba b. Abī Waqqāṣ to Abū Mūsā, his governor of Kūfa, with a letter ordering him to summon the Kufans to his support. Abū Mūsā consulted al-Sā'ib b. Mālik al-Ash'arī who advised him to follow 'Alī's order. He refused, however, concealed the letter, and threatened Hāshim with prison and death. Hāshim now sent a letter with al-Muḥill b. Khalīfa al-Ṭā'ī, informing 'Alī of Abū Mūsā's hostile attitude. Al-Muḥill assured 'Alī that the Kufans were ready to back him, but warned that Abū Mūsā would oppose him if he found supporters for that. 'Alī replied that Abū Mūsā was not trustworthy in his view and that he had intended to depose him, but al-Ashtar had interceded for him, claiming that the Kufans were satisfied with him. He now sent 'Abd Allāh b. al-'Abbās and Muḥammad b. Abī Bakr to Kūfa with a coarse letter to Abū Mūsā in which he called him a weaver's son (*ibn al-ḥā'ik*) and deposed him. In his place he appointed the Anṣārī Qaraẓa b. Ka'b of Khazraj.[112]

'Alī also learned in al-Rabadha of the takeover of Baṣra by the rebels and the death of Ḥukaym and his companions of 'Abd al-Qays and other Rabī'a. The news was brought by al-Muthannā b. (Bashīr b.) Maḥraba al-'Abdī. In a piece of poetry 'Alī lamented and praised Rabī'a, 'the

[108] Balādhurī, *Ansāb*, II, 239. [109] Ibn Ḥajar, *Iṣāba*, IV, 280–1.

[110] Ṭabarī, I, 3101. When 'Alī was preparing for his second campaign against Mu'āwiya at the beginning of the year 38/June 658 he recalled 'Umar b. Abī Salama from al-Baḥrayn to participate in the war. He replaced him with al-Nu'mān b. 'Ajlān al-Zuraqī. See 'Alī's letter quoted by al-Balādhurī (*Ansāb*, II, 158–9). Al-Nu'mān b. 'Ajlān was present at the battle of Ṣiffīn. The second campaign against the Syrians must thus be meant in the letter.

[111] Ṭabarī, I, 3139.

[112] So the account of Abū Mikhnaf quoted by Ibn Abi l-Ḥadīd, *Sharḥ*, IV, 9–10. According to al-Balādhurī's summary account (*Ansāb*, II, 234), which is also based on Abū Mikhnaf, Hāshim b. 'Utba himself returned to al-Rabadha. The account of Ibn Isḥāq, on the authority of his uncle 'Abd al-Raḥmān b. Yasār, according to whom 'Alī first sent Muḥammad b. Ja'far b. Abī Ṭālib and Muḥammad b. Abī Bakr to Kūfa (Ibn Abi l-Ḥadīd, *Sharḥ*, XIV, 8–9), is unreliable.

obedient', who had preceded him in battle and had obtained a lofty station by it.[113] Probably not much later 'Uthmān b. Ḥunayf arrived in al-Rabadha, his head and beard shorn. 'Alī consoled him while cursing Ṭalḥa and al-Zubayr for breaking their oath of allegiance.[114]

With Baṣra under the control of his opponents and Abū Mūsā in Kūfa trying to keep the people neutral, 'Alī's situation in al-Rabadha must have looked quite precarious. As he was about to leave, his son al-Ḥasan is reported to have expressed his fear to him that 'Alī would be killed in a wasted effort. 'Alī sent him off, insisting that he had no choice but to fight the opponents if he was to be faithful to the message of Muḥammad.[115]

'Alī's next halt was at Fayd, about midway on the route from Mekka to Kūfa, where a group of the Banū Ṭayyi' came to meet him. Their chief, Saʿīd b. 'Ubayd al-Ṭā'ī, promised him whole-hearted backing, and was killed fighting for him at Ṣiffīn.[116] It was probably at Fayd that 'Alī learned that Abū Mūsā was still holding on to the governorship in Kūfa, ordering the people to stay in their houses and warning them against participating in an inter-Muslim conflict (*fitna*),[117] and that his two emissaries had made no headway in summoning the Kufans to his support. He now sent his son al-Ḥasan and 'Ammār b. Yāsir to rally them.[118] Al-Ashtar, who must have been embarrassed by the conduct of Abū Mūsā, whom he had first installed as governor and then had recommended to 'Alī, now told 'Alī that he, al-Ashtar, had already sent a man to Kūfa who had accomplished nothing, and requested that 'Alī send him after al-Ḥasan and 'Ammār since the Kufans were most ready to obey him. Al-Ashtar entered Kūfa, gathered his supporters from various

[113] Balādhurī, *Ansāb*, II, 233–4.

[114] Ṭabarī, I, 3143, reported by Muḥammad b. al-Ḥanafiyya.

[115] Balādhurī, *Ansāb*, II, 236; Ibn Shabba, *Ta'rīkh al-Madīna*, 1256–8. The narrator, the Kufan Ṭāriq b. Shihāb al-Bajalī al-Aḥmasī (Ibn Ḥajar, *Tahdhīb*, III, 3–4) joined 'Alī in al-Rabadha coming from Iraq (see Ibn Abī Shayba, *Muṣannaf*, VIII, 138). Al-Ḥasan's appeal to 'Alī was also reported by Ibn al-'Abbās (Ibn 'Asākir, *'Alī*, III, 138).

[116] Ṭabarī, I, 3140. The report, transmitted by Abū Mikhnaf, goes back to al-Sha'bī, who placed the meeting at al-Rabadha. In his general account Abū Mikhnaf placed it, probably correctly, at Fayd (Balādhurī, *Ansāb*, II, 234).

[117] Abū Mūsā's position was clearly strict opposition to any fighting among Muslims, and came close to that of Ibn 'Umar and other neutrals in Mekka. He did not support 'Ā'isha and her party. The reports of the Kufan 'Uthmanid 'Abd al-Raḥmān b. Abī Laylā and of Ibn Isḥāq misrepresent his attitude in describing him as affirming that the *bay'a* of 'Uthmān was still binding him and 'Alī and that he would not fight (for 'Alī) until every one of the murderers of 'Uthmān was killed, wherever he was (Ṭabarī, I, 3139; Ibn Abi l-Ḥadīd, *Sharḥ*, XIV, 9). Abū Mūsā had, if reluctantly, given his *bay'a* to 'Alī and broke it only because of the Prophet's warning about *fitna*.

[118] Balādhurī, *Ansāb*, II, 234. There were, according to Abū Mikhnaf's account, conflicting reports as to whether Ibn al-'Abbās and Ibn Abī Bakr left or stayed on when the new emissaries arrived. According to the account of Abū Mikhnaf quoted by Ibn Abi l-Ḥadīd (*Sharḥ*, XIV, 10–11), 'Alī sent al-Ḥasan, 'Ammār, Zayd b. Ṣūḥān and Qays b. Sa'd b. 'Ubāda from Dhū Qār. The mention of Qays b. Sa'd here is, as pointed out by al-Balādhurī (*Ansāb*, II, 235), mistaken.

tribes, and seized the governor's palace by force while Abū Mūsā kept preaching in the mosque and al-Ḥasan and 'Ammār were arguing with him. When Abū Mūsā was informed by his men that they had been expelled from the palace, he himself tried to enter, but al-Ashtar ordered him out, calling him a hypocrite. The people tried to pillage Abū Mūsā's belongings but al-Ashtar stopped them.[119]

Al-Ḥasan now was able without difficulty to raise an army of between six thousand and seven thousand men.[120] They came from the whole range of tribes settled in Kūfa and were grouped in seven contingents (*asbā'*). Al-Ḥasan led them to Dhū Qār, not far east of Kūfa, where 'Alī had arrived in the meantime.

In Baṣra, there was more division along tribal lines. The presence of 'Ā'isha excited a powerful popular sense of obligation to stand up for, and protect, the 'Mother of the Faithful'.[121] Some of the religious leaders were more inclined to neutrality and preached abstention in the face of *fitna*, as had Abū Mūsā in Kūfa. Ka'b b. Sūr of Azd, *qāḍī* of Baṣra appointed by 'Umar, went around among his tribe urging them to stay neutral, but they insulted him, calling him a Christian carrying a cane, and insisted that they would not abandon the Mother of the Faithful. He had been a Christian before Islam. As they refused to listen to him, he withdrew into his house, intending to leave Baṣra. 'Ā'isha, however, visited him personally and persuaded him to join her followers.[122] 'Imrān b. Ḥuṣayn al-Khuzā'ī sent Ḥujayr b. Rabī'[123] to his people, the Banū 'Adī,[124] to press them to abstain from fighting on either side. They answered contemptuously: 'Do you order us to sit back from [protecting]

[119] Ṭabarī, I, 3153. In the *isnād* Nu'aym, misidentified in the indices to al-Ṭabarī as Nu'aym b. Ḥammād, is Nu'aym b. Ḥakīm al-Madā'inī (d. 148/765) (Ibn Ḥajar, *Tahdhīb*, X, 457).

[120] This figure given by the Kufan Shi'ite Salama b. Kuhayl (d. 121/739 or 122/740) (Khalīfa, *Ta'rīkh*, 184) is confirmed by a statement of Muḥammad b. al-Ḥanafiyya who was in the best position to know the exact number. He said that 'Alī's party left Medina with 700 men who were later joined by 7,000 men from Kūfa and by 2,000 others, mostly of Bakr b. Wā'il. Abū Mikhnaf and other sources speak of 10,000 to 12,000 Kufans (Balādhurī, *Ansāb*, II, 234; Ṭabarī, I, 3174).

[121] There was, however, also some opposition to backing a cause led by a woman. Abū Bakra al-Thaqafī, uterine brother of Ziyād b. Abīh, was ready to join Ṭalḥa and al-Zubayr, but when he found 'Ā'isha to be in command, he withdrew and stayed neutral, commenting that he had heard the Prophet say that a people whose affairs were run by a woman could not prosper (Mufīd, *Jamal*, 297; Ibn Abi l-Ḥadīd, *Sharḥ*, VI, 227, quoting al-Sha'bī; Abbott, *Aishah*, 175).

[122] Balādhurī, *Ansāb*, II, 238.

[123] Ḥujayr b. Rabī' al-'Adawī transmitted hadith from 'Imrān (Ibn Ḥajar, *Tahdhīb*, II, 215–16).

[124] The Banū 'Adī b. 'Abd Manāt of the tribal federation of al-Ribāb are meant. Wellhausen erroneously identified them as belonging to the Azd (*Skizzen*, VI, 139). Caetani thought the Banū 'Adī of Quraysh were meant and suggested that they were naturally devoted to 'Ā'isha because they remembered that 'Umar had fallen victim to the party of 'Alī now in power (*Annali*, IX, 108). In fact the Banū 'Adī of Quraysh failed to support 'Ā'isha and stayed neutral, although they had been prominent among the defenders of 'Uthmān's palace.

the treasure and inviolable consort of the Messenger of God? We will not do it.'[125] Al-Aḥnaf b. Qays, chief of the Banū Sa'd of Tamīm, personally inclined to 'Alī and was not prepared to break his oath of allegiance to him. He told Ṭalḥa and al-Zubayr that he would fight against neither the Mother of the Faithful nor the cousin of the Prophet and asked for leave to withdraw to Persia, Mekka, or somewhere outside Baṣra. Ṭalḥa and al-Zubayr, after some consideration, decided that he should stay close by so that they could observe his actions. He withdrew to the open country (*jalḥā'*) two parasangs from Baṣra together with four thousand or six thousand men.[126] When 'Alī stopped at al-Zāwiya near Baṣra, al-Aḥnaf sent word to him offering either to join him with just two hundred men of his family,[127] or to restrain four thousand swords from facing him. He evidently was ready to back 'Alī personally, but his tribesmen were inclining towards 'Ā'isha. 'Alī decided that he should try to keep as many as possible from joining his enemies.[128] Of other Tamīm, the Banū 'Amr, the Ḥanẓala except Yarbū', and the Banū Dārim except some of Mujāshi' fought for 'Ā'isha.[129]

As the two armies were facing each other and 'Alī appealed to the Basrans for concord, the Basran 'Abd al-Qays and Bakr b. Wā'il (Rabī'a), who had been the victims of Mekkan aggression, went over to him. They were led by 'Amr b. Marjūm al-'Abdī and Shaqīq b. Thawr al-Sadūsī respectively and numbered, according to Abū Mikhnaf, three thousand men. The Banū Qays b. Tha'laba of Bakr b. Wā'il, however, stayed with the opponents under their leader, Mālik b. Misma' al-Shaybānī.[130] These substantial defections evidently tipped the balance in favour of 'Alī.

The general command of the Basran army was given to al-Zubayr. 'Ā'isha insisted, however, that he should be acclaimed merely amir, not caliph. A decision on the caliphate would be made after the victory.[131] As the Basran army advanced from al-Furḍa and the Kufan army from al-Zāwiya, they met at the place where later the castle of Ziyād b. Abīh stood. They faced each other for three days, and a felt tent was pitched

[125] Balādhurī, *Ansāb*, II, 238; Ṭabarī, I, 3177.

[126] Ṭabarī, I, 3170–1; Balādhurī, *Ansāb*, II, 232.

[127] So the account in al-Mufīd, *Jamal*, 295. The other reports state that al-Aḥnaf offered to join 'Alī alone.

[128] Ṭabarī, I, 3174; Balādhurī, *Ansāb*, II, 237. Al-Mufīd's account (*Jamal*, 295) mentions a rivalry for the leadership of Tamīm between al-Aḥnaf and Hilāl b. Wakī' al-Ḥanẓalī, who insisted on backing the Mekkan rebels. Hilāl was killed in the battle of the Camel.

[129] Ibn Abi l-Ḥadīd, *Sharḥ*, IX, 320, quoting Abū Mikhnaf.

[130] Ṭabarī, I, 3174; Balādhurī, *Ansāb*, II, 237.

[131] Balādhurī, *Ansāb*, II, 229, 264. 'Abd Allāh b. al-Zubayr is quoted as suggesting to his father that 'Ā'isha wanted to give him the hard task and her kinsman (Ṭalḥa) the pleasant one (*ibid.*, 265–6). This quotation must be viewed with reserve since Ibn al-Zubayr is generally portrayed as an uncritical supporter of his aunt.

between them where 'Alī, al-Zubayr and Ṭalḥa met. On the third day, after noon, 'Alī raised the side of the tent and gave order to get ready for battle.[132]

In the exchanges before the battle, al-Zubayr's resolve seems to have been broken. The details of what happened, however, are obscure. 'Alī is said to have first sent Ibn al-'Abbās, instructing him to approach al-Zubayr, since Ṭalḥa was more recalcitrant. Ibn al-'Abbās questioned al-Zubayr in the name of 'Alī as to why he recognized him in the Ḥijāz but opposed him in Iraq. Al-Zubayr adamantly affirmed, however, that there was an unbridgeable gulf between them.[133] According to several reports, 'Alī himself reminded al-Zubayr of an incident in their childhood when the Prophet predicted that al-Zubayr would unjustly fight 'Alī. Remembering the incident, al-Zubayr swore that he would never fight 'Alī. His son 'Abd Allāh, however, accused him of cowardice. Al-Zubayr changed his mind again and, on 'Abd Allāh's advice, manumitted a slave in atonement for his broken oath.[134] The story is evidently legendary, and the detail about the manumission of the slave a duplicate of the report about Mu'āwiya's letter to al-Zubayr. It is not unlikely, however, that 'Alī's exhortations influenced al-Zubayr to reconsider his position. He may have recognized that he was merely being used as a pawn for the ambitions of 'Ā'isha and Ṭalḥa, who were clearly much more guilty of inciting the rebellion against 'Uthmān than was 'Alī. 'Ā'isha's insistence that he should be addressed only as amir may have brought home to him that she did not really favour his succession to the caliphate, to which he felt most entitled because of 'Uthmān's early preference for him and his own loyal support just before his death. To fight a bloody battle against the Prophet's cousin, pitting Muslims against Muslims, under such circumstances must have seemed both foolish and immoral to him. His son 'Abd Allāh, in contrast, stood much closer to his aunt 'Ā'isha and was determined to fight 'Alī in revenge for the blood of 'Uthmān.

There was obviously no room for negotiation and compromise. 'Ā'isha and her partisans wanted the removal of 'Alī and a *shūrā*. 'Alī considered himself the legitimate caliph, regardless of the broad Qurayshite opposition. While they accused him of being morally responsible for the violent death of 'Uthmān, he charged Ṭalḥa and 'Ā'isha. Neither side was interested in an investigation of who had actually wielded the sword.[135] The battle took

[132] Ṭabarī, I, 3174–5; Ibn Abī Shayba, *Muṣannaf*, VIII, 709–10.

[133] Jāḥiẓ, *Bayān*, III, 221–2.

[134] Ṭabarī, I, 3175–6; Balādhurī, *Ansāb*, II, 254–5; Ibn Abī Shayba, *Muṣannaf*, VIII, 719.

[135] Sayf's story about successful negotiations and agreement on the punishment of the murderers, which was then thwarted by the Saba'iyya and Nuffār who were in fear of their lives and therefore provoked the battle (Ṭabarī, I, 3155–8, 1362–3, 1381–3), is pure fiction not backed by any of the other sources.

place on Thursday, 15 Jumādā I 36/8 December 656[136] and lasted from noon to sunset. ʿAlī ordered a man of ʿAbd al-Qays to raise a copy of the Qur'ān between the battle lines and to appeal for adherence to its rules and for concord. When this man was hit by arrows and killed, ʿAlī gave the order to advance and fight.[137] This is widely reported with varying details, some legendary, and is in substance verisimilar. The Basrans had been talked into believing that they would fight the murderers of ʿUthmān and used 'revenge for ʿUthmān' as their battle cry. Their side were the aggressors, and ʿAlī wanted them to be seen as such. The Kufans had before the battle not seriously thought that their Basran Muslim brethren would fight them.[138]

The banner of ʿAlī's army was carried by his son Muḥammad b. al-Ḥanafiyya. When the latter wavered in front of the wall of lances of the enemy, ʿAlī took it out of his hands and led the assault.[139] Later he returned it to him. The fighting became fierce when al-Ashtar, leading the right wing of ʿAlī's army, killed Hilāl b. Wakīʿ b. Bishr al-Tamīmī of Dārim, the leader of the left wing of the Basrans.[140] Al-Zubayr left the battlefield quite early, apparently without having fought, and immediately set out on the route to the Ḥijāz. He is said to have been given protection by a man of Mujāshiʿ (of Dārim Tamīm). According to a report of Qatāda, al-Zubayr first went to the mosque of the Banū Mujāshiʿ asking for ʿIyāḍ b. Ḥammād, presumably to seek his protection. He was told that ʿIyāḍ was in Wādi l-Sibāʿ, and he went there in search of him.[141] Al-Aḥnaf b. Qays was alerted by some of his men that al-Zubayr was passing by. He remarked that al-Zubayr had led the Muslims to fight each other with the sword and now he was running away home. Three men followed al-Zubayr, and ʿAmr b. Jurmūz al-Mujāshiʿī killed him in the Wādi l-Sibāʿ. When Ibn Jurmūz after the battle came to see ʿAlī and announced himself as the slayer of al-Zubayr, ʿAlī, according to some reports preferred by Sunnite tradition, refused to see him and exclaimed: 'Announce hell-fire to the murderer of the son of Ṣafiyya.'[142] According to more credible accounts, Ibn Jurmūz, sent by al-Aḥnaf b. Qays with al-Zubayr's sword and head, was received by ʿAlī, who questioned him about the circumstances under which he had killed him. ʿAlī then unsheathed and looked at al-Zubayr's sword and commented that he

136 Thursday is given as the battle day by most sources. There is, however, a report by Qatāda that the two armies met on Thursday and that the battle took place on Friday (Khalīfa, *Ta'rīkh*, 184–5).

137 Balādhurī, *Ansāb*, II, 240.

138 The Basran Kulayb al-Jarmī, who visited the army of ʿAlī at Dhū Qār, describes the Kufans coming up to him laughing and expressing amazement, saying: 'Do you really think our Basran brethren will fight us?' (Ibn Abī Shayba, *Muṣannaf*, VIII, 705).

139 Ṭabarī, I, 3193.

140 Balādhurī, *Ansāb*, II, 241.

141 *Aghānī*, XVI, 131.

142 Al-Zubayr's mother was Ṣafiyya, daughter of ʿAbd al-Muṭṭalib.

knew it well; al-Zubayr had many a time fought in front of the Messenger of God but had come to an evil end.[143]

The men fighting were evidently at a loss to explain the desertion of al-Zubayr. Jawn b. Qatāda of Sa'd Tamīm, who was with al-Zubayr at the beginning of the battle, narrated that al-Zubayr became frightened when he learned that 'Ammār was participating on the side of 'Alī.[144] Other reports describe 'Ammār as encountering al-Zubayr in the battle.[145] 'Ammār was evidently introduced to explain al-Zubayr's conduct because of the hadith ascribed to Muḥammad stating that 'Ammār was of the righteous and predicting that he would be killed by the rebel party. Al-Zubayr had obviously known before that 'Ammār would be fighting with 'Alī. A battle-experienced and brave man, he cannot have fled in fear at the very beginning of the fight. It was serious misgivings about the justice of 'Ā'isha's cause that must have induced him to abandon it. He probably intended to withdraw completely from the conflict and therefore turned towards the Ḥijāz. It is less likely that he still thought of taking up the offer of Mu'āwiya. The Sa'd Tamīm, though formally neutral, were appalled by his desertion, as they considered him one of the main instigators of the conflict among the Muslims. They killed him as a man without honour rather than to please 'Alī.

Ṭalḥa was mortally wounded probably not much later. In command of the horsemen, he is said to have fought valiantly at first.[146] As the Kufans gained the upper hand, however, he turned back in a mêlée. Marwān hit him from behind with an arrow which pierced his sciatic vein (*nasā*) near the knee. The wound kept bleeding profusely while he and his companions tried at first to stanch and treat it. Continued attempts to stop the bleeding failed, and Ṭalḥa died in a house of the Banū Sa'd Tamīm or lying under a tree.[147]

The treacherous murder of Ṭalḥa by Marwān evidently was no spontaneous act. Marwān had already hinted his intention of also taking revenge among 'Ā'isha's partisans to the Umayyads who had deserted her army at Dhāt 'Irq. Yet he evidently waited until it was safe to predict that he would not be called to account by a victorious Mother of the Faithful. Having learned his lesson on the Day of the Palace, he stayed behind, biding his time without boastfully challenging the enemy. It was only

[143] See the accounts of Marwān b. al-Ḥakam and the Medinan Muḥammad b. Ibrāhīm b. al-Ḥārith al-Taymī quoted by al-Mufīd, *Jamal*, 387–90. Shi'ite tradition preferred these reports as proof that 'Alī did not forgive al-Zubayr.

[144] Ṭabarī, I, 3187–8; Balādhurī, *Ansāb*, II, 256–7. In the version of Ibn Sa'd (*Ṭabaqāt*, III/1, 77–8) 'Ammār is not mentioned.

[145] Ṭabarī, I, 3290; Balādhurī, *Ansāb*, II, 259.

[146] Balādhurī, *Ansāb*, II, 245.

[147] *Ibid.*, 246; Mufīd, *Jamal*, 383, 389. Marwān told 'Alī's grandson 'Alī Zayn al-'Ābidīn that he hit Ṭalḥa with two arrows.

after his deed that he was slightly wounded. He is said to have turned towards ʿUthmān's son Abān and told him: 'We have taken care of one of the murderers of your father for you.'[148]

With the two leaders killed, the defeat was sealed and the armed conflict could have been halted. The presence of ʿĀ'isha in her camel litter spurred her army on to a supreme, though senseless, effort to defend her. Ferocious fighting centred now around her camel and litter, which were protected by armoured plate, and continued for many hours. The men holding the camel's halter were killed one after the other. The first was the pious Kaʿb b. Sūr, who had a Qur'ān tied around his neck. Then a number of Qurayshites took over. The Umayyad ʿAbd al-Raḥmān b. ʿAttāb b. Asīd, called lord (*yaʿsūb*) of the Arabs or of Quraysh, was killed by al-Ashtar. ʿĀ'isha was particularly grieved by his death.[149] Ṭalḥa's son Muḥammad, known as a pious worshipper, is said to have taken the halter and been killed there.[150] Al-Aswad b. Abi l-Bakhtarī of Asad Quraysh was brought down to the ground but escaped unhurt. ʿAbd Allāh b. al-Zubayr took over and was attacked by al-Ashtar. According to the common account, the two men grappled with each other; Ibn al-Zubayr was wounded, but then they were separated.[151] According to al-Ashtar's own report, he rather struck Ibn al-Zubayr on the head with his sword and left him for dead.[152] Al-Aswad found him lying on the ground, laid him on his own horse, and took him off the battlefield to the house of a man of the Banu l-Ghabrā' of Azd.[153]

[148] Khalīfa, *Ta'rīkh*, 185; Balādhurī, *Ansāb*, II, 246.

[149] Ṭabarī, I, 3227–8. Al-Ṭabarī's identification of the Yaʿsūb al-ʿArab as Muḥammad b. Ṭalḥa is, as noted by Levi della Vida (in *Annali*, IX, 149), mistaken.

[150] Balādhurī, *Ansāb*, II, 243. [151] Ṭabarī, I, 3199–200.

[152] Al-Nuʿmān, *Sharḥ al-akhbār*, I, 397. Al-Ashtar explained that he was eager to kill Ibn al-Zubayr because he held him responsible for bringing out his aunt ʿĀ'isha in the campaign. The one whom he pulled to the ground and grappled with was, he said, ʿAbd al-Raḥmān b. ʿAttāb.

[153] So according to ʿAbd Allāh b. al-Zubayr's own report quoted by al-Mufīd, *Jamal*, 362. On the way whenever al-Aswad passed by some follower of ʿAlī, he put Ibn al-Zubayr off the horse. On one occasion he passed by a man who recognized Ibn al-Zubayr. He (the man?) attacked him, but missed. Another man wounded his horse. Al-Aswad delivered Ibn al-Zubayr safely to the house of the man of the Banu l-Ghabrā' who had two wives, one of Tamīm and one of Bakr. They washed his wound and dressed it with camphor. It oozed little blood and healed quickly.

ʿAbd al-Raḥmān b. al-Ḥārith b. Hishām of Makhzūm narrated that he, al-Aswad b. Abi l-Bakhtarī and ʿAbd Allāh b. al-Zubayr had made a pact in Baṣra that they would either kill ʿAlī in the battle or die. During the battle they were looking for their chance, but witnessed first the right wing and then the left wing of the enemy routing their opposites. ʿAbd al-Raḥmān then saw ʿAlī slay two men of Ḍabba successively. Eventually they were swept away in the general defeat. After the battle ʿAbd al-Raḥmān successfully avoided the armed patrols of ʿAlī (Mufīd, *Jamal*, 375). ʿAbd Allāh b. al-Zubayr, who escaped separately, met him by chance (Mufīd, (*ibid.*, 363), and they evidently returned together to the Ḥijāz. According to a report of al-Wāqidī, ʿAbd al-Raḥmān b. al-Ḥārith pledged allegiance to ʿAlī after the battle and then departed (*ibid.*, 413–14).

Thereafter common tribesmen took over. The Banū Ḍabba in particular took great pride in thus serving the Mother of the Faithful. Forty of their men are said to have been killed, one after the other, at the halter.[154] The slaughter came to a sudden halt when ʿAlī called for someone to hamstring the camel. According to one report, this was done by Bujayr b. Dulja, a Kufan of Ḍabba, who later said that he had been worried that none of his Basran kinsmen might survive.[155] Another report identifies the man as al-Musallim(?) b. Maʿdān of the Banū Shazan b. Nukra of ʿAbd al-Qays.[156] As the animal dropped down with its load, ʿAlī and his close companions were able to approach. ʿĀ'isha's brother Muḥammad, on ʿAlī's order, cut the straps fastening the litter to the animal's body and, with some helpers, carried it off. Muḥammad b. Ḥāṭib al-Jumaḥī narrated: 'I went with ʿAlī on the day of the Camel to the litter which looked like the spikes of a hedgehog from arrows. He banged at the litter and said: 'Surely, this Ḥumayrā' of Iram[157] wanted to kill me as she killed ʿUthmān b. ʿAffān.' Then her brother Muḥammad asked her: 'Has anything hit you?' She said: 'An arrow in the upper arm.' He put his hand inside [the litter], drew her towards himself, and pulled it out.'[158]

When ʿAlī faced ʿĀ'isha, he severely reproached her for the ruin she had brought on the Muslims. It was now her turn to sue humbly for peace. 'You have won the reign, Ibn Abī Ṭālib, so pardon with goodness.'[159] ʿAlī ordered her brother Muḥammad to escort her to town, where she was then lodged in the house of Ṣafiyya bt al-Ḥārith b. Ṭalḥa b. Abī Ṭalḥa of ʿAbd al-Dār.[160] There she stayed for a few days. Al-Ashtar bought an expensive camel and sent it to her to replace the one killed in the battle, but she would not accept it from him.[161]

Then ʿAlī sent ʿAbd Allāh b. al-ʿAbbās to order her to leave. According to his own account, Ibn al-ʿAbbās asked for permission to enter the house where she was staying but, being refused, entered without it. In the room, where ʿĀ'isha was concealed behind a screen, he did not find anything to sit on. Then he discovered at the side a saddle covered by a saddle rug (*ṭanfasa*). He spread out the rug and sat down on it. ʿĀ'isha asked him: 'Ibn ʿAbbās, what is this? You come to me in my home without my

[154] Ṭabarī, I, 3198. [155] *Ibid.*, 3204. [156] Balādhurī, *Ansāb*, II, 248.

[157] Ḥumayrā', 'little red one', was the pet name given by Muḥammad to ʿĀ'isha. Her enemies later used it as her nickname. Iram was the name of a legendary pre-Islamic Arabian tribe which had been destroyed. Pre-Islamic legend and poetry featured the male figure of the ill-omened Aḥmar or Uḥaymir of ʿĀd (or Thamūd), who brought misfortune and ruin down upon his own people. 'Ḥumayrā' of Iram' was meant to be a female equivalent. [158] Balādhurī, *Ansāb*, II, 250.

[159] Ṭabarī, I, 3186; Balādhurī, *Ansāb*, II, 250.

[160] Ṣafiyya's husband was ʿAbd Allāh b. Khalaf al-Khuzāʿī, appointed secretary of the *dīwān* of Baṣra by ʿUmar. He was killed fighting for ʿĀ'isha in the battle (Ibn Ḥajar, *Iṣāba*, VIII, 5–6, IV, 62).

[161] Ibn Abī Shayba, *Muṣannaf*, VIII, 705; Ṭabarī, I, 3227–8.

permission and you sit down on my belongings without my permission. You have contravened the Sunna.' Ibn al-'Abbās: 'We taught you and others the Sunna; we are more worthy of it than you. Your only home is the one where the Messenger of God left you and from which you departed wronging yourself, presumptious against your Lord, and disobedient towards your Prophet. When you return to it, I shall not enter without your permission, nor shall I sit down except on your order.' She began to weep, and he told her: 'The Commander of the Faithful has sent me to you to command you to leave Baṣra and to return to your home.' She said: 'And who is the Commander of the Faithful? The Commander of the Faithful was 'Umar.' Ibn al-'Abbās told her: "Umar used to be called Commander of the Faithful, but this one, by God, is 'Alī, the Commander of the Faithful in truth, as the Messenger of God called him thus. He, by God, is closer in kinship to the Messenger of God, earlier in submission [to Islam], more abounding in knowledge, and more forbearing (*aḥlamu ḥilman*) than your father and 'Umar.' As she protested, he assured her that her father's reign had been short in duration, but grave in outcome, of evident evil omen, and of clear misfortune. Yet she had taken advantage of it to reveal her hostility to the Prophet's kin. 'Ā'isha kept sobbing and declared defiantly: 'I shall, by God, leave you; there is no abode more loathsome to me than the one where you [pl.] are.' Ibn al-'Abbās questioned her: 'And why that? It is not because of any distress caused to you by us, nor any preference on our part over you and your father. We made you a Mother of the Faithful when you were the daughter of Umm Rūmān, and we made your father a Ṣiddīq when he was the son of Abū Quḥāfa.' 'Ā'isha: 'Do you claim to have benefited us through the Messenger of God?' Ibn al-'Abbās: 'And why should we not claim to have benefited you through someone who, if you had a single hair from him, you would claim to benefit through it and would boast by it. Yet we are of his flesh and blood, and you are merely one of nine stuffed beds which he left behind. Nor are you the one of them with the firmest root, the most verdant leaves, and the widest shade.' As he quoted some poetry illustrating his point, she fell silent and he left to inform 'Alī who expressed satisfaction with his conduct.[162] 'Ā'isha then requested, and was granted, a delay, but after a few days 'Alī pressed her, and she left for Medina accompanied by a group of Basran women and some men of her choice.[163]

Upon her arrival in Medina, first the 'Uthmanid Anṣārī poet Ka'b b. Mālik and then his daughter Kabsha in a group of women of the Anṣār visited her to greet her. Kabsha related 'Ā'isha's own account of her

[162] Al-Nu'mān, *Sharḥ al-akhbār*, I, 390–2; al-Majlisī, *Biḥār al-anwār* (Tehran/Tabriz, 1303–15/[1888–98]), VIII, 450–1. [163] Balādhurī, *Ansāb*, II, 249.

experiences in the battle. She claimed now that just before the battle she had stood up among the people and summoned them to a truce, the Book of God, and the Sunna, but nobody would listen to a word of her speech as they hastened to start the fighting; first one or two of 'Alī's followers were killed, then the battle lines drew near each other; the people showed no other concern than about her camel; some arrows entered the armoured litter, wounding her. As she showed the women the wound in her upper arm, all wept. She then described how every man taking hold of the halter of her camel was killed and how she vainly tried to drive her nephew 'Abd Allāh b. al-Zubayr away from it. The young men of Quraysh on their side, she commented, were inexperienced in war and thus became easy prey for slaughter by the enemy. After a short break in the fighting she saw the son of Abū Ṭālib personally engaged in fighting and heard him shout: 'The camel, the camel.' She said to herself: 'He wants, by God, to kill me.' Then he approached together with her brother Muḥammad, Mu'ādh b. 'Ubayd Allāh al-Tamīmī[164] and 'Ammār b. Yāsir, and they cut the straps holding the litter on the camel's back and carried it off as the men on her side dispersed. Next she heard the herald of 'Alī calling out: 'No one turning his back shall be pursued, no one wounded shall be killed, whoever throws away his arms is safe.'

She then was taken to the house of 'Abd Allāh b. Khalaf al-Khuzā'ī who had been killed in the battle and whose family were weeping for him. Everyone who had been hostile to 'Alī (*nāṣaba lah*) and had fled in fear now came to her. When she asked about Ṭalḥa and al-Zubayr, she was told that they had been killed. She was also told at first that her nephew 'Abd Allāh had been killed, and fell into even deeper grief. For three days she would not eat or drink anything, although her hosts were most hospitable and there was plenty of bread. She closed her account, stressing her remorse for having incited the revolt against 'Uthmān. The Muslims, she said, would never again have a caliph like him. He had been the greatest among them in gentleness (*ḥilm*), the most persevering in worship, the most generous in misfortune, and the one most protective of kinship ties.[165]

'Ā'isha's attitude towards 'Alī had evidently not changed much. When al-Nu'mān b. Bashīr came to see her some time later with a message from Mu'āwiya, now in open conflict with 'Alī, she received him well. Then she confided to him that she had heard the Prophet, in the presence of 'Umar's daughter Ḥafṣa, tell 'Uthmān three times that God would clothe

[164] Mu'ādh b. 'Ubayd Allāh al-Tamīmī fought in the battle on the side of the Mekkan rebels. He may have gone over to 'Alī before the end; his reports about the battle express admiration for him (Mufīd, *Jamal*, 364–5, 373–4).

[165] *Ibid.*, 378–80, quoting al-Wāqidī.

him in a garment which he should not take off when the hypocrites would want him to do so. Pleased but surprised, al-Nuʿmān asked her: 'Mother of the Faithful, where have you been in relation to this hadith?' She told him that she had forgotten it as if she had never heard it.[166]

Her defeat in the battle of the Camel put an end to ʿĀ'isha's political career and sealed the demise of the early patriarchal caliphate of Medina, which she had hoped to restore. After the death of Muʿāwiya, her nephew ʿAbd Allāh b. al-Zubayr was to make another attempt to revive it, but failed. The memory of the horrible carnage taking place around her litter in which so many men close to her lost their lives and of her own part as Mother of the Faithful in driving Muslims to kill Muslims must have haunted her. The numerous reports about her remorse and wish not to have lived to see that day certainly reflect the truth. The mood is well caught in the story narrated by the Kufan Jundab b. ʿAbd Allāh al-Azdī: ʿAmr b. al-Ashraf al-ʿAtakī of the Basran Azd took the halter of the camel, and no one could get close to him but that he would be struck down by his sword; then al-Ḥārith b. Zuhayr of the Kufan Azd, a Companion of the Prophet, came up to him, reciting:

> O our Mother, the best mother we know, do you not see how many a brave man is being smitten, and has his head and hand cut off?

'Then they exchanged two strikes, and I saw them digging up the earth with their legs before they died. Later I paid ʿĀ'isha a visit in Medina. She said: "Who are you?" I answered: "A man of the Azd. I live in Kūfa." She asked: "Were you present with us on the Day of the Camel?" I said yes, and she asked: "For us or against us?" I answered: "Against you." She asked: "Do you know the one who said: O our mother, the best mother we know?" and I said: "Yes, that was my cousin." Then she wept so that I thought she would not calm down again.'[167]

The losses were substantial on both sides, though obviously more grievous in ʿĀ'isha's camp. Quraysh, fighting for their caliphate and status as the sole ruling class, paid a heavy toll, affecting most of its clans. Among the dead[168] were of ʿAbd Shams: ʿAbd al-Raḥmān b. ʿAttāb b. Asīd; ʿAbd Allāh b. al-Walīd b. Yazīd b. ʿAdī b. Rabīʿa b. ʿAbd al-ʿUzzā; Muḥriz b. Ḥāritha b. Rabīʿa b. ʿAbd al-ʿUzzā; his cousin ʿAlī b. ʿAdī b. Rabīʿa, governor of Mekka under ʿUthmān; and ʿAbd al-Raḥmān, son of ʿUthmān's governor of Baṣra ʿAbd Allāh b. ʿĀmir b. Kurayz;[169] of

[166] Ibn Shabba, *Ta'rīkh al-Madīna*, 1068–9. Ḥafṣa confirmed ʿĀ'isha's report (*ibid.*, 1069–70).

[167] Ṭabarī, I, 3201. In Abū Mikhnaf's version of the story, 'the best mother' is replaced by 'the most uncaring (*aʿaqq*) mother' (Ibn Abi l-Ḥadīd, *Sharḥ*, I, 264).

[168] For the following list see in general the necrology for the year 36 H. in *Annali*, IX and Khalīfa, *Ta'rīkh*, 177–8, where some of the names and lineages need to be corrected.

[169] ʿAbd al-Raḥmān was born when his father was only thirteen years old (Ibn Manẓūr, *Mukhtaṣar*, XII, 285). He was thus nineteen years old when he was killed.

Nawfal: Muslim b. Qaraẓa b. 'Abd 'Amr b. Nawfal, brother of Mu'āwiya's wife Fākhita;[170] of Asad: al-Zubayr and 'Abd Allāh b. Ḥakīm b. Ḥizām, who carried the banner of 'Ā'isha's army and was killed by 'Adī b. Ḥātim al-Ṭā'ī and al-Ashtar;[171] of 'Abd al-Dār: 'Abd Allāh b. Musāfi' b. Ṭalḥa b. Abī Ṭalḥa; of Zuhra: al-Aswad b. 'Awf, brother of 'Abd al-Raḥmān b. 'Awf;[172] of Makhzūm: 'Abd al-Raḥmān b. al-Sā'ib b. Abi l-Sā'ib b. 'Ā'idh; 'Abd al-Raḥmān b. Abī Burda b. Ma'bad b. Wahb b. 'Amr b. 'Ā'idh, Ma'bad b. al-Zuhayr b. Abī Umayya b. al-Mughīra; of Taym: Ṭalḥa; his son Muḥammad; his brother 'Abd al-Raḥmān b. 'Ubayd ('Abd) Allāh b. 'Uthmān; and 'Abd al-Raḥmān b. Abī Salama b. al-Ḥārith;[173] of Jumaḥ: 'Abd Allāh b. Ubayy b. Khalaf b. Wahb; 'Abd Allāh b. Rabī'a b. Darrāj b. al-'Anbas;[174] 'Abd al-Raḥmān b. Wahb b. Asīd b. Khalaf; and Muslim b. 'Āmir b. Ḥumayl;[175] of Sahm: a son of Qays b. 'Adī b. Sa'd, the '*sayyid* of Quraysh in his time'; and of 'Āmir: 'Abd al-Raḥmān and 'Amr, sons of Ḥumayr b. 'Amr b. 'Abd Allāh b. Abī Qays; Abū Sufyān b. Ḥuwayṭib b. 'Abd al-'Uzzā b. Abī Qays;[176] 'Ubayd Allāh b. Anas b. Jābir b. 'Abada b. Wahb;[177] and 'Abd Allāh b. Yazīd b. al-Aṣamm.[178] The lowest figures of all the dead given are 2,500 for 'Ā'isha's army and 400 to 500 for 'Alī's.[179] These figures seem realistic. The heaviest losses were taken by the Basran Ḍabba and Azd.

As one after the other of his tribesmen was slain, 'Amr b. Yathribī al-Ḍabbī spurred them on with Rajaz verses of encouragement for 'Ā'isha

[170] Finding Muslim b. Qaraẓa's body among the dead on the battlefield, 'Alī sarcastically questioned whether it was perhaps kindness (*birr*) that had motivated this man to come forth against him. Muslim had, he explained, asked him to intervene with 'Uthmān in a claim he had against him in Mekka. 'Alī had pressed 'Uthmān until he conceded it to Muslim remarking: 'If it were not for you, I would not give it to him.' Now Muslim had met his death backing 'Uthmān (Mufīd, *Jamal*, 393). [171] Ṭabarī, I, 3202.

[172] Among the enemy dead on the battlefield 'Alī also found Ma'bad, the son of al-Miqdād b. al-Aswad ('Amr), confederate of Zuhra. Al-Miqdād, one of the earliest converts to Islam, had been a strong supporter of 'Alī even at the time of 'Uthmān's election, and Ma'bad's mother was a Hashimite. 'Alī expressed severe condemnation of Ma'bad's betrayal of his kinship ties while praising his father (Balādhurī, *Ansāb*, II, 264–5; Mufīd, *Jamal*, 392–3).

[173] Mentioned only by Khalīfa (*Ta'rīkh*, 186). He is not traceable elsewhere.

[174] Zubayrī, *Nasab*, 396; Ibn Abi l-Ḥadīd, *Sharḥ*, XI, 125. 'Alī commented on his dead body: 'This miserable one, it was not backing for 'Uthmān which made him go out. By God, 'Uthmān's view of him and of his father was not good' (Mufīd, *Jamal*, 396).

[175] He is mentioned only by Khalīfa (*Ta'rīkh*, 186) and is not traceable elsewhere.

[176] According to a report of Sa'īd b. Abī Hind, 'Alī tried to save Abū Sufyān b. Ḥuwayṭib, who appeared frightened in the battle, by inviting him to go over to his side. Abū Sufyān tried to do so, but a Basran offensive against 'Alī's position caught up with him. A Kufan of Hamdān attacked and slew him, failing to comprehend in time 'Alī's order to leave him (Mufīd, *Jamal*, 361). Abū Sufyān's father Ḥuwayṭib was, according to some reports, among those present at the burial of 'Uthmān (Zubayrī, *Nasab*, 426; see chapter 3, n. 291). His nephew Musāḥiq b. 'Abd Allāh b. Makhrama b. 'Abd al-'Uzzā was among the survivors of the battle; he offered his apologies to 'Alī and was pardoned by him (Mufīd, *Jamal*, 413, 416). [177] Zubayrī, *Nasab*, 434. [178] *Ibid.*, 439.

[179] Balādhurī, *Ansāb*, II, 264; Khalīfa, *Ta'rīkh*, 186; Ṭabarī, I, 3232.

not to worry. He killed three of ʿAlī's men, ʿIlbāʾ b. al-Haytham al-Sadūsī, Hind b. ʿAmr al-Jamalī and Zayd b. Ṣūḥān of ʿAbd al-Qays. ʿIlbāʾ and Zayd were known to have been early and vigorous supporters of ʿAlī.[180] The aged ʿAmmār is said to have confronted Ibn Yathribī. The latter attacked him with his sword, but it stuck in ʿAmmār's leather shield, and the Kufans hit him with arrows. As he fell to the ground he recited:

> If you kill me, I am Ibn Yathribī who killed ʿIlbāʾ and Hind al-Jamalī
> and then Ibn Ṣūḥān, followers of the religion of ʿAlī (*ʿalā dīn ʿAlī*).

He was taken captive and led before ʿAlī. Although he asked for his life, ʿAlī ordered him to be killed, the only captive in the battle whom he did not pardon.[181] When questioned about this, ʿAlī is said to have explained that Ibn Yathribī had killed three men who, he pretended, were followers of the 'religion of ʿAlī'. The religion of ʿAlī, the latter emphasized, was the religion of Muḥammad.[182] That ʿAlī's refusal of pardon was at least partly motivated by Ibn Yathribī's verse is not unlikely. He was ever sensitive to any suggestion that he did not observe and apply the Qurʾān and Muḥammad's precedent more faithfully than anyone else.[183] It was a weakness that would later prompt him to his most grievous mistake.

Other reports confirm the existence of the concept of a 'religion of ʿAlī' among the Basrans. Muḥammad b. al-Ḥanafiyya narrated that he attacked a man, but when he was about to stab him he said: 'I am a follower of the religion of ʿAlī b. Abī Ṭālib.' Ibn al-Ḥanafiyya understood what he meant and left him.[184] As the tide turned against the Basran Azd and they were forced to turn to flight they called out: 'We are followers of the religion of ʿAlī b. Abī Ṭālib', evidently in order to save their lives. A Kufan of the Banū Layth later lampooned them, condemning their disgraceful opinion.[185] He meant presumably both their dissimulation in claiming to be followers of ʿAlī and their attribution of a special religion to him.

The conflict thus had also a religious dimension. *Dīn ʿAlī* could at this

[180] Zayd b. Ṣūḥān's brother Sīḥān was also killed in the battle. The third brother, Ṣaʿṣaʿa b. Ṣūḥān, was a prominent figure among ʿAlī's followers and an eyewitness informant of al-Shaʿbī for events during ʿAlī's reign (Sezgin, *Abū Miḥnaf*, 137; al-Najāshī, *Rijāl*, ed. Mūsā al-Shabīrī al-Zanjānī (Qumm, 1407/[1987]), 203). ʿĀʾisha is reported to have used the formula 'may God have mercy on him' when she was informed of Zayd's death after the battle (Ibn Manẓūr, *Mukhtaṣar*, IX, 146).

[181] Ṭabarī, I, 3198–9.

[182] Ibn Durayd, *al-Ishtiqāq*, ed. ʿAbd al-Salām Muḥammad Hārūn (Baghdad, 1399/1979), 413.

[183] Levi della Vida evidently misinterpreted the explanation by suggesting that it reflects the same tendency as reports about ʿAlī's punishing ʿAbd Allāh b. Sabaʾ and his extremist (*ghulāt*) followers (in *Annali*, IX, 142). Here it is a question of imputing deviant doctrine to ʿAlī, not of preaching extremist doctrine in his name.

[184] Ibn Abī Shayba, *Muṣannaf*, VIII, 711.

[185] Ṭabarī, I, 3189–90.

stage have only a limited meaning, most likely the claim that 'Alī was the best of men after Muḥammad, his legatee (*waṣī*), and as such most entitled to lead the Community. This is probably implied in two lines which one of the Banū 'Adī recited as he was holding the halter of 'Ā'isha's camel:

> We are 'Adī, we seek (*nabtaghī*) 'Alī, carrying lances and Mashrafī swords, helmets, and twisted iron rings [of mail], we kill whoever opposes the legatee (*man yukhālifu l-waṣiyyā*).[186]

As this was said by a shaykh of the Banū 'Adī backing 'Ā'isha, the legatee cannot be 'Alī.[187] It is equally unlikely that some pro-'Alī poetry slipped inadvertently into the story which was transmitted by Abū Na'āma 'Amr b. 'Īsā b. Suwayd, a well-known scholar of the Banū 'Adī.[188] The legatee is here Abū Bakr whom 'Alī and his followers oppose in making war against his daughter. Abū Bakr was not normally, certainly in later times, considered the legatee of Muḥammad. He is called so here to counter the claim of the opponents that 'Alī was the *waṣī*.[189]

Fighting Muslim opponents in regular battle was a new experience in Islam. 'Alī could have treated his opponents on Abū Bakr's precedent as apostates and infidels and thus applied the common rules of warfare to them. Given the long-standing rank of his leading opponents in Islam, this was hardly a reasonable option. 'Alī ordered at the beginning of the battle that wounded or captured enemies should not be killed, those throwing away their arms should not be fought, and those fleeing from the battleground should not be pursued. Only captured weapons and animals were to be considered war booty. After the battle he ordered that no war prisoners, women or children were to be enslaved and that the property of slain enemies was to go to their legal Muslim heirs. As a compensation he paid 500 dirhams to each of his men out of the Basran treasury.[190] These rules were to become authoritative in Islam for the warfare against Muslim rebels (*bughāt*). While they were evidently accepted by most of his men without argument, a few radicals questioned his conduct. He is said to have told them that if they insisted on enslaving

[186] Balādhurī, *Ansāb*, II, 245–6.

[187] This was the interpretation of Levi della Vida, who translated the report without further comment ('Il califfato di 'Alī secondo il Kitāb Ansāb al-Ašrāf di al-Balāḏurī', *Rivista degli Studi Orientali*, 6 (1914–15), 427–507, at 444; *Annali*, IX, 155). The Shī'ite editor of Balādhurī, *Ansāb*, II, commented on the unexpected use of the term with a *sic* (*kadhā*).

[188] Ibn Ḥajar, *Tahdhīb*, VIII, 87.

[189] The expression *nabtaghī 'Aliyyan*, 'we seek, or desire, 'Alī', is in itself ambiguous. Here it evidently means we seek him to make him pay for the murder of 'Uthmān. It is to be compared to the complaint of 'Amr b. Yathribī: 'I strike them, but I do not see Abū Ḥasan ['Alī], that is indeed a pity' (Ṭabarī, I, 3199).

[190] Balādhurī, *Ansāb*, II, 261–2. Numerous relevant reports are quoted in Ibn Abī Shayba, *Muṣannaf*, VIII, 707–8, 710–11, 713, 718–21.

their opponents, they would have to draw lots for the possession of 'Ā'isha. The Kharijites later made it a point of their accusations against him that he was breaking the norms of Islam by denying his warriors their legal share of war booty.

The prisoners of war were set free by 'Alī after they pledged allegiance. Still on the battle day, 'Uthmān's sons Abān and Sa'īd were led as captives before 'Alī. One of those present suggested that he kill them, but 'Alī rebuked him, asking how he could kill these two men after having announced a general pardon. Turning towards the two captives he told them to abandon their delusion and to depart to wherever they wished. If they preferred they could stay with him, and he would honour their kinship ties. They answered that they would pledge allegiance and then depart. They evidently left for the Ḥijāz.[191]

Ṭalḥa's son Mūsā recalled how the prisoners, gathered together in the evening after the battle, were saying: 'Mūsā b. Ṭalḥa will be killed tomorrow.' The next morning, after he had prayed the first prayer, the prisoners were called. He was the first one to be led before 'Alī. The Commander of the Faithful asked him: 'Will you pledge allegiance? Will you join what the people have joined?' He answered: 'Yes.' After his pledge 'Alī told him to return to his family and property. When the others saw that he came out safely, they readily entered and pledged allegiance.[192] Mūsā became one of the heirs of Ṭalḥa's vast property.[193]

Musāḥiq b. 'Abd Allāh b. Makhrama al-'Āmirī al-Qurashī recounted that he and a group of Qurayshites, among them Marwān b. al-Ḥakam, agreed to offer 'Alī their apologies for their revolt against him. They realized that he was the most noble and forbearing man in his conduct after the Prophet and that they had wronged him. 'Alī received them and questioned them in a speech as to whether he had not been the man closest to the Prophet and most entitled to rule the people after him. When they assented, he reminded them that they had turned away from him to pledge allegiance to Abū Bakr; not wishing to split the ranks of the Muslim Community, he had refrained from opposing their choice; he had done the same when Abū Bakr appointed 'Umar to succeed him, even

191 Mufīd, *Jamal*, 382. Abān b. 'Uthmān is described by al-Balādhurī as the first one to take flight in the battle of the Camel (*Ansāb*, V, 120).

192 Ibn Abī Shayba, *Muṣannaf*, VIII, 716. There is a gap in the text of the report: Ibn Manẓūr, *Mukhtaṣar*, XXV, 290–1.

193 Al-Zubayrī, however, describes 'Imrān b. Ṭalḥa as the one who visited 'Alī after the battle of the Camel and requested that he return his father's property at al-Nashtāstaj to him. 'Alī treated him kindly, prayed for God's mercy for his father, and ordered that all the property with the crops which had been gathered from it be turned over to him (*Nasab*, 281–2). 'Imrān was, unlike Mūsā, a full brother of Muḥammad b. Ṭalḥa and perhaps the eldest surviving son. He does not seem to have participated in the battle.

though he knew that he was most entitled to the position of the Messenger of God; when 'Umar appointed him one of six candidates for the succession, they had pledged allegiance to 'Uthmān, but then criticized and killed him while he, 'Alī, remained sitting in his house. 'Then you came to me and pledged allegiance to me just as you pledged allegiance to Abū Bakr and 'Umar. Why then did you keep your pledge to them but not to me?' They begged him to act as Joseph had to his brothers and to pardon them, quoting Qur'ān XII 92. 'Alī took their pledge of allegiance and let them go.[194]

Some of 'Alī's enemies were able to avoid pledging allegiance. Concerning Marwān, there are conflicting reports. According to some, Marwān, having been pardoned, himself expressed eagerness to do homage and 'Alī accepted his pledge.[195] Abū Mikhnaf, in contrast, reported that Marwān, wounded in the battle, first found shelter among the 'Anaza. He then requested, and received, the protection of Mālik b. Misma' al-Shaybānī, who obtained 'Alī's pardon for him. When the people of Baṣra all pledged allegiance, 'Alī proposed that he also do so. Marwān refused, however, reminding him that he had already pardoned him. He would pledge allegiance only if forced to do so by 'Alī. The latter told him to his face that he would not force him, since whatever pledge he would give he would not fail to betray it. Marwān left to join Mu'āwiya in Syria.[196]

Regardless of whether he actually swore allegiance or not, 'Alī obviously could be under no illusion as to the value of the oath of a man such as Marwān. That he simply let him go shows how little he was prepared to adopt the new rules of the game of politics which, as a result of the civil war, came to prevail now in Islam. Surely neither Mu'āwiya nor Marwān himself would have hesitated to do away with so dangerous and vicious an enemy who had just revealed his hand by treacherously murdering one of the closest Companions of the Prophet after first threatening 'Alī with perdition.[197]

'Abd Allāh b. al-Zubayr, also wounded, had, as noted, found refuge in the house of a man of the Azd. He sent to his aunt 'Ā'isha to inform her of his whereabouts. She asked her brother Muḥammad to bring him to her. On the way the two men rebuked each other rudely concerning 'Uthmān.

[194] Mufīd, *Jamal*, 413–14, 416–17; al-Nu'mān, *Sharḥ al-akhbār*, I, 392–4.

[195] See in particular the report of Nāfi' (Ibn Sa'd, *Ṭabaqāt*, V, 26) which erroneously states that Marwān departed for Medina and stayed there until the accession of Mu'āwiya. The report contains other errors and seems on the whole unreliable. According to a report of the Shi'ite imam Ja'far al-Ṣādiq, Marwān himself told his grandfather 'Alī b. al-Ḥusayn that he willingly swore allegiance to 'Alī, who allowed him to go wherever he wished (Balādhurī, *Ansāb*, II, 262–3).

[196] Balādhurī, *Ansāb*, II, 263.

[197] See excursus 6 on Mūsā b. Ṭalḥa and the Umayyads.

Mu'āwiya's brother 'Utba b. Abī Sufyān, who first had been granted protection by 'Iṣma b. Ubayr of the Banū Taym of al-Ribāb, also moved to stay with 'Ā'isha. Informed of this, 'Alī did not interfere.[198] Neither of them presumably pledged allegiance, and 'Utba soon found his way to his brother in Damascus. Whether 'Abd Allāh b. 'Āmir b. Kurayz swore allegiance is not known. Well acquainted with Baṣra and having friends there, he may have found it easy to hide and abscond. He, too, went off to Syria.[199]

In his sermon to the Basrans, 'Alī chastized them for being the first subjects to break their oath of allegiance and split the ranks of the Community. He forgave them, however, and warned them against sedition (*fitna*). Then he received their renewed oath of allegiance. He wrote to Qaraẓa b. Ka'b, his governor of Kūfa, announcing the victory and praising the Kufans.[200] Preparing to set out for Kūfa, he appointed 'Abd Allāh b. al-'Abbās governor of Baṣra and attached Ziyād b. 'Ubayd (Abīh) to him as secretary.[201] It may have been at this same time that he appointed 'Umar b. Abī Salama governor of al-Baḥrayn and Qutham b. al-'Abbās governor of Mekka. The latter, however, is not mentioned among those present at the battle of the Camel and may have been sent by 'Alī from Medina or al-Rabadha after the Qurayshite rebels had departed from Mekka. The appointment of 'Abd Allāh b. al-'Abbās was resented by al-Ashtar, who had hoped to be rewarded with the governorship for

[198] Balādhurī, *Ansāb*, II, 263–4, quoting Abū Mikhnaf. According to 'Abd Allāh b. al-Zubayr's own account, he sent the owner of the house in which he first stayed to 'Ā'isha to inform her about him, telling him to avoid being seen by Muḥammad b. Abī Bakr. The man mentioned his concern to 'Ā'isha but she sent him to call her brother, whom she then asked to go and get their nephew. Ibn al-Zubayr was at first scared by the sight of Muḥammad and began to curse him. Muḥammad calmed him down, however, by informing him that he was sent by 'Ā'isha. It was at 'Ā'isha's house that he heard 'Uthmān being cursed openly and decided that he would not stay in a town where this was done. He took a camel from his companion (presumably the man with whom he had stayed) and left Baṣra, keeping away from the armed guards. Then he observed a man who, like himself, was trying to avoid being seen. It was his friend 'Abd al-Raḥmān b. al-Ḥārith b. Hishām. Further on he saw a man with a horse, which he recognized as his father's. He wanted to kill him, but 'Abd al-Raḥmān told him not to be hasty since the man could not slip away from them. It turned out to be al-Zubayr's slave. When 'Abd Allāh asked him where al-Zubayr was, he answered that he did not know. 'Abd Allāh, according to his account, then knew that his father had been killed (Mufīd, *Jamal*, 362–3).

[199] Ibn 'Asākir's eulogistic report describes 'Abd Allāh b. 'Āmir as appealing to al-Zubayr before the battle not to proceed and thus to save the Community of Muḥammmad. As al-Zubayr ignored his advice, Ibn 'Āmir left for Syria, presumably without fighting (Ibn Manẓūr, *Mukhtaṣar*, XII, 288). This is highly improbable. 'Abd Allāh b. 'Āmir would hardly have left his son to fight and die while running away himself. The same source also wrongly suggests that Ibn 'Āmir was not present at Ṣiffīn.

[200] Balādhurī, *Ansāb*, II, 264. The text of the letter quoted by al-Mufīd, *Jamal*, 403–4, is probably spurious. The date given, Rajab 36/Dec. 656–Jan. 657, cannot be correct.

[201] Balādhurī, *Ansāb*, II, 271.

his decisive part in the battle,[202] and there was evidently some murmuring among those critical of the privileged position of Quraysh at the fact that three of 'Alī's Hashimite kin were now holding governorships. 'Alī assured al-Ashtar that he was needed to deal with the Syrians, among whom there were many of his kin.

Leaving Baṣra, 'Alī was accompanied by the dignitaries of the town as far as Mawqū'. Al-Aḥnaf b. Qays and Sharīk b. al-A'war al-Ḥārithī of Dahy b. Ka'b continued on with him to Kūfa, but there is disagreement as to how far they went.[203] 'Alī entered Kūfa, according to al-Sha'bī, at the beginning of Rajab 36/24 December 656,[204] or, according to Abu l-Kanūd, on Monday 12 Rajab/ 2 January 657,[205] less than a month after the battle. He refused to reside in the governor's castle, calling it the castle of corruption (*qaṣr al-khabāl*) and chose to stay with his nephew Ja'da b. Hubayra al-Makhzūmī.[206] In his first sermon he took to task those who had failed to join his army. Sa'īd b. Qays al-Hamdānī and Sulaymān b. Ṣurad al-Khuzā'ī, two close supporters, were personally reprimanded by him for having stayed behind.[207]

202 Ṭabarī, I, 3162; see Ibn Abī Shayba, *Muṣannaf*, VIII, 706 for some differences in the report. Al-Ashtar is said to have commented: 'What for have we killed the old man in Medina?' and to have called for Madhḥij, his tribesmen, to leave with him. That he intended to join Mu'āwiya, as suggested by the reporter Kulayb al-Jarmī, is not likely. 'Alī, according to Kulayb, put his own date of departure forward in order to prevent al-Ashtar from leaving alone with his men. 203 Balādhurī, *Ansāb*, II, 271.

204 Minqarī, *Waq'at Ṣiffīn*, 80. Al-Sha'bī's statement that 'Alī stayed in Kūfa for seventeen months exchanging letters with Mu'āwiya and 'Amr b. al-'Āṣ must be understood as meaning that 'Alī continued to exchange letters with them until the end of the year 37/June 658 when he set out on his second campaign against them, not that he stayed in Kūfa for the whole period.

205 *Ibid.*, 3; Christian date adjusted for Monday. The alternative date given by al-Balādhurī (*Ansāb*, II, 273), Ramaḍān 36/Feb.–March 657, which apparently goes back to al-Zuhrī (see *ibid.*, 293 n. 1), is far too late. The reports give the impression that 'Alī stayed in Baṣra a very brief time. The earlier date given by al-Sha'bī seems not unreasonable.

206 Minqarī, *Waq'at Ṣiffīn*, 3, 5. Ja'da's mother Umm Hāni' was a sister of 'Alī (Zubayrī, *Nasab*, 39; Balādhurī, *Ansāb*, II, 41). In Abū Mikhnaf's report on 'Alī's return to Kūfa from Ṣiffīn he is described as entering the castle (Ṭabarī, I, 3349). In al-Balādhurī's account of the murder of 'Alī based on al-Wāqidī, Abū Mikhnaf and 'Awāna, it is affirmed, however, that he did not reside in the castle but in some houses with wooden roofs (*akhṣāṣ*) at the plaza known as Raḥbat 'Alī (Balādhurī, *Ansāb*, II, 492). He may have used the palace only for ceremonial purposes.

207 Balādhurī, *Ansāb*, II, 272–4; Minqarī, *Waq'at Ṣiffīn*, 4, 6–7. Sulaymān b. Ṣurad reported that he had complained to al-Ḥasan about the latter's failure to convey his excuses properly to his father. Al-Ḥasan told him that 'Alī was reproaching him, Sulaymān, while 'Alī himself had expressed misgivings at the battle about being responsible for bringing together the two hostile camps. According to another report al-Ḥasan told Sulaymān b. Ṣurad that 'Alī during the battle expressed the wish that he himself had died twenty years before (Balādhurī, *Ansāb*, II, 272–3; on 272, read *bi-'mri'in* for *bi-amrin qad*). These reports reflect the opposition of al-Ḥasan to the fighting.

Mu'āwiya and Ṣiffīn

With the conflict with the Mekkan Quraysh settled in his favour, 'Alī now could turn his attention to Mu'āwiya. Although seven months had passed since his accession, no relations had yet been established with the governor of Syria. To later viewers who saw his reign mainly in the light of his conflict with the Umayyad, this delay seemed entirely implausible and they invented various stories about early contacts. Sayf fabled that 'Alī sent Sahl b. Ḥunayf as his governor to Syria, but when the latter reached Tabūk he was turned back by the Syrian border guard since he had not been appointed by the legitimate caliph, 'Uthmān.[208] Others made up stories designed to illustrate the cleverness of Mu'āwiya, who met the overtures of 'Alī by sending back to him an empty sheet containing merely the address: 'From Mu'āwiya b. Abī Sufyān to 'Alī b. Abī Ṭālib.'[209] In fact 'Alī was, after his discussion with Ibn al-'Abbās, certainly aware that he could deal with Mu'āwiya only from a position of strength. At the same time the threat to his caliphate from 'Ā'isha, Ṭalḥa and al-Zubayr was evidently much more serious in his eyes. For Mu'āwiya, a late convert without early merit in Islam, could hardly aspire to the caliphate at this stage and was in no position to act against him on his own.

Mu'āwiya also initially saw that it was in his best interest to observe the developments and keep his options open. He had been joined, however, by 'Uthmān's brother al-Walīd b. 'Uqba who was urging him to take quick revenge for the caliph's blood. After his humiliating punishment for wine-drinking, al-Walīd had defiantly addressed the Banū Umayya, declaring his bonds of kinship severed for their lack of solidarity.[210] Was it for this reason that he forsook his brother in his hour of need? Now, in any case, he saw his chance to rally his Umayyad kin as their poetical spokesman and to get back at his many personal enemies. His first poetical admonition to Mu'āwiya and the Syrians was probably the following:

> By God, Hind will not be your mother if the day passes
> without the avenger taking revenge for 'Uthmān.
> Can the slave of the people kill the lord of his household
> and you [pl.] do not kill him? Would your mother were barren!

[208] Ṭabarī, I, 3087.

[209] Balādhurī, *Ansāb*, II, 211–12. In the version transmitted by Abū Mikhnaf 'and others', 'Alī's messenger to Mu'āwiya is identified as al-Miswar b. Makhrama. In reality al-Miswar, in solidarity with Quraysh, did not swear allegiance to 'Alī and seems to have stayed in Mekka throughout his caliphate. While in this version 'Alī is described as merely trying to induce Mu'āwiya to pledge allegiance, the other version, which Wahb b. Jarīr transmitted on the authority of Ṣāliḥ b. Kaysān, described 'Alī as trying to bribe Mu'āwiya with the offer of confirming him in his governorship.

[210] Zubayrī, *Nasab*, 139; Ibn Shabba, *Ta'rīkh al-Madīna*, 974.

Surely if we kill them no one can [legitimately] retaliate
for them, the wheels of fortune have turned on you.[211]

The 'slave of the people' was 'Amr b. al-'Aṣ, and the others to be killed with him were the Egyptian rebels who, al-Walīd assumed, had been working on behalf of their former governor. Calling 'Amr the slave who killed his master was a suitable response to the boasting match between 'Amr and 'Uthmān about the nobility of their fathers. 'Amr's mother, al-Nābigha, had indeed been a slave woman and prostitute. It was widely believed that 'Amr's real father was the Umayyad Abū Sufyān, who had claimed his paternity against the Sahmī al-'Aṣ b. Wā'il. Al-Nābigha was said to have judged in favour of al-'Aṣ because of his generous support of her, while Abū Sufyān was known as a miser. In looks, however, 'Amr resembled Abū Sufyān most.[212] The appeal to Mu'āwiya as the son of Hind, the proud Umayyad mother of Mu'āwiya, thus aimed at driving a wedge between him and his bastard half-brother, the mere slave of Umayya. Al-Walīd had a personal score to settle with 'Amr who had dared to divorce his sister in a show of anger at being deposed by 'Uthmān. An exemplary punishment of 'Amr, who had withdrawn to his estate in Palestine, would also have been the most convenient course for Mu'āwiya to demonstrate his right and will to retaliate for the murdered caliph.

At about the same time, al-Walīd addressed a poem to his brother 'Umāra who was living in Kūfa. Al-Walīd was evidently irked because his brother remained in the town from which he himself had been removed under ignominious circumstances, even after the Kufans had risen in rebellion against 'Uthmān. He wanted to pressure him into joining the Umayyad coalition which he hoped to gather around Mu'āwiya.

I have been given 'Amr in exchange for 'Uthmān when I lost
him, may God judge between a lord and the supporters of 'Amr!
Surely the best of mankind after three is the one slain by
the Tujībī who came from Egypt.
If my thought about my mother's son, 'Umāra, does not
deceive me, he will not seek blood-revenge and retaliation.
He will stay, when the duty of revenge for Ibn 'Affān is
with him, his tent pitched between al-Khawarnaq and al-Qaṣr.[213]

[211] *Aghānī*, IV, 177.

[212] See Ibn Abi l-Ḥadīd, *Sharḥ*, VI, 284–5, where he quotes the *Kitāb al-Ansāb* of Abū 'Ubayda. Abū Sufyān's paternity of 'Amr b. al-'Āṣ had been publicized by Ḥassān b. Thābit in a lampoon in response to 'Amr's lampoon of the Prophet. The account quoted by Ibn Abi l-Ḥadīd from al-Zamakhsharī's *Rabī' al-abrār* (*Sharḥ*, VI, 283; *Rabī' al-abrār*, ed. Salīm al-Nu'aymi (Baghdad, 1976), III, 548–50) that six men representing the major clans of Quraysh, including Abū Lahab, claimed the paternity is evidently a slanderous elaboration of the theme.

[213] Ṭabarī, I, 3064; Ibn Bakr, *Tamhīd*, 209. The first line is missing in al-Ṭabarī's version, and the response ascribed there to al-Faḍl b. al-'Abbās thus appears unmotivated. In the first line as quoted by Ibn Bakr *nāṣiri* must be read *nāṣirī*. A further line of the poem is quoted in Ibn Manẓūr, *Mukhtaṣar*, XXVI, 247.

Here, too, it is ʿAmr b. al-ʿAṣ who is seen as the man responsible for the murder of the caliph. ʿAmr's Egyptian supporters, in particular the Tujībī Kināna b. Bishr, have killed him. Al-Walīd's claim that ʿUthmān was the most excellent of mankind after Muḥammad, Abū Bakr and ʿUmar drew forth a response from a different quarter. Al-Ṭabarī attributes it to al-Faḍl b. ʿAbbās, great-grandson of Muḥammad's uncle Abū Lahab, but more likely it is by al-Faḍl's father al-ʿAbbās b. ʿUtba b. Abī Lahab. Al-ʿAbbās b. ʿUtba, as noted, was married to Āmina, daughter of al-ʿAbbās b. ʿAbd al-Muṭṭalib and seems to have acted as the poetical spokesman of the Banū Hāshim at this time, just as al-Walīd b. ʿUtba was the spokesman of the Banū Umayya. He answered al-Walīd:

> Do you claim a revenge of which you are not worthy, nor does
> it belong to you?
> Where does the son of Dhakwān, the [barbarian slave] from
> Ṣaffūriyya,[214] stand in relation to ʿAmr?
> Just like the daughter of the ass who attaches herself to her mother
> and forgets her father when she vies for superiority with the
> glorious.
> Surely, the best of mankind after Muḥammad is the legatee (*waṣī*)
> of the Prophet al-Muṣṭafā among those who take note,
> The first one who prayed and the brother of his Prophet,
> the first to fell the misguided at Badr.
> If the Helpers [Anṣār] had seen that your [pl.] cousin was wronged
> they would readily have helped him against being wronged.
> Sufficient blemish it is that they should beckon to kill him
> and would surrender him to the black hordes (*aḥābīsh*) from
> Egypt.[215]

Muʿāwiya, to be sure, was not tempted to follow the course urged upon him by his irate kinsman. He wanted at this stage above all to hold on to the rule of Syria. ʿUthmān had meant little to him, he had done nothing to aid him, and felt no personal obligation to seek revenge. Yet he immediately sensed the political utility of a claim of revenge for the blood of the wronged caliph, as long as he, Muʿāwiya, could decide on whom to pin the blame. He might well lock up Muḥammad b. Abī Ḥudhayfa and

[214] Dhakwān al-Ṣafūrī. Dhakwān, al-Walīd's grandfather, was said by some genealogists to have been a client of Umayya adopted by the latter as his son (Ibn al-Athīr, *Kāmil*, II, 152). According to al-Kalbī, Dhakwān was the son of a Jewish slave girl of Lakhm in Ṣaffūriyya (near Ṭabariyya in al-Urdunn) with whom Umayya had illicit intercourse. Umayya claimed him as his son and took him from his mother (Nuʿmān, *Sharḥ al-akhbār*, II, 119). Al-Walīd b. ʿUqba is thus called a barbarian (*ʿilj*) from Ṣaffūriyya in a boasting speech ascribed to al-Ḥasan b. ʿAlī in the *Kitāb al-Mufākharāt* of al-Zubayr b. Bakkār (quoted by Ibn Abi l-Ḥadīd, *Sharḥ*, VI, 293). In the poem al-Ṣafūrī presumably stands for al-Ṣaffūrī because of metrical necessity (*ibid.*, II, 116).

[215] Ṭabarī, I, 3065.

the Egyptian rebels who were rash enough to pass through his territory, but 'Amr b. al-'Āṣ was a different matter. Mu'āwiya was not convinced that nobody would claim blood-revenge for 'the slave who killed his master', as al-Walīd had put it. He was aware that 'Ā'isha had backed 'Amr against 'Uthmān and certainly did not want to stir up a quarrel with the Mother of the Faithful. Besides, 'Amr was no threat to him now and might soon become useful. Some pressure on him, however, could only be beneficial. Mu'āwiya left 'Amr alone on his estate in Palestine, but did not stop al-Walīd from pursuing his vendetta.

'Amr b. al-'Āṣ felt the heat. When he had first heard of the murder of 'Uthmān he had, so it was reported, proudly taken some of the credit for it, boasting: 'I am Abū 'Abd Allāh, surely, when I scratch a sore I scrape the scab before it heals (*idhā ḥakaktu qarḥatan naka'tuhā*).'[216] But he realized that to have a claim for blood-revenge pronounced against him by the spokesman of Umayya was not a matter to be taken lightly. 'Amr began to squirm and changed his tune. In a poem addressed to Mu'āwiya he distanced himself from the Egyptian rebels who were suspected of having acted on his behalf. Grave matters, he said, have reached us whose heavy weight made the camels (of the messengers) limp; they had been perpetrated by men of the basest rabble; yet matters would only get worse if they were not decisively dealt with. He therefore was stating publicly that these people had committed against 'us' crimes whose flames could not be extinguished except by killing them all, or banishing[217] them to the desert. Mu'āwiya must, he told him, publicize their offence in these two matters (the murder of 'Uthmān and the takeover of Egypt).

> Mu'āwiya, do not close your eyes, rise in the stirrup of
> the matter, act equitably or resign, there is no third choice.
> Will you undertake the grand matter and grasp the forelocks
> of opportunity in these hideous times?[218]

The grand matter that 'Amr wanted Mu'āwiya to undertake was the conquest of Egypt, in which he, 'Amr, no doubt expected to play his appropriate part.

In another piece of poetry meant for the world, in particular the Syrians, 'Amr again yammered about the grave matters that had reached him and which he fully accepted as true, having predicted them in advance. They were that al-Zubayr and Ṭalḥa had flung a shot with which they demolished the prop of the people ('Uthmān) and that 'Alī had been managing their affairs. Would 'Alī kill or hinder the killer? How

[216] Balādhurī, *Ansāb*, V, 74.
[217] 'Amr may well have added this milder alternative in the expectation that Mu'āwiya would be loath to put to death Muḥammad b. Abī Ḥudhayfa, who was a maternal cousin of his wife Fākhita (Ibn al-Athīr, *Kāmil*, III, 221).
[218] Ibn 'Asākir, *'Uthmān*, 308.

could it be hoped that he would aid the slain victim when he had already deserted 'our 'Uthmān'? He would, 'Amr predicted now, efface the traces of the crime for the murderers and walk barefoot or in sandals for them, whatever they wished.[219]

These lines are evidently early, before the rebellion of Ṭalḥa and al-Zubayr in the suite of 'Ā'isha. 'Amr thus did not have to choose between them and 'Alī and could picture the three eminent Companions as colluding in the murder of 'our 'Uthmān', with 'Alī now covering up their joint crime. His conversion to Islam having been motivated strictly by opportunism, 'Amr had never cared much for any of that lot, and the least that could be said about them now was that they were fools not to have looked for an alibi, as he had done with wise political foresight. Al-Zubayr, 'Amr realized, was more acceptable to the Umayyads than the other two, but had he not been sent by 'Umar to Egypt merely to deprive himself of the glory of being the sole conqueror and to keep an eye on his dealings? No, he would rather not see al-Zubayr succeed to the caliphate, and named him first among the murderers. Why should not he, 'Amr, and Mu'āwiya share the spoils of the Muslim conquests between themselves rather than have to surrender the better part to some pious figurehead in Medina? 'Amr was confident that the argument was good and would appeal to Mu'āwiya, though he might not yet be ready for it.

Mu'āwiya was, no doubt, carefully listening, but he did not follow either of 'Amr's two pieces of advice. Nor did he, for the time being, invite the new partisan of 'our 'Uthmān' to his court. The dead caliph's late warning that 'Amr's jubbah was full of lice ever since he had deposed him may still have been ringing in everybody's ears.

As the drama of the conflict between the great Companions in the Ḥijāz unfolded, al-Walīd b. 'Uqba saw the chance to cast the net of his vendetta wider. 'Alī was now vulnerable, and the Umayyad poet laureate was happy to join the Mekkan chorus condemning him as the chief culprit. He hated 'Alī, if anything, more than 'Amr, holding him responsible for the flogging he had received for drunkenness. Yet he was not yet ready to let 'Amr off the hook. In one of his poems he asked his audience to look at the division among the Anṣār and Quraysh, which had been caused by a gang among whom the Dhamīm and his companion were high up. The Dhamīm was Muḥammad b. Abī Bakr, and his companion, 'Amr b. al-'Āṣ. As will be seen, al-Walīd associated the two closely, thus suggesting that the son of Abū Bakr had been acting on behalf of 'Amr, stirring up the trouble in Egypt. Since 'Ā'isha was backing 'Amr in his conflict with 'Uthmān, this suggestion may not be entirely unfounded.

219 Ibn Bakr, *Tamhīd*, 180.

The third one high up among the gang, al-Walīd continued, was

> The companion of 'Uthmān who beckoned to killing him, while
> his scorpions [= malicious calumnies] kept crawling to us every day.
> Don't you see how 'Alī[220] today is showing off his excuses,
> while inside him lies concealed the crime he perpetrated?
> The ones who please me are Ka'b, Zayd b. Thābit, Ṭalḥa, and
> al-Nu'mān, may his withers not be cut!
> They restrained whoever of them blamed 'Uthmān, and the most blameworthy
> among the sons of whatever mothers (*banu l-'allāt*) is he who blames him.[221]

While thus turning 'Alī into the leader of the conspiracy, al-Walīd also managed to sneak the name of Ṭalḥa among the three long-standing Medinan 'Uthmanid loyalists Ka'b b. Mālik, Zayd b. Thābit and al-Nu'mān b. Bashīr, who had joined Mu'āwiya. Ṭalḥa, 'Uthmān's most vehement critic among the Early Companions, was now, after his volte-face, handed a clean record as having restrained the censurers of the caliph. Mu'āwiya and the Syrians were thus given to understand that they ought to co-operate with Ṭalḥa in his battle against 'Alī.

Again Mu'āwiya was not inclined to follow the advice of his fiery kinsman. The fact that 'Ā'isha and Ṭalḥa had put their bet on Baṣra rather than joining him made him suspicious. 'Ā'isha, it is true, had commended him to 'Uthmān and insisted that he, appointed by 'Umar, stay governor of Damascus. But would Ṭalḥa, a haughty and self-assured man, be content with a semi-independent Umayyad governor of this key province once he was in power? Mu'āwiya might not in the end be better off with him than with 'Alī. He decided rather to write to al-Zubayr inviting him to Damascus, even though it meant splitting the anti-'Alid coalition.

In spite of Mu'āwiya's apparent indifference to his admonitions, al-Walīd was now confident that his vendetta was on course. In another poem composed about the same time he threatened:

> So tell[222] 'Amr and the Dhamīm you both have done wrong
> by killing Ibn 'Affān in return for no one slain,
> And by charging Abū 'Amr ['Uthmān] with every grave misdeed
> upon no basis but empty rumour;
> Yet there you are – and God will surely attain his purpose –
> without having gained a farthing from your censure.

220 In the text Dulaym ('Ammār) has evidently been substituted, probably by Sayf b. 'Umar, for 'Alī. The same substitution was made, as will be seen, in the poem quoted next below. The sense in both cases requires 'Alī. 'Ammār certainly was least inclined to make excuses for the murder of 'Uthmān. 'Alī rightly distanced himself from any involvement in it.

221 Ibn 'Asākir, *'Uthmān*, 552–3; Ibn Bakr, *Tamhīd*, 205–6.

222 Reading *fa-qūlā* for *qūlā*. The beginning of the piece is presumably missing.

For if you have cut off your noses through Ibn Arwā[223]
and have done a thing that was not kind,
Surely we shall – while you are a clique in distress,
sustaining a matter of hatred and blood revenge –
Observe you on every day and night with a glance that guides
to what is inside the hearts,
Until we see what delights the eye and what will quench the
burning thirst.
They say 'Alī[224] clung to the recesses of his house, yet what
he did was not kind;
For his place was no hidden matter, nor was he unaware of
what had passed.
If he had said: 'Desist from him', they would have sheathed
their swords and turned away with lasting grief in their breasts.
But he closed his eyes, his path was their path, and
iniquity is the most evil path.
So every one has a debt of guilt to us, which we shall
count, and 'Alī's guilt for him is no small one.[225]

'Alī's victory at Baṣra spurred Mu'āwiya to action. He had no illusion about 'Alī's determination to remove him from his governorship and was equally determined to hold on to what he, having succeeded his brother Yazīd, considered Sufyanid hereditary property. 'Alī's presence in Iraq and Qays b. Sa'd's precarious control of Egypt exposed him to potential attack from two fronts. Mu'āwiya stepped up his propaganda, charging 'Alī with the murder of 'Uthmān and wrote the governor of Egypt a letter in the hope of drawing him, by threats and promises, to his side.[226] He accused him of having been one of the instigators of the rebellion and demanded that he repent 'if repentance from killing a believer is of any avail'. As for his master, Mu'āwiya had ascertained that he was the one

[223] Arwā is 'Uthmān's (and al-Walīd's) mother.

[224] Here, too, and in the final line 'Dulaym' has been substituted for "Alī', who is obviously intended.

[225] Ibn Bakr, *Tamhīd*, 206–7. A shorter version of this poem was quoted by al-Jāḥiẓ and attributed by him to Yaḥyā b. al-Ḥakam, the younger brother of Marwān (*ibid.*, 179; for *Abū Marwān* read *Akhū Marwān*). In this version "Alī' is correctly retained in place of 'Dulaym', and "Amr' and 'al-Dhamīm' are, certainly erroneously, replaced by 'Ṭalḥa' and 'al-Zubayr', which spoils the metre. The attribution to Yaḥyā b. al-Ḥakam is no doubt mistaken. Yaḥyā was at this time quite young, and his known poetry dates from a later period. He probably accompanied his brother Marwān to Baṣra and participated in the battle of the Camel (Ṭabarī, I, 3219; report by Sayf, who also mentions 'Abd al-Raḥmān b. al-Ḥakam as present). It is thus out of the question that he could have accused Ṭalḥa and al-Zubayr. Being closely associated with his brother, it is equally unlikely that he would have denounced 'Amr b. al-'Āṣ and Muḥammad b. Abī Bakr with whom Marwān had no serious quarrel since they, unlike 'Alī, were not in possession of 'our property'.

[226] Sahl b. Sa'd states in his account that Mu'āwiya wrote to Qays when 'Alī was in Kūfa (Ṭabarī, I, 3238). This is evidently too late to allow sufficient time for the developments before his replacement by Muḥammad b. Abī Bakr.

who enticed the people to revolt against ʿUthmān and induced them to kill him. None of the great of Qays' people were indeed innocent of ʿUthmān's blood. If Qays, however, could get himself around to joining the demand for revenge for ʿUthmān's blood and would follow Muʿāwiya, the reign of the two Iraqs (*al-ʿIrāqayn*, Kūfa and Baṣra) would be his when Muʿāwiya won and as long as he lived, and the rule of the Ḥijāz would belong to one of his kinsmen of Qays' choice.

Qays b. Saʿd was not ready to provoke a Syrian attack on Egypt and answered Muʿāwiya's deceit with his own. He politely distanced himself from having had any part in the murder of ʿUthmān, denied having knowledge of his master's involvement, and claimed that his clan had been the first to stand up for the caliph. Muʿāwiya's proposal that he follow him and the reward offered by him were a matter to be considered carefully. In the meantime he promised not to attack him or cause him trouble until further consideration.

Muʿāwiya realized that Qays was stalling and resorted again to threat. The likes of himself, he wrote bluntly, could not be cajoled by deceit, since the superior number of men was with him and the reins of the horses in his hand. By now Muʿāwiya was evidently under sufficient pressure from the east for Qays to answer equally bluntly. Was Muʿāwiya deluded enough to think that he could buy him so that he would forsake the one most worthy to rule, the most truthful and soundest in guidance, and the closest to the Messenger of God, in order to obey the one furthest from legitimate rule, the most perfidious and errant, and the one most remote from God and His Messenger?

Muʿāwiya gave up hope of winning over Qays b. Saʿd.[227] He now forged a letter from Qays to himself in which ʿAlī's governor declared his obedience to Muʿāwiya and his whole-hearted support of the fight in revenge for the wronged imam of right guidance and publicized it among his commanders. ʿAlī, informed by his spies, was upset and incredulous and summoned his sons and his nephew ʿAbd Allāh b. Jaʿfar for consultation. ʿAbd Allāh advised him to depose Qays, but ʿAlī countered that he could not believe the story. Then a letter arrived from the governor explaining his practical arrangements with the ʿUthmāniyya rebels who were gathered in Kharbitā. ʿAbd Allāh saw his suspicions confirmed and suggested that ʿAlī order Qays to fight the rebels. When ʿAlī did so, the governor wrote back pointing out the folly of attacking peaceful people who would then make common cause with the enemy. ʿAbd Allāh b. Jaʿfar now counselled ʿAlī to dismiss Qays and to send in his place Muḥammad b. Abī Bakr, ʿAbd Allāh's uterine brother, who would

[227] *Ibid.*, 3238–41; Balādhurī, *Ansāb*, II, 390–1.

take care of these people. Qays, he had learned, was saying that any reign that required killing his kinsman Maslama b. Mukhallad was an evil one. 'Alī now deposed Qays and sent the son of Abū Bakr.[228] The letter of appointment was written by 'Ubayd Allāh b. Abī Rāfi' on 1 Ramaḍān 36/21 February 657.[229] It was to prove a poor decision.

Muḥammad b. Abī Bakr seems to have had no trouble in reaching Egypt passing through territory of Mu'āwiya. Qays questioned him as to whether someone had influenced the Commander of the Faithful against him, but Ibn Abī Bakr denied this and assured him that he was welcome to stay in Egypt.[230] Qays was upset, however, and left for Medina. There Ḥassān b. Thābit came to see him. Ḥassān had earlier, as noted, joined Mu'āwiya in Damascus together with Ka'b b. Mālik and al-Nu'mān b. Bashīr, and the two Anṣārī poets had there composed their lengthy poems reproaching the Medinans for their failure to defend 'Uthmān and threatening them with revenge. They had refused, however, to put any blame on 'Alī. As they came more and more under Syrian pressure to join the chorus condemning the Prophet's cousin, Ḥassān is reported to have added to one of his poems the line:

> Would that the birds informed me
> what was the matter between 'Alī and Ibn 'Affān![231]

It may have been this pressure that induced Ḥassān, who remained 'Uthmanid, to leave Mu'āwiya and return to his home town. He insinuated to Qays b. Sa'd that 'Alī had ungratefully deposed him after he, Qays, had incurred permanent guilt by killing 'Uthmān. Qays showed him the door in anger and joined 'Alī's governor Sahl b. Ḥunayf as he was setting out to join 'Alī for the battle of Ṣiffīn.[232] When Sahl left Medina, 'Alī entrusted Qutham b. al-'Abbās with the governorship of the town in addition to that of Mekka.[233]

[228] Ṭabarī, I, 3243–5. The parallel report of al-Zuhrī (*ibid.*, 3241–2) is less reliable. Al-Zuhrī erroneously describes 'Alī as first sending al-Ashtar to replace Qays. The mission of al-Ashtar was later, after the battle of Ṣiffīn. [229] *Ibid.*, 3247.

[230] Qays b. Sa'd was married to Qurayba bt Abī Quḥāfa, paternal aunt of Muḥammad b. Abī Bakr (Thaqafī, *Ghārāt*, 219–20).

[231] According to Ibn 'Abd al-Barr, quoted by Ibn al-Athīr (*Kāmil*, III, 151), the line was added by the Syrians. (Ḥassān, *Dīwān*, II, 92).

[232] Ṭabarī, I, 3245; Balādhurī, *Ansāb*, II, 392. Al-Zuhrī, 'Awāna and Ṣāliḥ b. Kaysān narrated that Qays was frightened into leaving Medina and joining 'Alī by threats to his life from Marwān and al-Aswad b. Abi l-Bakhtarī and that Mu'āwiya took Marwān and al-Aswad to task for strengthening the cause of 'Alī through such a formidable opponent (Ṭabarī, I, 3245–6; Balādhurī, *Ansāb*, II, 300–1). Caetani accepted this version and concluded that Medina, just a few months after 'Alī's departure, was in fact dominated by the partisans of 'Uthmān and Mu'āwiya (*Annali*, IX, 325–6). In reality Marwān was in Syria at the time. There is no reason to doubt that Medina was solidly behind 'Alī.

[233] Balādhurī, *Ansāb*, II, 300. Sahl b. Ḥunayf had written to 'Alī that some people were joining Mu'āwiya, and asked him for permission to join him. 'Alī gave him permission. 'Alī's letter to him is quoted in *ibid.*, 157.

After his arrival in Kūfa 'Alī had appointed al-Ashtar governor of Mossul, Naṣībīn, Dārā, Sinjār, Hīt, 'Ānāt and whatever he would be able to conquer of Upper Mesopotamia (al-Jazīra). The western towns of the province, Ḥarrān, al-Raqqa, Edessa and Qarqīsiyā were firmly under the control of Mu'āwiya and were sheltering numerous 'Uthmanid refugees from Baṣra and Kūfa. In al-Raqqa, where al-Walīd b. 'Uqba had chosen his residence, Simāk b. Makhrama of the Banū 'Amr b. Asad, a refugee from Kūfa backed by seven hundred of his tribesmen, was in charge.[234] Mu'āwiya first sent al-Ḍaḥḥāk b. Qays al-Fihrī to meet the threat of al-Ashtar. As the latter advanced on Ḥarrān, al-Ḍaḥḥāk joined forces with Simāk, and they met al-Ashtar at Marj Marīnā between Ḥarrān and al-Raqqa. They fought until evening, and during the night al-Ḍaḥḥāk retreated to fortified Ḥarrān. Al-Ashtar pursued the Syrians, but they would not do battle with him. Mu'āwiya now sent 'Abd al-Raḥmān b. Khālid b. al-Walīd with a cavalry troop. Al-Ashtar departed and, finding al-Raqqa and Qarqīsiyā also fortified, returned to his territory.[235]

Also soon after his arrival in Kūfa, 'Alī asked Jarīr b. 'Abd Allāh al-Bajalī and al-Ash'ath b. Qays al-Kindī, 'Uthmān's governors of Hamadān and Ādharbayjān respectively, to pledge allegiance and recalled them. Both were distinguished leaders, and there was some uncertainty as to whether they would do homage to 'Alī. Jarīr complied, however, immediately. Al-Ash'ath, whose daughter was married to 'Uthmān's eldest son, 'Amr, resented 'Alī's demand for an accounting of the treasury of Ādharbayjān and is said to have thought of joining Mu'āwiya, but was persuaded by his people to stay in Kūfa.[236] Several Kufan clans of Kinda, however, were 'Uthmanid and left for Edessa (al-Ruhā) after 'Alī came to Kūfa.[237]

When 'Alī was looking for a suitable envoy to Mu'āwiya, Jarīr offered

[234] Minqarī, *Waq'at Ṣiffīn*, 146. Al-Balādhurī also mentions several 'Uthmanid refugees of Ju'fī (*Ansāb*, II, 297–8).

[235] Minqarī, *Waq'at Ṣiffīn*, 12–14. The poetry of Ayman b. Khuraym al-Asadī quoted there in which Mu'āwiya is addressed as Amīr al-Mu'minīn dates evidently from at least a year later. It mentions repeated raids by al-Ashtar but seems to imply that he was still alive.

[236] Minqarī, *Waq'at Ṣiffīn*, 21; Balādhurī, *Ansāb*, II, 296. 'Uthmān is said to have allowed al-Ash'ath b. Qays to take 100,000 dirhams annually from the land tax of Ādharbayjān for his personal use (Ṭabarī, I, 3440; see below, p. 276).

[237] According to Ibn al-Kalbī (*Nasab Ma'add wa l-Yaman al-Kabīr*, ed. Nājī Ḥasan (Beirut, 1988), I, 149–50), the Banu l-Arqam b. al-Nu'mān b. 'Amr b. Wahb, the Banū Khamar b. 'Amr b. Wahb, some of the Banu l-Ḥārith b. 'Adī b. Rabī'a and the Banu l-Akhram of Ḥujr b. Wahb left Kūfa when 'Alī arrived there, since they would not stay in a country where 'Uthmān was being reviled. The Banu l-Arqam had backed al-Ash'ath b. Qays during the *ridda* against the Muslims (see M. Lecker, 'Kinda on the Eve of Islam and during the *Ridda*', *Journal of the Royal Asiatic Society* (1994), 333–56, at 345). Mu'āwiya, according to Ibn al-Kalbī, settled these refugees in Mesopotamia, at first in Naṣībīn and then in Edessa, since he feared that they would corrupt the Syrians. They fought for him at Ṣiffīn.

himself, since he had good personal relations with the Umayyad. He suggested that he would be able to obtain Muʿāwiya's allegiance to ʿAlī on the basis that Muʿāwiya would be one of his governors and expressed the expectation that the Syrians, who mostly belonged to his people, would follow his call for obedience to ʿAlī. Al-Ashtar warned ʿAlī not to send Jarīr to the Syrians since he inclined to their side. ʿAlī decided, however, to send him with instructions to convey his letter to Muʿāwiya and to ask him only for his oath of allegiance, while giving him to understand that ʿAlī would not accept him as a governor.[238]

In his letter ʿAlī told Muʿāwiya that the public pledge of allegiance in Medina was binding on him in Syria. It had been given to ʿAlī by the same people who had pledged allegiance to Abū Bakr, ʿUmar and ʿUthmān, and when those present made a choice, it could not be rejected by those absent. The right of consultation (*shūrā*) belonged to the Muhājirūn and Anṣār. When they agreed on an imam, their choice was pleasing to God, and anyone opposing him could be fought to make him follow the path of the faithful. In attributing a right of consultation to the Anṣār, ʿAlī was in a way returning to the practice of Muḥammad, who had treated the Muhājirūn and the Anṣār in Medina on a par.

ʿAlī went on to state that Ṭalḥa and al-Zubayr had broken their pledge to him. This was equal to refusing it, and he had legitimately fought them. Muʿāwiya must now join the Muslims and pledge allegiance, otherwise ʿAlī would fight him. He, Muʿāwiya, had been talking a lot about the killers of ʿUthmān. He should defer them to the judgment of ʿAlī who would deal with him and them in accordance with the Book of God. In reality, ʿAlī charged, Muʿāwiya was playing a childish game of deceit. If he looked with his sound mind rather than his passion, he would find ʿAlī the one most innocent of the blood of ʿUthmān among Quraysh. ʿAlī reminded the Umayyad that he was a *ṭalīq*, one of those pardoned and set free by Muḥammad at the time of the conquest of Mekka, not a Muhājir, and thus was excluded from any *shūrā*.[239]

Jarīr handed ʿAlī's letter to Muʿāwiya and in a speech appealed to him and the Syrians to join the Muslims everywhere in pledging allegiance to ʿAlī. He told Muʿāwiya that it would not be proper for him to claim that

[238] Minqarī, *Waqʿat Ṣiffīn*, 27–8.

[239] *Ibid.*, 29–30. The term *ṭalīq*, freed captive, was generally applied to the Qurayshite former enemies of Islam who converted under duress at the time of the Muslim conquest of Mekka. They did not acquire the status of Muhājirūn even if they emigrated to Medina, since Muḥammad declared the gate of *hijra* closed after the conquest. Pro-Umayyad tradition tried to magnify Muʿāwiya's association with Muḥammad by describing him as one of the Prophet's scribes. His function as such was, however, hardly significant. No specific occasion on which he was called upon to write for Muḥammad is recorded.

'Uthmān had appointed him and had not deposed him, for God did not give a past ruler precedence over the present one.[240]

Mu'āwiya's response was dilatory: 'Let us consider, and I will explore the view of the people of Syria.' He was, no doubt, already determined to reject 'Alī's demand, but wanted to gain time to secure maximum support for his move and to mobilize his forces. At the next prayer in the mosque he addressed the people, appealing to their local Syrian patriotism. God had made the Holy Land the home of the prophets and His righteous worshippers; He had made the people of Syria dwell there because by His foreknowledge He knew their obedience and their sincerity to His vicegerents and executors of His commandment; He had made them a model of order for the Community, signposts on the path of everything good, through whom God restrained the disloyal and united the faithful. 'O God,' he prayed, 'support us against a people who awaken our sleepers, frighten those of us who feel safe, want to shed our blood, and to make our path insecure. God knows that we did not want to chastize them, nor to rip apart their screens, nor to make them tread on slippery ground. God, the Praiseworthy, has, however, dressed us in a cloth of nobility which we shall not take off voluntarily as long as an echo resounds, dew drops, and right guidance is recognized. Only rebelliousness and envy has induced them to oppose us, thus we ask God for help against them.' Then came the climax of his oration: 'You know that I am the vicegerent unto you of the Commander of the Faithful 'Umar b. al-Khaṭṭāb, that I am the vicegerent of the Commander of the Faithful 'Uthmān b. 'Affān, that I have never let anyone of you stand in a position of disgrace, and that I am the next-of-kin (*walī*) of 'Uthmān, who has been killed wrongfully. Yet God says: "If anyone is killed wrongfully, We give his next-of-kin authority, but let him not be extravagant in killing, surely he is being helped" [Qur'ān XVII 33]. I would like you to let me know what is in your hearts about the murder of 'Uthmān.' The people of Syria, or rather those present, all rose and responded, calling for revenge for the blood of 'Uthmān, and pledged allegiance to him on that basis.[241]

Mu'āwiya was satisfied for the moment. He was confident that if he continued whipping up their frenzy of patriotic self-righteousness, they would not pay much attention to God's commandment not to be extravagant in killing and would be ready to slaughter anyone charged with complicity by their commanders, whose most obedient servants, as he had assured them, they were. But he was not yet ready to hand Jarīr his answer. There never could have been any doubt that his loyalist followers

[240] *Ibid.*, 28–31. [241] *Ibid.*, 31–2.

in Damascus would back him to the hilt.[242] To be reassured he needed broader support.

Muʿāwiya immediately wrote to ʿAmr b. al-ʿAṣ. It was time to bury al-Walīd's silly private vendetta against someone who could be so useful for the Umayyad cause as the wily man of Quraysh, Muʿāwiya's unacknowledged bastard brother. Matters of high politics were now at stake where the ends justify the means. Muʿāwiya had just declared himself the next-of-kin of his somewhat remote cousin. ʿUthmān's brother must now stand back and dance to his, Muʿāwiya's, whistle. Muʿāwiya wrote to ʿAmr: 'You have heard what happened in the affair of ʿAlī, Ṭalḥa, and al-Zubayr. Now Marwān b. al-Ḥakam together with the rejectionists (*rāfiḍa*) of the people of Baṣra has joined us, and Jarīr b. ʿAbd Allāh has arrived for the pledge of allegiance to ʿAlī. I reserve myself for you until you arrive. Come here that I may discuss a matter with you.'[243]

ʿAmr was pleased to see that his versified advice had, as he expected, impressed Muʿāwiya, and followed the invitation. He was sure that he could now strike a bargain which would satisfy his own wishes. It would be Egypt for life or no deal. Muʿāwiya is said to have been somewhat reluctant, but his brother ʿUtba, one of the rejectionists now with him, urged him to accept.[244] ʿAmr swore allegiance to Muʿāwiya on the basis that he would back the Umayyad in his fight against ʿAlī, while Muʿāwiya would help him regain Egypt and guarantee him lifetime possession. ʿAmr made sure that the agreement was made public. He was too experienced not to know that the private promises of men such as his new master were worth no more than the paper on which they might or might not be written. Closer scrutiny of the agreement would reveal that Muʿāwiya's gain was not so moderate as might appear at first sight. For Muʿāwiya would not be able to keep his side of the bargain unless he not only kept Syria but was also in a position to dispose over Egypt. Implicitly ʿAmr had committed himself to secure, in his own interest, the

242 This is the impression created by most of the historical sources. There is, however, a report that, if Caetani's interpretation of it (*Annali*, X, 330) were correct, would imply that Muʿāwiya was not so popular in Damascus at the time as is commonly assumed. According to Abu l-Faraj al-Iṣfahānī (*Aghānī*, X, 151), Ziyād b. al-Ashhab al-Jaʿdī, a noble chief of ʿĀmir b. Ṣaʿṣaʿa settled in Damascus, visited ʿAlī and sought to bring about a settlement of the conflict between the caliph and Muʿāwiya on the basis that ʿAlī appoint him governor of Syria. Caetani understood the ambiguous text to mean that Ziyād asked to be appointed governor of Syria. In order to make such a proposal, Ziyād would have to have been confident that he could muster enough support in Damascus to force the Umayyad out of office. Most likely, however, Ziyād rather proposed to bring about a reconciliation between ʿAlī and Muʿāwiya on the basis that ʿAlī reappoint Muʿāwiya governor of Syria. ʿAlī, in any case, declined the offer.

243 Minqarī, *Waqʿat Ṣiffīn*, 34. Similarly Balādhurī, *Ansāb*, II, 285 where the text has 'a group of the people of Baṣra of those who reject ʿAlī and his cause'.

244 Minqarī, *Waqʿat Ṣiffīn*, 39–40; Balādhurī, *Ansāb*, II, 288.

caliphate for Mu'āwiya. This was, however, not to be spelled out in the agreement. The time was not yet ripe to let the cat out of the bag, which might have frightened some of the pious neutrals into 'Alī's camp.

The pact which turned the primary accused in the murder of the wronged caliph overnight into the official public prosecutor intrigued contemporary observers and early historians.[245] They narrated lengthy stories about the circumstances; they described in detail, and supported with appropriate poetry, 'Amr's conversations first with his sons 'Abd Allāh and Muḥammad and then with Mu'āwiya in which 'Amr confessed, or boasted, to be selling his religion for worldly gain. Much of this is evident fiction.[246] Yet 'Amr, so keen an observer of the foibles of others, was, no doubt, fully aware of the rot in his own guts. Al-Walīd's accusation of blood guilt had given him a rude scare and a sense of himself 'riding over abysses'. Unlike 'Uthmān he would not repent, however, but rather accept his role as the slave of Umayya which al-Walīd had assigned to him. As such he now felt in the driver's seat again.

The alliance between Mu'āwiya and 'Amr b. al-'Āṣ constituted a formidable political force. The Umayyad needed 'Amr for more than his expertise in affairs of Egypt and his backing among the military there. In the nearly two decades of his governorship of Syria, Mu'āwiya had developed a taste for despotism of the Roman Byzantine type. While endowed with a natural instinct for power and domination, his judgement of human nature was, contrary to his reputation, limited and primitive. He had come to understand that in statecraft, whenever bribery or intimidation would not reduce an opponent, murder, open or secret, was

245 Of modern western historians, Wellhausen commented on the pact as follows: 'Die Rache für Uthman war der Titel, worauf Muavia sein Recht der Erbschaft gründete. In welchem Sinne er sie unternahm, erhellt daraus, dass er sich dazu mit Amr b. Aç verbündete, der am giftigsten gegen Uthman gehetzt hatte. Pietät war nicht sein Motiv' (*Das Arabische Reich*, 85).

246 Al-Madā'inī's informant for his lengthy account (Balādhurī, *Ansāb*, II, 284–9) was 'Īsā b. Yazīd al-Laythī al-Kinānī, i.e. Ibn Da'b, a Medinan historian active at the 'Abbasid court in Baghdad who was widely accused of gross forgery (see on him al-Khaṭīb al-Baghdādī, *Ta'rīkh Baghdād* (Cairo, 1931), XI, 148–52). Quoting another lengthy report by him about an exchange of letters and poetry between 'Amr b. al-'Āṣ and Ibn al-'Abbās at Ṣiffīn, the Syrian authority Hishām b. 'Ammār al-Dimashqī commented (to al-Balādhurī): 'This story belongs to what was forged by this Ibn Da'b of yours' (Balādhurī, *Ansāb*, II, 307–10). Concerning the present account the same Hishām used to observe: 'This is a story with forged poetry which has come to us from the direction of Iraq.' Presumably he considered Ibn Da'b as the forger here also. The account on 'Amr's reaction to Mu'āwiya's invitation which Naṣr b. Muzāḥim assembled from his informants 'Umar b. Sa'd and Muḥammad b. 'Ubayd Allāh (Minqarī, *Waq'at Ṣiffīn*, 34–44) contains some of the same poetry and may, at least partly, also go back to Ibn Da'b. In substance, however, the Syrian historians' judgement of 'Amr's conduct was no less devastating than the Iraqis'. See the account transmitted by Hishām b. 'Ammār on the authority of al-Walīd b. Muslim in Balādhurī, *Ansāb*, II, 282–3.

the most convenient and effective means. The adherence of the first caliphs to the early Islamic prohibition of shedding Muslim blood had so far prevented him from following his inclination. He was still gnashing his teeth at the thought of al-Ashtar and the other Kufan rebels whom ʿUthmān had exiled to him in Damascus and then had not allowed him to deal with in the traditional Roman way of handling rebels. This, he trusted, would be different now that so much blood had been shed among Muslims in the internal war unleashed by his cousin Marwān.

ʿAmr b. al-ʿĀṣ, although hardly more troubled by scruples, was more resourceful and subtle in his means. With his incisive grasp of human motivation and foibles, his general contempt for men, it was a pleasure for him to bring out and expose by guile and trickery their defects, hypocrisy and folly. He was a master of planning, and playing on, political scenarios and manoeuvres and of clever manipulation of the public with specious arguments appealing to their hidden aspirations and greed. Muʿāwiya needed him at a time when his grip on power was not yet secure. He needed him also, though not so keenly, for his practical battle experience and sure judgement of military strategy and tactics. Personally a coward and lacking military competence, Muʿāwiya had an instinctive distrust of his own capable and popular military leaders who might pose a threat to his power. He knew he could trust ʿAmr at this stage since ʿAlī would never make a deal with him at Muʿāwiya's expense.

Al-Walīd did not find it difficult to accept the compromise forced on him by Muʿāwiya's alliance with ʿAmr and to turn his vendetta now fully on ʿAlī. In the end, it was ʿAlī, not ʿAmr, who had been responsible for his flogging, and why worry now about who was most responsible for the dead man's blood? Al-Walīd understood what Muʿāwiya would want to hear now. He wrote to him:

> Muʿāwiya, the withers of the reign have been cut off,
> and you are today the lord of what is in your hand.
> A letter has come to you from ʿAlī in his handwriting;
> this is the moment of decision, choose peace with him or make war on him.
> If you intend to give an answer to his letter,
> ignominy to the one dictating and the one writing it!
> But if you intend to reject his letter –
> for you will inevitably take some course –
> Then drop the Yemenite clan (*al-ḥayy al-Yamānī*) a word
> through which you will obtain the matter you are seeking.
> Tell them: 'The Commander of the Faithful has been struck
> by some men who were backed by his kin,
> Sorts of people, among them killer and instigator,
> without offence committed, and another despoiling him.
> I have been Commander of Syria before among you,

sufficient for me and you is the duty that is obligatory!
So come, by the One who anchored Mount Thabīr in its place,
we shall ward off a sea whose high waves cannot be turned back.'
Say little and much, there is today for the calamity no master but you,
so speak out clearly: 'I am not one you will dupe.'
Never let the reign go, the matter is moving forward
and seek what looks forbidding for you to reach.
For 'Alī will not wipe off [from your record] a swindle
as long as drinkers shall swallow water;
Nor will he accept what he does not want, and this
is a calamity for which one day women will stand wailing.
So fight with him, if you fight, the war of a free mother's son
and if not, then make a peace in which his scorpions will not be crawling.[247]

Al-Walīd was urging Mu'āwiya above all to hold on to Syria which, now that the sovereign caliph was removed, belonged to him as his property. Mu'āwiya thus must reject 'Alī's demand for his pledge of allegiance and fight him with all his power. Just as an afterthought al-Walīd mentioned the possibility of a peace in which "Alī's scorpions would not come crawling'. He was alluding to a peace agreement giving Mu'āwiya full independence without any right of 'Alī to interfere. But al-Walīd made clear that he did not expect 'Alī to agree to such a peace. In order to gain the backing of the people Mu'āwiya must tell the Yemenites that 'Uthmān had been murdered and despoiled by his kinsman 'Alī.

By the Yemenites al-Walīd probably did not mean the Syrian Kalb, who were not yet considered part of them. They were, in any case, safely allied to Mu'āwiya through marriage ties and could be counted on to obey his orders. Al-Walīd was referring to the Yemenites in Ḥimṣ and northern Syria, Sakūn and Sakāsik of Kinda, Ḥimyar, and Hamdān, whose support was crucial but still uncertain. They had come under Mu'āwiya's rule only under 'Uthmān and were people proud of their Yemenite identity and their leading part in the conquest of Syria as well as in the campaigns to Anatolia against Byzantium. They had, moreover, close ties to their numerous tribal brothers in Kūfa. There Yemenites of Kinda, Hamdān and Madhḥij were the most vigorous supporters of 'Alī aside from Rabī'a, who were not represented in Syria. The Northern Arabs, Muḍar, had been mostly hostile towards 'Alī in Iraq or lukewarm, and Mu'āwiya had no need to be concerned about those in Syria.

'Amr's advice to Mu'āwiya now agreed with al-Walīd's. He counselled him to pin the blame for 'Uthmān's murder on 'Alī and to seek, by whatever means, the backing of Shuraḥbīl b. al-Simṭ al-Kindī, son of the

[247] Ibn 'Asākir, *'Uthmān*, 552; Minqarī, *Waq'at Ṣiffīn*, 53–4, where the sequence of lines differs substantially. The version of Ibn 'Asākir has been followed in the translation here, but in some instances the readings of al-Minqarī's text have been preferred.

conqueror of Ḥimṣ al-Simṭ b. al-Aswad. Shuraḥbīl was not only, in succession to his father, an influential notable in Ḥimṣ, but also one of the pious ascetics (*nussāk*) of the town. His father and he were the only men of his clan, the Banū Muʿāwiya of Kinda, who had not renounced Islam and refused to pay the alms-tax to Abū Bakr during the *ridda*[248] and he was widely respected in Syria also outside his home town.

There had been some incident between Shuraḥbīl and Jarīr b. ʿAbd Allāh at the time of the conquest of Iraq under Saʿd b. Abī Waqqāṣ. He would thus not easily be influenced by Jarīr, especially if he were given to understand that ʿAlī intended to appoint Jarīr, if the latter were successful in his mission, his deputy in Ḥimṣ. Shuraḥbīl was indeed, as he admitted to Muʿāwiya, endowed with a big head but weak intelligence[249] and ʿAmr was confident that he could be duped. He suggested to Muʿāwiya to put up a few of his confidants, including some Yemenites, who would impress on Shuraḥbīl their conviction that ʿAlī had killed ʿUthmān.

Muʿāwiya thus wrote to Shuraḥbīl: 'Jarīr b. ʿAbd Allāh has come to us from ʿAlī with a horrific matter, so come.' Shuraḥbīl first consulted the Yemenites of Ḥimṣ on how to respond and found them divided in their opinion. ʿAbd al-Raḥmān b. Ghanm al-Ashʿarī[250], a Companion and close associate of Muʿādh b. Jabal,[251] advised him that the matter of ʿUthmān had been presented to them with the charge that ʿAlī had killed him. If ʿAlī had indeed done so, still the Muhājirūn and Anṣār had pledged allegiance to him, and they were the judges over the people. But if ʿAlī had not killed him, why should Shuraḥbīl take Muʿāwiya's word for it and ruin himself and his people? If he did not want Jarīr to benefit, Shuraḥbīl should himself go to ʿAlī and pledge allegiance for Syria and his people. Shuraḥbīl, however, insisted on going to Muʿāwiyaḍ. ʿIyāḍ al-Thumālī, an ascetic, sent him a poem also urging him to ignore the deception of Muʿāwiya, who hoped to set himself up as an imam and king over them and to expend the blood of the Banū Qaḥṭān (Yemenites) for the benefit of Lu'ayy b. Ghālib (Quraysh); rather, he should pledge allegiance to ʿAlī, the best man of Hāshim, 'who had a covenant incumbent on the neck of the people like the covenant of Abū Ḥafṣ (ʿUmar) and Abū Bakr'.[252]

When Shuraḥbīl arrived in Damascus, he was given a splendid welcome and honoured. Then Muʿāwiya received him and said: 'Shuraḥbīl,

[248] Ibn Manẓūr, *Mukhtaṣar*, X, 286–7. [249] See the anecdote in *ibid.*, 288.

[250] Minqarī, *Waqʿat Ṣiffīn*, 45, erroneously has al-Azdī. On him see Ibn Manẓūr, *Mukhtaṣar*, XV, 7–10.

[251] Muʿādh b. Jabal of Khazraj was governor in Yemen under Muḥammad and took a major part in the conquest of Syria. He was briefly governor of Ḥimṣ after the death of Abū ʿUbayda and died in the plague of ʿAmwās. [252] Minqarī, *Waqʿat Ṣiffīn*, 44–6.

Jarīr b. ʿAbd Allāh summons us to swear allegiance to ʿAlī, and ʿAlī would be the best man if he had not killed ʿUthmān b. ʿAffān. I have reserved my opinion for you. I am merely a man of the people of Syria, I am pleased with whatever they are pleased with, and loathe whatever they loathe.' Shuraḥbīl answered: 'Let me go out and consider the matter.' As he went out, the men who had been set up to speak to him met him, and every one assured him that ʿAlī had killed ʿUthmān. He returned in anger to Muʿāwiya and told him: 'Muʿāwiya, the people will accept nothing but that ʿAlī has killed ʿUthmān. By God, if you pledge allegiance to him, we shall drive you out of Syria or kill you.' Muʿāwiya did not mind the boastful threat and meekly repeated: 'I am merely one of the people of Syria.' Shuraḥbīl: 'Send this man back then to his master.'

Shuraḥbīl then went to see Ḥuṣayn b. Numayr, chief of Sakūn, and asked him to send for Jarīr. When the latter arrived he took him to task for trying to pull the wool over their eyes and singing the praise of ʿAlī who was the murderer of ʿUthmān. Jarīr defended himself and suggested that Shuraḥbīl had fallen victim to greed of worldly power and to a grudge he had held against him from the time of Saʿd b. Abī Waqqāṣ. Muʿāwiya learned of their meeting and sent for Jarīr to restrain him from debating with his subjects in private. Jarīr, however, tried once more to influence Shuraḥbīl by sending him a poem with an appeal to his good sense: the accusations against ʿAlī were nothing but falsehood and slander; ʿAlī was the sole legatee of the Messenger of God among his people and the knight closest to him about whom proverbs were coined.

Jarīr's letter threw Shuraḥbīl into doubt, and Muʿāwiya had to send his confidants once more with false testimony and fake documentary evidence to impress on him the monstrosity of ʿAlī's crime. When they had brought him around and whetted his determination, one of the ascetics of Ḥimṣ of Bāriq, his sister's son, made a last desperate attempt to influence him. He lampooned him as a feeble-minded Yemenite duped and bribed by the son of Hind, whose arrow would certainly kill him in the end. Shuraḥbīl was convinced now that this man was the envoy of the devil and that God was trying his heart. He swore that he would drive out the author of this poetry by force unless he ran away from him in time. The man fled to Kūfa from where he had originally come and pledged allegiance to ʿAlī.

Muʿāwiya realized that he must keep Shuraḥbīl occupied lest he begin reflecting again and asked him to tour the towns of Syria and tell the people the truth about ʿAlī which he had ascertained. Shuraḥbīl started in Ḥimṣ, where he preached: 'O people, surely ʿAlī has killed ʿUthmān b. ʿAffān. Then some people rose up in anger on his behalf, but he killed them. He defeated all and overcame the land, so that only Syria is left.

Now he is putting his sword on his shoulder, ready to wade with it through the floods of death until he will come to you, unless God intervenes with some event. We do not find anyone stronger to fight him than Muʿāwiya, so strive and rise up.' The people responded to his summons, except for some pious ascetics who stood up and said: 'Our houses will be our tombs, and our mosques. You know best what you think.' As he continued to make his round through the towns of Syria and the people everywhere accepted his message, the poet al-Najāshī, Qays b. ʿAmr of the Banu l-Ḥārith b. Kaʿb, sent him a poem. Al-Najāshī was an old friend of his and now a poetical spokesman for ʿAlī; later, some time after Ṣiffīn, ʿAlī punished him for wine-drinking, the common vice of poets. Al-Najāshī suggested to Shuraḥbīl once more that he had deviated not for religion's sake, but for hatred of Jarīr and a rancour which had crept between Saʿd (b. Abī Waqqāṣ) and Jarīr; Shuraḥbīl had then been a poor helper when Bajīla had reason to censure Quraysh; now he was misjudging another matter on the basis of hearsay which no one with a sound mind could accept. The poem came too late to change Shuraḥbīl's mind.[253]

Soon after Jarīr's arrival in Damascus Muʿāwiya also received a poem by Kaʿb b. Juʿayl, a bard of Taghlib. The Banū Taghlib were mostly living in the northern Mesopotamian borderland of Syria and Iraq, and Muʿāwiya was, no doubt, heartened by this backing, although it presumably did not represent the opinion of all of Taghlib. ʿAlī had, in fact, strong backing at Ṣiffīn from part of Taghlib, probably from Baṣra, who were fighting under the command of Kurdūs b. Hāni' al-Bakrī.[254] Ibn Juʿayl opened his poem thus:

> I see Syria loathing the reign of Iraq,
> and the people of Iraq loathing her.
> Each one hates his partner
> and considers all that as religion.
> When they throw blame at us we throw at them
> and we lend them the like of what they lend us.
> They said: ʿAlī is an imam for us,
> so we said: We are pleased with Ibn Hind, we are pleased.
> They said: We think you should obey him,
> but we said: Surely, we do not think we should obey.
> Before we do that the tragacanth must be stripped of its leaves,

[253] *Ibid.*, 46–51.

[254] See the poetry in *ibid.*, 486–7. Kurdūs b. Hāni' was the son of Hāni' b. Qabīṣa, the leader of all of Rabīʿa in the battle of Dhū Qār (see W. Caskel, *Ǧamharat an-nasab: Das genealogische Werk des Hišām ibn Muḥammad al-Kalbī* (Leiden, 1966), II, indexes s.v. Hāni' b. Qabīṣa). Evidently for this reason Kurdūs was called by Khālid b. al-Muʿammar al-Sadūsī the son of the chief of Taghlib (*Kurdūs ibn Sayyid Taghlib*) (Minqarī, *Waqʿat Ṣiffīn*, 487.) The statement of H. Kindermann (*EI* suppl. art. 'Taghlib') that Taghlib fought at Ṣiffīn for Muʿāwiya must be modified.

there will be strikes and thrusts to settle matters.
Each one is pleased with what he has,
seeing the lean thing in his hand as fat.

Ibn Ju'ayl went on to lampoon 'Alī who, once blameless, was today sheltering the offenders and lifting the *lex talionis* from the murderers. When questioned about his involvement in the crime, he obfuscated his answer claiming that he was neither pleased nor angry; neither was he of those who forbade nor of those who ordered. Yet inevitably he must belong to one or the other side.[255]

Although matters in Syria had clearly gone well for Mu'āwiya, with the war-drum now being beaten throughout his land and cries of revenge for the wronged caliph resounding everywhere, he was not yet ready to send 'Alī's envoy home empty-handed. He went to see Jarīr in his lodgings and told him that he had come upon an idea. His proposal was that 'Alī concede Syria and Egypt and their revenue to him and that he agree not to impose on him allegiance to anyone after 'Alī's death. On these conditions Mu'āwiya was prepared to recognize his reign and to address him as caliph. Jarīr agreed to convey Mu'āwiya's message to 'Alī together with a letter of his own.[256]

Mu'āwiya's personal visit to Jarīr was motivated by the need to keep his initiative strictly secret. Had his offer to 'Alī become known to the public, the fraudulence of his claim of revenge for the murdered caliph would have become patent to all and the carefully staged mobilization campaign would have ground to a halt. The major historical accounts know nothing about Mu'āwiya's excursion into secret diplomacy. It is confirmed, however, by a poem by al-Walīd b. 'Uqba who was evidently close enough to the top to get wind of what was going on.[257] Al-Walīd was clearly appalled. It was not so much that his own vendetta, which had already suffered the blow of the deal with 'Amr, was again to be sacrificed to some higher interests of state. He himself had hinted at an acceptable peace settlement under which 'Alī would have to recognize the complete independence of Umayyad Syria. Yet now Mu'āwiya was conditionally offering to recognize 'Alī's overlordship. Al-Walīd still saw 'Alī's scorpions creeping, but now he described them as snakes. He wrote:

Mu'āwiya, surely Syria is your Syria, so hold on
to your Syria, do not let the snakes come in to you,
And protect her with legions and lances,

255 Minqarī, *Waq'at Ṣiffīn*, 56–7; al-Mubarrad, *al-Kāmil*, ed. W. Wright (Leipzig, 1974–92), I, 184–5, where the lines of reproach to 'Alī are omitted. In line five the version of al-Mubarrad seems clearly preferable and has been adopted.

256 Minqarī, *Waq'at Ṣiffīn*, 52; (pseudo-)Ibn Qutayba, *al-Imāma wa l-siyāsa*, ed. Muḥammad Maḥmūd al-Rāfi'ī (Cairo, 1322/1904), I, 157.

257 Al-Walīd b. 'Uqba is usually described as staying in al-Raqqa before the battle of Ṣiffīn. It seems likely, however, that he spent at least much of the time at the court in Damascus.

do not be faint with dried up forearms.
Surely, ʿAlī is watching what you will answer him,
so present him with a war that will turn the forelocks hoary.
If not, make peace, certainly in peace there is repose
for him who does not desire war, so choose, Muʿāwiya!
Surely, a letter which you, Ibn Ḥarb, have written
out of greed will drive disasters towards you.
You have asked ʿAlī in it what you will not obtain,
and if you obtained it, it would last only some nights.
You would face from him that after which
there is no survival, so do not fill yourself with hopes.
Will you strike the like of ʿAlī with a ruse?
Sufficient is what you have tasted before.
Were his claws once to cling to you, he would
deal out to you, Ibn Hind, what you have been dealing out.[258]

Al-Walīd's reaction suggests that the overture was not entirely a delaying tactic. As such Muʿāwiya later no doubt would have liked it to be seen by posterity. His hopes that ʿAlī would accept cannot have been high. Al-Walīd's pointed reference to the greed out of which Muʿāwiya's proposal was born may hint at more than the obvious. Muʿāwiya's demand for Egypt and its revenue was evidently not made in order to fulfil his commitment to ʿAmr b. al-ʿĀṣ. If ʿAlī were to hand over Egypt voluntarily to him and make peace, ʿAmr's services would no longer be needed, and the slave could go. ʿAmr thus can hardly have been behind the proposal, and, if aware of it, must have been keenly conscious of his impotence.

As al-Walīd expected, ʿAlī rejected Muʿāwiya's proposal. He wrote to Jarīr that Muʿāwiya was seeking independence and was playing for time in order to test the mood of the Syrians. Al-Mughīra b. Shuʿba in Medina had suggested to him, ʿAlī, that he appoint Muʿāwiya over Syria, but he had refused to do so. God should not see him taking the deceivers for helpers. Either Muʿāwiya would unconditionally pledge allegiance or Jarīr should return home.[259]

Jarīr still stayed on with Muʿāwiya, and suspicions were spreading in Kūfa that he was disloyal. ʿAlī finally sent him word to insist on an immediate decision in the choice between war and peace. Jarīr showed Muʿāwiya ʿAlī's letter, and the Umayyad promised his decision at the next council session (*majlis*). Having reassured himself of the support of the Syrians, he told Jarīr in public session: 'Return to your master, Jarīr', and handed him his declaration of war. He wrote:

[258] Minqarī, *Waqʿat Ṣiffīn*, 52–3. The last line is perhaps an addition. It is lacking in the version in Ibn Abi l-Ḥadīd, *Sharḥ*, III, 84–5.
[259] Minqarī, *Waqʿat Ṣiffīn*, 52; (pseudo-)Ibn Qutayba, *Imāma*, I, 157–8.

By my life, if the people were pledging allegiance to you and you were innocent of the blood of ʿUthmān you would be like Abū Bakr, ʿUmar, and ʿUthmān, may God be pleased with them all. But you incited the Muhājirūn against ʿUthmān and induced the Anṣār to desert him, so the ignorant obeyed you and the feeble became strong through you. The people of Syria accept nothing but to fight you until you surrender to them the killers of ʿUthmān. If you do, there will be a *shūrā* among the Muslims. The people of Ḥijāz used to be the judges over the people holding the right in their hands, but since they abandoned i t, the right is now in the hands of the people of Syria. By my life, your argument against me is not like your argument against Ṭalḥa and al-Zubayr since they pledged allegiance to you and I have not pledged allegiance to you. Nor is your argument against the Syrians like your argument against the Basrans, since the Basrans [at first] obeyed you, and the Syrians did not. As for your nobility in Islam and your close kinship with the Messenger of God and your place among Quraysh, I do not deny them.

Muʿāwiya then appended the poem of Kaʿb b. Juʿayl to his letter.[260]

Unlike Muʿāwiya's secret letter, this one bore the handwriting of his adviser ʿAmr. Aimed primarily at the ears of his Syrian followers, it was a masterpiece of war propaganda. It was they who insisted on fighting ʿAlī; Muʿāwiya was just one of them. Appealing to their sense of chauvinist patriotism, Muʿāwiya assured them that only they among the Muslims were now left on the moral high ground, since all others, including the supporters of the Mother of the Faithful, had sullied their honour by pledging allegiance to the instigator of ʿUthmān's murder; after their victory, there would be a *shūrā* about the caliphate, but it would be their *shūrā*, not that of the people of Ḥijāz with their guilty consciences. The Syrians, hearing themselves raised in their Islamic ranking above all the venerable old Companions of the Prophet, must have been almost stunned by the prospect.

Muʿāwiya himself was convinced that he could live with such a *shūrā*. The result would be a foregone conclusion, and most likely it would not even be needed. For in general Muʿāwiya was no friend of the principle of *shūrā* when one of his perceived vital interests was at stake. Later during his reign he would impose his dissolute son Yazīd as the successor without even a notional Syrian *shūrā*. The letter made clear that Muʿāwiya had now taken up ʿAmr b. al-ʿĀṣ' earlier suggestion and, in pursuit of it, was already aspiring to the caliphate.[261]

ʿAlī answered Muʿāwiya's letter, refuting his assertions point for point: with respect to Muʿāwiya's claim that ʿAlī's wrong-doing (*khaṭīʾa*)

[260] (Pseudo-)Ibn Qutayba, *Imāma*, I, 166–7; Mubarrad, *Kāmil*, I, 184, where the crucial sentence about the Syrians now being entitled to the *shūrā* instead of the people of Ḥijāz is missing (see Minqarī, *Waqʿat Ṣiffīn*, 56, n. 2). That it was part of Muʿāwiya's letter is evident from ʿAlī's answer.

[261] Contrary to the view of Caetani and Levi della Vida (*Annali*, IX, 256).

towards 'Uthmān had spoiled Mu'āwiya's pledge of allegiance for him, he affirmed that he was only one of the Muhājirūn acting as they had done; he had not killed 'Uthmān, so the *lex talionis* did not apply to him; Mu'āwiya's raving lies about 'Alī in the matter of 'Uthmān were based on neither eyewitness knowledge nor certain information; regarding Mu'āwiya's claim that the Syrians were now the judges over the people of Ḥijāz, 'Alī challenged him to name a single member of Quraysh in Syria who could be accepted in a *shūrā* or was eligible for the caliphate – if he were to claim that, the Muhājirūn and Anṣār would call him a liar.

As for your statement: Hand over the killers of 'Uthmān, what are you in relation to 'Uthmān? You are merely a man of the Banū Umayya, and the sons of 'Uthmān are more entitled to that than you. But if you claim that you are more powerful than they to seek retaliation for the blood of 'Uthmān, enter under my obedience and then bring the people before me for judgment, and I shall put you and them on the road to justice. As for your distinction between Syria and Baṣra and between [you and] Ṭalḥa and al-Zubayr, by my life, the matter there is in every way the same because it was a general pledge of allegiance in which neither a second view may be taken nor an option renewed.

Finally 'Alī suggested that if Mu'āwiya had been able to deny 'Alī's excellence in Islam, his kinship with the Prophet, and his nobility among Quraysh, he would not have failed to do so.

'Alī then asked al-Najāshī to respond to the poetry of Ka'b b. Ju'ayl, and al-Najāshī produced, in accordance with convention, a poem in the same rhyme and metre. He warned Mu'āwiya against false dreams about the future: 'Alī was coming to them with the people of Ḥijāz and of Iraq who had already defeated the host of al-Zubayr and Ṭalḥa and the band of perjurers. Addressing the 'misguider from Wā'il', Ka'b b. Ju'ayl, he said: 'You have made 'Alī and his followers the equal of Ibn Hind, are you not ashamed?' and went on to eulogize 'Alī as the foremost of mankind after the Messenger.[262]

'Alī's sounder arguments could not conceal the fact that Jarīr's mission had been a failure. Mu'āwiya had been able to detain him for weeks, if not months, secure the backing of northern Syria by duping Shuraḥbīl b. al-Simṭ during his stay, and send him back with a splendid sample of specious war propaganda. Suspicion of Jarīr's loyalty was now widely expressed, and al-Ashtar, who had warned against sending him, accused him in front of 'Alī: 'By God, Commander of the Faithful, if you had sent me to Mu'āwiya I would have done better for you than this one who loosened the noose around his neck and stayed with him until he [Mu'āwiya] left no door unopened from which he hopes for ease and none

[262] Minqarī, *Waq'at Ṣiffīn*, 57–9.

unshut from which he fears grief.' Jarīr defended himself: 'By God, if you had gone to them, they would have killed you, for they assert that you are one of the murderers of 'Uthmān', and he attempted to scare him by mentioning 'Amr, Dhu l-Kalā' and Ḥawshab Dhū Ẓulaym. Al-Ashtar answered confidently: 'If I had gone to him, Jarīr, I would, by God, not have lacked an answer for them, and their charge would not have weighed on me. I would have carried him on a course where he would have had no time to reflect.' Jarīr: 'Then go to them.' Al-Ashtar: 'Now that you have spoiled them, and the evil has taken root among them?'[263]

Al-Ashtar was right; 'Alī had made a serious mistake in sending Jarīr. He had earlier correctly judged that he could deal with Mu'āwiya, if he did not wish to reappoint him, only from a position of strength. Yet when he was, after the victory in Baṣra, in a position of strength, he sent Jarīr who considered himself a friend of Mu'āwiya and believed he might cajole him into submission. Al-Ashtar, a *bête noire* for Mu'āwiya ever since he had been exiled to Damascus by 'Uthmān, would have been the right man to deal with him and force him with blunt threats to reply immediately. Mu'āwiya could, at this time, not have killed or imprisoned him on a charge of complicity in the murder of 'Uthmān as he probably would have done with Ibn al-'Abbās when 'Alī was still impotent in Medina. To touch al-Ashtar at this stage would have brought the fury of the Yemenites of Ḥimṣ and northern Syria down on him and sealed his fate. Later on he could safely poison him and boast of it. But at this time, with his flank to the north not yet secured, matters looked different. It is a moot question whether he would have capitulated immediately or tried to resist with the backing of Damascus and Kalb. But his chances of survival in power would have looked poor.

According to the account of al-Sha'bī, al-Ashtar directly accused Jarīr before 'Alī of hostility and cheating and suggested that 'Uthmān had bought his faith with the governorship of Hamadān; the Commander of the Faithful should imprison him and his like until matters were settled with the wrongdoers.[264] As an 'Uthmanid al-Sha'bī had no liking for al-Ashtar, and there may be some doubt regarding his reliability here. In the poem that al-Ashtar addressed to Jarīr he made light of the threats of 'Amr, Mu'āwiya, Dhu l-Kalā' and Ḥawshab Dhū Ẓulaym but did not threaten or accuse him. Jarīr, however, felt let down and uncomfortable in Kūfa now and left for Qarqīsiyā. He is said to have written to Mu'āwiya who welcomed him,[265] but he did not fight for him at Ṣiffīn. Several members of his clan, Qasr of Bajīla, joined him, and only nineteen men of Qasr fought for 'Alī at Ṣiffīn, while of Aḥmas of Bajīla seven hundred

[263] *Ibid.*, 59–60; Ṭabarī, I, 3255–6.
[264] Minqarī, *Waq'at Ṣiffīn*, 60; Balādhurī, *Ansāb*, II, 277. [265] Ṭabarī, I, 3205.

participated in the battle. ʿAlī in anger at the desertion wanted to burn Jarīr's house, but Jarīr's grandson told him that some of the property belonged to others. ʿAlī then went to burn and destroy the house of Thuwayr b. ʿĀmir, a noble man who had joined Jarīr.[266]

It was evidently an ugly quarrel at a time when solidarity was needed, and al-Zibriqān b. ʿAbd Allāh, a bard of Sakūn of Kinda, expressed his concern about what he heard of Jarīr and Mālik (al-Ashtar). He suggested that ʿAmr b. al-ʿĀṣ had been stirring up this enmity and that they were not acting like experienced men. Probably correctly, he judged that Jarīr had been sincere to his imam, but this was said before he deserted.[267]

Having gained broad allegiance in Syria, Muʿāwiya hoped to draw some of the religious aristocracy in the holy cities to his side by a campaign of letters. ʿAmr is said to have advised him against it, but he persisted. ʿAlī's taunt that there was in Syria not a single Qurayshite eligible for a *shūrā* and the caliphate must have irked him, and spurred him to try his luck. He wrote a general letter to the people of Medina and Mekka and individual letters to the most prominent neutrals ʿAbd Allāh b. ʿUmar, Saʿd b. Abī Waqqāṣ and Muḥammad b. Maslama.[268] If reliably reported, these letters consisted of clumsy intimidation and accusations of having failed to back the murdered caliph, and false promises, much in the general style of Muʿāwiya's political epistles. He was particularly eager to win over ʿUmar's son ʿAbd Allāh, whose favour would obviously have greatly strengthened his cause. He assured him that he would have preferred that the Community had agreed on him before any other Qurayshite after the murder of ʿUthmān, but then had remembered his desertion of the caliph[269] and his criticism of his supporters and had changed his mind. Ibn ʿUmar's opposition to ʿAlī had, however, eased his ill feelings against him, and Muʿāwiya appealed to him to back the campaign on behalf of revenge for the wronged caliph, for he did not wish to reign (*imāra*) over him but wanted the reign for him. Only if he declined would there be a *shūrā* among the Muslims.[270] It was widely rumoured that ʿAbd Allāh b. ʿUmar would not accept the caliphate unless it were presented to him on a platter, and Muʿāwiya evidently felt that he must lure him with more than just the promise of *shūrā* with which he tried to deceive the others. The answers of the three pacifist neutrals were indignant rejections. On behalf of the people of the holy cities al-Miswar

[266] Minqarī, *Waqʿat Ṣiffīn*, 60–1; Balādhurī, *Ansāb*, II, 277.
[267] Minqarī, *Waqʿat Ṣiffīn*, 62.
[268] *Ibid.*, 62–4, 71–7; (pseudo-)Ibn Qutayba, *Imāma*, I, 161–2.
[269] Ibn ʿUmar had in fact been among the defenders of the palace.
[270] Minqarī, *Waqʿat Ṣiffīn*, 71–2; (pseudo-)Ibn Qutayba, *Imāma*, I, 163.

b. Makhrama wrote to him that he was looking in the wrong place for support; what had he, a *ṭalīq* whose father had been the leader of the hostile Confederates (*al-aḥzāb*, Qur'ān Sūra XXXIII), to do with the caliphate?[271]

Mu'āwiya did, however, get the backing of a member of 'Umar's family without having to deceive him with false promises. 'Ubayd Allāh b. 'Umar, the threefold murderer, had been, after his pardon, granted an estate near Kūfa, later known as Kuwayfāt Ibn 'Umar, by 'Uthmān, who wanted him to be out of sight in Medina. When 'Alī came to Kūfa, 'Ubayd Allāh discreetly asked him for amnesty through some mediators, since 'Alī had previously opposed his pardon. 'Alī again refused, insisting that he was obliged to apply the *lex talionis* and kill him if he got hold of him. Al-Ashtar, one of the mediators, informed 'Ubayd Allāh, who promptly fled to Mu'āwiya.[272] Mu'āwiya was evidently uplifted by his arrival and, according to a somewhat legendary report, tried to induce him to accuse and denigrate 'Alī in public, but 'Ubayd Allāh would not do so.[273]

'Ubayd Allāh did, however, participate as one of the leaders of Mu'āwiya's army in the battle of Ṣiffīn. The Syrians were proud of his presence and shouted: 'With us is the good one, son of the good, son of 'Umar b. al-Khaṭṭāb.' The followers of 'Alī answered back: 'With you is the abominable one, son of the good.'[274] Mu'āwiya asked him to lead his heavily armoured elite troop (*shahbā'*) against the Rabī'a whom he saw as the staunchest supporters of 'Alī. According to the Syrian Yazīd b. Yazīd b. Jābir al-Azdī, 'Ubayd Allāh was warned by a client that Mu'āwiya was intentionally exposing him to mortal danger. If he were to win, Mu'āwiya would get the rule, and if he were killed, he would be rid of him. His wife Baḥriyya, daughter of the great leader of Rabī'a at the battle of Dhū Qār, Hāni' b. Qabīṣa, also told him that he would certainly be killed and that this was what Mu'āwiya wanted. 'Ubayd Allāh insisted on obeying his amir and was killed.[275] At least four men claimed to have slain him. He had had with him the sword of 'Umar, named Dhu l-Wishāḥ, which he had inherited.[276] After the surrender of Iraq, Mu'āwiya pressed the Bakr b. Wā'il in Kūfa for it. They told him that one of their men in Baṣra, Muḥriz b. al-Ṣaḥṣaḥ of the Banū 'Ā'ish b. Mālik b. Taym al-Lāt b. Tha'laba had killed him. He sent to Baṣra and took the sword away from him[277] and sent it to 'Abd Allāh b. 'Umar

271 (Pseudo-)Ibn Qutayba, *Imāma*, I, 162–3. In Minqarī, *Waq'at Ṣiffīn*, 62 the answer is, less plausibly, ascribed to 'Abd Allāh b. 'Umar and is addressed to Mu'āwiya and 'Amr jointly. 272 Balādhurī, *Ansāb*, II, 295–6. 273 Minqarī, *Waq'at Ṣiffīn*, 82–4.
274 Balādhurī, *Ansāb*, II, 305; Minqarī, *Waq'at Ṣiffīn*, 293.
275 Ibn Sa'd, *Ṭabaqāt*, V, 10–11. 276 Ibn Manẓūr, *Mukhtaṣar*, XV, 348.
277 Minqarī, *Waq'at Ṣiffīn*, 298; Ṭabarī, I, 3314–15; Balādhurī, *Ansāb*, II, 325.

in order to ingratiate himself with the harmless son of the illustrious caliph.[278]

As war hysteria, enflamed by public outcries for revenge for the wronged caliph, engulfed Syria, the Syrian Qur'ān readers, who had so far opposed any idea of fighting Muslims, felt under increasing pressure to fall in line. A group of them, led by Abū Muslim al-Khawlānī, went to see Muʿāwiya and questioned him as to why he was making war on ʿAlī when he lacked his rank as a Companion, Emigrant, and his close kinship with Muḥammad and merits in Islam. Muʿāwiya told them modestly that he was not claiming a rank in Islam similar to ʿAlī's, but did they know that ʿUthmān had been wrongfully killed? They answered: 'Certainly', and he continued: 'Then let him surrender to us his murderers so that we can kill them in revenge, and there will be no fight between us and him.' They asked him to write a letter to ʿAlī which one of them would take to him. Abū Muslim al-Khawlānī went with Muʿāwiya's letter and addressed ʿAlī, assuring him that he preferred him as a ruler to anyone else. 'Surely ʿUthmān has been killed wrongfully as a Muslim whose blood is sacred. Hand his murderers to us, and you will be our amir.' ʿAlī asked him to return on the next morning to receive his reply to the letter.

As the news of his mission spread in Kūfa, ʿAlī's followers (*shīʿa*) wore their weapons and filled the mosque, shouting: 'We all have killed ʿUthmān.' The next day ʿAlī handed over his answer for Muʿāwiya. Abū Muslim said to him: 'I have seen a people over whom you have no command.' ʿAlī: 'Why is that?' Abū Muslim: 'The people learned that you wanted to surrender to us the murderers of ʿUthmān. So they started an uproar, gathered, and wore their armour claiming that they all had killed ʿUthmān.' ʿAlī: 'By God, I never for a moment intended to hand them to you. I have carefully looked at this matter head and tail; I do not see that I should hand them to you or anyone else.' Abū Muslim left with his letter, commenting: 'Now the fighting will be sweet.'[279]

Muʿāwiya had commenced his letter to ʿAlī[280] with praise to God who

[278] Ibn Manẓūr, *Mukhtaṣar*, XV, 351. According to the report of Nāfiʿ, Ibn ʿUmar's client, Muʿāwiya bought the sword from the slayer. This statement was presumably meant to absolve Ibn ʿUmar from any charge of accepting extorted property and is certainly unreliable. Muʿāwiya, never a chivalrous opponent, wanted to teach Rabīʿa a lesson not to challenge the Vicegerent of God on earth. He had vowed during the battle to enslave their women and kill their captive warriors (Minqarī, *Waqʿat Ṣiffīn*, 294). Only the terms of the surrender prevented him four years later from following his vindictive instincts.

[279] Minqarī, *Waqʿat Ṣiffīn*, 85–6.

[280] The text of the letters of Muʿāwiya and ʿAlī was given to Abū Rawq ʿAṭiyya b. al-Ḥārith al-Hamdānī, early Kufan Qur'ān commentator and historian (see on him Sezgin, *Abū Miḥnaf*, index s.v. ʿAṭiyya b. al-Ḥārith) in the time of the governorship of al-Ḥajjāj by the son of ʿAmr b. Salima (read thus instead of ʿUmar b. Maslama in Minqarī, *Waqʿat Ṣiffīn*, 85; see Sezgin, *Abū Miḥnaf*, 200). ʿAmr b. Salima al-Arḥabī was a governor under ʿAlī (Balādhurī, *Ansāb*, II, 161), took part in the negotiations leading to the surrender of

had elected Muḥammad as His messenger to creation and had chosen helpers for him through whom He supported him; these helpers were ranked with Him according to their merits in Islam; the most excellent in his practice of Islam, and the most sincere to God and His Messenger, was his *khalīfa* after him, then the *khalīfa* of his *khalīfa*, and the third was the wronged *khalīfa*, 'Uthmān. Then he had addressed 'Alī:

Yet each one you envied, and against each one you revolted. We knew that from your looking askance, your offensive speech, your heavy sighing, and your holding back from the caliphs. To each one of them you had to be led as the male camel is led by the wood stick through its nose in order to give your pledge of allegiance while you were loath. Then you were consumed by envy towards no one more than towards your cousin 'Uthmān, who was most entitled among them to your refraining from that because of his kinship and marriage ties with you. Yet you cut the bonds of kinship with him, denigrated his virtues, incited the people against him in secret and openly, until camels were urged on with bits and noble horses were led towards him, arms were borne against him in the sanctuary of the Messenger of God, and he was killed while you were with him in the same place, hearing the frightful screams. Yet you do not even try to deflect the suspicion and accusation in his respect from yourself by word or act. I swear truthfully that had you stood up in this affair of his even a single time restraining the people from him, the people with us would not have considered anyone equal to you, and it would have wiped out in their opinion everything they witnessed of your avoidance of 'Uthmān and your rebellion against him. Another matter through which you are suspect in the eyes of the supporters of 'Uthmān is your giving shelter to his murderers. They are your backbone, your helpers, your hand, and your entourage. It has been mentioned to me that you disavow blood guilt for him. If you are truthful, give us power over his murderers that we may kill them for him, and we shall be the quickest people to join you. If not, there is nothing for

al-Ḥasan b. 'Alī to Mu'āwiya (Ibn Sa'd, *Ṭabaqāt*, VI, 118–19; Balādhurī, *Ansāb*, III, 40–2; Ṭabarī, I, 2524–5), and was a major informant of Abū Rawq. Nothing is known about his son. Both 'Amr b. Salima and Abū Rawq belonged to the Yemenite tribal aristocracy in Kūfa and were not sectarian Shi'ites. The letters are almost certainly authentic and, like 'Uthmān's letters to the Mekka pilgrims and the Syrians, of capital interest for the history of the time. Caetani commented on the letter ascribed to Mu'āwiya suggesting that it, though not written by Mu'āwiya at that moment and in this form, certainly reflected the view of the Umayyad party hostile to 'Alī. He suspected exaggeration and literary retouching (*Annali*, IX, 254) – as if Mu'āwiya and 'Amr had not been able to write articulate and persuasive Arabic. The letters were meant for public consumption. Neither Mu'āwiya nor 'Alī were so naïve as to believe that they could influence each other with this rhetoric. 'Alī's answer was in Caetani's rendering reduced to a few lines. Djaït commented that it seemed fabricated since it reflected later Shi'ite argumentation. The correspondence between 'Alī and Mu'āwiya quoted in the *Waq'at Ṣiffīn* is, he asserted, in general certainly apocryphal. Abū Mikhnaf quoted nothing of it, while al-Balādhurī reproduced the most important letters in the same terms as Naṣr b. Muzāḥim (*La Grande Discorde*, 243, n. 2). Yet al-Balādhurī received the letters from (Hishām) al-Kalbī on the authority of Abū Mikhnaf from Abū Rawq al-Hamdānī (Balādhurī, *Ansāb*, II, 277). It was al-Ṭabarī who suppressed this material in his quotations of Abū Mikhnaf because he found it unpalatable from his Sunnite perspective.

you and your companions but the sword. By the One beside whom there is no god, we shall seek the murderers of ʿUthmān on the mountains and in the deserts, on land and on sea, until God kills them, or our spirits join God.[281]

It was a clever caricature, ridiculing ʿAlī's claim to be the most meritorious Companion of Muḥammad. The point about ʿAlī's presence in Medina at the time of the murder reveals the hand of ʿAmr, who had prudently sneaked away after bringing the kettle to a boil by his talk of ʿUthmān riding over abysses.

ʿAlī began his answer by mentioning the 'brother of Khawlān' who had brought him Muʿāwiya's letter in which he mentioned God's bounty upon Muḥammad. Then he recalled the violent opposition of Muḥammad's own people towards their prophet, their calling him a liar, their instigation of the Arabs to war against him until the cause of God had become victorious in spite of their rancour. His tribe (*usra*), the closest of his people, had been the most violent against him except for those whom God had protected; now Muʿāwiya was coming and brazenly proposing to inform them about God's favour to His prophet and to them; Muʿāwiya was in this like one carrying dates to Hajar or the trainee challenging his trainer to a duel.

You have mentioned that God chose for him helpers among the Muslims through whom He backed him, and that they were in their ranking with Him according to their merits in Islam. The most excellent, you asserted, in Islam and the most sincere to God and His Messenger were the *khalīfa*, and the *khalīfa* of the *khalīfa*.[282] By my life, their station in Islam is indeed great, and the loss of them a grievous wound in it, may God have mercy on them and reward them with the best reward. You mentioned further that ʿUthmān was third in excellence. If ʿUthmān was indeed doing good, God will recompense him for it, and if he was doing evil, he will meet a Lord most merciful for whom no sin is too great to be forgiven. By God, I am full of hope, when God will reward mankind in accordance with their merits in Islam and their sincerity to God and His Messenger, that our share in that will be the most ample.[283] Surely, when Muḥammad called for faith in God and for proclamation of His unity we, the people of his house (*ahl al-bayt*), were the first to have faith in him and to hold true what he brought. We continued for lengthy years when no one in a living quarter of the Arabs worshipped God but us. Our people then wanted to kill our prophet and to destroy our base. They plotted against us and carried out deeds. They kept provisions from us, withheld drinking water, spread fear among us, set up guards and spies on us, forced us unto a rugged mountain, burned the fire of war against

[281] Minqarī, *Waqʿat Ṣiffīn*, 86–7; Balādhurī, *Ansāb*, II, 278–9. The variants are insignificant.

[282] In the text of al-Balādhurī 'his [Muḥammad's] *khalīfa* and the *khalīfa* of his *khalīfa*' (*Ansāb*, II, 279).

[283] In the text of al-Balādhurī: 'our share will be the most ample of any family (*ahl bayt*) among the Muslims' (*ibid.*, 280).

us, and wrote a compact among themselves not to eat or drink with us, nor to intermarry or trade with us. We should not be safe among them until we surrendered the Prophet so that they would kill and torture him.

'Alī continued to describe the persecution of the Prophet's family by Quraysh, and noted:

As for those of Quraysh who accepted Islam thereafter, they were spared the trials we were in, for among them were the protected confederates, or the clansmen whose clan would defend them so that no one would transgress against them as the people had transgressed against us in order to destroy us. They were in a place of asylum and safety from being killed.[284] So that was as God wanted it. Then he ordered His messenger to emigrate and allowed him thereafter to fight the polytheists. Whenever matters got tough and the battle cry was sounded, he used to put the people of his house up in the front rank and protected his Companions from the heat of the lances and the sword. Thus 'Ubayda [b. al-Ḥārith b. al-Muṭṭalib] was killed at Badr, Ḥamza on the day of Uḥud, Ja'far and Zayd [b. Ḥāritha][285] on the day of Mu'ta. The one whose name I would mention, if I so wished, more than once sought for the sake of God the same martyrdom they sought, yet their terms were expedited, while his death was delayed. God is now the renderer of bounty to them, their benefactor for the good works which they performed before. For I have not heard of anyone, nor have I seen anyone among the people, who was more sincere to God in his obedience to His Messenger, or more submissive to His Messenger in obedience to his Lord, or more steadfast in hardship and distress, and at the time of stress, and in the places of adversity with the Prophet than these few whom I named to you, even though there was much good among the Emigrants which we recognize, may God reward them for their best of works.

Then came the passage for which al-Ṭabarī presumably suppressed the correspondence:

You mentioned my envy of the caliphs, my holding back from them, and my rebellion against them. As regards rebellion, God forbid that there was. As for my holding back from them, and my being loath of their affair, I do not apologize for that to the people, because, when God took away His Prophet, Quraysh said: 'From us an amir', and the Anṣār said: 'From us an amir.' Then Quraysh said: 'From us is Muḥammad, so we are entitled to "this matter."' The Anṣār recognized that and surrendered to them the reign and the authority. Yet if they deserved it through Muḥammad to the exclusion of the Anṣār, then the people closest to Muḥammad are more entitled to it than they. If not, the Anṣār surely have the greatest portion in it among the Arabs. Thus I do not know whether my companions feel blameless for either having taken my right, or having wronged

[284] 'Alī evidently had 'Uthmān in particular in mind.

[285] The mention of the Muttalibid 'Ubayda and Muḥammad's freedman Zayd among the *ahl al-bayt* is quite incompatible with 'later Shi'ite argumentation'. For the later Shi'ites these men were not members of the Prophet's Family.

the Anṣār. I do not know that my right was taken, but I left it to them, may God pass over their doing.[286]

As for your mention of the affair of 'Uthmān and my incitement against him, you have heard what 'Uthmān did. The people then did with him what you have seen and know. I surely was in isolation from it, unless you want to incriminate me falsely; accuse me then as you see fit. In regard to those who killed 'Uthmān, I have fully considered this matter head and tail, and I do not see that I should surrender them to you or to anyone else.[287] By my life, if you will not pull back from your transgression and your dissent, you will get to know them shortly when they will seek you and will not impose on you to seek them on land or on sea, in mountain or plain.

Finally, 'Alī reminded Mu'āwiya:

Your father came to me when the people put up Abū Bakr as their ruler and said: 'You are more entitled to "this matter" after Muḥammad; I back you in this against whoever opposes you. Stretch out your hand that I pledge allegiance to you.' But I did not do it. You know that your father said this and desired it, and that then it was I who declined because the people were still close to infidelity and I feared division among the people of Islam. Thus your father was more ready to recognize my right than you. If you recognize my right which your father recognized, you will come to your good senses. But if you will not, God will let us dispense with you.[288]

'Alī's answer was resounding and set the record straight. Apart from some hyperbole and rhetorical embellishment, it stated the plain truth. It is true that Mu'āwiya's letter forced him to bring into the open what he would have preferred not to touch upon at this time. He first praised the conduct of Abū Bakr and 'Umar unconditionally, but, when challenged to account for his slowness and reluctance in backing them, he realized that there was nothing to gain from hiding the facts. He sensed that the truth in history, as in personal life, sometimes hurts, but also liberates those willing to accept it; he had certainly been cheated out of his right at the *falta*, not just by the norms of the Book, but also by the traditional Arab tribal order; none other than Abū Sufyān, Mu'āwiya's father, had attested it; now he was being accused by his son of envy, when it was his own people Quraysh, as 'Umar had told Ibn al-'Abbās, who could not

[286] The section from 'Quraysh said' to here is not contained in al-Balādhurī's version (*ibid.*, 281). It could thus be a later Shi'ite addition. More likely, however, al-Balādhurī preferred to suppress it. He thus had to pull the argument about Abū Sufyān forward. The formulation of that argument suggests that it came at the end as the climax. The point that the Anṣar, too, had been wronged at the Saqīfa was also very likely part of 'Alī's argumentation.

[287] The text of the version of al-Balādhurī has here: 'I do not know any killer of him specifically. I have considered the matter head and tail, but I do not see that it would be possible for me to surrender to you those with me whom you have accused or placed under suspicion' (*ibid.*, 281–2).

[288] Minqarī, *Waq'at Ṣiffīn*, 88–91; Balādhurī, *Ansāb*, II, 279–83.

bear that Hāshim should have the imamate in addition to Prophethood; let the admirers of Abū Bakr and 'Umar be hurt by the truth; he had no quarrel any more with the two patriarchs and could sincerely lament their loss for Islam; if their old followers were now ready to back the impostor Mu'āwiya, they would do so at their own risk.

The position on both sides had been fully set forth, and war was inevitable. 'Alī called a council of the Islamic ruling elite, which for him meant, as in the time of Muḥammad, Muhājirūn and Anṣār on an equal footing. When he asked them for their advice, they all urged him to lead them to *jihād* against the deceivers. First Hāshim b. 'Utba spoke, describing the enemies as wholly motivated by worldly greed. 'Ammār b. Yāsir, who as a client of Quraysh had been excluded from the supreme advisory council under the early caliphs in spite of his early rank in Islam, advised speedy action before the fire of the offenders should be in full flame. Then Qays b. Sa'd spoke, assuring 'Alī that *jihād* against these people was dearer to him than against the Turks and Byzantines. He expressed great bitterness about their mistreatment of the faithful. In particular he took up the grievance of the Anṣār, which Ḥassān had vented under Abū Bakr, that they had appropriated the *fay'* of the Anṣār and treated them as their servants (*qaṭīn*). Several senior Anṣār, among them Khuzayma b. Thābit and Abū Ayyūb al-Anṣārī, intervened, questioning Qays as to why he spoke out of turn before the shaykhs of his people. He apologized to them and recognized their excellence, adding that his blood had boiled over remembering the Confederates (*aḥzāb*) of the time of the Prophet. The Anṣār then decided that Sahl b. Ḥunayf should speak for all of them. He assured 'Alī that they were with him equally in peace and war and advised him to appeal for the support of the people of Kūfa which would be crucial for him.[289]

The Kufans were less united in their support of the war. Whatever they might think of Mu'āwiya, they realized that, as ever in war with its chess-game ethics, they and their Syrian brethren would pay the price in blood long before their respective leaders. Some felt that in contrast to the Basrans, who had broken their oaths of allegiance, Mu'āwiya and the Syrians, who had never given theirs, should not be attacked, even though Abū Bakr had set the precedent of treating non-recognition of the caliph as apostasy. Al-Ashtar himself was quoted as telling his clan, al-Nakha', confidentially that the war against the Syrians would be morally more delicate than Baṣra because there was no *bay'a* binding them.[290] For those

[289] Minqarī, *Waq'at Ṣiffīn*, 92–4.

[290] Ibn Abī Shayba, *Muṣannaf*, VIII, 711. The report betrays its 'Uthmanid origins, however, in ascribing to al-Ashtar the confession that the Community had attacked and murdered its best man.

still remembering their former freedom and tribal autonomy, it must have been an attractive argument.

As ʿAlī appealed to the Kufans: 'March against the enemies of God, march against the remnants of the Confederates, the murderers of the Muhājirūn and the Anṣār', a man of the Banū Fazāra, Arbad b. Rabīʿa, stood up and shouted: 'Do you want to make us march against our Syrian brothers to kill them for you, as you went with us to our Basran brothers and we killed them? By God, that we shall not do.' When al-Ashtar stood up and asked: 'Who will take care of this man, O people?', the Fazārī fled, pursued by a crowd. They caught up with him in the horse-market and beat and trampled him to death. ʿAlī came and enquired who had killed him. They told him: 'Hamdān and a medley of people.' He decided that the man had been killed in factional strife (*qatīl ʿimmiyya*) with the killer unknown and that the blood-money should be paid by the treasury. Abū ʿIlāqa al-Taymī of Taym Rabīʿa commented on his death in verse:

> I seek refuge with my Lord that my death should be
> as Arbad died in the market of work horses.
> The Hamdān took turns in beating him with their sandals,
> when one hand was raised from him another hand came down.[291]

When the meeting resumed, al-Ashtar stood up and assured ʿAlī of the loyalty of the Kufans, distancing himself from the words of 'this miserable traitor'. All the people, he said, were ʿAlī's followers (*shīʿa*) who wished him to lead them against his enemy. The situation was evidently saved, and ʿAlī concluded with the conciliatory comment: 'The path is joined, and the people are equal in the truth. Whoever renders his opinion in sincere advice to the common people has done his duty.'[292]

Not all opponents of the war and doubters, however, were satisfied. ʿAbd Allāh b. al-Muʿtamm of ʿAbs, a Companion and prominent leader of his tribe in the conquest of Iraq[293] and Ḥanẓala b. al-Rabīʿ of Tamīm, known as al-Kātib because he was proficient in writing and had written a letter for the Prophet,[294] came to see ʿAlī together with a crowd of Ghaṭafān (to whom ʿAbs belonged) and Tamīm. Both offered their advice not to fight the Syrians since the outcome of the war was uncertain, but to write to Muʿāwiya again; others agreed with them. ʿAlī answered that those disobedient to God would inevitably be the losers whoever won in battle. He believed, he said, to be hearing the words of people who were not ready 'to back what is proper and to reject the reprehensible'. One of his loyalist supporters, Maʿqil b. Qays al-Yarbūʿī al-Riyāḥī (Yarbūʿ belonging

[291] Minqarī, *Waqʿat Ṣiffīn*, 54–5. In al-Balādhurī's version of the two lines (*Ansāb*, II, 293) those beating Arbad are identified as 'our Qur'ān readers' instead of the Hamdān.

[292] Minqarī, *Waqʿat Ṣiffīn*, 95.

[293] See Ibn Ḥajar, *Iṣāba*, IV, 132; Ṭabarī, indices, s.v.

[294] Ibn Ḥajar, *Iṣāba*, II, 43–4.

to Tamīm), stood up and said: 'Commander of the Faithful, surely these men have not come to you with sincere advice, but with fraud. Beware of them, for they are closer to the enemy.' His police chief, Mālik b. Ḥabīb al-Yarbū'ī, chimed in: 'Commander of the Faithful, I have learned that this man Ḥanẓala keeps writing to Mu'āwiya. Hand him over to us in order that we arrest him until the end of your campaign and your return.' Two men of 'Abs, 'Ayyāsh b. Rabī'a and Qā'id b. Bukayr, also told 'Alī that they had heard that their tribesman 'Abd Allāh b. al-Mu'tamm was writing to Mu'āwiya, and asked for permission to arrest him till the end of the campaign. The two accused men protested: 'This is the recompense of those who consider carefully and advise you [pl.] about yourselves and your enemy.' 'Alī told them: 'Let God judge between me and you; I entrust you to Him and seek His help against you. Go wherever you want.'

Ḥanẓala's attitude in particular evidently worried 'Alī because of the Prophet's reliance on him, and he sent for Ḥanẓala again to ask him whether he was for or against him. Ḥanẓala replied that he was neither for nor against. On 'Alī's question what he wanted to do now, he said: 'I shall go to Edessa [al-Ruhā], for it is a place of escape [from both sides] and hold out there until the matter is over.' The elite of his clan, the Banū 'Amr of Tamīm, were angry at this, but he told them: 'You will not seduce me from my faith. Leave me, I know better than you.' They threatened that they would not let his slave wife (*umm walad*) and his children go with him, or might even kill him. Others of his people came to his defence and drew their swords. He asked them to give him time and locked himself in his house; at night he fled to Mu'āwiya. He was followed by twenty-three of his people. Ibn al-Mu'tamm also joined Mu'āwiya, taking with him thirteen of his tribe. Both of them refrained from fighting for Mu'āwiya, however, and stayed neutral between the two parties.

When Ḥanẓala fled, 'Alī ordered his house to be destroyed; Bakr b. Tamīm, the overseer (*'arīf*) of Tamīm, and Shabath b. Rib'ī al-Tamīmī did so. Ḥanẓala complained bitterly in a poem about the two of them and in another incited Mu'āwiya to kill and punish the Anṣār whom he, as a good Mudarite, seems to have held particularly responsible for the discord in the Community.[295]

'Adī b. Ḥātim al-Ṭā'ī, chief of Ṭayyi', also advised 'Alī to give letters and messengers another chance before marching. Zayd b. Ḥiṣn (or Ḥuṣayn)[296] al-Ṭā'ī, one of the burnous-wearing legal experts (*min aṣḥāb*

[295] Minqarī, *Waq'at Ṣiffīn*, 95–8.

[296] Both Ḥiṣn and Ḥuṣayn occur frequently in the sources. The text of al-Minqarī has here Ḥuṣayn. The manuscripts of al-Balādhurī's *Ansāb al-ashrāf*, however, consistently offer the reading Ḥiṣn. In his edition, al-Maḥmūdī regularly changed it to Ḥuṣayn (see his note, *Ansāb*, II, 364). Here the reading Ḥiṣn will be preferred throughout.

al-barānis al-mujtahidīn) and later a prominent Kharijite, contradicted him, affirming that if they were in any doubt about the justice of their war, it would not become proper through delay. No one could be in doubt, however, that the enemy was seeking blood unjustly. Another man of Ṭayyi' protested: 'Zayd b. Ḥiṣn, do you disparage the words of our chief 'Adī b. Ḥātim?' Zayd defended himself: 'You do not know the title of 'Adī better than I, but I will not stop saying the truth even if it irks the people.' 'Adī generously repeated 'Alī's words that whoever sincerely offered his considered opinion did his duty.[297] Bāhila, who were not numerous in Kūfa but had many kinsmen in Syria, were not eager to fight the Syrians. 'Alī told them bluntly: 'I call God to witness, you loathe me and I loathe you. So take your stipends and go to fight the Daylamites.'[298]

Others were urging 'Alī to speed up his campaign before the enemy was fully prepared. Yazīd b. Qays al-Arḥabī and Ziyād b. al-Naḍr al-Ḥārithī, both leaders of Yemenite tribes, may have been the first to report that their men and equipment were ready and to ask 'Alī that he order the men through heralds to move out to their army camp at al-Nukhayla, two miles from Kūfa. 'The expert of war (*akhu l-ḥarb*)', Yazīd b. Qays[299] told 'Alī, 'is not one who tarries in aversion or wastes time in sleeping, nor one who delays, or seeks advice when opportunity presents itself, nor one who postpones today's war to the morrow or after.' Ziyād b. al-Naḍr joined in asking 'Alī to lead them against their enemy. On the same occasion 'Abd Allāh b. Budayl b. Warqā' al-Khuzā'ī, representing Muḥammad's Companions, warned 'Alī not to expect his enemies to change course since they were driven by old hatred and rancour against him. Turning to the people he asked: 'How could Mu'āwiya pledge allegiance to 'Alī when 'Alī has killed his brother Ḥanẓala, his maternal uncle al-Walīd, and his grandfather 'Utba in a single stand?'[300] These people, he suggested, could be straightened out only by the lances and swords. 'Alī now gave order to al-Ḥārith b. 'Abd Allāh al-Hamdānī, known as al-Ḥārith al-A'war, to summon the people to their war camp at al-Nukhayla.[301]

Two of 'Alī's activist followers, Ḥujr b. 'Adī al-Kindī and 'Amr b. al-Ḥamiq al-Khuzā'ī, went around the town cursing the Syrians and proclaiming their dissociation (*barā'a*) from them. 'Alī called them and asked them to stop. They were not to behave as execrators and vilifiers, but ought to describe the evil conduct of the enemy and pray to God that

[297] Minqarī, *Waq'at Ṣiffīn*, 99–100. [298] *Ibid.*, 116.

[299] According to others, this was said by 'Abd Allāh b. Budayl al-Khuzā'ī.

[300] Ḥanẓala b. Abī Sufyān, al-Walīd b. 'Utba b. Rabī'a, brother of Mu'āwiya's mother Hind, and his father 'Utba b. Rabī'a b. 'Abd Shams were all killed at Badr. The latter was, according to the common account, slain by the Muttalibid 'Ubayda b. al-Ḥārith before he himself was killed.

[301] Minqarī, *Waq'at Ṣiffīn*, 102–3; Balādhurī, *Ansāb*, II, 294.

He would guide them to the right path and spare blood on both sides. They accepted his reprimand and promised to abide by his advice.[302]

The religious class, Qur'ān reciters and others, were for the most part among 'Alī's most vigorous supporters. The disciples of 'Abd Allāh b. Mas'ūd, however, were reserved. As 'Alī was ready to set out on his campaign, a group of them, among them 'Abīda b. Qays al-Salmānī of Murād and his companions, told him that they would go along but remain a separate group and then judge which side were the transgressors, against whom they would fight. 'Alī praised their attitude as according with religion and good sense. Another group of them, some four hundred men led by Rabī' b. Khuthaym al-Thawrī, said they were in doubt about the rightness of this war in spite of their recognition of 'Alī's excellence, and begged him to send them to some frontier town. He sent them to al-Rayy to face the Daylamites and tied a banner for them.[303]

There was also some trouble caused by tribal rivalry between the Yemenites and Rabī'a in Kūfa. 'Alī had removed al-Ash'ath b. Qays from the joint command of the Kufan Kinda and Rabī'a and given it to Ḥassān b. Maḥdūj of Dhuhl. Several Yemenite chiefs, among them al-Ashtar, 'Adī b. Ḥātim al-Ṭā'ī, Zaḥr b. Qays al-Ju'fī and Hāni' b. 'Urwa al-Murādī, went to see 'Alī suggesting that the leadership of al-Ash'ath, scion of the chiefs of Kinda, could be given only to someone like him and that Ḥassān was not his peer. The Rabī'a became incensed for their man Ḥassān, holding him no less noble than the Kinda chief. The poet al-Najāshī, himself a Yemenite, took their side and expressed his satisfaction with whatever pleased 'Alī, the legatee of the Messenger of God. Sa'īd b. Qays al-Hamdānī warned the Yemenites that they would do worse under Mu'āwiya where they would face Muḍar. The Yemenites, however, were not satisfied, and Ḥassān proposed that al-Ash'ath should have the flag of Kinda and he the flag of Rabī'a. Al-Ash'ath declined, suggesting that whatever belonged to one of them equally belonged to the other.

Mu'āwiya learned of the quarrel and consulted Mālik b. Hubayra, the leader of Kinda in Syria and a friend of al-Ash'ath. They found a bard of Kinda who composed a poem putting the Kinda of Iraq to shame for accepting the disgrace of their chief and sent it to the Yemenites in 'Alī's army. Shurayḥ b. Hāni' al-Ḥārithī now warned them that their Syrian kinsman was merely trying to stir up trouble between them and Rabī'a. Ḥassān planted the flag in the house of al-Ash'ath, and 'Alī offered to return the command to him. Again al-Ash'ath declined, protesting his loyalty, but accepted 'Alī's proposal that he take the command of his right wing.[304]

[302] Minqarī, *Waq'at Ṣiffīn*, 103–4. [303] *Ibid.*, 115. [304] *Ibid.*, 137–40.

'Alī had written to some of his governors to join him for the campaign. From Iṣfahān came Mikhnaf b. Sulaym al-Azdī, great-grandfather of the historian Abū Mikhnaf. He had appointed al-Ḥārith b. al-Ḥārith b. al-Rabī' and Sa'īd b. Wahb, both of his people, as his deputies in Iṣfahān and Hamadān respectively.[305] While 'Alī stayed at al-Nukhayla, 'Abd Allāh b. al-'Abbās arrived with the Basrans. He had appointed Abu l-Aswad al-Du'alī to lead the prayers in his absence and put Ziyād b. Abīh in charge of the land tax. The Basrans were grouped in five contingents. Bakr b. Wā'il were led by Khālid b. al-Mu'ammar al-Sadūsī, 'Abd al-Qays by 'Amr b. Marjūm (var. Marḥūm) al-'Abdī, Azd by Ṣabra b. Shaymān, Tamīm, Ḍabba and al-Ribāb by al-Aḥnaf b. Qays, and the Ahl al-'Āliya (the highlands of Ḥijāz) by Sharīk b. al-A'war al-Ḥārithī.[306]

In Syria the preparations for war also went ahead. After his return from Kūfa, Abū Muslim al-Khawlānī took the bloody shirt of 'Uthmān which Mu'āwiya's sister Umm Ḥabība was said to have sent from Medina and toured the garrison towns in Syria with it, inciting the people to revenge. Ka'b b. 'Ujra al-Anṣārī, *qāḍī* of Damascus, is also described as having done his utmost to stir up popular sentiment.[307]

In spite of this war propaganda, enthusiasm for fighting their Iraqi brethren was certainly not universal among the Syrians. According to the Basran Abū Bakr al-Hudhalī, 'Amr b. al-'Āṣ, in order to spur them on, belittled the strength of the enemy who, he asserted, were divided and weakened by the battle of the Camel, with the Basrans opposed to 'Alī. When Mu'āwiya learned of the build-up of 'Alī's army, he was worried, delayed his own march, and began writing letters to all whom he thought to be opposed to 'Alī and upset by the murder of 'Uthmān and appealed for their help. Al-Walīd b. 'Uqba became impatient and wrote to him:

> Inform Mu'āwiya b. Ḥarb:
>   You surely are blamed by a trustworthy brother.
> You have spent the time like a confined camel stallion in
>   lust, braying in Damascus, but do not move.
> Surely, you and your letter-writing to 'Alī
>   are like a woman tanner whose hide is worm-eaten.
> Every mounted troop gives you hope for the caliphate
>   as it hits hard the ground towards the ruins of Iraq.
> The fellow of blood-revenge is not one who hesitates,
>   rather the seeker of vengeance is the brute.
> If you were the slain, and he were alive,
>   he would bare his sword, neither lax nor averse,
> Nor shrinking from blood crimes, even

[305] *Ibid.*, 104–5.
[306] *Ibid.*, 117; Balādhurī, *Ansāb*, II, 293, 295. It was also reported that of the Basran Azd only 'Abd al-Raḥmān b. 'Ubayd together with less than ten men participated.
[307] Balādhurī, *Ansāb*, II, 291.

confessing them, nor tiring or sitting still.
Your people have been destroyed in Medina,
and are lying felled as if they were dry stalks.[308]

When Mu'āwiya five years later entered Kūfa in triumph, he called on al-Walīd to ascend the pulpit which had once to be washed of his vomit and recite these lines to the humiliated enemy. He himself then quoted the line of Aws b. Ḥajar, the pre-Islamic bard of Tamīm:

Many a one wonders at what he sees of our deliberation,
yet when war pushes him, he will not utter a word.[309]

The brute was celebrating victory.

Once al-Walīd had publicly declared the caliphate the war prize, he could take up Marwān's old contention: The caliphate is the property of Umayya, they would fight for it. He remembered the weapons and communal camels (*ibl al-ṣadaqa*)[310] in 'Uthmān's palace which 'Alī had seized. Speaking for Umayya, he addressed Hāshim who were now collectively guilty:

Banū Hāshim, return the arms of your sister's son,
do not loot them, his loot is not licit.
Banū Hāshim, do not hasten to invite retaliation,
the same to us are his murderers and his plunderer.
Banū Hāshim, how could there be negotiation between us
when his sword is with 'Alī and his noble horses.
They killed him in order to be in his place
just as once Chosroes was betrayed by his Marzpans.
I surely shall travel to you in a boundless host
whose noise and turmoil will deafen the ear.[311]

Al-'Abbās b. 'Utba b. Abī Lahab answered for Hāshim:

Do not ask us for the arms, for they are lost;
their owner threw them away in the battle's fright.
You likened him to Chosroes, indeed he was like him,
alike with Chosroes his manners and his hordes.[312]

308 Ṭabarī, I, 3257–8. The poem is quoted with variants and different sequence of lines in Balādhurī, *Ansāb*, II, 290–1; Ibn Manẓūr, *Mukhtaṣar*, XXVI, 347–8; and elsewhere. The version of al-Ṭabarī has been translated here, but 'caliphate' (*khilāfa*) has been substitued for 'amirate' (*imāra*) with most other versions. Al-Walīd was certainly luring Mu'āwiya with hopes for the caliphate. He was amir already.

309 Ibn Manẓūr, *Mukhtaṣar*, XXVI, 3478. That Mu'āwiya quoted the line of Aws b. Ḥajar on this occasion seems more likely than that he sent it to al-Walīd as a reply on an otherwise empty scroll, as the anecdote in Ṭabarī, I, 3258 has it.

310 See *Aghānī*, IV, 168.

311 The fullest version, nine lines, is quoted in *ibid.*, 176. The partial translation is based on this version except that in line 3 (l. 6 of the *Aghānī* version) *najā'ibuh* has been substituted for *ḥarā'ibuh*. For other versions see Balādhurī, *Ansāb*, V, 104 and the references given in the annotation there.

312 *Aghānī*, IV, 177. Abu l-Faraj's alternative identification of the poet as al-Faḍl b. al-'Abbās is, no doubt, mistaken.

In order to concentrate his forces for the invasion of Iraq, Muʿāwiya had to secure his borders to the north and west. He concluded a truce with the Byzantine emperor, making gifts and paying tribute. ʿAlī, he could be sure, would not try to make common cause with the enemy of Islam against him. Egypt was now less of a worry since the capable Qays b. Saʿd had been replaced by Muḥammad b. Abī Bakr. The latter, though deeply devoted to ʿAlī, was a man of no political skill. A month after his arrival he wrote to the seceders in Kharbitā with whom Qays had made peaceful arrangements and demanded that they either enter into obedience or leave the country. They refused, asking for time to consider the developments in the imminent battle between ʿAlī and Muʿāwiya, and took precautions for resistance. Ibn Abī Bakr did not attack them until after Ṣiffīn.[313] But having been antagonized by him, they were now a thorn in his side.

The son of Abū Bakr also engaged, certainly before the battle of Ṣiffīn, in a public slanging match with Muʿāwiya, the text of which was suppressed by al-Ṭabarī because, he suggested, the common people (*ʿāmma*) would not bear hearing it.[314] It was, however, preserved by al-Balādhurī and other sources. Muḥammad b. Abī Bakr addressed Muʿāwiya as the Seducer (*ghāwī*), son of Ṣakhr, and went on to compare him, the accursed son of the accursed, who had never failed to seek ruin for the religion of God and now was sheltering the remnants of the Confederates, with ʿAlī, the first one to respond to the Prophet's summons to Islam, his brother and cousin, who was ever in the forefront of his followers, his legatee, and father of his offspring, who was now backed by the Anṣār whom God had praised. Ibn Abī Bakr did not fail to mention ʿAmr b. al-ʿĀṣ, Muʿāwiya's partner in his game of fraud and deception. They would find out to whom the lofty outcome would belong; God was watching Muʿāwiya.

Muʿāwiya, no doubt assisted by ʿAmr, answered in kind. He addressed his letter to the detractor from his own father: Muḥammad, son of Abū Bakr. Having spotted the weak point in Muḥammad's family record with respect to the legatee of the Prophet, he hammered away at it. In Muḥammad's discourse, he said, there was rebuke of his father:

> You mentioned the right of Ibn Abī Ṭālib, his ancient merits, his close association with the Prophet of God, his support of him, and his consolation of him in every situation of fear and horror. Your argument against me is with another's excellence, not yours; so give praise to a God who diverted excellence from you and gave it to another. We, and your father with us, during the lifetime of the Prophet used to consider the right of Ibn Abī Ṭālib binding upon us, and his excellence surpassing us. Yet when God chose for His Prophet what He had in

313 Ṭabarī, I, 3248. 314 *Ibid.*

store for him, after He had completed for him what He had promised him and had made manifest his summons and victorious his argument, He took him to Himself. Then your father and his Fārūq ['Umar][315] were the first to snatch it [the succession] (*ibtazzahū*) and to oppose him. On that the two of them agreed and cooperated. Then they summoned him to themselves, but he was slow, keeping away from them and tarrying in relation to them. At that time both had designs against him and intended great offence (*arādā lahu l-'aẓīm*), but he pledged allegiance and surrendered to them. They would not let him share in their reign, nor did they make him privy to their secret until they died and their rule passed away. Then their third one rose after them, 'Uthmān b. 'Affān, following in their straight path, and acting in accordance with their conduct, but you and your master blamed him until the remotest of the sinful people would covet his life. You both concealed and displayed your hatred and your spite until you attained your desires in regard to him.

Mu'āwiya went on to ridicule the son of Abū Bakr who would challenge a giant of political wisdom (*ḥilm*) such as himself, whose reign Muḥammad's father, Abū Bakr, had facilitated, built and raised to lofty heights.

If what we are about is not sound, then your father was the first one to be about it. If it was injustice, then your father founded it, and we are his partners. We followed his guidance and imitated his action. If your father had not preceded us to it and considered him unsuitable for the rule,[316] we would not oppose Ibn Abī Ṭālib and would submit to him. But since we saw your father do that, we follow his example and imitate his action. So blame your father as you see fit or quit.[317]

Inadvertently the son of Abū Bakr had exposed himself to another brilliant sample of that facetious brainwash with which the potentates of this world like to entertain their credulous subjects and to lead them by their noses. Shooting for the caliphate now, what better way could Mu'āwiya take than to posture as the true preserver and restorer of the building raised high by Abū Bakr and his Fārūq? Had their stunning success not come from keeping that subversive mole 'Alī at bay and from allowing him no share in their government and secret planning? Mu'āwiya was committed to following their wisdom and guidance to save the caliphate from Abū Bakr's deviant son and his master. 'Uthmān, their unfortunate third man, was still needed to secure the apostolic succession,

[315] The formulation is noteworthy. Was it Abū Bakr who gave 'Umar his famous epithet? In the version of al-Balādhurī (*Ansāb*, II, 396) the pronoun of *Fārūquhū* refers to Muḥammad. The text of what follows is clearly toned down and rhetorically weakened in al-Balādhurī's version in order to make it more acceptable from a Sunnite perspective. The text of al-Mas'ūdī corroborates that of al-Minqarī. For a discussion of various reports on the origins of 'Umar's epithet see S. Bashear, 'The Title ⟨*Fārūq*⟩ and its Association with 'Umar I', *Studia Islamica*, 72 (1990), 47–70.

[316] The passage 'and considered him unsuitable for the rule' is taken from al-Balādhurī's version (*Ansāb*, II, 397).

[317] Minqarī, *Waq'at Ṣiffīn*, 118–20; Balādhurī, *Ansāb*, II, 393–7; Mas'ūdī, *Murūj*, III, 197–201, paras. 1790–1.

which would now lead from the most faithful friend of the Prophet and his two illustrious Companions to their most loyal servant, if merely a reformed *ṭalīq*, and eventually to his slightly debauched son and slaughterer of the Prophet's grandson. Once more the lice in ʿAmr's jubbah must have tickled him as he pictured Ibn Abī Bakr and ʿAlī as starting the campaign of vilifying ʿUthmān that led to his sorry end.

For later Sunnites Muʿāwiya's letter could not appear so amusing as it did to his contemporaries. Did Muʿāwiya really mean it when he said that in the time of the Prophet they all had recognized ʿAlī's superior merit and precedence or was he merely engaging in legitimate war guile? Al-Ṭabarī had good reason to judge this letter as unsuitable for the ears of the common people. It was better to forget the testimony of the 'scribe of the Prophet' and to stick to that of ʿUmar's son ʿAbd Allāh received in Aḥmad b. Ḥanbal's *Musnad*: 'We used to count, when the Messenger of God was alive and his Companions plentiful: Abū Bakr, ʿUmar, ʿUthmān, and then we were silent.'[318]

With Muḥammad b. Abī Bakr facing difficulty in Egypt, Muʿāwiya could leave the protection of his western border to three minor local Palestinian commanders.[319] He had just been troubled by news that Nātil b. Qays, chief of Judhām, had overpowered Palestine and taken possession of the treasury. ʿAmr advised him, however, to let Nātil consume his loot and to congratulate him, since he was not fighting for a religious cause.[320] Muʿāwiya did so, and Nātil commanded Lakhm and Judhām for him at Ṣiffīn.[321] When Muʿāwiya learned that ʿAlī was personally leading his army, he decided, on ʿAmr's advice, to take the command of the Syrians.[322]

ʿAlī set out from al-Nukhayla probably early in Dhu l-Ḥijja 36/late May 657.[323] As governor of Kūfa in his absence he appointed Abū Masʿūd ʿUqba b. ʿAmr al-Anṣārī of ʿAwf b. al-Ḥārith b. al-Khazraj, a veteran of Badr.[324] This was a risk, since Abū Masʿūd, in contrast to Ḥudhayfa b. al-Yamān, had been strongly opposed to the Kufan revolt against ʿUthmān's governor Saʿīd b. al-ʿĀṣ[325] and evidently inclined to neutralism. ʿAlī further ordered his police chief, Mālik b. Ḥabīb al-Yarbūʿī, to round up anyone trying to stay behind.[326] He moved via Muẓlim Sābāṭ to

[318] Ibn Ḥanbal, *Musnad*, II, 14. See also W. Madelung, *Der Imam al-Qāsim ibn Ibrāhīm und die Glaubenslehre der Zaiditen* (Berlin, 1965), 226.

[319] Minqarī, *Waqʿat Ṣiffīn*, 128. Of the three named, only Sumayr (Samīr ?) b. Kaʿb b. Abi l-Ḥimyarī is otherwise known as a participant in the early conquests (Ṭabarī, I, 2158 (Sayf b. ʿUmar)). [320] Ṭabarī, II, 210–1.

[321] Ibn Manẓūr, *Mukhtaṣar*, XXVI, 96. [322] Ṭabarī, I, 3256–7.

[323] The date given by Abu l-Kanūd, 5 Shaw./27 March (Minqarī, *Waqʿat Ṣiffīn*, 131), is about two months too early. It could not have taken ʿAlī two and a half months to reach Ṣiffīn. [324] Ibn Ḥajar, *Iṣāba*, IV, 252. [325] Ṭabarī, I, 2934.

[326] Minqarī, *Waqʿat Ṣiffīn*, 121, 131. Mālik is reported to have beheaded a man who stayed behind (*ibid.*, 140).

al-Madā'in, and from there to al-Anbār and along the eastern bank of the Euphrates to al-Raqqa. From al-Madā'in he sent Ma'qil b. Qays al-Riyāḥī at the head of three thousand men to take the northern route via Mossul, Naṣībīn and Ra's al-'Ayn with instructions to rejoin him at al-Raqqa.[327]

On the way 'Alī was asked by some of his men to write Mu'āwiya and his followers another letter inviting them to recognize him and give up their error. He addressed it to Mu'āwiya and the Quraysh with him, reminded them of their duty as Muslims to accept the command of the most virtuous and meritorious among them, and called upon them to follow the Book of God, the Sunna of His Prophet, and to spare the blood of this Community. Mu'āwiya answered with a quote of poetry implying that only the lance and sword could rule between them.[328]

Near Qarqīsiyā 'Alī's vanguard, under the command of Ziyād b. al-Naḍr and Shurayḥ b. Hāni', came up from behind. They had made their way from Kūfa along the western bank of the Euphrates. When they reached 'Ānāt, they learned that 'Alī had taken the route on the eastern bank and that Mu'āwiya was approaching from Damascus. As the people of 'Ānāt prevented them from crossing the river, they turned back and crossed it at Hīt. They wanted to get back at the people of 'Ānāt, but these fortified their town, so they went on to join the main army.

In al-Raqqa Simāk b. Makhrama closed the gates and fortified the town as 'Alī's army approached. 'Alī stayed outside and asked the hostile people to provide a boat bridge over the river for his army. When they refused, he turned towards Jisr Manbij upstream in order to cross there. Al-Ashtar, however, shouted some threats at the occupants of the fortress, and, aware that he was not inclined to joking, they decided to provide the bridge. The whole army now crossed the river.[329]

As 'Alī moved from al-Raqqa westward towards Ṣiffīn, he again dispatched his vanguard under Ziyād b. al-Naḍr and Shurayḥ b. Hāni'. They met Abu l-A'war Sufyān b. 'Amr al-Sulamī[330] with a Syrian detachment at Sūr al-Rūm and, after failing to persuade him to submit, informed 'Alī. The latter sent al-Ashtar with horsemen to join them, with the order not to attack first. The Syrians attacked in the evening and then

[327] Balādhurī, *Ansāb*, II, 296. [328] Minqarī, *Waq'at Ṣiffīn*, 151.

[329] *Ibid.*, 151–2; Ṭabarī, I, 3259–60; Balādhurī, *Ansāb*, II, 297–8.

[330] On Abu l-A'war al-Sulamī see the article by H. Lammens in *EI*, reprinted in the second edition. Lammens says of him that he 'does not seem to have belonged to the closest circle of the Prophet'. In fact he was, as a confederate of Abū Sufyān, one of the most vigorous enemies of Muḥammad (see M. J. Kister, 'O God, Tighten thy Grip on Muḍar . . .: Some Socio-economic and Religious Aspects of an Early Ḥadith', *Journal of the Economic and Social History of the Orient*, 24 (1981), 242–73, at 258–9). He is named among those cursed by Muḥammad in his *qunūt* (Ibn Abī Shayba, *Muṣannaf*, II, 215).

withdrew. The next morning al-Ashtar attacked, and a well-known Syrian knight, ʿAbd Allāh b. al-Mundhir al-Tanūkhī, was killed by a young man of Tamīm, Ẓubyān b. ʿUmāra. Al-Ashtar sent to Abu l-Aʿwar, challenging him to a duel. Abu l-Aʿwar faulted al-Ashtar for having driven ʿUthmān's governors out of Iraq and for having denigrated the caliph, and claimed that he was now sought for the murder of ʿUthmān. He had, so he told the messenger, no need for duelling with al-Ashtar and sent him away without allowing him to set the record straight. Al-Ashtar commented: 'He was concerned about his life.' The two detachments remained the rest of the day facing each other. The following morning ʿAlī arrived with the main army. The Syrians left under the cover of night.[331] This was, according to al-Balādhurī's account, in the second half (*li-layālin baqīna*) of Dhu l-Ḥijja 36/after 5 June 657.[332]

When ʿAlī's army put up their camp, they found the watering place at the Euphrates occupied by Abu l-Aʿwar and the Syrians, who prevented them from reaching the water. They looked for another watering place nearby but could not find one. As they complained to ʿAlī, he sent Ṣaʿṣaʿa b. Ṣūḥān to tell Muʿāwiya that he and his men had come not wishing to fight him before proper warning, summons and argument; Muʿāwiya's cavalry and foot soldiers had, however, started fighting them; now they were trying to prevent his men from obtaining water. He asked Muʿāwiya to order his companions to give them access to the water until they had fully considered their conflict; if it pleased Muʿāwiya, however, he could let them fight it out about the water rather than the matter for which they had come. Muʿāwiya consulted his advisers, and al-Walīd b. ʿUqba urged him to deprive the enemy of water as they had done with ʿUthmān whom, he claimed, they had kept without cold water and soft food for forty days. ʿAmr b. al-ʿĀṣ, in contrast, advised him to let them get at the water, since they would certainly fight for it. Al-Walīd repeated his words, and ʿAbd Allāh b. Saʿd b. Abī Sarḥ joined him, suggesting that the enemy would be forced to retreat in disgrace. 'Keep them from the water, may God keep them from it on the Day of the Resurrection.' Ṣaʿṣaʿa intervened: 'God, powerful and lofty, will keep it on the Day of the Resurrection from the sinful unbelievers and drinkers of wine like you and like this profligate', meaning al-Walīd. They exploded, vilifying and threatening him, but Muʿāwiya restrained them, reminding them that he was an envoy. As he was about to leave, Ṣaʿṣaʿa asked Muʿāwiya for his answer, who said: 'My

[331] Minqarī, *Waqʿat Ṣiffīn*, 152–6; Ṭabarī, I, 3261–4.

[332] Balādhurī, *Ansāb*, II, 299. Other sources, including Abū Mikhnaf, speak of the start of the fighting at Ṣiffīn at the beginning of Dhu l-Ḥijja/10 May. There is, however, little information about fighting before the interruption during the month of Muḥ/June–July. It seems unlikely that it could have continued for a whole month without any memorable events.

decision will come to you.' He ordered his cavalry to back up Abu l-A'war in preventing the enemy from reaching the water.[333]

It was, as 'Amr readily realized, a silly blunder. For nothing would more quickly turn these men, most of whom were hardly eager to fight their Syrian brethren, into furious lions than to deprive them of drinking water. As it happens with despots, Mu'āwiya was carried away by his own propaganda that these were the murderers of 'Uthmān who should be made to die of thirst. Mu'āwiya got some versified support from a man of Sakūn, al-Salīl b. 'Amr.[334] An ascetic of Hamdān, al-Mu'arrā b. al-Aqbal, backed the view of 'Amr b. al-'Āṣ, his friend, and told Mu'āwiya that this was the beginning of oppression (*jawr*) since there were slaves, hired servants and weak innocent persons in the camp of the enemy. Mu'āwiya vented his anger on 'Amr. The Hamdānī now bid a scathing poetical farewell to Ibn Hind and, during the night, joined 'Alī.[335]

'Alī did not have to rouse his men into action. After they had been without water for a day and a night, al-Ash'ath b. Qays came to him asking for permission to attack and requesting that 'Alī order al-Ashtar to join with his horsemen. They would, he said, not turn back before they either had water or were dead; 'Alī consented.[336] Twelve thousand men volunteered, and they swooped down on Abu l-A'war and his men. The presence of 'Amr b. al-'Āṣ with the Syrian cavalry did not stop them. The enemy were driven off and left to count their losses. Al-Ashtar had personally killed seven and al-Ash'ath five.[337] The Day of the Euphrates remained one of the more pleasant memories for the Kufans and Basrans. At first they said they would not allow the Syrians to get water. 'Alī ordered them, however, to take their needful and return to their camp.[338] He was still eager to try persuasion.

For two days the armies stayed facing each other. Then 'Alī called the Anṣārī Abū 'Amra Bashīr b. 'Amr b. Miḥṣan, Sa'īd b. Qays of Hamdān and Shabath b. Rib'ī of Tamīm, instructing them to see Mu'āwiya and to summon him to God, obedience and community. Shabath b. Rib'ī asked him whether he would not tempt Mu'āwiya by offering him a government and a position of prestige with him, but 'Alī told them to argue with Mu'āwiya and discover his views. Abū 'Amra first gave Mu'āwiya a sermon about the transitoriness of this world and the account which the Almighty would take of his work. He appealed to him not to split the unity of this Community and not to shed their blood in communal strife. Mu'āwiya was not impressed and interrupted his discourse: 'Why don't you recommend that to your master?' Abū 'Amra replied: 'My master is

333 Ṭabarī, I, 3269–9; Minqarī, *Waq'at Ṣiffīn*, 160–2.
334 Minqarī, *Waq'at Ṣiffīn*, 162–3. 335 *Ibid.*, 163–4. 336 *Ibid.*, 166. 337 *Ibid.*, 174.
338 Ṭabarī, I, 3269; Minqarī, *Waq'at Ṣiffīn*, 162.

not like you. My master is the one most entitled among creation to 'this matter' by his excellence, religion, early merit in Islam, and close kinship with the Messenger of God.' Mu'āwiya: 'What does he say then?' Abū 'Amra: 'He orders you to fear God and to respond to the summons of your cousin to what is right. That is soundest for you in your worldly affairs and best for your end.' Mu'āwiya: 'Shall we allow 'Uthmān's blood to be spilled for nothing? No, by God, I shall never do that.'

Now Sa'īd b. Qays went forward to speak, but Shabath b. Rib'ī impatiently broke in: 'Mu'āwiya, I have understood your answer to Ibn Miḥṣan. By God, what you intend and seek is not obscure to us. Surely, you found nothing with which to deceive the people, to attract their sympathy, and to win their sincere obedience but your assertion: Your imam has been killed wrongfully, so we seek revenge for his blood, and a bunch of simpletons responded to you. We know that you held back from aiding him, wishing him to be killed for the sake of this station which you now have come to seek. Yet many an aspirant and seeker of a matter is prevented by God with His power, or perhaps he may obtain his wish and beyond his wish. By God, there is no good for you in that in either case. If what you hope escapes you, you will truly be in the worst condition of all the Arabs. If you attain what you wish, you will not attain it without incurring the burning hell-fire from your Lord. So fear God, Mu'āwiya, leave what you are set upon, and do not dispute the reign of those entitled to it.'

Mu'āwiya now felt uncomfortable. He sensed that Shabath had, with but slight exaggeration, uncovered his true motivation and was worried about the impact such subversive talk might have on his own people. He must show himself to be that giant of political sagacity that 'Amr had recently depicted him to be, and serve up some of his Umayyad arrogance. After giving God due laud and praise, he said: 'Surely, the first thing by which I know your foolishness and the light weight of your judgement (*ḥilm*) is your cutting in on the discourse of this respected noble man, the lord of his people. Then afterwards you concerned yourself with what you have no knowledge of. You lied and spoke basely, you boorish, crude bedouin (*A'rābī jilf jāfī*), in everything you mentioned and described. Go away [pl.] from me, there can be nothing between me and you but the sword.' Forgetting his own courtesy in his anger, he would not listen to what that 'respected noble lord of his people' might have to say; but then, what was that one compared to himself who was just growing into his new prospective role as God's Vicegerent on earth? As the envoys departed, Shabath, a daredevil not impressed by Mu'āwiya's flight into the realm of lofty politics, had the last word: 'Do you think you can frighten us with the sword? I swear by God that it will quickly be carried to you.'[339]

There was now daily skirmishing until the end of Dhu l-Ḥijja/18 June. 'Alī would send one of his noble chiefs with a small troop and Mu'āwiya would match them. They were afraid of mass destruction should the two armies meet. One day al-Ashtar went forward with a group of Qur'ān readers, and there was hard fighting. An unknown giant of a man came forward from the Syrians, challenging to a duel. No one dared meet him but al-Ashtar. They exchanged a few strokes, then al-Ashtar killed him. It turned out to be Sahm b. Abi l-'Ayzār of the Banū Zāra of Azd. One of his men swore he would kill his killer or himself be killed. Al-Ashtar turned back to face him, but as the man was in front of his horse his companions rushed forward and saved him.[340]

At the beginning of Muḥarram 37/19 June 657 a truce was agreed for the month in the hope that a peaceful settlement might be reached. Again envoys went back and forth between the two camps. 'Alī sent 'Adī b. Ḥātim al-Ṭā'ī, Yazīd b. Qays al-Arḥabī, Shabath b. Rib'ī al-Tamīmī and Ziyād b. Khaṣafa al-Taymī of Taym Rabī'a. The discussion did not go any better than the previous time. Mu'āwiya accused the Ṭā'ī chief of having been one of the instigators of the revolt against 'Uthmān and one of his murderers and told him that he hoped he would be one of those killed in revenge. Shabath and Ziyād b. Khaṣafa countered with the suggestion that he stop engaging in idle talk and respond to their proposals. Yazīd b. Qays then praised the virtues and merits of their master and appealed to Mu'āwiya to return to concord, community and obedience. Mu'āwiya answered that the community to which they were summoning him was on his side. Obedience to their master he did not deem proper since their master had killed the caliph, had split the community, and was sheltering his murderers. 'Your master claims that he did not kill him, so we do not throw that back at him. Don't you see the murderers of our master, don't you know that they are companions of your master? Let him surrender them to us, so that we may kill them in revenge for him. Then we shall respond to your summons to obedience and community.' Shabath asked him incautiously: 'Would it please you, Mu'āwiya, if you were given power over 'Ammār to kill him?' Mu'āwiya saw his chance. He could now make another show of his Umayyad arrogance to the 'boorish bedouin'. 'What would prevent me from that? By God, if I had power over Ibn Sumayya, I would kill him not for 'Uthmān; I

[339] Ṭabarī, I, 3270–2; Minqarī, *Waq'at Ṣiffīn*, 186–8.
[340] Ṭabarī, I, 3272–3; Minqarī, *Waq'at Ṣiffīn*, 195–6.

would be his killer for Nātil, the client of 'Uthmān.' Shabath expressed astonishment and swore that Mu'āwiya would not reach 'Ammār.

As they left, Mu'āwiya called Ziyād b. Khaṣafa back. He was aware that Rabī'a, so far the most loyal followers of 'Alī, might play a crucial part in the battle. As a good Umayyad merchant, he must try bribery. Addressing the 'brother of Rabī'a' he said: 'Surely 'Alī has cut the bonds of kinship to us and sheltered the killers of our companion. I ask you for help against him with your family and your tribe. In that case you have the pact and covenant of God that I shall appoint you, when I win, over whichever of the two cities you prefer.' The brother of Rabī'a answered quoting the Qur'ān: 'Truly, I stand upon evidence from my Lord, for the bounty He has bestowed on me; I will not be a helper of the criminals' (VI 57, XXVIII 17) and stood up to leave. He could hear Mu'āwiya commenting to 'Amr b. al-'Āṣ who was sitting next to him: 'One of us cannot say a word to anyone of them and get a good response. What is with them, may God cut off their hands and feet in evil. Their hearts are all like the heart of a single man.'[341]

Mu'āwiya sent the Qurayshite Ḥabīb b. Maslama al-Fihrī, Shuraḥbīl b. al-Simṭ al-Kindī and Ma'n b. Yazīd b. al-Akhnas al-Sulamī as his envoys to 'Alī. Ḥabīb b. Maslama addressed the Prophet's cousin: "Uthmān was a rightly-guided (*mahdī*) caliph who acted in accordance with the Book of God and submitted to the commandment of God. Yet you [pl.] found his life annoying and his death too slow, so you assaulted and killed him. Hand over the murderers of 'Uthmān to us if you claim that you did not kill him, in order that we kill them in retaliation for him. Then resign the reign of the people, so there will be a *shūrā* among them, and the people will appoint to the rule whomever they agree upon.' 'Alī told him to shut up since he was neither here nor there in respect to the right of deposing anyone. They exchanged some threats, and 'Alī sent him packing.

Shuraḥbīl told 'Alī that he would have the same speech for him as his companion, and asked whether he had a different answer for him. 'Alī answered that for him and his remaining companion he had another answer. He recounted to them the story of the caliphate, how the people had chosen Abū Bakr as caliph and he had chosen 'Umar as his successor, both of whom had followed good conduct and had acted justly in the Community. 'We were angry at them that they assumed the rule over us, as we are the Family of the Messenger of God, but we forgave them for that. Then 'Uthmān assumed the reign and committed things for which the people reproached him. They went to him, killed him, and then came

[341] Ṭabarī, I, 3274–7; Minqarī, *Waq'at Ṣiffīn*, 196–200.

to me while I kept away from their affairs.' The people had then asked him to accept the pledge of allegiance; he had at first declined, but then accepted when they told him that the Community would not be satisfied with anyone but him; then he had been surprised by the desertion of two men who had first pledged allegiance to him. The opposition of Mu'āwiya was rather of someone without previous merit in the faith, without previous sincerity in Islam, a *ṭalīq*, son of a *ṭalīq*, a confederate of the Confederates, who, together with his family, never ceased to be an enemy of God's Messenger and the Muslims until they entered Islam against their will. 'Alī summoned them now to the Book of God, the Sunna of His Prophet, to the extirpation of falsehood and the revival of the principles of the faith. The two men said: 'Testify that 'Uthmān was wrongfully killed.' He answered: 'I do not say that he was wrongfully killed, nor do I say that he was killed as a wrong-doer.' They declared that they dissociated themselves from anyone who would not affirm that 'Uthmān was killed wrongfully, and left. 'Alī quoted Qur'ān Sūra XXVII 80-1: 'You will not make the dead to hear, nor will you guide the blind out of their error. You will make to hear only him who believes in Our signs; they are the Muslims'; he told his men that those could not be more serious in their falsehood than they were in their truth and obedience to their Lord.[342]

As the sun set on the last day of Muḥarram/18 July 657, 'Alī ordered Marthad b. al-Ḥārith al-Jushamī to proclaim to the Syrians that they had failed to respond to his summons to the Book of God and had persisted in their falsehood. The time for battle had arrived.[343] During the first seven days of Ṣafar/19–25 July, from Wednesday to Tuesday, prominent leaders on both sides were dispatched to fight each day, with only a small retinue, as in a tournament. On the fourth day Muḥammad b. al-Ḥanafiyya met 'Ubayd Allāh b. 'Umar, who challenged him to a duel. Muḥammad accepted, but 'Alī, on being informed about the identity of the duellers, called his son back and offered to duel with 'Ubayd Allāh himself. 'Umar's son answered that he had no need to duel with him, and turned back. Muḥammad asked him why he had prevented him from duelling with 'Ubayd Allāh. 'Alī answered: 'If you had duelled with him, I would have had hope that you would kill him, but I was not sure that he might not have killed you.' Muḥammad said: 'Father, would you duel with this offender? By God, if his father had asked you to duel, I would not have wished you to accept.' 'Alī told him: 'My son, do not say anything but good about his father.' Then the opposing parties separated for the day.

On the fifth day 'Abd Allāh b. al-'Abbās and al-Walīd b. 'Uqba met.

[342] Ṭabarī, I, 3277–9; Minqarī, *Waq'at Ṣiffīn*, 200–2.
[343] Ṭabarī, I, 3281–2; Minqarī, *Waq'at Ṣiffīn*, 203.

There was heavy fighting, then Ibn al-ʿAbbās came close to al-Walīd. The latter began to curse the Banū ʿAbd al-Muṭṭalib and said to Ibn al-ʿAbbās, who had read ʿUthmān's letter to the Mekka pilgrims on his behalf: 'Ibn ʿAbbās, you [pl.] have cut the bonds of kinship and killed your imam. How do you view what God is doing with you? You have not been given what you sought; you have not obtained what you were hoping. God willing, He shall annihilate you and aid us against you.' Ibn al-ʿAbbās sent him a challenge to single combat, but al-Walīd, ever surer of his foul mouth than of his skill at arms, declined.[344] Abū Shamir b. Abraha b. al-Ṣabbāḥ, present in Muʿāwiya's army, had heard and seen enough. He and a group of Syrian Qur'ān readers joined ʿAlī that day. Abū Shamir was later killed in the battle.[345]

The all-out battle of Ṣiffīn began on Wednesday, 8 Ṣafar/26 July. According to al-Shaʿbī, Abū Mikhnaf and al-Wāqidī, representing the main historical tradition, it continued 'for three days and nights', until Friday at noon.[346] There is a variant report, however, going back to ʿAbd al-Raḥmān b. Abzā, who fought on ʿAlī's side, that it lasted four days, until Saturday morning.[347] The sources offer a profusion of detail about the battle events, part of it legendary, reflecting the epic character of this crucial conflict in early Islamic history, but the major lines of development are difficult to disentangle. If the first day, Wednesday, passed without major events, as the traditional accounts affirm,[348] it must seem likely that the battle continued until Saturday, since all the major developments as described in the sources can hardly be crowded into a single day. This is not the place, however, to pursue the question in detail.

On Thursday ʿAbd Allāh b. Budayl was in command of the right wing of ʿAlī's army, facing Ḥabīb b. Maslama on Muʿāwiya's left wing. Ibn Budayl advanced well towards Muʿāwiya's pavilion. Muʿāwiya now ordered his elite troops to stand against him, and at the same time sent word to Ḥabīb b. Maslama to attack with all his forces. ʿAlī's right wing, consisting mainly of Yemenites, was pushed back, leaving Ibn Budayl with two hundred and fifty or three hundred Qur'ān readers cut off, and then completely disintegrated. ʿAlī sent Sahl b. Ḥunayf with the Anṣār to back them up, but they, too, were pushed by the Syrians towards the centre. Muḍar in the centre also gave way, and ʿAlī was forced to move towards the left wing, which was composed mainly of Rabīʿa. They stood firm, and ʿAlī now sent al-Ashtar to rally the retreating men on the right. Al-Ashtar, backed by Madhḥij and Hamdān, succeeded in restoring the

[344] Ṭabarī, I, 3285–6; Minqarī, *Waqʿat Ṣiffīn*, 221–2.
[345] Minqarī, *Waqʿat Ṣiffīn*, 222, 369. In both passages Shamir should be read Abū Shamir.
[346] Ṭabarī, I, 3327; Minqarī, *Waqʿat Ṣiffīn*, 369; Balādhurī, *Ansāb*, II, 318, 323.
[347] Khalīfa, *Ta'rīkh*, 193–4.
[348] Ṭabarī, I, 3287–9; Minqarī, *Waqʿat Ṣiffīn*, 230; Balādhurī, *Ansāb*, II, 305.

right wing and, driving back the Syrians, in the afternoon reached Ibn Budayl and his men, who were relieved to learn that 'Alī was alive. Against al-Ashtar's advice Ibn Budayl again pushed forward towards Mu'āwiya, eager to take revenge for his brother Abū 'Amr. He was surrounded, however, and killed with several of his companions.[349]

The day had evidently gone well on the whole for Mu'āwiya. He decided to concentrate his assault now on the Rabī'a on 'Alī's left wing. If they gave way, Syrian victory would be close. He asked 'Ubayd Allāh b. 'Umar to take the command of his heavily armed elite, the *shahbā'*, and to lead the attack. 'Ubayd Allāh seems to have been surprised that he was chosen for the task, presumably feeling that some member of the Umayyad family, who were the prime claimants of revenge, would have been more appropriate. He went ahead, however, in spite of warnings from his client and his wife, daughter of the distinguished leader of Rabī'a Hāni' b. Qabīṣa. Already facing Rabī'a were the strong Ḥimyar of Ḥimṣ under their leader, Dhu l-Kalā' Samayfa' b. Nākūr, known as the king of Ḥimyar. Under the impact of the first onslaught, the ranks of Rabī'a were shaken. The Syrians drew back and then returned for a second assault. Rabī'a stood firm, except for a few who turned to leave. Khālid b. al-Mu'ammar al-Sadūsī, the commander of Rabī'a, followed them, but seeing the banners of Rabī'a standing firm, exhorted the retreating men to return.[350]

Ziyād b. Khaṣafa, leader of the Kufan Rabī'a, appealed to 'Abd al-Qays to join the fray, as otherwise no Bakr b. Wā'il would be left after this day. The 'Abd al-Qays followed his appeal, and soon Dhu l-Kalā' and 'Ubayd Allāh b. 'Umar were both killed.[351] The tide turned, and the Syrians were

[349] Ṭabarī, I, 3289–99; Minqarī, *Waq'at Ṣiffīn*, 233–4, 245–7. According to Ibn al-Kalbī, 'Abd Allāh b. Budayl's brother 'Abd al-Raḥmān was also killed in the battle (Ibn Ḥajar, *Iṣāba*, IV, 39–40). This is apparently confirmed by a line of poetry by the Anṣārī al-Ḥajjāj b. Ghaziyya (Balādhurī, *Ansāb*, II, 320). According to Abū Mikhnaf's account, however, he was killed at the beginning of the battle of the Camel (Ibn Abi l-Ḥadīd, *Sharḥ*, IX, 111).

[350] Ṭabarī, I, 3312–3; Minqarī, *Waq'at Ṣiffīn*, 291. The account portrays Khālid b. al-Mu'ammar clearly in an unfavourable light as being among those ready to flee first. Khālid is said to have defended himself, explaining that he merely wanted to hold the men back from fleeing. Like al-Ash'ath b. Qays, his loyalty to 'Alī is put in doubt by the main tradition, probably because both men were prominent among those in favour of accepting the Syrian truce offer. Khālid is reported to have been accused by some of his tribesmen, including Shaqīq b. Thawr al-Sadūsī, of writing secretly to Mu'āwiya. 'Alī challenged him about the truth of these allegations but accepted his oaths that they were false (Ṭabarī, I, 3310–11; Minqarī, *Waq'at Ṣiffīn*, 287–8). Khālid is said to have been the first to submit to Mu'āwiya in the name of Rabī'a when al-Ḥasan b. 'Alī negotiated his peace agreement with the Umayyad (Balādhurī, *Ansāb*, III, 39).

[351] The apparent statement of Ibn Shabba (*Ta'rīkh al-Madīna*, 654) that both 'Ubayd Allāh and his full brother Zayd al-Aṣghar were killed at Ṣiffīn rests on a faulty reading of the dual *qutilā*. The text is taken from Ibn Sa'd (*Ṭabaqāt*, III/1, 190) where the singular *qutila* is used. Zayd al-Aṣghar is nowhere mentioned as present at the battle.

pushed back towards their camp. Mu'āwiya fled from his pavilion and sheltered in one of the tents of his army.[352] Elsewhere on the battlefield that day 'Ammār b. Yāsir, said to have been above ninety years old, and Hāshim b. 'Utba b. Abī Waqqāṣ were killed fighting for 'Alī. In the evening, as the armies pulled back, Baḥriyya, 'Ubayd Allāh's wife, accompanied by some servants, rode on a mule to her people in 'Alī's camp. In true tribal spirit she congratulated them that God had not disgraced their faces, something she would not have wished to see. They welcomed the daughter of their great chief and let her take the body of her dead husband. She ordered her servants to dig a grave, buried him, and left, reciting two lines of an elegy by Ka'b b. Ju'ayl for him.[353] The loss of 'Ubayd Allāh b. 'Umar was a political, though no personal, blow for Mu'āwiya, and it is unlikely that he wanted to get rid of him, as his family suspected. Although he had joined Mu'āwiya merely because 'Alī would not uphold 'Uthmān's pardon of his triple murder, he had been the single proof in the Umayyad's claim to represent the glorious early caliphate against the subversive mole 'Alī. Mu'āwiya's men had proudly celebrated his presence, hailing him as 'the good one, son of the good'. His disappearance made it patent to everyone that Quraysh, after their defeat by 'Alī, were even less inclined to back Mu'āwiya.[354]

The death of Dhu l-Kalā' was a different matter. Mu'āwiya is reported to have told his confidants: 'I am happier about the killing of Dhu l-Kalā' than I would be if I had conquered Egypt.' Dhu l-Kalā', 'king of Ḥimyar',

[352] Minqarī, *Waq'at Ṣiffīn*, 306–7. He is said to have sent to Khālid b. al-Mu'ammar, promising him the government of Khurāsān if he would not continue. Khālid therefore did not press on. This is, no doubt, part of the slander campaign against Khālid by his critics. That Mu'āwiya fled at one point during the battle and then turned back is, however, well attested and was later admitted by him himself.

[353] Balādhurī, *Ansāb*, II, 326.

[354] Wellhausen created an entirely false impression about the character of the battle of Ṣiffīn by asserting that 'Alī's brother 'Aqīl and sons of the caliphs Abū Bakr and 'Umar fought on the side of the Syrians (*Das arabische Reich*, 52). 'Aqīl did not fight at Ṣiffīn (see below, p. 263–4). By son(s) of Abū Bakr Wellhausen probably meant 'Abd al-Raḥmān. The latter was not present at Ṣiffīn, but was later in 'Amr's army conquering Egypt. His sister 'Ā'isha had sent him, not to fight, but to protect the life of their brother Muḥammad (see below, p. 268). 'Abd al-Raḥmān later remained a major opponent and critic of Mu'āwiya's conduct, denounced the arbitration, refused to countenance Mu'āwiya's recognition of Ziyād as his father's bastard son, and withheld his pledge of allegiance from Yazīd despite Mu'āwiya's attempt to bribe him (Abbott, *Aishah*, 178–9, 189, 194–6). The family of 'Umar (Āl 'Umar) were widely recognized as neutral in the conflict between 'Alī and Mu'āwiya. When al-Nu'mān b. Bashīr was sent by Mu'āwiya with a message to 'Ā'isha and met two men on his way near Tabūk, he identified himself, according to his own account, as a client of 'Umar b. al-Khaṭṭāb as a precaution, until he discovered that they were partisans of 'Uthmān (Ibn Shabba, *Ta'rīkh al-Madīna*, 1067–8). Even more telling for the lack of support for the *ṭalīq* Mu'āwiya from the religious establishment in Medina was the absence of the sons of the caliph 'Uthmān at Ṣiffīn.

had taken a major part in the conquest of Syria and seems to have entertained hopes of restoring a Himyarite kingdom in Damascus under Islam. Muʿāwiya disliked him because he used to 'contradict him and was obeyed by the people' in Ḥimṣ.[355] Dhu l-Kalāʿ had, however, strongly backed Muʿāwiya's war policy before Ṣiffīn both in his advisory council and in fiery public speeches. Muʿāwiya might thus have expressed some appreciation. Yet loyalty is in the eyes of the despot a one-way street. The Ḥimyar of Ḥimṣ had lost, probably on the previous day, another one of their prominent figures, Ḥawshab Dhū Ẓulaym, chief of Alhān.[356] The death of their two leaders marked the beginning of the long-term decline of their political prestige.[357]

The battle thus remained in the balance and the slaughter continued. It could have been settled in a moment by a duel between the two main contenders. This was variously proposed by ʿAlī and by some of Muʿāwiya's followers, but Muʿāwiya, the chess king, would have none of it. Appalled by the massive losses of his people, Abraha b. al-Ṣabbāḥ al-Ḥimyarī, grandson of the last ruling Himyarite, proposed in a speech to them that the two leaders should fight it out and they would back whoever killed his opponent. When Muʿāwiya heard this he withdrew behind the lines and told those with him: 'I think Abraha is afflicted in his mind.' The Syrians backed Abraha, however, affirming that he was among the best in religion, sound opinion and fortitude. As Muʿāwiya continued to refuse single combat, ʿUrwa b. Dāwūd al-Dimashqī of the Banū ʿĀmir offered to duel with ʿAlī in his stead. ʿAlī was told by his companions not to bother with this dog who was not his peer, but ʿAlī countered that he was on this day no more enraged against Muʿāwiya than against this man. He met him and cleft him in two. A cousin of ʿUrwa who sought to avenge him did not fare much better.[358]

The princes of the house of Umayya also preferred to let others do the fighting in revenge for their kinsman. Muʿāwiya seems to have seen the incongruity between their words and action, and vainly tried to persuade them to take a prominent part in the battle. He is said to have asked Marwān to lead a troop of horsemen of Kalāʿ and Yaḥṣub against

[355] See Madelung, 'Apocalyptic Prophecies', 183–4; Minqarī, *Waqʿat Ṣiffīn*, 303.

[356] That Ḥawshab was killed on the same day as ʿAbd Allāh b. Budayl seems evident from the account in Minqarī, *Waqʿat Ṣiffīn*, 400–1. In the lines attributed to al-Ashtar in *ibid.*, 264, which imply that Dhu l-Kalāʿ was killed before Ḥawshab, *qablahū* should perhaps be read *baʿdahū*.

[357] Another prominent man of Ḥimṣ killed in the battle of Ṣiffīn was ʿAmr b. al-Ḥaḍramī, stabbed by Saʿīd b. Qays al-Hamdānī (Khalīfa, *Taʾrīkh*, 194; Balādhurī, *Ansāb*, II, 322). He was an early settler in Ḥimṣ under Abū ʿUbayda and probably belonged to the prestigious family of clients of Ḥarb b. Umayya (Ibn Ḥajar, *Iṣāba*, V, 4–5).

[358] Minqarī, *Waqʿat Ṣiffīn*, 457–9. ʿUrwa b. Dāwūd al-Dimashqī is enumerated by Khalīfa (*Taʾrīkh*, 194) among the prominent Syrians killed at Ṣiffīn.

al-Ashtar. Marwān advised him coldly to ask ʿAmr b. al-ʿĀṣ, who was in his generous pay. If he wanted him, Marwān, to act he should first make him ʿAmr's equal in pay or make ʿAmr his equal in deprivation. ʿAmr, he said, would have a splendid position if Muʿāwiya won, and if he were defeated, flight would be easy for him.[359]

An appeal by Muʿāwiya that one of his kinsmen seek a duel among the Quraysh of Iraq was also met with derision by al-Walīd b. ʿUqba and Marwān.[360] Muʿāwiya's brother ʿUtba, however, proposed a duel with Jaʿda b. Hubayra, and Muʿāwiya approved, acknowledging that Jaʿda, as a Makhzumite with a Hashimite mother, was a noble peer. ʿUtba went out in the morning and called for Jaʿda to come forward. ʿAlī allowed Jaʿda to meet him, and the people gathered to listen to their discourse. ʿUtba challenged Jaʿda, suggesting that he was fighting merely because of his love for his maternal uncle (ʿAlī) and his paternal uncle (ʿUmar) b. Abī Salama, governor of al-Baḥrayn. 'We, by God, would not claim that Muʿāwiya has a better right to the caliphate than ʿAlī, were it not for his affair with ʿUthmān. But Muʿāwiya has a better right to Syria, because the people of Syria are pleased with him, so excuse us for her. For, by God, there is no man of any strength in Syria who is not more serious than Muʿāwiya in fighting, nor is there in Iraq anyone more serious than ʿAlī in war. We are more obedient to our master than you to yours. How abominable it is for ʿAlī to be in the hearts of the Muslims the most worthy of people [to rule] over the people, but when he attains authority he annihilates the Arabs.'

Jaʿda answered: 'As for my love for my maternal uncle, if you had one like him you would forget your father [Abū Sufyān]. As for Ibn Abī Salama, no greater one in rank could be found, and *jihād* is preferable to me to government. As for the superior excellence of ʿAlī over Muʿāwiya, no two men disagree about that. As for your satisfaction with Syria, you were satisfied with her yesterday, but we did not accept it. As for your statement that there is not a man in Syria more serious [in warfare] and no man in Iraq equal in seriousness to ʿAlī, this is how it should be. For ʿAlī is moved by his certitude, while Muʿāwiya is held back by his doubting; and the resolution of the people of truth is better than the endeavour of the people of falsehood. As for your assertion: 'We are more obedient to

[359] Minqarī, *Waqʿat Ṣiffīn*, 439.

[360] Al-Balādhurī describes a meeting of ʿUtba b. Abī Sufyān, al-Walīd b. ʿUqba 'and others' in the presence of Muʿāwiya at Ṣiffīn in which ʿUtba referred to the Umayyads killed by ʿAlī at Badr. Muʿāwiya suggested that they ought to thrust their spears at him, seeking revenge. Al-Walīd then rose and improvised a poem in which he made fun of Muʿāwiya's proposition. He described ʿAlī as a snake at the bottom of the valley for whose bite there was no physician and recalled that ʿAlī called out for Muʿāwiya in the battle but Muʿāwiya, though made to hear, failed to respond (*Ansāb*, 4/1, 117–18).

Mu'āwiya than you to 'Alī', by God, we do not ask him when he keeps silent, nor do we contradict him when he speaks. As for killing the Arabs, God has prescribed killing and fighting, and whoever is killed by the truth goes to God['s judgment].' 'Utba was incensed now and hurled abuse at Ja'da, who did not answer and turned away. They were both ready to fight. 'Utba gathered all his men and horses and came forward with a retinue of Sakūn, Azd and Ṣadif. Ja'da also prepared with every means at his disposal. They met, and for a while the men stood firm. Ja'da himself fought on that day, but 'Utba became frightened, abandoned his horsemen, and fled speedily to Mu'āwiya. The Iraqi poets al-Najāshī and al-A'war al-Shannī had a splendid opportunity to lampoon him and praise Ja'da.[361]

It remained for 'Amr b. al-'Āṣ, as commander of the Syrian cavalry, to supervise the overall Syrian battle conduct and occasionally to intervene in the fighting. He did so with due circumspection but not much personal distinction. When he took command of Ḥimyar and Yaḥṣub to lead them against al-Ashtar, the latter struck him in the face with his lance. Protected by his visor, he was not wounded, but feeling dazed by the impact, he turned back to the camp, holding his face. A youth of Yaḥṣub sped up to him and took the banner from his hands, appealing to Ḥimyar to stand firm. Al-Ashtar called his son Ibrāhīm: 'Take the banner from him, a boy for a boy.' The two young men met and fought for a while until the Yaḥṣubī fell dead. The Yemenites blamed Mu'āwiya for giving their command to someone who ran away from battle, and demanded that only one of their own should be appointed to lead them. Mu'āwiya conceded this to them.[362]

After the crucial, but indecisive, day, the battle continued through the night which was remembered as the night of the rumble (*laylat al-harīr*). The fighting was now mostly by sword, and the number of dead mounted. Advancing for a time, 'Alī recovered many of the dead from his army.[363] Unlike him, Mu'āwiya did not allow the enemy to pick up their dead or to bury them.[364] Nu'aym b. Suhayl b. al-'Ulayya al-Bajalī, fighting on the Syrian side, found his cousin Nu'aym b. al-Ḥārith b. al-'Ulayya among the Iraqi dead and asked Mu'āwiya for permission to bury him. Mu'āwiya answered that these people were not worthy of being buried since they had prevented a public burial for 'Uthmān. When Nu'aym threatened to join the enemy, he angrily told him to do what he pleased. Nu'aym buried his cousin.[365]

361 Minqarī, *Waq'at Ṣiffīn*, 462–6. 362 *Ibid.*, 439–42. 363 *Ibid.*, 369.

364 There is, however, a report that 'Amr b. al-'Āṣ agreed to a proposal by 'Alī to interrupt the fighting so that each side could get its dead from the other side and bury them: Balādhurī, *Ansāb*, II, 383. 365 Ṭabarī, I, 3302–3.

When morning came, the balance seemed to be slowly moving in 'Alī's favour. Towards noon some of the Syrians facing the centre of 'Alī's army raised copies of the Qur'ān tied to the heads of their lances. The fighting stopped.

Arbitration, Kharijite revolt, and end

The raising of the Qur'ān copies signified an appeal to settle the conflict on the basis of the Holy Book. The Syrians shouted at the same time: 'Let the Book of God judge between us and you. Who will protect the border towns of the people of Syria after they are all gone, and who will protect the border towns of the people of Iraq after they are all gone?'[366] It could be seen as an offer of surrender. Mu'āwiya had so far refused to submit to the Qur'ān, at least on 'Alī's terms, and had insisted that only the sword could judge between them. He had promised his followers that he would lead them to Iraq and pursue the murderers of 'Uthmān wherever they would seek to hide. When 'Amr b. al-'Āṣ realized that the Syrians could not win the battle and that the enemy was gradually gaining the upper hand, he advised Mu'āwiya to adopt the stratagem. The latter agreed, no doubt, with some reluctance.

In 'Alī's army the stratagem, as 'Amr had hoped, immediately caused confusion and discord. 'Alī exhorted his men to continue fighting. Mu'āwiya, 'Amr and their chief supporters were, he warned, not men of religion and the Qur'ān but were raising it for deception and fraud. To many of the Qur'ān readers, however, the appeal to the Scripture proved irresistible. Had they not marched against their Syrian brethren in order to teach them respect for the Qur'ān? How could they now reject their offer to submit to the judgment of the Holy Book? Two leaders of a group of Qur'ān readers who then became leading Kharijites, Mis'ar b. Fadakī of Tamīm and Zayd b. Ḥiṣn al-Ṭā'ī, threatened 'Alī: "Alī, respond to the Book of God since you have been summoned to it. If not, we shall hand you over to these people or we shall do with you as we did with Ibn 'Affān. We are obliged to act in accordance with the Book of God, and we accept it.' Facing open mutiny, 'Alī gave in to their demand that he recall al-Ashtar, who had advanced far towards the Syrian camp and sensed victory close at hand. Al-Ashtar refused at first to respond and had to be warned that the army would abandon him. His reproaches to the men that they were relinquishing the battle as he was hoping for victory and were allowing themselves to be duped for worldly motives were answered with curses. 'Alī had to restore order by affirming that he had accepted that the

[366] Ṭabarī, I, 3329; Balādhurī, *Ansāb*, II, 323.

Qur'ān be made the judge between the two parties. Al-Ash'ath b. Qays came up to him and assured him that the men of the army were pleased to respond to the offer of the opponents and offered to meet Mu'āwiya and enquire about the meaning of their appeal to the Qur'ān. Mu'āwiya proposed to him that each side choose a representative to arbitrate the conflict in accordance with the Book of God and that both parties agree to abide by their joint verdict. Al-Ash'ath welcomed the proposal without further question, and the majority of 'Alī's army immediately declared their acceptance.[367]

As the implications of Mu'āwiya's proposal became evident, however, a substantial minority dissented. According to the account of al-Sha'bī, a group of about four thousand men of insight and pious worshippers objected to the principle of arbitration. They evidently realized that Mu'āwiya was not sincerely submitting to the Qur'ān but intended a game of political wheeling and dealing between two representatives of the opposing parties which would allow him to hold on to power. Another, smaller, group abstained from either backing or opposing the proposal. The group opposed to the arbitration came to 'Alī and demanded that he resume the war. 'Alī, according to al-Sha'bī, was in favour of this. Those in favour of arbitration, however, insisted that the proposal was only right, fair and just. Al-Ash'ath b. Qays and the Yemenites were most outspoken in their opposition to a return to war. 'Alī pointed out to the opponents of arbitration that they were in a minority and that the majority would be tougher against them if they resumed the war than the Syrians and would jointly with these wipe them out. He, 'Alī, was not pleased with what had happened, but he inclined to the majority in fear that they would suffer senseless loss of life. Then he recited the line of the pre-Islamic poet Durayd b. al-Ṣimma:

> I am only one of Ghaziyya; when they go astray,
> I go astray, and when they are rightly guided, I am guided.

The opponents of arbitration went away in anger. Some of them left for Kūfa before the agreement was signed. Others stayed on, saying: 'Perhaps he will repent and turn back.'[368]

Al-Ash'ath b. Qays, who was the most active and prominent advocate of truce and arbitration, evidently represented the strong peace sentiment of the majority of the Yemenites, especially Kinda. More crucial for 'Alī was probably the attitude of Rabī'a. They had borne the brunt of the battle, had thwarted Mu'āwiya's hopes for victory, and had suffered, besides the Yemenites, the most substantial losses. When 'Alī consulted their chiefs, one of them, Ḥurayth b. Jābir al-Ḥanafī, spoke in favour of

[367] Ṭabarī, I, 3329–33. [368] Balādhurī, *Ansāb*, II, 338–9.

continuing the war. Kurdūs b. Hāni' al-Bakrī and al-Ḥuḍayn b. al-Mundhir al-Raqāshī al-Rabaʿī, the youngest one among them, expressed their unconditional support of ʿAlī, with the former evidently inclining to the truce proposal, and the latter favouring resumption of the war. Khālid b. al-Muʿammar al-Sadūsī, who had held the general command of Rabīʿa, backed the truce and was supported by Shaqīq b. Thawr al-Sadūsī. They probably represented the majority sentiment. The Bakr b. Wā'il displayed hostility to al-Ḥuḍayn when his stand became known, and ʿAlī had to intervene in order to conciliate between them.[369] The chief of Bajīla, Rifāʿa b. Shaddād, also spoke in favour of the truce, arguing that the Syrians, after fighting and killing, were now accepting what they had been asked to accept. If they were to go back on their agreement, ʿAlī's followers would be able to resume the war with renewed vigour.[370] The number of Bajīla present, however, was insignificant.

Among those opposed, to varying degrees, to the truce were, apart from al-Ashtar, ʿAdī b. Ḥātim, chief of Ṭayyi', ʿAmr b. al-Ḥamiq, leader of Khuzāʿa,[371] and al-Aḥnaf b. Qays of Saʿd Tamīm. Tamīm had not been prominent in most of the fighting at Ṣiffīn, and their losses seem to have been lighter than those among the Yemen and Rabīʿa. Partly because of this they may have been more ready to continue the war in the hope of victory. Saʿīd b. Qays, chief of Hamdān, is said to have wavered between acceptance and rejection of the truce.[372]

The decision hung in the balance for some time while ʿAlī consulted his commanders. The Syrians, who were evidently eager to have the truce which was, under the circumstances, clearly favourable to them, urged Muʿāwiya to press the case for it. Muʿāwiya asked ʿAbd Allāh b. ʿAmr b. al-ʿĀṣ, who had the reputation of a pious man, to address ʿAlī's army. His appeal to the common interest of both sides in ending the conflict was answered, however, by Saʿīd b. Qays with a reminder that so far ʿAlī's army had fought for the rule of the Qur'ān to which the Syrians were now summoning.[373] Muʿāwiya also persuaded Maṣqala b. Hubayra of the Banū Shaybān of Rabīʿa to try to influence all of Rabīʿa, by means of a poem, to accept the truce.[374] In the Syrian army, only Busr b. Abī Arṭāh is said to have objected strongly to the arbitration and threatened that he would join the Iraqis. Muʿāwiya made light of his threat, however, well knowing that Busr was not a man to back ʿAlī.[375]

Immediately after the fighting stopped, evidently before the agreement on arbitration, Muʿāwiya made another attempt to reach a direct settlement with ʿAlī, regardless of his public claim of retaliation for ʿUthmān. He wrote to ʿAlī that if both of them had known what extent the

[369] Minqarī, *Waqʿat Ṣiffīn*, 484–8. [370] *Ibid.*, 488. [371] *Ibid.*, 482. [372] *Ibid.*, 484.
[373] *Ibid.*, 483. [374] *Ibid.*, 486. [375] *Ibid.*, 504.

destruction caused by their war would reach, they would presumably not have inflicted it on each other; yet though they had been deprived of their sound minds in starting the war, it remained for them to repent of their past folly and to restore what was left. He reminded 'Alī that he had previously asked him for possession of Syria on the basis that he would not owe obedience to him, and appealed to him now for what he had appealed to him yesterday. 'Alī, he suggested, was hoping for survival just as he, Mu'āwiya, was hoping for it, and must be fearing what Mu'āwiya feared from the fighting; their armies had been weakened, and their men were gone, yet they were both of 'Abd Manāf, and neither of them had superior merit over the other by which a proud man could be humbled or a free man enslaved.

'Alī answered the letter point for point. If he were killed in the cause of God and brought to life seventy times, he would not falter in his strength on behalf of God and the *jihād* against the enemies of God; he, 'Alī, had not been deficient in his sound mind and did not repent of what he had done. As for Mu'āwiya's demand for Syria, he would not give him today what he refused him yesterday; as for their equality in fear and hope, Mu'āwiya was as deep in doubt as he, 'Alī, was in certitude – and the Syrians were not more eager in their pursuit of this world than the people of Iraq were in pursuit of the other world; they were indeed both descended from the same forefather, 'Abd Manāf, but Umayya was not like Hāshim, Ḥarb not like 'Abd al-Muṭṭalib, Abū Sufyān not like Abū Ṭālib, nor was a Muhājir like a *ṭalīq*, or a rightful claimant like a false pretender. 'In our hands is the superior merit of prophethood through which we have humbled the proud and given pride to the humble.'[376]

In the face of the strong peace sentiments of the majority of his army, 'Alī decided to accept, against his own judgement, the arbitration proposal. His public display of reluctance merely strengthened the resolve of the peace party who, after initial victory, felt now in a position to dictate the terms. 'Alī evidently was convinced that the arbitration would fail, and put up little resistance. Two groups of Qur'ān readers of both sides first met between the lines to discuss the procedure. They agreed to 'revive what the Qur'ān revived and to deaden what the Qur'ān deadened'. The Syrians then proposed 'Amr b. al-'Āṣ as their arbitrator. Al-Ash'ath and the Iraqi Qur'ān readers led by Zayd b. Ḥiṣn al-Ṭā'ī and Mis'ar b. Fadakī proposed Abū Mūsā al-Ash'arī. When 'Alī objected that he did not wish to nominate Abū Mūsā, they countered that they would not be satisfied with anyone but him since he had warned them of what they had fallen into. The discussion thus turned into open criticism of

[376] *Ibid.*, 470–1; Mas'ūdī, *Murūj*, III, 201–2, para. 1792–3; (pseudo-)Ibn Qutayba, *Imāma*, I, 191–2.

'Alī's previous war policy. 'Alī pointed out that he could not trust Abū Mūsā, who had opposed him, had encouraged the people to desert him, and then fled from him. Only after some months had 'Alī granted him a pardon. He proposed appointing 'Abd Allāh b. al-'Abbās. They answered that there was no difference between himself and Ibn al-'Abbās; they wanted someone who was equally distant from both 'Alī and Mu'āwiya. 'Alī now proposed al-Ashtar. Al-Ash'ath reacted strongly against his Yemenite rival: 'Is there anyone but al-Ashtar who has set the earth aflame?' It was al-Ashtar's judgement, he asserted, that had pitted the Muslims against each other with their swords in order to achieve 'Alī's and his own desires.

'Alī now gave in, and Abū Mūsā, who was living in retreat at 'Urḍ, between Tadmur and al-Ruṣāfa in Syrian territory,[377] was sent for. Abū Mūsā readily accepted his role as arbitrator. Both al-Ashtar and al-Aḥnaf b. Qays vainly tried to persuade 'Alī to change his mind. Al-Ashtar suggested that he was the man to block 'Amr's designs and was prepared to kill him. Al-Aḥnaf argued that Abū Mūsā was indecisive and superficial, no match for a wily opponent such as 'Amr. If 'Alī did not want to appoint him, al-Aḥnaf, arbitrator, he should put him at least in second or third place so that he could untie the knots that 'Amr would try to tie, and that he would tie firmer knots for 'Alī.[378] Yet the peace party wanted none but Abū Mūsā.

As the text of the arbitration agreement was drawn up, another problem arose. Mu'āwiya objected to the title 'Commander of the Faithful' being attached to 'Alī's name, remarking that if he, Mu'āwiya, recognized 'Alī to be Commander of the Faithful, he would not have fought him. 'Amr b. al-'Āṣ, who was visiting 'Alī's camp for the negotiations, proposed that only the name and the father's name be mentioned, since 'Alī was amir of his followers but not of the Syrians. Al-Aḥnaf b. Qays advised 'Alī not to omit the title since he feared if he omitted it now he would never get it back. Rather than allowing that, the people should resume fighting. 'Alī thus at first on that day refused to remove the title. Then al-Ash'ath asked him to omit it since God would not want distress to be caused by it. 'Alī agreed, recalling the precedent set by Muḥammad at al-Ḥudaybiyya when he allowed the title 'Messenger of God' to be omitted from the treaty on the demand of the polytheists. 'Amr pretended to be offended: 'Praise the Lord, in this example we are likened to the infidels, yet we are believers.' 'Alī told him: 'Ibn al-Nābigha, when were you ever anything but a friend to the reprobate and an enemy to the Muslim? Are you not just like your [slave] mother

[377] Minqarī, *Waq'at Ṣiffīn*, 500; Yāqūt, *Buldān*, III, 644–5.
[378] Ṭabarī, I, 3333–4; Minqarī, *Waq'at Ṣiffīn*, 409–501.

who bore you?' 'Amr rose and said: 'No assembly room will ever bring me and you together again after this day.' 'Alī: 'Surely, I hope that God will cleanse my assembly room from you and the likes of you.'[379] Some of 'Alī's followers had strong feelings about the matter. A group of them came with their swords on their shoulders and said: 'Commander of the Faithful, order us to do whatever you wish.' Sahl b. Ḥunayf calmed them down, repeating the story of Muḥammad's precedent at al-Ḥudaybiyya.[380]

The arbitration agreement was written and signed in duplicate on Wednesday, 15 Ṣafar 37/2 August 657, four days after the cessation of hostilities.[381] It reflected primarily the sentiments of the peace party. The two sides committed themselves to adhere to the Book of God. The two arbitrators, who were named, were to follow strictly the rules of the Qur'ān. Whatever they could not find a rule for in the Qur'ān, they were to apply 'the just, uniting and not dividing, sunna', evidently meaning good practice acceptable to both sides. What they were to judge was not specified. They were bound, however, to judge among the Community rightly so as not to throw them into division and war. This was obviously the primary concern of the peace party, who were otherwise prepared to give the arbitrators a free hand. They were to make their judgment by Ramaḍān, seven months after the agreement, but might either advance or defer the date.[382] They should meet at a place equidistant from Damascus and Kūfa, but could meet elsewhere by mutual agreement. No one was allowed to attend their meeting except by their choice, and they were free to choose the witnesses who would sign their decision. The text quoted by al-Minqarī contained a clause, missing in other versions, that the two sides were absolved from any judgment not agreeing with God's revelation.[383] If the clause was part of the original document, it was presumably added at 'Alī's instance. Even without it, it was clear, however, that any decision in conflict with the Qur'ān would be *eo ipso* invalid.

There was plainly a deplorable lapse in 'Alī's leadership at this trying but crucial time. He permitted the majority of his army to impose their will on him as if he were a tribal shaykh, as implied in his quotation of Durayd b. al-Ṣimma, rather than the Commander of the Faithful. It is

[379] Ṭabarī, I, 3334–5; Minqarī, *Waq'at Ṣiffīn*, 508–9. [380] Minqarī, *Waq'at Ṣiffīn*, 509.

[381] The date is given in both versions of the text quoted by al-Minqarī (*Waq'at Ṣiffīn*, 507–8, 511) and is confirmed by al-Ṭabarī (I, 3340). Abū Mikhnaf, however, according to al-Balādhurī (*Ansāb*, II, 337–8), gave the date as 'Friday in Ṣafar'; and the Basran Abū 'Amr b. al-'Alā', quoted by Abū 'Ubayda, mentioned Friday, 17 Ṣafar 37/4 Aug. 657. Of the two versions of the text given by al-Minqarī, the shorter one (*Waq 'at Ṣiffīn*, 510–11; Ṭabarī, I, 3339) is basically reliable as shown by M. Hinds, 'The Ṣiffīn Arbitration Agreement', *JSS*, 17 (1972), 92–129, at 93–129.

[382] The text of the various versions disagrees on whether the date could only be advanced or only deferred or both. [383] Minqarī, *Waq'at Ṣiffīn*, 511.

true that the raising of the Qur'ān copies by the Syrians put him in a difficult position. He could not simply ignore the gesture and had to ascertain its significance. Yet once it became evident that Muʿāwiya was not submitting to the Qur'ān but was proposing to use it as a political football in order to hold on to power, ʿAlī had to resume the battle. This was evidently harder now that the fighting had been stopped by false hopes for a peaceful settlement, but there were a sufficient number of prominent leaders such as al-Ashtar, al-Aḥnaf b. Qays and ʿAdī b. Ḥātim who were ready and eager to go on with the war to definite victory. It is quite unlikely that any substantial part of his men were, whatever the rhetoric, at this point prepared to desert to Muʿāwiya. Al-Ashʿath b. Qays was no traitor, although he had been reluctant from the beginning to fight his own people on the Syrian side.[384] It was ʿAlī's own deference to the majority sentiment in his army, after having made clear his preference for resumption of the battle, that encouraged the peace party to make a show of their strength and to question openly ʿAlī's judgement in starting the campaign itself. ʿAlī's former experience of seeing the people 'turn away from him' seems to have haunted him and to have paralysed his resolve.

Later, when ʿAlī approached Kūfa, he enquired about the opinion of the judicious there about his conduct. He was told that they thought he had allowed the massive army gathered by him to disperse and had destroyed the firm fortress built by him; they were questioning when he might be able to assemble again the dispersed and to rebuild what he had destroyed. If indeed part of his army had disobeyed him, he should have fought on with those obeying him until victory or death. ʿAlī countered that it was they, not he, who had dispersed and destroyed. He had thought of fighting on with the loyal minority, since he was not sparing with his own life; but looking at al-Ḥasan and al-Ḥusayn, he had realized that if they perished the offspring of Muḥammad would be cut off from the Community. He had also been concerned for the lives of his nephew ʿAbd Allāh b. Jaʿfar and his non-Fatimid son Muḥammad who had come along only for his sake. If he were to meet the enemy again, these charges of his would not again be in his army.[385]

The latter point may be viewed with some sympathy. ʿAlī was an exceptionally brave man, and his lack of resolve after the battle of Ṣiffīn cannot be explained by either cowardice or plain defeatism. If he sincerely lost faith in the loyalty of the bulk of his army, concern for the only surviving grandsons of the Prophet and other members of his family was a reasonable motive not to resume a suicidal fight. The blame that may attach to his decision to retreat is minor. His acceptance of the

[384] Hinds is mistaken, however, in suggesting that al-Ashʿath did not take part in the battle of Ṣiffīn ('The Ṣiffīn Arbitration Agreement', 93). [385] Ṭabarī, I, 3346–7.

arbitration proposal, in contrast, was a serious and unjustifiable political blunder. He could have arranged a simple military truce with Mu'āwiya. He could have withdrawn from the battlefield without any agreement. Arbitration on Mu'āwiya's terms was the worst option.

'Alī realized fully that arbitration on the basis of the Qur'ān with 'Amr b. al-'Āṣ as one of the arbitrators could only end in failure. Whatever the agreement voiced about the independence of the arbitrators and their sole obligation to judge in accordance with the Qur'ān in the interest of peace for the whole Community, it was obvious that 'Amr was not a free agent but a stooge of Mu'āwiya acting solely for his benefit. 'Alī thus foresaw that he would inevitably have to repudiate any agreement of the arbitrators if they were able to reach one. He acted out of spite in permitting al-Ash'ath and the peace party to set the terms of the agreement, thinking to teach them a lesson about their illusory hopes for an honourable settlement with Mu'āwiya. It was not the case, as the defenders of 'Alī's conduct later claimed, that he acted under duress from his disloyal followers.[386] For as soon as he had accepted their demands to end the war, they were in no position to dictate his relations with Mu'āwiya. Even if a few had gone over to the enemy, it would have mattered little.

It was not so much the terms of the agreement dictated by the peace party, unfavourable as they were for 'Alī, as the principle of arbitration itself that was objectionable. How could 'Alī, after steadfastly refusing men such as Mu'āwiya and 'Amr b. al-'Āṣ public office under his reign, now allow them to sit as judges over the Qur'ān? The arbitration agreement both undermined the conviction among his own loyal followers that they had been fighting for a righteous cause and encouraged the Syrians to believe that the fraudulent claims of Mu'āwiya had a credible basis in the Qur'ān. It thus handed Mu'āwiya a moral victory even before it caused the disastrous split in the ranks of 'Alī's men. On this basis Syrian propaganda could later celebrate Ṣiffīn as a victory for Mu'āwiya although militarily it had been close to a defeat. Mu'āwiya and 'Amr, to be sure, knew as well as 'Alī that the arbitration was bound to end in failure. But Mu'āwiya gained time to consolidate his grip on Syria and would attempt to draw the maximum propagandistic benefit out of the negotiations.

When al-Ashtar was called to sign the agreement, he refused to do so, declaring that he was in no doubt that the enemy was misguided and that the peace party was merely caving in out of moral lassitude. Al-Ash'ath protested and demanded that he sign since he, al-Ashtar, could not

[386] See, for instance, the argument of Ibn al-'Abbās, Balādhurī, *Ansāb*, II, 337.

dispense with the backing of the people. The latter angrily countered that he could certainly dispense with al-Ash'ath in this world and the hereafter. Al-Ash'ath, he added, was in his eyes no better, nor was his blood more sacred, than the men whose blood God had shed through his sword. Al-Ash'ath paled. Then al-Ashtar added that he was satisfied with what 'Alī had done and that he saw no guidance except in following him.[387]

Al-Ash'ath took the text of the agreement and read it out before each banner of the two armies. The Syrians were all satisfied. When he read it to the 'Anaza, who numbered four thousand men in 'Alī's army, two young brothers, Ma'dān and Ja'd, came forward with the call: 'No judgment except God's.' Attacking the Syrian battle line, they were killed. They were said to have been the first ones to raise the Kharijite battle cry. Among the Murād, Ṣāliḥ b. Shaqīq, one of their chiefs, voiced his disapproval. The Banū Rāsib of Azd similarly objected to the arbitration of men in the religion of God. When al-Ash'ath read the agreement to the Tamīm, 'Urwa b. Ḥudayr, known by his mother's name as 'Urwa b. Udayya, came forward exclaiming: 'Will you appoint men as arbitrators in the affairs of God? No judgment but God's. Where are our dead, Ash'ath?' Then he charged at al-Ash'ath with his sword and, missing him, hit the hind part of his horse with a light blow, causing it to bolt. 'Urwa's companions shouted: 'Control your hand', and he turned back. As al-Ash'ath's men and many Yemenites stood up in anger on his behalf, al-Aḥnaf b. Qays, Jāriya b. Qudāma, Ma'qil b. Qays al-Riyāḥī, Mis'ar b. Fadakī al-'Anbarī, Shabath b. Rib'ī and other chiefs of Tamīm went to him to offer their apologies; he accepted them.[388]

After the battle, the remaining dead were buried. On the Syrian side Ḥābis b. Sa'd al-Ṭā'ī, a chief of the Banū Ṭayyi' in Ḥimṣ, had been killed. His body was found by his Kufan nephew Zayd, son of 'Adī b. Ḥātim, who said to his father: 'This is, by God, my maternal uncle.' His father confirmed his identity and cursed Ḥābis. Zayd repeatedly called out, asking who had killed him. Finally a man of Bakr b. Wā'il came forth and acknowledged having slain him. Zayd asked him about the circumstances and then pierced him with a lance, killing him. His own father attacked him, cursing him and his mother, and threatened to surrender him to the Bakr. Zayd rode off swiftly and joined Mu'āwiya, who received him with open arms. There was some murmuring among 'Alī's followers against 'Adī b. Ḥātim, who had been one of his closest associates. 'Adī apologized to 'Alī for Zayd's offence; he affirmed that he would kill him if he found him, and 'Alī praised him for his loyalty.[389]

387 Minqarī, *Waq'at Ṣiffīn*, 511–12; Ṭabarī, I, 3338.

388 Minqarī, *Waq'at Ṣiffīn*, 512–13; Ṭabarī, I, 3338–9; Balādhurī, *Ansāb*, II, 336, 339.

389 Minqarī, *Waq'at Ṣiffīn*, 521–4; Balādhurī, *Ansāb*, II, 306, according to whose account Zayd's revenge and desertion occurred during the battle.

The prisoners on both sides were released. 'Amr b. al-'Āṣ is said to have earlier advised Mu'awiya to kill his Iraqi prisoners of war. When 'Alī released his Syrian captives, however, Mu'āwiya expressed relief that he had not done so and reciprocated.[390] Two days after the conclusion of the agreement both sides departed from the battlefield.[391]

'Alī took the route along the western bank of the Euphrates to Hīt where he crossed the river. He stayed a night at Ṣandawdā' and continued on to Kūfa via al-Nukhayla. On the way the deep rift in his army became fully apparent as supporters and opponents of the arbitration agreement cursed and hit each other with whips. 'No judgment but God's' became the motto of the opponents, who accused the supporters of having acted dishonourably in the matter of God by appointing human arbitrators, while these condemned the opponents as deserters of their imam and their community. Witnessing the division among his men, 'Alī is said to have confessed in verse that he had made a slip (*'athra*) for which he need not apologize. He rather would act intelligently and continue firmly so as to mend the rift.[392] Yet the schism proved too serious. As he entered Kūfa and dismissed his army in Rabī' I 37/August–September 658,[393] some twelve thousand men seceded and withdrew to Ḥarūrā' outside the town in protest against the arbitration, fully prepared to fight for their cause. They chose Shabath b. Rib'ī al-Tamīmī as their military leader and 'Abd Allāh b. al-Kawwā' al-Yashkurī of Bakr b. Wā'il as leader of their prayers. Among them were evidently also many who had initially advocated the truce or accepted arbitration and now recognized their mistake. The choice of Shabath b. Rib'ī may indicate that the presence of Tamīm among 'the first Ḥarūriyya' was substantial. According to Ṣāliḥ b. Kaysān even al-Aḥnaf b. Qays was among them,[394] but his reliability here is doubtful. Prominent among the seceders was also the Yemenite Yazīd b. Qays al-Arḥabī, 'Alī's former governor of al-Madā'in.[395] No longer recognizing 'Alī as their imam, the rebels committed themselves to a *shūrā* after victory. In the meantime their oath of allegiance was to God on the basis of 'ordering what is proper and prohibiting what is reprehensible'.[396]

In Kūfa 'Alī reprimanded his interim governor Abū Mas'ūd al-Anṣārī who, during his absence, had encouraged the deserters of 'Alī's army to come out by promising them safety and had in his sermons criticized the

[390] Ṭabarī, I, 3339–40; Minqarī, *Waq'at Ṣiffīn*, 518–19. The note of al-Minqarī that 'Alī released his Syrian prisoners except those who had killed one of his men or had been captured for a second time, in which case they would be killed, evidently does not apply to the situation at Ṣiffīn. It probably refers to the later Syrian raids.

[391] Balādhurī, *Ansāb*, II, 337. [392] *Ibid.*, 342.

[393] Muḥammad b. al-Sā'ib al-Kalbī gives as the date of 'Alī's return to Kūfa 20 Rab. I 37/5 Sept. 657 (*ibid.*, 345–6). This seems rather late. [394] *Ibid.*, 342.

[395] Ṭabarī, I, 3352. [396] *Ibid.*, 3349; Balādhurī, *Ansāb*, II, 342.

rebels against ʿUthmān. ʿAlī called him a chicken and an old man who had lost his sound mind, but Abū Masʿūd defended himself, reminding ʿAlī that the Prophet had promised him paradise. He left for a pilgrimage and continued admonishing the people to hold on to the Community.[397]

To mediate with the seceders, ʿAlī first sent ʿAbd Allāh b. al-ʿAbbās, advising him to stall for time in replying to their questions and in arguing with them until he would join him. Ibn al-ʿAbbās was drawn, however, into debate by them, and he questioned them as to why they resented arbitration, since God stipulated the appointment of two arbitrators in the case of a serious conflict between husband and wife (Sūra IV 35). The seceders answered that in this case, where God prescribed arbitration, it was licit for the people to judge, but in matters where God had stated His rule, such as the punishment of a hundred lashes for the fornicator and the cutting off of the hand for the thief, His rule was binding. Ibn al-ʿAbbās gave as another example the judgment of 'two men of integrity (*dhawā ʿadl*)' stipulated by the Qurʾān in the case of compensation for illicit killing of game by a pilgrim in the state of sanctity (Sūra V 95). The seceders countered that these cases could not be compared to one involving the shedding of blood of Muslims; furthermore, did Ibn al-ʿAbbās consider ʿAmr b. al-ʿĀṣ a 'man of integrity' after he had fought them and shed their blood? God had laid down His judgment concerning Muʿāwiya and his party that they be killed unless they turned back; they had been summoned to the Book of God and had rejected it; a peace settlement of Muslims with non-Muslims was not licit after the revelation of the Sūra of Renunciation except with Christians and Jews if they paid tribute (*jizya*).[398] The seceders thus unequivocally denounced Muʿāwiya and the Syrians as infidels. They stood their ground, and the weak arguments of Ibn al-ʿAbbās evidently made little impact.[399]

ʿAlī had sent Ziyād b. al-Naḍr to the camp of the seceders to investigate which of their leaders enjoyed the most prestige among them, and Ziyād reported that most of them assembled around Yazīd b. Qays. ʿAlī now went to visit Yazīd in his pavilion and performed his ablution and prayer there. He apparently had no difficulty in regaining Yazīd's allegiance and appointed him governor of Iṣfahān and Rayy. Then he went out to where Ibn al-ʿAbbās was debating with the seceders and interrupted his discourse. He addressed them, reminding them that they had wished to respond to the Syrian appeal to the Qurʾān while he had warned against it. When they had persisted in their view, he had stipulated that the

[397] Ibn Abī Shayba, *Muṣannaf*, VIII, 728. [398] Ṭabarī, I, 3351–2.

[399] According to the main report, none of the seceders followed the appeal of Ibn al-ʿAbbās to return to Kūfa. Other accounts reported that 2,000 or 4,000 men did so (Balādhurī, *Ansāb*, II, 349).

arbitrators strictly follow the judgment of the Qur'ān. If they failed to do so, their judgment would not be binding. When the seceders asked whether he considered the arbitration of men in cases of bloodshed licit, he suggested that he had not agreed to the arbitration of men but to the arbitration of the Qur'ān. The Qur'ān, however, was in writing and did not speak. It was thus for men to pronounce it. They asked him why he had agreed to a fixed term for the truce, and he answered that it was in the hope that God might restore peace in the Community during the truce. 'Alī then appealed to them to return to their town, and all of them did so.[400]

Abū Mikhnaf added to this account of 'Umāra b. Rabī'a and Jundab b. 'Abd Allāh al-Azdī that the Kharijites themselves reported their answer to 'Alī. They told him that they had indeed done what he described, but this had been an act of infidelity on their part for which they repented before God. 'So repent as we have repented, and we shall pledge allegiance to you. If not we shall oppose you.' 'Alī had responded with a general declaration: 'I repent to God and ask His forgiveness from every sin.' They then pledged allegiance to him on the basis that he would resume the war after six months, while they would collect the land tax and fatten their riding animals.[401]

Full accord, however, was not restored. When the seceders returned to Kūfa, there was antagonism between the more radical among them and those Kufans who championed the arbitration agreement. The radicals now claimed that 'Alī had repented and affirmed that the arbitration was an act of infidelity and a sinful error (*ḍalāl*). They were, so they affirmed, only waiting for their animals to be fattened before they headed for Syria. 'Alī was forced to distance himself from this claim, stating that he had not gone back on the agreement and did not consider it a sinful error. While many of the 'first Ḥarūriyya', including their chosen leaders Shabath b. Rib'ī and 'Abd Allāh b. al-Kawwā', accepted this, some of them resumed their public condemnation of the arbitration agreement.[402] They interrupted 'Alī's sermons in the mosque with their battle cry 'No judgment but God's'. 'Alī commented on it, affirming that it was a word of truth by

[400] Ṭabarī, I, 3352–3. [401] *Ibid.*, 3353; Balādhurī, *Ansāb*, II, 349.

[402] Balādhurī, *Ansāb*, II, 356. Veccia-Vaglieri's suggestion that 'Alī somehow went back on concessions he had made to the seceders ('Il conflitto 'Alī–Mu'āwiya e la secessione Khārigita riesaminati alla luce di fonti ibāḍite', *Annali Istituto Orientale di Napoli*, NS 4 (1952), 1–94, at 42–7; 'Ḥarūrā' in *EI* (2nd edn) is not well founded. 'Alī had committed himself to resuming the war against Mu'āwiya but obviously only if the arbitration, as he expected, would not lead to a sound judgment based on the Qur'ān. This was evidently sufficient for the moderate seceders to return to obedience. He could not have promised to break the arbitration agreement, and this is not even claimed by the Ibāḍī sources. The radicals, especially those who themselves had confessed their repentance of their initial support of the arbitration, now wanted to force a similar confession on him and the majority of the community.

which they sought falsehood.[403] They were effectively repudiating government (*imra*), yet an amir was indispensable in the conduct of religion.[404] Basically agreeing with their position, however, he hesitated to let the tribes act against them. He ordered that they be neither excluded from the mosques nor deprived of their share of the *fay'* revenue. They should be fought only if they started fighting.[405]

Faced with this discord among the Kufans, 'Alī put off the preparations for the arbitration. Ramaḍān passed, and in early Shawwāl/mid-March 658 an envoy from Mu'āwiya, Ma'n b. Yazīd b. al-Akhnas al-Sulamī,[406] arrived to complain about the delay. Mu'āwiya, he reported, had fulfilled his obligations, and 'Alī must now fulfil his without letting himself be swayed by 'the bedouins (*a'ārīb*) of Bakr and Tamīm'.[407] 'Alī now gave orders to proceed with the arbitration. He sent four hundred men under the command of Shurayḥ b. Hāni' al-Ḥārithī as an escort for his arbitrator to Dūmat al-Jandal. Since he had little trust in Abū Mūsā, he also sent 'Abd Allāh b. al-'Abbās along as his personal representative. Ibn al-'Abbās was to lead the prayers of the Kufans and to manage their affairs. He also carried on the correspondence between 'Alī and his arbitrator. 'Amr b. al-'Āṣ arrived at Dūmat al-Jandal with an escort of four hundred Syrians.

Among the Kufans there were evidently doubts whether Abū Mūsā al-Ash'arī would stand up to 'Amr b. al-'Āṣ and back the cause of 'Alī. Shurayḥ b. Hāni' is said to have told Abū Mūsā that he would have to make up for his previous failure to support 'Alī, and Abū Mūsā commented that people who doubted his integrity should not be sending him to defend their case. Shurayḥ then changed his attitude and praised him in order to strengthen his prestige. The poet al-A'war al-Shannī, however, warned Shurayḥ in a poem that Abū Mūsā was a man without astuteness or incisive judgement, no match for the cunning 'Amr. If the two were to judge in accordance with right guidance they would be followed, but if they judged according to false inclination, they would end up in bitter conflict. Al-Najāshī, who was a friend of Abū Mūsā, expressed his faith in him and encouraged him to crush 'Amr with his thunderbolts.[408] Even while Abū Mūsā was in Dūmat al-Jandal, al-A'war al-Shannī and al-Ṣalatān sent poetry to him. The latter, a poet of 'Abd al-Qays, declared that he would never agree to depose 'Alī on the basis of a judgement by Abū Mūsā and 'Amr.[409]

[403] Ṭabarī, I, 3361–2. [404] Balādhurī, *Ansāb*, II, 352, 361, 377.
[405] Ṭabarī, I, 3362–3; Balādhurī, *Ansāb*, II, 352.
[406] He was a Companion and was killed at Marj Rāhiṭ fighting for al-Ḍaḥḥāk b. Qays (Ibn Manẓūr, *Mukhtaṣar*, XXV, 150–2).
[407] Ṭabarī, I, 3353; Balādhurī, *Ansāb*, II, 346–50. [408] Minqarī, *Waq'at Ṣiffīn*, 534–5.
[409] *Ibid.*, 537–8.

As soon as 'Alī's decision to send Abū Mūsā became known, two Kharijites, Zur'a b. al-Burj al-Ṭā'ī and Ḥurqūṣ b. Zuhayr al-Sa'dī,[410] came to him protesting and urging him to forgo the arbitration and to lead them to fight against their enemies. 'Alī countered that he would have liked to do that but they had disobeyed him. A treaty had therefore been written and confirmed between the two parties, and they were bound by it in accordance with Qur'ān Sūra XVI 91. Ḥurqūṣ stated that this was a sinful act for which 'Alī must repent. 'Alī denied that it was sinful, maintaining that it was merely an unsound opinion and weakness in action against which he had warned them. Zur'a b. al-Burj now intervened, declaring that if 'Alī would not abandon the arbitration of men concerning the Book of God, he would fight him, seeking the face and pleasure of God by that. Rebuking him, 'Alī foretold his death, but Zur'a answered that death would be pleasant to him. 'Alī told him that if he were fighting for something rightful, death in rightness would be a consolation for this world. The devil had, however, deluded him. Both men should fear God since there was no good in their fighting for a portion of this world. The two left proclaiming 'No judgment but God's'.[411]

The radical opponents of the arbitration now met in the house of 'Abd Allāh b. Wahb al-Rāsibī.[412] They all agreed that they could no longer stay in this unjust city and must leave for a place where they could assemble to denounce and fight the misguided innovations of its people. They decided to choose a leader among themselves. Zayd b. Ḥiṣn al-Ṭā'ī, Ḥurqūṣ b. Zuhayr, Jamra[413] b. Sinān al-Asadī and Shurayḥ b. Awfā al-'Absī all declined the leadership. 'Abd Allāh b. Wahb al-Rāsibī, known as Dhu l-Thafināt because of the callosities on his forehead and hands from his many prostrations in worship, accepted it reluctantly. They pledged allegiance to him on 10 Shawwāl 37/21 March 658.[414] Then, after Abū Mūsā's departure for the arbitration,[415] they met in the house of Shurayḥ b. Awfā, who proposed that they occupy al-Madā'in, expel the inhabitants, and invite their Basran brethren to join them. Zayd b. Ḥiṣn suggested that if they departed as a group they would be pursued; rather, they should leave individually and in secret. They were sure to be prevented from entering al-Madā'in and should rather go to Jisr

410 So the report of Abū Mikhnaf on the authority of 'Awn b. Abī Juḥayfa (Ṭabarī, I, 3360). In two reports of al-Sha'bī, Shurayḥ b. Awfā al-'Absī, Farwa b. Nawfal al-Ashja'ī, 'Abd Allāh b. Shajara al-Sulamī, Jamra b. Sinān al-Asadī, 'Abd Allāh b. Wahb al-Rāsibī and Zayd b. Ḥiṣn al-Ṭā'ī are named aside from these two (Balādhurī, *Ansāb*, II, 359, 361).

411 Ṭabarī, I, 3360–1.

412 According to al-Sha'bī's account, they met in the house of either 'Abd Allāh b. Wahb or Zayd b. Ḥiṣn (Balādhurī, *Ansāb*, II, 359, see also 363).

413 Jamra is the name given by al-Balādhurī. In al-Ṭabarī it appears as Ḥamza.

414 Al-Balādhurī (*Ansāb*, II, 363) gives the date as Friday night, 20 Shawwāl. This would be 22 March 658.

415 Balādhurī, *Ansāb*, II, 363.

al-Nahrawān, east of the Tigris, and invite the Basrans to meet them there. This proposal met with approval, and ʿAbd Allāh b. Wahb wrote to their Basran brethren informing them of their decision and urging them to join them. The Basrans responded positively to his letter.

The first to leave were Shurayḥ b. Awfā and Zayd b. Ḥiṣn. ʿAdī b. Ḥātim's son Ṭarafa[416] also intended to join the rebels. His father pursued him but was unable to catch up with him. When Ṭarafa reached al-Madā'in, he decided to return. On his way back he was met at Sābāṭ by ʿAbd Allāh b. Wahb with twenty horsemen. ʿAbd Allāh wanted to kill him, but ʿAmr b. Mālik al-Nabhānī and Bishr b. Zayd al-Bawlānī[417] prevented him. ʿAdī b. Ḥātim sent to Saʿd b. Masʿūd, ʿAlī's governor of al-Madā'in, warning him of the rebels' approach. Saʿd secured the gates of al-Madā'in and rode out to meet them. There was some fighting at al-Karkh, but during the night ʿAbd Allāh b. Wahb crossed the Tigris and reached al-Nahrawān safely.[418] About two thousand men gradually assembled there.

Some of those attempting to join were caught and imprisoned by their people. Among them were al-Qaʿqāʿ b. Qays al-Ṭā'ī, uncle of the later Kharijite poet al-Ṭirimmāḥ, ʿAbd Allāh b. Ḥakīm al-Bakkā'ī[419] and Kaʿb b. ʿUmayra.[420] ʿItrīs b. ʿUrqūb al-Shaybānī, a companion of ʿAbd Allāh b. Masʿūd, was pursued by Ṣayfī b. Fushayl al-Shaybānī and some of his men but escaped.[421] ʿAlī was informed that Sālim b. Rabīʿa al-ʿAbsī intended to leave. He had him brought before him and persuaded him to stay.[422]

After the Kharijites left Kūfa, ʿAlī's followers offered him a renewed oath of allegiance on the basis that they would be friends of those he befriended and enemies of those he took as enemies. ʿAlī stipulated adherence to the Sunna of the Prophet in the oath. When he asked Rabīʿa b. Shaddād al-Khathʿamī, who had fought for him in the battles of the Camel and Ṣiffīn and was the carrier of the banner of Khathʿam, to pledge allegiance on the basis of the Book of God, the Sunna of the Messenger of God, Rabīʿa suggested: 'On the sunna of Abū Bakr and ʿUmar.' ʿAlī objected that if Abū Bakr and ʿUmar had been acting on anything but the Book of God and the Sunna of his Messenger, they would have been remote from the truth. Rabīʿa pledged allegiance to him, but ʿAlī told him

416 Al-Balādhurī is probably mistaken in insisting that it was ʿAdī b. Ḥātim's son Zayd who joined the Kharijites (*Ansāb*, II, 364). He argues that Ṭarafa was killed fighting for ʿAlī at al-Nahrawān. According to Abū Mikhnaf's account, Ṭarafa was killed there fighting on the side of the Kharijites (Ṭabarī, I, 3384). In either case he must be the one who initially tried to join the Kharijites. Zayd had earlier joined Muʿāwiya.

417 Nabhān and Bawlān were clans of Ṭayyi'.

418 Ṭabarī, I, 3366–7.

419 *Ibid.*, 3367. Bakkā' was a tribe of ʿĀmir b. Ṣaʿṣaʿa.

420 Balādhurī, *Ansāb*, II, 364.

421 *Ibid.*, 363.

422 Ṭabarī, I, 3367.

that he foresaw his death on the side of the rebels. Rabīʿa was in fact killed at al-Nahrawān among the Basran Kharijites.[423]

The conflict about the arbitration thus brought a wider dogmatic schism to the fore. The Kharijites objected to the personal allegiance to the imam expressed in the formula offered by the partisans of ʿAlī that they would be friends of those he befriended and enemies of those he took as enemies. They accused them of emulating the Syrians in their infidelity when they pledged allegiance to Muʿāwiya on the basis of their likes and dislikes.[424] For the Kharijites allegiance was not bound to a person, but to adherence to the Book and the Sunna of the righteous, the Prophet, Abū Bakr and ʿUmar. They were evidently critical of ʿAlī's claim of his specific right to the imamate on the basis of his early merits and close kinship with Muḥammad. Early merit could be lost at any time by an infraction of the divine law, as it was lost by ʿUthmān, and kinship with the Prophet was irrelevant in their eyes. Against ʿAlī's claims they stressed their own adherence to the sunna of Abū Bakr and ʿUmar, overlooking that this sunna entailed the privileged status of Quraysh, which they as political egalitarians rejected.

The formula of the new oath of allegiance for ʿAlī matched the invocation that Muḥammad was reported to have made for him at Ghadīr Khumm: 'O God, be a friend of whomever he [ʿAlī] befriends and an enemy of whomever he takes as an enemy.'[425] It was most likely about this time that ʿAlī had the hadith of Ghadīr Khumm proclaimed in public. The hadith is introduced in many of its versions by the statement that ʿAlī one day appealed to the crowd assembled on the square (*raḥaba*) in front of the mosque of Kūfa, asking those who had heard the words of the Prophet at Ghadīr Khumm to testify. Twelve or thirteen Companions came forward and witnessed that they had heard words in which Muḥammad affirmed that ʿAlī was the patron (*mawlā*) of everyone whose patron Muḥammad was and an invocation on behalf of his cousin. ʿAlī thus unequivocally claimed a religious authority superior to that of Abū Bakr and ʿUmar.

The Basran Kharijites, some five hundred men under the leadership of Misʿar b. Fadakī, departed as a group. They were pursued by Abu l-Aswad al-Duʾalī,[426] who caught up with them at al-Jisr al-Akbar. They

[423] *Ibid.* [424] *Ibid.*, 3350.

[425] For versions of the hadith of Ghadīr Khumm containing this invocation, see the references in Wensinck, *Concordance*, s.v. *walī*. The ambiguity of the pronouns in the invocation allows the interpretation of ʿAlī either as the subject or the object of 'befriending and taking as an enemy'. The translation chosen here agrees with the formula of the oath offered to ʿAlī by his partisans.

[426] That Abu l-Aswad was sent after them by Ibn al-ʿAbbās, as Abū Mikhnaf's report has it (Ṭabarī, I, 3367), is probably incorrect. Ibn al-ʿAbbās was at the time in Dūmat al-Jandal for the arbitration. He presumably left Abu l-Aswad in charge of Baṣra.

faced each other until nightfall, and Misʿar escaped with his companions in the darkness. Then they continued on to al-Nahrawān. On their way there the Basran Kharijites are said to have started the practice of interrogating and killing people for their views.[427] According to one report, they murdered ʿAbd Allāh b. Khabbāb b. al-Aratt and others just before they reached al-Nahrawān.[428] Most likely, however, these murders occurred some months later when ʿAlī was ready to set out for Syria. Otherwise ʿAlī could hardly have ignored their activity and asked them to join his army without taking account of the offences committed by them.

In the meantime the two arbitrators were meeting at Dūmat al-Jandal. Since they reported to their respective patrons in Kūfa and Damascus and received instructions from them, the negotiations must have lasted some weeks and probably extended to early Dhu l-Qaʿda 37/mid-April 658. The Kufan escort was evidently most eager to learn immediately about the developments of the discussions and pressed Ibn al-ʿAbbās to inform them about the contents of ʿAlī's letters when they were delivered by his messenger. Ibn alʿAbbās reprimanded them and pointed out that the Syrians were self-disciplined and did not interfere with the messages exchanged between Muʿāwiya and his arbitrator.[429] The Syrians could obviously trust ʿAmr not to betray the interests of Muʿāwiya. In Kūfa doubts about Abū Mūsā's loyalty to ʿAlī grew in the course of the meetings, and al-Ṣalatān al-ʿAbdī composed, as noted, his poem affirming that he would never depose ʿAlī on the basis of a verdict by Abū Mūsā and ʿAmr. As the tension among the Kufans grew, the two arbitrators agreed to keep their discussions strictly confidential.[430]

The story of the arbitration has been much discussed in light of the contradictory information provided by the sources about date, place, procedure and outcome. That there were actually two meetings, one at Dūmat al-Jandal and the other at Adhruḥ, was suggested early on by Caetani[431] and strongly backed by Veccia-Vaglieri. More recently Djaït has again argued that there was only one meeting, at Adhruḥ, probably in Muḥarram 38/June–July 658.[432] On closer examination of the early

[427] *Ibid.*, 3368. [428] *Ibid.*, 3374–5.

[429] *Ibid.*, 3354; Minqarī, *Waqʿat Ṣiffīn*, 533–4. The report clearly implies that Muʿāwiya was not present at Dūmat al-Jandal, contrary to some reports and the assumption of most modern scholars, including Veccia-Vaglieri ('Il conflitto', 48–9). Muʿāwiya was present at Adhruḥ, and this fact evidently influenced some reports about Dūmat al-Jandal. The arbitration agreement suggested that the arbitrators would meet without the presence of their respective patrons. [430] Minqarī, *Waqʿat Ṣiffīn*, 538.

[431] *Annali*, X, 30–1.

[432] *La Grande Discorde*, 276. Djaït suggests that only the Syrian delegation came to Dūmat al-Jandal in Ramaḍān 37, while ʿAlī, occupied with the Kharijites, failed to send a delegation. This was also the view of H. Lammens (*Etudes sur le règne du Calife Omaiyade Moʿâwia 1er* (Paris, 1908), 126–9).

reports it seems clear that there were two meetings between Abū Mūsā and 'Amr. However, only the first one, at Dūmat al-Jandal, was an attempt to implement the arbitration agreement. As it failed, 'Alī considered the truce void and resumed hostilities. The second meeting, at Adhruḥ, was, as will be seen, convened solely on Mu'āwiya's initiative. Since Abū Mūsā was at that time no longer the recognized representative of 'Alī, who ignored the meeting, the proceedings were not part of the arbitration. The Kufan historical tradition focused its attention on the meeting at Dūmat al-Jandal, which was the only one relevant to 'Alī and the Kufans. Though largely ignoring the meeting at Adhruḥ, it incorporated some of the events there, especially the famous final scene, into its account of the earlier meeting. The Medinan tradition generally focused on the meeting at Adhruḥ, but also included details of the meeting at Dūmat al-Jandal in its account.

Veccia-Vaglieri suggested that the question to be examined by the arbitrators at Dūmat al-Jandal was whether 'Uthmān had been killed wrongfully or not.[433] They reached the verdict that he was killed wrongfully, but kept it secret. As it became known, however, 'Alī denounced it as contrary to the Qur'ān, while the Syrians received it enthusiastically and pledged allegiance to Mu'āwiya as caliph. This is only partly accurate. The task of the arbitrators according to the agreement of Ṣiffīn was to settle the conflict among the Muslims comprehensively, not just to examine 'Uthmān's innocence or guilt. That question was presumably put on the table first by 'Amr b. al-'Āṣ because he rightly expected that he could easily reach agreement with Abū Mūsā about it. A verdict that 'Uthmān was killed wrongfully and that Mu'āwiya was his next-of-kin who could legitimately claim revenge for his blood would cement Syrian support for the Umayyad and weaken the position of 'Alī. 'Amr no doubt realized that he could not get much more from Abū Mūsā and that the arbitration would inevitably fail.

Abū Mūsā was a neutralist sincerely concerned to restore peace in the Muslim Community. He saw the admission, in general terms, that 'Uthmān had been killed wrongfully as a conciliatory gesture which, he hoped, would somehow be reciprocated by 'Amr in the vital question of the leadership of the Community. It was hardly his view that 'Alī should hand over men such as al-Ashtar, who had established and backed Abū Mūsā as governor of Kūfa, to Mu'āwiya for blood-revenge. He was also, at this time, not prepared to accuse 'Alī, or simply to depose him as caliph to make room for someone else. He would probably have been satisfied to let 'Alī stay on as caliph if he accepted Mu'āwiya as governor of Syria and

[433] 'Il conflitto', 26–31.

Mu'āwiya recognized him. Ideally he would have liked a *shūrā* composed of the religious aristocracy in which 'Alī might be included. His favourite candidate, however, was 'Abd Allāh b. 'Umar. Abū Mūsā, himself an early Companion, was certainly not prepared to accept Mu'āwiya, a *ṭalīq*, as caliph. Mu'āwiya could be allowed, however, to remain governor of Syria since he was well liked by his army.

The verdict that 'Uthmān was killed wrongfully thus was a political deal, not based on a judicial investigation. Abū Mūsā presumably justified it in his mind with the argument already used by 'Ā'isha that 'Uthmān had repented of any wrongdoing he had committed. A judicial examination, however, would first have had to establish whether Niyār 'the Evil' had been wrongfully killed; for 'Uthmān's violent death had been precipitated by the murder of Niyār. It is true that either the murderer or his master Marwān would have been subject to the *lex talionis* rather than 'Uthmān, who was probably opposed to the murder. In this sense it could be held that 'Uthmān had not been rightfully killed. He had, however, prevented legal retaliation by refusing to investigate the murder, presumably aware or suspecting that his cousin Marwān was behind it. 'Alī's judgment that 'Uthmān's violent death was neither wrongful nor rightful thus was substantially correct. Abū Mūsā should have been particularly wary of agreeing to a blank declaration of 'Uthmān's innocence since the proposal came from 'Amr, the foremost agitator against 'Uthmān and the first target of al-Walīd b. 'Uqba's vendetta. He was probably naïve enough to believe that 'Amr now sincerely regretted his former conduct. The sentence, judicially a misjudgment, became political and, for Sunnites, religious dogma with disastrous long-term effects for Islam.

Once the initial agreement on 'Uthmān's innocence had been reached, it was 'Amr's strategy to block any agreement on either 'Alī retaining the caliphate or on a *shūrā*. He probably did not press the case for a caliphate of Mu'āwiya seriously at this point, since the latter had not yet put forward a formal claim. A *shūrā*, as favoured by Abū Mūsā, would have meant electing one of the neutrals. This might at this time still have been acceptable to Mu'āwiya, but only if his permanent rule of Syria was guaranteed. Such a guarantee could obviously not be given by Abū Mūsā. It was thus best to let the negotiations collapse. The agreement that 'Uthmān had been killed wrongfully would, 'Amr trusted, cause further division among 'Alī's followers and dissuade any of the pious neutrals from turning to his side.

The details of the discussions at Dūmat al-Jandal are uncertain. Much of what is reported about them seems to refer rather to Adhruḥ since

Mu'āwiya appears already as a serious candidate for the caliphate. That the caliphate itself was discussed, however, is evident from the poem of al-Ṣalatān. It is certain that the meeting, contrary to Veccia-Vaglieri's assumption, broke up in disarray without agreement.[434] As the failure of the negotiations, Abū Mūsā's concessions and 'Amr's intransigence became known, the Kufans present reacted with fury. Shurayḥ b. Hāni' attacked 'Amr b. al-'Āṣ with his whip. One of 'Amr's sons hit back at Shurayḥ before they were separated by the people. Shurayḥ later used to say that his only regret was not having used his sword instead of his whip.[435] Abū Mūsā was disgraced and fled to Mekka. 'Amr and the Syrians, in contrast, departed triumphantly to Mu'āwiya and greeted him as Commander of the Faithful.[436] Before the end of Dhu l-Qa'da 37/April–May 658 Mu'āwiya received the general pledge of allegiance of the Syrians as caliph.[437]

When Ibn al-'Abbās and Shurayḥ reported to 'Alī, he denounced the conduct of both arbitrators. Preaching to the Kufans, he reminded them of his warnings about both men and the arbitration; now these two arbitrators, whom they had chosen, had thrown the rule of the Qur'ān behind their backs, had judged without sound argument or accepted precedent, and in the end had disagreed between themselves. He called on his followers to prepare to march to Syria and to assemble in their military camp on Monday.[438] As it became known that Mu'āwiya had accepted the oath of allegiance as caliph, 'Alī broke off all relations and correspondence with him. He introduced a curse on Mu'āwiya, 'Amr, Abū l-A'war al-Sulamī, Ḥabīb b. Maslama, 'Abd al-Raḥmān b. Khālid b. al-Walīd, al-Ḍaḥḥāk b. Qays and al-Walīd b. 'Uqba in the invocation of the morning prayer (*qunūt*).[439] This followed the practice of Muḥammad

[434] Veccia-Vaglieri attributed undue significance to the agreement of the two arbitrators 'to say nothing' mentioned by al-Minqarī (*Waq'at Ṣiffīn*, 538). Read in context, it merely means that the two arbitrators, after hearing al-Ṣalatān's poem, agreed to keep their proceedings secret. Once it was clear that they were unable to reach an agreement there was no longer any reason to maintain secrecy.

[435] Ṭabarī, I, 3359; Minqarī, *Waq'at Ṣiffīn*, 546. There had already been a clash between Shurayḥ and 'Amr at the beginning of the meetings when Shurayḥ conveyed a message from 'Alī appealing to 'Amr not to back the traitors and oppressors. 'Amr sarcastically queried whether he had ever accepted any advice from 'Alī. Shurayḥ countered that Abū Bakr and 'Umar, who were better than 'Amr, had consulted 'Alī and acted on his advice. 'Amr responded haughtily that the likes of himself would not talk to the likes of Shurayḥ. The latter belittled 'Amr's father and mother, and they parted in enmity (Ṭabarī, I, 3357–8; Minqarī, *Waq'at Ṣiffīn*, 542–3).

[436] Ṭabarī, I, 3359; Minqarī, *Waq'at Ṣiffīn*, 546.

[437] Ṭabarī, I, 3396, II, 199.

[438] *Ibid.*, I, 3368; Balādhurī, *Ansāb*, II, 365–6.

[439] Ṭabarī, I, 3360. Al-Minqarī (*Waq'at Ṣiffīn*, 552) mentions Abū Mūsā al-Ash'arī in place of Abu l-A'war.

of calling a curse upon some of his enemies in the *qunūt*.[440] Mu'āwiya retaliated by introducing a curse on 'Alī, Ibn al-'Abbās, al-Ashtar, al-Ḥasan and al-Ḥusayn.[441]

After his call for resumption of the war with Mu'āwiya, 'Alī wrote to the Kharijites assembled at al-Nahrawān, addressing his letter to Zayd b. Ḥiṣn and 'Abd Allāh b. Wahb as their leaders. Again he denounced the two arbitrators who had failed to act in accordance with the sunna and to carry out the rule of the Qur'ān. He invited them to join him and to fight their common enemy on the same basis as they had done before. The Kharijites answered that he was standing up not on behalf of God, but of himself. If he testified that he had committed an act of infidelity and repented, they would reconsider their relations with him; otherwise they would continue to oppose him. When 'Alī read their letter, he despaired of gaining their support. He decided, however, to leave them and to carry out his campaign to Syria.[442]

'Alī was evidently eager to set out on the campaign as quickly as possible, before Mu'āwiya could gather all his forces. He instructed Ibn al-'Abbās to mobilize the Basrans. According to Abū Mikhnaf's account,[443] only 1,500 men there joined al-Aḥnaf b. Qays at first. After a second appeal by Ibn al-'Abbās, 1,700 Basrans were recruited by Jāriya b. Qudāma.[444] In Kūfa 'Alī is said to have ordered the tribal chiefs to register their warriors, the sons of warriors old enough to fight, slaves and clients, and thus to have assembeld an army of 65,000.[445] This figure is, no doubt, greatly inflated, and many must have ignored the new call to arms. In a speech 'Alī urged the Kufans to fight a people without merit in Islam who would rule them like Chosroes and Heraclius.[446] He was informed that his men wished him first to subdue the Kharijites before moving against the Syrians. When he told them, however, that the war against 'a people who would be tyrants and kings and would take the worshippers of God for

[440] See Wensinck, 'Ḳunūt', *EI*; Kister, 'O God, Tighten Thy Grip on Muḍar', 252–73. Kister's suggestion (271) that 'Alī's adherents probably disapproved of his invocation against Mu'āwiya, considering it perhaps as *bid'a*, is based on a report (Ibn Abī Shayba, *Muṣannaf*, II, 209) of the 'Uthmanid al-Sha'bī, a servant of the Umayyad government (see F. Krenkow's article on him in *EI*) who cannot be presumed to be speaking for the followers of 'Alī. The historical accounts do not suggest that there was any opposition to the cursing in Kūfa. While the majority of the Kufans were not eager to fight the Syrians, public opinion was at this time, after the failure of the arbitration, outraged by the conduct of 'Amr b. al-'Aṣ and strongly opposed to Mu'āwiya.

[441] Ṭabarī I 3360. Al-Minqarī, (*Waq'at Ṣiffīn*, 552) names Qays b. Sa'd in place of al-Ashtar. Most likely Qays b. Sa'd was substituted for al-Ashtar after the latter's murder by Mu'āwiya. [442] Ṭabarī, I, 3368–9; Balādhurī, *Ansāb*, II, 461, 467.

[443] On the authority of Abu l-Waddāk al-Hamdānī.

[444] Al-Balādhurī (*Ansāb*, II, 367) speaks of 3,000 or 5,000 or more under the command of Jāriya b. Qudāma. [445] Ṭabarī, I, 3370–2. [446] *Ibid.*, 3369–70.

servants' was more important than the Kharijites, they all assured him of their obedience and loyalty.[447]

'Alī moved north via Shāhī and Dabāhā to the east bank of the Euphrates and al-Anbār. He had received disturbing news about the murder of 'Abd Allāh b. Khabbāb b. al-Aratt, his pregnant wife and Umm Sinān al-Ṣaydāwiyya by the Kharijites, and sent al-Ḥārith b. Murra[448] to investigate their conduct and to question them. Then he learned that they had met and killed his envoy. His men turned to him, pleading that they could not leave their families and property behind at the mercy of such people and urged him to fight them first. They were backed by al-Ash'ath b. Qays, who evidently preferred fighting the Kharijites rather than the Syrians since there were few, if any, Yemenites among them. While this was evidently the sentiment of the majority, there were, however, others who had been prepared to fight the Syrians but left when 'Alī decided to deal with the internal rebels first.[449] 'Alī now sent Qays b. Sa'd b. 'Ubāda ahead to al-Madā'in to join forces with his governor, Sa'd b. Mas'ūd al-Thaqafī. As he caught up with them, 'Alī sent to the Kharijites demanding the surrender of the murderers. If they did so he would leave them alone until he had fought the Syrians in the hope that they would change their minds in the meantime and return to the course of right. They answered defiantly that all of them had killed these people and all considered the shedding of their and 'Alī's partisans' blood licit.

Then Qays b. Sa'd addressed them, impressing on them the magnitude of their crimes; but 'Abd Allāh b. Shajara countered by stating that the truth had illuminated them and that they would not adhere to Qays' party unless their opponents brought them someone like 'Umar b. al-Khaṭṭāb. Qays told them that he knew no one in his party like 'Umar except for their master 'Alī and asked them whether they knew someone like him in their own ranks. He entreated them not to destroy their lives. Abū Ayyūb al-Anṣārī also pleaded with them, suggesting that there was no cause for division between them now. Why would the Kharijites wish to fight 'Alī's supporters? They answered: 'If we were to swear allegiance to you today, you would agree to arbitration tomorrow.' He told them not to engage in a rebellion now in fear of what might happen tomorrow.

[447] *Ibid.*, 3572–3.

[448] Abū Mikhnaf's account names al-Ḥārith b. Murra al-'Abdī. This is, as al-Balādhurī points out (*Ansāb*, II, 368), a mistake, since al-Ḥārith b. Murra al-'Abdī was killed in Sind several years later. Al-Dīnawarī gives his *nisba* as al-Faq'asī (*Annali*, I, 127, 240–1). This may, however, be merely a guess.

[449] Balādhurī, *Ansāb*, II, 485.

ʿAlī addressed them once more and tried to justify his conduct in regard to the arbitration, which they had forced upon him. He asked them by what right they considered it licit for them to leave their community, to draw their swords against their own people, to investigate their views, and to spill their blood. The Kharijites called to each other not to speak to their opponents but to prepare to meet their Lord and go to paradise. Both sides drew up in battle order. ʿAlī gave Abū Ayyūb a banner of safe conduct for anyone wishing to surrender, and the latter shouted that anyone who came to this banner or departed for Kūfa or al-Madāʾin and had not committed a murder would be safe. 'We have no need to shed your blood after we strike the killers of our brethren.'[450] Misʿar b. Fadakī with a thousand men sought refuge at Abū Ayyūb's banner. Farwa b. Nawfal al-Ashjaʿī declared that he did not know now why they should fight ʿAlī and that he needed more time to reflect on his proper conduct. He left with five hundred horsemen for al-Bandanījayn and al-Daskara east of al-Nahrawān. Between one hundred and three hundred men went over to ʿAlī. ʿAbd Allāh b. (Abi) l-Ḥawsāʾ al-Ṭāʾī withdrew with three hundred men, Ḥawthara b. Wadāʿ with another three hundred, and Abū Maryam al-Saʿdī with two hundred. Out of four thousand men only one thousand eight hundred or one thousand five hundred stayed with ʿAbd Allāh b. Wahb.[451]

ʿAlī gave the order to let the Kharijites attack. They were greatly outnumbered by ʿAlī's followers, said to have been fourteen thousand,[452] and fought desperately without hope of survival. The battle thus turned into a one-sided massacre. ʿAbd Allāh b. Wahb, Zayd b. Ḥiṣn, Jamra b. Sinān, ʿAbd Allāh b. Shajara and Shurayḥ b. Awfā were killed. Four hundred wounded were found among the dead on the battlefield. ʿAlī ordered them to be handed over to their tribes for medical care. On ʿAlī's side only seven or, according to another report,[453] twelve or thirteen men were killed. ʿAdī b. Ḥātim found his son Ṭarafa among the dead and buried him. As ʿAlī heard that some of his men were burying their dead kin, he gave order to depart immediately. He showed no sympathy for those men who had once been his vigorous supporters and now had become his bitter enemies.

The date of the battle of al-Nahrawān is given by al-Balādhurī as 9 Ṣafar 38/17 July 658.[454] Al-Ṭabarī, following Abū Mikhnaf, reported it under the year 37 but argued that it occurred in 38, in which year most

[450] Ṭabarī, I, 2277–80.
[451] Balādhurī, *Ansāb*, II, 371: reading *wa-yuqāl* for *yuqāl*. The number of 1,800 for the Kharijite horsemen alone would be quite unreasonable since Jamra b. Sinān, the commander of their cavalry, is then described as commanding only 300 horsemen (Ṭabarī, I, 3380–1). [452] Balādhurī, *Ansāb*, II, 371. [453] Khalīfa, *Taʾrīkh*, 197.
[454] Balādhurī, *Ansāb*, II, 362.

sources dated it.[455] Modern historians have generally accepted the date given by al-Balādhurī and viewed the battle as contemporaneous with the conquest of Egypt by Muʿāwiya and ʿAmr, which according to al-Wāqidī and al-Kindī took place in Ṣafar 38. It is, however, quite unlikely, and incompatible with various reports, that Muʿāwiya could have undertaken the invasion of Egypt at the very time when he expected the second incursion of ʿAlī's army from the east. There is good evidence, as will be seen, that the battle of al-Nahrawān took place, in accordance with Abū Mikhnaf's account, in the year 37, most likely early in Dhu l-Ḥijja/mid-May 658.

The massacre of the Kharijites at al-Nahrawān was the most problematic event in ʿAlī's reign. From the perspective of ordinary statecraft it was a reasonable, even necessary, act. These men were rebels, violators of their oath of allegiance, provocatively spurning the public order, openly threatening to shed the blood of any Muslim, including their own kin, who would not join them. ʿAlī, eager to resume the battle with his real enemy Muʿāwiya, would have preferred to ignore them for the time being and to deal with them after his campaign to Syria. They were too numerous, however, and he could not overlook the possibility that they might, in their reckless mood, be tempted to seize Kūfa in the absence of the bulk of the army. With any temporary accommodation now precluded by the murder of his messenger, he saw himself compelled once more to give in to the demands of those most reluctant to fight the Syrians in his army and to move against the rebels first.

Yet these rebels were, like himself, sincere and uncompromising upholders of the rule of the Qurʾān. Some of their leaders had backed him on that basis earlier during the scandalous reign of ʿUthmān. They and he basically agreed in their view of the futility of arbitration in the conflict with Muʿāwiya. Although some of them had initially pressed him to accept it, they had come to recognize their mistake and had repented it as an act of infidelity. They would have been among his most vigorous allies in the war against the distorters of the rule of the Qurʾān. He ought to have made every effort to regain their allegiance even if it meant putting off the Syrian campaign. This was, it is true, not an easy task in view of their radicalism which precluded compromise. ʿAlī could not agree to either of their demands, that he attest his own infidelity in accepting the arbitration, or that he treat Muslim opponents as infidels. He could not simply condone the murders that some of them had committed. Patient argument with them, however, might have gradually won over most, if not all, of them. His first task would have been to restore a consensus

[455] Ṭabarī, I, 3387–9.

among the Qur'ān readers, or at least the activists among them, who were his natural allies. It was the haste with which he sought to resume the war with Mu'āwiya that forced him to resort to counterproductive threats and violence against his former followers. The battle of al-Nahrawān sealed the division between Shī'a and Kharijites.

The weakness of his support now became quickly apparent. 'Alī wanted to proceed immediately from al-Nahrawān to Syria. His men complained that their arrows were used up, their swords dulled, their spearheads had fallen off their lances, and urged him to return to Kūfa so that they might restore their equipment and replenish their forces. Again al-Ash'ath b. Qays was their spokesman, and 'Alī gave in. When they reached al-Nukhayla, he ordered that they stay in their camp there to get ready for the war and only occasionally visit their wives and families. Within days his army melted away, leaving but a few of the leaders with him. 'Alī realized that he had lost control over them and entered Kūfa, abandoning the campaign.[456]

The initiative now rested with Mu'āwiya. Informed of 'Alī's war preparations after the failure of the arbitration, he had hastily assembled a Syrian army outside Damascus. Ḥabīb b. Maslama is said to have advised him to take again his defensive position at Ṣiffīn, while 'Amr proposed that he invade 'Alī's territories in northern Mesopotamia. While still hesitating, Mu'āwiya learned that 'Alī had turned off his route to Syria in order to subdue the rebels in his own ranks. He was pleased and waited for further developments. Then information arrived that 'Alī had killed the rebels and that his army had compelled him to defer his campaign to Syria. A letter from 'Umāra b. 'Uqba b. Abī Mu'ayṭ confirmed the disarray of 'Alī's army and the deep division and antagonism among the Kufans.

Mu'āwiya now called al-Ḍaḥḥāk b. Qays and instructed him to attack the bedouin Arabs loyal to 'Alī in the desert west of Kūfa, to fight minor troop detachments of the enemy army, but to avoid any major force sent against him. He gave him between three thousand and four thousand horsemen. Al-Ḍaḥḥāk crossed the desert, killing the bedouins he met and carrying off their property and reached al-Tha'labiyya[457] on the pilgrimage route from Kūfa to Mekka. There he attacked the pilgrims, presumably as they were returning from Mekka, and robbed them of their belongings. He turned north on the pilgrimage route and met 'Amr b. 'Umays b. Mas'ūd al-Dhuhlī, nephew of 'Abd Allāh b. Mas'ūd, at al-Quṭquṭāna. He

[456] *Ibid.*, 3385–6.

[457] In his letter to his brother 'Aqīl, 'Alī mentioned Wāqiṣa and Sharāf, both on the pilgrimage route north of al-Tha'labiyya, as being passed through by al-Ḍaḥḥāk in his raid (Thaqafī, *Ghārāt*, 331–2). Wāqiṣa is also named in the accounts of al-Balādhurī (*Ansāb*, II, 437) and al-Ṭabarī (I, 3447).

murdered him and a number of his companions. 'Alī appealed to the Kufans to avenge the blood of 'Amr b. 'Umays and their compatriots. At first they ignored him, but then Ḥujr b. 'Adī responded with four thousand horsemen, taking up the pursuit of the Syrians. In the desert of al-Samāwa, in Kalbite territory, Imru' ul-Qays b. 'Adī al-Kalbī, who had marriage ties with 'Alī and his sons, aided him, and his tribesmen acted as guides in the desert. He caught up with al-Ḍaḥḥāk near Tadmur. They fought for a while, and nineteen Syrians were killed as against two men of Ḥujr. In the cover of night the Syrians fled.[458]

This type of ordinary brigandage, highway robbery and murder now became a regular feature of the raids that Mu'āwiya dispatched into 'Alī's territories, marking a new low in the character of inter-Muslim warfare. In a sermon al-Ḍaḥḥāk later, as governor of Kūfa in 55/674-5, boasted of his murder of 'Amr b. 'Umays as a heroic deed. The Kufan (Abu l-Kanūd) 'Abd al-Raḥmān b. 'Ubayd (al-Azdī) sarcastically commended him on his final brave stand outside Tadmur, which he had witnessed.[459]

Some time after al-Ḍaḥḥāk's raid, 'Alī received a letter from his elder brother 'Aqīl in which he mentioned an extra-seasonal pilgrimage (*'umra*) he had recently performed. On his way he had met 'Abd Allāh b. Sa'd b. Abī Sarḥ with some forty young men, sons of *ṭalīqs*, heading west from Qudayd.[460] Perceiving evil intent in their faces, he asked them whether they were joining Mu'āwiya out of their undisguisable old grudge against Islam, and there was an exchange of insults. When he arrived in Mekka, he heard the people talking about the raid of al-Ḍaḥḥāk on al-Ḥīra and how he had carried off whatever he wished of their property and returned safely to Syria. Upon hearing this, he imagined that 'Alī must have been deserted by his followers. He asked 'Alī if he intended to fight to the death and offered to join him with his sons and cousins to share his fate.

In his answer to 'Aqīl, 'Alī made light of Ibn Abī Sarḥ, whom he described as a diehard enemy of Muḥammad and the Qur'ān, and he disparaged Quraysh, who had cut their kinship ties to him, connived to deprive him of his right, and handed it to one who was not equal to him in kinship to the Prophet and early merit in Islam. Against al-Ḍaḥḥāk, he assured his brother, he had sent a strong troop of Muslims who had

458 Thaqafī, *Ghārāt*, 416–26; Balādhurī, *Ansāb*, II, 437–8.

459 Thaqafī, *Ghārāt*, 336–8; Balādhurī, *Ansāb*, II, 438–9. The raid of al-Ḍaḥḥāk b. Qays is reported by al-Ṭabarī (I, 3347) under the year 39, two years too late. Caetani followed his dating (*Annali*, X, 287–9). Al-Balādhurī confirms that this was the first of the raids ordered by Mu'āwiya (*Ansāb*, II, 437), and Ibn A'tham al-Kūfī (*al-Futūḥ* (Hyderabad, 1968–75), IV, 36–8), whose account is based on Abū Mikhnaf's, affirms that it took place immediately after the arbitration (at Dūmat al-Jandal).

460 It is unknown where 'Aqīl resided at this time. Ibn Abi l-Ḥadīd argues in favour of Medina (*Sharḥ*, X, 250), but Syria seems also possible. Qudayd is near Mekka. 'Towards the west' evidently meant Syria.

punished him in his flight. He declared his intention to pursue the *jihād* against the desecrators (*muḥillūn*) until he met God. A multitude of backers could not increase his strength, nor their desertion his solitude, since he was in the right, and God was with the right. As for ʿAqīl's offer to join him with his sons and cousins, he had no need of that and did not wish them to perish if he should perish. ʿAqīl should not imagine that his mother's son, even if the people were to abandon him, would be so humbled as to implore for help or meekly submit to injustice.[461]

Lammens accepted ʿAqīl's letter as authentic,[462] yet described him as ʿAlī's '*ennemi acharné*'.[463] ʿAqīl is reported to have visited ʿAlī in Kūfa and asked him for money. It is to be noted in this regard that ʿAqīl had owned a house there which he sold to al-Walīd b. ʿUqba during the latter's governorship.[464] He had thus presumably been on the pension register of Kūfa. ʿAlī refused to give him money from the *fay*' revenue, but is said to have offered him money from his personal estate at Yanbuʿ. ʿAqīl then left for Damascus, and was given a large sum of money by Muʿāwiya. This was probably before the battle of Ṣiffīn. It is not known whether Muʿāwiya gave him this money because he now was on the pension register of Syria, or simply as a bribe. As noted by Lammens,[465] one of ʿAqīl's wives was Muʿāwiya's aunt. The reports about his relations with Muʿāwiya are anecdotal and describe him as treating the Umayyad and his prominent companions with exceeding disdain. There is no sound evidence that he ever backed Muʿāwiya against his brother ʿAlī. Veccia-Vaglieri's suggestion that 'the estrangement between the two brothers probably had political causes' is quite unfounded.[466]

Muʿāwiya next turned his eyes on Egypt. Here the government of Muḥammad b. Abī Bakr was in serious trouble. As noted, Muḥammad had antagonized the ʿUthmanid seceders gathered at Kharbitā with

[461] Thaqafī, *Ghārāt*, 434–5; *Aghānī*, XV, 46; Balādhurī, *Ansāb*, II, 74–5. The letters give the impression of being basically authentic. They must, in any case, be quite early. ʿAqīl's letter was conveyed by (Abu l-Kanūd) ʿAbd al-Raḥmān b. ʿUbayd al-Azdī, who had participated in Ḥujr's pursuit of al-Ḍaḥḥāk b. Qays and must have met ʿAqīl in Mekka or visited him soon afterwards. ʿAqīl was thus evidently well informed about the desertion of the Kufans and feigned out of courtesy that he merely imagined that ʿAlī must have been left in the lurch by them. The transmitter of the letters in al-Thaqafī's account, the Kufan Abū Sulaymān Zayd b. Wahb al-Juhanī (d. after 82/701 or in 96/714-5) collected a book of ʿAlī's speeches (see Thaqafī, *Ghārāt*, 34 n. 5; Sezgin, *Abū Miḥnaf*, 209–10) and presumably obtained the text of the letters from Abu l-Kanūd. Abū Mikhnaf transmitted the letters on the authority of Sulaymān b. Abī Rāshid from Abu l-Kanūd (*Aghānī*, XV, 46; for *Ibn Abi l-Kanūd* read *Abu l-Kanūd*). It is evident from the letters that ʿAbd Allāh b. Saʿd b. Abī Sarḥ was still alive at this time and that his presence at the battle of Ṣiffīn is probably not a fiction as suggested by C. H. Becker, ("Abd Allāh b. Saʿd', *EI*).

[462] *Moʿâwia*, 175.

[463] *Ibid.*, 112.

[464] *Aghānī*, IV, 182.

[465] *Moʿâwia*, 175.

[466] See "Aḳīl b. Abī Ṭālib', *EI* (2nd edn).

whom his predecessor, Qays b. Sa'd, had arranged a working relationship. The successful resistance of the Syrians to 'Alī at Ṣiffīn encouraged them to raise their heads in opposition to the governor. Muḥammad sent an army under al-Ḥārith b. Jumhān al-Ju'fī against the rebels, who were still being led by Yazīd b. al-Ḥārith al-Kinānī. Al-Ḥārith b. Jumhān was defeated and killed.[467] A second army sent by the governor under the command of a Kalbite, Ibn Muḍāhim, fared no better. Ibn Muḍāhim was killed by the seceders.[468]

The leadership of the seceders was now taken over by a more renowned man, Mu'āwiya b. Ḥudayj al-Sakūnī, who attracted others into the 'Uthmanid camp.[469] Maslama b. Mukhallad also resumed his campaign for revenge for 'Uthmān independently of the group at Kharbitā. Both men had fought for Mu'āwiya at Ṣiffīn[470] and now evidently returned to Egypt. The initially independent Egyptian 'Uthmanid movement became more pro-Mu'āwiya. 'Alī was aware of the weakness of Muḥammad b. Abī Bakr's position and thought of replacing him with either Qays b. Sa'd or al-Ashtar. He had, after returning from Ṣiffīn, appointed Qays his police chief and promised him the governorship of Ādharbayjān after the arbitration. Al-Ashtar had returned to his governorship of Upper Mesopotamia. Immediately after the arbitration 'Alī summoned him from Naṣībīn[471] and sent him to Egypt to take over from Ibn Abī Bakr, whom he described to him as a young man inexperienced in war and political affairs. That he dispensed with al-Ashtar just as he was about to set out on his second campaign to Syria reflects the importance of Egypt in his planning.

Mu'āwiya learned of al-Ashtar's appointment through his spies. He bribed a tax collector to attempt to murder him. Al-Ashtar sought to avoid Syrian territory, travelling by boat from the Ḥijāz to al-Qulzum on the Egyptian Red Sea coast.[472] There he was hospitably received by Mu'āwiya's tax collector, who served him a poisoned honey drink, killing him.[473] Mu'āwiya boasted about the murder of his old enemy and 'Amr is

467 Al-Ḥārith b. Jumhān al-Ju'fī had fought for 'Alī at Ṣiffīn (Minqarī, *Waq'at Ṣiffīn*, 154, 254–5). 'Alī presumably sent him to Egypt to aid Muḥammad b. Abī Bakr. However, in the accounts of al-Balādhurī and al-Thaqafī, in contrast to al-Ṭabarī's, his *nisba* is given as al-Balawī instead of al-Ju'fī. It is thus possible that he is not identical with 'Alī's supporter at Ṣiffīn.

468 Ṭabarī, I, 3248; Balādhurī, *Ansāb*, II, 398; Thaqafī, *Ghārāt*, 254–5.

469 According to al-Balādhurī's account (*Ansāb*, II, 398), Mu'āwiya b. Ḥudayj was persuaded to act as leader of the Egyptian 'Uthmāniyya by Mu'āwiya b. Abī Sufyān. If the latter did so, it was in breach of his truce agreement with 'Alī.

470 See Minqarī, *Waq'at Ṣiffīn*, index on both men.

471 Al-Ashtar named Shabīb b. 'Āmir al-Azdī to replace him in Upper Mesopotamia (Thaqafī, *Ghārāt*, 258).

472 Balādhurī, *Ansāb*, II, 399.

473 Ṭabarī, I, 3392–3; Thaqafī, *Ghārāt*, 254–60. There are different reports on the murder of al-Ashtar (Thaqafī, *Ghārāt*, 262–3).

quoted as commenting that God has armies in honey.[474] It was probably Mu'āwiya's first murder by poison, but certainly not his last. In public he congratulated his followers, assuring them: "'Alī b. Abī Ṭālib had two right hands. One of them was cut at Ṣiffīn', meaning 'Ammār b. Yāsir, 'and the other today', meaning al-Ashtar.[475]

The loss of al-Ashtar, a most loyal and capable, if not always submissive, supporter, was a severe blow to 'Alī. He did not conceal his grief and expressed his highest praise for him to the shaykhs of his clan al-Nakha' who visited him.[476] He wrote to Muḥammad b. Abī Bakr, who had been disturbed by the mission of al-Ashtar, reassuring him that he had not acted out of impatience with his war effort or dissatisfaction with his seriousness. If he had removed him from his present authority, he would have appointed him to one that was lighter for him to bear and more pleasing. Then he praised the man whom he had appointed over Egypt as one sincere to him, severe against his enemies, who had met his death with 'Alī well pleased with him; he prayed that God would be pleased with him and double his reward. 'Alī asked Ibn Abī Bakr to be steadfast towards his enemy and ready for war. In his answer Muḥammad b. Abī Bakr assured 'Alī of his firm loyalty.[477]

After the raid of al-Ḍaḥḥāk b. Qays, Mu'āwiya consulted his senior commanders and 'Amr about his plans to seize Egypt. 'Amr b. al-'Āṣ, eager to obtain his promised prize, advised him to expedite a large army to Egypt immediately. The Egyptians agreeing with their views would then flock to them and aid them against their enemy. Mu'āwiya preferred first to write both to their partisans in Egypt, encouraging them to stand firm with assurances of his aid, and to the opponents, trying to weaken their resolve by promises and intimidation. If necessary, they would still have the option to make war on them. 'Amr told him to do as he saw fit. He, 'Amr, was still convinced that matters would end up in fierce fighting.

Mu'āwiya then wrote a letter to Maslama b. Mukhallad and Mu'āwiya b. Ḥudayj jointly. He praised them for their noble stand in seeking revenge for the blood of the wronged caliph, promised them the early support of the friends of God on earth and from Mu'āwiya's realm, and urged them to carry on their *jihād* and to summon those who were still

[474] Kindī, *Wulāt*, 23. [475] Ṭabarī, I, 3394.

[476] Thaqafī, *Ghārāt*, 264–5. The report that 'Alī was pleased to be rid of al-Ashtar, transmitted by the 'Uthmanid al-Sha'bī from 'Abd Allāh b. Ja'far b. Abī Ṭālib (Kindī, *Wulāt*, 23; Ibn al-Athīr, *Kāmil*, III, 296), is tendentious. 'Abd Allāh b. Ja'far, half-brother of Muḥammad b. Abī Bakr, had recommended the removal of Qays b. Sa'd from the governorship and the appointment of Ibn Abī Bakr, which proved to be a serious mistake. He evidently had no liking for al-Ashtar who now had to be sent in a vain attempt to salvage the situation. That it was he who advised 'Alī in the first place to send al-Ashtar, as he claimed, is quite unlikely.

[477] Ṭabarī, I, 3315–16; Thaqafī, *Ghārāt*, 267–70; Balādhurī, *Ansāb*, II, 400.

keeping aloof from their guidance. The letter was taken by Mu'āwiya's client Subay' b. Mālik al-Hamdānī to Maslama. After reading it he handed it to the messenger and asked him to show it to Ibn Ḥudayj and then bring it back so that he could answer it for both of them. Ibn Ḥudayj was satisfied, and Maslama wrote to Mu'āwiya that they were hoping for the reward of God in fighting those who had revolted against their imam. They had not set out on this course seeking material gain and had not expected his aid now offered to them. He asked Mu'āwiya, however, to send his horses and men quickly to ensure victory.[478] Although the 'Uthmāniyya in Egypt had gained strength after Ṣiffīn and the arbitration, they were evidently not ready to take the offensive against the governor on their own.

Mu'āwiya received the letter in Palestine where he had moved in order to direct matters from nearby. He gave 'Amr the command of six thousand men[479] to invade Egypt. As 'Amr was entering his former province, the Egyptian 'Uthmāniyya joined him. He halted and wrote a letter to Muḥammad b. Abī Bakr, warning him to leave in order to save his life. The people of Egypt, he claimed, were united in repudiating his rule and regretted having followed him. 'Amr preferred not to mention to his former ally the murder of 'Uthmān, to which he had incited him. He attached a letter from Mu'āwiya, however, who accused Muḥammad b. Abī Bakr of having been the most vicious rebel against 'Uthmān and the shedder of his blood. Now he was pretending to the rule of a country, the bulk of whose people were supporters of Mu'āwiya and his views. Mu'āwiya was writing to him only, he added, because he was loath to mutilate and kill a Qurayshite. Yet God would never save Ibn Abī Bakr from retaliation wherever he would be.

Muḥammad b. Abī Bakr sent the two letters to 'Alī with a note describing his dangerous situation, as his own followers were failing him. He asked 'Alī to supply him with auxiliaries and money if he cared to keep Egypt. 'Alī wrote to him to stand firm, to fortify his city and to dispatch Kināna b. Bishr, known for his loyalty and toughness, against the enemy. He, 'Alī, would send him a mounted army of support. He made light of the letters from Mu'āwiya and 'Amr and instructed Ibn Abī Bakr to send them a suitable response. Ibn Abī Bakr answered Mu'āwiya that he would not apologize to him in the matter of 'Uthmān; Mu'āwiya was just trying to intimidate him with his mention of mutilation, as if he were sincere and concerned for him; he held out hope that he could defeat the enemy; if not, God would punish them for their wrong-doing and killing of the faithful. To 'Amr he replied that his concern for his safety was a lie; those

[478] Ṭabarī, I, 3396–400; Thaqafī, *Ghārāt*, 270–6.
[479] According to al-Wāqidī's account, 'Amr's army numbered 4,000 men (Ṭabarī, I, 3406).

Egyptians who were repudiating his rule and regretted having followed him were merely the followers of ʿAmr and the devil; he would continue to put his trust in God.

Muḥammad b. Abī Bakr took the offensive with an army of only two thousand men. He sent Kināna b. Bishr ahead with his vanguard. ʿAmr dispatched one detachment after another against Kināna, drawing him ever closer, and then had him surrounded at al-Musannāt by Muʿāwiya b. Ḥudayj with the Egyptian ʿUthmāniyya, followed by the bulk of the Syrians. Completely outnumbered, Kināna and his men were killed. As the news reached Muḥammad b. Abī Bakr, he was deserted by all his men. He went off to hide in a ruin while ʿAmr occupied the capital, al-Fusṭāṭ. Muʿāwiya b. Ḥudayj searched for Ibn Abī Bakr and was directed by some peasants to his hiding place. They seized him, nearly dead of thirst, and intended to take him to al-Fusṭāṭ. When the news of his capture reached ʿAmr, Muḥammad's brother ʿAbd al-Raḥmān b. Abī Bakr, having been sent by ʿĀ'isha to ʿAmr's army on a mission to save their brother's life,[480] intervened on his behalf. ʿAmr gave orders to Muʿāwiya b. Ḥudayj to bring the son of Abū Bakr alive to him. Ibn Ḥudayj was incensed that ʿAmr would kill his kinsman Kināna b. Bishr, Tujīb being a subtribe of Sakūn, while demanding of him that he spare the life of the Qurayshite Ibn Abī Bakr. He refused his captive water, using as pretext the false accusation spread by Umayyad propaganda that the rebels had prevented ʿUthmān from drinking water. After an angry exchange he killed the son of Abū Bakr, put him inside the carcass of a donkey, and burned him in it. When ʿĀ'isha heard of her brother's miserable end, she was seized with violent grief, and she included a curse on Muʿāwiya and ʿAmr in the *qunūt* of her prayers. She took charge of her brother's dependants and brought up his son al-Qāsim, who became one of the leading religious scholars of Medina.[481] ʿAmr reported to Muʿāwiya about his victory and the death of Muḥammad b. Abī Bakr and Kināna b. Bishr in a letter. Again he merely mentioned that the two had persisted in their error and said nothing about the revenge for ʿUthmān.[482]

ʿAlī had, when receiving Ibn Abī Bakr's appeal for help, addressed the Kufans, calling for immediate action and asking for volunteers to gather at al-Jaraʿa between Kūfa and al-Ḥīra. He went there himself on the following day but was joined by fewer than a hundred men. Returning to Kūfa, he sent for the tribal leaders and upbraided them for their inaction.

[480] Ibn Manẓūr, *Mukhtaṣar*, XIV, 281; Abbott, *Aishah*, 179–80.

[481] Ṭabarī, I, 3400–6; Thaqafī, *Ghārāt*, 276–85. According to al-Wāqidī's account, Ibn Abī Bakr went into hiding in the house of Jabala b. Masrūq. Muʿāwiya b. Ḥudayj surrounded the house, and Ibn Abī Bakr was killed fighting (Ṭabarī, I, 3406–7). On ʿĀ'isha's taking charge of her brother's daughter Qurayba and son al-Qāsim, see Abbott, *Aishah*, 209.

[482] Ṭabarī, I, 3407; Thaqafī, *Ghārāt*, 288–9.

Mālik b. Ka'b al-Arḥabī came forward to back him, and Alī ordered his herald to summon the people to march to Egypt under his command. It still took a month[483] before a small army of two thousand men had assembled outside Kūfa and were sent off by 'Alī. Five days later 'Alī received the news, from both al-Ḥajjāj b. Ghaziyya al-Anṣārī from Egypt and his spy 'Abd al-Raḥmān b. al-Musayyab al-Fazārī coming from Syria, that Muḥammad b. Abī Bakr had been killed. He sent 'Abd al-Raḥmān b. Shurayḥ al-Yāmī to recall Mālik b. Ka'b.

The date of 'Amr's victory at al-Musannāt is given by al-Wāqidī as Ṣafar 38/July–August 658.[484] Al-Kindī mentions as the date of Ibn Abī Bakr's death 14 Ṣafar 38/23 July 658,[485] probably too early. 'Amr b. al-'Āṣ had camped in Egypt for a period of between one and two months before the battle. 'Alī is quoted as telling the Kufans that he had tried for more than fifty days to mobilize an army in support of their Egyptian brethren.[486] The battle presumably took place no earlier than the end of Ṣafar 38/early August 658. Al-Kindī dates the beginning of 'Amr's second governorship of Egypt from Rabī' I 38/August–September 658.[487]

'Alī was deeply distressed by the loss of his foster-son Muḥammad b. Abī Bakr as well as that of Egypt, and showed it in public. In a sermon he took credit for his own eagerness to face the enemy, while blaming the Kufans for their failure to obey him. In a letter informing 'Abd Allāh b. al-'Abbās of the conquest of Egypt and the death of Ibn Abī Bakr he bitterly complained about the lack of support from his people; if it were not for his desire to die as a martyr, he would prefer not to stay on a single day with them. His cousin answered him, praying for God's support and suggesting that he treat his subjects kindly, since they might change their attitude in the future. 'Alī evidently now regretted having entrusted Ibn Abī Bakr with the governorship of Egypt, describing him again as an inexperienced young man (*ghulām ḥadath*). He revealed that he had thought of appointing Hāshim b. 'Utba who, he suggested, would not have left the field open for 'Amr b. al-'Āṣ and his helpers and would not have died without his sword in his hand. This, he added, was not meant as a reproach of Muḥammad b. Abī Bakr, who had sacrificed his life and fulfilled his duty.[488] Questioned about his deep grief for the son of Abū Bakr, he explained that he had been his foster-son, a brother to his own sons. 'I was a father to him and considered him my child.'[489]

Frustrated by his loss of authority, 'Alī devoted his energies to teaching

[483] Thaqafī, *Ghārāt*, 294. [484] Ṭabarī, I, 3407.
[485] Kindī, *Wulāt*, 31. Al-Kindī's statement that Ibn Abī Bakr's governorship lasted five months is completely mistaken. [486] Ṭabarī, I, 3412; Thaqafī, *Ghārāt*, 297.
[487] Kindī, *Wulāt*, 31. [488] Ṭabarī, I, 3411–13; Thaqafī, *Ghārāt*, 295–301.
[489] Thaqafī, *Ghārāt*, 301.

those of his followers eager to listen to him. While still in a state of grief and depression about the conquest of Egypt, he was visited by five of his close followers, ʿAmr b. al-Ḥamiq, Ḥujr b. ʿAdī, Ḥabba b. Juwayn al-ʿUranī al-Bajalī, al-Ḥārith al-Aʿwar al-Hamdānī and ʿAbd Allāh b. Sabaʾ al-Hamdānī, and was asked about his views concerning Abū Bakr and ʿUmar. ʿAlī reproached them: 'Is your mind free for that when Egypt has just been conquered and my followers (*shīʿatī*) have been killed there? I shall issue a letter for you in which will be described what you have questioned me about. I ask you to safeguard my rights which you have squandered before. Therefore read it to my followers and be helpers unto the truth.'[490]

The contents of the letter agreed substantially with what he had written Muʿāwiya about his relations with the first two caliphs. ʿAlī described the mission of the Prophet, the disaster that struck both his close kin and the whole Community with his death, and the conflict over the reign after him. He affirmed that he had been surprised and greatly disturbed to see the people turning away from the Prophet's family and thronging to Abū Bakr to pledge allegiance to him; he had withheld his hand for a time, considering himself more entitled to the position of the Messenger of God among the people than anyone who might assume it; then the apostasy of some of the people had induced him to put the cause of Islam above his own interest; he pledged allegiance to Abū Bakr, assisted him in overcoming the apostates, and backed him with sincere advice; he had neither been convinced, nor had he been without hope, that Abū Bakr would eventually turn the rule over to him. Had it not been for the special bond between Abū Bakr and ʿUmar, he would not have thought that Abū Bakr might divert the reign from him; just before his death, however, Abū Bakr sent for ʿUmar and appointed him his successor; he, ʿAlī, had obeyed and sincerely backed ʿUmar, and ʿUmar's conduct was pleasing and blessed with good success; when ʿUmar was about to die, he had been confident that he would not divert the rule from him, but ʿUmar made him one of six candidates, and they turned out to be most strongly opposed to his rule. This was because he had argued with Abū Bakr at the time of the Prophet's death, telling Quraysh: 'We, the Prophet's Family, have a better right to 'this matter' than you so long as there is among us one who recites the Qurʾān, knows the Sunna, and adheres to the religion

[490] Thaqafī, *Ghārāt*, 302–3; Balādhurī, *Ansāb*, II, 382–3. Al-Balādhurī states that ʿAlī then gave them a letter to be read at all times to his followers for their benefit. Ibn Sabaʾ had a copy of it but altered it. Al-Balādhurī omitted the text of the letter, commenting that it did ʿAlī no good. The text is preserved by al-Thaqafī. In Ibn Abi l-Ḥadīd's quotation from al-Thaqafī's book the text is introduced as a speech by ʿAlī given after the killing of Muḥammad b. Abī Bakr (*Sharḥ*, VI, 94). The introductory statement may have been suppressed because of the mention of ʿAbd Allāh b. Sabaʾ in it.

of the truth.' The people thus feared that if he were to rule them they would have no share in the reign for their lifetime, and they agreed unanimously to divert the reign to 'Uthmān and to deprive him of it in the hope that they would have it in turn; they demanded that he pledge allegiance, or they would fight him, and he had done so under constraint. One of them had told him: 'Ibn Abī Ṭālib, surely you are covetous of "this matter."' He had answered: 'You are more covetous, yet more remote. Am I the most covetous when I ask for my heritage and my right of which God and His Messenger have made me the most worthy, or you who strike my face to keep me from it?' They were dumbfounded.

'Alī then prayed for God's help against Quraysh who had cut their kinship ties to him, defrauded him of his right, lowered his high station, and colluded to dispute a right to which his title was prior to theirs; when he looked around, he could not see anyone prepared to assist or defend him except for his own family; he was wary of bringing ruin down on them and therefore suppressed his anger.

Next he reminded the faithful how they had become enraged against 'Uthmān and had come to Medina and killed him; then they had approached him, 'Alī, in order to pledge allegiance to him; he had at first resisted, but in the end they had pressed him hard, assuring him that they would be satisfied with none but him, and he had accepted. Then 'Alī recounted the story of his reign, the rebellion of Ṭalḥa and al-Zubayr, the refusal of the Syrians to respond to his summons, the mutiny of his army at Ṣiffīn, the failure of the arbitrators to judge in accordance with the Qur'ān and their disagreement, the rebellion of the Kharijites, and the desertion of most of the Kufans from his second campaign to Syria. Finally he appealed to them to do their duty in defence of Islam, as their enemies were seizing their cities, killing his followers, and raiding their lands.[491]

About this time, soon after the loss of Egypt, 'Alī became embroiled in an angry exchange with his cousin 'Abd Allāh b. al-'Abbās. While preparing for his second campaign to Syria, he had appointed Ibn al-'Abbās leader of the pilgrimage to Mekka, as he had done the previous year at Ṣiffīn.[492] Evidently because of this mission 'Abd Allāh was not present at the battle of al-Nahrawān. Leaving for Mekka, he put Abu l-Aswad al-Du'alī in charge of the congregational prayers in Baṣra and Ziyād b. Abīh in charge of the land tax. A quarrel erupted between the two during his absence, and Abu l-Aswad satirized Ziyād in a poem.

[491] Thaqafī, *Ghārāt*, 303–22.

[492] Al-Ṭabarī (I, 3390) states erroneously that 'Abd Allāh's brother 'Ubayd Allāh, governor of Yemen, was leader of the pilgrimage in the year 37. Khalīfa correctly names 'Abd Allāh (*Ta'rīkh*, 192).

Ziyād answered with ugly insults, and Abu l-Aswad composed a further lampoon. When ʿAbd Allāh b. al-ʿAbbās returned, Ziyād complained about Abu l-Aswad. ʿAbd Allāh severely scolded the latter, comparing him to a camel, for improperly injuring the honour of free men, and sent him off.[493]

Abu l-Aswad now wrote ʿAlī a letter in which he praised him for his trustworthiness with regard to the *fay'* of the Muslim Community, which he amply distributed to them, while abstaining from taking anything that belonged to them for himself. His cousin, in contrast, was partaking of the money under his control without ʿAlī's knowledge. He, Abu l-Aswad, was unable to conceal that from him and was therefore seeking his advice. In his reply ʿAlī thanked him for his sincerity to his imam and informed him that he would write to Ibn al-ʿAbbās without mentioning Abu l-Aswad's letter. He wrote to Ibn al-ʿAbbās that he had received news about him which, if true, implied that Ibn al-ʿAbbās had disgraced his trustworthiness, disobeyed his imam and cheated the Muslims. He asked him to provide an account for the public money under his control. Ibn al-ʿAbbās answered that the information that had reached him was false and that he was correctly administering and preserving whatever was under his control. ʿAlī wrote back insisting on an exact account of his revenue from the non-Muslims (*jizya*), its sources and his expenditure. Ibn al-ʿAbbās was deeply hurt by this show of persistent distrust in him, who had backed ʿAlī most loyally under trying circumstances. He replied that he recognized the extreme seriousness with which ʿAlī viewed the report he had received about his embezzling the money of the Basrans. He swore that he preferred to meet God with all the gold found above and under the earth in his hands to having spilled the blood of the Community for the sake of gaining power and dominion. 'Send whomever you want to your province, I am leaving.' When ʿAlī read the letter, he commented incredulously: 'Has Ibn ʿAbbās perhaps not participated with me in shedding this blood?'[494]

Ibn al-ʿAbbās' allusion to spilled blood has been interpreted by Veccia-Vaglieri as a criticism of the massacre of the Kharijites at al-Nahrawān which, she suggested, was the prime cause of his defection.[495] That Ibn al-ʿAbbās regretted al-Nahrawān, where he had not been

[493] This background to the quarrel between Ibn al-ʿAbbās and Abu l-Aswad is provided only by Ibn Aʿtham (*Futūḥ*, IV, 72–3). The report of Abu l-Kanūd, on whom the other accounts are based, begins with ʿAbd Allāh's scolding of Abu l-Aswad with largely the same words. Ibn Aʿtham's further account (*ibid.*, 74–5) evidently condenses that of Abu l-Kanūd and describes Ibn al-ʿAbbās as merely retiring to his house in Baṣra. ʿAlī then wrote to him reproaching him for his angry reaction and restored him to his office. This latter part is obviously not reliable in the light of Abu l-Kanūd's account.

[494] Balādhurī, *Ansāb*, II, 169–71. [495] 'Il conflitto', 77.

present, is not unlikely. This is also implied in a chronologically flawed remark by al-Balādhurī[496] that 'Abd Allāh b. al-'Abbās, some time after the Syrian conquest of Egypt, disagreed with 'Alī at al-Nahrawān and left for Mekka. Ibn al-'Abbās was later, as noted by Veccia-Vaglieri,[497] held in high esteem and consulted in legal matters by the Kharijites. Yet his angry remark in the letter was hardly prompted by al-Nahrawān. Rather he was reminding 'Alī that he, a man without personal ambition for government, had always backed him out of solidarity and even soiled his hands with Muslim blood in the battles of the Camel and Ṣiffīn for 'Alī's sake, with which he would have to face his Lord; did he deserve 'Alī's distrust of his word and his lending credence to some slanderous insinuations against him?

Ibn al-'Abbās now left for Mekka in an unambiguous protest demonstration. He secured the backing first of the Banū Hilāl to whom he had kinship ties through his mother, Lubāba bt al-Ḥārith. Al-Ḍaḥḥāk b. 'Abd Allāh al-Hilālī, whom he had appointed police chief, offered him personal protection (*ajārahū*), and 'Abd Allāh b. Razīn b. Abī 'Amr, Qabīṣa b. 'Abd 'Awf and others came to back him. Hilāl were soon joined by Hawāzin, Sulaym and all other tribes of Qays. Ibn al-'Abbās was also accompanied by Sinān b. Salama b. al-Muḥabbiq al-Hudhalī, al-Ḥuṣayn b. Abi l-Ḥurr al-'Anbarī and al-Rabī' b. Ziyād al-Ḥārithī. He now took possession of the treasury, filled sacks with the money, said to have amounted to 6,000,000 dirhams, and took off, accompanied by his protectors. The other tribes set out after them in the desert high ground (*ṭaff*). The Qays warned them that they would fight to defend Ibn al-'Abbās. There was evidently not much eagerness to start a quarrel about the money. First Ṣabra b. Shaymān al-Huddānī of Azd explained to his people that Qays were their brethren in Islam and their neighbours in Baṣra, while their share in the money, if it were returned, was minimal. Then Bakr b. Wā'il and 'Abd al-Qays also decided to remain neutral. Only Tamīm were ready to fight, but al-Aḥnaf b. Qays told them that some of those refusing to fight were more remote in kinship to Qays than they, and abandoned them. Tamīm now chose another chief to lead them and there were some blows exchanged that left a few wounded but no dead. The neutrals intervened, putting Tamīm to shame by boasting that in leaving this money to the cousins of Tamīm they were more generous than the latter. They all left, and Ibn al-'Abbās continued on to Mekka accompanied by a few men of Qays, among them al-Ḍaḥḥāk b. 'Abd Allāh and 'Abd Allāh b. Razīn. On the way Ibn al-'Abbās handed out money to the poor, whether they begged for it or not. In Mekka he bought three

496 Balādhurī, *Ansāb*, II, 405. 497 'Il conflitto', 78.

Ḥijāzī slave girls of mixed race from Ḥabtar,[498] the client of the Banū Ka'b, for 3,000 dinars.[499]

The report, going back to Abu l-Kanūd, describes the profligacy of Ibn al-'Abbās in drastic terms, and there may be reasonable doubts about some aspects of it. It seems hardly likely that all of Qays would have defended Ibn al-'Abbās if he had simply carried off the whole contents of the treasury of Baṣra, and even less likely that the rest of the Basran tribes would have so easily acquiesced to it. Ṣabra b. Shaymān's argument that the share of Azd would be minimal if the money were returned indicates that either the treasury was exceptionally low at the time or only a small portion was carried off. The figure of 6,000,000 dirhams is probably fanciful. Ibn al-'Abbās himself later insisted in his letter to 'Alī that what he had taken was only part of his entitlement. The Basran historian Abū 'Ubayda maintained that he took the accumulated provisions (*arzāq*) to which he was entitled.[500] It is plain, however, that he intended to make a show of defiance towards 'Alī.

'Alī was informed about Ibn al-'Abbās' action by the same Abu l-Kanūd who narrated the whole story of the conflict between the two cousins of the Prophet. Abu l-Kanūd describes himself at this point as an assistant (*min a'wān*) of Ibn al-'Abbās in Baṣra. 'Alī reacted by quoting Qur'ān Sūra VII 175: 'Recite to them the story of him to whom We gave Our signs, but he withdrew from them and Satan followed him, and he became one of the seduced.' Then he wrote to Ibn al-'Abbās, noting the trust he had placed in him; in no one of his family had he confided more deeply for his comfort, support and reliability than in Ibn al-'Abbās; yet when times had turned grim – the enemy raising his head, the Community becoming discordant and restive – Ibn al-'Abbās had turned his back on his cousin, deserted and cheated him in the most abominable manner; he had snatched the money of the people and run away with it to the Ḥijāz as if he had taken possession of his inheritance from his father and mother; now he was eating and drinking from forbidden money, buying slave women and marrying them – all with the property of orphans, widows and fighters for the cause of God. 'Alī demanded that Ibn al-'Abbās return the money to the people, otherwise he would have to punish him with all severity whenever he got hold of him; if his own sons al-Ḥasan or al-Ḥusayn had committed anything like this, they would have found no clemency from him. Ibn al-'Abbās answered 'Alī, briefly acknowledging the receipt of his letter in which he had magnified Ibn al-'Abbās' breach

[498] This, rather than Ḥabīra (Balādhurī, *Ansāb*, II, 174), is the reading of the better manuscripts. Ibn 'Abd Rabbih, *al-'Iqd al-farīd*, ed. Mufīd Muḥammad Qumayḥa and 'Abd al-Majīd al-Tarḥīnī (Beirut, 1983), V, 105 gives the name as 'Aṭā' b. Jubayr.

[499] Balādhurī, *Ansāb*, II, 171–4.

[500] Ṭabarī, I, 3454–5.

of trust regarding the money he had seized from the treasury of Baṣra. He assured 'Alī that his right in God's treasury (*bayt māl Allāh*) was greater than the amount he had taken.

'Alī next wrote Ibn al-'Abbās an angry letter in which he expressed amazement at his belief that he had a right to a greater share in God's treasury than any other Muslim. In reality he was now living in sin. Again he mentioned what he had heard about Ibn al-'Abbās' buying slave girls from Medina and al-Ṭā'if, choosing them for himself yet paying with the money of others. 'Alī assured him that he would never have considered any of the money taken by Ibn al-'Abbās as licit for himself to leave as inheritance to his offspring. How could Ibn al-'Abbās then be pleased with it, since he was consuming forbidden property? Yet he would have to repent of his wrong-doing. Ibn al-'Abbās answered this time even more curtly: 'By God, if you will not spare me your fables, I shall carry it [the money] to Mu'āwiya so that he can fight you with it.' 'Alī now left him alone.[501]

So far the account of Abu l-Kanūd. From the exchange of letters it is evident that the conflict was about the share of the 'money of God', the *fay'*, to which Ibn al-'Abbās was entitled. The Kufan traditionist Abū Bakr b. Abī Shayba, evidently trying to excuse Ibn al-'Abbās, explained that he considered the *fay'* licit for himself on the basis of an 'interpretation' (*ta'wīl*) of Qur'ān Sūra VIII 42 which gave the Prophet's kin a share in the fifth of the Muslim war booty. The explanation went in the right direction, yet Ibn al-'Abbās did not need to 'interpret' the Qur'anic text which is quite unambiguous as was the parallel verse Sūra LIX 7 specifically concerning the *fay'*. Ibn al-'Abbās thus was in a strong position and could with good conscience tell 'Alī to keep his fables to himself. He justly maintained all his life that Abū Bakr and 'Umar had deprived the Prophet's kin of their Qur'anic right.

'Alī, in contrast, asserted that Ibn al-'Abbās and he himself were not entitled to a different share of the *fay'* than any other Muslim. He did so evidently on the precedent set by Abū Bakr, who treated the Qur'anic text as no longer valid after the Prophet's death. The same position had been taken by 'Umar, who had tried to make up partially for the loss suffered by the Prophet's kin by according them higher shares in the pension system. 'Uthmān had revalidated the Qur'anic rule for the benefit of his own Umayyad kin as the house of the 'Vicegerent of God'. This was indeed interpretation of the Qur'ān rather than acceptance of its rule, and it had raised a storm of public protest. 'Alī was bending backwards to follow the sunna of the two popular successors of the Prophet, which

[501] Balādhurī, *Ansāb*, II, 174–6; Ibn 'Abd Rabbih, *'Iqd*, V, 106–7.

'Uthmān, contrary to his commitment at the time of his election, had so flagrantly broken.[502]

Ibn al-'Abbās' protest action was thus not only motivated by his resentment of 'Alī's display of distrust in him, but by his dissatisfation with 'Alī's policy of dealing out strictly equal shares from the *fay'* to those entitled. In his letter to al-Ḥasan after 'Alī's death he went so far as to state: 'You know that the people turned away from your father 'Alī and went over to Mu'āwiya only because he equalized the share from the *fay'* amongst them and treated them all the same in regard to their stipends (*'aṭā'*); this weighed heavily upon them.'[503] 'Alī's refusal to make a payment from the *fay'* to his brother 'Aqīl had, as noted, induced the latter to take money from Mu'āwiya. Later Maṣqala b. Hubayra al-Shaybānī, a prominent chief of Rabī'a and 'Alī's governor of Ardashīrkhurra, defected to Mu'āwiya unable to pay the public treasury for debts incurred. He declared that if his debt had been owed to Mu'āwiya or to 'Uthmān, they would have waived it. 'Uthmān had, he added, allowed al-Ash'ath b. Qays to pocket 100,000 dirhams annually from the land tax of Ādharbayjān.[504]

'Alī's refusal to make financial concessions to the nobility and tribal chiefs evidently left them vulnerable to bribery by Mu'āwiya. According to a Syrian report, Mu'āwiya, after receiving the pledge of allegiance as caliph and hearing of the battle of al-Nahrawān, sent letters to the leading men in Kūfa, among them al-Ash'ath b. Qays, making them promises and offers of money in order to induce them to incline to his side and to show themselves reluctant to follow 'Alī in his campaign against Syria. Mu'āwiya later used to say that after Ṣiffīn he made war on 'Alī without armies and without exertion.[505]

[502] This attitude of 'Alī was noted by his great-grandson Muḥammad al-Bāqir. He told Ibn Isḥāq that 'Alī during his reign in Iraq followed the conduct of Abū Bakr and 'Umar in respect to the Qur'anic portion of the Prophet's kin. 'Alī did so, he explained, because he was loath to be accused of contravening the practice of the two caliphs (Ibn Shabba, *Ta'rīkh al-Madīna*, 217).

[503] Ibn Abi l-Ḥadīd, *Sharḥ*, XVI, 23; Ibn A'tham, *Futūḥ*, IV, 149. Quite similar was the judgement of Fuḍayl b. al-Ja'd quoted by al-Madā'inī: The strongest reason for the Arabs' withdrawal of their support from 'Alī was that he did not give preference to anyone, however noble, in the distribution of money and failed to bribe the chiefs of the tribes as kings do (Ibn Abi l-Ḥadīd, *Sharḥ*, II, 197). The pro-'Alid Mu'tazilite Abū Ja'far al-Iskāfī asserted that 'Alī's distribution of the contents of the treasury in Medina immediately after his accession giving equal shares to everybody was the first cause of the opposition to him. Al-Iskāfī supported this claim with a lengthy fictitious account of the developments after 'Alī's *bay'a* (Ibn Abi l-Ḥadīd, *Sharḥ*, VII, 37–43).

[504] Ṭabarī, I, 3440; Balādhurī, *Ansāb*, II, 416; Thaqafī, *Ghārāt*, 364.

[505] Balādhurī, *Ansāb*, II, 383. Caetani's comment on this report that 'the tradition favourable to 'Alī naturally attributes every setback suffered by him to the malevolent stratagems of enemies and not to the shortcomings and weakness of the caliph' (*Annali*, X, 108) is quite out of place. The report is purely Syrian, pro-Umayyad, and probably reliable.

With the charge that 'Alī equalized the *fay'* shares among the Muslims, Ibn al-'Abbās was presumably referring to his handing out of the surplus in the treasury among those entitled on equal terms. He had done so on his accession in Medina and seems to have continued the practice throughout his caliphate.[506] It is unlikely that he interfered with the inequality of the stipends and pensions set by 'Umar and paid out of the *fay'*. Since the *fay'* from the conquered land under 'Umar's settlement belonged to the conquerors rather than the government, 'Alī was evidently intent on spreading the benefits equally and exclusively to all those entitled. 'Umar had, however, regularly granted concessions of dead land in Arabia and other territories not part of *fay'* land to the Qurayshite nobility and tribal leaders. There is no evidence that 'Alī granted any such concessions, although he also did not interfere with the concessions made by his predecessors, including 'Uthmān. He does not even seem to have touched the oasis of Fadak which 'Uthmān had granted to Marwān.

Ibn al-'Abbas did not stay long in Mekka. When 'Abd Allāh b. 'Āmir al-Ḥaḍramī, sent by Mu'āwiya, arrived in Baṣra to stir up trouble there, Ibn al-'Abbās was already in Kūfa with 'Alī. Nothing is known as to how the reconciliation was brought about. 'Alī could evidently ill afford to lose the backing of his politically experienced cousin whose brothers Qutham and 'Ubayd Allāh were his governors in the Ḥijāz and Ṣan'ā'. 'Abd Allāh b. al-'Abbās, on his part, fully appreciated and admired 'Alī's personal qualities and his deep devotion to Islam, in spite of his anger at the treatment he had met with and his disapproval of some aspects of his cousin's policies. 'Alī did not replace him as governor in Baṣra. Ziyād b. Abīh, whom Ibn al-'Abbās left in charge in preference to Abu l-Aswad al-Du'alī, continued to act as his deputy. Not even al-Ḍaḥḥāk b. 'Abd Allāh al-Hilālī, Ibn al-'Abbās' police chief who had aided him in his raid of the treasury, was dismissed or punished. Some time after the failure of Ibn al-Ḥaḍramī's mission, Ibn al-'Abbās returned to Baṣra and resumed the governorship. Only al-Ya'qūbī reports that Ibn al-'Abbās, on 'Alī's insistence, restored all or a major part of the money he had taken from the treasury and later used to say that no exhortation ever made a greater impression on him than 'Alī's on this occasion.[507] Although the report seems generally unreliable, it is possible that Ibn al-'Abbās returned some of the money to allow 'Alī to save face. He presumably obtained, however, some commitment from the caliph henceforth not to interfere in his administration of Baṣra.

[506] Balādhurī, *Ansāb*, II, 131–6; Ibn 'Asākir, *'Alī*, III, 180–8; Ibn Abi l-Ḥadīd, *Sharḥ*, II, 198–203. [507] Ya'qūbī, *Ta'rīkh*, II, 242.

Abu l-Kanūd's dramatic account of the quarrel between the two cousins of the Prophet and his failure to mention their reconciliation has led early historians to the assumption of a permanent defection of Ibn al-ʿAbbās from ʿAlī. Aware that Ibn al-ʿAbbās was still governing Baṣra in the later years of ʿAlī's reign, al-Madāʾinī placed this defection shortly before ʿAlī's murder. He assumed, on the basis of some early reports, that Ibn al-ʿAbbās was present in Kūfa, in order to console ʿAlī about the death of Muḥammad b. Abī Bakr, at the time of Ibn al-Ḥaḍramī's activity in Baṣra.[508] Al-Madāʾinī's account was accepted by ʿUmar b. Shabba, al-Balādhurī,[509] and al-Ṭabarī, who reported the defection of Ibn al-ʿAbbās under the year 40/660.[510] The independent Basran historian Abū ʿUbayda, on the other hand, maintained that Ibn al-ʿAbbās did not leave Baṣra permanently before the death of ʿAlī but departed only after al-Ḥasan's surrender of the caliphate to Muʿāwiya. At that time he took some money from the treasury which he claimed as his salary.[511] Among modern authors, Caetani[512] and Veccia-Vaglieri recognized that the conflict reported by Abu l-Kanūd must have occurred early in the year 38/late summer 658, before Ibn al-Ḥaḍramī's mission. They tended to assume that Ibn al-ʿAbbās' defection at that time was final and that reports showing him later still governing Baṣra must be unreliable. Veccia-Vaglieri suggested that he later, some time after his break with ʿAlī, returned to Baṣra and emptied the treasury.[513] All this is quite untenable.

Several months after his success in Egypt, Muʿāwiya decided to send ʿAbd Allāh b. ʿĀmir al-Ḥaḍramī, the Umayyad client, to Baṣra with the mission to subvert ʿAlī's government and to draw the town to his own side. ʿAlī's setbacks had strengthened the cause of the ʿUthmanid party everywhere, and the time seemed ripe to test the ground in the town that had so vigorously backed ʿĀʾisha's revolt. Muʿāwiya told Ibn al-Ḥaḍramī that most of the people of Baṣra shared the Umayyad abhorrence of ʿUthmān's murder. They were full of rancour against ʿAlī because of the losses they had suffered at his hands and were yearning for someone who would summon and lead them in seeking revenge for ʿUthmān's blood. He instructed him to alight among Muḍar, to keep away from Rabīʿa, and to covet the friendship of the Azd who would all be with him except for a

[508] Ṭabarī, I, 3414; Thaqafī, *Ghārāt*, 387.

[509] Balādhurī, *Ansāb*, II, 176. Al-Balādhurī held, however, that Ibn al-ʿAbbās was in Kūfa at the time of Ibn al-Ḥaḍramī's mission because of his quarrel with ʿAlī, not because of the death of Muḥammad b. Abī Bakr (*ibid.*, 426–7).

[510] Ṭabarī, I, 3453–6.

[511] *Ibid.*, 3456. Abū ʿUbayda also reported Ibn al-ʿAbbās's earlier temporary departure to Mekka, stating that he took his accumulated salary from the treasury (*ibid.*, 3454–5).

[512] *Annali*, X, 195–206.

[513] 'Il conflitto', 77–8; "Abd Allāh b. al-ʿAbbās', *EI* (2nd edn).

few, and these would not oppose him.[514] Ibn al-Ḥaḍramī's departure was delayed because Mu'āwiya was troubled by the astrological signs of the night before. Mu'āwiya now wrote to 'Amr b. al-'Āṣ in Egypt seeking his advice. 'Amr endorsed the plan with enthusiasm. His usual political judgement failed him on this occasion.

Following Mu'āwiya's instructions, Ibn al-Ḥaḍramī alighted among the Tamīm. The Banū Mujāshi', who had before treacherously killed al-Zubayr, offered him protection.[515] When he addressed the chiefs of the Basrans and tried to incite them to revenge against 'Alī as the murderer of 'Uthmān, al-Ḍaḥḥāk b. 'Abd Allāh al-Hilālī, the police chief of Ibn al-'Abbās, stood up and warned him against inciting the Basrans once more to fight each other so that Mu'āwiya would become their amir and Ibn al-Ḥaḍramī his assistant (*wazīr*); a single day with 'Alī and the Prophet was better than affliction with Mu'āwiya and the house of Mu'āwiya on earth as long as the earth would last. Then 'Abd Allāh b. Khāzim of Sulaym rose and told al-Ḍaḥḥāk to keep silent since he was not entitled to speak for the common people (*'āmma*). He assured Ibn al-Ḥaḍramī that they were all his helpers and would do whatever he wished. Al-Ḍaḥḥāk b. 'Abd Allāh ridiculed his self-importance, and they insulted each other.

Then a Qurayshite, 'Abd al-Raḥmān b. 'Umayr b. 'Uthmān of Abū Bakr's clan Taym, intervened, taking the side of Ibn al-Ḥaḍramī, who, he said, was seeking to unite, rather than divide, them; he proposed that they read the letter from Mu'āwiya which he had brought along. The letter was opened and read to them. Mu'āwiya addressed them as the Commander of the Faithful. He described 'Uthmān as a paragon of good conduct, justice, fairness to the oppressed and love for the weak, who had been killed as a Muslim, in the ritual state of a pilgrim, thirsty, and fasting, and summoned them to revenge. He did not mention 'Alī, but his aim was clear enough. In return for their righteous stand, he promised them that he would treat them in accordance with the Book, would give them their stipends doubly every year, and would not carry off any of their *fay'* from them. Many of the Basran chiefs were taken in by this rhetoric and called out: 'We hear and obey.' There was no unanimity, however, among those

[514] Thaqafī, *Ghārāt*, 375; Balādhurī, *Ansāb*, II, 423. The narrator in al-Thaqafī's account, 'Amr b. Miḥṣan, accompanied Ibn al-Ḥaḍramī on his way to Baṣra but seems to have left him soon after his arrival there, perhaps returning to Mu'āwiya. He is obviously not the Anṣārī 'Amr b. Miḥṣan b. 'Amr of al-Najjār whose son Abū 'Amra Bashīr was a prominent supporter of 'Alī and was killed at Ṣiffīn. He may rather be 'Amr b. Miḥṣan b. Ḥurthān al-Asadī, brother of 'Ukkāsha b. Miḥṣan, a confederate of 'Abd Shams (see Ibn Ḥajar, *Iṣāba*, V, 14 and IV, 256). He is also quoted by al-Thaqafī (*Ghārāt*, 510) reporting on the pilgrimage in Mekka in the year 39/660.

[515] See Jarīr's lampoon of Mujāshi' in Ṭabarī, I, 3418.

present, and al-Aḥnaf b. Qays went off commenting: 'As for me, I will have no camel, female or male, in this.' 'Amr b. Marjūm of 'Abd al-Qays warned them not to break their oath of allegiance lest a disaster strike and annihilate them.[516]

In a further meeting Ibn al-Ḥaḍramī appealed to the Basran chiefs for help against Ziyād b. 'Ubayd (Abīh), whom Ibn al-'Abbās had left in charge of the town as his deputy. Ṣuḥār b. 'Ayyāsh[517] al-'Abdī, who opposed his own tribe 'Abd al-Qays in their backing of 'Alī, eagerly offered their support with their swords and hands. He had, it was said, written to Mu'āwiya before and invited him to take advantage of the situation in Baṣra as the governor Ibn al-'Abbās was absent, and Mu'āwiya had answered him, promising prompt action. Al-Muthannā b. Maḥraba al-'Abdī, however, countered Ṣuḥār's offer, telling Ibn al-Ḥaḍramī that if he would not return to where he came from, they would get at him with their swords, hands, arrows and spear heads; would they abandon the cousin of their Prophet to obey a party tyrant? Ibn al-Ḥaḍramī realized that it was time to seek, in accordance with Mu'āwiya's instructions, the help of the Azd. He appealed to their chief, Ṣabra b. Shaymān, reminding him of the stand of his people in seeking revenge for 'Uthmān. Ṣabra answered cautiously: 'If you come and alight at my house, I shall back and protect you.' Ibn al-Ḥaḍramī apologized: 'The Commander of the Faithful Mu'āwiya has ordered me to alight among his people, the Muḍar.' Ṣabra replied coolly: 'Do what he ordered you', and left him. Ibn al-Ḥaḍramī had offended the Azd by choosing to stay with their rivals, the Tamīm. They, the Azd, had borne the brunt of the losses in the battle of the Camel, while the Tamīm partly remained neutral and partly fought half-heartedly. Now the would-be Commander of the Faithful showed his preference for 'his people Muḍar'.

Ziyād was still residing in the governor's palace, but was getting frightened as Ibn al-Ḥaḍramī's following increased. He sent for al-Ḥuḍayn b. al-Mundhir and Mālik b. Misma', the chiefs of Rabī'a, and asked them to grant him protection until he received the orders of the Commander of the Faithful. Al-Ḥuḍayn immediately promised him protection. Mālik, who had previously failed to back 'Alī, pretended that he would first have to consult his men. Ziyād realized that he could not trust him and sent – it was said on the advice of Abu l-Aswad al-Du'alī – for Ṣabra b. Shaymān. The latter readily offered to protect him and the public treasury if he would stay in his house. Ziyād moved at night to Ṣabra's house, taking

[516] Thaqafī, *Ghārāt*, 378–85; Balādhurī, *Ansāb*, II, 424–5.

[517] The reading "Abbās' instead of 'Ayyāsh in some sources, including al-Thaqafī's *Ghārāt*, is probably mistaken. See Caskel, *Ǧamharat an-nasab*, index s.v. Ṣuḥār b. 'Aiyāš.

along the treasury. Ṣabra insisted that he should not appear to be hiding; he provided a police force for him and set up a pulpit and ceremonial chair in the mosque of the Huddān for him to lead the Friday prayer. He justified his political turn to his people by explaining that on the day of the Camel they had said: 'We defend our city, obey our Mother, and support our wronged caliph.' They had stood firm when the other people fled, and the best of them had been killed; today Ziyād was their protected guest, and they did not have to fear from 'Alī what they feared from Mu'āwiya.[518] He evidently meant Mu'āwiya's partiality towards Muḍar.

Ziyād now wrote to Ibn al-'Abbās, who was still staying in Kūfa, about what had happened and asked him to inform 'Alī and to seek his instructions. Ibn al-Ḥaḍramī in the meantime was urged by his supporters of Tamīm and Qays to occupy the governor's palace. As he was getting ready to move, the Azd rode out in force and warned his supporters that they would not permit anyone to occupy the palace with whom they were not pleased. Ibn al-Ḥaḍramī's supporters, however, refused to give up their aim. Al-Aḥnaf b. Qays intervened and lectured Ibn al-Ḥaḍramī's friends that they had no better right to the governor's palace than their opponents nor the right to impose a governor on them whom they did not want. As they turned back, al-Aḥnaf reassured the Azd that nothing would be done against their will, and they also departed.[519]

Ibn al-Ḥaḍramī began to act as a governor, collecting taxes in the area controlled by his followers. Much of his support, however, was lukewarm. The Banū Tamīm, seeing that the Azd were vigorously defending Ziyād, sent to them proposing that they both expel their respective protégés and wait to see which of the two Commanders of the Faithful would prevail. The Azd replied, however, that this would have been acceptable before they had granted protection to their man; expelling him now would in their eyes be equal to allowing him to be killed; they had granted him protection only out of generosity. This was a hint that the Tamīm had been backing Ibn al-Ḥaḍramī in order to ingratiate themselves with Mu'āwiya, the presumptive victor in the battle for the caliphate.

The rivalry between the Azd and Tamīm in Baṣra had its repercussions also in Kūfa. The Tamimite Shabath b. Rib'ī urged 'Alī to send someone of Tamīm to summon his Basran kinsmen back to obedience and not to give the Azd 'Umān, 'the remote [in kinship] and odious', authority over them. 'Surely,' he addressed 'Alī, 'a single one of your people is better for you than all others.' Mikhnaf b. Sulaym of Azd countered: 'Surely, the remote and odious are those who disobey God and oppose the Commander of the Faithful, and they are your people. The dear and close ones are

[518] Thaqafī, *Ghārāt*, 393. [519] *Ibid.*, 485–91; Balādhurī, *Ansāb*, II, 425–9.

those who obey God and back the Commander of the Faithful, and they are my people. A single one of them is better for the Commander of the Faithful than ten of your people.' ʿAlī had to hush them; he reminded them that Islam had come in order to curb mutual hatred and bickering. He took, however, the advice of Shabath and called Aʿyan b. Ḍubayʿa al-Mujāshiʿī to question him about the conduct of his people in Baṣra who were assaulting his official together with Ibn al-Ḥaḍramī. Aʿyan apologized for them and offered to take care of them. ʿAlī sent him forthwith to Baṣra with a letter of instructions to Ziyād to let Aʿyan deal with his people and to fight them only if he failed to persuade them.

Aʿyan had no difficulty in drawing most of his people to his side, but there were some diehard supporters of Ibn al-Ḥaḍramī. He moved with his converts to face them and tried all day to preach good sense into them, but they answered with affronts. As he left in the evening for his travel baggage, ten men, thought to be Kharijites, followed him and hit at him with their swords while he was in bed, not expecting trouble. He ran away naked, but they caught up with him and killed him. Ziyād was ready to attack Ibn al-Ḥaḍramī in revenge together with the Azd and other supporters, but the Tamīm now sent a message to the Azd, declaring that they had touched neither their guest to whom they had promised protection, nor his money, nor anyone who disagreed with them; why would the Azd want to make war on them and their protected guest? When the Azd received the message, they did not want to fight.[520] Aʿyan, to be sure, belonged to Tamīm.

Ziyād wrote to ʿAlī, this time directly, informing him of what had happened and requesting that he send Jāriya b. Qudāma, who, he said, had a sharp mind, was obeyed among his tribe, and was tough on the enemies of the Commander of the Faithful. Jāriya, himself a Basran Tamimite, had remained in Kūfa after ʿAlī's abortive campaign against the Syrians.[521] ʿAlī now sent him to Baṣra with fifty men of Tamīm and a tough letter to the Basrans, threatening those who persisted in their rebellion with perdition. When Jāriya read the letter to them, the Azd and others were ready to fight. The next day they returned Ziyād to the governor's palace. Jāriya was unable to persuade the hard core of Ibn

[520] Thaqafī, *Ghārāt*, 394–410; Balādhurī, *Ansāb*, II, 428–9.

[521] The date of Ibn al-Ḥaḍramī's subversive activity could be determined more accurately if it were known whether Jāriya's mission to Baṣra occurred before or after his battle with the Kharijite leader Abū Maryam al-Saʿdī, which is dated in Ram. 38/Feb. 659 (Balādhurī, *Ansāb*, II, 485–6). On balance it seems more likely that the battle took place later, since the reports suggest that Muʿāwiya sent Ibn al-Ḥaḍramī soon after his conquest of Egypt. Jāriya seems to have stayed permanently in Kūfa during the last years of ʿAlī's reign. He was there at the beginning of Busr b. Abī Arṭāh's raid of the Ḥijāz and Yemen.

al-Ḥaḍramī's partisans to relinquish Mu'āwiya's envoy and had to seek the help of the Azd. There was fighting, and Ibn al-Ḥaḍramī and his followers were defeated and sought refuge in the fortified house of Sunbīl al-Sa'dī, a pre-Islamic Persian castle. When Jāriya ordered firewood to be piled up around the building, the Azd declared that they would have nothing to do with arson, and that those were his people. 'Ajlā', the Ethiopian mother of 'Abd Allāh b. Khāzim al-Sulamī, came to get her son, the chief of Ibn al-Ḥaḍramī's cavalry. She called him from in front of the castle, baring her head and breasts, and threatened to undress. Ibn Khāzim finally came out, and she took him away. Ibn al-Ḥaḍramī and seventy of his followers were burned alive in the castle. Among them was the Taymī Qurayshite 'Abd al-Raḥmān b. 'Umayr b. 'Uthmān.

Ibn al-Ḥaḍramī had vainly asked both Jāriya and Ziyād, later recognized as Mu'āwiya's half-brother, for a letter of safe conduct. Mu'āwiya's emissary could hardly expect clemency after Mu'āwiya had poisoned al-Ashtar and 'Amr b. al-'Āṣ had washed his hands of his former ally Muḥammad b. Abī Bakr and allowed him to be burned. There is no word about Mu'āwiya's reaction. It is unlikely that he felt much grief for the loyal Umayyad client. The chess-king knows which of his pawns are expendable. Jāriya b. Qudāma was thenceforth known as 'the Burner (*al-muḥarriq*)'.[522]

In Sha'bān 38/January 659, according to al-Wāqidī,[523] the meeting of the two arbitrators, Abū Mūsā al-Ash'arī and 'Amr b. al-'Āṣ, at Adhruḥ in northern Jordan took place. There is no circumstantial evidence either to confirm or to deny this dating. The Kufan tradition virtually ignored the event. For it, the arbitration had ended with the failure of the two men to agree at Dūmat al-Jandal and with 'Alī's denunciation of their conduct and repudiation of his own arbitrator. 'Alī no longer considered Abū Mūsā his representative nor did he appoint anyone else to represent him. The Medinan tradition, in contrast, saw Adhruḥ as the main event in the arbitration. At Adhruḥ some of the major representatives of the Medinan religious aristocracy, who had not been invited to Dūmat al-Jandal, were present with hopes of reaching agreement on the future of the caliphate.

Adhruḥ was a show of strength by Mu'āwiya. The meeting was held on his territory and he attended it himself with his top Syrian advisers. He was already firmly acknowledged as caliph in Syria and obviously had no intention of relinquishing his claim to the universal rule of the faithful. Yet in order to attract the neutral religious aristocracy to attend the show, he and 'Amr must have made them concrete promises of a *shūrā*. At Dūmat al-Jandal the two arbitrators had been unable to reach agreement

[522] Thaqafī, *Ghārāt*, 401–12; Balādhurī, *Ansāb*, II, 429–35. [523] Ṭabarī, I, 3360.

because 'Amr had adamantly refused to accept either the nomination of Abū Mūsā's favourite, 'Abd Allāh b. 'Umar, or a *shūrā*. The quarrel between them had evidently not been serious enough to prevent 'Amr from persuading Abū Mūsā that this time he would negotiate in earnest and was prepared for compromise. Abū Mūsā foolishly allowed himself to be turned into a tool of Mu'āwiya's imperial aspirations, although he no longer was legally representing 'Alī. The second-generation religious aristocracy, mostly sons of caliphs and of the most prominent Companions, were equally duped. 'Abd Allāh b. 'Umar, 'Abd al-Raḥmān b. Abī Bakr, 'Abd Allāh b. al-Zubayr, 'Abd al-Raḥmān b. al-Aswad b. 'Abd Yaghūth of Zuhra, 'Abd al-Raḥmān b. al-Ḥārith b. Hishām of Makhzūm, Abu l-Jahm b. Ḥudhayfa of 'Adī and al-Mughīra b. Shu'ba all attended.[524] Only Sa'd b. Abī Waqqāṣ, member of 'Umar's electoral council, refused to join in spite of the strong urging of his son 'Umar. He evidently saw through the fraud.

Mu'āwiya and 'Amr cannot seriously have expected that the Islamic aristocracy and Abū Mūsā would endorse Mu'āwiya's claim to the caliphate. Mu'āwiya, it is true, sent Abū Mūsā a handwritten note in which he pointed out to him that 'Amr had already recognized him as caliph on certain conditions and promised Abū Mūsā that, if he backed his caliphate on the same conditions, he would give his two sons the governorships of Kūfa and Baṣra; for himself, Abū Mūsā, every door would be open and every request would be satisfied. Such attempts at bribery were, however, a matter of routine with Mu'āwiya, and he was hardly surprised that Abū Mūsā rejected the offer indignantly. Mu'āwiya indeed later showed his appreciation for the substantial services Abū Mūsā had unintentionally rendered him, even though Abū Mūsā consistently rejected his claim to the caliphate while an arbitrator.[525] For Mu'āwiya's and 'Amr's purposes it was sufficient that these men, Abū Mūsā and the prominent Medinan Islamic aristocracy, accepted their invitation to attend the meeting, thus implicitly recognizing that the future of the caliphate would depend on Mu'āwiya and 'Amr rather than 'Alī. This was a considerable coup, especially since the Ḥijāz, their home base, was still nominally under the rule of 'Alī. The Holy Cities were, however, heavily dependent on Egypt for their provisions, and the

524 According to al-Zubayr b. Bakkār, Abū Mūsā and 'Amr b. al-'Āṣ agreed specifically to invite the following five men for consultation: 'Abd Allāh b. al-Zubayr, 'Abd Allāh b. 'Umar (reading thus instead of 'Amr), Abu l-Jahm b. Ḥudhayfa, Jubayr b. Muṭ'im and 'Abd al-Raḥmān b. al-Ḥārith b. Hishām (Ibn Abi l-Ḥadīd, *Sharḥ*, XX, 113–14).

525 Ibn Sa'd, *Ṭabaqāt*, IV/1, 82–3. Caetani's comment that the tradition insidiously insinuates that Abū Mūsā was bought by Mu'āwiya, or secretly agreed with him (*Annali*, X, 54), is obviously baseless. There is no reason to doubt that the report goes back to Abū Mūsā's son Abū Burda.

conquest of that province by Mu'āwiya had, in the eyes of the Ḥijāzīs, decisively shifted the balance of power in his favour. During the meetings 'Amr evidently pretended for some time to be open to a discussion of different candidates for the caliphate. He is reported to have countered Abū Mūsā's backing for 'Abd Allāh b. 'Umar by proposing his own son 'Abd Allāh, a man with a more credible record in Islam than himself. Abū Mūsā rejected him as a partisan in the conflict. 'Amr also brought up the name of Muḥammad's maternal nephew 'Abd al-Raḥmān b. al-Aswad al-Zuhrī, who was known for his high standing with 'Ā'isha. Abū Mūsā countered, as 'Amr presumably expected, that neither 'Abd al-Raḥmān, nor his father al-Aswad, had the merit of *hijra*.[526] 'Amr even talked privately to 'Abd Allāh b. 'Umar, evidently with the aim of eliciting from him a reaffirmation that he would accept only if there were unanimity in his favour. Mu'āwiya, according to a dubious report, was seriously concerned and almost burst into the room where the two were conversing. The doorkeeper, however, reassured him that they failed to agree and that Ibn 'Umar declined to accept the caliphate.[527]

The famous final public scene of the arbitration, in which 'Amr played his crude trick of deception on Abū Mūsā – breaking his private commitment to depose Mu'āwiya in favour of a *shūrā* and provoking a match of insults – was stage-managed from the beginning. The very insolence of 'Amr's conduct was intended as a slap in the face, not for 'Alī, who had already denounced the arbitration, but for 'Abd Allāh b. 'Umar and the other Medinan dreamers of *shūrā*. Mu'āwiya was triumphant. As Abū Mūsā returned to Mekka in indignation, the reconfirmed caliph invited his prominent guests in the evening for a farewell party together with his Syrian high command. He knew that this was the time to give free rein to his Umayyad arrogance, and addressed them: 'Whoever wants to speak about 'this matter', let him now display his horn against us.' It was the son of 'Umar b. al-Khaṭṭāb whom he was challenging. He went on: 'Surely, we are more worthy of it than he and his father.' Who was the plebeian 'Umar b. al-Khaṭṭāb to appoint him, Mu'āwiya, to govern what was the property of the house of Abū Sufyān? And Syria, the Land of Emigration (*muhājar*) of Abraham, was clearly destined to rule the empire of Islam; the son of 'Umar and his sort were henceforth to stick to their business of arguing about the minutiae of the Prophet's Sunna and to leave high politics to the experts, such as himself and 'Amr b. al-'Āṣ.

[526] Zubayrī, *Nasab*, 262. According to the less reliable Ṣāliḥ b. Kaysān, it was Abū Mūsā who proposed 'Abd al-Raḥmān b. al-Aswad (Balādhurī, *Ansāb*, II, 344). 'Amr no doubt tried to have Abū Mūsā admit that a Companion without *hijra* was acceptable so that he would be in a better position to push the case of Mu'āwiya.

[527] Balādhurī, *Ansāb*, II, 345. The source is Ṣāliḥ b. Kaysān.

'Abd Allāh b. 'Umar, according to his own account, loosened his garment in order to speak up and tell Mu'āwiya that those who had fought his father Abū Sufyān on behalf of Islam were more worthy of 'this matter' than he. But then he kept silent, fearing that his words might divide the Community, cause bloodshed and be used to misrepresent his views. God's promise of paradise was dearer to him than that. After he left for his residence, Mu'āwiya's counsellor Ḥabīb b. Maslama visited him and asked him why he had not responded to Mu'āwiya's challenge, and Ibn 'Umar told him the reason. Ḥabīb commented: 'You have protected yourself.'[528]

Ibn 'Umar's claim to have kept silent out of concern for the concord of the Community would have been more credible if he had remained in Medina. After he had accepted Mu'āwiya's invitation and thus admitted his interest in the caliphate, his silence at the disparagement of his father's memory was a distinct display of cowardice. Where Mu'āwiya's carrot had failed to work, his big stick did so. The son of the imposing Commander of the Faithful was intimidated. He made his case, if anything, worse, by hinting that he had gone to Syria only at the behest of his sister Ḥafṣa. His father had evidently been right in judging him unfit for the caliphate on the grounds that he could not even divorce his wife.

Yet in Ibn 'Umar's defence it must be added that Ḥabīb b. Maslama's allusion to his having saved his own life by keeping silent was realistic. Mu'āwiya was now assured that Ibn 'Umar did not pose a threat to him and ceased to view him as a potential opponent. Not that otherwise Mu'āwiya would have touched him at this time. But later, when he made arrangements for his son Yazīd to succeed, he might well have murdered Ibn 'Umar as a precaution, as he murdered others who might stand in his son's way. His judgement was right; Ibn 'Umar quickly pledged allegiance to Yazīd and pressed his sons to do so.[529] He realized that times had changed since the beginning of 'Alī's reign when he could with impunity insist on a *shūrā* before he would do homage. At that time he had not been worried that his action might cause further division in the Community.

For Mu'āwiya, Adhruḥ was a distinct success even though the Islamic aristocracy had failed to recognize his claim to the caliphate. He had demonstrated to his Syrian followers that this religious aristocracy was

[528] Ṭabarī, I, 3343; Bukhārī, *Ṣaḥīḥ*, *Maghāzī*, XXIX. Al-Zuhrī preferred to omit Mu'āwiya's boastful claim to be more worthy of the caliphate than 'Umar and his son (Ṭabarī, I, 3343). Caetani identified 'Umar's daughter and Mother of the Faithful Ḥafṣa as 'Alī's wife and presumably on that basis tried to discredit the report as pro-'Alid (*Annali*, X, 423). There is nothing pro-'Alid in it, nor is there any reason to doubt that it goes back to Ibn 'Umar. Quite unrealistic is Caetani's suggestion that Ibn 'Umar could easily have won general backing if he had more actively intrigued on his own behalf.

[529] Ibn Sa'd, *Ṭabaqāt*, IV/1, 134.

politically impotent and irrelevant. In the future they would not even be consulted in important affairs of state any more. The Syrians were jubilant about his and 'Amr's conduct. Mu'āwiya's court poet Ka'b b. Ju'ayl celebrated 'Amr's primitive stratagem as the victory of Luqmān's proverbial wisdom over the trickery of Abū Mūsā who was trying to cheat Mu'āwiya out of his inheritance from Muḥammmad.[530]

In the last two years of 'Alī's reign the Inter-Muslim War deteriorated into its final, most vicious stage. The initiative was now with the Umayyad. In spite of the serious disarray on 'Alī's side, Mu'āwiya, while asserting that his opponent had been deposed and he had been recognized as the sole caliph in the arbitration, did not dare to mount an all-out offensive and anxiously avoided even minor engagements with the enemy army. In order to reinforce his claim to the universal rule of the Muslims, he rather relied on surprise attacks on the civilian population, killing those who would not recognize him as caliph, looting and ravaging. The purpose was to undermine 'Alī's reign by terrorizing and intimidating his subjects in concert with his campaign of bribery among the tribal chiefs in 'Alī's army. The early historians referred to these attacks collectively as 'the raids (*ghārāt*)'. Al-Ṭabarī reported them, except for the last one, that of Busr b. Abī Arṭāh in the Ḥijāz and Yemen, under the year 39/659-60.[531] Those that can be dated took place in fact either earlier or in the year 40/660–1. There seems to have been a relative lull in activity in 39/659–60, though some of the undatable events presumably occurred during that year.

The first of the raids, that of al-Ḍaḥḥāk b. Qays, had, as described, occurred at the end of the year 37/May–June 658. The second one was probably that of the Anṣārī al-Nu'mān b. Bashīr.[532] Mu'āwiya had earlier, even before Ṣiffīn, sent him together with Abū Hurayra on a propaganda mission to 'Alī to ask for the surrender of the killers of 'Uthmān. 'Alī had at that time confronted al-Nu'mān and questioned him as to why he was one of the three or four Anṣār breaking ranks with his people and opposing him. Al-Nu'mān appears to have been embarrassed by this direct question and answered that he was merely hoping to bring about a peace between 'Alī and Mu'āwiya and would, if 'Alī saw otherwise, stay with him. When Abū Hurayra returned empty-handed to Syria, al-Nu'mān remained with 'Alī for a month[533] pretending to be on his side, but then

[530] Minqarī, *Waq'at Ṣiffīn*, 549. [531] Ṭabarī, I, 3444–8.

[532] Al-Balādhurī enumerates al-Nu'mān's raid as the third one after that of Sufyān b.'Awf but states that according to some his raid occurred before Sufyān's (*Ansāb*, II, 447).

[533] The accounts of al-Thaqafī (*Ghārāt*, 447) and al-Balādhurī (*Ansāb*, II, 445) speak of several months (*ashhuran*). This is not possible, since al-Nu'mān was with the Syrians in the battle of Ṣiffīn. Ibn Abi l-Ḥadīd's parallel account (*Sharḥ*, II, 302) gives one month (*shahran*).

fled clandestinely. At ʿAyn al-Tamr he was seized, however, by the governor, Mālik b. Kaʿb al-Arḥabī, who intended at first to seek instructions from ʿAlī about what to do with him. As al-Nuʿmān implored him not to inform ʿAlī, Mālik consulted the Anṣārī Qaraẓa b. Kaʿb who was collecting the land tax nearby for ʿAlī. Qaraẓa suggested that he let him quietly escape. Mālik now gave al-Nuʿmān two days to disappear and threatened to cut his head off if he found him thereafter.

When Muʿāwiya, two or three months after the raid of al-Ḍaḥḥāk b. Qays,[534] asked for a volunteer to attack along the bank of the Euphrates, al-Nuʿmān came forward, evidently eager to take revenge on Mālik b. Kaʿb. Muʿāwiya gave him a detachment of two thousand men and instructed him to avoid the towns and large assemblies of men, not to attack any garrison (*maslaḥa*),[535] to raid the people along the bank of the Euphrates and to return quickly. Al-Nuʿmān approached ʿAyn al-Tamr, where Mālik b. Kaʿb was in command of a garrison of a thousand men. Since most of these were on leave in Kūfa, and only a hundred[536] men remained with him, Mālik asked Mikhnaf b. Sulaym al-Azdī, who was in charge of tax collection along the Euphrates up to the territory of Bakr b. Wāʾil, for assistance. Mikhnaf sent his son ʿAbd al-Raḥmān or ʿAbd Allāh with fifty men. They arrived in the evening as Mālik and his men were barely holding back the Syrian attack on ʿAyn al-Tamr. The Syrians thought large enemy reinforcements were arriving and withdrew. Mālik pursued them, and one of his men and three Syrians were killed. ʿAlī is said to have sent ʿAdī b. Ḥātim al-Ṭāʾī to track down al-Nuʿmān; ʿAdī almost reached Qinnasrīn before turning back.[537]

At an unknown date Muʿāwiya sent Zuhayr b. Makḥūl of the Banū ʿĀmir al-Ajdar of Kalb to the desert of al-Samāwa west of the Euphrates to collect the alms-tax there. Most of the nomads in this region were of Kalb, and Muʿāwiya, who had a marriage alliance with Kalb, evidently hoped to extend his sway over them. When ʿAlī learned of this, he sent three men, Jaʿfar b. ʿAbd Allāh al-Ashjaʿī, ʿUrwa[538] b. al-ʿUshba of ʿAbd Wadd of Kalb and al-Julās b. ʿUmayr of the Banū ʿAdī b. Janāb of Kalb, acting as the scribe, to collect the alms-tax from the Kalb and Bakr b. Wāʾil obeying him. They met Zuhayr in the territory of Kalb, fought with

[534] Reading *baʿda dhālik* in the account of al-Thaqafī, *Ghārāt* 499, and Ibn Abi l-Ḥadīd, *Sharḥ*, II, 303, for *qabla dhālik* which makes no sense. Alternatively *dhālik* would have to be understood as referring to al-Nuʿmān's actual raid rather than al-Ḍaḥḥāk's. If al-Nuʿmān's raid is to be dated two or three months after that of al-Ḍaḥḥāk, it occurred around Rab. I or Rab. II 38/Aug.–Sept. 658.

[535] Thus the text in al-Balādhurī, *Ansāb*, II, 447. According to the text of al-Thaqafī, *Ghārāt*, 449, Muʿāwiya rather ordered him to attack only garrisons.

[536] According to al-Thaqafī's account only thirty.

[537] Balādhurī, *Ansāb*, II, 445–8; Ṭabarī, I, 3444–5; Thaqafī, *Ghārāt*, 445–59.

[538] In al-Thaqafī's account (*Ghārāt*, 461–2) he is named ʿAmr rather than ʿUrwa.

him, and were defeated. Ja'far b. 'Abd Allāh was killed and al-Julās escaped. Ibn al-'Ushba returned to 'Alī and was accused by him of cowardice and running away out of partisanship for his Kalbite tribesman Zuhayr; in his anger 'Alī hit him with his whip (*dirra*). Zuhayr had in fact put Ibn al-'Ushba on a horse after having defeated him. When Ibn al-'Ushba defected and joined Mu'āwiya, 'Alī had his house destroyed. Al-Julās eventually returned to Kūfa, having exchanged his silk jubbah for the woollen garment of a shepherd.[539]

This success among the Kalb of al-Samāwa may have encouraged Mu'āwiya to seek to bring the Kalb of Dūmat al-Jandal under his rule also. These had so far abstained from pledging allegiance to either 'Alī or Mu'āwiya. The latter now sent Muslim b. 'Uqba al-Murrī to summon them to his obedience and to pay their alms-tax to him. They resisted, however, and Muslim laid siege to the oasis. 'Alī recalled Mālik b. Ka'b from 'Ayn al-Tamr, ordering him to appoint a deputy commander of the garrison, and sent him with a thousand horsemen to Dūmat al-Jandal. They took Muslim by surprise, and there was some inconclusive fighting. The next day the Syrians left. Mālik b. Ka'b stayed for a few days, summoning the inhabitants to allegiance to 'Alī. They insisted, however, that they would not pledge allegiance until all the people agreed on an imam, and Mālik departed without pressing them.[540]

The Syrian raids on Mesopotamia and Iraq having had little success, Mu'āwiya decided to test the ground in the Ḥijāz. Probably in the year 39/659–60[541] he dispatched 'Abd Allāh b. Mas'ada b. Ḥakama al-Fazārī with one thousand seven hundred men to Taymā' with instructions to collect the alms-tax from the bedouin Arabs whom he passed, to take the pledge of allegiance for Mu'āwiya from those who obeyed, and to put those who refused to the sword. From Taymā' he was to proceed to Medina and Mekka, doing the same and reporting every day on his actions and plans. A large number of his people of Fazāra joined him. When 'Alī learned of this, he ordered al-Musayyab b. Najaba al-Fazārī to pursue Ibn Mas'ada with a strong force. Al-Musayyab was also joined by a large number of his kinsmen of Fazāra. He moved via al-Janāb to Taymā' where he caught up with Ibn Mas'ada. They engaged in battle

539 Balādhurī, *Ansāb*, II, 465–6.

540 *ibid.*, 467; Thaqafī, *Ghārāt*, 462–4. 'Alī and his sons al-Ḥasan and al-Ḥusayn had married daughters of Imru' ul-Qays b. 'Adī b. Aws al-Kalbī during the caliphate of 'Umar (Balādhurī, *Ansāb*, II, 194–5; see also excursus 7). Imru' ul-Qays seems to have been the chief of the Kalb in Dūmat al-Jandal at this time (see the editor's note in Thaqafī, *Ghārāt*, 815–7).

541 Al-Ṭabarī (I, 3446) gives the date as the year 39/659–60. It is, in any case, unlikely that Mu'āwiya would have ordered a raid on Medina and Mekka before Adhruḥ. The raid, on the other hand, probably took place before the dispute about the leadership of the pilgrimage of the year 39/April 660.

immediately, and fought until nightfall. Al-Musayyab struck Ibn Mas'ada three times, wounding him, but intentionally did not kill his tribal brother and encouraged him to escape. Ibn Mas'ada and some of his men sought shelter in the fortress of Taymā', while the rest of them fled headlong to Syria. The camels they had gathered as alms-tax were looted by bedouins. The men in the fortress were besieged for three days. Then firewood was piled up around the wall and kindled. Threatened by perdition, the besieged men of Fazāra looked down on al-Musayyab, calling: 'Musayyab, your people!' Al-Musayyab ordered the fire to be extinguished and arranged for their escape during the night.[542] 'Abd al-Raḥmān b. Shabīb al-Fazārī suggested to al-Musayyab that they be pursued. When al-Musayyab refused, Ibn Shabīb accused him of having cheated the Commander of the Faithful in favour of the enemy.

'Alī, according to al-Balādhurī's account, confined al-Musayyab for some days and reproached him for unduly protecting his people.[543] Al-Musayyab apologized, and the Kufan nobles interceded on his behalf. 'Alī tied him, however, to a pillar in the mosque or, according to others, imprisoned him. Then he called and forgave him, and entrusted him jointly with 'Abd al-Raḥmān b. Muḥammad al-Kindī with the collection of the alms-tax in Kūfa. After a time he investigated their accounts and found nothing against them. He now praised both men highly.[544]

After these failures of his attempts to expand his sway in Arabia, Mu'āwiya hoped to use the pilgrimage at the end of the year 39/April–May 660 for gaining recognition as the legitimate caliph in Mekka. Mekka, the home town of Quraysh who had been the first to oppose 'Alī, would be, he

[542] According to the account of al-Balādhurī, 'Abd al-Raḥmān b. Asmā' al-Fazārī, who had valiantly fought the Syrians before, now let them escape through a breach in the wall and on to the road to Syria.

[543] 'Alī had presumably little sympathy for 'Abd Allāh b. Mas'ada al-Fazārī in particular. The latter had as a boy been among the captives of the Muslims from Fazāra and had been given by Muḥammad as a slave to Fāṭima. She had manumitted him, and he had been brought up by her and 'Alī. He joined Mu'āwiya, however, fought for him at Ṣiffīn, and is said to have become one of the most vigorous enemies of 'Alī (Ibn Manẓūr, *Mukhtaṣar*, XIV, 41).

[544] Balādhurī, *Ansāb*, II, 449–51; Ṭabarī, I, 3446–7. Al-Ṭabarī (I, 3447) quotes a further report of al-Wāqidī and Abū Ma'shar on the authority of the Mekkan Ibn Abī Mulayka (d. 118/736), according to which Mu'āwiya himself went forth, and reached the river Tigris in the year 39/659-60 before turning back. Caetani considered this report, in spite of its meagreness in detail, as of great importance in proving the new ardour and strength of Mu'āwiya who could move across the whole of Mesopotamia without a blow being struck and the impotence of 'Alī whose dominion was confined to the environs of Kūfa and *perhaps* Baṣra and Fārs (*Annali*, X, 289–90). It is safe to assume that the report is false and reflects the ignorance of the Ḥijāzī tradition about Syria and Iraq in this period. The Kufan tradition knows nothing about such a move by Mu'āwiya. Given his extreme caution with respect to his personal safety, it is hardly conceivable that he would suddenly have exposed himself to such danger.

assumed, more inclined to co-operate with him than Medina and other parts of Arabia. He secretly summoned Yazīd b. Shajara of Madhḥij, one of his northern Syrian army leaders. Yazīd was known as a pious worshipper and, firmly 'Uthmanid, had fought for Mu'āwiya at Ṣiffīn. Mu'āwiya confided to him that he was sending him to the Sanctuary of God and to his own tribe, 'my protected homeland (*bayḍatī*) which has split from me'. Its governor was, he asserted, 'one of those who killed 'Uthmān and shed his blood' and in overthrowing him there would be 'satisfaction for me and you' and an act pleasing to God; Yazīd should move to Mekka where he would find the people in the pilgrimage season. He should summon them to obedience to Mu'āwiya; if they accepted, he should keep his hands off them, but if they refused, he should declare war on them (*nābidhhum*); he should not fight them, however, before making clear to them that he was acting on the orders of Mu'āwiya, for Mu'āwiya considered them as his own root and tribe and preferred their survival; then he should pray with the people and take charge of the pilgrimage season.[545]

Qutham b. al-'Abbās, 'Alī's governor of Mekka, had had no more to do with the murder of 'Uthmān than had his brothers 'Abd Allāh and 'Ubayd Allāh. The latter's infant sons were to be murdered by Busr b. Abī Arṭāh under Mu'āwiya's instructions soon thereafter. The official Umayyad propaganda line that the Banū Hāshim were collectively guilty of the murder of 'Uthmān was now paying dividends. Although duped by it, Yazīd b. Shajara nevertheless had misgivings about the use of violence in the Sanctuary during the Holy Month of the pilgrimage. He told Mu'āwiya that he was prepared to proceed only if he were given a free hand to act at his own discretion in bringing about a peaceful accord; if Mu'āwiya would be satisfied with nothing but violence (*ghashm*), the use of the sword and terrorizing the innocent, he should look for someone else. Mu'āwiya pulled back and assured him that he fully trusted his views and conduct. He gave him an army of three thousand men, who were not informed of the aim of their mission before leaving Syria. They moved via Wādi l-Qurā and al-Juḥfa, bypassing hostile Medina, and reached Mekka on 10 Dhu l-Ḥijja/27 April.

When Qutham b. al-'Abbās learned that the Syrians had reached al-Juḥfa, he addressed the Mekkans, informing them of the threat and asking them to speak out openly whether they were prepared to resist them together with him. As no one spoke at first, he declared that they had made their intentions clear and descended from the pulpit, ready to leave the town. Then Shayba b. 'Uthmān b. Abī Ṭalḥa of 'Abd al-Dār, who was

[545] Thaqafī, *Ghārāt*, 504–5.

in charge of the office of Doorkeeper (*ḥijāba*) of the Kaʿba,[546] stood up and assured him that the people were behind him and the caliph, his cousin, and would obey his orders. Qutham, however, had no faith in them and insisted that he would leave Mekka to hide in a ravine. Then the Anṣārī Abū Saʿīd al-Khudrī, a personal friend of Qutham, arrived from Medina and urged the governor not to leave, since he had learned from the pilgrims arriving in Medina from Iraq that the Kufans were expediting a detachment with Maʿqil b. Qays al-Riyāḥī to Mekka. Qutham showed Abū Saʿīd a letter from ʿAlī in which he informed him that he had been notified by a spy that the enemy was sending a troop to Mekka to interfere with the pilgrimage. ʿAlī was sending Maʿqil b. Qays in order to chase them out of the Ḥijāz and urged Qutham to remain steadfast in adversity until he arrived. When Abū Saʿīd had read the letter, Qutham told him that this letter was of no benefit to him since he had learned that the Syrian horse troops would precede Maʿqil, who would not be arriving before the pilgrimage was over. Abū Saʿīd nonetheless kept urging him to stay on and thus to earn the appreciation of his imam and the people. The enemy would certainly hesitate to assault the Sanctuary whose inviolability had ever been observed in the Jāhiliyya and Islam. Qutham decided to stay.

When Yazīd b. Shajara arrived in Mekka, he ordered a herald to proclaim to the people that all would be safe except those who attempted to interfere in 'our work and authority'. Quraysh, Anṣār, Companions and pious people all hastened to bring about a peaceful accord between the two sides. Both were in fact gratified by their efforts – Qutham because he did not trust the Mekkans, and Yazīd because he was a man inclined to ascetic worship who was loath to commit evil in the Sanctuary. Yazīd addressed the Mekkans suggesting that he had been sent to pray with the people, order the proper and prohibit the reprehensible. He realized that the governor disliked what he had come for and was loath to pray with him, while he and his men hated to pray with the governor. If Qutham agreed both of them should forgo the leadership of the prayers and leave the choice of a prayer leader to the people of Mekka. If Qutham refused, however, he would refuse too, and, he added ominously, he was in a position to carry him off to Syria since there was no one to protect him. He asked Abū Saʿīd al-Khudrī to act as a go-between, and Qutham readily agreed. The people chose Shayba b. ʿUthmān as their imam, and he prayed with them; Yazīd then speedily departed. Maʿqil's horsemen arrived after the pilgrimage was over, were informed of the departure of the Syrians, and pursued them. At Wādi l-Qurā they captured ten of them who had tarried while the others left. Yazīd b. Shajara was informed

[546] The Banū ʿAbd al-Dār were traditionally in charge of the office of Doorkeeper of the Kaʿba while the Banū Hāshim were in charge of providing the pilgrims with water (*siqāya*).

but would not turn back to give battle. Ma'qil returned via Dūmat al-Jandal to Kūfa with his captives.[547]

Mu'āwiya was now under pressure from his followers to seek the release of the ten prisoners. He instructed al-Ḥārith b. Numayr al-Tanūkhī, who had been the commander of the vanguard of Yazīd b. Shajara's army, to invade Upper Mesopotamia and to seize some of 'Alī's partisans. Al-Ḥārith moved via Ṣiffīn to the region of Dārā; from there he carried off eight men of Taghlib loyal to 'Alī. Some men of Taghlib who had earlier defected from 'Alī's side to join Mu'āwiya now asked for their release. When Mu'āwiya refused, they renounced their obedience to him also. A chief of Taghlib loyal to 'Alī, 'Utba b. al-Wa'l, gathered his men and, crossing the Euphrates at Jisr Manbij, attacked Syrian territory, seizing much booty. He addressed a defiant poem to Mu'āwiya, proudly proclaiming that he had raided just like the son of Ṣakhr had done. Mu'āwiya sent to 'Alī proposing an exchange of their captives, and 'Alī agreed.[548]

After this exchange 'Alī thought that Mu'āwiya would abstain from further raids. About a month later, however, Mu'āwiya mounted a much more serious assault by sending Sufyān b. 'Awf b. al-Mughaffal al-Azdī al-Ghāmidī to al-Anbār.[549] According to Sufyān's own account, Mu'āwiya called him and told him that he was sending him with a strong army to raid along the bank of the Euphrates. Sufyān was to cross the river at Hīt. If he found a garrison there, he should attack them. Otherwise he should move on to al-Anbār and, if he did not encounter enemy troops there, proceed to al-Madā'in and then turn back. He should not get close to Kūfa. If he attacked al-Anbār and al-Madā'in, this would have the same effect as attacking Kūfa and would instil fear in the hearts of the people of Iraq and embolden those inclining towards the Syrians. Mu'āwiya instructed Sufyān to invite all those fearing attacks to join the Syrians, to destroy the villages he passed by, to kill all he met who did not agree with his opinion, and to loot property, for that was similar to killing and most painful to the heart.[550]

Sufyān found Hīt, on the west bank of the Euphrates, deserted by its garrison and inhabitants, who had learned of his approach and had crossed over to the east bank. He passed by Ṣandawdā' on the west bank, which was equally deserted, and moved on to al-Anbār on the east side. The people there had also been warned, and the commander of the

[547] *Ibid.*, 504–12; Balādhurī, *Ansāb*, II, 461–4; Ibn A'tham, *Futūḥ*, IV, 38–45; Ṭabarī, I, 3448.

[548] Balādhurī, *Ansāb*, II, 469–70; Ibn A'tham, *Futūḥ*, IV, 45–7; Ibn al-Athīr, *Kāmil*, III, 319. According to the account of Ibn A'tham, 'Alī, rather than Mu'āwiya, took the initiative in seeking the exchange.

[549] Ibn A'tham, *Futūḥ*, IV, 47. On the basis of this report the raid of Sufyān b. 'Awf is to be dated in summer of the year 40/660.

[550] Thaqafī, *Ghārāt*, 464–7.

garrison, Ashras b. Ḥassān al-Bakrī, had moved out to meet him. Sufyān questioned some boys of the town about the strength of the garrison and learned that there were five hundred men, but that many of them were dispersed. He now ordered an attack on foot, to be followed immediately by cavalry. Aware of the superior enemy force, Ashras had given his remaining men the choice of joining him in a fight to death or leaving under cover of those choosing to resist. He was killed together with some thirty of his men. Sufyān had the town thoroughly looted, tearing anklets from women's legs and necklaces from their necks, and then speedily left for Syria without proceeding to al-Madā'in. In his own account he proudly stated that he had never carried out a cleaner (*aslam*) and more pleasing raid. Mu'āwiya had praised him highly and assured him that he would appoint him to any office he desired. He concluded his account with the remark that it was not long before the people of Iraq came in droves fleeing to Syria.[551]

'Alī was, according to Abū Mikhnaf, informed about the raid on al-Anbār by a local peasant (*'ilj*). He appealed from the pulpit to the Kufans to avenge the death of Ashras and drive the enemy out of Iraq. As there was no immediate response, he walked on foot to al-Nukhayla, followed by the people and a group of chiefs (*ashrāf*). They promised him that they would take care of the enemy for him. Though not convinced of their sincerity, he returned to Kūfa and ordered Sa'īd b. Qays al-Hamdānī to pursue the Syrians with eight thousand men, having been given to understand that the enemy army was massive. The delay caused by assembling such a strong army may have aided Sufyān to escape untouched. Sa'īd b. Qays moved along the Euphrates and reached 'Ānāt. From there he dispatched Hāni' b. al-Khaṭṭāb al-Hamdānī with a detachment. The latter tracked the enemy as far as the region of Qinnasrīn but did not catch up with them. When Sa'īd b. Qays returned to Kūfa without success, 'Alī was ill. He wrote an angry letter to be read to the Kufans in which he severely castigated them for their failure to respond to his call for *jihād*. This, he complained, exposed him to talk of Quraysh and others that 'Alī was a brave man but knew nothing about warfare.[552]

The commander of the garrison of Hīt was Kumayl b. Ziyād al-Nakha'ī, an early Shi'ite supporter of 'Alī. He had left his post at the time of Sufyān's raid with most of his men and gone in the direction of Qarqīsiyā because he had been informed that people had assembled there intending to attack Hīt, and he wanted to strike them first. When Sufyān approached Hīt, the inhabitants and remaining fifty men of the garrison, as noted,

551 *Ibid.*, 468. 552 *Ibid.*, 464–82; Balādhurī, *Ansāb*, II, 441–3; Ṭabarī, I, 3445–6.

abandoned the town, crossing the river to the east bank. 'Alī wrote him a stern letter reprimanding him for dereliction of his duty and refused to accept his excuses. He left him, however, in his post. Not long afterwards Kumayl received a note from Shabīb b. 'Āmir al-Azdī[553] from Naṣībīn notifying him that, according to the information of a spy, Mu'āwiya was sending 'Abd al-Raḥmān b. Qabāth b. Ashyam al-Kinānī[554] in the direction of Upper Mesopotamia. Shabīb did not know whether the raid was directed towards Naṣībīn or the Euphrates region and Hīt. Kumayl saw a chance to recover the favour of 'Alī and immediately set out with four hundred horsemen to meet the raiders, leaving his six hundred foot soldiers in Hīt. He was advised to seek instructions from 'Alī but refused, in order to avoid delay. Ibn Qabāth, he learned, had passed al-Raqqa in the direction of Ra's al-'Ayn and had reached Kafartūthā. Kumayl rode speedily to Kafartūthā where he hit upon Ibn Qabāth and Ma'n b. Yazīd al-Sulamī with two thousand four hundred Syrians. He evidently took them by surprise and scattered their army killing a large number while losing two of his men. Afraid that they might reassemble for another attack, he forbade pursuing the enemy in order to keep his men together. When Shabīb b. 'Āmir arrived from Naṣibīn with six hundred horsemen and foot soldiers, he found that Kumayl had already routed the raiders, and congratulated him.[555] Shabīb went on to pursue the Syrians and to invade Syrian territory. He crossed the Euphrates at Jisr Manbij and sent his cavalry to attack the region of Ba'labakk. When Mu'āwiya ordered Ḥabīb b. Maslama to meet Shabīb, the latter withdrew and raided the region of al-Raqqa, where he looted cattle, horses and weapons. 'Alī sent letters to Kumayl and Shabīb, praising them and commending their action. He instructed Shabīb, however, not to loot cattle and personal property except for horses and weapons.[556]

In the year after al-Nahrawān, 'Alī was also faced with the hostile activity of a number of Kharijite splinter groups. Al-Balādhurī mentions five such rebel groups and gives the dates of their defeat. They were small bands which posed no serious military threat but were deeply determined to follow the example of their brethren killed at al-Nahrawān and to seek martyrdom for what they saw as their righteous cause. The first rebel group of two hundred men was led by Ashras b. 'Awf al-Shaybānī. He

553 Shabīb b. 'Āmir was the ancestor of Juday' b. 'Alī al-Kirmānī, the rival of Naṣr b. Sayyār in Khurāsān in the late Umayyad age (Balādhurī, *Ansāb*, II, 469; Ibn A'tham, *Futūḥ*, IV, 50).

554 On 'Abd al-Raḥmān's father Qabāth b. Ashyam see Caskel, *Ǧamharat an-nasab*, II, index s.v.

555 According to the account of Ibn A'tham (*Futūḥ*, IV, 50–2), Shabīb and Kumayl rather joined forces before the battle and then defeated the Syrians. Shabīb lost four of his men.

556 Balādhurī, *Ansāb*, II, 473–6.

had evidently belonged to the Kharijites who withdrew just before the fighting at al-Nahrawān to al-Daskara. From there he now made an approach towards al-Anbār. ʿAlī sent al-Abrash b. Ḥassān with three hundred men against him, and Ashras was killed in Rabīʿ I 38/August–September 658.[557]

Next came the rebellion of Hilāl b. ʿAlqama and his brother Mujālid of Taym al-Ribāb. They moved with over two hundred men east to Māsābadhān, summoning others to their cause. Against them ʿAlī sent Maʿqil b. Qays al-Riyāḥī, who killed all the rebels in Jumādā I 38/October 658.[558] Then followed the rising of the Kufan al-Ashhab (or al-Ashʿath) b. Bashīr al-Qaranī of Bajīla with a hundred and thirty (or a hundred and eighty) men. He retraced the tracks of Hilāl b. ʿAlqama, performed prayers for him on the battlefield where he had been killed, and buried the dead whom he still found. ʿAlī dispatched Jāriya b. Qudāma or Ḥujr b. ʿAdī after him. Al-Ashhab and his followers were killed at Jarjarāyā in Jumādā II 38/November 658.[559] Saʿīd (or Saʿd) b. Qafal al-Taymī of Taym Allāh b. Thaʿlaba b. ʿUkāba of Rabīʿa mounted an uprising in al-Bandanījayn with two hundred followers. As he moved towards al-Madā'in, ʿAlī instructed his governor there, Saʿd b. Masʿūd al-Thaqafī, to take action against them. The governor met the rebels at Qanṭarat al-Darzījān, and Ibn Qafal and his men were killed in Rajab 38/December 658.[560]

Abū Maryam al-Saʿdī of Saʿd Tamīm had, as noted, left the Kharijite battle lines before the fighting at al-Nahrawān together with two hundred men. He made his way to Shahrazūr where he stayed for several months, inciting his followers to revenge for the martyrs of al-Nahrawān and successfully summoning others to the Kharijite cause. Then he moved with a following of four hundred men to al-Madā'in and from there on towards Kūfa. His followers were mostly clients and non-Arabs (*ʿajam*). According to al-Madā'ini, the only Arabs among them, aside from himself, were five men of the Banū Saʿd. As they approached Kūfa, ʿAlī sent a message to him suggesting that he pledge allegiance to him, ʿAlī, on the basis that he could enter Kūfa and join those who would not fight either for or against him. Abū Maryam answered that there could be nothing between them but war. ʿAlī now sent Shurayḥ b. Hāni' with seven hundred men against the rebels. Shurayḥ repeated ʿAlī's offer to Abū Maryam and received the reply: 'You enemies of God, shall we pledge allegiance to ʿAlī and stay among you while your imam oppresses us? You have killed ʿAbd Allāh b. Wahb, Zayd b. Ḥiṣn, Ḥurqūṣ b. Zuhayr, and our righteous brethren.' Then the rebels shouted their battle cry 'No judgment but God's' and attacked. Shurayḥ's army turned to

557 *Ibid.*, 481. 558 *Ibid.*, 482. 559 *Ibid.*, 483. 560 *Ibid.*, 484.

flee, and he withdrew with two hundred men to a nearby village. Some of his other men rejoined him there, while the rest returned to Kūfa where rumours spread that Shurayḥ had been killed. 'Alī now went forth himself. He sent Jāriya b. Qudāma with five hundred men as his vanguard and followed him with another two thousand. When Jāriya came face to face with his tribesman Abū Maryam, he addressed him: 'Woe to you, are you pleased with exposing yourself to being killed with these slaves? By God, when they feel the pain of iron, they will abandon you.' Abū Maryam answered: 'We have heard a wondrous Qur'ān which guides to the right path. We believe in it and shall not associate any partner with our Lord.' Then 'Alī arrived and invited them once more to pledge allegiance. They refused and attacked him, wounding a number of his men. Then they were killed, except for fifty of them who asked for a letter of safety and were granted it; another forty were found wounded. 'Alī ordered them to be taken to Kūfa and to be treated there; then he allowed them to go to any country they wished. The battle took place in Ramaḍān 38/February 659.[561] No further Kharijite revolts are recorded during 'Alī's reign.

The last months before 'Alī's assassination in Ramaḍān 40/January 661 were marked by a renewed intensification of the conflict with Mu'āwiya. 'Alī was as intent as ever on undertaking another campaign against the Umayyad in Syria and seems to have found sufficient backing to plan it for the spring. Partly perhaps in order to forestall this attack by opening a second front, Mu'āwiya expedited a major force under Busr b. Abī Arṭāh to the Ḥijāz and Yemen.[562]

561 *Ibid.*, 485–6.

562 Al-Ṭabarī, in contrast, reported the conclusion of a truce between 'Alī and Mu'āwiya, after a lengthy exchange of letters, in the year 40/660–1, according to which 'Alī was to keep Iraq and Mu'āwiya Syria (Ṭabarī, I, 3452–3). The report, attributed to the Kufan Abū Isḥāq al-Sabī'ī, is obviously untenable since 'Alī was killed when Busr was still raiding Arabia. Caetani, however, considered it 'absolutely secure' and argued that it proved how deeply the disgraced 'Alī had fallen, who now was forced to accept the 'good reasons' of Mu'āwiya for not recognizing him as caliph. 'Alī's renunciation of his previous pretences, according to Caetani, thus constituted his moral suicide, making it reasonable that one of his followers, disgusted with the man, would have assassinated him (*Annali*, X, 329–30). It is difficult to see why the truce would have been less discreditable for Mu'āwiya, who would have had to renounce his noble claim of revenge for the wronged caliph at a time when he, according to Caetani, could freely move across Iraq without meeting any resistance. According to Abū Isḥāq's report, it was Mu'āwiya who proposed the truce to 'Alī.

Wellhausen suggested that 'Abū Isḥāq' in the *isnād* of the report should be read Ibn Isḥāq and that the truce, concluded early in the year 40/660, was subsequently broken by 'Alī when Mu'āwiya adopted the title caliph and received the pledge of allegiance of the Syrians in Jerusalem (*Das arabische Reich*, 64). In reality Mu'āwiya had claimed the title caliph long before and had been acclaimed as such by the Syrians. 'Alī could hardly have taken the formal ceremony in Jerusalem as an issue over which to break the truce.

The early Kufan historian Abū Rawq al-Hamdānī described the background of Busr b. Abī Arṭāh's raid as follows: in the Yemen the partisans of ʿUthmān (*shīʿat ʿUthmān*) after his murder were at first leaderless and disorganized, and pledged allegiance to ʿAlī. ʿAlī's governor of Ṣanʿāʾ was at that time ʿUbayd Allāh b. al-ʿAbbās and his governor of al-Janad Saʿīd b. Nimrān al-Hamdānī al-Nāʿiṭī.[563] As matters were turning against ʿAlī – Muḥammad b. Abī Bakr having been killed in Egypt and the Syrians carrying out regular raids on ʿAlī's territories – the ʿUthmāniyya in the Yemen also raised their heads, demanding revenge for the blood of ʿUthmān, and withheld their alms-tax. ʿUbayd Allāh wrote to some of their leaders questioning them about their new conduct, but they answered defiantly that they had always disapproved of the murder of ʿUthmān and wished to fight those who had revolted against him. When ʿUbayd Allāh imprisoned them, they wrote to their companions in al-Janad who rose against Saʿīd b. Nimrān and expelled him from the town. The ʿUthmāniyya from Ṣanʿāʾ joined the rebels there, as did others who did not hold their views but wanted to withhold their alms-tax.

ʿUbayd Allāh now consulted with Saʿīd b. Nimrān and the partisans of ʿAlī. He argued that the opponents were close to them in strength so that they could not be sure to win if they fought them. On his suggestion, the two governors wrote to ʿAlī apprising him of the situation and seeking his instructions. ʿAlī was angered by their inaction and sent them a stern order to invite the rebels back to obedience and, if they refused, to fight them.

According to Ibn al-Kalbī, ʿAlī then addressed Yazīd b. Qays al-Arḥabī of Hamdān, telling him reproachfully: 'Don't you see what your people are doing?' Yazīd assured him that in his opinion his people were basically loyal to the Commander of the Faithful and suggested that ʿAlī either send him to the Yemen to bring them into line or that he write them a letter and wait for their response. ʿAlī then wrote the rebels a personal letter urging them to return to obedience, in which case they would be treated justly; but if they failed to do so, he threatened to send an army of horsemen to crush the refractory. He sent the letter with a man of Hamdān. As the rebels failed to give an answer for some time, the messenger told them that when he departed from Kūfa, the Commander of the Faithful had been ready to dispatch Yazīd b. Qays with a massive army. ʿAlī was restrained merely by the expectation of their reaction. The ʿUthmāniyya now protested: 'We shall hear and obey if he removes these two men, ʿUbayd Allāh and Saʿīd, from us.' The messenger returned to ʿAlī and informed him of this. As it turned out, the rebels had, on hearing

[563] It is not known when ʿAlī replaced Saʿīd b. Saʿd b. ʿUbāda as governor of al-Janad with Saʿīd b. Nimrān.

that 'Alī was prepared to send Yazīd b. Qays, addressed a poem to Mu'āwiya urging him to send quick relief, otherwise they would pledge allegiance to 'Alī. Mu'āwiya immediately ordered Busr b. Abī Arṭāh to proceed towards the Yemen.[564]

From the Syrian side, 'Abd al-Raḥmān b. Mas'ada al-Fazārī reported the following during the caliphate of 'Abd al-Malik: as the year 40/summer 660 began, the people of Syria were telling each other that 'Alī was trying to mobilize the people of Iraq, but they would not respond to his summons since their sympathies were divided and schism prevailed among them. He, Ibn Mas'ada, and a group of Syrians thus went to see al-Walīd b. 'Uqba and told him: 'The men do not doubt that the people of Iraq are in disagreement in regard to 'Alī. Go to your companion and press him to move with us against them before they reunite after their division or the corrupt state in which their master finds himself in relation to them is repaired.' Al-Walīd assured them that he had talked to Mu'āwiya again and again and had admonished and reproached him in that regard until he had become annoyed with him and disgusted by the sight of him. He swore that he would not fail to convey to him what they had come for. When he informed Mu'āwiya, the latter admitted them to his presence and asked them about their concern. They told him about the mood of the people, urged him to take advantage of the situation and attack the enemy before it might change, and to move against them before they moved against him. His opponent would certainly have attacked him already were it not for the division among his men. Mu'āwiya answered them gruffly that he could dispense with their opinion and their advice; when he needed them he would call upon them. He was, he said, not so eager to annihilate the people they mentioned that he would put his army at risk not knowing which side would be struck by calamity. He warned them to beware of accusing him of slowness; he was pursuing the most effective means of destroying the enemy by sending continuous raids against them; as a result the nobles (*ashrāf*) of Iraq, seeing God's favour for Mu'āwiya, were arriving every day on their camels, increasing the strength of the Syrians and diminishing the power of the enemy. His visitors left satisfied with the excellence of his view. Mu'āwiya immediately sent for Busr b. Abī Arṭāh, ordering him to raid Medina and Mekka and to move on as far as Ṣan'ā' and al-Janad where he had partisans (*shī'a*) whose letter had just arrived. As Busr reviewed his troops at Dayr Murrān outside Damascus, al-Walīd b. 'Uqba grumbled: 'We have made our view clear to Mu'āwiya that he should move to Kūfa, but he sends an army to Medina. We are with him like the one who said: "I point out [the

[564] Thaqafī, *Ghārāt*, 592–8.

dim star] al-Suhā to her, and she shows me the moon."' When this reached Muʿāwiya, he was furious and commented: 'By God, I am inclined to chastize this idiot (*aḥmaq*) who is no good at sound planning and understands nothing about the proper management of affairs.' But then he refrained from punishing him.[565]

Muʿāwiya's own understanding of the proper management of affairs was revealed by his choice of Busr b. Abī Arṭāh to lead the new raid into Arabia. The previous campaign, under the command of the pious Yazīd b. Shajara, had not borne the fruits that the Umayyad caliph was seeking. Yazīd had insisted on being given discretion in his conduct in order to avoid bloodshed in the Holy City and ended up losing a few of his own men as captives. Busr, Muʿāwiya was sure, would not be plagued by such scruples. If he had ordered him to herd all his opponents together and burn them in the Sanctuary, he would have been pleased to comply. Muʿāwiya instructed Busr to chase and intimidate the people on his way to Medina, and to loot the property of all who would not enter into Umayyad obedience. When he entered Medina, he should frighten the inhabitants into panic, threatening that they would have no pardon nor excuse with him; then, when they expected that he would kill them, he should leave off; he should terrorize and expel the people between Medina and Mekka, but should not touch the Mekkans. In Ṣanʿā' he should back Muʿāwiya's partisans against ʿAlī's officials and supporters; he should kill whoever abstained from pledging allegiance to Muʿāwiya and seize whatever he could find of their property.[566] As Busr's commission became known, Maʿn b. Yazīd b. al-Akhnas al-Sulamī (or his brother ʿAmr) and Ziyād b. al-Ashhab al-Jaʿdī intervened with Muʿāwiya, asking him not to give his commander authority over Qays; otherwise Busr would, they suggested, kill Qays in revenge for the Banū Fihr (Quraysh) and Kināna killed by the Banū Sulaym when Muḥammad entered Mekka. Muʿāwiya realized that he could not afford to ignore the wishes of these influential men and told Busr that he had no rule over Qays.[567]

Busr departed for Dayr Murrān where he reviewed his troops. He threw out four hundred men and continued on to Arabia with two thousand six hundred. Moving towards Medina, he stopped at every watering place to seize the camels belonging to the local tribes and had his men ride them while sparing their horses, which they led along. When they reached the next watering place, they would release the camels they had and seize the fresh ones available there.

As he approached Medina, ʿAlī's governor, Abū Ayyūb al-Anṣārī, fled

565 *Ibid.*, 598–601. 566 Balādhurī, *Ansāb*, II, 453–4; Thaqafī, *Ghārāt*, 600.

567 A. A. Bevan (ed.), *The Naḳā'iḍ of Jarīr and al-Farazdaḳ* (Leiden, 1905–12), 716–17; *Aghānī*, IV, 131–2.

for Kūfa. Busr entered the town without resistance and delivered a blistering sermon of vituperation and menaces to the Anṣār, threatening to massacre them all. Finally his kinsman and stepfather, Ḥuwayṭib b. 'Abd al-'Uzzā al-'Āmirī, intervened by ascending the pulpit to him and implored him: 'These are your people and the Helpers of the Messenger of God, not the killers of 'Uthmān.' Fortunately Busr remembered his master's voice and calmed down. He summoned the people to pledge allegiance to Mu'āwiya and burned the houses of the fugitives Zurāra b. Jarwal of the Banū 'Amr b. 'Awf, Rifā'a b. Rāfi' al-Zuraqī, 'Abd Allāh b. Sa'd of 'Abd al-Ashhal and Abū Ayyūb al-Anṣārī. When the Banū Salima came to offer their pledge, he questioned them about Jābir b. 'Abd Allāh, who had gone into hiding, and threatened them with collective punishment if they failed to bring him along. Jābir, under pressure from his people, sought the advice of Umm Salama, the Mother of the Faithful favourably disposed to 'Alī. She urged him to pledge allegiance to save his own and his people's blood. She assured him that she had asked her own nephew[568] to pledge allegiance even though she knew that it was a pledge of misguidance (*bay'at ḍalāla*).[569] When Busr left the Medinans a few days later, he told them that he had pardoned them although they were not worthy of it; he hoped that God would have no mercy on them in the hereafter. He appointed Abū Hurayra to rule them in his absence and warned them not to oppose him.

From Medina Busr moved on to Mekka, killing and looting on the way. This time 'Alī's governor of the Holy City, Qutham b. al-'Abbās, fled immediately, and there was a mass exodus of the inhabitants. Those remaining behind chose Shayba b. 'Uthmān al-'Abdarī, who had been acceptable to Yazīd b. Shajara, as their amir. A delegation of Qurayshites came out to meet Busr. He reviled them and assured them that if he were left to act in accordance with his own inclination, he would not leave a living soul of them walking on earth. They begged him to have mercy on his own people and tribe, and he said no more.

In Mekka Busr murdered several descendants of Abū Lahab.[570] He probably did not consider this a violation of Mu'āwiya's instruction not to touch the Mekkans, since the caliph had evidently also ordered him to kill every Hashimite on whom he could lay his hands as they were collectively guilty of the murder of 'Uthmān. The unfortunate descendants of Muḥammad's uncle, cursed together with his wife in the Qur'ān, after the victory of Islam had thrown in their lot with their clan Hāshim without

[568] So according to Jābir's own report (Thaqafī, *Ghārāt*, 606). According to 'Awāna's account, Umm Salama said that she ordered her own son 'Umar b. Abī Salama and her son-in-law 'Abd Allāh b. Zam'a (b. al-Aswad of Asad Quraysh) to pledge allegiance (Ṭabarī, I, 2451). [569] Thaqafī, *Ghārāt*, 603–6. [570] *Aghānī*, X, 45.

being fully accepted by them; now they became the first victims, as the *ṭalīq*s, their pre-Islamic allies, took over to rule in the name of Islam. The sources, reticent about the fate of this branch of Muḥammad's kin, do not even identify them individually. Was the poet al-ʿAbbās b. ʿUtba, who had so aptly answered al-Walīd b. ʿUqba's attack on ʿAmr b. al-ʿĀṣ, among them?

In Mekka Abū Mūsā al-Ashʿarī had gone into hiding, but was discovered and brought before Busr. He had written a letter to the Yemenites warning them that Muʿāwiya was sending a cavalry troop that put to death anyone refusing 'to affirm [the result of] the arbitration (*man abā an yuqirra bi l-ḥukūma*)'. Remembering how well pleased Muʿāwiya was with Abū Mūsā for having allowed himself to be fooled twice by ʿAmr b. al-ʿĀṣ, Busr said, as he saw him unable to conceal his fear of being killed: 'I surely would not do that to the Companion of the Messenger of God', and let him go.[571]

After circumambulating the Kaʿba and praying two *rakʿa*s, Busr ascended the pulpit and in his sermon gave due praise to God who had 'humiliated through killings and expulsions our enemy, this son of Abū Ṭālib, who is now in the region of Iraq in dire straits and distress. God has afflicted him for his offence and abandoned him for his crime, so that his companions have dispersed full of spite against him, and He has given the reign to Muʿāwiya who is demanding vengeance for the blood of ʿUthmān. So pledge allegiance to him and do not create a path [of vengeance] against yourselves.' The Mekkans meekly pledged allegiance. The Umayyad Saʿīd b. al-ʿĀṣ, however, absconded rather than doing homage to the new Vicegerent of God. Busr sought him but could not find him.[572] Saʿīd was still not convinced of the wisdom of pinning the guilt for the murder of ʿUthmān on the Hashimite kinsmen of Umayya, descendants of their common ancestor ʿAbd Manāf. His son ʿAmr was to be the first victim when the Umayyads, under ʿAbd al-Malik, began to murder each other for the succession to the throne.

Busr's next aim was al-Ṭāʾif. Here al-Mughīra b. Shuʿba was in control of his people, Thaqīf. Ever a shrewd opportunist, al-Mughīra had so far successfully kept out of the civil war but had attended the meeting of the arbitrators at Adhruḥ as an observer. Seeing the balance of power moving in favour of the Umayyad, he decided that it was time to climb on the bandwagon. He wrote Busr a letter congratulating him on his mission and praising his sound opinion in treating the subversives (*murīb*) with severity and the people of intelligence (*uli l-nuhā*) with generosity. He encouraged him to proceed in his virtuous conduct, since God would only

571 Ṭabarī, I, 3451. 572 Thaqafī, *Ghārāt*, 608–9.

increase His goodness towards the people of good, and concluded with the prayer that God place both of them among those who command the proper, aim for the just, and remember God frequently. Then he came out to welcome Mu'āwiya's general. Busr was aware that he had been denied authority over Thaqīf, but he did not want to let them get off without a good scare. He told al-Mughīra: 'Mughīra, I want to investigate (*asta'riḍ*) your people.' Al-Mughīra pretended to be alarmed: 'I pray to God that he may guard you from this. Assuredly, it has reached me ever since you set forth, how severe you are against the enemies of the Commander of the Faithful 'Uthmān, and your view in that is most praiseworthy. But if you treat your enemy and your friend alike you are sinning against your Lord and entice your enemy against you.' Busr was impressed by this argument and did not harm anyone in al-Ṭā'if.[573]

While in al-Ṭā'if Busr sent a detachment to Tabāla with orders to kill the partisans of 'Alī there. According to an anecdote quoted by al-Thaqafī, they were miraculously saved by the selfless exertion of Manī' al-Bāhilī who was sent by the Syrian commander in Tabāla to seek Busr's pardon for them. Busr delayed his pardon in the hope that the captives would be killed before it would reach Tabāla. The messenger, however, continuously rode by day and night, and thus arrived just in time, before the execution. According to Ibn A'tham's account the captives were all killed.[574]

When Busr left al-Ṭā'if, al-Mughīra b. Shu'ba accompanied him for a while before taking leave. As he passed through the territory of the Banū Kināna, Busr chanced upon the two minor sons of 'Ubayd Allāh b. al-'Abbās, 'Abd al-Raḥmān and Qutham. Their mother was Umm Ḥakīm Juwayriya, daughter of Qāriẓ (or Qāriṭ) b. Khālid of Kināna, a confederate of the Banū Zuhra of Quraysh. 'Ubayd Allāh had therefore entrusted his two sons to a man of Kināna so that they would experience life in the desert in accordance with custom among the noble families of Quraysh. When Busr seized the two boys and threatened to kill them, their Kinānī guardian took his sword and went out to face Busr. Mu'āwiya's general angrily questioned him: 'We did not want to kill you, so why do you expose yourself to being killed?' The Kinānī in true bedouin spirit answered: 'Yes, I shall be killed in protection of my guest (*dūna jārī*). That will exonerate me better before God and the people.' Then he struck at the captors with his sword until he was killed. Busr had the two boys led before him and slaughtered them with a knife. A group of women of Kināna came, and one of them told the savage: 'You kill the

[573] *Ibid.*, 609–10; Ibn A'tham, *Futūḥ*, IV, 62. The Thaqīf are reported to have told Busr that he had no authority over them since they were the very core of Qays (Bevan (ed.), *Naḳā'iḍ*, 717; *Aghānī*, IV, 132).

[574] Thaqafī, *Ghārāt*, 610–11; Ibn A'tham, *Futūḥ*, IV, 62.

men, but what for do you kill the children? By God, it was not the practice for them to be killed either in the Time of Ignorance (*jāhiliyya*) or in Islam. By God, surely a regime which can find strength only by killing the meek, the humble, and the tottering old, by denying mercy and cutting the bonds of kinship is a regime of evil.' Busr, now fully furious, shouted: 'By God, I wish to put the sword among you [f. pl.].' Though challenged by the woman to do so, he refrained, recalling that his master had declared Kināna off limits for him.[575]

Entering South Arabian territory, Busr was no longer confined by Mu'āwiya's restrictions. In Tathlīth he murdered the pious ascetic Ka'b b. 'Abda Dhi l-Ḥabaka al-Nahdī, who had been whipped and exiled from Kūfa to Rayy for his criticism of 'Uthmān's conduct but later had been pardoned by him.[576] In Najrān he killed 'Abd Allāh (al-Aṣghar) b. 'Abd al-Madān al-Ḥārithī, chief of the Banu l-Ḥārith, his son Mālik and his brother Yazīd b. 'Abd al-Madān. 'Abd Allāh, scion of one of the distinguished houses of the Arabs (*buyūtāt al-'Arab*), had led a delegation of his people to Muḥammad to offer their submission and had been given by him the name 'Abd Allāh to replace his pre-Islamic name 'Abd al-Ḥajar. After the Prophet's death he had tried to keep his people from joining the Apostasy. His daughter 'Ā'isha was married to 'Ubayd Allāh b. al-'Abbās, whom he aided in the government of Yemen.[577] Then after killing Mālik, Busr gathered the people of Najrān and addressed them: 'You bands of Christians and brethren of monkeys, by God, if I should get to hear from you what I dislike, I shall return to you with action that will cut off your offspring, devastate your fields, and ruin your houses. So be careful, careful.'[578]

In the Yemen Busr first attacked the Arḥab of Hamdān and killed the partisans of 'Alī including Abū Karib, a noble chief of Hamdān.[579] The Hamdān then fortified themselves on the mountain of Shibām. They defiantly shouted: 'Busr, we are Hamdān, and this is Shibām.' Busr pretended not to pay any attention to them and departed. When they returned to their villages he overpowered them, killed the men, and enslaved the women. They were said to have been the first Muslim women to be sold into slavery.[580]

[575] Thaqafī, *Ghārāt*, 614–16. [576] Balādhurī, *Ansāb*, II, 455, V, 40.

[577] Ibn Ḥajar, *Iṣāba*, IV, 98; Ibn al-Kalbī, *Nasab Ma'add*, I, 271–2.

[578] Thaqafī, *Ghārāt*, 616–17.

[579] *Ibid.*, 617–18; Ibn A'tham, *Futūḥ*, IV, 63. An Abū Karib of Hamdān is mentioned as an official of 'Uthmān in charge of guarding the treasury shortly before the caliph's death (Ṭabarī, I, 3020, 3046). It is uncertain whether he is identical with this partisan of 'Alī killed by Busr.

[580] Bevan (ed.), *Naḳā'iḍ* 717; *Aghānī*, IV, 132; Ibn al-Athīr, *Usd al-ghāba*, I, 180; al-Ṣafadī, *al-Wāfī bi l-wafayāt*, ed. H. Ritter et al. (Istanbul/Wiesbaden, 1931–), X, 130–1.

Of 'Alī's two governors of Yemen, only Sa'īd b. Nimrān seems to have put up some, albeit ineffective, resistance to the invaders. Then both governors fled to Kūfa.[581] 'Ubayd Allāh b. al-'Abbās left as his deputy the Thaqafite 'Amr b. Arāka who vainly tried to prevent Busr from entering Ṣan'ā'. Mu'āwiya's general killed him and many others in the town. Then a delegation from Ma'rib arrived to make their submission. Busr murdered all of them except one, who was allowed to bring his people the gruesome news. From Ṣan'ā' Busr made an excursion to Jayshān where the partisans of 'Alī were strong. They came out to fight him, but were defeated and massacred. Those remaining fortified themselves against him, and he returned to Ṣan'ā'. Altogether Busr is said, no doubt with some exaggeration, to have killed thirty thousand men in his raid of Arabia.[582]

Busr then received a letter from Wā'il b. Ḥujr, a noble lord (*qayl*) of Ḥaḍramawt, who assured him that half of Ḥaḍramawt was 'Uthmanid and invited him to come there, since there was no one to hinder him.[583] Busr readily followed the invitation and was welcomed by Wā'il with a gift of money and cloth. When Wā'il asked him what he intended to do with the people of Ḥaḍramawt, he answered that he wanted to kill a quarter of them. Wā'il advised him, if he wished to do that, to start with 'Abd Allāh b. Thawāba, who deemed himself safe from being killed. 'Abd Allāh b. Thawāba was another great lord of Ḥaḍramawt and Wā'il's enemy. He lived in an impregnable fortress built by the Abyssinians when they first occupied South Arabia. Busr advanced to the foot of the castle and courteously invited the lord to come down to him. Unsuspectingly, Ibn Thawāba descended and was received with the command: 'Strike his neck.' He asked Busr: 'Do you want to kill me?' and Mu'āwiya's general assured him: 'Yes.' On his request he was given permission to perform a prayer. Then he was led before Busr and beheaded. Busr confiscated his property and seized together with it the third that belonged to his sister. Mu'āwiya later graciously returned the third to her.[584]

Busr's further plans to kill a quarter of the population of Ḥaḍramawt were cut short by reports of the approach of an enemy relief army under Jāriya b. Qudāma. 'Alī's reaction to Busr's invasion of Arabia had been

[581] Thaqafī, *Ghārāt*, 619–20. [582] *Ibid.*, 640.

[583] According to the account of Fuḍayl b. Khadīj, Wā'il had been with 'Alī in Kūfa although he was secretly 'Uthmanid. He asked 'Alī for leave to visit his country in order to settle his property affairs there, promising to return quickly. 'Alī was unaware of his inclination and permitted him to go. When he learned of Wā'il's treason and collusion with Busr, he arrested his two sons (*ibid.*, 630–1). Wā'il b. Ḥujr had sided with the Muslims during the *ridda* and led the members of his tribe in the fight against the apostate Kinda chief al-Ash'ath b. Qays (Lecker, 'Kinda on the Eve of Islam', 344).

[584] Thaqafī, *Ghārāt*, 629–31.

slow. The Kufan sources, as usual, describe him as at first vainly trying to stir his followers to revenge before Jāriya volunteered. It is likely, however, that ʿAlī, at a time when he was building up his forces for a third campaign to Syria, was reluctant to divert some of them to a sideshow. He had reacted angrily to the lack of initiative of his governors in Yemen in countering the rebellion of the local ʿUthmāniyya and was evidently inclined to let them fend for themselves in warding off the Syrian attack. Reports of the brutal savagery of Muʿāwiya's general now forced him to act. Jāriya set out from Kūfa with a thousand men and recruited another thousand in Baṣra, presumably mostly from his tribe, Saʿd Tamīm. Afterwards ʿAlī sent another two thousand men under Wahb b. Masʿūd al-Khathʿamī from Kūfa who joined Jāriya b. Qudāma in the Ḥijāz. Jāriya was to have the general command. ʿAlī gave him strict instructions not to harm Muslims or non-Muslims protected by treaty, not to confiscate property or riding animals even if their own mounts were worn out and they were forced to continue on foot, and to perform their prayers regularly.

Jāriya moved quickly through the Ḥijāz to Yemen passing by the towns, the fortified places, and stopping nowhere. As he reached the Yemen, the ʿUthmanid partisans in power fled, seeking shelter in the mountains. They were now persecuted and killed by the partisans of ʿAlī. Jāriya left them to settle accounts, avoided the towns, and pressed on to Ḥaḍramawt in pursuit of Busr. On his approach the latter immediately fled like a thief, without giving battle.[585] In this he followed, no doubt, Muʿāwiya's instructions rather than his own preference. The purpose of Busr's raid was not to conquer and occupy any part of the country permanently, but to terrorize and intimidate by causing maximum damage to the populace with a minimum loss of Syrian soldiers. On his return Busr is said to have proudly announced to his master that he had led his army killing the caliph's enemy and looting without losing a single man.[586]

Afraid that he might get caught between an oncoming and a pursuing enemy army, Busr decided not to retreat through the Ḥijāz, and took an eastern route through the Jawf towards the territory of the Tamīm. Learning of this, Jāriya b. Qudāma commented that he was heading for a people who knew how to defend themselves. Jāriya stayed in Jurash for a month to allow his men a time for rest. It was there that he was informed of the assassination of ʿAlī.[587]

As Jāriya expected, Busr did not challenge the main body of Tamīm even though they seized some of his loot.[588] At al-Falaj, however, he hit

[585] *Ibid.*, 621–32. [586] *Ibid.*, 639. [587] *Ibid.*, 624, 633, 638, 640.
[588] Ibn Abi l-Ḥadīd, *Sharḥ*, II, 16.

upon a group of the Banū Sa'd (of Tamīm) who had alighted there among the Banū Ja'da. He attacked them, killing some and carrying off others as captives.[589] Then he moved on to al-Yamāma. Here the people had remained neutral in the civil war under their amir, al-Qāsim b. Wabara.[590] Busr threatened to assault the Banū Ḥanīfa, but a son of their renowned former chief Mujjā'a b. Murāra offered to accompany him to Mu'āwiya in order to make peace with him on behalf of his people. This was presumably after 'Alī's death, and the Banū Ḥanīfa were prepared to pledge allegiance to the Umayyad caliph. Busr, however, wanted to punish them for their former neutrality and took the son of Mujjā'a along as he returned through the desert of al-Samāwa to Syria.[591] He advised Mu'āwiya to kill him, but Mu'āwiya was now in a mood for peace. He accepted his submission and confirmed him as the chief of his people.[592]

The outrages committed by Busr in his raid of Arabia produced shock in Kūfa and aided 'Alī in his efforts to mount a new offensive against Mu'āwiya. The Kufans blamed each other for their past inaction, and a group of tribal nobles (*ashrāf*) came to see 'Alī and urged him to appoint one of them as their commander to lead an army against this man. 'Alī reassured them that the man he had sent against Busr would not return without having expelled him or one or the other of them having been killed; they should stand up and get ready for his summons for the campaign to Syria. Sa'īd b. Qays al-Hamdānī, Ziyād b. Khaṣafa and Wa'la b. Maḥdūj al-Dhuhlī[593] gave speeches declaring their unreserved loyalty to the Commander of the Faithful. Suwayd b. al-Ḥārith al-Taymī of Taym al-Ribāb urged him to order each of the chiefs of his *shī'a* to gather his companions, to incite them to participation in the campaign by reading them the Qur'ān and warning them of the consequences of treason and disobedience. Ḥujr b. 'Adī al-Kindī now quickly assembled four thousand men, Ziyād b. Khaṣafa al-Bakrī two thousand, Ma'qil b. Qays al-Riyāḥī also two thousand, and 'Abd Allāh b. Wahb al-Saba'ī[594] about a thousand. When 'Alī asked for a tough, reliable commander who

[589] Bevan (ed.), *Nakā'iḍ*, 717; *Aghānī*, IV, 132.

[590] Al-Qāsim b. Wabara seems otherwise unknown.

[591] Thaqafī, *Ghārāt*, 639.

[592] *Ibid.*, 643; Ibn Abi l-Ḥadīd, *Sharḥ*, II, 16–17. The name of the son of Mujjā'a b. Murāra is not given. He may be identical with Mujjā'a's son Sirāj, a transmitter of hadith recognized as a Companion of the Prophet (Ibn Ḥajar, *Iṣāba*, III, 67). The report that Busr passed through Mekka on his way back before turning to al-Yamāma (Thaqafī, *Ghārāt*, 638) is evidently mistaken. After Busr's departure from Mekka on his way to the Yemen, Qutham b. al-'Abbās seems to have quickly regained control of the town (*ibid.*, 620–1).

[593] The text of *ibid.*, 637, has Wa'la b. Makhdū'. For his identity see the editor's footnote 4 on that page.

[594] Reading thus for al-S-m-nī (Balādhurī, *Ansāb*, II, 478). He may be identical with Ibn Saba', later accused of having been the founder of extremist Shi'ism.

would recruit the men dispersed in the *sawād* and bring them to Kūfa for the campaign, Saʿīd b. Qays suggested Maʿqil b. Qays al-Riyāḥī, and Maʿqil was dispatched with this mission. As he arrived in al-Daskara, he learned that Kurds were raiding Shahrazūr. He attacked them and pursued them into the mountains of Jibāl. When he was finished with his recruitment and reached al-Madā'in on his way to Kūfa, news of ʿAlī's death reached him.

Ziyād b. Khaṣafa volunteered to raid Syrian territory along the banks of the Euphrates and then to return speedily to join the general campaign. The damage inflicted by him was presumably limited since ʿAlī ordered him not to wrong anyone, to fight only those attacking him, and not to interfere with the bedouins (*aʿrāb*). Muʿāwiya sent ʿAbd al-Raḥmān b. Khālid b. al-Walīd against him, but Ziyād eluded him, turning back. While he stayed in Hīt waiting for ʿAlī and his army, he learned of his assassination.[595]

In preparation for his campaign, ʿAlī had written to Qays b. Saʿd b. ʿUbāda, now governor of Ādharbayjān, instructing him to appoint ʿUbayd Allāh b. Shubayl al-Aḥmasī as his deputy and to proceed speedily to Kūfa. A large mass of Muslims, he wrote, was assembled there now submitting to his command and ready to move against the desecrators (*muḥillūn*); ʿAlī was delaying departure merely in expectation of Qays' arrival. The date of the campaign had in fact been set for the end of winter 40/661.[596]

On Friday, 17 Ramaḍān 40/26 January 661, as he entered the mosque of Kūfa to perform the morning prayer, ʿAlī was met by his assassin with the words: 'The judgment belongs to God, ʿAlī, not to you', and was struck on the head with a poisoned sword. The attacker was ʿAbd al-Raḥmān b. ʿAmr b. Muljam al-Murādī, a Kharijite from Egypt, of Ḥimyar by male descent but counted among Murād because of his maternal kinship, and a confederate of the Banū Jabala of Kinda. He had come to Kūfa with the aim of killing ʿAlī in revenge for the Kharijite leaders slain at al-Nahrawān and had found two local Kharijite accomplices, Shabīb b. Bujra of Ashjaʿ and Wardān b. al-Mujālid of Taym al-Ribāb. Shabīb's sword thrust had missed ʿAlī and hit the wooden frame of the door or the arch. He ran away but was caught near the gates of Kinda by a man from Ḥaḍramawt called ʿUwaymir. The Ḥaḍramī seized Shabīb's sword and was pressing him to the ground when other pursuers approached, shouting to each other to seize the man with the sword. Fearing for his own life, he threw the sword away and ran off; Shabīb escaped in the crowd. Wardān fled to his home where he was killed by his

[595] *Ibid.*, 478–9; Thaqafī, *Ghārāt*, 637–8. [596] Balādhurī, *Ansāb*, II, 480.

kinsman 'Abd Allāh b. Najaba b. 'Ubayd after confessing his involvement. Ibn Muljam was caught, it was said, by the Hashimite al-Mughīra b. Nawfal b. al-Ḥārith who hit him in the face with a coat (*qaṭīfa*) and forced him to the ground. He was led before 'Alī, who ordered that, if he died from his wound, Ibn Muljam should be put to death in retaliation. If he survived, he would decide on how to treat him. Two days later, in the night before Sunday, 19 Ramaḍān/28 January 'Alī died. His body was washed by his sons al-Ḥasan, al-Ḥusayn, Muḥammad b. al-Ḥanafiyya, and by his nephew 'Abd Allāh b. Ja'far. The same men together with 'Ubayd Allāh b. al-'Abbās buried him. Ibn Muljam was now killed in accordance with his instruction. Shabīb b. Bujra later revolted against Mu'āwiya's governor al-Mughīra b. Shu'ba and attacked people near Kūfa. The governor sent a mounted troop against him, and he was killed.[597]

'Alī was assassinated at a time when his fortunes, after the lengthy crisis following Ṣiffīn, the failed arbitration and al-Nahrawān, seemed on the ascendant. The mood in Kūfa and Baṣra had changed in his favour as Mu'āwiya's vicious conduct of the war, especially in Busr's Arabian campaign, had revealed the true nature of his reign. The Kufans and Basrans were now ready to fight the Syrians for their independence, if not for the glory of 'Alī. The outcome of a third Syrian campaign could not be seen as a foregone conclusion. The Syrians had certainly gained in confidence since Ṣiffīn and now had their backs towards Egypt free. Yet experience had so far shown that, whenever Syrians and Iraqis met in battle on roughly equal terms, it was the Syrians who usually gave way first. The Iraqis, resuming the war with the bitter resolve of outwitted political underdogs, might well have triumphed militarily this time.

'Alī's rule, to be sure, had not gained popularity in Kūfa during his lifetime. The loyalist following that he built up during the final years of his reign, consisting of men convinced that he was the best of Muslims after the Prophet and the only one entitled to rule them, remained a small minority. The town was deeply divided in its attitude towards him. What united the majority now was rather their distrust of, and opposition to, Mu'āwiya and his Syrian cohorts.

Umayyad highhandedness, misrule and repression were gradually to turn the minority of 'Alī's admirers into a majority. In the memory of later generations 'Alī became the ideal Commander of the Faithful. In face of the fake Umayyad claim to legitimate sovereignty in Islam as God's Vicegerents on earth, and in view of Umayyad treachery, arbitrary and divisive government, and vindictive retribution, they came to appreciate his honesty, his unbending devotion to the reign of Islam, his

597 *Ibid.*, II, 487–96; Ṭabarī, I, 3456–64.

deep personal loyalties, his equal treatment of all his supporters, and his generosity in forgiving his defeated enemies. They were now prepared to forget the harsh edges of his rule and his at times grave errors of judgement, which had divided his followers, and rather blamed their ancestors for failing to support him unconditionally. The more radical among them extolled him, surrounding him with an aura of impeccability and supernatural qualities. Such views were far from his own mind. For although he, with some justification, had claimed to know the Prophet's message and practice better, and to be more sincerely devoted to Islam than anyone after Muḥammad, he was well aware of, and admitted, some of his human failings and was concerned with making amends for them. It was, in the end, largely the same qualities that brought about both the failure of his reign and his elevation to a much-revered saintly hero in Islam. His *duʿāba* noted by ʿUmar, his 'foolishness' in refusing to engage in the new game of political treachery, unscrupulous manoeuvring and clever opportunism that was then taking root in the government of Islam, deprived him of success in his life, but also raised him in the eyes of his admirers into a paragon of the virtues of a pristine, uncorrupted Islam as well as of pre-Islamic Arab chivalry.

Conclusion

Restoration of the Community and despotic kingship

The death of 'Alī, in the midst of preparations for a fresh campaign to Syria, left the course of the civil war in suspense. The succession of his eldest son, al-Ḥasan, Muḥammad's grandson, went ahead without dispute. Presumably following the precedent of the Prophet, 'Alī had declined to nominate a successor before his death. He had, however, on many occasions expressed his conviction that only the Prophet's *ahl al-bayt* were entitled to rule the Community; and al-Ḥasan, whom he had appointed his legatee,[1] must have seemed the obvious choice. A speech defect which slowed his tongue evidently did not disqualify him.[2] In fact, he was generally considered an effective orator.

In the congregational mosque of Kūfa al-Ḥasan announced the death of his father whom he described as a man whose acts were unrivalled and would forever remain so, who had fought together with the Messenger of God, protecting him with his own life. Muḥammad had sent him forward bearing his flag with Jibrā'īl on his right side and Mikā'īl on his left, and he had not turned back until God gave him victory. He had died this night, the same night in which Jesus, son of Mary, had been raised to heaven and in which Joshua, son of Nūn, the legatee of Moses, had passed away. He had left no silver and no gold behind except for 700 dirhams of his stipend, with which he wanted to buy a servant for his family.

Then al-Ḥasan was choked by tears, and the people wept with him. He resumed: 'O people, whoever knows me, knows me, and whoever does not know me, I am al-Ḥasan, the son of Muḥammad. I am the son of the bringer of good tidings, the son of the warner, the son of the summoner to God, powerful and exalted, with His permission; I am the shining lamp. I am of the Family of the Prophet from whom God has removed filth and

[1] Balādhurī, *Ansāb*, II, 497, 504.

[2] Abu l-Faraj al-Iṣfahānī, *Maqātil al-Ṭālibiyyīn*, ed. Aḥmad Ṣaqr (Cairo, 1949), 49–50. Veccia-Vaglieri misunderstood the text as meaning that he inherited the defect from 'one of his uncles' ('al-Ḥasan b. 'Alī', *EI*(2nd edn)). The 'uncle ('*amm*)' is Moses.

whom He has purified, whose love He has made obligatory in His Book when He said: 'Whosoever performs a good act, We shall increase the good in it' (XLII 23). Performing a good act is love for us, the Family of the Prophet.' Then 'Ubayd Allāh b. al-'Abbās, the governor of Ṣan'ā' who had fled to Kūfa, stood up and summoned the people to pledge allegiance to al-Ḥasan. They did so, acknowledging that he was the one best entitled and dearest to them.[3]

This show of loyalty to the dead Commander of the Faithful and praise of his *jihād* on behalf of Islam concealed for the moment the deep discord prevailing between father and son. By nature pacifist and conciliatory, al-Ḥasan had for some time been uneasy and even openly critical with regard to 'Alī's militant pursuit of his cause, the basic justice of which, however, he did not doubt. He had felt a genuine sympathy, even admiration, for his uncle 'Uthmān with his aristocratic bearing and aversion to bloodshed, and thought that his father should have done more to try to save him. 'Alī's defiant stand in face of the opposition of the old religious establishment and the majority of Quraysh had frightened him, and he had begged him to abandon his course of confrontation and conflict. The continuation and broadening of the brutal civil war after his father's surprise victory at Baṣra had filled him with horror. Mu'āwiya, he realized, was nothing but a scoundrel. Yet could the attempt to remove him justify the massive bloodletting among Muslims which carried away friend and foe alike and led to ever-deepening hatred between kinsmen once united in tribal brotherhood?

The supreme leadership position into which his birth as the Prophet's grandson was now propelling him had no attraction for him. As for himself, he could just as well have walked away to a desert retreat, something he had earlier proposed that his father do. He understood, however, that it would have been unforgivable for him simply to abandon his father's followers to the vindictive instincts of Mu'āwiya, who had just displayed his true colours in the utter brutality of Busr b. Abī Arṭāh's raid. If he wanted to be remembered in history as the restorer of a semblance of concord and peace in the Community founded by his grandfather, he must at least seek an honourable peace with a general amnesty.

The pledge of allegiance to al-Ḥasan included, in addition to the usual backing for the Book of God and the Sunna of the Prophet, the commitment to make war on whomever al-Ḥasan declared war on and to

[3] Abu l-Faraj, *Maqātil*, 51–2; Balādhurī, *Ansāb*, III, 28. The Medinan tradition generally describes Qays b. Sa'd b. 'Ubāda as the one who proposed al-Ḥasan for the succession and as the first to pledge allegiance (see Ṭabarī, II, 1; Balādhurī, *Ansāb*, III, 28: Ṣāliḥ b. Kaysān). The Kufan tradition giving prominence to 'Ubayd Allāh b. al-'Abbās is probably more reliable.

keep the peace with whomever he made peace. This was, to be sure, merely the formula that ʿAlī had demanded of his followers and which had been denounced by the Kharijites. It is said, however, to have immediately raised suspicions among the Kufans that al-Ḥasan did not intend to carry out the campaign to Syria prepared by his father.[4] Given his record of opposition to fighting, such suspicion was not unreasonable. The prominent part now played by ʿUbayd Allāh b. al-ʿAbbās, who had recently been reprimanded by ʿAlī for his failure to put up any resistance to Busr as governor of Ṣanʿāʾ,[5] may have contributed to the doubts.

For fifty days or two months after his accession, al-Ḥasan remained passive, not dispatching anyone against Muʿāwiya nor even mentioning a campaign or war.[6] The army mobilized by his father evidently became restive. Then a letter from ʿAbd Allāh b. al-ʿAbbās arrived from Baṣra, stirring him to action. Ibn al-ʿAbbās addressed him as the son of the Messenger of God and told him that the Muslims who had appointed him their leader after his father were now disapproving of his inaction towards Muʿāwiya and his failure to demand his right.

Get ready for war, fight your enemy, coax your companions, appoint the men of distinguished houses and nobility to offices, for you buy their hearts with that. Follow the practice of the imams of justice (*aʾimmat al-ʿadl*) of conjoining hearts [*taʾlīf al-qulūb*, i.e. by paying bribes to influential men] and restoring concord among the people. And know that war is deceit (*khudʿa*) and that you are at liberty with that while you are at war, so long as you do not deprive a Muslim of a right that belongs to him. You know that the people turned away from your father ʿAlī and went over to Muʿāwiya only because he equalized among them in regard to the *fay*ʾ and gave to all the same stipend. This weighed heavily upon them.

Ibn al-ʿAbbās went on to remind al-Ḥasan that his enemies were those who had made war on God and His Messenger before; when God had rendered His religion triumphant, they had outwardly professed the faith and recited the Qurʾān while privately mocking its verses; they performed the duties of Islam while loathing them; when they saw that in this religion only the pious prophets and those virtuous in learning enjoyed prestige, they had stamped themselves outwardly with the characteristics of the righteous so that the Muslims would think well of them, while inwardly they were turning their backs on the Signs of God; al-Ḥasan was now afflicted with these people, their sons, and their likes, whose arrogant transgression had merely increased with time. Ibn al-ʿAbbās appealed to him to fight them and not to accept a foul compromise (*daniyya*) with them; his father had accepted the arbitration in respect of his right only under constraint and knowing that he would be found the most worthy of

[4] Balādhurī, *Ansāb*, III, 29; Ṭabarī, II, 1, 5. [5] Thaqafī, *Ghārāt*, 619–20.
[6] Balādhurī, *Ansāb*, III, 29; Ibn Aʿtham, *Futūḥ*, IV, 148.

the reign if the arbitrators judged justly; when they judged according to their whim, he had gone back to his previous position and remained determined to fight these people until his term came and he passed on to his Lord. 'So consider, Abū Muḥammad, may God have mercy on you, and never relinquish a right to which you are more entitled than anyone else, even if death should intervene.'[7]

Ibn A'tham's account describes al-Ḥasan's reaction to the letter as one of joy, as he now knew that Ibn al-'Abbās was pledging allegiance to him and commanding him to do his duty in respect to the right of God. This was no doubt far from al-Ḥasan's mind. If he was partly pleased by this token of moral support from his uncle, who surely had already pledged allegiance to him, he was by no means convinced by his argument for war. If he himself did not desire the death of others for the sake of his right to rule, why indeed should he be prepared to sacrifice his own life for it? He must seek an accommodation with Mu'āwiya.

Al-Ḥasan now wrote a letter to the Umayyad, addressed thus: 'From the servant of God, Commander of the Faithful, al-Ḥasan to Mu'āwiya b. Ṣakhr.' Muḥammad, he wrote, had been sent by God as a sign of mercy to all the worlds, and as a warner to everyone alive; he had conveyed God's message, and God had manifested the truth through him, obliterated polytheism, buttressed the faithful, given glory to the Arabs, and honoured Quraysh in particular through him; when he died, the Arabs had contended with each other for his authority, but Quraysh had told them: 'We are his tribe, his family (*usra*), his close followers; it is not licit for you to dispute the authority of Muḥammad over the people and his right with us.' The Arabs had recognized the soundness of their argument and surrendered the authority to them.

Then we argued with Quraysh as they had argued with the Arabs, but Quraysh did not treat us with justice as the Arabs treated them. . . . When we, the Family (*ahl al-bayt*) of Muḥammad and his close followers, argued with them and sought fairness from them, they removed us and united in wronging and boycotting us. . . . We were then amazed by those who jumped on us in regard to our right and the authority of our Prophet, even though they were men of virtue and early merit in Islam. Yet we refrained from contending with them within Islam, fearing for the faith lest the hypocrites and the Confederates (*aḥzāb*) would find a breach through which to enter and work corruption as they wished. Today let men marvel, Mu'āwiya, at your jumping on a right of which you are not worthy, neither by any known excellence in the faith, nor any praiseworthy deed in Islam. Rather you are the son of one of the Confederates, the son of the most hostile man of Quraysh towards the Messenger of God. Yet God has frustrated your hopes.

[7] Ibn A'tham, *Futūḥ*, IV, 149–50; Ibn Abi l-Hadīd, *Sharḥ*, XVI, 23–4; Balādhurī, *Ansāb*, III, 29, 3 (Dūrī), 51.

After ʿAlī had passed away, continued al-Ḥasan, the Muslims had appointed him to succeed, and he begged God not to increase His bounty to him in this passing world by decreasing His bounty to him in the hereafter; he was moved to writing to Muʿāwiya merely by the wish of doing justice to him before God; there would, if Muʿāwiya did as al-Ḥasan proposed, be immense fortune for him and benefit for the Muslims.

> Give up persevering in falsehood and enter into my allegiance as the people have done, for you know that I am better entitled to 'this matter' than you before God and in the eyes of everyone who is ready to return to obedience and whoever has a repentant heart. Fear God, abandon rebellion, and spare the blood of the Muslims, for, by God, there is no good for you in meeting Him with more of their blood on your hands than you shall already meet Him with. Enter into peace and obedience, do not contest the rule of those entitled to it . . . so that you may restore concord. But if you refuse all else and persist in your arrogant transgression, I shall rise up against you with the Muslims and ask God to judge between us, for He is the best of judges.[8]

The letter was delivered to Muʿāwiya by Jundab b. ʿAbd Allāh al-Azdī, ʿAlī's early follower, and al-Ḥārith b. Suwayd al-Taymī of Taym al-Ribāb.[9]

Muʿāwiya was aware of al-Ḥasan's peaceful disposition and knew from his spies that he was not about to attack. As Muʿāwiya equally wished to avoid another all-out confrontation with the Kufans and Basrans, there was no sense in trying to threaten and intimidate the grandson of the Prophet. His usual stratagem of pinning guilt for the blood of ʿUthmān on his opponents, which he had employed so successfully, at least for Syrian home consumption, with respect to ʿAlī, might now be hazardous, since even his countrymen presumably knew that al-Ḥasan had been among the defenders of the palace in Medina. The proper course would be to treat him with dignified condescension, to cajole and dupe him with false promises.

Muʿāwiya reversed the salutation: 'From the servant of God, Commander of the Faithful, to al-Ḥasan b. ʿAlī.' Acknowledging his letter, he approved fully of al-Ḥasan's praise of Muḥammad; mentioning the Prophet's death and the strife of the Muslims after him, al-Ḥasan had, however, explicitly accused the Ṣiddīq Abū Bakr, the Fārūq ʿUmar, the Amīn Abū ʿUbayda, the Disciple (*ḥawārī*) of the Messenger (al-Zubayr), the righteous Emigrants and Helpers. 'I disliked that on your part, for surely you are in my eyes and those of the people not suspected, neither a wrongdoer nor base, and I would love sound speech and kindly mention on your part.'

[8] Abu l-Faraj, *Maqātil*, 55–7; Ibn Abi l-Ḥadīd, *Sharḥ*, XVI, 24–5.
[9] Ibn Abi l-Ḥadīd, *Sharḥ*, XVI, 25; Ibn Aʿtham, *Futūḥ*, IV, 152.

Muʿāwiya then lectured al-Ḥasan that the Community, when they differed after their Prophet's death, did not ignore the excellence of his family, their early merit and kinship with him, their station in Islam and among its people; rather, the whole Community had recognized the closeness of Quraysh to the Prophet and had chosen Abū Bakr as the one who accepted Islam first, knew God best, was dearest to Him, and strongest in His cause; this had been the view of the men of intelligence, faith, excellence, and concern for the Community, who were unjustly accused by al-Ḥasan's kin; if the Muslims had found among these anyone of equal competence who could have taken his place and would have protected the sanctuary of the Muslims as he did, they would not have turned the right to rule away from them.

Muʿāwiya's present position, he went on, in relation to al-Ḥasan was the same as that of Abū Bakr after the Prophet's death; if he knew that al-Ḥasan was more efficient than he in controlling and leading the subjects, more effective than he in collecting money, and more skilful in deceiving the enemy, Muʿāwiya would readily respond to his summons since he saw him worthy of that; but he knew that he had been longer in office, was more experienced in the affairs of the Community, more skilled in statecraft, and older in age; it was therefore more appropriate that al-Ḥasan should acknowledge that the station for which he was asking recognition belonged to him, Muʿāwiya; if he entered under his obedience, the reign would belong to him afterwards; whatever amount there was now in the treasury of Iraq, he could take away with him to wherever he wished; the land tax of any province of Iraq he desired would belong to him as a subsidy for his expenses; a man in his trust could collect it and deliver it to him every year; he would be protected from all harm – matters would not be decided without him, nor would he be disobeyed in any matter he was seeking in obedience to God.

Delivering Muʿāwiya's letter to al-Ḥasan, Jundab b. ʿAbd Allāh warned his imam: 'This man is going to march against you. Take the initiative to move against him first so that you battle him on his homeground. Even so there is no way that he could touch you before witnessing a battle greater than the Day of Ṣiffīn.' Al-Ḥasan answered that he would act according to his advice, but, Jundab added, 'then he abstained from consulting me and acted as if oblivious to my words.'[10]

Al-Ḥasan in fact did not reply to Muʿāwiya's letter. He realized that his extravagant promises were fraudulent and was, in any case, not interested

[10] Abu l-Faraj, *Maqātil*, 57–9; Balādhurī, *Ansāb*, III, 31–2. The version of Muʿāwiya's letter quoted by Ibn Abi l-Ḥadīd on the authority of al-Madāʾinī (*Sharḥ*, XVI, 25) contains a sharp attack on ʿAlī accusing him of the murder of ʿUthmān and of usurping power without a *shūrā*.

in them. Aware of the Umayyad's personal cowardice, he seems to have hoped that if he ignored Muʿāwiya, the latter would also leave him alone. Muʿāwiya now sent a more threatening letter. 'Be warned of placing your hopes in the hands of a rabble and despair of finding a weak spot in our armour. But if you turn away from your course and pledge allegiance to me, I shall keep what I have promised and fulfil what I stipulated to you . . . Then the caliphate will be yours after me, for you are the most worthy of it.' Al-Ḥasan's answer was feeble: 'Your letter has arrived in which you mention what you mention. I abstained from answering it lest I might commit a transgression (*abghī*) against you. I seek refuge with God to ward that off. So follow the right and you shall know that I am worthy of it. May guilt stick to me, if I should speak and lie.'[11]

Muʿāwiya was now convinced that he would be able to swallow Iraq without doing battle. Writing to his governors and commanders to mobilize, he gave praise to God who had taken care of their enemy and the killers of their caliph for them and, in His kindness and beneficent management, had granted ʿAlī b. Abī Ṭālib one of His servants, who by stealth had dealt him a mortal blow, killing him; now his companions were left divided and discordant, and letters from their nobles and commanders had been coming to him, asking pardon for themselves and their tribes. 'So make haste to come to me when this letter of mine reaches you, with your soldiers, your resolve, and your good equipment, for you shall, praise be to God, obtain your revenge and attain your hope, and God shall ruin the people of rebellion and aggression.'[12]

This time Muʿāwiya did not need to be asked to take part in the campaign. When ʿAmr b. al-ʿĀṣ saw his sudden determination to march himself, he observed mockingly: 'Muʿāwiya knows, by God, that the lion ʿAlī has perished, treacherously killed by male camel foals.'[13] Leaving al-Ḍaḥḥāk b. Qays al-Fihrī as his deputy in Damascus,[14] he set out with his full army, said to have numbered sixty thousand men,[15] and crossed the Euphrates at Jisr Manbij. Only now was al-Ḥasan stirred to react. He sent Ḥujr b. ʿAdī to his local governors ordering them to get ready to march and addressed the Kufans with a lukewarm war speech: God had prescribed the *jihād* for his creation and called it a loathsome duty (*kurh*, Qurʾān II 216); he had been informed that Muʿāwiya, having learned that they intended to march against him, had now begun moving against

[11] Abu l-Faraj, *Maqātil*, 59–60.
[12] *Ibid.*, 60. According to al-Balādhurī's account (*Ansāb*, III, 30) Muʿāwiya had his army assembled already before al-Ḥasan sent his first letter and made his gloating comment on ʿAlī's death in a speech. He further stated that Kūfa was now governed by his son who was young, inexperienced and ignorant in warfare.
[13] Balādhurī, *Ansāb*, III, 37: reading *suqūb* for *sughūb*. Young male camels were proverbial for their vileness. [14] *Ibid.*, 36. [15] Ibn Aʿtham, *Futūḥ*, IV, 153.

them; therefore he asked them to assemble in their war camp at al-Nukhayla where they would look into the matter.

At first there was no response. Some of the tribal chiefs, in the pay of Muʿāwiya, were evidently not eager to move. ʿAdī b. Ḥātim stood up and scolded them, asking whether they would not respond to their imam and the son of the Prophet's daughter? Turning to al-Ḥasan he assured him of their obedience, and immediately left for the war camp. Then other loyal supporters of his father, Qays b. Saʿd, Maʿqil b. Qays and Ziyād b. Khaṣafa, joined in reproaching and rousing the people to follow ʿAdī's example. Al-Ḥasan praised them and later joined them at al-Nukhayla, where the men were assembling in large numbers. He appointed al-Mughīra b. Nawfal b. al-Ḥārith b. ʿAbd al-Muṭṭalib as his deputy in Kūfa with instructions to incite the people to war and send any laggers on to join the army.

At Dayr ʿAbd al-Raḥmān, al-Ḥasan halted for three nights to wait for more men to arrive. He summoned ʿUbayd Allāh b. al-ʿAbbās and appointed him commander of his vanguard of twelve thousand men with orders to move along the Euphrates to Maskin. There he was to detain Muʿāwiya until al-Ḥasan arrived with the main army. ʿUbayd Allāh should not fight the enemy unless attacked and should consult with Qays b. Saʿd and Saʿīd b. Qays, who would be second and third in command if he were killed. ʿUbayd Allāh moved via Shīnwar and Shāhī along the west bank of the Euphrates and on to al-Fallūja and Maskin.[16]

The choice of ʿUbayd Allāh b. al-ʿAbbās over the warlike Qays b. Saʿd and Saʿid b. Qays reflected al-Ḥasan's continued reluctance to be drawn into a battle. He still was hoping to reach a peace settlement with Muʿāwiya. ʿUbayd Allāh, he knew, was fully aware of his feelings and would, as in his governorship in the Yemen, do everything to avoid fighting. Al-Ḥasan did not even ask ʿAbd Allāh b. al-ʿAbbās, who had urged him to pursue the war against Muʿāwiya with vigour, to join his army with the Basrans.[17]

Meanwhile al-Ḥasan moved north via Ḥammām ʿUmar and Dayr Kaʿb to Sābāṭ near al-Madāʾin. There he gave a sermon during the morning prayer in which he avowed that he prayed to God to be the most sincere of His creation to His creation; he held no grudge nor hatred against any Muslim, nor did he desire evil and harm to anyone; whatever they hated in community was better than what they loved in schism. He was, so he assured them, looking after their best interest, better than they themselves;

[16] Abu l-Faraj, *Maqātil*, 62–3; Balādhurī, *Ansāb*, III, 32–3.

[17] Wellhausen's assumption that ʿAbd Allāh b. al-ʿAbbās, rather than ʿUbayd Allāh, was the confidant of al-Ḥasan who betrayed him first to make his peace with Muʿāwiya (*Das arabische Reich*, 66–70) is mistaken.

and he appealed to them not to contravene whatever orders he gave them nor to answer back to him.[18]

His men looked at each other and concluded, probably rightly: 'He intends to seek a truce with Mu'āwiya and to surrender the reign to him; he is weak and confounded.' A storm broke loose.[19] They overran and looted his pavilion, seizing even the prayer rug from underneath him. Then 'Abd al-Raḥmān b. 'Abd Allāh b. Ja''āl al-Azdī attacked him, pulling his tunic off his shoulders and leaving him undressed, clinging to his sword. Al-Ḥasan called for his horse and rode off surrounded by his servants and a few of his partisans who warded off those seeking to reach him, all the while reproaching him and calling him a weakling for what he had said. He asked his friends to summon Rabī'a and Hamdān, the tribes most loyal to his father. They surrounded him and shoved the people away from him. Some others, however, were mingling among them; and as they were passing by Muẓlim Sābāṭ, al-Jarrāḥ b. Sinān, a man of the Banū Naṣr b. Qu'ayn of Asad b. Khuzayma with Kharijite leanings, grasped the reins of his mount, shouting: 'God is greatest, Ḥasan, you have associated partners with God as your father did before you.' Then he struck his thigh with a pick-axe and cleft it open. Al-Ḥasan hit at him with his sword while clasping him, and both fell to the ground. 'Abd Allāh b. al-Ḥiṣl[20] jumped upon al-Jarrāḥ, tearing the pick-axe out of his hands and hit his belly with it, while Ẓubyān b. 'Umāra al-Tamīmī threw himself on him and cut his nose off. Then others joined in, crushing his face and head with baked bricks until he was dead. Al-Ḥasan was carried on a stretcher to al-Madā'in where he stayed with the governor Sa'd b. Mas'ūd al-Thaqafī to cure his wound.[21]

Mu'āwiya had advanced from Jisr Manbij via al-Raqqa, Naṣībīn, and Mossul to al-Akhnūniyya (later Ḥarba)[22] near Maskin, everywhere calming the populace and granting amnesty. When 'Ubayd Allāh also arrived there with the Kufan vanguard, Mu'āwiya sent 'Abd al-Raḥmān

[18] According to the version of al-Madā'inī quoted by Ibn Abi l-Ḥadīd (*Sharḥ*, XVI, 26), al-Ḥasan quoted his father 'Alī as stating: 'Do not loathe the reign of Mu'āwiya.' This is obviously quite incredible.

[19] Kufan 'Uthmanid tradition, represented by al-Sha'bī and 'Awāna, narrated that the mutiny was rather provoked by a false announcement that Qays b. Sa'd had been killed (al-Dhahabī, *Siyar a'lām al-nubalā'*, ed. Shu'ayb al-Arna'ūṭ and Ḥusayn Asad (Beirut, 1981–8), III, 263–4, 269). The story is blatant anti-Shi'ite fiction. The Kufan supporters of the 'Alids are depicted as so fickle and undisciplined that, when receiving adverse news, they vented their frustration on their own imam, who had thus good reason to abandon them to Mu'āwiya.

[20] Al-Madā'inī gives his name as 'Ubayd Allāh al-Ṭā'ī (Ibn Abi l-Ḥadīd, *Sharḥ*, XVI, 26).

[21] Abu l-Faraj, *Maqātil*, 63–4; Balādhurī, *Ansāb*, III, 34–6. The story quoted by al-Balādhurī and al-Ṭabarī (II, 2) that Sa'd b. Mas'ūd's young nephew al-Mukhtār b. Abī 'Ubayd advised him to fetter al-Ḥasan and buy his pardon from Mu'āwiya through this treacherous act is certainly anti-Mukhtār slander.

[22] See Yāqūt, *Buldān*, I, 167.

b. Samura b. Ḥabīb b. ʿAbd Shams to the Kufans to tell them that he had received letters from al-Ḥasan asking for a truce and that he had come for that purpose and had ordered his men to stay the fight. Muʿāwiya asked the Kufans not to attack until he concluded his negotiations with al-Ḥasan. His claim was probably untrue, but he had good reason to believe that he could intimidate al-Ḥasan to surrender. The Kufans gave his envoy the lie and reviled him. Next Muʿāwiya sent ʿAbd al-Raḥmān to visit ʿUbayd Allāh privately, and the envoy swore to him that al-Ḥasan had asked Muʿāwiya for a truce. Muʿāwiya was offering ʿUbayd Allāh 1,000,000 dirhams, half of the amount to be paid immediately, the other half in Kūfa, if he went over to him. Aware of al-Ḥasan's inclination to a peaceful settlement which would spare Muslim blood, ʿUbayd Allāh accepted and deserted at night to Muʿāwiya's camp. Muʿāwiya was greatly pleased and kept his promise to him.[23]

While ʿUbayd Allāh was thus received by Muʿāwiya with open arms, he saw Busr b. Abī Arṭāh in his presence. He asked Muʿāwiya: 'Did you order this accursed one to kill my two sons?' The caliph answered: 'By God, I did not, and I loathed it.' This was less than a half-truth; for while Muʿāwiya had probably not ordered the slaughter of the two boys, he certainly had instructed him to kill all Hashimites he could lay his hands on. It is inconceivable that Busr would have dared to kill any descendants of ʿAbd Manāf, his master's kin, without such explicit authorization. Muʿāwiya had not punished or reprimanded Busr for the act which he now claimed to have loathed, but rather had rewarded him for his atrocities by appointing him commander of his vanguard. Busr had thus reason to be furious at this display of hypocrisy at his expense. He threw his sword down before him, exclaiming: 'Take it from me. You have ordered me to knock the people with it and I obeyed your command. Now you tell this one what you just said when he was only yesterday your enemy and I your sincere helper and backer against him.' Muʿāwiya told him: 'Take your sword back. Surely you are feeble-minded when you throw your sword in front of a man of the Banū Hāshim whose sons you have killed.' This was empty flattery, for Muʿāwiya knew well that ʿUbayd Allāh b. al-ʿAbbās was not one to carry out blood-revenge for his sons. As Busr, humiliated, picked up his sword, ʿUbayd Allāh bragged: 'By God, I was not going to kill Busr for one of my sons; he is too base, vile, and despicable for that. By God, I do not see that I would obtain revenge for the two of them except through Yazīd and ʿAbd Allāh, the sons of Muʿāwiya.' Muʿāwiya merely laughed and commented: 'What is

[23] Balādhurī, *Ansāb*, III, 37–8; Abu l-Faraj, *Maqātil*, 64–5.

the offence of Yazīd and ʿAbd Allāh? By God, I did not order, know, or desire it.'[24]

The Kufans waited next morning in vain for ʿUbayd Allāh to come out and lead their morning prayer. Then Qays b. Saʿd took over and, in his sermon, harshly condemned him, his father and his brother, from whom nothing good had ever come; al-ʿAbbās had gone out to fight his nephew, the Prophet, at Badr, had been captured by the Anṣārī Abu l-Yusr Kaʿb b. ʿAmr and been ransomed; ʿAbd Allāh, appointed governor of Baṣra by the Commander of the Faithful ʿAlī, had stolen the money of God and the Muslims and bought slave girls with it, claiming that was legitimate for him; this one had run away as governor of Yemen from Busr b. Abī Arṭāh leaving his two sons to be killed, and now he did the same here. The men shouted: 'Praise be to God that He has removed him from us; stand up with us against our enemy.' Qays was their man.[25]

Muʿāwiya thought that the desertion of ʿUbayd Allāh had broken the spirit of the enemy and sent Busr with troops to persuade them to surrender. Qays attacked and drove him back. The next day Busr attacked with larger forces but was again defeated. Muʿāwiya now wrote to Qays offering bribes and extending him an invitation, but Qays answered that he would never meet him except with a lance between them. In his next letter Muʿāwiya called him a Jew, son of a Jew, who courted being killed for a prize that would never be his. He suggested that if the party dear to Qays were victorious, he would be deposed and replaced, and if the party odious to him won he would be tortured and killed; his father had already shot arrows in a vain fight only to be deserted by his people and to perish in Ḥawrān as an outcast. In reply Qays called Muʿāwiya an idol (*wathan*), son of a Mekkan idol. 'You entered Islam under duress, stayed in it out of fear, and left it voluntarily without faith preceding or hypocrisy occurring as a novelty on your part.' Qays' father had fought an honest battle, hitting his target, but someone 'whose dust you cannot cleave[26] and whose ankle you do not reach' had incited opposition to him; it was a cause shunned by many; Muʿāwiya had called him a Jew, son of a Jew, 'but you and the people know that I and my father are of the Helpers of the religion which you have left and the enemies of the religion which you have joined.' Muʿāwiya was reduced to silence. ʿAmr b. al-ʿĀṣ suggested that he answer, but he confessed that he was

[24] Balādhurī, *Ansāb*, II, 459–60, quoting the account of Hishām al-Kalbī. The story appears in variant versions in many sources. See Thaqafī, *Ghārāt*, 661–3; *Aghānī*, XV, 47.

[25] Abu l-Faraj, *Maqātil*, 65.

[26] 'To cleave someone's dust' was metaphorical for 'to contest with, to overtake'. Qays was reducing Muʿāwiya, who had boasted of being superior to ʿUmar, to his proper size.

afraid that Qays' next reply might be worse than this one.[27] As the news of the mutiny against al-Ḥasan and of his having been wounded arrived, however, both sides refrained from fighting in order to await further developments.

Muʿāwiya now sent ʿAbd Allāh b. ʿĀmir b. Kurayz and ʿAbd al-Raḥmān b. Samura as his envoys to al-Ḥasan. Ibn ʿĀmir implored al-Ḥasan to spare the blood of the Community of Muḥammad. Muʿāwiya, he said, was obstinate, and he therefore appealed to al-Ḥasan to beware of obstinacy lest the people perish between the two of them; Muʿāwiya would appoint him his successor and give him whatever he wished. ʿAbd al-Raḥmān b. Samura spoke to him in the same vein. The argument about saving Muslim blood evidently met al-Ḥasan's own sentiments. He accepted the overture in principle and sent ʿAmr b. Salima al-Hamdānī al-Arḥabī and his own brother-in-law Muḥammad b. al-Ashʿath al-Kindī back to Muʿāwiya as his negotiators, together with the envoys of the latter. Muʿāwiya then wrote a letter addressing him humbly: 'To al-Ḥasan b. ʿAlī from Muʿāwiya b. Abī Sufyān.' He stated that he was making peace with him on the basis that the reign would belong to al-Ḥasan after him. He swore solemnly by God and the Messenger Muḥammad that he would not commit any wrong against, or seek to harm him. He would give him 1,000,000 dirhams from the treasury (*bayt al-māl*) annually, and the land tax of Fasā and Darābjird would belong to him; al-Ḥasan was to send his own tax agents to collect it and could do with the two tax districts whatever he pleased. The letter was witnessed by the four envoys and dated in Rabīʿ II 41/August 661.

When al-Ḥasan read the letter he commented: 'He is trying to appeal to my greed for 'a matter' which, if I desired it, I would not surrender to him.' Then he sent ʿAbd Allāh b. al-Ḥārith b. Nawfal b. al-Ḥārith b. ʿAbd al-Muṭṭalib, whose mother Hind was Muʿāwiya's sister, to the Umayyad, instructing him: 'Go to your uncle and tell him: If you grant safety to the people I shall pledge allegiance to you.' Muʿāwiya now gave him a blank sheet with his seal at the bottom of it, inviting him to write on it whatever he wished. Al-Ḥasan wrote that he was making peace with Muʿāwiya, surrendering the reign over the Muslims to him on the basis that he act in it according to the Book of God, the Sunna of His Prophet and the conduct of the righteous caliphs. He stipulated that Muʿāwiya should not be entitled to appoint his successor but that there should be an electoral council (*shūrā*); the people would be safe, wherever they were, with respect to their person, their property and their offspring; Muʿāwiya

[27] Balādhurī, *Ansāb*, III, 39–40; Abu l-Faraj, *Maqātil*, 65–6. According to the version of Abu l-Faraj Muʿāwiya wanted to answer the letter but ʿAmr persuaded him not to do so.

would not seek any wrong against al-Ḥasan secretly or openly, and would not intimidate any of his companions. The letter was witnessed by ʿAbd Allah b. al-Ḥārith and ʿAmr b. Salima and conveyed by them to Muʿāwiya for him to take cognizance of its contents and to attest his acceptance.[28]

Muʿāwiya now moved with his army from Maskin to Kūfa where he first camped between al-Nukhayla and the store-house for provisions. Al-Ḥasan and Qays b. Saʿd also returned with their men to al-Nukhayla. Before leaving al-Madā'in al-Ḥasan addressed his men with a sermon in which he quoted Qur'ān IV 19: 'Perhaps you hate something, though God will put in it much good.' As he met Muʿāwiya in Kūfa, he and ʿAmr b. Salima al-Hamdānī pledged allegiance in public. Muʿāwiya demanded: 'Get up and apologize.' At first al-Ḥasan declined, but Muʿāwiya insisted. Al-Ḥasan reminded the people that he and his brother al-Ḥusayn were the only grandsons of the Prophet; Muʿāwiya had contested a right that belonged to al-Ḥasan who ceded it to him in the best interest of the Community and for the sake of sparing their blood. 'You have pledged allegiance to me on the basis that you make peace with whomever I make peace. I have deemed it right to make peace with him and have pledged allegiance to him, since I considered whatever spares blood as better than whatever causes it to be shed. I desired your best interest and what I did should be an argument against whoever covets the reign.'[29]

In his own speech to the Kufans at al-Nukhayla, Muʿāwiya laid out his vision of proper government. He told them that, after duly considering matters, he had recognized that people would behave well only under three conditions: they must meet their enemy in his country, for if they did not attack him there, he would attack them; the stipends and provisions must be distributed at the proper time; expeditions to nearby territories should last six months, those to remote areas a year. Then he reminded them that he had stipulated conditions, made promises to them, and raised their desires. He had done so merely wishing to extinguish the fire of insurrection, to cut short the war, to cajole the people and calm them. According to the more drastic versions of the speech he stated that his promises to al-Ḥasan and anyone else were but

[28] Balādhurī, *Ansāb*, III, 40–2. Ibn Aʿtham gives a slightly longer version (*Futūḥ*, IV, 159–60).

[29] Balādhurī, *Ansāb*, III, 42–3. Al-Balādhurī quotes other versions of al-Ḥasan's speech (*ibid.*, 43–4). Many of his men openly denounced him for his surrender to Muʿāwiya. Sufyān b. Abī Laylā al-Hamdānī addressed him as the humiliator of the faithful (*mudhill al-mu'minīn*). Ḥujr b. ʿAdī told him: 'You have blackened the faces of the faithful.' He defended himself invariably with the argument that he was seeking to spare their blood (Abu l-Faraj, *Maqātil*, 67–8; Balādhurī, *Ansāb*, III, 44–6).

dirt under his feet which he would not keep.[30] Then he shouted: 'God's protection is dissolved from anyone who does not come forth and pledge allegiance. Surely, I have sought revenge for the blood of 'Uthmān, may God kill his murderers, and have returned the reign to those to whom it belongs in spite of the rancour of some people. We grant respite of three nights. Whoever has not pledged allegiance by then will have no protection and no pardon.' The people hastily came from every direction to pledge allegiance.[31]

No keen observer of the game of politics could have been in doubt that Mu'āwiya ever had had any intention of fulfilling his exorbitant promises made for the noble purpose of shortening the war. Yet it was not a newly discovered sense of honesty that induced him now to disavow them publicly as fraud. The presence of a massive Syrian army whose chauvinistic patriotism he had fanned to fever pitch with vows of revenge for the wronged caliph forced him to reveal his hand more quickly than he, generally inclined to caution, might otherwise have done. Yet since he would need them again, he could not afford to confess that his vows of vengeance, too, had been mere war fraud, and had to proceed with the game of make-believe.

According to Ibn A'tham's account, there were immediate protests and abuse, and Mu'āwiya, fearing the outbreak of riots, regretted his words.[32] This is not confirmed by the more reliable sources and is probably fiction. In the mosque of Kūfa, shortly afterwards, Mu'āwiya also boasted of his brutishness in order to please his kinsman al-Walīd b. 'Uqba who had disgraced himself there. While still camping outside Kūfa, however, Mu'āwiya faced a Kharijite rebellion led by Farwa b. Nawfal al-Ashja'ī. Farwa had been staying with five hundred Kharijites at Shahrazūr while refraining from attacks on 'Alī and al-Ḥasan. He had no doubts now that it was legitimate to fight Mu'āwiya and entered Kūfa with his men. Mu'āwiya sent a Syrian cavalry troop against them, but they were beaten back by the rebels. Al-Ḥasan had already left for Medina together with his brother al-Ḥusayn and his cousin 'Abd Allāh b. Ja'far, accompanied by Mu'āwiya as far as Qanṭarat al-Ḥīra. Ever eager to find others to fight his wars, Mu'āwiya now sent after al-Ḥasan, ordering him to return and fight the Kharijites. Al-Ḥasan, who had reached al-Qādisiyya, wrote back: 'I have abandoned the fight against you, even though it was my legal right, for the sake of peace and

[30] Abu l-Faraj, *Maqātil*, 69; Ibn A'tham, *Futūḥ*, IV, 164; Balādhurī, *Ansāb*, III, 44, 48. According to the account of Abu l-Faraj, the Kufan traditionist Abū Isḥāq al-Sabī'ī, who reported having himself heard Mu'āwiya's words, added the comment: 'He was, by God, utterly perfidious (*wa-kāna wa llāhi ghaddāran*).' Abū Isḥāq would have been eight years old at the time if, as he claimed, he was born in the year 33/653–4 (Ibn Ḥajar, *Tahdhīb*, VIII, 63).
[31] Balādhurī, *Ansāb*, III, 46–7.
[32] Ibn A'tham, *Futūḥ*, IV, 164.

reconciliation of the Community. Do you think I shall fight together with you?'[33]

The caliph now turned to the Kufans, threatening that if they would not take care of their turbulent brethren, he would withdraw his pardon of them. He had, he told them, not fought them that they might pray, fast, perform the pilgrimage, and give alms, since they were doing that already. Rather, he had fought them in order to command them as their amir, and God had granted him that against their will.[34] The Kharijites in turn asked the Kufans to leave them alone since they were fighting their enemy Muʿāwiya. If they won, the Kufans would be rid of him, and if Muʿāwiya won, they would be rid of the Kharijites. Blinded by their hatred of the Kharijites, the Kufans insisted on fighting them. The Kharijites commented: 'May God have mercy on our brethren of al-Nahrawān. They knew you best, people of Kūfa.' As Farwa b. Nawfal was seized by his people Ashjaʿ, the Kharijites chose ʿAbd Allāh b. (Abi) l-Ḥawsā' al-Ṭā'ī as their leader, and were killed together with him.[35]

When the Basrans heard of al-Ḥasan's surrender and of Muʿāwiya's conduct in Kūfa, they rioted and declared that they would not accept the rule of the new caliph. ʿAbd Allāh b. al-ʿAbbās is not mentioned; he must have left them immediately after al-Ḥasan's resignation. Ḥumrān b. Abān of the Banu l-Namir b. Qāsiṭ of Rabīʿa, ʿUthmān's client whom he had banished to Baṣra, rose in revolt and seized control of the town. Muʿāwiya at first intended to send a man of the Banu l-Qayn, who had a blood claim against the Basrans, to subdue them.[36] Either ʿUbayd Allāh or ʿAbd Allāh b. al-ʿAbbās[37] advised him against this, however, and Muʿāwiya decided to send Busr b. Abī Arṭāh. Busr arrived in Baṣra in Rajab 41/November 661 and evidently had no difficulty in quelling the insurrection of Ḥumrān. He lived up to his reputation as child murderer by threatening to kill the sons of Ziyād b. Abīh who was still holding out in Iṣṭakhr against Muʿāwiya's reign. In this instance, however, the show may have been staged, for Muʿāwiya was convinced that he would be able

[33] Balādhurī, *Ansāb*, III, 46; Ibn Abi l-Ḥadīd, *Sharḥ*, XVI, 14–15 (al-Madā'inī).

[34] Ibn Abi l-Ḥadīd, *Sharḥ*, XVI, 15; Abu l-Faraj, *Maqātil*, 70.

[35] Ṭabarī, II, 9–10.

[36] At the beginning of al-Ḥasan's reign, Muʿāwiya is said to have sent a man of Ḥimyar to Kūfa and a man of (al-)Qayn to Baṣra as spies. Both men were seized and killed. This was presumably the reason for Muʿāwiya's choice. Both al-Ḥasan and ʿAbd Allāh b. al-ʿAbbās are said to have complained to Muʿāwiya who rejected their charges (Abu l-Faraj, *Maqātil*, 52–4).

[37] Most of the sources name here ʿUbayd Allāh b. al-ʿAbbās. In the Ṭabarī edition (II, 11) ʿAbd Allāh was chosen by the editor against the MSS as in other passages. In the present case a confusion with ʿAbd Allāh seems not unlikely. ʿAbd Allāh could have been in the presence of Muʿāwiya if he left Baṣra immediately after the surrender of al-Ḥasan. For him to give advice to Muʿāwiya concerning Baṣra would obviously be more reasonable than for ʿUbayd Allāh to do so.

to buy Ziyād, his bastard brother, though for no small price. When Ziyād's uterine brother Abū Bakra intervened to save his nephews, Busr told him that he was acting under Mu'āwiya's instructions, but allowed him to intercede with the Commander of the Faithful. Mu'āwiya immediately ordered the release of Ziyād's sons. After prolonged haggling with Ziyād over the spoils of 'money of the Muslims' put aside in his governorship, he allowed him to swallow them up and then crowned his bribe with his formal recognition of Ziyād as his father's son. Ziyād was now ready to deliver his former allies, who proved less venal than he, to Mu'āwiya's knife.

The year 41 of the *hijra* came to be known as *'ām al-jamā'a*, the year of the Community. The *fitna*, Inter-Muslim War, was over, and the unity of the Community under a single caliph was restored. Yet it was not the old Community that was resurrected. The universal brotherhood of Islam, the respect for the sanctity of Muslim blood legislated by the Prophet, would not return. The schisms torn open in the war would not heal, but rather deepened and hardened. Umayyad government, whose legitimacy was, as noted by Wellhausen, founded on the claim of revenge for the caliph 'Uthmān, kept pitting Muslims against Muslims, inciting suspicion, mistrust, hatred and constant strife. Not until the caliphate of the pious 'Umar II was a short-lived attempt made to bring about a broad reconciliation between the factions rather than governing by provocation, repression and oppression.

The caliphate itself was transformed. Sunnite tradition recognized the profound change and attributed to the Prophet the prediction that the successorship to prophethood (*khilāfat al-nubuwwa*) would last after him for thirty years to be followed by 'biting kingship' (*mulk ladūd*). No longer was the principle of *sābiqa*, early merit and service in the cause of Islam, acknowledged as the criterion for the choice of the successor of the Prophet. Instead, swords and soldiers' boots, the natural prop of despotism, determined thenceforth the identity of the Vicegerent of God on earth. The true implications of 'Uthmān's adopted title Vicegerent of God, of being above rather than subject to Islam – from which he personally had shied away in the end – were now fully realized by Mu'āwiya and his successors. The caliph became counterpart and successor to the Roman–Byzantine emperor. He took over the old crown lands conquered by the Muslim armies as his divine right. He ruled Muslims as his subjects, absolute lord over their life and death, himself above the law and the *lex talionis*, killing at discretion whomever he saw as a potential threat to his power.

In a wider historical perspective, Islam was now taken over by the state. Just as three centuries earlier Roman–Byzantine despotism had appropriated Christianity, strangled its pacifist religious core, and turned it into a tool of imperial domination and repression, so it now appropriated Islam, strangling its spirit of religious brotherhood and community and using it as an instrument of repressive social control, exploitation and military terrorization. The Roman emperor, in pagan times deified in order to exact worship from his subjects, had since Constantine become head of the Christian church, the Vicar of Christ on earth, a Christ transformed from a Saviour and brother of man into a grim Pantocrator and Judge. The Umayyad caliph, rival and successor of the Roman emperor in all but name, became the Vicegerent of God on earth, a God who now primarily commanded absolute obedience and unquestioning submission to His arbitrary Decree and Ordainment.

The Arabs had now what most of them had dreaded and vigorously resisted for so long. They had lost their freedom and tribal autonomy and become subjects of a state in the form of traditional kingship introduced through the back door of Islam. The first step had, as noted, already been taken when Abū Bakr turned the religious obligation of giving alms into an assessable and enforceable tax. The final step was taken under Muʿāwiya, when the duty to obey the Commander of the Faithful was made enforceable under pain of death, rather than imprisonment and deportation as it had been under the early caliphs. They had now, as ʿAlī had warned them, the rule of Caesar and Chosroes. Those still remembering their former freedom and their brotherhood and respect for Muslim life under the Prophet and the early caliphs might wonder what Umayyad state Islam had in common with the message preached by Muḥammad. Seeing the odious little impostor posturing as the Vicegerent of God on earth, they could well believe that their Prophet had pronounced the hadith attributed to him: 'When you see Muʿāwiya on my pulpit, kill him!'

It remains to take a brief look at the career and fate of some of the surviving actors in the story of the early caliphate under the new Umayyad kingdom. Muḥammad's grandson al-Ḥasan retired permanently to Medina and tried to keep aloof from political involvement for or against Muʿāwiya. In spite of his resignation, however, he was still considered the chief of the Prophet's house by the Banū Hāshim and the partisans of ʿAlī, who pinned their hopes on his eventual succession to the Umayyad. According to the general account of al-Baladhūrī (*qālū*), al-Ḥasan, on the basis of his treaty with Muʿāwiya, sent his tax collectors to Fasā and Darābjird. The caliph had, however, instructed ʿAbd Allāh b. ʿĀmir, now again governor of Baṣra, to incite the Basrans to protest that this money belonged to them by right of their conquest and that their stipends were being diminished. According to some they chased al-Ḥasan's tax collectors out of the two provinces. Muʿāwiya thus confined himself to the payment of 1,000,000 or 2,000,000 dirhams (annually) which he took from the land tax of Iṣfahān and elsewhere.[38] All this is surely fiction. Muʿāwiya had stipulated the land tax of Fasā and Darābjird in his offer to al-Ḥasan in order to test the resolve of al-Ḥasan and the Basrans to continue to uphold ʿUmar's ruling, vigorously supported by ʿAlī, that the *fay*ʾ from the conquered lands belonged to the conquerors. His ulterior motive was to assert the sole right of government to tax and to restrict the garrison towns' right to receive payment of stipends arbitrarily set by the authorities. Al-Ḥasan was fully aware of this. He had rejected Muʿāwiya's offer and in his own peace proposal had made no stipulation for any financial compensation. That he would now send tax collectors from Medina to Iran, after just having made plain that he would not join Muʿāwiya in fighting the Kharijites, is entirely incredible.

Hardly more plausible is that Muʿāwiya would, under the circumstances, send al-Ḥasan annually 1,000,000 or 2,000,000 dirhams, to which he was not even contractually obliged, since al-Ḥasan had not accepted his offer. Muʿāwiya might have paid him a princely salary for a time if the grandson of the Prophet had joined him and propped up the legitimacy of his regime by unequivocal support as his crown prince. But as he observed al-Ḥasan's determination to retire to Medina and his consistent assertion that he had resigned only to spare Muslim blood, not in recognition of Muʿāwiya's superior qualifications for the caliphate, he lost all interest in continuing to cajole him. Muʿāwiya's Syrian propaganda machine now turned against him with insinuations that he was plotting to overthrow the government. This is reflected in the report of ʿAbd al-Raḥmān b. Jubayr b. Nufayr al-Ḥaḍramī, an ʿUthmanid loyalist from Ḥimṣ,[39] that his father reproached al-Ḥasan: 'The people say that you want the caliphate.' Al-Ḥasan answered: 'The skulls of the Arabs were in my hand; they were ready to make peace with whomever I concluded peace and to make war on whomever I declared war, yet I abandoned it, seeking instead the face of God. Would I now want it through the people of the Ḥijāz?'[40]

Disappointed in his hopes that the Prophet's grandson would bolster the legitimacy of his regime by lending his moral support, Muʿāwiya proposed strengthening his ties with Muḥammad's Family by marrying his granddaughter Umāma, ʿAlī's widow. Umāma was the daughter of Abu l-ʿĀṣ b. al-Rabīʿ of ʿAbd Shams and Muḥammad's eldest daughter, Zaynab.[41] ʿAlī had married her some time after Fāṭima's death, and she

[38] Balādhurī, *Ansāb*, III, 47. [39] See Madelung, 'Apocalyptic Prophecies', 145–7, 178.

[40] Balādhurī, *Ansāb*, III, 49, variant: through the goats (*atyās*) of the Ḥijāz.

[41] Abu l-ʿĀṣ b. al-Rabīʿ was Zaynab's maternal cousin. She bore him also a son, ʿAlī, who died, however, as a boy.

had borne him a son, Muḥammad al-Awsaṭ. After 'Alī's death, her paternal cousin 'Abd al-Raḥmān b. Muḥriz b. Ḥāritha b. Rabī'a had taken her to Medina. Mu'āwiya now ordered his governor Marwān b. al-Ḥakam to convey his marriage proposal to her. Umāma can hardly have been pleased by the offer from a ruler who continued the practice of public cursing of her murdered husband and father of her son. She gave the right to decide on her remarriage to the Hashimite al-Mughīra b. Nawfal b. al-Ḥārith b. 'Abd al-Muṭṭalib, who had briefly been governor of Kūfa under al-Ḥasan's reign. Having made sure that she was giving him a completely free hand, al-Mughīra himself married her, with a dowry of 400 dinars. Marwān informed Mu'āwiya, who instructed him to leave her alone since she was most entitled to decide about herself. The caliph, however, judged al-Mughīra's conduct as sufficiently suspicious that he later exiled (*sayyara*) him from Medina to nearby Wādi l-Ṣafrā'. There both he and the Prophet's granddaughter died. They had a son, Yaḥyā.[42]

Mu'āwiya's largesse among the Banū Hāshim was mostly confined to al-Ḥasan's cousin 'Abd Allāh b. Ja'far b. Abī Ṭālib, who, after 'Alī's death and al-Ḥasan's abdication, had abandoned all political ambition. 'Abd Allāh paid regular visits to Mu'āwiya and was granted by him 1,000,000 dirhams annually, which he spent in entertaining and making lavish gifts to poets, singers and musicians in Medina.[43] Mu'āwiya's motivation in voluntarily heaping these sums on a Hashimite to whom he owed nothing was similar, though in a cruder form, to 'Umar's motivation in courting and elevating al-'Abbās and his son 'Abd Allāh, while keeping 'Alī, the recognized chief of Hāshim, strictly on a par with the other senior Companions. 'Abd Allāh b. Ja'far, who neither had a political following nor engaged in subversive religious teaching as did Ibn al-'Abbās, was no threat to the Umayyad regime. Rather, he conformed to the image of the Prophet's kin that Mu'āwiya sought to portray for the public. At best, they were greedy profligates, bon vivants and philanderers, unsuited for the serious business of government, which required the management of the glorious dynasty.

Umayyad propaganda is thus reflected in the ill-informed account of al-Zuhrī on the negotiations between al-Ḥasan and Mu'āwiya, which was quoted by al-Ṭabarī in preference to the Kufan reports. Al-Zuhrī described al-Ḥasan as eager to take all that he could get for himself from Mu'āwiya and then 'to enter the Community'.[44] It was, according to his account, al-Ḥasan who first addressed Mu'āwiya and enumerated the conditions on which he would obey him. Mu'āwiya received his letter after he had sent al-Ḥasan a blank sheet with his seal under it for him to

[42] Balādhurī, *Ansāb*, I, 400. [43] Madelung 'The Hāshimiyyāt', 18–22.
[44] Ṭabarī, II, 3.

stipulate his conditions. The greedy al-Ḥasan now doubled his previous demands. Muʿāwiya retained al-Ḥasan's original letter. When the two met they quarrelled about which of the two letters was valid and, in the end, having outwitted the double-crosser, Muʿāwiya fulfilled none of the conditions.[45] Al-Zuhrī's story is blatant defamation of Muḥammad's grandson, while describing Muʿāwiya, along the common Umayyad propaganda line, as the sly fox (*dāhiya*). It confirms, however, both the existence of two agreements and that Muʿāwiya fulfilled the conditions of neither.

Tendentious reporting turned al-Ḥasan also into a voluptuous sensualist who spent his fortune and life in marrying and divorcing countless women and maintaining an immense harem. The fanciful and often hostile anecdotal material supporting this image deserves little credit. The number of his reliably recorded marriages is smaller than for the Umayyad ʿUthmān.[46] As heir to ʿAlī's property, including the *ṣadaqāt*, real estate, of the Prophet in Medina which ʿUmar had turned over to al-ʿAbbās and ʿAlī,[47] al-Ḥasan was obviously a man of substantial wealth, although not comparable to the enormous riches of some of the prominent Companions such as Ṭalḥa and al-Zubayr, now in the hands of their heirs, and of the Umayyad princes. Receiving also one of the highest stipends under ʿUmar's pension system, he could easily afford the high lifestyle of the Qurayshite nobility in Medina without any princely subsidies from Muʿāwiya. His pursuit of women was not more covetous than that of most of his class and less frivolous than that of many.

It is thus evident that the explanation that Lammens in his character assassination of al-Ḥasan[48] offered for the joy manifested by Muʿāwiya

[45] *Ibid.*, 5–6. Al-Zuhrī also reported, again reflecting Umayyad propaganda, that Qays b. Saʿd, not al-Ḥasan, stipulated amnesty for himself and the followers of ʿAlī in his truce agreement without asking for any money. Muʿāwiya generously agreed to his conditions (*ibid.*, 8).

[46] See excursus 7 on the marriages and children of al-Ḥasan. In her article on al-Ḥasan in the *EI* (2nd edn) Veccia-Vaglieri states as a fact that after his move to Medina 'as before, he went from one marriage to another, so earning for himself the title of *al-Miṭlāḳ*, 'the Divorcer.' He had 60 or 70 or 90 wives and 300 or 400 concubines. This life of sensual pleasures does not appear, however, to have aroused much censure.' These figures are entirely absurd. In a similar vein, H. Halm writes: 'Al-Ḥasan kehrte nach Madina zurück und lebte dort bis zu seinem Tode als reicher Grandseigneur . . . das einzig Bemerkenswerte, das die Quellen noch über ihn zu berichten wissen, sind seine zahlreichen Ehen und seine große Nachkommenschaft.' (*Der schiitische Islam: Von der Religion zur Revolution*, (Munich, 1994), 20). According to the best sources, al-Ḥasan's children amounted to seven or eight sons and six daughters. These numbers were by the standards of the Qurayshite nobility both before and in early Islam not unusually large and smaller than for ʿUthmān or Marwān.

[47] Among al-Ḥasan's sons, the eldest, Zayd b. al-Ḥasan, inherited the *ṣadaqāt* of the Prophet, while the second, al-Ḥasan b. al-Ḥasan, inherited control of the *ṣadaqāt* of ʿAlī (Mufīd, *Irshād*, 176, 178; Zubayrī, *Nasab*, 46).

[48] *Moʿâwia*, 147–54.

over the death of the Prophet's grandson in 49/669 or 50/670 – to wit that 'the prolongation of his days became onerous for the finances of the Umayyads'[49] – does not hold water. The cause of Mu'āwiya's joy was that the death of al-Ḥasan removed a hurdle to his appointment of his son Yazīd to the succession, which he was eagerly promoting at the time. For while it is true that al-Ḥasan was innocuous enough and hardly harboured any intentions of reclaiming the caliphate,[50] many of the disaffected, smarting under the divisive Umayyad despotism, had not forgotten Mu'āwiya's recognition of al-Ḥasan as his legitimate successor and al-Ḥasan's stipulation of a *shūrā*. This situation also lends credibility to the reports that al-Ḥasan was poisoned by his wife Ja'da, daughter of al-Ash'ath b. Qays,[51] at the instigation of Mu'āwiya. These reports are not, as often suggested, accepted only by Shi'ite sources, but also by the major Sunnite historians al-Wāqidī, al-Madā'inī, 'Umar b. Shabba, al-Balādhurī and al-Haytham b. 'Adī.[52] According to Abū Bakr b. Ḥafṣ, great-grandson of Sa'd b. Abī Waqqāṣ and highly respected Medinan Sunnite transmitter from 'Urwa b. al-Zubayr, it was generally believed at the time that Mu'āwiya poisoned both al-Ḥasan and Sa'd b. Abī Waqqāṣ, who died in the same year.[53] Al-Ṭabarī suppressed these reports not, as

49 *Ibid.*, 153. In order to make his argument more plausible, Lammens increased the sum demanded and received by al-Ḥasan under the treaty to over 5,000,000 dirhams in addition to the revenue of 'a district of Persia' (*ibid.*, 149). His source, al-Dīnawarī, does not mention any demand of 5,000,000 dirhams, only the revenue of al-Ahwāz. Mu'āwiya, according to Lammens, kept word in everything he had promised. Al-Dīnawarī, in spite of his strong pro-Umayyad and anti-Shi'ite bias, states nothing of this sort. The passage to which Lammens (149 n. 3) refers describes Mu'āwiya as vainly asking 'Amr b. al-'Āṣ for a contribution from the treasury of Egypt because of the exhaustion of his financial resources through gifts to his visitors from the Ḥijāz and Iraq.

50 Contrariwise, the pro-Umayyad account of al-Dīnawarī suggests that al-Ḥasan regretted his surrender when Ḥujr b. 'Adī urged him in Medina to resume the war against Mu'āwiya (al-Dīnawarī, *al-Akhbār al-ṭiwāl*, ed. V. Guirgass (Leiden, 1888–1912), I, 233–4).

51 According to al-Haytham b. 'Adī, it was rather the daughter of Suhayl b. 'Amr of 'Āmir Quraysh who poisoned al-Ḥasan for a bribe of 100,000 dinars from Mu'āwiya (Balādhurī, *Ansāb*, III, 59). Al-Wāqidī, quoted by al-Dhahabī (*Siyar*, III, 274), reported that according to one of his informants a servant of al-Ḥasan offered him a poisoned drink at the instigation of Mu'āwiya.

52 The generally pro-Umayyad 'Awāna also seems to imply that Mu'āwiya had a hand in al-Ḥasan's demise when he describes him as instructing Marwān, just before al-Ḥasan's death, to inform him as quickly as possible when it happened. Marwān did so, and Mu'āwiya thus could surprise 'Abd Allāh b. al-'Abbās with the news (Ibn Abī Uṣaybi'a, *'Uyūn al-anbā' fī ṭabaqāt al-aṭibbā'*, ed. A. Müller (Cairo, 1299/1882), I, 118–19). The report, however, erroneously suggests that Marwān was at that time governor of Medina. Lammens interpreted it as agreeing with reports that al-Ḥasan's mortal illness lasted two months (*Mo'âwia*, 152–3). This interpretation is in conflict, however, with 'Awāna's point that Mu'āwiya wanted to surprise Ibn al-'Abbās with the news. Ibn al-'Abbās would have been among the first to know of a mortal illness afflicting al-Ḥasan.

53 Balādhurī, *Ansāb*, I, 404: *kānū yarawna annahū sammahumā*; Abu l-Faraj, *Maqātil*, 73. Abū Bakr b. Ḥafṣ is 'Abd Allāh b. Ḥafṣ b. 'Umar b. Sa'd b. Abī Waqqāṣ (Ibn Ḥajar, *Tahdhīb*, V, 188–9). He was thus a grandson of 'Umar b. Sa'd, the leader of the Kufan army which slaughtered al-Ḥusayn and his entourage at Karbalā'.

suggested by Lammens, because he considered them insignificant,[54] but because he saw them as potentially dangerous for the faith of the common people (*'awāmm*). For the same reason he suppressed the reports about Mu'āwiya's recognition of Ziyād as his bastard brother.[55]

The burial of al-Ḥasan in Medina nearly provoked fighting between the Hashimites and Umayyads. According to the account of 'Urwa b. al-Zubayr, al-Ḥasan instructed his family before his death to bury him with his grandfather Muḥammad. If they feared evil, however, they should bury him with his mother Fāṭima. When they proposed interring him next to Muḥammad, Marwān interfered, declaring: ''Uthmān will not be buried in Ḥashsh Kawkab and al-Ḥasan here.'[56] The Banū Hashim and Banū Umayya assembled, each group with their supporters, brandishing their weapons. Abū Hurayra, this time taking the side of the Prophet's Family, asked Marwān: 'Will you prevent al-Ḥasan from being buried in this place when I have heard the Messenger of God say about him and his brother al-Ḥusayn that they are the lords of the youth (*sayyidā shabāb*) of the inmates of Paradise?' Marwān told him: 'Leave us alone. The hadith of the Messenger of God would be lost if nobody but you and Abū Sa'īd al-Khudrī had preserved it. You have become a Muslim only at the siege of Khaybar.' Abū Hurayra protested that he had indeed accepted Islam at Khaybar, but that he then stayed constantly with the Prophet and knew everyone whom he loved and whom he hated, for whom he prayed and whom he cursed. When 'Ā'isha saw the men and weapons, she feared evil would occur and said: 'The apartment is mine. I shall not permit anyone to be buried in it.' Muḥammad b. al-Ḥanafiyya suggested to his brother al-Ḥusayn: 'If he had given testamentary instruction (*awṣā*) to be buried here, we would so bury him, even facing death. But he has made it conditional saying 'unless you fear evil'. What evil could be greater than what you see?' Al-Ḥasan then was buried next to his mother in the cemetery of Baqī' al-Gharqad.[57] Marwān now joined

54 Lammens, *Mo'âwia*, 149.

55 See Wellhausen, *Das arabische Reich*, 76. The adoption of Ziyād as his brother, in flagrant violation of the law of Islam, was generally considered by religious scholars as one of the most scandalous of Mu'āwiya's acts.

56 The Marwanids deeply resented that 'Uthmān was not buried together with his predecessors next to the Prophet. 'Umar II recounted that the caliph al-Walīd inspected the mosque of Medina while he was governor. At the Prophet's tomb he inquired whether Abū Bakr and 'Umar were buried with him and then asked where the Commander of the Faithful 'Uthmān was buried. The governor suspected that he intended to remove the remains of Abū Bakr and 'Umar, and explained that 'Uthmān had been killed and was buried at a time of revolt. The caliph calmed down (Ibn Shabba, *Ta'rīkh al-Madīna*, 113–14).

57 Balādhurī, *Ansāb*, III, 60–2; Ibn Abi l-Ḥadīd, *Sharḥ*, XVI, 13–14. Since 'Alī had buried Fāṭima secretly at night, there was disagreement about the location of her tomb. According to some reports she was buried in her home which adjoined and was later

those carrying the bier and, when questioned, paid tribute to a man 'whose forbearance (*ḥilm*) weighed mountains.'[58] The Umayyad governor Saʿīd b. al-ʿĀṣ led the funeral prayer.

Muʿāwiya's joy about the death of the Prophet's grandson was slightly dampened by worries about who would now be recognized as the leader of the Banū Hāshim. The thought that the politically experienced and astute ʿAbd Allāh b. al-ʿAbbās might take the place of the passive pacifist bothered him. According to one report, he commented to Ibn al-ʿAbbās when visiting Mekka: 'How amazing that al-Ḥasan drank a Ṭā'ifī honey drink with glue water (*mā' rūma*) and died from it!' Ibn al-ʿAbbās answered: 'If al-Ḥasan perished, your term will not be deferred.' Muʿāwiya: 'And you are today the lord of your people.' Ibn al-ʿAbbās realized that he was getting on dangerous ground and reassured the caliph: 'So long as Abū ʿAbd Allāh [al-Ḥusayn] remains, surely not.'[59] According to other reports, Muʿāwiya offered his condolences to Ibn al-ʿAbbās, adding: 'May God not cause you grief (*yasū'uka*).' Ibn al-ʿAbbās replied: 'God will not cause me grief, Commander of the Faithful, so long as He leaves you alive.' Muʿāwiya ordered a gift of 100,000 dirhams for him.[60] This cousin of the Prophet had learned how to deal with 'the men of this world'. He preferred to continue his religious teaching.

Qays b. Saʿd b. ʿUbāda pledged allegiance to Muʿāwiya in the presence of al-Ḥasan. He asked the latter if he was absolved from his pledge to him, and al-Ḥasan said yes. A chair was pulled up for him, a massive figure, in front of Muʿāwiya's throne. The caliph asked him: 'Will you pledge allegiance, Qays?' He answered yes and placed his hand on his thigh without stretching it towards Muʿāwiya. The caliph bent down from his throne to touch his hand, which Qays would not raise.[61] Qays withdrew to Medina where he lived in retirement and died towards the end of Muʿāwiya's reign in 59/679 or 60/680.[62] Muʿāwiya had obviously no use for the incorruptible 'Jew, son of a Jew' who had governed Egypt for ʿAlī with such wise restraint. A Ziyād, who could be bought to keep his subjects under control by ruthless exploitation of their divisions, as he had done before for ʿAlī, suited him better. Yet Qays escaped the fate of

incorporated into the Prophet's mosque (Ibn Shabba, *Ta'rīkh al-Madīna*, 106–8). According to another report al-Ḥasan had tried to arrange for his burial next to Muḥammad some time before his death. Marwān informed Muʿāwiya, who instructed him to prevent this by all means, just as ʿUthmān's burial next to the Prophet had been prevented (Balādhurī, *Ansāb*, II, 62). Another version asserted that ʿĀ'isha incited the Umayyads to prevent the burial next to the Prophet (Abu l-Faraj, *Maqātil*, 75).

[58] Balādhurī, *Ansāb*, III, 66–7; Abu l-Faraj, *Maqātil*, 75–6.

[59] Balādhurī, *Ansāb*, III, 62–3. [60] *Ibid.*, 63–4; Ibn Abi l-Ḥadīd, *Sharḥ*, XVI, 11.

[61] Balādhurī, *Ansāb*, III, 50; Abu l-Faraj, *Maqātil*, 72.

[62] Ibn Saʿd, *Ṭabaqāt*, VI, 34–5; Ṣafadī, *Wāfī*, XXIV, 284.

his equally incorruptible Medinan compatriot Muḥammad b. Maslama, who fell victim to a Syrian murderer.

Having acquired the sole rule over the world of Islam, Muʿāwiya carried on successfully bribing, cheating, extorting, intimidating and murdering his way through his reign in order to consolidate his grip on money and power and to secure the succession of his unattractive son. Lacking Islamic legitimacy, his regime required the claim of revenge for the wronged caliph as its permanent legitimizing seal. Regular public cursing of ʿAlī in the congregational prayers thus remained a vital institution, which was not abolished until sixty years later by the pious ʿUmar II. During the pilgrimage, it became sunna for the caliphs to vilify ʿAlī on the day of ʿArafa. After the caliphate of ʿUmar II, ʿAbd Allāh b. al-Walīd, grandson of ʿUthmān, publicly reminded the caliph Hishām, as he stood on the pulpit at ʿArafa: 'Commander of the Faithful, this is the day on which the caliphs deemed it desirable to curse Abū Turāb [ʿAlī].' Hishām told him that he had not come there to revile and curse anyone.[63] Marwān, the architect of Umayyad dynastic rule, clearly recognized the importance of the cursing as a tool of government. He told ʿAlī's grandson ʿAlī b. al-Ḥusayn privately: 'No one [among the Islamic nobility] was more temperate (*akaff*) towards our master than your master.' The harmless son of al-Ḥusayn asked him: 'Why do you curse him then from the pulpits?' He answered: 'Our reign would not be sound without that (*lā yastaqīmu l-amru illā bi-dhālik*).'[64]

Particularly useful for Muʿāwiya's purposes was the public cursing of ʿAlī in Kūfa where, he hoped, it would bring out into the open the latent opposition to Umayyad rule, thus facilitating his measures of repression. When he appointed al-Mughīra b. Shuʿba governor of Kūfa in Jumādā 41/September–October 661, he instructed him: 'Never desist from abusing and censuring ʿAlī, from praying for God's mercy and forgiveness for ʿUthmān, from disgracing the followers of ʿAlī, from removing them and refusing to listen to them, and never cease praising the partisans of ʿUthmān, may God be pleased with him, bringing them close to you, and listening to them.'[65] Al-Mughīra punctiliously carried out these instructions, although he, an opportunist more inclined to political intrigue than confrontation, had little sympathy for Muʿāwiya's policy of provoking violence. Ḥujr b. ʿAdī acted as the spokesman for the partisans of ʿAlī. Whenever he heard the governor abusing ʿAlī and praying for ʿUthmān in the mosque, he stood up, quoting Qur'ān IV 135: 'Stand up in justice as witnesses unto God' and gave witness that the one whom they censured

[63] Balādhurī, *Ansāb*, V, 116.
[64] *Ibid.*, II, 184–5; Ibn ʿAsākir, *ʿAlī*, III, 98–9; Ibn Abi l-Ḥadīd, *Sharḥ*, XIII, 100.
[65] Ṭabarī, II, 112.

and blamed was more worthy of excellence and the one whom they vindicated and extolled was more worthy of censure. Al-Mughīra would warn him of the wrath of the ruler but then left him alone.

Al-Mughīra's son Muṭarrif is reported to have narrated how his father vainly attempted to persuade Muʿāwiya to change his policy. He had pleaded that the Commander of the Faithful had now reached an advanced age. If he were to make a show of justice and spread goodness by displaying concern for his Hashimite kin and by strengthening his bonds with them, since he had no longer anything to fear from them, he would gain from that lasting fame and reward. Muʿāwiya had answered: 'Far from it, would it were so. What fame can I hope for that would last? The brother of Taym [Abū Bakr] reigned, acted justly, and did what he did. Yet as soon as he perished, his fame perished, except for someone occasionally saying: Abū Bakr. Then the brother of ʿAdī [ʿUmar] reigned, strove, and put his shoulder to the wheel for ten years, but as soon as he perished, his fame perished, except for someone occasionally mentioning: ʿUmar. Yet Ibn Abī Kabsha [Muḥammad's nickname among his Mekkan enemies][66] is loudly advertised every day five times: "I testify that Muḥammad is the Messenger of God." What work could endure and what fame could last after that? No, by God, there is nothing but burying, burying.' Al-Mughīra, who had before always praised the sharp mind of Muʿāwiya to his son, now confessed to him that he was the most infidel and abominable of men.[67]

Al-Mughīra went on cursing ʿAlī and extolling ʿUthmān until the end of his governorship in the year 50/670 and ignored Ḥujr's protests, which were becoming more and more insolent. His entourage urged him to take action against the troublemaker and to restore his authority, warning him that his lenience would infuriate the caliph. He told them that Ḥujr would certainly be killed by his successor, whom he would treat with the same insolence; he, al-Mughīra, did not wish to lose the other world by shedding the blood of the best men of this city for the sake of securing Muʿāwiya's power in this world.[68]

Al-Mughīra's successor was Ziyād, now recognized as Muʿāwiya's bastard brother, who had already held the governorship of Baṣra for some

[66] The Abū Kabsha, from whom the nickname was derived, was Wajz b. Ghālib of Khuzāʿa, father of Qayla, the paternal grandmother of Muḥammad's mother Āmina bt. Wahb b. ʿAbd Manāf al-Zuhrī. Abū Kabsha was said to have deviated from the religion of his people and to have worshipped the star Sirius (*al-shiʿrā*) (Zubayrī, *Nasab*, 261–2).

[67] Ibn Abi l-Ḥadīd, *Sharḥ*, V, 129–30, quoting the *Muwaffaqiyyāt* of al-Zubayr b. Bakkār. The story is in this form certainly fictitious. As Ibn Abi l-Ḥadīd correctly observes, however, al-Zubayr b. Bakkār cannot be accused of Shiʿite or pro-ʿAlid views. His story rather reflects the image of Muʿāwiya among early Sunnite Muslim historians before al-Ṭabarī who, out of anti-Shiʿite sentiments, covered up some of the more scandalous aspects of his career.

[68] Ṭabarī, II, 113–14.

time. He was, as Muʿāwiya expected, determined to restore law and order and ready to kill in order to make his point. He already had the blood of some Basran Kharijites on his hands. These executions could, however, be justified on the grounds that they had openly declared war on the Community and were a threat to the life of peaceful Muslims. The Kufan partisans of ʿAlī with whom he wanted to deal now were, though loudly denouncing God's Vicegerent on earth, neither engaged in armed rebellion nor endangering the life of any Muslim. Ziyād thus had to provoke an incident to justify bloody repression. The occasion was provided by pebbles thrown at his deputy in the mosque. Ziyād came hurriedly from Baṣra and delivered a sermon threatening Ḥujr with exemplary punishment. Then he sent his police chief to summon him to the governor. Ḥujr was surrounded by his followers who answered for him that he would not respond to the summons. Ziyād next sent some men along with the police chief, but they received the same answer. The governor turned to the tribal chiefs, thundering that they were with him in body only, while their brothers, sons and tribes were with Ḥujr, and threatened to bring down outside forces on them. They hastened to assure him of their loyalty to him and the Commander of the Faithful and of their opposition to Ḥujr, and he charged them with bringing their tribes under control. Then he ordered the police chief with his men to tear out the poles (*ʿumud*) of the market booths and to attack the mutineers with them until they surrendered Ḥujr. Ḥujr's supporters were unarmed except for Abu l-ʿAmarraṭa and no one was killed, although ʿAmr b. al-Ḥamiq was hit over the head with a pole and fell. Abu l-ʿAmarraṭa, himself hit with a pole, struck Yazīd b. Ṭarīf with his sword, bringing him to the ground.[69]

Ḥujr b. ʿAdī escaped and for a while found shelter moving from one tribal quarter to another. Then he surrendered voluntarily after he had obtained a guarantee of safety from Ziyād with the condition that he would send him to Muʿāwiya for judgment. When he appeared before the governor, Ziyād told him that he could not expect pardon after God had placed him in his power. He imprisoned him and swore that he would have killed him immediately were it not for his guarantee.[70] Then he had Abū Mūsā al-Ashʿarī's son Abū Burda, chief of one of the four quarters of Kūfa, draw up a letter of accusation in which he testified: 'Ḥujr b. ʿAdī has renounced obedience, departed from the Community, cursed the caliph, has incited to war and rebellion, gathered the masses to himself summoning them to break their oaths of allegiance and to overthrow the

[69] *Ibid.*, 114–20.
[70] *Ibid.*, 126–7. According to ʿAwāna, Ziyād swore: 'By God, I shall be most eager to cut the thread of his neck.'

Commander of the Faithful Muʿāwiya. He has committed a manifest act of infidelity towards God (*kafara bi llāhi kafratan ṣalʿāʾ*).' The harmless mutiny artificially provoked by the governor was thus presented as a dangerous armed rebellion and incitement to civil war and the denunciation of the caliph as apostasy from Islam, the only offence apart from murder and adultery for which the law allowed the death penalty.

The signature of the four government-appointed heads of quarters was not sufficient in the governor's eyes. He summoned the *ashrāf*, Qurayshites and tribal chiefs, to do their duty and thus gathered seventy signatures. The witness of al-Sarī b. Waqqāṣ al-Ḥārithī was written down although he was absent in his tax district. Shurayḥ b. Hāniʾ al-Ḥārithī, who did not testify, learned that his testimony had been recorded. He came forward denying it and denouncing the forgery. The *qāḍī* Shurayḥ b. al-Ḥārith, whose testimony would evidently have been most useful for the governor, was asked by him about Ḥujr but testified that the accused had been most assiduously fasting and praying. Ziyād added his name anyway among the witnesses.[71] The *qāḍī* now wrote to Muʿāwiya that his testimony recorded by Ziyād was false and that he testified that Ḥujr was of those who perform the prayer, give alms, frequent the pilgrimage and *ʿumra*, order what is proper and prohibit what is reprehensible, whose blood and property were inviolable. The caliph commented to Ziyād's two messengers, who had conveyed the indictment with a triumphant covering letter from the governor: 'This one, it seems to me, has removed himself from your testimony.'[72] Then he went back to business.

Ḥujr wrote to him from prison assuring him that he and his companions stood by their pledge of allegiance to him and that only their enemies had testified against them. The caliph ruled that the testimony of Ziyād – whose fraudulence had just been brought home to him – was more truthful. In the end, he released six of the fourteen accused because their Syrian kinsmen asked him for their pardon. He refused the request of Mālik b. Hubayra al-Sakūnī of Kinda for the life of Ḥujr. The eight men were offered pardon if they would declare their dissociation from ʿAlī and curse him; they refused, and six were executed. The remaining two now asked the executioners to send them to the Commander of the Faithful, promising to say about ʿAlī whatever the caliph said. Led before

[71] Wellhausen, trying to picture Ziyād as the tough but correct governor who merely did 'was seines Amtes war' (*Die religiös-politischen Oppositionsparteien im alten Islam* (Berlin, 1901), 25, 60), summarizes these reports, stating (59) that some of the witnesses disavowed their signatures after at first eagerly giving them. In a footnote he concedes, without mentioning Ziyād, that the names of the witnesses, or at least some of them, were not written by these. This is a distinct misrepresentation of his source, Abū Mikhnaf, who rather portrays Ziyād as an unscrupulous and malicious forger.

[72] Ṭabarī, I, 137.

Mu'āwiya, Karīm b. 'Afīf al-Khath'amī appealed to him: 'Fear God, Mu'āwiya, you will be transferred from this passing abode to the other, permanent abode and will then be asked what you desired by killing us and why you shed our blood.' Mu'āwiya: 'What do you say about 'Alī?' He answered: 'I say about him what you say: I dissociate from the religion of 'Alī with which he professed obedience to God.' Mu'āwiya did not want to keep his commitment, but now Shamir b. 'Abd Allāh of the Banū Quḥāfa (of Khath'am) asked him for the life of his kinsman. Mu'āwiya granted it to him, but insisted on keeping him in prison for a month. Every other day he sent a messenger to tell him that he held Iraq too precious to allow someone like him to stay there. Shamir b. 'Abd Allāh, however, kept pressing him, and Mu'āwiya released the prisoner on condition that he would not enter Kūfa during his reign. Karīm chose to live in Mossul, ever declaring that, should Mu'āwiya die, he would return to the city. He died a month before Mu'āwiya.

When the other surviving convict, 'Abd al-Raḥmān b. Ḥassān al-'Anazī, was led before the Commander of the Faithful, Mu'āwiya asked him: 'Now, brother of Rabī'a, what do you say about 'Alī?' He replied: 'Leave me and do not ask me, for that is better for you.' Mu'āwiya: 'By God, I shall not leave you until you tell me about him.' He said: 'I witness that he was of those who make mention of God often, who command what is right, who act with justice, and forgive the people.' Mu'āwiya: 'What do you say about 'Uthmān?' He answered: 'He was the first one to open the gate of oppression and bolted the doors of the right.' Mu'āwiya: 'You have killed yourself!' 'Abd al-Raḥmān: 'Rather I have killed you – yet there are no Rabī'a in this valley.' He meant that there were no Rabī'a among the Syrians who could ask for his life or avenge his blood. The Vicegerent of God now sent him to Ziyād and wrote to the governor: 'This 'Anazī is the worst one you have sent me . . . Kill him in the worst fashion.' Ziyād sent him to Quss al-Nāẓif, where he was buried alive.[73]

It was plain murder barely disguised under an absurd charge of apostasy from Islam. Abū Bakr had set a precedent in the War of the Apostasy, but he had rendered licit war on tribes refusing to recognize his succession to the Prophet and to pay the alms-tax to him, not judicial murder of men who recognized the caliph while denouncing his actions. Under the existing law and practice mutineers and rebels not guilty of

[73] *Ibid.*, II, 141–3. Wellhausen summed up the latter part of Abū Mikhnaf's report as follows: Mu'āwiya freed six of the accused on the intercession of his loyal supporters, but he refused the intercession of Mālik b. Hubayra for Ḥujr. He even offered him and the other prisoners pardon if they dissociated from 'Alī. Two of them did so and saved their lives, even though they withdrew their dissociation afterwards. The other six were executed. On this basis Wellhausen judged that Mu'āwiya dealt mildly with the accused (*Oppositionsparteien*, 58–9).

murder could be imprisoned and deported, their houses could be destroyed, but they could not be killed. When Muʿāwiya had first consulted his Syrian advisers on what to do with the accused, Yazīd b. Asad al-Bajalī thus had suggested dispersing them in the towns of Syria where their bullies (*ṭawāghīt*) would take care of them for him.[74] For Muʿāwiya, however, the principle that the ruler must have authority to kill and pardon his subjects at his own discretion without being subject to the *lex talionis* was a vital tool of government. He had been waiting long for an occasion to establish it. Roman state ideology and tyranny triumphed thus over Arab tribal law and Islam.

The shock was predictably profound. Muʿāwiya found it again convenient to resort to the ruler's privilege of putting the blame on his underlings and subjects. Even ʿĀ'isha who, after the disastrous miscarriage of her previous public ventures generally kept aloof of political involvement, felt that she could not remain silent in spite of her aversion to ʿAlī and his partisans. She is said to have sent the noble Makhzumite ʿAbd al-Raḥmān b. al-Ḥārith b. Hishām to Muʿāwiya to intercede for Ḥujr and his companions, but he arrived only after the execution. He asked the Umayyad what had become of the forbearance (*ḥilm*) of Abū Sufyān. Muʿāwiya told him that it had departed from him ever since the forbearing men of his people such as ʿAbd al-Raḥmān shunned him, and the son of Sumayya (Ziyād) had induced him to act. According to another report Muʿāwiya paid ʿĀ'isha a visit during the pilgrimage. ʿĀ'isha asked him: 'Do you feel secure that I am not sheltering someone to kill you?' He answered: 'I have entered a house of safety.' ʿĀ'isha: 'Don't you fear God for the murder of Ḥujr and his companions?' Muʿāwiya: 'It is not I who murdered him. Those who testified against him have killed him.'[75] The Basran ʿUthmanid al-Ḥasan al-Baṣrī counted the killing of Ḥujr as one of the four pernicious crimes (*mūbiqa*) committed by Muʿāwiya.[76]

Muʿāwiya's murders were not confined, however, to opponents of his despotic regime. Out of jealousy, he also poisoned one of his own outstanding military leaders, ʿAbd al-Raḥmān b. Khālid b. al-Walīd. ʿAbd al-Raḥmān had participated with his father, who was widely recognized as the real conqueror of Syria, in the battle on the Yarmūk. Muʿāwiya appointed him governor of Ḥimṣ, presumably as a Qurayshite counter-balance to the powerful Himyarite presence there. He led several of the Syrian summer campaigns against the Byzantines and was prominent in Muʿāwiya's war against ʿAlī at Ṣiffīn and elsewhere. His military excellence and popularity with the northern Syrian army worried Muʿāwiya, however, and on one occasion he abruptly dismissed

[74] Ṭabarī, II, 137. [75] *Ibid.*, 145. [76] *Ibid.*, 146.

him as commander. This provoked an exchange in which ʿAbd al-Raḥmān, a proud Makhzumite, suggested that had they been in Mekka, Muʿāwiya would not have dared to treat him in this high-handed manner.[77]

As Muʿāwiya prepared to pave the way for the succession of his son Yazīd, he is said to have addressed the Syrian leaders with the remark that the Commander of the Faithful was getting old and wished to appoint a successor over them. When he asked them whom they would consider suitable, they named ʿAbd al-Raḥmān b. Khālid.[78] The caliph fell silent, and ʿAbd al-Raḥmān's fate was sealed. After he returned from the regular summer campaign to Anatolia in 46/666, one of his slaves served him a poisoned drink prepared by Muʿāwiya's Christian physician Ibn Uthāl at the instigation of the caliph. Having thus easily disposed of the potential rival,[79] Muʿāwiya commented some time later to his court poet Kaʿb b. Juʿayl who had glorified ʿAbd al-Raḥmān in numerous panegyrics: 'Poets know no loyalty. ʿAbd al-Raḥmān was a friend to you, but as soon as he died you forgot him.' Kaʿb denied this and quoted some lines which he had said after ʿAbd al-Raḥmān's death. In them he had praised the Sword of Islam, ʿAbd al-Raḥmān's father, as the conqueror of Damascus, Baʿlabakk and Ḥimṣ and as the one who had established Muʿāwiya b. Ḥarb there.[80] Muʿāwiya must have felt pleased with his own achievement.

ʿAbd al-Raḥmān's nephew Khālid b. al-Muhājir b. Khālid learned of the murder in Mekka where he was residing. His father, al-Muhājir, had fought at Ṣiffīn on the side of ʿAlī against Muʿāwiya and his own brother ʿAbd al-Raḥmān; Khālid thus had a poor opinion of his murdered uncle. After a time, however, ʿUrwa b. al-Zubayr stirred him into seeking revenge against the Christian poison-mixer. He took his client Nāfiʿ, a tough man, along to Damascus where they ambushed and killed Ibn Uthāl as he left Muʿāwiya's palace. The caliph immediately guessed that Khālid b. al-Muhājir was behind the deed. When Khālid was apprehended and led before him, he accused him of having killed his physician. Khālid answered: 'I killed the one ordered, the one who ordered remains.' Muʿāwiya: 'God's curse upon you. By God, if he had only once pronounced the confession of faith, I would kill you for him.' Since Ibn Uthāl was a Christian, the *lex talionis* did not apply. Later Muʿāwiya

[77] Balādhurī, *Ansāb*, 4/1, 104.

[78] Lammens misrepresented Muʿāwiya's loaded question as a debate among his followers and saw in it evidence for some form of parliamentary organization in which the Syrian Arabs under his reign discussed their common interests (*Moʿâwia*, 6–7).

[79] Like his poisoning of al-Ashtar, Muʿāwiya's sudden murder of ʿAbd al-Raḥmān b. Khālid gave rise to a proverbial saying. According to Abū ʿUbayd al-Qāsim b. Sallām, Muʿāwiya observed to one of his slave girls: 'Slay instantly and be rid of whom you loathe (*aqʿiṣ ʿanka man takrah*)' (Ibn Abī Uṣaybiʿa, *ʿUyūn*, I, 118). The proverb is missing in the edited version of Abū ʿUbayd's *Kitāb al-Amthāl* (ed. ʿAbd al-Majīd ʿĀbidīn and Iḥsān ʿAbbās (Khartoum, 1958)).

[80] Zubayrī, *Nasab*, 325.

ordered a hundred lashes for Nāfiʿ while merely imprisoning Khālid. He imposed blood money of 12,000 dirhams on the Banū Makhzūm.[81] They retaliated for the vile murder of their battle hero, the son of the Sword of Islam, by solidly backing the counter-caliph ʿAbd Allāh b. al-Zubayr against Muʿāwiya's son.[82]

While Muʿāwiya thus appeared to be successfully scheming for the future reign of the Sufyanid house, there remained a weak link in his Machiavellian armour. For so long as the legitimacy of the dynasty was founded on succession to the rights of the wronged caliph, it was difficult to conceal that there were others with a better title to rule than ʿUthmān's remote kinsman whom he had always kept at some distance. The Sufyanid had successfully tamed and satisfied ʿUthmān's poet brother al-Walīd b. ʿUqba, whose unrestrained demands for vendetta could at an early stage have easily spoiled his stratagems. He had, so he trusted, neutralized the murdered caliph's unambitious eldest son ʿAmr by marrying his daughter Ramla to him. ʿUthmān's cousin Marwān b. al-Ḥakam, the architect of the Umayyad kingdom, was a different matter. Muʿāwiya vainly hoped to control his aspirations by appointing him governor of Medina. Marwān never made any secret of his determination to restore the Banū Abi l-ʿĀṣī to their rightful heritage in place of the Sufyanids. He really meant himself, as was plain from the fact that he himself had sacrificed his cousin ʿUthmān when it became apparent that otherwise he, Marwān, would have to be sacrificed. Muʿāwiya could not be in doubt that the rules of sound statecraft would have required him to do away with Marwān in the interest of the safety of the Sufyanid reign.

81 *Aghānī*, XV, 13. According to this account, Muʿāwiya put half of the amount in the public treasury and pocketed the other half personally. This remained Umayyad practice with respect to blood-money for non-Muslims under treaty protection until ʿUmar II abolished the ruler's taking a share for himself.

82 Lammens argued against any involvement of either Muʿāwiya or Ibn Uthāl in the murder of ʿAbd al-Raḥmān (*Moʿâwia*, 3–14). In order to defend Muʿāwiya's record of tolerance towards his Christian subjects, he tried to identify the physician Ibn Uthāl with the Christian bishop of Ḥimṣ, who according to Theophanes was burned to death under Muʿāwiya, and accepted from al-Ṭabarī's account, which he otherwise rejected, the detail that Muʿāwiya appointed Ibn Uthāl tax collector of Ḥimṣ. The Makhzumite murderer of Ibn Uthāl, according to Lammens' theory, merely took advantage of the anti-Christian sentiment of the Muslim masses in order to curry favour with them and to cause trouble for the tolerant Muʿāwiya. Lammens conceded that Muʿāwiya had good reason for concern about the popularity of ʿAbd al-Raḥmān, which could have prompted him 'to forestall eventualities so menacing for the future of his dynasty'. He nevertheless rejected the two reports about Muʿāwiya's responsibility for the murder as containing contradictory details. The basic reliability of the report about Khālid b. al-Muhājir, however, is not invalidated by al-Ṭabarī's report which mistakenly identifies ʿAbd al-Raḥmān's son Khālid as the avenger of his father. Khālid b. al-Muhājir's part is confirmed by al-Zubayrī (*Nasab*, 327). That Khālid would have come from Mekka to Syria to murder Ibn Uthāl merely in order to please the anti-Christian Muslims of Ḥimṣ seems hardly plausible.

Yet he was entirely helpless in dealing with this kinsman, whose evil genius and sheer calculated malice inspired him with a mixture of fascination, admiration and fear.

Marwān first tried to incite ʿAmr b. ʿUthmān to seek the reign. When ʿAmr complained of an illness, Marwān visited him regularly and stayed on while all other visitors left. ʿAmr's wife Ramla became suspicious and listened in on their conversation through a hole which she had pierced in the wall. She heard Marwān say: 'These people [meaning the Banū Ḥarb b. Umayya] have seized the caliphate only in the name of your father. What prevents you from rising to claim your right? Surely we have more men than they.' Then he enumerated the male descendants of Abu l-ʿĀṣī, matching each one against a descendant of Ḥarb. There were several more of the former. Ramla used the occasion of her husband's pilgrimage to visit her father in Syria and inform him. She said: 'He went on enumerating the surplus of men of Abu l-ʿĀṣī over the Banū Ḥarb, even counting my two sons ʿUthmān and Khālid from ʿAmr. I wished they had died.' Muʿāwiya wrote to Marwān with an appropriate quotation of poetry, adding: 'I testify, Marwān, that I have heard the Messenger of God say: "When the children of al-Ḥakam reach thirty men, they shall appropriate the money of God in turns, employ the religion of God for deceit, and take the worshippers of God as slaves."' Marwān answered with delight: 'Muʿāwiya, truly I am father of ten, brother of ten, and paternal uncle of ten.'[83]

Marwān cared less about the female offspring of Abu l-ʿĀṣī. At the suggestion of Muʿāwiya, he readily got rid of his niece, a daughter of his brother Yaḥyā. He invited her for a visit and had a well dug and covered over with mats. She fell into it on her way, and the well became her grave. She and another woman, Umm Saʿīd al-Aslamiyya, had spent much time in the disreputable company of the bisexual singer al-Dalāl and are described as the most shameless of women. Particularly disgraceful was that they rode out together on horses and raced each other so that their anklets showed.[84] When it came to public morality, the murderer of Ṭalḥa wanted to be seen as a good Muslim.

Marwān was unable to stir ʿAmr into claiming his title to the Umayyad caliphate. His arguments were more successful with ʿAmr's half-brother Saʿīd b. ʿUthmān. When Muʿāwiya in the year 56/676 imposed the pledge of allegiance for his son Yazīd, the Medinan Umayyads Marwān, Saʿīd b. al-ʿĀṣ and ʿAbd Allāh b. ʿĀmir complied reluctantly while expressing

[83] Zubayrī, *Nasab*, 109–10; Balādhurī, *Ansāb*, 4/1, 46, 58. The hadith is quoted by Ibn Ḥanbal (*Musnad*, III, 80) with Abū Saʿīd al-Khudrī as the first transmitter. As a good Sunnite, Ibn Ḥanbal suppressed the name of al-Ḥakam and substituted *Abī Fulān* (for Abi l-ʿĀṣī?). [84] *Aghānī*, IV, 64.

their disapproval.[85] The Anṣār of Medina, too, had no reason to be pleased with the crown prince, since he had encouraged the poet al-Akhṭal to lampoon them. Soon a ditty in *urjūza* form made its rounds on the tongues of boys, slaves and women: 'By God, Yazīd'll not get it, before the blade'll get his head. The amir after him will be Saʿīd.' Marwān, Muʿāwiya's governor, presumably was not eager to stop the seditious rhymes from circulating. The caliph questioned Saʿīd b. ʿUthmān about them when he visited him in Damascus for the purpose of seeking high office.[86] Saʿīd proudly answered: 'What is there to be disapproved of in that? Surely, my father is more excellent than Yazīd's father, my mother is more excellent than his mother, and I am better than he. We have put you in office and have not dismissed you. We have honoured our bonds of kinship with you and have not cut them. Thus our reign has come into your hands, yet you have debarred us from it altogether.' Muʿāwiya could not fail to perceive Marwān's prompting. He told him: 'You have said the truth in stating that your father is better than I and that your mother is better than his, for your mother is of Quraysh,[87] and his mother is a woman of Kalb. Yet sufficient it is for a woman to be of their decent women. As for your statement that you are better than he, by God, it would not please me to have a rope strung between me and Iraq with the likes of you.' Then he sent Saʿīd to ʿUbayd Allāh b. Ziyād[88] in Baṣra, ordering the latter to appoint the boastful rival of his son commander of the war in Khurāsān. Muʿāwiya may have hoped that he would be killed there. When Saʿīd instead conquered Samarqand, he deposed him in fear that he would claim the caliphate. Saʿīd returned to Medina with some fifty sons of Soghdian princes and chiefs who had been surrendered to him as hostages. He mistreated them by taking away their precious clothes, which he gave to his slaves, then dressing them in wool and forcing them to do hard labour. They conspired to kill him in a walled garden where they were working with shovels; then they killed themselves. Marwān came too late to rescue his nephew, as they had locked the entrance to the garden.[89] The caliph had one descendant of Abu l-ʿĀṣī less to worry about.

When Muʿāwiya deposed Marwān from the governorship of Medina to appoint Saʿīd b. al-ʿĀṣ, probably in 49/669, Marwān decided it was time

[85] *Ibid.*, XVIII, 71.
[86] According to al-Ṭabarī's account (al-Madāʾinī), Saʿīd asked Muʿāwiya for the governorship of Khurāsān (Ṭabarī, II, 177). From al-Balādhurī's report it would appear that he rather expected a governorship in Iraq.
[87] Saʿīd's mother was the Makhzumite Fāṭima bt al-Walīd. On this basis Saʿīd could also claim to be more noble than his elder brother ʿAmr whose mother was Azdite.
[88] The account (Balādhurī, *Ansāb*, V, 118) anachronistically names Ziyād. He had died three years before. [89] *Ibid.*, 117, 119; Ṭabarī, II, 179.

to teach his overbearing kinsman a lesson and set out, uninvited, for Damascus. His brother ʿAbd al-Raḥmān, who was in Damascus, advised him to wait until he, ʿAbd al-Raḥmān, could test the atmosphere. If Muʿāwiya had dismissed him in anger, he should visit him alone; if not, he might visit him in company. ʿAbd al-Raḥmān aroused the caliph's displeasure first by his boastful entry and then by uncautiously alluding to the line in which the pro-ʿAlid poet al-Najāshī had lampooned Muʿāwiya for his headlong flight at Ṣiffīn. Muʿāwiya paid him back by alluding to ʿAbd al-Raḥmān's nightly escapade of scaling the wall to pay a visit to Marwān's wife, ʿUthmān's daughter Umm Abān. Thus put to shame, ʿAbd al-Raḥmān inquired meekly: 'Commander of the Faithful, what has induced you to depose your cousin? Is it for an offence which necessitated indignation, or out of an opinion which you deemed suitable, or for a design through which you seek the best interest?' Muʿāwiya affirmed it was the latter. ʿAbd al-Raḥmān commented: 'There is nothing wrong with that,' and left.

When he informed his brother, Marwān flew into a rage and scolded him for being a weakling. 'Do you make allusions to the man which anger him, and when he takes revenge, you flinch from him?' Then he donned his robe of honour, mounted his horse, and girded on his sword – he knew how to impress his unwarlike kinsman – and made his entrance to Muʿāwiya. When the caliph saw him and recognized the anger in his face, he addressed him obligingly: 'Welcome, Abū ʿAbd al-Malik, you come to visit us just as we were longing for you.' Marwān: 'No, by God, I am not visiting you for that reason. I have never come to you but to find you disrespectful and aloof. By God, you do not treat us with justice and do not requite us properly. The early merit (*sābiqa*) among the Banū ʿAbd Shams belonged to the family of Abu l-ʿĀṣī.' Marwān realized that it was the proper occasion to mention his grandfather rather than his father who had been outlawed by the Prophet. 'The marriage tie with the Messenger of God belonged to them, the caliphate was among them. They maintained their bonds with you, Banū Ḥarb, and honoured you, set you up in high office and did not depose you or prefer others above you. Then, when you were established in office and the reign devolved on you, you displayed nothing but preference for others, evil treatment of us, and vicious cutting of kinship ties. But just you wait, the sons of al-Ḥakam and his sons' sons have already reached twenty and some, and before long they will have reached forty. At that time a man will come to know where he stands in relation to them, for they will lie in wait to requite good and evil.'

Muʿāwiya was not yet quite softened up and started arguing: 'I have deposed you for three matters, any one of which would have made your dismissal inevitable. The first one is that I gave you power over ʿAbd Allāh b.ʿĀmir when there was between you [the enmity] which there is, yet you were unable to get satisfaction from him.[90] The second one is your loathing of the affair of Ziyād, and the third one is that my daughter Ramla asked for your help against her husband ʿAmr, but you would not assist her.' Marwān answered him: 'As for Ibn ʿĀmir, I do not ask for assistance in my own jurisdiction, but when the footing is equal, he knows where he stands.[91] As for my loathing the affair of Ziyād, the rest of the Banū Umayya loathed it, but then God placed much good in that which we hated [Qur'ān IV 19]. As for Ramla's request for help against ʿAmr, by God, a year and more may go by while the daughter of ʿUthmān is staying with me, yet I would not lift a dress of hers.' He was hinting that the daughter of the Commander of the Faithful had merely been seeking his assistance to obtain sexual gratification from her husband.

Muʿāwiya lost his temper: 'You son of a gecko, you are not yet there.' Marwān answered coldly: 'That is so now. But, by God, I am father of ten, brother of ten, and uncle of ten, and my sons are close to completing the number. When they reach it, you shall know where you stand in relation to me.' Muʿāwiya was now reduced to quoting poetry by which he hinted at Marwān being a weak bird with numerous chicks and himself being a hawk with few offspring. By the time Marwān ended his discourse, the Commander of the Faithful was like clay in his hand and submissive. He bargained: 'You shall be content; I return you to your office.' Jumping up, Marwān easily trumped his mercenary deck: 'Not at

[90] In the version of al-Balādhurī this point reads: 'You came to me when ʿAbd Allāh b. ʿĀmir was in my hands and he had owned up that he owed me one million dirhams, but you snatched him away from me' (*Ansāb*, 4/1, 65). Muʿāwiya evidently wanted to fleece ʿAbd Allāh b. ʿĀmir after his dismissal from the governorship of Baṣra in 44/664. According to the account of al-Ṭabarī (II, 69) the caliph demanded his property in ʿArafa and his houses in Mekka. He also wanted to stir up enmity among his Umayyad kin, and apparently vainly tried to get Marwān to put pressure on Ibn ʿĀmir. Muʿāwiya's crude policy of *divide et impera* among his kinsmen seems to have had the effect of uniting them against him. Later he attempted to stir up trouble between Saʿīd b. al-ʿĀṣ and Marwān who were at odds because Saʿīd had earlier refused to back Marwān's war on ʿAlī. Muʿāwiya ordered Saʿīd b. al-ʿĀṣ, while he was governor of Medina, to demolish the house of Marwān or, according to al-Wāqidī's account, to confiscate his property and turn his estates, including Fadak, into domanial land (*ṣāfiya*). Saʿīd failed to carry out the order even when Muʿāwiya repeated it. Then Muʿāwiya reappointed Marwān governor and ordered him to demolish the house of Saʿīd. Marwān was prepared to carry out his instructions, but when Saʿīd showed him Muʿāwiya's earlier letters he refrained and admitted that Saʿid had acted more honourably than he. Saʿīd, according to al-Wāqidī, sent Muʿāwiya a courteous note putting him to shame for trying to incite hatred between his kinsmen (Ṭabarī, II, 164–5; Balādhurī, *Ansāb*, 4/1, 33).

[91] In the account of al-Balādhurī, Marwān's answer is quoted thus: 'As for Ibn ʿĀmir, his kinship to me and to you is equal, and I have no better right over him than you. If you would abandon voluntarily his debt to you, [it would be praiseworthy]. But if not, I shall guarantee for what he has owned up that he owed you' (*Ansāb*, 4/1, 65).

all, by God and your life, you shall not see me return to it ever,' and walked out.[92]

'Abd al-Raḥmān b. Sīḥān b. Arṭāh al-Muḥāribī was a confederate of the Banū Ḥarb living in Medina, a gifted poet and an excellent entertainer, full of unusual stories and anecdotes about the Arabs, their battle-days and their poetry. His panegyrics for his masters made him a valuable prop for the regime. His weak spot was the common vice of poets – wine, which he copiously consumed in the company of members of the ruling class, especially Umayyads. Saʿīd b. al-'Āṣ during his governorship of Medina questioned him about a line of poetry in which he described himself as swaying from intoxication. Ibn Sīḥān protested his innocence of either drinking or describing wine in his poetry and pointedly quoted a piece in which he boasted of his confederation with Ḥarb which led him to the peaks and summits of nobility. As he haughtily walked out, Saʿīd's son 'Amr remarked to his father: 'If you ordered this dog to be beaten two hundred lashes, it would be the best for him.' Saʿīd countered: 'My dear son, shall I beat him when he is a confederate of Ḥarb b. Umayya and Mu'āwiya is caliph in Syria? He would hardly be pleased about it.' When Mu'āwiya met Saʿīd during his pilgrimage in Minā, he told him: 'Ah Saʿīd, your idiot ordered you to beat my confederate two hundred lashes? By God, if you gave him one lash, I would give you two.' Saʿīd: 'And why that? Have you not lashed your confederate 'Amr b. Jabala?' Mu'āwiya: 'He is my flesh which I eat and do not give to eat.'[93]

Mu'āwiya's unguarded and uncalled-for bragging gave Marwān a chance to teach him another lesson with a brilliant piece of mischief. It was many years later, after Mu'āwiya, in Dhu l-Qa'da 58/September–October 678,[94] had once again deposed Marwān and appointed his own nephew al-Walīd b. 'Utba b. Abī Sufyān governor of Medina. The new governor, fond of a good drink in his hours of privacy, discovered an agreeable boon companion in 'Abd al-Raḥmān b. Sīḥān and regularly sent for him to join his carousing. Abu l-Zinād, a Medinan counted among the most reliable early traditionists,[95] recounted the incident. Ibn

[92] *Aghānī*, XII, 72–3. The account goes back to al-Haytham b. 'Adī on the authority of Ṣāliḥ b. Ḥassān (al-Naḍrī?) (Ibn Ḥajar, *Tahdhīb*, IV, 384–5). A shorter, less colourful version is presented by al-Balādhurī (*Ansāb*, 4/1, 65–6) quoting al-Madā'inī on the authority of Mu'āwiya's great-grandson Ḥarb b. Khālid b. Yazīd. In this version Mu'āwiya is described in the end as commending his daughter when she confessed that she wished her sons were 'in the sea' and suggesting that the Sufyanids were too badly afflicted with the opposition of Marwān for her to mend it by trying to behave like a man. The anecdote reflects Sufyanid resentment at being dislodged from the throne by the Marwanids.

[93] *Aghānī*, II, 87–8; Balādhurī, *Ansāb*, 4/1, 97–8, 133–4.

[94] Ṭabarī, II, 181.

[95] Abu l-Zinād 'Abd Allāh b. Dhakwān (d. 130/747-8) was a client of one of the daughters of Shayba b. Rabī'a b. 'Abd Shams or of the family of 'Uthmān. His father was said to have been a brother of Abū Lu'lu'a, the assassin of 'Umar (Ibn Ḥajar, *Tahdhīb*, V, 203–4).

Sīḥān had some time in the past offended Marwān by insults, but more recently had eulogized him and received his obligatory reward. He did not expect that the treacherous man might still want to harm him; Marwān had in fact his eyes on bigger prey than the harmless poet. He hid his men in ambush for him in the mosque at night. When Ibn Sīḥān came out at dawn, thoroughly tipsy, from the adjoining governor's palace through the ruler's stall (*maqṣūra*) of the mosque, Marwān and his assistants jumped on him. The proper witnesses were at hand, Muḥammad b. ʿAmr and ʿAbd Allāh b. Ḥanẓala, two pious Qur'ān readers who used to pass their nights with vigils in the mosque. The unsuspecting victim was asked to recite the first Sūra of the Qurʾān but was too drunk to comply. He was then turned over to the chief of police,[96] who imprisoned him. When the governor awoke, he learned the news, which had spread through the town like wildfire. He realized that Marwān was after him and that he would not have bothered Ibn Sīḥān if he had departed drunk from anyone else. He decided that nothing would save him from potential disgrace in the eyes of the Medinans except inflicting the legal flogging on the offender. The chief of police carried out his order to flog him, and then the governor released him.

Ibn Sīḥān stayed at home for some time, ashamed to face the people. The Makhzumite ʿAbd al-Raḥmān b. al-Ḥārith b. Hishām, with whom he used to sit, came to visit him together with his sons. He brought some fine clothes along for him and proposed that he go out and show himself in the mosque as if nothing had happened. Then he should go to the Commander of the Faithful, who would reward him and order his legal punishment to be rescinded. In the mosque he reclined together with the highly respected Makhzumite against a pillar, and some of the people now said: 'He was not beaten,' while others insisted: 'I have seen him being beaten,' or: 'He has been punished with lashes.' He remained a few days and then travelled to the caliph in Damascus. First he visited the crown prince Yazīd and drank with him. Yazīd talked to his father about him. He was summoned to the caliph and reported his story and what Marwān had done to him. Muʿāwiya commented: 'May God disfigure al-Walīd, how feeble-minded he is. Is he not ashamed to beat you for his own drinking? As for Marwān, I did not think he would go to such lengths of meanness towards you in spite of your good opinion and friendship towards him. He wanted to lower al-Walīd in my esteem but he has not succeeded. Rather he has put himself in a rank we used to deem beneath him; he has become a policeman.' Then he dictated to his secretary a letter to al-Walīd, reprimanding him for meting out a punishment to Ibn Sīḥān which had merely acquainted the people of Medina with his own

96 Literally his chief of police (*Aghānī*, II, 82). Perhaps Marwān's former chief of police is meant.

consumption of forbidden drink. He ordered him to annul his punishment, to lead him around in the mosque and to inform the people that his chief of police had transgressed and wronged him and that the Commander of the Faithful had revoked his punishment. Had not Ibn Sīḥān recited the following poetry? And Muʿāwiya quoted at length a panegyric in praise of ʿAbd Shams. Al-Walīd was to present Ibn Sīḥān with 400 sheep and 30 milk camels of the kind raised in al-Sayyāla. Muʿāwiya personally gave the wronged poet 500 dinars, and Yazīd added 200. The governor faithfully carried out his instructions, but when he invited the poet to join him for a party, he received the reply: 'By God, I shall never taste a drink with you again.' Muʿāwiya also wrote to Marwān, reproaching him for what he had done to Ibn Sīḥān and for his ulterior motives.[97]

Marwān presumably did not even bother to answer. Abu l-Zinād implied in his account that he, Marwān, wanted to get at the governor, al-Walīd, and that Muʿāwiya, seeing through his game, thwarted him by merely reprimanding his nephew. In reality Marwān wanted to get at the caliph himself and at the Sufyanid regime. He achieved exactly what he intended. Not only did he make Muʿāwiya swallow his boast that only he was allowed to touch his poet confederate, he also exposed the Commander of the Faithful to the Medinan public as the protector of his drunkard family members and clients against the obligatory punishment imposed by the religious law. The annulment of Ibn Sīḥān's penalty by the caliph did not thwart Marwān, but rather disgraced a corrupt regime which charged an obedient chief of police with transgression and set aside the unimpeachable testimony of two highly respected Qur'ān readers.

Muʿāwiya's successor Yazīd was soon to reap the fruits. He was never able to shake off the image of a wine-bibber unworthy of his office in Medina. The open rebellion of the Medinans, not so much in favour of ʿAbd Allāh b. al-Zubayr as against Yazīd, opened the second, critical phase of the second civil war. Marwān insidiously encouraged Ibn al-Zubayr to claim the caliphate against his Umayyad kinsman. He knew what he was doing. For his designs the paramount task was to overthrow the Sufyanid regime in Syria. He was sure that he would then be able to cope with Ibn al-Zubayr in Mekka. Thus he went on ostensibly backing the counter-caliph until the Syrians were ready to drop the Sufyanids. The scenario he had set for himself long ago in murdering Ṭalḥa now was put on stage. As his propagandists presented him as the first avenger of the wronged caliph, the Syrians realized that they had found their man. He need not reveal to them that his careful planning of scenarios went

[97] *Aghānī*, II, 82–3; Balādhurī, *Ansāb*, 4/1, 135–6. The other reports, in which Marwān himself is described as ordering the beating of Ibn Sīḥān and then being forced by Muʿāwiya to annul the punishment (*Aghānī*, II, 81–2, 83–4), are secondary and unreliable.

back further to when he threw his elderly cousin to the wolves in the interest of the Umayyad caliphate, which now finally became his caliphate. That had been truly high politics, to be appreciated only by the most refined connoisseurs of the art. The Syrians, crude soldiery that they were, might not have properly understood it.

To the distant observer Marwān's takeover of the throne could appear miraculous. Wellhausen quotes the anonymous author of the *Continuatio Byzantia Arabica A. DCCXLI*: 'Marvan (insidiose ab Almidina pulsus) post modica temporis intervalla aliquantis de exercitu consentientibus deo connivente provehitur ad regnum.'[98] To the insider with a keen mind there was nothing to marvel at. Had not Marwān told everyone who cared, including Muʿāwiya, what would happen when 'the descendants of Abu l-ʿĀṣī reached forty men'? It was just a matter of time. Marwān was also as good as his word in treating the members of the deposed house of Abū Sufyān, who, as he painted it, had not properly honoured their kinship ties to the Banū Abi l-ʿĀṣī. As he stood at the tomb of the last Sufyanid caliph who had just been buried, he asked his Syrian entourage: 'Do you know whom you have buried?' They answered: 'Yes, Muʿāwiya b. Yazīd.' He countered: 'Rather you have buried Abū Laylā.' Abū Laylā, the dead caliph's agnomen (*kunya*), was also the nickname for a weakling. They loved it, and a bard of the Banū Fazāra said:

> Do not be deceived, for 'the matter' has become disputed,
> and the reign after Abū Laylā belongs to the conqueror (*li-man ghalaba*).[99]

As soon as he had secured his succession, Marwān married Umm Khālid Fākhita, the widow of Yazīd and mother of the latter's sons Muʿāwiya, Khālid, ʿAbd Allāh al-Akbar and Abū Sufyān. It was, as Wellhausen observed, 'less an alliance than a seizure of an inheritance'.[100] Marwān succeeded where Muʿāwiya had failed, as Nā'ila, ʿUthmān's proud widow, broke her front teeth rather than surrender to his demands. It took Marwān only months before he violated his agreements on the succession of his stepson Khālid and of ʿAmr b. Saʿīd al-Ashdaq in order to appoint his own sons ʿAbd al-Malik and ʿAbd al-ʿAzīz. In this respect, it is true,

98 *Das arabische Reich*, 114; T. Mommsen (ed.), *Chronica Minora Saec. IV. V. VI. VII.*, II (Berlin, 1894), 346. Wellhausen backed the miraculous nature of the event: 'Without his own achievement, without even having desired it himself, Marwān through his expulsion from Medina came unto the throne in Damascus.' An astounding misjudgement of a great historian.

99 Balādhurī, *Ansāb*, 4/1, 356.

100 *Das arabische Reich*, 114. Lammens contradicted Wellhausen, suggesting that Marwān aimed above all at strengthening his alliance with 'the senior branch of the Umayyad family' ('L'avènement des Marwanides', *Mélanges de la Faculté Orientale de l'Université St Joseph de Beyrouth*, 12 (1927), 43–147, at 67). In reality it was Marwān's lifelong contention that the Sufyanids were not the senior branch of the Umayyads but rather had usurped the primary rights of the Banū Abi l-ʿĀṣī.

Muʿāwiya had, at least partly, outdone him by declaring his agreements with al-Ḥasan invalid war fraud in a matter of days, though he had to wait well over a decade before he could appoint his son Yazīd to the succession.

Marwān then systematically undertook to humiliate his stepson Khālid b. Yazīd in public. It had been his practice to seat him together with himself on his throne until one day, when Khālid moved to take his usual place, he rebuked him: 'Get off, son of a . . .' Renowned for his foul language (*faḥḥāsh*),[101] he used a drastic obscenity to describe Khālid's mother, the queen, as a whore: 'I have never found any sound mind in you.' The youthful Khālid, no great hero, walked off in anger and went to his mother. He reproached her: 'You have disgraced me and have lowered my head by marrying this man,' and he told her what had happened.

This time the chess-king had gone too far. The rules of the royal game allow the king to sacrifice his queen, to let her be butchered by the enemy to save his own skin, to replace her by a pawn or to double up on her whether she approves or not. Had not Yazīd, Umm Khālid's former royal spouse, paired her off with Umm Miskīn, great-granddaughter of the caliph ʿUmar as his second queen, just in order to vex her and then had rubbed her wounded pride with lines of poetry mocking her for bewailing her divinely ordained 'fate' (*qadar*)?[102] Umm Khālid had learned the rules of the royal game the hard way. Yet which rule-book had ever allowed the king to revile his lady in the lewdest language of the street to please the vulgar taste of his pawns, knights, bishops and rooks? Had the chess-master overlooked the formidable weaponry with which the game equipped the queen for her thankless part? What if she, too, for once broke the rules and turned against her own husband instead of serving and humouring his every whim? Woe then to the chess-king, that useless drone. Fākhita had seen enough of the whole ilk.

She told her son calmly not to talk about the matter to anyone, to conceal from Marwān that he had informed her, and to keep visiting her as usual; she would take care of the matter for him. As a slight suspicion crept up in his mind, Marwān asked her whether Khālid had told her anything about him that day. She answered that he had not told her anything. Marwān insisted: 'Has he not complained to you about me and mentioned my belittling him and what I told him?' The queen: 'Commander of the Faithful, you are too lofty in the eyes of Khālid, and his veneration for you is too great for him to tell me anything about you or to be offended by anything you say. You are in the position of a father to him.' Marwān was reassured and believed that the lady had spoken the truth. It was his second, bigger, mistake. Inveterate despiser of women, he did not deem them capable of war guile, except perhaps for the benefit of a lover. Whom

[101] See Lammens, 'L'avènement', 91. [102] Zubayrī, *Nasab*, 155; *Aghānī*, XVI, 88.

the gods want to destroy, they strike with blindness. Did he not see that the lady was of ʿAbd Shams, if not of Umayya?[103] Woe to the drone of Umayya from the lioness of ʿAbd Shams.

When the time for a siesta came, Marwān made his third, fatal, misstep. He repaired to the queen's chamber which, unbeknown to him, had turned into a lions' den. As he fell peacefully asleep, the doors were shut. The lioness pounced on her prey. She put a pillow stuffed with feathers on his face and sat on top of it, placing that part of her body which he had so crudely defamed squarely on his nose and mouth. Her slave girls happily joined her, excited about the break in their tedious routine. The Commander of the Faithful had hardly time to reflect that not even his rival in Mekka, the master-wrestler ʿAbd Allāh b. al-Zubayr, could have cast off the solid weight of a furious queen and a dozen well-built royal slave girls before he suffocated.[104] The game was over, check-mate by his own lady; *shāh māt*, the shah is dead. To the end he had put into practice the counsel which he had, to no avail, preached to his pious cousin ʿUthmān: 'To persist in wrongdoing for which you can ask God's forgiveness is better than repentance compelled by fear.' His Graeco-Roman gods, jealous of his stupendous success, begrudged him the time for repentance without fear before they shoved him off into the nether world of shadows.

This story of Marwān's end, although transmitted with prestigious chains of authority[105] and so widely attested that even al-Ṭabarī could not avoid quoting it, has found little favour among modern western scholars. Wellhausen, a historian with a sense of humour, summed it up in a sentence, adding: 'So according to al-Wāqidī.'[106] *Nāqilu l-kufri laysa bi-kāfir*: the reporter of unbelief is no unbeliever. Serious historians mostly either rebutted its credibility or simply ignored it.[107] Lammens, doyen of modern Umayyad historiography, confessed: 'Mais avec Nöldeke, j'hésite à admettre le rôle tragique que prête à cette femme la tradition.'[108]

[103] Fākhita was the daughter of Abū Hāshim b. ʿUtba b. Rabīʿa b. ʿAbd Shams (Zubayrī, *Nasab*, 155).

[104] Ibn Saʿd, *Ṭabaqāt*, V, 29–30; Ṭabarī, II, 576–7; *Aghānī*, XVI, 90; Balādhurī, *Ansāb*, V, 145, 159.

[105] The version of Ibn Saʿd, on which the above presentation is mainly based, is introduced by the *isnād* Mūsā b. Ismāʿīl – Juwayriya b. Asmāʾ – Nāfiʿ.

[106] *Das arabische Reich*, 114.

[107] Only R. Sellheim, *Der zweite Bürgerkrieg im Islam* (Wiesbaden, 1970), 104, admits the possibility that Marwān may have lost his life because of his treachery towards the Sufyanids, 'if the tradition is reliable'.

[108] 'L'avènement', 91. In a footnote Lammens quoted, somewhat grudgingly, Nöldeke's suggestion that the story was a fable planted by the Sufyanids. A plausible guess; the Sufyanids had reason to be angry at Marwān. It clashed, however, with Lammens' theory of an alliance between Marwān and 'the senior branch of the family'. Lammens added that the adversaries of the Umayyads were in a hurry to adopt the fable. There were obviously plenty of those, though Lammens probably had mainly wicked Shiʿites in mind.

He continued: 'On ne voit pas 'Abdalmalik, si impitoyable contre Aśdaq, inquiéter les auteurs et les complices prétendues du meurtre de son père.'[109] Lammens then chose for Marwān from the modes of death offered on al-Mas'ūdī's palette that of the plague.[110] Excellent choice; there is nothing dishonourable for a great king and war hero to succumb to the great reaper. It could also explain why the tradition has not preserved any of the obligatory royal deathbed scenes with wise recommendations to the successor and good counsel to the close ones. Who would expect such forward-looking thoughts from anyone, even a moral giant, grappling with the plague?

G. Rotter, re-examining matters more recently, was even more positive about the facts: the story of Umm Khālid's crime had been invented quite early. Yet even al-Mas'ūdī, who otherwise displayed a strong penchant for such anecdotes, felt obliged to honour the truth and to point out that several of the sources available to him accepted that Marwān died of the plague or by natural death. Death by plague was indeed the most probable version since the first wave of the scourge reached Syria in that spring. Were there any truth to the murder story, Rotter concluded, 'Abd al-Malik would surely not have allowed 'the murderess' to get away with it.[111]

Faced with such a consensus and incisive reasoning of the serious historians, the defender of the pillow story may be prepared to capitulate. Why should not for once the semi-Shi'ite al-Mas'ūdī have the edge in veracity over the faithful Sunnite al-Ṭabarī? Yet, on second thoughts, one may soon begin to wonder about the motivation behind that remarkable unanimity with which western critical historians, so intent on portraying the architect of the Umayyad reign as a great statesman and soldier, have either refuted or buried the story. Could not the same realization that the grotesque scene simply will not fit into the picture of an exemplary statesman, soldier and Umayyad *dāhiya* have already plagued his successor, 'Abd al-Malik, and given rise to the other colours on al-Mas'ūdī's palette? Even murder by poisoning by his wife angry at the treatment of her son would be more palatable. The reader may forgive being dragged once more to the deathbed scene.

Her victory achieved, the queen stood up, ripped the neck opening of her dress, and ordered her slave girls and servants to tear their dresses. Then, as was the custom, the wailing cries of the women resounded

[109] *Ibid.*, 91. Al-Ashdaq was 'Abd al-Malik's cousin 'Amr b. Sa'īd. 'Abd al-Malik slaughtered him with his own hands after 'Amr's revolt in which he claimed the throne as rightfully his under the agreement concluded by Marwān at the time of his accession.

[110] *Ibid.*, 96. Al-Mas'ūdī offered the following choices from his sources: plague, natural death, suffocation by Fākhita, poisoned milk administered by her (*Murūj*, III, 288–9).

[111] G. Rotter, *Die Umayyaden und der zweite Bürgerkrieg (680–692)* (Wiesbaden, 1982), 162–3.

through the palace: 'The Commander of the Faithful has suddenly died.'[112] The sources do not try to penetrate the mind of the deceased caliph's son 'Abd al-Malik as he heard, or was informed of, the commotion, and leave it to the imagination of the observer to read his thoughts. The first lightning to flash through his mind was no doubt that he had become God's Vicegerent on earth. The destiny of mankind rested now on his wise decision making. What did he make of the wailing of the women? It probably took him only moments to realize what had happened. His father had been fit and healthy a moment earlier, and heart attack was not much heard of in those hardier times. What should he do? Grip his sword and in righteous filial wrath avenge his father by cutting off the head of his treacherous stepmother? 'Abd al-Malik had gone through Marwān's schooling long enough to know that a nobleman, not to mention a king, must not soil his hands with the blood of a woman, like an ordinary soldier. He remembered that his father had had to build an ingenious trap to get rid of his misbehaved niece. He could, of course, have the offender dealt with in some other way, by his servants; the choices of the king to kill, torture or otherwise punish are infinite. But what then? Would not punishment bring out into public daylight what ought better remain forever concealed behind the walls of the queen's chamber? 'Abd al-Malik was well aware of what every ordinary politician and public official knows, that in the make-believe world of the Great Game appearances often count for more than facts. He shuddered thinking what might happen if the facts became public. A minor Khurasanian bard's immortal lines describing the end of the kingdom of Umayya – the dead body of Yazīd lying in his pleasure palace at Hawwārīn with a cup next to his pillow and a wine skin whose nose was still bleeding – came to his mind and their devastating effect as the governors everywhere withdrew their support.[113] Had it not been for the resolute action of his father, the House of Umayya might indeed have collapsed. The lampoon poets would now have a feast picturing the ignominious end of the great avenger of the wronged founder under a pillow with the crushing weight of an angry queen and her slave girls. The enemies, the counter-caliph in Mekka, the Basrans and the Kufans, would triumph, the Syrians be demoralized. Even the most loyal of them might decide that it was time to change sides to Ibn al-Zubayr as many had done after Yazīd's death. No, this was definitely the occasion for a cover-up. He must play the part offered him by the cunning murderess and pretend to believe that the caliph had died of a sudden fatal disease. 'Abd al-Malik realized that it would probably be impossible to prevent

[112] Ibn Sa'd, *Ṭabaqāt*, V, 30. [113] Wellhausen, *Das arabische Reich*, 105.

the spread of rumour; women are, after all, talkative. But then most people, those who count, would perhaps privately listen to, but not seriously believe, their gossip. People prefer to take the truth from their kings, at least so long as these know how to save face.

It began to dawn on the new Commander of the Faithful that the lioness had acted not just in blind fury, but in cold calculation. She was not so foolish as to risk her own life just to be rid of her unpleasant spouse. In fact, she was now safer from the king's retribution than any murderer hired by him would have been. He recognized that '*cette femme*' to whom the tradition attributed '*le rôle tragique*' could not be an ordinary woman. 'Abd al-Malik looked again. The lioness, though short in size,[114] was of 'Abd Shams;[115] how could his father have ignored it? It was check-mate, no doubt about it. But then, that was his father's game which he had lost. His own game had only just begun, thanks to the pounce of the lioness. There was not much sentimentality about blood ties in 'Abd al-Malik – something he could scarcely have inherited from his father. Suddenly he sensed relief, even a touch of gratitude, insofar as gratitude is allowed to kings. As long as Marwān had been alive, treacherous schemer that he was, 'Abd al-Malik could never have been sure of his succession to the throne. Might his father not at any time have replaced him as crown prince by another of his 'ten sons'?[116] 'Abd al-Malik appreciated now that letting the offender get away with murder may at times be more useful to the sovereign than exercising his privilege to kill and execute at discretion. Time to celebrate the accession. *Le roi est mort. Vive le roi!*

All fiction, the critical historians will judge, and rightly so. History, even if it were an exact science rather than a gamble on probabilities and plausibilities, would leave many gaps to be filled only by imagination, which enjoys the colourful. Others in the past, frustrated by our inability to penetrate the veil and to discover what really happened, have already filled its pages with a myriad of anecdotes. This may easily create the illusion in the mind of the critical historian that plain prosaic reports, be they in the news media or in their historical antecedents, are more likely

114 Her nickname was Ḥabba because of her small stature (Balādhurī, *Ansāb*, V, 159).

115 Wellhausen in a footnote (*Das arabische Reich*, 114) corrected the error of A. Müller that Fākhita was 'a proud bedouin woman' and described her instead as 'a Qurayshite'. He underestimated her also in suggesting that she took revenge simply for Marwān's perfidious treatment of her son. Lammens similarly thought that Fākhita might have been furious on behalf of her son and concealed Marwān's insult to his queen ('L'avènement', 90–1). She was, no doubt, well aware that her action would not return the caliphate to the young Khālid and that her sensitive son was, in any case, not suited for the caliphate. Her disgust with Marwān, Umayyad royalty and its amusements most likely ran deeper than that.

116 Marwān, according to al-Zubayrī, had in fact, not just in metaphor, ten sons and ten daughters (*Nasab*, 160–1).

than anecdotes to be plain, not manipulated fact. The good anecdote tells what could, and, stripped of its literary dressing, may well have happened, just as the good plain report does. Plague or lioness? You may try to balance the probability of the evidence, and perhaps one or the other side will eventually preponderate. But will you be able to prove it to anyone but the convinced? In the end the choice may be a mere matter of taste. If you prefer the king's truth, enjoy stories about great heroes, Roman-style statesmen, tough soldiers and *dāhiya*s, you will opt for the plague and perhaps, after much argument, you may convince yourself that you have found the real truth. If you are satisfied with poetical truth, conceding that it may at times be truer to life than the king's truth, and do not wish to go on forever weighing imponderables, choose the lioness and you may cut all further argument short with a sceptical yet confident

Se non e vero e ben trovato.

Excursuses

1 THE BURIAL OF MUḤAMMAD

The traditional Sunnite account of the burial of Muḥammad stresses that the preparations for the funeral were begun only after the general pledge of allegiance (*bayʿa*) had been given to Abū Bakr on Tuesday, the day following the Prophet's death. This chronology is reflected in Ibn Isḥāq's arrangement of the events in his *Sīra*. After reporting Muḥammad's death some time after the morning prayer on Monday, Ibn Isḥāq narrates, on the authority of Abū Hurayra, that ʿUmar addressed the Muslims assembled at the gate of the mosque, denying the death of Muḥammad; he threatened 'the hypocrites' who claimed that the Prophet was dead with punishment after he returned from 'his temporary absence'. Later Abū Bakr arrived and, after having taken a look at Muḥammad's body in ʿĀ'isha's apartment, contradicted ʿUmar and confirmed the Prophet's death. Ibn Isḥāq next presents the story of the Saqīfat Banī Sāʿida. The Muhājirūn, gathered around Abū Bakr, learned that the Anṣār had assembled in the Saqīfa to decide on the succession. The Muhājirūn joined them, and Abū Bakr was elected in a tumultuous scene.

Ibn Isḥāq then reports, on the authority of Anas b. Mālik, that the general *bayʿa* took place the following day in the mosque. ʿUmar spoke first, before Abū Bakr, apologizing to the people for his mistaken denial of Muḥammad's death. He then introduced Abū Bakr and asked the people to pledge allegiance to him. After the general *bayʿa* Abū Bakr gave a brief inaugural speech. Only then does Ibn Isḥāq return to the dead Muḥammad, stating: 'When the *bayʿa* had been given to Abū Bakr, the people proceeded to prepare for the funeral (*jahāz*) of the Messenger of God on Tuesday.'[1] Ibn Isḥāq's arrangement of events was also adopted by al-Ṭabarī and later authors such as Ibn Kathīr.[2] The latter categorically affirms that the Companions were occupied with the *bayʿa* of Abū Bakr for the remainder of Monday (after Muḥammad's death) and part of

[1] Ibn Hishām, *Sīrat sayyidinā*, 1018. [2] Ibn Kathīr, *Bidāya*, V, 244ff.

Tuesday. Only when it was completed did they begin with the preparation of the funeral 'following the instructions of Abū Bakr al-Ṣiddīq in everything which was problematical for them'.[3]

The motive behind the insistence on this chronology is evidently to avoid the impression that Abū Bakr's election was decided while the kin of the Prophet were busy with the funeral preparations and to show Abū Bakr in complete control of the arrangements for the burial. Al-Zuhrī, representative of the Medinan school of Sunnite tradition, stated: 'Abū Bakr and the Companions of the Messenger of God gave leave (*khallā bayna*) to al-'Abbās, 'Alī, al-Faḍl b. al-'Abbās and the rest of the family, and thus it was they who wrapped him in his grave cloths (*ajannūhu*).'[4] The question had evidently already become a point of Sunnite dogma, and Ibn Isḥāq firmly supported the orthodox Medinan position.

Ibn Isḥāq then quotes Ibn al-'Abbās' account of the washing of Muḥammad's body together with 'Ā'isha's counter-report[5] and a short notice attributed to the 'Alid 'Alī b. al-Ḥusayn (Zayn al-'Ābidīn) on the three cloths in which he was wrapped. He continues with a report on the digging of the grave with the *isnād* Ḥusayn b. 'Abd Allāh (b. 'Ubayd Allāh b. al-'Abbās) *'an* 'Ikrima *'an* Ibn 'Abbās. There were two gravediggers available, the Emigrant Abū 'Ubayda b. al-Jarrāḥ, who followed the Mekkan practice, and the Helper Abū Ṭalḥa Zayd b. Sahl, who dug according to the Medinan practice, making a niche (*yalḥad*). Al-'Abbās called two men and sent one of them to Abū 'Ubayda and the other to Abū Ṭalḥa while praying to God to make the choice for the Prophet. The one sent to Abū Ṭalḥa found him, and thus Abū Ṭalḥa dug the grave with the niche according to the Medinan practice.

Ibn Isḥāq continues, again insisting that all this happened on Tuesday: 'When the preparations for the funeral of the Messenger of God were completed on Tuesday, he was laid on his bed (*sarīr*) in his house.' The Muslims had been in disagreement concerning his burial, some suggesting that he be buried in his mosque, others wishing that he be buried with his Companions (in the Baqī' cemetery). Abū Bakr settled the matter saying: 'I have heard the Messenger of God state: "No prophet has ever died but

[3] *Ibid.*, 260. [4] Balādhurī, *Ansāb*, I, 570.

[5] See above, pp. 26–7. The Hashimite 'Abd Allāh b. al-Ḥārith b. Nawfal (Babba) described the washing as follows: when the Prophet had died, 'Alī locked the door of the room. Al-'Abbās came together with the Banū 'Abd al-Muṭṭalib and stood at the door. 'Alī began to say: 'Dearer than my father and mother, your smell is sweet alive and dead', and a sweet odour rose, the like of which they had never experienced. Al-'Abbās said to 'Alī: 'Stop wailing like a woman and get on [pl.] with your fellow!' 'Alī asked that al-Faḍl be sent in to him. The Anṣār said: 'We implore you by our share in the Messenger of God', and they let in Aws b. Khawalī, who was carrying a jug in one of his hands. 'Alī washed the body, moving his hand under the shirt while al-Faḍl held the garment on him and the Anṣārī carried the water (Ibn Sa'd, *Ṭabaqāt*, II/2, 62–3).

that he was buried where he died."' The grave was thus dug under the bed of Muḥammad. Then the people entered and performed their prayers. No one acted as imam during the prayers. The Prophet was buried in the night of (Tuesday to) Wednesday.[6]

This section clearly does not continue the report of Ibn al-ʿAbbās on the digging of the grave. The place of the grave must have been chosen before the gravediggers were sent for. Ibn al-ʿAbbās evidently did not report anything about this decision, and Ibn Isḥāq therefore supplied the information from other accounts without mentioning an *isnād*. The omission of an *isnād* quickly resulted in the attribution of Ibn Isḥāq's elaborations to Ibn al-ʿAbbās. Al-Balādhurī and Ibn Māja quoted Ibn Isḥāq's account from the story of the two gravediggers to the end with his *isnād* going back to Ibn al-ʿAbbās.[7] Ibn Ḥanbal was more judicious. He quoted Ibn Isḥāq's report on the washing of the body together with the story of the gravediggers under his *isnād* to Ibn al-ʿAbbās, but without Ibn Isḥāq's elaborations.[8] Ibrāhīm b. Ismāʿīl b. Abī Ḥabīb took the elaborations of Ibn Isḥāq and claimed to have heard them from Dāwūd b. al-Ḥusayn from ʿIkrima from Ibn al-ʿAbbās.[9]

The story of the disagreement about the place of burial and Abū Bakr's decision was widely reported, among others by ʿĀ'isha,[10] so that Ibn Isḥāq evidently considered mention of an *isnād* unnecessary. In contrast to the account of Ibn al-ʿAbbās, the majority of these reports also describe the Muslims or Abū Bakr, rather than al-ʿAbbās, as deciding to send for the two gravediggers after disagreement about the appropriate practice.[11]

Ibn Isḥāq then describes the burial. He quotes ʿĀ'isha, who stated: 'We did not know that the Messenger of God was being buried until we heard the sound of the shovels in the middle of the night of [Tuesday to] Wednesday.'[12] The next section, reported without *isnād*, is again based on Ibn al-ʿAbbās as is evident from the similarity with the report about the washing of the Prophet.[13] ʿAlī, al-Faḍl b. al-ʿAbbās, Qutham b.

[6] Ibn Hishām, *Sīrat sayyidinā*, 1019–20; Ṭabarī, I, 1832.

[7] Balādhurī, *Ansāb*, I, 573–4; Ibn Māja, *Sunan*, ed. Muḥammad Fu'ād ʿAbd al-Bāqī ([Cairo] 1395/1975), *Janā'iz, bāb* 65, quoted by Ibn Kathīr, *Bidāya*, V, 266–7.

[8] Ibn Kathīr, *Bidāya*, V, 260–1. Ibn Kathīr, however, quotes the end of Ibn Isḥāq's elaborations somewhat freely, following the story of the two gravediggers, all with his *isnād* going back to Ibn al-ʿAbbās (*ibid.*, 265).

[9] Ibn Saʿd, *Ṭabaqāt*, II/2, 71. On Ibrāhīm b. Ismāʿīl (d. 165/781-2) see Ibn Ḥajar, *Tahdhīb*, I, 104–5. It is not impossible that Dāwūd b. al-Ḥusayn (al-Umawī, d. 135/752-3, Ibn Ḥajar, *Tahdhīb*, III, 181–2) had already made the false claim. Both traditionists are specifically described as unreliable in their transmission from ʿIkrima from Ibn al-ʿAbbās.

[10] Ibn Saʿd, *Ṭabaqāt*, II/2, 71; Balādhurī, *Ansāb*, I, 573–4; Ibn Kathīr, *Bidāya*, V, 266–8.

[11] Ibn Saʿd, *Ṭabaqāt*, II/2, 72–5; Ibn Kathīr, *Bidāya*, V, 266, 268.

[12] Ṭabarī, I, 1832–3.

[13] The report is quoted by Ibn Māja with Ibn Isḥāq's *isnād* going back to Ibn al-ʿAbbās (*Sunan, Janā'iz, bāb* 65).

al-ʿAbbās and Shuqrān descended into the tomb. Aws b. Khawalī again begged ʿAlī for permission to descend and was allowed to join them. Shuqrān placed a blanket (*qaṭīfa*) of the Prophet in the grave to be buried with him.[14]

There are other relevant reports of Ibn al-ʿAbbās which Ibn Isḥāq ignored and which significantly change the chronology and the implications of his complete account. According to Ibn al-ʿAbbās it was his father al-ʿAbbās who first contradicted ʿUmar when he denied Muḥammad's death and claimed that his spirit had been temporarily raised to heaven like that of Moses. Al-ʿAbbās urged the people to proceed with burying the Prophet, since his body would begin to smell like any other corpse; if it were as they were saying (that Muḥammad was not really dead), it would be easy for God to open his tomb and bring him out.[15]

Contrary to the chronology of the Medinan school, Ibn al-ʿAbbās also reported that the Prophet was lying in state on his bed from sunset (*ḥīna zāghat al-shams*) on Monday until sunset on Tuesday. The people prayed at the side of his bed which was standing next to the edge of his grave. When they were ready to bury him, the bed was inclined at the foot end and was lowered from there into the tomb. Al-ʿAbbās, al-Faḍl, Qutham, ʿAlī and Shuqrān descended into the grave.[16] The washing of the body and the digging of the grave thus took place on Monday, while Abū Bakr and ʿUmar were busy at the Saqīfat Banī Sāʿida.

There can be little doubt that the chronology given by Ibn al-ʿAbbās is essentially correct. Regardless of whether al-ʿAbbās or Abū Bakr, or both, put an end to ʿUmar's attempt to deny Muḥammad's death, there was no reason to delay the preparations of the burial. For the close kin to take charge of the preparations was customary and no permission from Abū Bakr and the Companions was required. The decision to bury Muḥammad in his house was not made by Abū Bakr, but by his kin. The reason for it was obviously the insecurity of the situation in Medina and the desire to keep control over the arrangements. Had Abū Bakr been in command, he would no doubt have wished the Prophet to be buried in al-Baqīʿ with his relatives and martyred Companions and would have led the funeral prayers as Muḥammad had done for them. The hadith that Abū Bakr is reported to have quoted to justify the burial at the place of Muḥammad's death is fiction. It may well belong to the early efforts, furthered by ʿĀʾisha, to show Abū Bakr as the recipient of Muḥammad's

[14] Ibn Hishām, *Sīrat sayyidinā*, 1020; Ṭabarī, I, 1833.

[15] ʿAbd al-Razzāq, *Muṣannaf*, V, 433–5; Ibn Saʿd, *Ṭabaqāt*, II/2, 53-4; Balādhurī, *Ansāb*, I, 567. The report was evidently not meant to counter the common account that it was Abū Bakr's intervention that silenced ʿUmar. This account was also confirmed by Ibn al-ʿAbbās (ʿAbd al-Razzāq, *Muṣannaf*, V, 436–7).

[16] Ibn Saʿd, *Ṭabaqāt*, II/2, 70.

instructions about what should be done after his death. After the general *bay'a* on the Tuesday morning, Abū Bakr evidently did not wish to force a showdown with the Prophet's kin, who refused to swear allegiance to him, and to change their arrangements. There is consensus that no one led the funeral prayers.[17] It is doubtful whether Abū Bakr and 'Umar even went to pay their last respects to the Prophet. Only a late and patently fabricated report describes them as entering with the Emigrants and addressing a few words to the dead body.[18]

The mention of Aws b. Khawalī and of the two gravediggers thus takes on a distinctly polemical aspect. While Muḥammad's kin went to prepare his burial, the Mekkan Emigrants ran off busily engaging in their political machinations. Only the Anṣār showed some concern, and Aws b. Khawalī was allowed to join the kin. When al-'Abbās sent for the gravediggers, the Mekkan Emigrant Abū 'Ubayda could not be found, presumably because he was occupied with Abū Bakr and 'Umar scheming to seize power. The Anṣārī, Abū Ṭalḥa, was available, and thus the Prophet was buried in a grave dug in conformity with Medinan practice. God's choice in response to the prayer of al-'Abbās thus could be understood as a reminder to the Anṣār that Muḥammad had been, through his great-grandmother Salmā bt 'Amr, one of them.

2 THE INHERITANCE OF MUḤAMMAD

In its general formulation, the hadith ascribed by Abū Bakr to the Prophet that prophets do not have heirs was manifestly in conflict with the letter and spirit of the Qur'ān.[19] The Hashimite 'Abbās b. 'Abd Allāh b. Ma'bad, great-grandson of al-'Abbās b. 'Abd al-Muṭṭalib, reported about the meeting of Fāṭima and al-'Abbās with Abū Bakr on the authority of an unidentified Ja'far as follows: 'Fāṭima came to Abū Bakr demanding her inheritance and al-'Abbās came to demand his inheritance; with them came 'Alī. Abū Bakr said: "The Messenger of God has said: We do not have heirs, whatever we leave is alms. Whatever sustenance the Prophet provided, it is now my responsibility." 'Alī countered, quoting

[17] The irregularity in the burial of Muḥammad and the motivation of the Prophet's kin have been essentially correctly seen by Caetani (*Annali*, II/1, 519–20, 529–33). Later Caetani seems to have moved away from his view under the influence of Lammens, who held that the burial of Muḥammad in the place where he died and without a funeral prayer was in conformity with the 'barbaric' practices of the time, these being abandoned only later in Islam under Christian influence (*ibid.*, III, 90–1). Lammens' view is untenable. Concerning the early Islamic burial practices see I. Grütter, 'Arabische Bestattungsbräuche in frühislamischer Zeit', *Der Islam*, 31 (1954), 147–73, 32 (1955), 79–104, 168–94.

[18] Ibn Sa'd, *Ṭabaqāt*, II/2, 69; Balādhurī, *Ansāb*, I, 574–5.

[19] The hadith is considered unauthentic by I. Hrbek, 'Muḥammads Nachlass und die Aliden', *Archív Orientální*, 18 (1950), 143–9, at 146.

the Qur'ān: "Solomon became David's heir (XXVII 16) and Zachariah said [in his prayer: give me a next-of-kin] who will inherit from me and inherit from the family of Jacob (XIX 6)." Abū Bakr said: "This is so, and you, by God, know the same as I know." ʿAlī replied: "This is the Book of God speaking." Then they stopped talking and departed.'[20]

A way to avoid controversy was to argue that by saying 'We' the Prophet did not mean the prophets in general but only himself. The hadith was thus transmitted from al-Zuhrī with the comment: 'By that the Messenger of God meant himself (*yurīdu bi-dhālika rasūlu llāhi nafsah*).'[21] In other versions of the hadith, however, Muḥammad is quoted as expressly explaining 'We' as the prophets (*maʿshar al-anbiyāʾ*). Sunnite apologists were thus challenged to find another explanation for the ostensible conflict between Qur'ān and Abū Bakr's hadith.

The Sunnite traditionalist historian Ibn Kathīr angrily rejects what he calls an argument of the Rāfiḍa (Shiʿites), one of whom in his ignorance tried to counter Abū Bakr's hadith with the two Qur'anic verses about Solomon and Zachariah. The verse about Solomon inheriting from David referred only to kingship (*mulk*) and prophethood, not to inheritance of property. David had, according to numerous exegetes, as many as a hundred children; if the verse referred to inheritance of property, it would not have been confined to mentioning Solomon. Likewise Zachariah prayed for a son who would inherit his prophethood and spiritual leadership of the Banū Isrāʾīl. He could not have meant inheritance of property, since he was himself a poor carpenter living on the work of his own hands.[22]

Another way to justify the confiscation of Muḥammad's estates in Medina, Khaybar and Fadak was to claim that they had not been his personal property, but rather belonged to the Muslim community and were merely assigned to his discretionary use for his lifetime. This concept is reflected in another hadith ascribed to Abū Bakr according to which he had heard Muḥammad say: 'This [land] is merely a morsel (*ṭuʿma*) which God gave me to eat, and when I die it will belong to the Muslims (*kāna bayna l-Muslimīn*).'[23]

According to a report of ʿĀʾisha, the caliph ʿUmar made a distinction

[20] Ibn Saʿd, *Ṭabaqāt*, II/2, 86.

[21] *Ibid.*, 85. The Companions who reported the hadith in this version are listed as ʿUmar, ʿUthmān, ʿAlī, al-Zubayr, Saʿd and al-ʿAbbās. It is evidently based on the report about ʿUmar demanding and receiving the assurance of the most prominent Companions, including ʿAlī and al-ʿAbbās, that they all knew the statement of Muḥammad (see above, pp. 62–3). [22] Ibn Kathīr, *Bidāya*, V, 290.

[23] Ibn Saʿd, *Ṭabaqāt*, II/2, 86; Ibn Shabba, *Taʾrīkh al-Madīna*, 210–11, where Fāṭima is quoted as having reported that Abū Bakr justified his withholding of Fadak with this hadith. She replied: 'You and the Messenger of God know best. I shall not ask you again after this session.'

between private property of Muḥammad and state property merely assigned to him for his use. He surrendered Muḥammad's estates in Medina to 'Alī and al-'Abbās. The former quickly usurped the rights of the latter (*ghalabahū 'alayhā*). 'Umar retained the estates of Khaybar and Fadak, however, maintaining that they had been assigned to the Prophet for his needs and emergencies and that they were now at the disposal of the ruler of the Muslims (*amruhumā ilā man waliya l-amr*).[24] Muḥammad's land property in Medina is usually described as consisting of seven gardens which the Jew Mukhayrīq of the Banu l-Naḍīr or the Banū Qaynuqā', who was killed in the battle of Uḥud, left to him by will.[25] Al-Wāqidī claimed that the Prophet constituted them as an endowment in the year 7 of the *hijra*.[26] 'Umar may have found it difficult to maintain that the land of the Banu l-Naḍīr was communal property of the Muslims since Abū Bakr had made a gift from his share to his daughter 'Ā'isha.[27] There is mention of two other estates of Muḥammad coming from the property of the Banū Qurayẓa located in 'Āliyat al-Madīna.[28] From 'Ā'isha's report it is evident that Abū Bakr's confiscation of Muḥammad's possessions was not based on a claim that they had in fact been state property.

Caetani presented the question of Muḥammad's inheritance thus: in deciding that all of Muḥammad's possessions should become public property and that the income accruing from them should go entirely to the Muslims, Abū Bakr was interpreting the will of the Prophet expressed many times during his life.[29] In his later life Muḥammad had made highly arbitrary use of the revenue of Fadak. When his widows and Fāṭima – the latter at the instigation of her husband 'Alī – laid claim to the inheritance of Fadak, the righteous spirit of Abū Bakr revolted against such pretence and he proffered a statement of Muḥammad denying his daughter any right to the revenue of Fadak, which was rather to be dedicated to the common benefit of the Muslims.[30] Muḥammad, according to Caetani, did not own any land in Medina except his domicile.[31] On this basis Caetani held that in the time of Muḥammad communist tendencies prevailed in land ownership.[32] The Qur'ān (LIX 6), however, stated clearly that the land taken from the Banu l-Naḍīr belonged to the Prophet, to be used at

[24] Ibn Ḥanbal, *Musnad*, I, 6–7; Ibn Shabba, *Ta'rīkh al-Madīna*, 207.
[25] Balādhurī, *Futūḥ*, 18; Ibn Shabba, *Ta'rīkh al-Madīna*, 173–6; Wensinck, *Muhammad and the Jews of Medina*, trans. W. Behn (Freiburg, 1975), 26–7; *Annali*, II/1, 688. According to another report, the Prophet's estates in Medina came from the land of the Banu al-Naḍīr, and he distributed the land left by Mukhayrīq after the battle of Uḥud among the Muslims (Ibn Shabba, *Ta'rīkh al-Madīna*, 175).
[26] Ibn Shabba, *Ta'rīkh al-Madīna*, 175. [27] See above, p. 51.
[28] Ibn Shabba, *Ta'rīkh al-Madīna*, 187. [29] *Annali*, II/1, 521. [30] *Ibid.*, II/1, 686.
[31] *Ibid.*, II/1, 688. It is difficult to see how this 'clearly results from the whole question', as Caetani asserts. [32] *Ibid.*, V, 526.

his discretion, not to the Muslim community.

The disallowance of any inheritance from Muḥammad by Abū Bakr evidently soon gave rise to the numerous traditions that the Prophet had died without any personal possessions. 'Ā'isha is quoted as reporting that when the Messenger of God died he did not leave a dinar, a dirham, a slave or slave girl, a sheep, or a camel. Ibn al-'Abbās is said to have added that Muḥammad had left his armour as a pawn with a Jew for thirty measures (*ṣā'*) of barley.[33] In reality, no doubt, everyone, especially the widows, simply appropriated all they could.

3 THE MARRIAGES OF 'UTHMĀN B. 'AFFĀN*

'Uthmān is said to have recounted to his son 'Amr that before Islam and his marriage with Muḥammad's daughter Ruqayya, he was promiscuous with women (*kuntu mustahtiran bi l-nisā'*).[34] He was probably married, however, to Umm Ḥakīm Asmā', daughter of the Makhzumite chief Abū Jahl b. Hishām, Muḥammad's leading enemy, and had a son, al-Mughīra, by her. While Asmā' is mentioned only by al-Balādhurī[35] among the wives of 'Uthmān, al-Mughīra is enumerated among his sons also by other sources.[36] Al-Mughīra was presumably named after Abū Jahl's grandfather al-Mughīra b. 'Abd Allāh, the early chief of Makhzūm. Asmā' was divorced by 'Uthmān, most likely at the time of his conversion to Islam. He would then have been under pressure from her father, and perhaps also from Muḥammad, to separate from her. Asmā' was then married to the Makhzumite al-Walīd b. 'Abd Shams b. al-Mughīra, her father's cousin. 'Uthmān's son al-Mughīra was evidently still a child and thus was brought up by his mother and her kin. He may well be, as has been suggested,[37] the al-Mughīra b. 'Uthmān who is mentioned by al-Suddī among the pagan Mekkans attacked by the Muslims at al-Nakhla in the year 2/623, at which time he escaped.[38] Since there is no further mention of him, it is likely that he died as a pagan before the Muslim conquest of Mekka. That 'Uthmān's marriage with Asmā' must have been early in his life is also indicated by the fact that he married Umm

33 Ibn Sa'd, *Ṭabaqāt*, II/2, 87; *Annali*, II/1, 521.

* In addition to the sources quoted by Caetani, *Annali*, VIII, 298–307, see in particular Balādhurī, *Ansāb*, V, 11–13, 105–6 and Zubayrī, *Nasab*, 104–12.

34 Ibn 'Asākir, *'Uthmān*, 20.

35 Balādhuri, *Ansāb*, V, 105. Muṣ'ab al-Zubayrī does not mention Asmā' among 'Uthmān's wives nor al-Mughīra among his sons. In his notice on Asmā' bt Abī Jahl he mentions only her marriage to the Makhzūmite al-Walīd b. 'Abd Shams (*Nasab*, 312).

36 Ibn Qutayba, *Ma'ārif*, 198; Mas'ūdī, *Murūj*, III, 75, para. 1577.

37 Pellat in Mas'ūdī, *Murūj*, VII, index s.v. al-Mughīra b. 'Uthmān.

38 See Ṭabarī, I, 1277 and Ṭabarī, *Jāmi'*, II, 196. Al-Mughīra b. 'Uthmān is not mentioned in Ibn Isḥāq's account of the raid of al-Nakhla. On the basis of the identity of the pagans named in the two accounts it is evident that the caravan was essentially Makhzumite.

'Abd Allāh Faṭima, her daughter with al-Walīd b. 'Abd Shams, during the caliphate of 'Umar. Al-Walīd b. 'Abd Shams had been killed fighting under Khālid b. al-Walīd in the battle of al-'Aqrabā' in 12/633.[39] The date of the death of Asmā' bt Abī Jahl is not known.

According to 'Uthmān's own account he had first, before knowing of Muḥammad's prophetic mission, been moved by the beauty of Ruqayya and by his jealousy of 'Utba b. Abī Lahab, to whom Muḥammad had given her in marriage, and for that reason sought a meeting with the Prophet.[40] He became converted to Islam and immediately married her after she was divorced by 'Utba at his father's demand. She accompanied 'Uthmān during his migrations to Abyssinia and to Medina. Because of Ruqayya's illness, Muḥammad permitted 'Uthmān to stay at home during the campaign to Badr in 2/624. Ruqayya died before Muḥammad's return. After a miscarriage she had, probably in Abyssinia, borne 'Uthmān a son, 'Abd Allāh, known as the elder 'Abd Allāh (al-Akbar). According to most sources he died, after a cock had pecked him in one of his eyes, at the age of six in Jumādā I 4/October–November 625.[41]

After his return from Abyssinia to Mekka 'Uthmān married Ramla, daughter of Shayba b. Rabī'a b. 'Abd Shams. Her father Shayba b. Rabī'a was a prominent member of the pagan Qurayshite nobility and was killed together with his brother 'Utba in the battle of Badr. 'Uthmān must have been proud to be able to marry her, presumably with the consent of her father. He paid a dowry of 30,000 or 40,000 dirhams for her.[42] She migrated to Medina with 'Uthmān and is counted among the Muhājirāt. When her father was slain at Badr, Abū Sufyān's wife Hind bt 'Utba lampooned her for her betrayal of her kin. Most of the sources conceal the fact that she was married to 'Uthmān at the same time as Ruqayya.[43] Muḥammad, it is known, after the conquest of Mekka intervened to prevent the marriage of 'Alī with Juwayriya, daughter of Abū Jahl, insisting that the daughter of the 'enemy of God' should not be conjoined with the Prophet's daughter Fāṭima. At the time of 'Uthmān's marriage to Ramla, Muḥammad was probably in no position to raise objections, if he had any.

'Uthmān had three daughters with Ramla: Umm Abān, Umm 'Amr and 'Ā'isha. They were probably born during Muḥammad's lifetime, and 'Uthmān gave them in marriage early on in his caliphate. He married

[39] Zubayrī, *Nasab*, 330. [40] Ibn 'Asākir, *'Uthmān*, 20.

[41] Ibn Sa'd, *Ṭabaqāt*, III/1, 37; Ṭabarī, I, 1453; *Annali*, I, 588. In his biography of Ruqayya, Ibn Sa'd (*Ṭabaqāt*, VIII, 24) states that 'Abd Allāh died at the age of one or two, years before Ruqayya's own death. [42] Balādhurī, *Ansāb*, V, 13.

[43] Ibn 'Abd al-Barr, as quoted by Ibn al-Athīr (*Usd al-ghāba*, V, 457), stated expressly that Ramla emigrated together with her husband 'Uthmān b. 'Affān to Medina. In the edition of Ibn 'Abd al-Barr's *Istī'āb* (II, 730), however, 'Uthmān b. Maẓ'ūn is substituted. See also the discussion of Ibn Ḥajar, *Iṣāba*, VIII, 86.

Umm Abān to Marwān b. al-Ḥakam,[44] Umm 'Amr to Sa'īd b. al-'Āṣ,[45] and 'Ā'isha to al-Ḥārith b. al-Ḥakam. 'Ā'isha was later married and divorced by 'Abd Allāh b. al-Zubayr.[46] Ramla was still alive and married to 'Uthmān when he was killed.

Shortly after Ruqayya's death 'Umar b. al-Khaṭṭāb offered his daughter Ḥafṣa, who had recently been widowed, to 'Uthmān in marriage. The latter promised to consider the matter but after a few days rebuffed 'Umar with the excuse that he was not ready to marry at present. Muḥammad now intervened to marry Ḥafṣa himself while offering 'Uthmān his own daughter Umm Kulthūm.[47] 'Uthmān married her in Rabī' I 3/August–September 624, five months after the battle of Badr. She had been married to 'Utayba b. Abī Lahab, but the marriage had not been consummated before he was forced by his father to divorce her. She died childless in Sha'bān 9/November–December 630.[48]

In Medina, most likely while Muḥammad was alive, 'Uthmān married Fākhita bt Ghazwān. Her brother 'Utba b. Ghazwān b. Jābir of Māzin of Qays 'Aylān, a confederate of the Banū Nawfal, converted to Islam at an early date in Mekka and migrated to Abyssinia and Medina; later, under 'Umar, he became the founder and first governor of Baṣra.[49] Fākhita is not mentioned among the Muhājirāt and may have come to Medina some time after her brother. 'Uthmān presumably married her in order to support her. She bore him a son, 'Abd Allāh, called the younger (al-Aṣghar).[50] He was presumably born after the death of Ruqayya's son and therefore given the same name. He also died young, before 'Uthmān's accession to the caliphate. Fākhita survived 'Uthmān as his wife and was later married to Abū Hurayra.[51]

After the conquest of Mekka in 8/630 'Uthmān married a daughter of his second-degree cousin Khālid b. Asīd b. Abi l-'Īṣ b. Umayya, providing a dowry of 40,000 dirhams.[52] Khālid b. Asīd converted to Islam at the time of the conquest and was killed in the battle of al-'Aqrabā' in 12/633.

[44] Balādhurī, *Ansāb*, V, 106; Ibn Ḥabīb, *al-Muḥabbar*, ed. I. Lichtenstaedter (Hyderabad, 1942), 56. Marwān's brother 'Abd al-Raḥmān in a line of poetry aired his love for her (Zubayrī, *Nasab*, 161). The marriage probably took place after Marwān's return from 'Abd Allāh b. Sa'd's expedition to Ifrīqiya in 27/647 when 'Uthmān also gave him 500,000 dirhams of the *khums* of the booty (Ya'qūbī, *Ta'rīkh*, II, 191; *Annali*, VII, 193).

[45] Zubayrī, *Nasab*, 112; Balādhurī, *Ansāb*, V, 106; Ibn Ḥabīb, *Muḥabbar*, 55.

[46] Balādhurī, *Ansāb*, V, 106; Zubayrī, *Nasab*, 112 where the text *tazawwajat . . . 'Uthmān b. al-Ḥārith fa-waladat lah* is corrupt and should be read *tazawwajat . . . al-Ḥārith b. al-Ḥakam fa-waladat lahū 'Uthmān b. al-Ḥārith*. See Zubayrī, *Nasab*, 170. Ibn Ḥabīb, *Muḥabbar*, 55.

[47] Ibn Sa'd, *Ṭabaqāt*, VIII, 56–8. Reports that it was 'Uthmān who proposed to marry Ḥafṣa and that 'Umar declined his offer (Ibn 'Asākir, *'Uthmān*, 31–2) are obviously mistaken.

[48] Ibn Sa'd, *Ṭabaqāt*, VIII, 25. [49] *Ibid.*, III/1, 69, VII/1, 1–3.

[50] On Ibn Qutayba's list 'Abd Allāh al-Akbar appears as the son of Fākhita, and 'Abd Allāh al-Aṣghar as the son of Ruqayya (*Annali*, VIII, 301). This is certainly erroneous.

[51] Balādhurī, *Ansāb*, V, 100. [52] *Ibid.*, V, 13.

'Uthmān's aim in marrying her evidently was to strengthen his family ties with the most prominent Umayyads. Nothing further is known about Khālid b. Asīd's daughter. Most likely she soon died childless.

Jundab b. 'Amr b. Ḥumama of the Banū Daws of Azd came to Medina as a Muhājir. When he joined the campaign for the conquest of Syria he gave his daughter Umm 'Amr in custody to the caliph 'Umar with the instruction that, should anything happen to him, 'Umar should marry her to an equal. 'Umar used to call her 'my daughter', and she called him 'my father'. When Jundab was killed as a martyr, the caliph asked for someone to marry 'the beautiful corpulent one (*al-jamīla al-jasīma*)'.[53] 'Uthmān married Umm 'Amr bt Jundab and later used to say that he found in her everything he loved in a woman.[54] She bore him four sons, 'Amr, Abān, Khālid and 'Umar, and a daughter, Maryam (al-Kubrā). 'Amr, Abān and 'Umar survived 'Uthmān and had offspring. Khālid was killed in an accident during his father's reign, but also left children.[55] 'Uthmān gave Maryam in marriage to 'Abd al-Raḥmān b. al-Ḥārith b. Hishām al-Makhzūmī, nephew of Abū Jahl. Later, according to Muṣ'ab al-Zubayrī, she was married to 'Abd al-Malik b. Marwān.[56] Umm 'Amr bt Jundab seems to have died before 'Uthmān.

Probably not much later, during the caliphate of 'Umar, 'Uthmān married Umm 'Abd Allāh Fāṭima bt. al-Walīd b. 'Abd Shams b. al-Mughīra al-Makhzūmī with a dowry of 30,000 dirhams.[57] She was, as noted, the daughter of his pre-Islamic wife Umm Ḥakīm Asmā' bt Abī Jahl, who had married al-Walīd. The latter accepted Islam at the conquest of Mekka and was killed in the battle of al-'Aqrabā'. From Fāṭima bt al-Walīd, 'Uthmān had two sons, al-Walīd and Sa'īd, and a daughter, Umm Sa'īd, called Umm 'Uthmān by Muṣ'ab al-Zubayrī.[58] Both al-Walīd and Sa'īd survived their father and al-Walīd had offspring. 'Uthmān, while caliph, gave Umm Sa'īd, or Umm 'Uthmān, in marriage

[53] So al-Balādhurī (*ibid.*) Abu l-Faraj al-Iṣfahānī gives the reading 'the beautiful noble (*al-ḥasība*) one' (*Aghānī*, I, 153).

[54] Balādhurī, *Ansāb*, V, 13; *Aghānī*, I, 153–4, with further detail.

[55] Balādhurī, *Ansāb*, V, 116–17; Zubayrī, *Nasab*, 119. It was the caliph 'Uthmān, according to al-Zubayrī, who took the initiative to offer his daughter to the Makhzumite.

[56] Zubayrī, *Nasab*, 111–12, 308; Ibn Ḥabīb, *Muḥabbar*, 55. Al-Balādhurī states that Maryam al-Kubrā was married to Sa'īd b. al-'Āṣ after the death of her sister Umm 'Amr and that only after his death did she marry 'Abd al-Raḥmān b. al-Ḥārith, and died before him (*Ansāb*, V, 106). Sa'īd b. al-'Āṣ, however, did not die until the years 57–9/677–9, and it is uncertain whether 'Abd al-Raḥmān survived him. According to Muṣ'ab al-Zubayrī (*Nasab*, 180) and Ibn Sa'd (*Ṭabaqāt*, V, 20), Sa'īd b. al-'Āṣ rather married Maryam al-Ṣughrā, 'Uthmān's daughter by Nā'ila, after the death of her sister Umm 'Amr. This seems on balance more likely.

[57] Balādhurī, *Ansāb*, V, 13. That 'Uthmān married Fāṭima after Umm 'Amr is to be inferred from the fact that her sons were younger than 'Uthmān's eldest surviving son, 'Amr.

[58] *Nasab*, 104, 112.

to the Umayyad ʿAbd Allāh b. Khālid b. Asīd, brother of his above-mentioned wife, and paid for his debts.[59] It is not known whether ʿUthmān at that time was still married to ʿAbd Allāh's sister. Fāṭima bt al-Walīd either died or, less likely, was divorced before ʿUthmān's death.

After the death of the caliph ʿUmar, ʿUthmān proposed to marry his daughter Fāṭima bt ʿUmar. The exceptionally high dowry of 100,000 dirhams which he offered may have been intended to placate her family for his earlier slight to ʿUmar and Ḥafṣa when he declined to marry her. ʿAbd Allāh b. ʿUmar, full brother of Ḥafṣa, insisted, however, on the prior right of Fāṭima's paternal cousin, and she was married to ʿAbd al-Raḥmān b. Zayd b. al-Khaṭṭāb.[60] ʿUthmān may have been particularly interested in this daughter of ʿUmar since her mother was the Makhzumite Umm Ḥakīm bt al-Ḥārith b. Hishām, to whose brother ʿAbd al-Raḥmān he then gave his own daughter Maryam. Fāṭima bt ʿUmar cannot have been more than nine years old at this time, since ʿUmar had only married her mother in 14/635 after her previous husband, Khālid b. Saʿīd b. al-ʿĀṣ, had been killed in the battle of Marj al-Ṣuffar.[61] It is possible that Fāṭima bt al-Walīd had recently died and that ʿUthmān was eager to renew once more his close ties with the family of Abū Jahl.

In the year 28/648-9, seven years before his death, ʿUthmān married Nā'ila, daughter of the Christian Kalbite chief al-Farāfiṣa b. al-Aḥwaṣ.[62] Saʿīd b. al-ʿĀṣ had married her sister Hind bt al-Farāfiṣa. When ʿUthmān learned of this, he wrote to Saʿīd instructing him that, if Hind had a sister, he convey ʿUthmān's marriage proposal to her. Saʿīd sent to her father who asked her brother Ḍabb to accompany and present her to the caliph, since Ḍabb was a Muslim. ʿUthmān gave her a dowry of 10,000 dirhams and Kaysān Abū Sālim and his wife Rummāna, a slave woman from Kirmān, as presents.[63] Nā'ila bore ʿUthmān at least four daughters, Maryam (al-Ṣughrā), Umm Khālid, Arwā, Umm Abān (al-Ṣughrā), and perhaps a fifth one, Umm al-Banīn. The mother of the latter was Nā'ila according to al-Wāqidī,[64] but according to Ibn Saʿd,[65] a concubine (*umm walad*). An isolated report of Hishām al-Kalbī that ʿUthmān also had a son, ʿAnbasa, by Nā'ila[66] is probably unreliable. Maryam (al-Ṣughrā) was married to the Umayyad ʿAmr b. al-Walīd b.

[59] *Ibid.*, 112. [60] Balādhurī, *Ansāb*, V, 13. [61] Zubayrī, *Nasab*, 303, 349–50.

[62] Ṭabarī, I, 2827; *Annali*, VII, 231–2.

[63] Balādhurī, *Ansāb*, V, 11–12; *Aghānī*, XV, 70–1; *Annali*, VII, 303–4. Saʿīd b. al-ʿĀṣ was probably in charge of the alms-tax of Kalb at the time. The sources quoted by Caetani, *Annali*, VII, 232, mention al-Walīd b. ʿUqba as the one arranging the marriage of Nā'ila with ʿUthmān and put him in charge of the *ṣadaqāt* of Kalb. Al-Walīd b. ʿUqba, however, was governor of Kūfa then. In the account in *Aghānī*, XV, 70–1, Saʿīd b. al-ʿĀṣ is erroneously described as governor of Kūfa at this time. [64] Ṭabarī, I, 3056–7.

[65] *Ṭabaqāt*, III/1, 37; so also Ibn Shabba, *Ta'rīkh al-Madīna*, 953. [66] Ṭabarī, I, 3056.

'Uqba b. Abī Mu'ayṭ. She is described as uncouth (*sayyi'at al-khuluq*) and as provoking the reproach of her husband.[67] If the reports of Muṣ'ab al-Zubayrī and Ibn Sa'd that she was married to Sa'īd b. al-'Āṣ after the death of her sister Umm 'Amr[68] are reliable, 'Amr b. al-Walīd, who outlived Sa'īd b. al-'Āṣ, must have divorced her. Umm Khālid was married by 'Abd Allāh b. Khālid b. Asīd after the death of her sister Umm Sa'īd (Umm 'Uthmān).[69] Arwā married Khālid b. al-Walīd b. 'Uqba b. Abī Mu'ayṭ,[70] brother of 'Amr b. al-Walīd. Umm Abān (al-Ṣughrā) did not marry.[71] Umm al-Banīn, according to al-Wāqidī[72] and Ibn Sa'd,[73] married the Sufyanid 'Abd Allāh b. Yazīd b. Abī Sufyān. According to al-Balādhurī[74] and Ibn Ḥazm,[75] however, Yazīd b. Abī Sufyān had no offspring. According to Ibn Ḥabīb, Umm al-Banīn was rather married to Abū Sufyān b. 'Abd Allāh b. Khālid b. Asīd.[76] A son of 'Abd Allāh b. Khālid b. Asīd named Abū Sufyān does not seem to be known otherwise. Muṣ'ab al-Zubayrī is probably mistaken in stating that she did not marry.[77] Nā'ila became famous among 'Uthmān's wives for her courageous stand in trying to defend her husband against his murderers and for her letter inciting Mu'āwiya to revenge. She refused a marriage proposal by Mu'āwiya and tore out two of her front teeth in order to put an end to his importunity.[78]

Certainly also during his caliphate 'Uthmān married Umm al-Banīn Mulayka, daughter of 'Uyayna b. Ḥiṣn b. Ḥudhayfa b. Badr al-Fazārī. Her father was the chief of Fazāra, a rough and tough bedouin, grandson of Ḥudhayfa b. Badr, famous tribal leader and battle hero in the war of Dāḥis. 'Uyayna at first vigorously fought the Muslims, then joined them just before the conquest of Mekka, remaining a pagan at heart. In the delegation of Fazāra that announced the formal conversion of the tribe to Muḥammad in the year 9/630-1, 'Uyayna was conspicuously absent.[79] After Muḥammad's death he participated in the *ridda*, actively backing the false prophet Ṭalḥa (Ṭulayḥa). He was caught and brought before Abū Bakr, who pardoned him. Immensely proud of his tribal nobility, it was evidently his ambition to marry his daughter Umm al-Banīn to the head of the Muslim community. According to an anecdote he had offered her first to Muḥammad, thereby upsetting 'Ā'isha.[80] Later he seems to have tried to get her married off to 'Umar. When he once rudely scolded his son-in-law 'Uthmān, the latter told him: 'If it had been 'Umar, you would not have this audacity.'[81]

[67] Balādhurī, *Ansāb*, V, 12, 106. [68] See above, n. 56.
[69] Zubayrī, *Nasab*, 112; Ibn Ḥabīb, *Muḥabbar*, 55.
[70] Zubayrī, *Nasab*, 112; Ibn Ḥabīb, *Muḥabbar*, 55. [71] Zubayrī, *Nasab*, 112.
[72] Ṭabarī, I, 3036–7. [73] *Ṭabaqāt*, III/1, 37. [74] *Ansāb*, 4/1, 6.
[75] Ibn Ḥazm, *Jamhara*, 111. [76] Ibn Ḥabīb, *Muḥabbar*, 55. [77] *Nasab*, 112.
[78] Balādhurī, *Ansāb*, V, 12–13; see above p. 349. [79] *Annali*, II/1, 291.
[80] Ibn Ḥajar, *Iṣāba*, V, 55. [81] *Ibid.*, 56.

'Uthmān, in any case, married Umm al-Banīn with a dowry of 500 dinars[82] and put up with her father's and her own bedouin mentality. 'Uyayna did not miss the opportunity to visit his daughter at night during Ramaḍān while she was with the caliph. 'Uthmān invited him to the fast-breaking dinner, but 'Uyayna excused himself on the grounds that he was fasting. On 'Uthmān's astonished question why anyone would fast at night, he explained that he considered day and night alike and found fasting at night less burdensome upon himself. The caliph smiled.[83] According to another story reported by al-Madā'inī,[84] Sālim (b. Musāfi') b. Dāra of the Banū 'Abd Allāh b. Ghaṭafān was wounded by Zumayl b. Ubayr of Fazāra after a quarrel and was carried to 'Uthmān in Medina. The caliph ordered his physician to attend to his wound. When the latter proposed to treat it with medicine rather than by surgery, the daughter of 'Uyayna, in true tribal solidarity with Fazāra, bribed him to sprinkle poison on the wound, killing Sālim.

Umm al-Banīn bore 'Uthmān a son, 'Abd al-Malik, who died in childhood.[85] Hishām Ibn al-Kalbī mentioned a second son of 'Uthmān by her, named 'Utba.[86] According to some sources, 'Uthmān repudiated Umm al-Banīn during the siege of his palace. Reporting this, al-Madā'inī commented that there was in her the same crudeness (*jafā'*) as in her father 'Uyayna. When the latter heard of the statement of the Prophet that the tribes of Muzayna, Juhayna, Aslam and Ghifār were more virtuous (*khayr*) than Tamīm, Asad, 'Āmir and Ghaṭafān (to whom Fazāra belonged), he countered: 'To be with these in hell-fire is preferable to me than to be with those in paradise.' When this reached Umm al-Banīn, she exclaimed: 'By God, my father is not far from the truth (*mā ab'ada Abī*).'[87] Umm al-Banīn is mentioned prominently, however, among those who helped to bury the murdered caliph clandestinely. Muṣ'ab al-Zubayrī names her and Nā'ila as the two wives who inherited from 'Uthmān.[88] Only Ibn Sa'd, as noted, mentions an anonymous concubine of 'Uthmān, according to him the mother of Umm al-Banīn bt 'Uthmān.

The pattern of marriages of 'Uthmān and of his daughters clearly

[82] Balādhurī, *Ansāb*, V, 13. The sequence in which 'Uthmān's payments of dowries to his wives are listed there appears to be chronological. The marriage with Umm al-Banīn is mentioned after 'Uthmān's proposal to Fāṭima bt 'Umar after 'Umar's death. This seems to confirm that the marriage took place during 'Uthmān's caliphate. Neither 'Uyayna nor 'Uthmān could have had any interest in the marriage before his reign.

[83] Balādhurī, *Ansāb*, V, 106; Ibn Shabba, *Ta'rīkh al-Madīna*, 1056–7.

[84] Balādhurī, *Ansāb*, V, 15. Further details about the feud are provided by Ibn Shabba, *Ta'rīkh al-Madīna*, 1057–63.

[85] This is stated by al-Mas'ūdī (*Murūj*, III, para. 1577) and implied by al-Ṭabarī (I, 3056). Muṣ'ab al-Zubayrī is probably mistaken in stating that he died as an adult (*rajulan*) but childless (*Nasab*, 104).

[86] Ṭabarī, I, 3056.

[87] Balādhurī, *Ansāb*, V, 100.

[88] *Nasab*, 112.

reflect his desire, especially when he was older, to strengthen his ties with the old-established Mekkan aristocracy. Aside from his own clan, ʿAbd Shams, he courted Makhzūm, in particular the family of Abū Jahl. He was evidently eager to restore the ties broken when he was forced to divorce Abū Jahl's daughter on his conversion to Islam. His overtures to Makhzūm bore fruit at the time of the *shūrā* election when Makhzūm strongly backed his candidacy against ʿAlī's.[89]

ʿUthmān's kinship, through his grandmother, with the Banū Hāshim did not mean much to him. His personal pride was presumably flattered by having been given two daughters of the Prophet. After both of them died, he made no effort to maintain marriage ties with Muḥammad's clan. He lacked any sense of solidarity with the new Islamic nobility based on *sābiqa* and merit in religion which ʿUmar had attempted to establish. With none of the families of prominent Muslim leaders, Abū Bakr, ʿUmar, the five members of the *shūrā*, or any of the Anṣār, did he forge marriage ties. His proposal to marry ʿUmar's daughter Fāṭima presumably was, as noted, influenced primarily by her maternal Makhzumite nobility. The pious ʿAbd Allāh b. ʿUmar may have acted partly out of an awareness of this motivation when he refused the proposal. Of the two tribal leaders whose daughters ʿUthmān married during his caliphate, one was a Christian and the other a nominal convert, making light of Islamic ritual and faith.

With regard to ʿUthmān's Umayyad kin, it is noteworthy that he did not establish marriage bonds with Muʿāwiya. His relations with Abū Sufyān and his numerous descendants were clearly not as close as with the other branches of the clan, even if the obscure reports about a marriage of his daughter Umm al-Banīn to an ʿAbd Allāh b. Yazīd b. Abī Sufyān should be reliable. It was Muʿāwiya who later, as caliph, gave his daughter Ramla in marriage to ʿAmr, ʿUthmān's eldest surviving son and presumptive successor.[90]

The data about ʿUthmān's marriages are also relevant to the question of ʿUthmān's age. If he married Nā'ila seven years before his death and had at least four daughters by her, it is hardly likely that he reached the age of eighty-two years given by most sources, not to mention eighty-six, eighty-eight, ninety or ninety-five years given by some. More reasonable would be the age of seventy-five years mentioned Abū Maʿshar. The age of sixty-three given by Sayf b. ʿUmar is arbitrarily chosen to make ʿUthmān and the other early caliphs all die miraculously at the same age as Muḥammad.[91]

[89] See above, p. 71. [90] Zubayrī, *Nasab*, 106.
[91] For the information about the age of ʿUthmān given in the various sources see *Annali*, VIII, 258–60.

4 DOMANIAL LAND IN IRAQ UNDER 'UMAR

All evidence adduced by Caetani for his assertion that 'Umar gave concessions from *fay'* land in Iraq[92] is unsound. The case of al-Rufayl or Ibn al-Rufayl,[93] a landed magnate (*dihqān*) who co-operated with the Muslim conquerors, does not concern ownerless domanial land. Al-Rufayl had stayed on his estate during the conquest. When he later converted to Islam, 'Umar allowed him to keep his land with the obligation of continuing to pay the land tax (*kharāj*). This did not affect the status of his land, since all those who had remained on their land at the time of the conquest had been recognized as its *de facto* owners in return for payment of *kharāj*.

The case of Sa'īd b. Zayd,[94] 'Umar's brother-in-law, is highly doubtful. Sa'd b. Abī Waqqāṣ is described as having, on 'Umar's order, granted land to him which turned out to belong to (Ibn) al-Rufayl. When the latter complained, 'Umar rescinded the land concession to Sa'īd. If the report is sound, this would have occurred during the time of the conquest, before 'Umar had decreed the general immobilization of agricultural land.

The case of 'Umar's land concession (*iqṭā'*) to 'Alī[95] concerned land at Yanbu' in Arabia. It was evidently ownerless dead land. Such land grants of previously uncultivated land had been made by Muḥammad. According to 'Urwa b. al-Zubayr, Abū Bakr conceded such land at al-Jurf three miles north of Medina to his father, al-Zubayr.[96] 'Umar also owned land there[97] which must have been granted by Abū Bakr or Muḥammad. The case of Khuthaym al-Qārī[98] likewise concerns land in Arabia near (Dhu) l-Marwa. Contrary to Caetani's note, 'Umar declined to grant Khuthaym the land he requested.

The case of 'Umar's land grant to Abū 'Abd Allāh Nāfi' on the bank of the Tigris for the purpose of grazing his horses also concerned unused land. 'Umar sought an assurance that it was not taxable agricultural land (*arḍ al-jizya*) nor irrigated by water coming from agricultural land.[99]

The report of Mūsā b. Ṭalḥa that 'Umar granted land to five Companions quoted by Yaḥyā b. Ādam[100] rests on a faulty transmission. In the reliable parallel versions quoted by al-Balādhurī,[101] Abū 'Ubayd,[102]

[92] *Annali*, V, 404. [93] Yaḥyā, *Kharāj*, 42.
[94] *Ibid.* [95] *Ibid.*, 57.
[96] *Ibid.*; Balādhurī, *Futūḥ*, 13, 21. Abū Yūsuf rather reports that al-Jurf was land belonging to the Banu l-Naḍīr and was granted to al-Zubayr by Muḥammad (Abū Yūsuf, *Kitāb al-Kharāj*, (Cairo, 1352/[1933], 61). [97] Yāqūt, *Buldān*, II, 7.
[98] Ibn Sa'd, *Ṭabaqāt*, V, 343. [99] Yaḥyā, *Kharāj*, 11, 57–8. [100] *Ibid.*, 57.
[101] *Futūḥ*, 273.
[102] Abū 'Ubayd al-Qāsim b. Sallām, *Kitāb al-Amwāl*, ed. Muḥammad Harrās (Cairo, 1968), 393.

and Ibn Shabba,[103] it is ʿUthmān who made these land grants. Mūsā b. Ṭalḥa categorically affirmed in several of his reports that ʿUthmān was the first to grant *iqṭāʿ*s in the *sawād*. As a contemporary and son of one of the beneficiaries of ʿUthmān's new policy, he must be considered a key witness in the question.

The later Muslim authors and jurists supportive of government interest generally favoured the view that the *ṣāwāfī* could be used freely at the caliph's discretion. Sayf b. ʿUmar thus also asserts, on the basis of a lengthy report attributed by him to ʿĀmir al-Shaʿbī (d. 103/721), another highly authoritative witness, that ʿUmar granted *iqṭāʿ*s in the *sawād*.[104] Yet the same al-Shaʿbī according to reliable reports stated that Muḥammad, Abū Bakr and ʿUmar did not grant *iqṭāʿ*s from (cultivated) land and that ʿUthmān was the first one to grant and sell such land.[105] The examples quoted by Sayf on al-Shaʿbī's authority are no doubt fabricated. Ṭalḥa's estate was granted by ʿUthmān, as attested by his son Mūsā as well as by al-Shaʿbī.[106] Jarīr b. ʿAbd Allāh, chief of Bajīla, received his estate along the Euphrates from ʿUthmān. When ʿUmar withdrew the *iqṭāʿ* initially conferred on Bajīla collectively, he is reported to have rewarded Jarīr with 80 dinars.[107] Sayf's story that ʿUmar ordered ʿUthmān b. Ḥunayf to give Jarīr land for his sustenance is an invention not supported by any other source. Under the circumstances, the other names mentioned by Sayf, al-Ribbīʿ b. ʿAmr al-Asadī, Abū Mufazzir al-Tamīmī and Abū Mūsā al-Ashʿarī, cannot inspire confidence.

Hārūn al-Rashīd's chief judge Abū Yūsuf states that in Iraq all land of the Persian king (Kisrā), his nobles (*marāziba*), and his household was (suitable for) fiefs (*qaṭāʾiʿ*);[108] the imam should grant *iqṭāʿ*s to whomever he wished and leave no land without owner and cultivation.[109] The only examples of land grants by ʿUmar mentioned by Abū Yūsuf concern Arabia.[110] For Iraq he cites land grants by ʿUthmān.[111] Abū ʿUbayd al-Qāsim b. Sallām likewise does not mention any grants of agricultural land in Iraq by ʿUmar. He justifies the land grants by ʿUthmān as coming from ownerless land which ʿUmar had set aside as *ṣawāfī* (*aṣfāhā*).[112]

Both Abū Yūsuf and Abū ʿUbayd support their argument with a report by the Kufan ʿAbd al-Malik b. Abī Ḥurra al-Ḥanafī on the authority of his father, according to which ʿUmar had set aside (*aṣfā*) the land of the Persian king (*arḍ Kisrā*), land whose owners had fled, and several other categories as *ṣawāfī*, and their register (*dīwān*) was burned by the people

[103] Ibn Shabba, *Taʾrīkh al-Madīna*, 1020–1.
[104] Ṭabarī, I, 2376. [105] Yaḥyā, *Kharāj*, 58; Ibn Shabba, *Taʾrīkh al-Madīna*, 1019.
[106] Balādhurī, *Futūḥ*, 273. [107] Yaḥyā, *Kharāj*, 29, 30. [108] Abū Yūsuf, *Kharāj*, 57.
[109] *Ibid.*, 58, 61. [110] *Ibid.*, 61–2. [111] *Ibid.*, 62.
[112] Abū ʿUbayd, *Amwāl*, 399–400.

at the time of the battle of (Dayr) al-Jamājim in 83/702.[113] The report was certainly formulated at a late date and has no source value for the time of 'Umar.[114] In reality 'Umar surveyed the *sawād* as a whole, set the rates of taxation, and placed the land under administration by the governor and garrison of Kūfa. The setting aside and registration of the *ṣawāfī* took place during the caliphate of Mu'āwiya.

5 NOTES ON THE SOURCES FOR THE CRISIS OF THE CALIPHATE OF 'UTHMĀN

The most reliable history of the crisis of 'Uthmān's caliphate was provided by al-Wāqidī. The sources quoted by him, many of them eyewitness or first-hand reports, span the whole range of political attitudes towards the events. Among them are the 'Alids 'Umar b. 'Alī b. Abī Ṭālib, his sons, Muḥammad and 'Alī, and the pro-'Alī 'Abd Allāh b. al-'Abbās. There are the representatives of the originally pro-'Uthmān, but later disillusioned, Qurayshite clan of Zuhra, al-Miswar b. Makhrama, his client Abū 'Awn,[115] 'Abd al-Raḥmān b. al-Aswad b. 'Abd Yaghūth,

[113] Abū Yūsuf, *Kharāj*, 57 ('Abd Allāh b. Abī Ḥurra in the text should presumably be read 'Abd al-Malik b. Abī Ḥurra. In Abū Yūsuf's version there is no separate mention of the father Abū Ḥurra); Abū 'Ubayd, *Amwāl*, 399; Balādhurī, *Futūḥ*, 272–3. The report was partly translated and accepted as reliable by D. C. Dennett, *Conversion and Poll Tax in Early Islam* (Cambridge, 1950), 26.

[114] Abū Ḥurra al-Ḥanafī is described in one of the versions of the report quoted by al-Balādhurī (*Futūḥ*, 272) as 'the best informed man about this *sawād*'. 'Abd al-Malik b. Abī Ḥurra is otherwise known only as a transmitter of Shi'ite reports about the last period of 'Alī's reign to Abū Mikhnaf (Ṭabarī, I, 3270, 3361, 3363, 3383; Sezgin, *Abū Miḥnaf*, 192). His main source for these reports, which he narrates without *isnād*, was probably information received from his father who is mentioned as a messenger from 'Alī to the rebel Banū Nājiya (Ṭabarī, I, 3440, for Abū Jurra read Abū Ḥurra; Thaqafī, *Ghārāt*, 364). Abū Ḥurra must have been quite young then if he was still alive after the battle of Dayr al-Jamājim. The reports were no doubt formulated by 'Abd al-Malik, not by his father.

The transmitter of 'Abd al-Malik's report about the *sawād* was the Kufan 'Abd Allāh b. al-Walīd b. 'Abd Allāh b. Ma'qil al-Muzanī (Ibn Ḥajar, *Tahdhīb*, VI, 69), who handed it on in variant versions but regularly with the formula *aṣfā 'Umar*. He evidently had a specific interest in ascribing the later caliphal policy concerning the *ṣawāfī* to 'Umar. Abū Yūsuf quoted a similar report by him on the authority of an unnamed 'man of the Banū Asad', who, he said, was more knowledgeable about the *sawād* than anyone he had ever met (*Kharāj*, 57; al-Madanī should be read al-Muzanī). Abū Yūsuf, himself equally interested in legitimizing 'Abbasid practice, added a further report about 'Umar's having set aside various categories of crown land, which he had heard from 'one of the old shaykhs of the people of Medina' (*ibid.*, 57–8).

[115] Abū 'Awn *mawlā* al-Miswar seems to be the same as Abū 'Awn, the father of Shuraḥbīl b. Abī 'Awn, although this cannot be definitely proven. Shuraḥbīl b. Abī 'Awn is not mentioned in the biographical dictionaries. While usually transmitting from his father, he is also al-Wāqidī's informant for an important report of the Egyptian Yazīd b. Abī Ḥabīb on the authority of Abu l-Khayr (Ṭabarī, I, 2999). He thus appears to have been a historian in his own right.

and the family of Sa'd b. Abī Waqqāṣ.[116] The clan of Makhzūm, similarly disillusioned, is also represented.[117] The pro-'Uthmān but anti-Marwanid family tradition of al-Zubayr is provided by Abū Ḥabība, client of al-Zubayr, and Mūsā b. 'Uqba, client of the Āl al-Zubayr. On the part of the Anṣār, there was the tradition of the distinguished Medinan family of 'Amr b. Ḥazm of the Banu l-Najjār, in the end distinctly anti-'Uthmān, and the vital and highly reliable testimony of Muḥammad b. Maslama of the Banū 'Amr b. 'Awf of Aws, a supporter of 'Uthmān until shortly before the end and thereafter a neutral who either did not pledge allegiance to 'Alī or would not back him in war. 'Uthmanid also was the testimony of 'Uthmān b. Muḥammad al-Akhnasī,[118] grandson of al-Mughīra b. al-Akhnas al-Thaqafī, who was killed defending the palace of 'Uthmān. Pro-Marwanid were Abū Ḥafṣa, freedman of Marwān, who boasted that he started the civil war, and Ṭalḥa's son Mūsā who, following his father's volte-face from giving active leadership to the rebels to persecuting them as murderers of the caliph, became an ideological supporter of the Umayyads.[119] 'Uthmanid and pro-Umayyad was also Yūsuf, the son of 'Abd Allāh b. Salām al-Isrā'īlī.[120] Caetani's description of al-Wāqidī as a tendentious pro-'Alid source[121] is entirely baseless. It is unfortunate that al-Ṭabarī suppressed much of al-Wāqidī's history of the crisis because he found it repugnant.[122] Some of the suppressed material is to be recovered from al-Balādhurī's *Ansāb al-ashrāf*. The value of al-Balādhurī's quotations is diminished, however, by his practice of condensing reports, sometimes radically,[123] and of omitting *isnāds*.

Al-Ṭabarī's other main source, Sayf b. 'Umar's account, is a late Kufan 'Uthmanid and anti-Shi'ite concoction without source value for the events. The *isnāds* are largely fictitious. The contents and tendentiousness of his account have been briefly analysed by Wellhausen.[124] Recent attempts to rehabilitate Sayf b. 'Umar[125] have done little to invalidate the substance

[116] Descendants of Sa'd b. Abī Waqqāṣ were Ismā'īl b. Muḥammad b. Sa'd (*ibid.*, 2979) and 'Āmir b. Sa'd (*ibid.*, 2981).

[117] 'Abd Allāh b. 'Ayyāsh b. Abī Rabī'a (*ibid.*, 3000) and his grandson 'Abd al-Raḥmān b. 'Abd al-'Azīz (*ibid.*, 3021).

[118] *Ibid.*, 3022.

[119] *Ibid.* On Mūsā b. Ṭalḥa and his pro-Umayyad stance see further excursus 6.

[120] Ṭabarī, I, 3023. 'Abd Allāh b. Salām is frequently quoted in Syrian sources extolling 'Uthmān and lamenting his death.

[121] *Annali*, VIII, 147, 150 and throughout.

[122] Ṭabarī, I, 2965, 2980.

[123] See, for instance, the report of 'Abd al-Raḥmān b. al-Aswad which takes up two-and-a-half pages in al-Ṭabarī (I, 2977–9) but is reduced to five lines by al-Balādhurī (*Ansāb*, V, 65).

[124] *Skizzen*, VI, 120–1, 124–5, 133–5. Parts of Sayf b. 'Umar's account not preserved by al-Ṭabarī are quoted by Ibn 'Asākir, *'Uthmān*, and Ibn Bakr, *Tamhīd*.

[125] See in particular A. Noth, 'Der Charakter der ersten grossen Sammlungen von Nachrichten zur frühen Kalifenzeit', *Der Islam*, 17 (1971), 168–88; A. Noth, *The Early Arabic Historical Tradition: A Source-critical Study*, (Princeton, 1994), 4–14; E. Landau-Tasseron, 'Sayf Ibn 'Umar in Medieval and Modern Scholarship', *Der Islam*, 67 (1990), 1–26.

of Wellhausen's judgement. Sayf preserved, however, some contemporary poetry by 'Uthmān's uterine brother al-Walīd b. 'Uqba and others, which is of considerable interest.[126]

Al-Ṭabarī's informant for another historical tradition repeatedly quoted by him, Ja'far b. 'Abd Allāh al-Muḥammadī, is to be identified as a descendant of Muḥammad b. al-Ḥanafiyya, Abū 'Abd Allāh Ja'far b. 'Abd Allāh Ra's al-Midhrā b. Ja'far al-Thānī b. 'Abd Allāh b. Ja'far b. Muḥammad.[127] He is an Imāmī Shi'ite author considered highly reliable as a traditionist. Al-Ṭabarī presumably heard traditions from him while he stayed in Kūfa. His constant *isnād* is 'Amr b. Ḥammād b. Ṭalḥa and 'Alī b. Ḥusayn b. 'Īsā – Ḥusayn b. 'Īsā – his father.[128] Of these, 'Amr b. Ḥammād al-Qannād (d. 222/837) is known as a Kufan Shi'ite (*rāfiḍī*) counted reliable as a transmitter[129] and Ḥusayn b. 'Īsā is perhaps al-Ḥusayn b. 'Īsā b. Muslim al-Kūfī, described by the Sunnite hadith critics as transmitting objectionable traditions (*munkar al-ḥadīth*).[130] The source is thus solidly Kufan Shi'ite. 'Īsā occasionally gives his own account but more often quotes further sources. Twice his transmitter is Muḥammad b. Isḥāq, who is quoted by al-Ṭabarī in another instance through a different *isnād*.[131] These quotations show that Muḥammad b. Isḥāq's sources and his grasp of the events were far inferior to al-Wāqidī's. Noteworthy is that Ibn Isḥāq's uncle 'Abd al-Raḥmān b. Yasār considered the letter intercepted by the Egyptian rebels to be written by 'Uthmān.[132] The details of his report, however, do not inspire confidence. Completely muddled and unreliable is the report quoted by Ibn Isḥāq with the *isnād* Yaḥyā b. 'Abbād (b. 'Abd Allāh b. al-Zubayr) – 'Abd Allāh b. al-Zubayr – his father.[133] It certainly does not go back to 'Abd Allāh b. al-Zubayr, who as a young man prominently involved in the events had a solid knowledge of them and would not have ascribed it to his father. Most likely his grandson Yaḥyā b. 'Abbād made it up from some scraps of information from him. Probably more reliable is the third report of Ibn Isḥāq going back to the Makhzumite Abū Bakr (b. 'Abd al-Raḥmān) b. al-Ḥārith b. Hishām.[134] Altogether the transmission of Ja'far al-Muḥammadī is of little source value.

The Syrian and Egyptian historical school traditions, to which Caetani gave some prominence in his discussion, contribute little sound information. The 'Syrian' report presented in the time of 'Umar II by Abū Ḥubaysh Sahm al-Azdī, who is described as the last eyewitness of the events,[135] is

[126] See Ibn 'Asākir, '*Uthmān*, 306–9, 544–55. A good deal of this poetry is probably authentic.
[127] Najāshī, *Rijāl*, 120; Ibn 'Inaba, '*Umdat al-ṭālib fī ansāb āl Abī Ṭālib*, ed. Muḥammad Ḥasan Āl al-Ṭāliqānī (Najaf, 1380/1961), 354.
[128] The *isnād*, in Ṭabarī, I, 2985, Ja'far – 'Amr – Muḥammad b. Isḥāq is obviously incomplete.
[129] Ibn Ḥajar, *Tahdhīb*, VIII, 22–3. [130] *Ibid.*, II, 364. [131] Ṭabarī, I, 3003.
[132] *Ibid.*, 2983–4. [133] *Ibid.*, 2986–9. [134] *Ibid.*, 3003–4.
[135] Ibn 'Asākir, '*Uthmān*, 422–5; *Annali*, VIII, 227–30.

pro-Umayyad fiction. Characteristic for its Umayyad tendentiousness is that Ṭalḥa, together with al-Zubayr, appears as one of the supporters of ʿUthmān before his death. Highly valuable and authentic is, in contrast, ʿUthmān's letter to the Syrians preserved by the Syrian school tradition, which was entirely misunderstood and misjudged by Caetani as a 'traditionist product of much later times'.[136]

The lengthy comprehensive account which the Egyptian ʿAbd Allāh b. Lahīʿa ascribed to Yazīd b. Abī Ḥabīb[137] reflects a far-reaching ignorance of the historical situation. Thus it describes al-Walīd b. ʿUqba as the governor of Kūfa at the time of the rebellion. Its description of the murder of ʿUthmān is partly based on the Syrian report of Abū Ḥubaysh al-Azdī. It is safe to assume that the whole account was made up by Ibn Lahīʿa, not by Yazīd b. Abī Ḥabīb, who had a sound grasp of the historical situation, as is evident from his report quoted by Shuraḥbīl b. Abī ʿAwn.[138]

Al-Balādhurī's *Ansāb al-ashrāf* and Ibn Shabba's *Ta'rīkh al-Madīna* provide some material from early sources ignored by al-Ṭabarī. Ibn Shabba quotes numerous ʿUthmanid traditions missing in other sources and, in contrast to al-Balādhurī, avoids reports about ʿUthmān's wrongdoings.[139] The reports of the pro-ʿAlid Kufan Abū Mikhnaf quoted by al-Balādhurī, in one passage jointly with ʿAwāna,[140] are vital for the events in Kūfa. For events in Medina Abū Mikhnaf seems to have occasionally had the same reports as were available to al-Wāqidī, so that al-Balādhurī could combine their narrations. A closer examination of their relationship, however, is hampered by al-Balādhurī's frequent omission of *isnād*s. Abū Mikhnaf's main account of the action of the Egyptian rebels[141] reveals the vagueness and faultiness of his knowledge of the developments in Medina. Thus he was not aware that the rebels during their first campaign did not enter Medina but stayed at Dhū Khushub. The letter from ʿUthmān to the rebels quoted by Abū Mikhnaf in which the caliph promises them general redress of their grievances[142] is a fake.

Reports by the Basran traditionist school represented by Abū Naḍra al-ʿAbdī, al-Ḥasan al-Baṣrī and Muḥammad b. Sīrīn are ʿUthmanid anti-Kufan, but not anti-ʿAlid, in tendency and mostly hagiographical. There was little first-hand information available. Strongly ʿUthmanid and fictitious are the reports transmitted by Abū Naḍra from Abū Saʿīd

[136] *Annali*, VIII, 240–1. See above, p. 91 with n. 59.

[137] Ibn ʿAsākir, *ʿUthmān*, 425–32; *Annali*, VIII, 227–30. [138] See above, n. 115.

[139] The characterization of Ibn Shabba as 'pro-ʿAlid' and 'with Shiʿite inclinations', put forward by E. L. Petersen (*ʿAlī and Muʿāwiya*, 92 n. 45 and p. 151), is no longer sustainable after the publication of his *Ta'rīkh al-Madīna*.

[140] Balādhurī, *Ansāb*, V, 36. [141] *Ibid.*, 62–6. [142] *Ibid.*, 64.

mawlā Abī Usayd.[143] The stories of 'Uthmān's client Waththāb transmitted by al-Ḥasan al-Baṣrī about an alleged meeting of 'Uthmān with al-Ashtar and Waththāb's presence at the murder of 'Uthmān[144] are probably unreliable. Al-Balādhurī quotes a lengthy account of the crisis and the murder of 'Uthmān by the Basran historian Wahb b. Jarīr b. Ḥāzim, who attributed it with an *isnād* to the Medinan al-Zuhrī.[145] Much of the basic information probably goes back to al-Zuhrī, but the composition is that of Wahb b. Jarīr or perhaps of his father. It contains some serious misconceptions, e.g. that the Egyptian rebels arrived at Dhū Khushub at the beginning of the year 35/July 655 and that al-Zubayr and Ṭalḥa jointly controlled the situation in Medina during the final siege.[146]

Both al-Balādhurī and Ibn Shabba cite a lengthy account of the crisis attributed to the early Medinan authority Sa'īd b. al-Musayyab.[147] Its real author was Ismā'īl b. Yaḥyā al-Taymī, a descendant of the caliph Abū Bakr and notorious as a forger of hadith.[148] Ismā'īl b. Yaḥyā gave his account the *isnad* Muḥammad b. Abī Dhi'b – al-Zuhrī – Sa'īd b. al-Musayyab. This was presumably after the death of Ibn Abī Dhi'b in 158/775 or 159/776. Ismā'īl narrated it to the Damascene Muḥammad b. 'Īsā (b. al-Qāsim) b. Sumay' al-Umawī (d. 204/819–20 or 206/821–2), who passed it on suppressing the name of his informant, evidently because of his bad reputation as a transmitter. Al-Balādhurī, Ibn Shabba and Ibn 'Asākir,[149] who quote the account *in extenso*, thus report it with an *isnād* omitting Ismā'īl b. Yaḥyā. The account, impressive in its apparent knowledge of detail, was quoted also in other works including Ibn 'Abd Rabbih's *al-'Iqd al-farīd*.[150] It was well known, however, that Ismā'īl b. Yaḥyā was the author of the account and that Ibn Sumay' suppressed his name.[151] Its authorship by a descendant of Abū Bakr explains the prominence of the part of Muḥammad b. Abī Bakr in the account. He is described as having been appointed governor of Egypt by 'Uthmān to replace 'Abd Allāh b.

[143] Abū Usayd is the Medinan Mālik b. Rabī'a al-Sā'idī, a veteran of the battle of Badr (Ibn Ḥajar, *Tahdhīb*, X, 15–16; Ibn Ḥajar, *Iṣāba*, VI, 13–14). Ibn al-Munkadir names him among the supporters of 'Uthmān in the palace (Ibn Shabba, *Ta'rīkh al-Madīna*, 1280).

[144] Ṭabarī, I, 2989–91; Balādhurī, *Ansāb*, V, 92–3; Ibn Sa'd, *Ṭabaqāt*, III/1, 50.

[145] Balādhurī, *Ansāb*, V, 88–92. [146] See above, p. 104.

[147] Balādhurī, *Ansāb*, V, 25–6, 67–71; Ibn Shabba, *Ta'rīkh al-Madīna*, 1157–61, 1302–6.

[148] Al-Dhahabī, *Mīzān al-i'tidāl* (Cairo, 1325/[1907]), I, 117–18; Ibn Ḥajar al-'Asqalānī, *Lisān al-mīzān* (Hyderabad, 1329–31/[1911–13]), I, 441–2. His full lineage is Ismā'īl b. Yaḥyā b. 'Ubayd Allāh b. Ṭalḥa b. 'Abd Allāh b. 'Abd al-Raḥmān b. Abī Bakr. The descendants of his great-grandfather Ṭalḥa b. 'Abd Allāh lived in the desert in a place called Ḥādhat al-Uṭum on the right side of the route from Medina to Mekka (Zubayrī, *Nasab*, 289). [149] Ibn 'Asākir, *'Uthmān*, 421–4.

[150] See the references given in Balādhurī, *Ansāb*, V, annotation to pp. 25 and 67. Caetani summarized the version of Ibn 'Asākir in *Annali*, VIII, 245–7.

[151] Ibn Ḥajar, *Tahdhīb*, IX, 390–1.

Sa'd on the demand of the Egyptian rebels. In the forged letter of 'Uthmān to 'Abd Allāh b. Sa'd intercepted by the rebels, the governor of Egypt was ordered to ignore the letter of appointment of Muḥammad b. Abī Bakr and to kill him surreptitiously. This story was evidently meant to justify Muḥammad b. Abī Bakr's hatred of 'Uthmān. Ibn Abī Bakr is further described as having ordered the Egyptians to beat and kill the caliph. All this and many other details are fiction in conflict with the early reliable reports.

6 MŪSĀ B. ṬALḤA AND THE UMAYYADS

The title to vengeance for Marwān's murder of Ṭalḥa would have primarily belonged to Ṭalḥa's son Mūsā since the eldest son, Muḥammad, had also been killed in the battle of the Camel. Mūsā b. Ṭalḥa, a transmitter of hadith and pious enough later to be considered by some as the expected Mahdi, was not the man to take up the pre-Islamic duty, especially against so intimidating a clan as the Umayya. He was clearly pleased to be granted his father's inheritance by 'Alī in exchange for his pledge of allegiance and does not seem to have joined Mu'āwiya before 'Alī's death. When he visited the Umayyad later, Mu'āwiya asked him politely whether he might cheer him with good tidings and then quoted what he had heard the Prophet say: 'Ṭalḥa is among those who have fulfilled their vow (*man qaḍā naḥbah*).'[152] The expression in Qur'ān XXXIII 23 to which he alluded was said to refer to the Muslim martyrs killed in the battle of Uḥud, in which Ṭalḥa had greatly distinguished himself. Mūsā was evidently well pleased and responded in due time by narrating a story in which he pictured Mu'āwiya as lecturing the Early Companions, including his own father Ṭalḥa, in the presence of 'Uthmān about their duty to back the latter and as putting 'Alī, the only one objecting to his wise counsel, in his proper place.[153] Mūsā and his brothers Isḥāq and Ismā'īl were the first Qurayshites to sign Ziyād's letter of indictment declaring Ḥujr b. 'Adī an infidel for rebellion against Mu'āwiya.[154]

Mūsā did not shun his father's murderer in Medina. On one occasion Marwān, ever mischievous, praised Ṭalḥa in the presence of Mūsā and 'Abd Allāh b. al-Zubayr, whereas he mentioned al-Zubayr without a good word about him. Ibn al-Zubayr took him up on this, remarking that Abū Muḥammad (Ṭalḥa) was certainly worthy of his praise but that he

[152] Ibn Sa'd, *Ṭabaqāt*, III/1, 155–6.
[153] Ṭabarī, I, 2948; Ibn Shabba, *Ta'rīkh al-Madīna*, 1090–1, where Mūsā b. Ṭalḥa is missing in the *isnād*. Ibn Shabba quotes several secondary versions of Mūsā's story (1091–5).
[154] Ṭabarī, II, 132.

knew of someone about whom no good was ever mentioned. Marwān: 'And who is that?' Ibn al-Zubayr: 'Your father.' Marwān jumped towards him and the two exchanged blows until Mūsā intervened. Ibn al-Zubayr rebuked him: 'Let me strike out an eye of the son of the outcast of the Messenger of God.'[155] Without Mūsā's intervention he might well have succeeded, for he was, in contrast to Marwān, a formidable wrestler.

Later, when challenging Ibn al-Zubayr's counter-caliphate, Marwān found it expedient to publicize his murder of Ṭalḥa among the Syrians as proof that he, not Muʿāwiya, had been the first one to avenge ʿUthmān.[156] The Syrians must have been surprised, since so far they had been told that Ṭalḥa was a praiseworthy man who had defended ʿUthmān against his critics[157] and had fought ʿAlī. They seem to have been impressed, however, by Marwān's credentials and preferred him to Ibn al-Zubayr who had just put forward his own claim to being the true avenger of the blood of the wronged caliph.[158]

Mūsā was evidently not much affected by this quarrel during the second *fitna*. Khālid b. Shumayr, Basran admirer of ʿAbd Allāh b. ʿUmar, reported that Mūsā was among the Kufans who fled to Baṣra during the inter-Muslim conflict in order to escape the impostor (*kadhdhāb*) al-Mukhtār. Ibn Shumayr and other Basrans frequented his circle, as many people thought that he was the Mahdi. The subject of *fitna* was discussed, and Mūsā gave vent to his horror of inter-Muslim warfare. In the end he asked God to have mercy upon ʿAbd Allāh b. ʿUmar who, he thought, was still steadfastly clinging to the commitment the Prophet had imposed on him. 'By God,' he concluded, 'the Quraysh were unable to provoke him [to fighting] in their first *fitna*.' Ibn Shumayr felt that Mūsā was casting aspersion on the conduct of his own father, who at that time had allowed himself to be killed.[159]

Marwān's son ʿAbd al-Malik married Mūsā's daughter ʿĀ'isha, who bore him his son Bakkār.[160] ʿAbd al-Malik's brother Bishr b. Marwān, while governor of Kūfa for his brother, found Mūsā a convenient go-between in dealing with the religious class. Bishr himself enjoyed drinking and preferred the company of poets. He sent Mūsā money for distribution among the Kufan Qur'ān readers (*qurrā'*) in order to keep them well disposed, but not all of them would accept the bribe.[161] ʿAbd al-Malik's uncouth other son, the caliph al-Walīd, told Mūsā, who was by then an old man, to his face: 'Whenever you pay me a visit, I feel like

155 Balādhurī, *Ansāb*, V, 203–4. 156 See esp. *ibid.*, 134–5.
157 See above, p. 189. 158 Balādhurī, *Ansāb*, V, 128.
159 Ibn Saʿd, *Ṭabaqāt*, V, 120–1; Ibn Manẓūr, *Mukhtaṣar*, XXV, 290.
160 Ibn Saʿd, *Ṭabaqāt*, V, 120; Zubayrī, *Nasab*, 286. 161 Balādhurī, *Ansāb*, V, 170.

killing you, were it not that my father informed me that Marwān killed Ṭalḥa.' Nothing is reported about Mūsā's reaction.[162]

7 THE MARRIAGES AND CHILDREN OF AL-ḤASAN B. 'ALĪ

The first marriage of al-Ḥasan was probably with Salmā, or Zaynab, daughter of the renowned Kalbite chief Imru' ul-Qays b.'Adī b. Aws b. Jābir b. Ka'b b. 'Ulaym. Imru' ul-Qays, a Christian, came from the Syrian desert to Medina in order to offer his conversion to Islam to the caliph 'Umar. 'Umar was so pleased with him that he immediately appointed him amir over all those of Quḍā'a (to whom Kalb belonged) who would accept Islam. As he departed, 'Alī together with his sons al-Ḥasan and al-Ḥusayn came forth to meet him and proposed establishing marriage ties with him. Imru' ul-Qays consented and gave his daughters al-Muḥayyāh, Salmā and al-Rabāb in marriage to the three members of the Prophet's family respectively.[163]

This must have happened at the time of the Muslim conquest of Palestine at the beginning of 'Umar's reign. Al-Ḥasan and al-Ḥusayn, born in the years 3/624–5 and 4/626 respectively, were evidently too young for the wedding to have taken place immediately. Nothing further is known about Salmā. Al-Muḥayyāh is listed among 'Alī's wives and bore him a daughter, who died as a child.[164] Al-Rabāb bore al-Ḥusayn his favourite daughter, Sukayna, and, after he was killed at Karbalā', spent a year in grief at his grave; she refused to remarry. According to Sukayna, al-Ḥasan had made reproaches to al-Ḥusayn with regard to her mother, but al-Ḥusayn expressed his deep love for both his wife and daughter in two lines of poetry.[165] In the later years of 'Alī's reign, Imru' ul-Qays and his kin were referred to as the 'in-laws (*aṣhār*) of al-Ḥusayn'.[166] Al-Ḥasan may never actually have married Salmā, or may have divorced her before this time.

Probably soon after 'Alī's arrival in Kūfa, al-Ḥasan married Ja'da, daughter of the Kinda chief al-Ash'ath b. Qays. 'Alī evidently was eager at this time to establish an alliance with the powerful Yemenite tribal coalition in Kūfa. He proposed to Sa'īd b. Qays al-Hamdānī that the latter give his daughter Umm 'Imrān in marriage to al-Ḥasan. Sa'īd b. Qays consulted al-Ash'ath, who suggested that he marry his daughter to

[162] Ibn Manẓūr, *Mukhtaṣar*, XXV, 289. 'Abd al-Malik is quoted as telling 'Abd al-Raḥmān b. Abī Laylā: 'Were it not that my father told me on the day of Marj Rāhiṭ that he killed Ṭalḥa, I would not leave a single one of the Banū Taym on the surface of the earth but would kill all of them' (Ibn Shabba, *Ta'rīkh al-Madīna*, 1170).

[163] Ibn Ḥajar, *Iṣāba*, I, 116–17; *Aghānī*, XIV, 164; Balādhurī, *Ansāb*, II, 194–5, who gives the name Zaynab in place of Salmā. [164] *Annali*, X, 380. [165] *Aghānī*, XIV, 163.

[166] Thaqafī, *Ghārāt*, 426.

his own son Muḥammad, who was her cousin. Saʿīd b. Qays did so, and al-Ashʿath invited al-Ḥasan for a meal. When al-Ḥasan asked for a drink of water, al-Ashʿath ordered his daughter Jaʿda to serve him. Then he told al-Ḥasan that he had been served by a girl, his own daughter, who had never before served any man. Al-Ḥasan informed his father, who told him to marry her. According to another report, ʿAlī had initially asked al-Ashʿath to mediate the marriage between Saʿīd b. Qays' daughter and al-Ḥasan. Al-Ashʿath, however, asked Saʿīd to marry her to his own son. When ʿAlī accused him of treachery, al-Ashʿath told him that he would pair al-Ḥasan with 'one who is not below her' and gave him his own daughter Jaʿda.[167] Jaʿda is commonly accused of having poisoned al-Ḥasan at the instigation of Muʿāwiya. Although childless, she evidently was not divorced by him. After his death she was married to Ṭalḥa's son Yaʿqūb and bore him offspring.[168]

Probably also soon after his arrival in Kūfa, before the battle of Ṣiffīn, al-Ḥasan married Umm Bashīr (in some sources Umm Bishr), daughter of the Anṣārī Abū Masʿūd ʿUqba b. ʿAmr b. Thaʿlaba of Khazraj, one of those early Medinan Muslims who had pledged allegiance to Muḥammad at al-ʿAqaba before the *hijra*. Abū Masʿūd had settled in Kūfa at an early stage and was among those opposed to the Kufan rebellion against ʿUthmān. ʿAlī evidently hoped to draw him to his side and presumably arranged the marriage of his daughter to al-Ḥasan. Then he appointed him governor of Kūfa during his absence for the campaign to Ṣiffīn. Abū Masʿūd, however, took a neutralist position and obstructed ʿAlī's war effort. After his return to Kūfa, ʿAlī, as noted, chided him, and Abū Masʿūd left in anger for a pilgrimage.

Umm Bashīr bore al-Ḥasan Zayd, probably his eldest son,[169] and a daughter, Umm al-Ḥusayn.[170] According to al-Mufīd, there was another daughter, Umm al-Ḥasan,[171] but this seems erroneous. Umm al-Ḥusayn was later married to ʿAbd Allāh b. al-Zubayr and had children. Umm Bashīr was married also to ʿAbd al-Raḥmān b. ʿAbd Allāh b. Abī Rabīʿa al-Makhzūmī and to Saʿīd b. Zayd b. ʿAmr b. Nufayl and had with them a son and a daughter respectively.[172] The sequential order of these marriages is uncertain.

After his abdication and return to Medina, al-Ḥasan married Khawla, daughter of the Fazāra chief Manẓūr b. Zabbān. Previously she had been married to Ṭalḥa's pious son Muḥammad, who was killed in the battle of

[167] Balādhurī, *Ansāb*, III, 14–5.

[168] Abu l-Faraj, *Maqātil*, 73; Balādhurī, *Ansāb*, III, 15. Al-Balādhurī's statement that she was later married to al-ʿAbbās and ʿAbd Allāh b. al-ʿAbbās is obviously anachronistic.

[169] It cannot be excluded that one of al-Ḥasan's sons by a slave mother was born before him.

[170] In some sources her name is given as Umm al-Ḥasan or Umm al-Khayr or Ramla.

[171] Mufīd, *Irshād*, 176. [172] Zubayrī, *Nasab*, 47–50.

the Camel, and had two sons and a daughter by him. She is said either to have been given in marriage to al-Ḥasan by ʿAbd Allāh b. al-Zubayr, who was married to her sister Tumāḍir, or to have herself given the choice to al-Ḥasan, who then married her. Upon hearing this, her father declared that he was not someone to be ignored with respect to his daughter. He came to Medina and planted a black flag in the mosque of the Prophet. All Qaysites (Fazāra belonged to the large Northern Arab tribal association claiming descent from Qays ʿAylān) present in Medina assembled under it in solidarity with him. He was asked: 'Where are you going? She has been married by al-Ḥasan b. ʿAlī, and there is no one like him', but he would not accept the *fait accompli*. Al-Ḥasan now surrendered her to him, and he took her away to Qubāʾ. She reproached him, quoting the hadith: 'Al-Ḥasan b. ʿAlī will be the lord of the youth among the inmates of paradise.' He told her: 'Wait here, if the man is in need of you, he will join us here.' Al-Ḥasan came to them accompanied by his brother al-Ḥusayn, his cousin ʿAbd Allāh b. Jaʿfar and his uncle ʿAbd Allāh b. al-ʿAbbās and took her back, marrying her this time with the approval of her father.[173] Khawla bore al-Ḥasan his son al-Ḥasan. A report leaves it open whether she was still married to him or divorced when he died. She did not marry again and put off her veil.[174]

In Medina al-Ḥasan married Ḥafṣa, the daughter of ʿAbd al-Raḥmān b. Abī Bakr. Al-Mundhir b. al-Zubayr b. al-ʿAwwām was in love with her, and spread a false rumour about her conduct. As a result, al-Ḥasan divorced her. The report characterizes him in this context as *miṭlāq*, evidently meaning here: ready to divorce on insubstantial grounds. Next ʿĀṣim, the son of ʿUmar b. al-Khaṭṭāb, married her. Al-Mundhir falsely accused her before him, and he also divorced her. Then al-Mundhir proposed marriage to her, but she refused, saying: 'He has tried to destroy my reputation.' He pursued her with further proposals, and she was advised to marry him so that it would become patent to everybody that he had falsely accused her. She did so, and the people realized that he had lied about her and what his motive had been. Al-Ḥasan now proposed to ʿĀṣim that they visit her. They asked al-Mundhir for permission to see her. After consulting his brother ʿAbd Allāh b. al-Zubayr, al-Mundhir gave them permission to visit her in his presence. She paid more attention to ʿĀṣim than to al-Ḥasan and spoke more freely with him. Al-Ḥasan told al-Mundhir to take her hand, and her two former husbands left. The report adds that al-Ḥasan loved her and had divorced her only because of al-Mundhir's slander. According to Ḥafṣa's nephew ʿAbd Allāh b. Muḥammad b. ʿAbd al-Raḥmān (known as Ibn Abī ʿAtīq), al-Ḥasan later

[173] *Aghānī*, XI, 56–7. [174] *Ibid*., 57.

repeatedly asked him to go along to al-ʿAqīq, where she lived, and would converse with her for a long time.[175]

Al-Ḥasan married, also in Medina, Ṭalḥa's daughter Umm Isḥāq. She is described as extremely beautiful but of bad character. Thus she is said to have been pregnant and given birth without telling her husband.[176] Muʿāwiya had asked her brother Isḥāq b. Ṭalḥa in Damascus to give her in marriage to his son Yazīd. Isḥāq told him that he was going to Medina; if Muʿāwiya sent a messenger to him there, he would conclude the marriage contract. After Isḥāq had left, his brother ʿĪsā b. Ṭalḥa visited Muʿāwiya. When the caliph told him about Isḥāq's promise, ʿĪsā offered to give Umm Isḥāq immediately in marriage. He concluded the marriage contract with Yazīd without consulting her. In the meantime Isḥāq had arrived in Medina and contracted her marriage to al-Ḥasan. It was not exactly known which of the two contracts was earlier, and Muʿāwiya advised his son to leave the matter. Her marriage with al-Ḥasan was now consummated, and she bore him his son Ṭalḥa, who later died childless.[177] Even after his accession to the caliphate Yazīd continued to harbour a grudge against Isḥāq b. Ṭalḥa for his betrayal and ordered his general Muslim b. ʿUqba, when he sent him to suppress the revolt in Medina, to kill him if he got hold of him. Isḥāq escaped, however, and Muslim was only able to destroy his house.[178] In spite of her alleged bad character, al-Ḥasan at the time of his death expressed satisfaction with Umm Isḥāq and recommended to his brother al-Ḥusayn that he marry her. She bore al-Ḥusayn's daughter Fāṭima.[179] Presumably still later she was married to Abū Bakr's great-grandson Ibn Abī ʿAtīq ʿAbd Allāh, to whom she also bore a daughter, Āmina.[180]

Al-Ḥasan further married in Medina Hind, daughter of Suhayl b. ʿAmr of ʿĀmir Quraysh. She had been married first to the Umayyad ʿAbd al-Raḥmān b. ʿAttāb b. Asīd, who was killed in the battle of the Camel, and then to ʿAbd Allāh b. ʿĀmir b. Kurayz. When the latter divorced her, Muʿāwiya wrote to Abū Hurayra in Medina to contract her marriage with his son Yazīd. On his way to meet her, Abū Hurayra met al-Ḥasan who inquired where he was going. When Abū Hurayra explained his mission, al-Ḥasan suggested that he mention him, al-Ḥasan, to her. Abū Hurayra did so, and Hind asked him to make the choice for her; Abū Hurayra chose al-Ḥasan. Some time later ʿAbd Allāh b. ʿĀmir came to Medina and complained to al-Ḥasan that his former wife had a deposit belonging to

[175] Balādhurī, *Ansāb*, III, 22–3. On Ibn Abī ʿAtīq see the article by C. Pellat in *EI* (2nd edn).
[176] *Aghānī*, XVIII, 203.
[177] According to al-Mufīd (*Irshād*, 176), Umm Isḥāq was also the mother of al-Ḥasan's son al-Ḥusayn (al-Ḥasan) al-Athram and his daughter Fāṭima. According to al-Zubayrī and al-Balādhurī, these two were borne by slave mothers.
[178] Zubayrī, *Nasab*, 282–3.
[179] *Aghānī*, XVIII, 203.
[180] Zubayrī, *Nasab*, 50; Ibn Saʿd, *Ṭabaqāt*, III/1, 152.

him in her possession. Al-Ḥasan allowed him to see her in his presence. As Ibn ʿĀmir looked at her sitting in front of him, he softened up towards her, and al-Ḥasan suggested: 'Shall I relinquish her to you? I think you could not find a better husband to make remarriage licit (*muḥallil*)[181] for you than myself.' Ibn ʿĀmir insisted: 'My deposit.' She produced two boxes filled with jewels. Ibn ʿĀmir took a handful out of each one and left the rest to her. Later she used to comment about her three husbands: 'The lord (*sayyid*) of all of them was al-Ḥasan; the most generous of them was Ibn ʿĀmir; and the one dearest to me was ʿAbd al-Raḥmān b. ʿAttāb.'[182]

Doubts may perhaps arise about the reliability of the first part of the account, which is related by al-Madāʾinī without *isnād* as a hearsay report (*balaghanī*), since it seems to duplicate the story about Muʿāwiya's failed attempt to arrange for the marriage of his son Yazīd with Umm Isḥāq bt Ṭalḥa. Basically the account is probably reliable. Al-Ḥasan had no children with Hind. Since she is accused by al-Haytham b. ʿAdī of having murdered al-Ḥasan, she was presumably still married to him when he died.

Al-Ḥasan's other children were probably all borne by slave women. Some sources suggest that the mother of ʿAmr b. al-Ḥasan was either a woman of Thaqīf or a slave.[183] ʿAmr is described as a pious man and had two sons and a daughter. If his mother had been a freeborn woman of Thaqīf, her name and lineage would almost certainly have been remembered. Al-Ḥasan's other sons were, according to al-Zubayrī: al-Qāsim and Abū Bakr, both childless and killed with their uncle al-Ḥusayn at Karbalāʾ; ʿAbd al-Raḥmān, died childless; and al-Ḥusayn al-Athram, who had offspring only through his daughters. Al-Balādhurī mentions a further son, ʿAbd Allāh.[184] According to Ibn ʿInaba, however, ʿAbd Allāh was the same as Abū Bakr.[185] Al-Mufīd in fact mentions only ʿAbd Allāh, and al-Zubayrī only Abū Bakr. In Abū Mikhnaf's list of those killed at Karbalāʾ, however, ʿAbd Allāh is mentioned separately from Abū Bakr. Abū Mikhnaf lists three sons of al-Ḥasan as being killed with al-Ḥusayn and gives the names of their killers.[186] Late sources add to the sons of al-Ḥasan three more names, Ismāʿīl, Ḥamza and Yaʿqūb, none of whom is said to have had children.[187]

Al-Ḥasan's daughters from various slave women were: Umm ʿAbd Allāh, who married her cousin ʿAlī b. al-Ḥusayn (Zayn al-ʿĀbidīn) and bore him several sons including the Shiʿite imam Muḥammad al-Bāqir; Fāṭima, who is not known to have married; Umm Salama, who was

[181] After a threefold divorce, the law required that the divorced wife must be married to another husband before the divorcer could remarry her.

[182] Balādhurī, *Ansāb*, III, 20–1.

[183] *Ibid.*, 73. Both al-Zubayrī and al-Mufīd state that ʿAmr's mother was of slave origin (*umm walad*).

[184] *Ibid.*

[185] Ibn ʿInaba, *ʿUmdat al-ṭālib*, 68.

[186] Ṭabarī, II, 387.

[187] Ibn ʿInaba, *ʿUmdat al-ṭālib*, 68.

married to ʿAmr b. al-Mundhir b. al-Zubayr b. al-ʿAwwām, but had no children; and Ruqayya, who is not known to have married.[188]

In the reports about al-Ḥasan's marriages quoted above, al-Ḥasan comes across as endowed with both a concern for dignified propriety and a spirit of forbearing conciliatoriness, an important aspect of the *ḥilm* of the true *sayyid*. In no way does his readiness to divorce reflect an inordinate appetite for sexual diversion. He divorces the granddaughter of Abū Bakr, when she is falsely accused by al-Mundhir b. al-Zubayr, out of a sense of propriety even though he still loves her. When the slanderous nature of the accusation becomes patent after al-Mundhir's marriage with her, al-Ḥasan visits the couple, but quickly forgives his rival, recognizing that he had lied out of love for her. He shows his continued affection for her by paying her visits in the proper company of her nephew. His sense of propriety is presumably also involved in his reproaches to his younger brother al-Ḥusayn, whose display of exuberant and indulgent love for the bedouin girl al-Rabāb he must have considered improper for a grandson of the Prophet. Al-Ḥasan humours the furious anger of the Fazāra chief Manẓūr b. Zabbān at having been ignored in his daughter's marriage to him, although the father had evidently no longer any real rights as her guardian since she had been previously married. Having returned her to her father, al-Ḥasan demonstrates the seriousness of his wish to marry her and his respect for the father by bringing the leading members of the Prophet's house along to visit the proud bedouin shaykh. Al-Ḥasan readily offers to divorce the daughter of Suhayl b. ʿAmr when he notices signs of renewed love for her in the behaviour of her former husband, ʿAbd Allāh b. ʿĀmir.

In striking contrast with these relatively realistic reports, there is a group of others which portray a rather different image of the Prophet's grandson. These reports and descriptions are for the most part vague, lacking in names, concrete specifics and verifiable detail; they appear to be spun out of the reputation of al-Ḥasan as a *miṭlāq*, now interpreted as a habitual and prodigious divorcer, some clearly with a defamatory intent. Most of the early reports of this type were narrated by al-Madā'inī.

Al-Madā'inī thus reported: 'It has reached us that al-Ḥasan, whenever he wanted to divorce a woman, would sit down with her and say: "Would it please you if I gave you such and such?" She would answer: "Whatever you wish", or: "Yes." He would tell her: "It belongs to you." Then he would get up and send her the money which he had mentioned together

[188] According to the Shiʿite genealogist al-ʿUmarī, Umm Salama was married to ʿUmar, son of ʿAlī Zayn al-ʿĀbidīn, and Ruqayya was married to ʿAmr b. al-Mundhir b. al-Zubayr (*ibid.*, 68, n. 2).

with her divorce.'[189] On the authority of the Basran Muḥammad b. Sīrīn, al-Madā'inī narrated that al-Ḥasan asked a man for the hand of his daughter. The man gave her in marriage to him and told him: 'I know that you are ill-tempered and a divorcer (*ghaliq ṭulaqa*), but you are the most excellent of mankind in lineage and the one with the most noble grandfather and house.'[190] According to another story, al-Ḥasan married a Yemenite woman and then sent her 10,000 dirhams together with her divorce. She commented with a quotation of poetry: 'Small chattel from a parting beloved.' Al-Ḥasan remarked: 'If I ever took any woman back, I would take this one back.'[191] In another version of this story, reported by Suwayd b. Ghafala, the Yemenite woman is identified as a woman of Khath'am. When 'Alī was killed and al-Ḥasan succeeded him, she congratulated him: 'May the caliphate please you.' He answered: 'You have expressed malicious joy at the murder of 'Alī', and pronounced her thrice divorced. She swore that she had not intended that, and he sent her 20,000 dirhams. Then she quoted the poetry about the parting beloved.[192]

Al-Madā'inī narrated, on the authority of the Anṣārī 'Abd Allāh b. Abī Bakr b. Muḥammad b. 'Amr,[193] that al-Ḥasan proposed to marry a woman of the Banū Shaybān, but was told that she held the views of the Kharijites. He commented: 'I would hate to clasp a live coal of hell-fire to my chest.'[194] The report does not suggest that al-Ḥasan married the woman, but al-Madā'inī, in his enumeration of al-Ḥasan's spouses, counts his marriage with 'a woman of the Banū Shaybān of the Āl Hammām b. Murra', retelling the story and asserting that he divorced her.[195] Ibn Qutayba narrated in his book on poetry that the poet 'Amr b. al-Ahtam al-Minqarī had a daughter called Umm Ḥabīb, who was married by al-Ḥasan on the assumption that she was as good-looking as her brother. When he found her to be ugly, he divorced her.[196] The story was also known to al-Madā'inī, who enumerates a daughter of 'Amr b. al-Ahtam among al-Ḥasan's spouses.[197] Al-Diyārbakrī, a late source, quotes Ibn Sīrīn as describing the following fairy-tale wedding: 'Al-Ḥasan married a woman. He sent her a hundred slave girls and with each one of them a thousand dirhams.'[198]

Muḥammad al-Kalbī seems to have been the first one to spread the claim that the number of al-Ḥasan's wives amounted to ninety. He reported on the authority of Abū Ṣāliḥ: 'Al-Ḥasan married [*aḥṣana*, lit.

[189] Balādhurī, *Ansāb*, III, 20. [190] *Ibid.*, 18; Ibn Abi l-Ḥadīd, *Sharḥ*, XVI, 21.
[191] Balādhurī, *Ansāb*, III, 25. [192] Dhahabī, *Siyar*, III, 262.
[193] On him see Ibn Ḥajar, *Tahdhīb*, V, 164–5. [194] Balādhurī, *Ansāb*, III, 14.
[195] Ibn Abi l-Ḥadīd, *Sharḥ*, XVI, 21.
[196] Ibn Qutayba, *al-Shi'r wa l-shu'arā'*, ed. M. J. de Goeje (Leiden, 1904), 402.
[197] Ibn Abi l-Ḥadīd, *Sharḥ*, XVI, 21.
[198] Al-Diyārbakrī, *Ta'rīkh al-khamīs* (Cairo, 1302/[1984], II, 324.

protected] ninety women'. 'Alī said: 'Al-Ḥasan married and divorced so much that I feared he would bring the enmity of [many] tribes down on us.'[199] The theme of 'Alī's worry was further elaborated in the following report ascribed to the Shi'ite imam Ja'far al-Ṣādiq on the authority of his father. Afraid of arousing the enmity of the tribes, 'Alī addressed the Kufans: 'Oh people of Kūfa, do not give your women in marriage to al-Ḥasan, for he is a habitual divorcer (*miṭlāq*).' A man of Hamdān answered back: 'By God, we shall let him marry. Whomever he is pleased with, let him keep her; whomever he dislikes, let him divorce her.'[200] The figure of ninety wives was picked up by al-Madā'inī. He enumerated all the women mentioned above, including the dubious cases of the daughter of 'Amr b. al-Ahtam, the woman of Thaqīf, mother of 'Amr, and the woman of Shaybān, and then concluded: 'I have counted the spouses of al-Ḥasan b. 'Alī, and they were seventy women.' The number seventy in the text is probably to be read ninety, a common misreading in Arabic script.[201] It is safe to assume that al-Madā'inī was unable to name even a single wife of al-Ḥasan aside from the eleven whom he actually mentioned and five of whom must be considered as uncertain or highly doubtful. Al-Diyārbakrī quoted him as relating that al-Ḥasan married ninety women 'in the lifetime of his father' alone.[202]

The unreliability of all these tales and reports requires no detailed discussion. It may be noted that the three known marriages of al-Ḥasan concluded during his father's lifetime were arranged by the latter as the head of the house, as was the custom. They were evidently concluded by 'Alī as political alliances. 'Alī could thus have been critical of al-Ḥasan if he considered him responsible for the breakdown of the marriage with the Kalbite Salmā. That he would have warned the Kufans in general against al-Ḥasan as a marriage partner is inconceivable. Al-Ḥasan presumably was in no position to choose his own marriage partners as long as his father was alive, just as 'Alī had been unable to choose his wives during the lifetime of Muḥammad. Since al-Ḥasan had little sympathy for his father's political aspirations, he evidently also viewed these arranged marriages in a different light than 'Alī.

199 Balādhurī, *Ansāb*, III, 25.
200 Dhahabī, *Siyar*, III, 267, 262.
201 Ibn Abi l-Ḥadīd, *Sharḥ*, XVI, 21–2. The only woman in al-Madā'inī's list not mentioned elsewhere is a 'daughter' of 'Alqama b. Zurāra (*imra'a min banāt 'Alqama b. Zurāra*). The latter was a chief of Dārim Tamīm killed in a tribal conflict long before Islam. Al-Ḥasan cannot have married one of his daughters. Presumably a descendant is meant and some anecdote is connected with her marriage to al-Ḥasan.
202 Diyārbakrī, *Ta'rīkh al-khamīs*, II, 324. Al-Madā'inī's own assertion that al-Ḥasan married ninety women is also reported by al-Dhahabī (*Siyar*, III, 267).

Bibliography

Abbott, N., *Aishah the Beloved of Mohammed*, Chicago 1942.
Studies in Arabic Literary Papyri, I, Chicago 1957.
'Abd al-Jabbār, *al-Mughnī*, XX, ed. 'Abd al-Ḥalīm Maḥmūd and Sulaymān Dunyā, Cairo n.d.
'Abd al-Razzāq al-Ṣan'ānī, *al-Muṣannaf*, ed. Ḥabīb al-Raḥmān al-A'ẓamī, [Beirut 1390–2/1970–2], 11 vols.
Abū Bakr b. al-'Arabī, *al-'Awāṣim min l-qawāṣim fī taḥqīq mawqif al-ṣaḥāba ba'd wafāt al-nabī*, ed. Muḥibb al-Dīn al-Khaṭīb, Cairo 1387/1968.
Abū Dāwūd, *Sunan*, Cairo 1292/[1875].
Abu l-Faraj al-Iṣfahānī, *Kitāb al-Aghānī*, [Būlāq 1285/1868], 20 vols.
Maqātil al-Ṭālibiyyīn, ed. Aḥmad Ṣaqr, Cairo 1949.
Abū 'Ubayd al-Qāsim b. Sallām, *Kitab al-Amthāl*, ed. 'Abd al-Majīd 'Ābidīn and Iḥsān 'Abbās, Khartoum 1958.
Kitāb al-Amwāl, ed. Muḥammad Khalīl Harrās, Cairo 1968.
Abū Yūsuf, *Kitāb al-Kharāj*, Cairo 1352/[1933].
Al-Azraqī, *Akhbār Makka*, ed. F. Wüstenfeld, in *Chroniken der Stadt Mekka*, I, Leipzig 1858.
Al-Balādhurī, *Ansāb al-ashrāf*, I, ed. Muḥammad Ḥamīd Allāh, Cairo 1959.
Ansāb al-ashrāf, II and III, ed. Muḥammad Bāqir al-Maḥmūdī, Beirut 1974.
Ansāb al-ashrāf, V, ed. S. D. F. Goitein, Jerusalem 1936.
Ansāb al-ashrāf, 3, ed. 'Abd al-'Azīz al-Dūrī, Wiesbaden 1978.
Ansāb al-ashrāf, 4/1, ed. Iḥsān 'Abbās, Wiesbaden 1979.
Futūḥ al-buldān, ed. M. J. de Goeje, *Liber expugnationis regionum*, Leiden 1866.
Bashear, S., 'The Title ⟨*Fārūq*⟩ and its Association with 'Umar I', *Studia Islamica*, 72 (1990), 47–70.
Bevan, A. A. (ed.), *The Naḳā'iḍ of Jarīr and al-Farazdaḳ*, Leiden 1905–12.
Blachère, R., *Le Coran*, Paris 1957.
Al-Bukhārī, *Ṣaḥīḥ*, Cairo 1312/[1894].
Caetani, L., *Annali dell' Islam*, Milan 1905–26, 10 vols.
Caskel, W., *Ǧamharat an-nasab: Das genealogische Werk des Hišām ibn Muḥammad al-Kalbī*, Leiden 1966, 2 vols.
Colpe, C., 'Das Siegel der Propheten', *Orientalia Suecana*, 33–5 (1984–6), 71–83.
Das Siegel der Propheten, Berlin 1990.
Crone, P. and Hinds, M., *God's Caliph: Religious Authority in the First Centuries of Islam*, Cambridge 1986.
De Goeje, M. J., *Mémoire sur la conquète de la Syrie*, Leiden 1900.

Dennett, D. C., *Conversion and Poll Tax in Early Islam*, Cambridge 1950.
Al-Dhahabī, *Mīzān al-iʿtidāl*, Cairo 1325/[1907], 3 vols.
Siyar aʿlām al-nubalāʾ, ed. Shuʿayb al-Arnaʾūṭ and Ḥusayn Asad, Beirut 1981–8, 24 vols.
Taʾrīkh al-islām, Cairo 1367–69/[1948–50], parts 1–6.
Al-Dīnawarī, *al-Akhbār al-ṭiwāl*, ed. V. Guirgass, Leiden 1888–1912, 2 vols.
Al-Diyārbakrī, *Taʾrīkh al-khamīs*, Cairo 1302/[1984], 2 vols.
Djaït, H., *La Grande Discorde : religion et politique dans l'Islam des origines*, Paris 1989.
Donner, F., *The Early Islamic Conquests*, Princeton 1981.
Encyclopaedia of Islam, Leiden 1913–38.
Encyclopaedia of Islam, 2nd edition, Leiden 1954–.
Friedmann, Y., 'Finality of Prophethood in Sunni Islam', in *Jerusalem Studies in Arabic and Islam*, 7 (1986), 177–215.
Goldziher, I., *Muhammedanische Studien*, Halle 1889–90, 2 vols.
Grütter, I., 'Arabische Bestattungsbräuche in frühislamischer Zeit', *Der Islam*, 31 (1954), 147–73; 32 (1955), 79–104, 168–94.
Guillaume, A., *The Life of Muhammad: A Translation of [Ibn] Isḥāq's Sīrat Rasūl Allāh*, London 1955.
Halm, H., *Der schiitische Islam: Von der Religion zur Revolution*, Munich 1994.
Al-Hamdānī, *al-Iklīl*, II, ed. Muḥammad b. ʿAlī al-Akwaʿ al-Ḥiwālī, Baghdad 1980.
Ṣifat Jazīrat al-ʿArab, ed. D. H. Müller, Leiden 1884–91.
Ḥassān b. Thābit, *Dīwān*, ed. W. N. ʿArafat, London 1971, 2 vols.
Hasson, I., 'Contributions à l'étude des Aws et des Ḫazraǧ', *Arabica*, 36 (1989), 1–35.
Hinds, M., 'The Murder of the Caliph ʿUthmān', *International Journal of Middle East Studies*, 3 (1972), 450–69.
'The Ṣiffīn Arbitration Agreement', *Journal of Semitic Studies*, 17 (1972), 92–129.
Hrbek, I., 'Muhammads Nachlass und die Aliden', *Archív Orientální*, 18 (1950), 143–9.
Ibn ʿAbd al-Barr, *al-Istīʿāb fī maʿrifat al-aṣḥāb*, Hyderabad 1336/[1918], 2 vols.
Ibn ʿAbd al-Ḥakam, *Futūḥ Miṣr wa-akhbāruhā*, ed. C. C. Torrey, New Haven 1922.
Ibn ʿAbd Rabbih, *al-ʿIqd al-farīd*, ed. Mufīd Muḥammad Qumayḥa and ʿAbd al-Majīd al-Tarḥīnī, Beirut 1983, 8 vols.
Ibn Abi l-Ḥadīd, *Sharḥ nahj al-balāgha*, ed. Muḥammad Abu l-Faḍl Ibrāhīm, [Cairo] 1959–64, 20 vols.
Ibn Abī Shayba, *al-Muṣannaf*, ed. Saʿīd Muḥammad al-Laḥḥām, Beirut 1409/1989, 9 vols.
Ibn Abī Uṣaybiʿa, *ʿUyūn al-anbāʾ fī ṭabaqāt al-aṭibbāʾ*, ed. A. Müller, Cairo 1299/1882, 2 vols.
Ibn ʿAsākir, [*Taʾrīkh Madīnat Dimashq*:] *Tarjamat al-imām ʿAlī b. Abī Ṭālib*, ed. Muḥammad Bāqir al-Maḥmūdī, Beirut 1975, 3 vols.
Taʾrīkh Madīnat Dimashq: ʿUthmān b. ʿAffān, ed. Sukayna al-Shihābī, Damascus 1984.
Ibn Aʿtham al-Kūfī, *al-Futūḥ*, Hyderabad 1968–75, 8 vols.
Ibn al-Athīr, *al-Kāmil fi l-taʾrīkh*, ed. C. J. Tornberg, Leiden 1851–76, 12 vols.
Usd al-ghāba fī maʿrifat al-ṣaḥāba, [Cairo 1285–87/1869–71], 4 vols.
Ibn Bakr, Muḥammad b. Yaḥyā, *al-Tamhīd wa l-bayān fi maqtal al-shahīd ʿUthmān*, ed. Maḥmūd Yūsuf Zāyid, Beirut 1963.

Ibn Durayd, *al-Ishtiqāq*, ed. 'Abd al-Salām Muḥammad Hārūn, Baghdad 1399/1979.
Ibn Ḥabīb, *al-Muḥabbar*, ed. I. Lichtenstaedter, Hyderabad 1942.
Ibn Ḥajar al-'Asqalānī, *Fatḥ al-bārī*, Cairo 1319–29/[1901–11], 13 vols.
al-Iṣāba fi tamyīz al-ṣaḥāba, Cairo 1323–25/[1905–7], 8 vols.
Lisān al-Mīzān, Hyderabad 1329–31/[1911–13], 6 vols.
Tahdhīb al-tahdhīb, Hyderabad 1325–27/[1907–9], 12 vols.
Ibn Ḥanbal, *Musnad*, [Cairo] 1313/1895, 6 vols.
Ibn Ḥazm, *Jamharat ansāb al-'Arab*, ed. E. Lévi-Provençal, Cairo 1948.
Ibn Hishām, *Sīrat sayyidinā Muḥammad rasūl Allāh*, ed. F. Wüstenfeld, *Das Leben Muhammeds nach Muhammed Ibn Ishâk*, Göttingen 1859–60.
Ibn 'Inaba, *'Umdat al-ṭālib fī ansāb āl Abī Ṭālib*, ed. Muḥammad Ḥasan Āl al-Ṭāliqānī, Najaf 1380/1961.
Ibn al-Kalbī, *Nasab Ma'add wa l-Yaman al-kabir*, ed. Nājī Ḥasan, Beirut 1988, 2 vols.
Ibn Kathīr, *al-Bidāya wa l-nihāya*, Cairo 1351/1932, 14 vols.
Ibn Māja, *Sunan*, ed. Muḥammad Fu'ād 'Abd al-Bāqī, [Cairo] 1395/1975.
Ibn Manẓūr, *Mukhtaṣar Ta'rīkh Madīnat Dimashq li-Ibn 'Asākir*, ed. Rūḥiyya al-Naḥḥās et al. Damascus 1984–90, 29 vols.
Ibn Qutayba, *al-Ma'ārif*, ed. Tharwat 'Ukāsha, Cairo 1960.
al-Shi'r wa l-shu'arā', ed. M. J. de Goeje, Leiden 1904.
(pseudo-)Ibn Qutayba, *al-Imāma wa l-siyāsa*, ed. Muḥammad Maḥmūd al-Rāfi'ī, Cairo 1322/1904, 2 vols.
Ibn Sa'd, *Kitāb al-Ṭabaqāt al-kabīr*, ed. E. Sachau et al., Leiden 1905–40, 9 vols.
Ibn Samura, *Ṭabaqāt fuqahā' al-Yaman*, ed. Fu'ād Sayyid, Cairo 1957.
Ibn Shabba, *Ta'rīkh al-Madīna al-munawwara*, ed. Fahīm Muḥammad Shaltūt, Qumm 1410/[1989–90].
Al-Jāḥiẓ, *al-Bayān wa l-tabyīn*, ed. 'Abd al-Salām Muḥammad Hārūn, Cairo 1367/1948, 4 vols.
Khalīfa, *Ta'rīkh*, ed. Akram Ḍiyā' al-'Umarī, Damascus 1977.
al-Khaṭīb al-Baghdādī, *Ta'rīkh Baghdād*, Cairo 1931, 14 vols.
Al-Kindī, *Kitāb al-Wulāt wa-Kitāb al-Quḍāt*, ed. R. Guest, London 1912.
Kister, M. J., 'O God, Tighten Thy Grip on Muḍar . . .: Some Socio-economic and Religious Aspects of an Early Ḥadīth', *Journal of the Economic and Social History of the Orient*, 24 (1981), 242–73.
'. . . *illā bi-ḥaqqihi*, A Study of an Early *Ḥadīth*', *Jerusalem Studies in Arabic and Islam*, 5 (1984), 33–52.
'The Market of the Prophet', in *Studies in Jāhiliyya and Early Islam*, Variorum Reprints, London 1980; first published in *Journal of the Economic and Social History of the Orient*, 8 (1965), 272–6.
'Notes on an Account of the Shura Appointed by 'Umar b. al-Khattab', *Journal of Semitic Studies*, 9 (1964), 320–6.
Lammens, H., 'L'avènement des Marwanides', *Mélanges de la Faculté Orientale de l'Université St Joseph de Beyrouth*, 12 (1927), 43–147.
Le Berceau de l'Islam: l'Arabie occidentale à la veille de l'Hégire, Rome 1914.
Etudes sur le règne du Calife Omaiyade Mo'âwia Ier, Paris 1908.
Fāṭima et les Filles de Mahomet, Rome 1912.

'Le triumvirat Abou Bakr, 'Omar et Abou 'Obaida', *Mélanges de la Faculté Orientale de l'Université St Joseph de Beyrouth*, 4 (1910), 113–44.

Landau-Tasseron, E., 'Sayf Ibn 'Umar in Medieval and Modern Scholarship', *Der Islam*, 67 (1990), 1–26.

Lazarus-Yafeh, H., *Some Religious Aspects of Islam*, Leiden 1981.

Lecker, M. *The Banū Sulaym: A Contribution to the Study of Early Islam*, Jerusalem 1989.

'The Estates of 'Amr b. al-'Āṣ in Palestine: Notes on a New Negev Arabic Inscription', *Bulletin of the School of Oriental and African Studies*, 52 (1989), 24–37.

'Kinda on the Eve of Islam and during the *Ridda*', *Journal of the Royal Asiatic Society*, 1994, 333–56.

'Muḥammad at Medina: A Geographical Approach', *Jerusalem Studies in Arabic and Islam*, 6 (1985), 29–62.

Muslims, Jews and Pagans: Studies in Early Islamic Medina, Leiden 1995.

Levi della Vida, G., 'Il califfato di 'Alī secondo il Kitāb Ansāb al-Ašrāf di al-Balāḏurī', *Rivista degli Studi Orientali*, 6 (1914–15), 427–507, 923–7.

Al-Mad'aj, 'A. M. M., *The Yemen in Early Islam 9–233/630–847: A Political History*, London 1988.

Madelung, W., 'Apocalyptic Prophecies in Ḥimṣ in the Umayyad Age', *Journal of Semitic Studies*, 30 (1986), 141–85.

'The Hāshimiyyāt of al-Kumayt and Hāshimī Shi'ism', *Studia Islamica*, 70 (1989), 5–26.

Der Imam al-Qāsim ibn Ibrāhīm und die Glaubenslehre der Zaiditen, Berlin 1965.

Al-Majlisī, *Biḥār al-anwār*, Tehran/Tabriz 1303–15/[1888–98], 14 vols.

Al-Maqrīzī, *al-Nizā' wa l-takhāṣum fīmā bayn Banī Umayya wa-Banī Hāshim*, ed. G. Vos, *Die Kämpfe und Streitigkeiten zwischen den Banū Umajja und den Banū Hāšim*, Leiden 1888.

Massignon, L., *La Mubâhala de Médine et l'hyperdulie de Fatima*, Paris 1955.

Al-Mas'ūdī, *Murūj al-dhahab*, ed. C. Pellat, Beirut 1968–79, 7 vols.

Al-Māwardī, *al-Aḥkām al-sulṭāniyya*, ed. R. Enger, Bonn 1853.

Al-Minqarī, Naṣr b. Muzāḥim, *Waq'at Ṣiffīn*, ed. 'Abd al-Salām Muḥammad Hārūn, Cairo 1382/[1962].

Mommsen, T. (ed.), *Chronica Minora Saec. IV.V.VI.VII.*, II, Berlin 1894.

Al-Mubarrad, *al-Kāmil*, ed. W. Wright, Leipzig 1974–92, 3 vols.

Al-Mufīd, *al-Irshād*, ed. Kāẓim al-Mūsawī al-Miyāmawī, Tehran 1377/[1957-8].

al-Jamal wa l-nuṣra li-sayyid al-'itra fī ḥarb al-Baṣra, ed. 'Alī Mīr Sharīfī, Qumm 1413/[1993].

Muranyi, M., 'Ein neuer Bericht über die Wahl des ersten Kalifen Abū Bakr', *Arabica* 25 (1978), 233–60.

Al-Murtaḍā, *al-Fuṣūl al-mukhtāra min al-'Uyūn wa l-maḥāsin*, Najaf 1365/[1946], 2 vols.

Muslim, *Ṣaḥīḥ*, Būlāq 1290/[1873].

Al-Najāshī, *Rijāl*, ed. Mūsā al-Shabīrī al-Zanjānī, Qumm 1407/[1987].

Nöldeke, T. and Schwally, F., *Geschichte des Qorāns*, Leipzig 1909–38, 3 vols.

Noth, A., 'Der Charakter der ersten grossen Sammlungen von Nachrichten zur frühen Kalifenzeit', *Der Islam* 17 (1971), 168–88.

The Early Arabic Historical Tradition: A Source-critical Study, Princeton 1994.
'Eine Standortbestimmung der Expansion (*Futuḥ*) unter den ersten Kalifen (Analyse von Tabari I, 2854–2846)', *Asiatische Studien*, 63 (1989), 120–35.
Al-Nu'mān, al-Qāḍī, *Sharḥ al-akhbār fī faḍā'il al-a'imma al-aṭhār*, ed. Muḥammad al-Ḥusaynī al-Jalālī, Qumm n.d., 3 vols.
Paret, R., 'Der Plan einer neuen, leicht kommentierten Koranübersetzung', in R. Paret (ed.), *Orientalistische Studien Enno Littmann zu seinem 60. Geburtstag*, Leiden 1935, 121–30.
Petersen, E. L., *'Alī and Mu'āwiya in Early Arabic Tradition*, Copenhagen 1964.
Puin, G., *Der Dīwān von 'Umar ibn al-Haṭṭāb: Ein Beitrag zur frühislamischen Verwaltungsgeschichte*, Bonn 1970.
Rotter, G., *Die Umayyaden und der zweite Bürgerkrieg (680–692)*, Wiesbaden 1982.
Al-Ṣafadī, *al-Wāfī bi l-wafayāt*, ed. H. Ritter et al., Istanbul/Wiesbaden 1931–, 22 vols (so far).
Sauvaget, J. and Cahen, C., *Introduction to the History of the Muslim East: A Bibliographical Guide*, Berkeley, CA/London 1965.
Schmucker, W., 'Die christliche Minderheit von Nağrān und die Problematik ihrer Beziehungen zum frühen Islam', in *Studien zum Minderheitenproblem im Islam*, Bonner Orientalistische Studien, Neue Serie, ed. O. Spies, XXVII/1, Bonn 1973, 183–281.
Untersuchungen zu einigen wichtigen bodenrechtlichen Konsequenzen der islamischen Eroberungsbewegung, Bonn 1972.
Sellheim, R., *Der zweite Bürgerkrieg im Islam*, Wiesbaden, 1970.
Sezgin, F., *Geschichte des arabischen Schrifttums*, Leiden 1967–84, 9 vols. (so far).
Sezgin, U., *Abū Miḥnaf: Ein Beitrag zur Historiographie der umaiyadischen Zeit*, Leiden 1971.
Sharon, M., 'Ahl al-Bayt – People of the House', *Jerusalem Studies* in *Arabic and Islam*, 8 (1986), 169–84.
Black Banners from the East, Jerusalem 1983.
'Notes on the Question of Legitimacy of Government in Islam', *Israel Oriental Studies*, 10 (1980), 116–23.
'The Umayyads as Ahl al-Bayt', *Jerusalem Studies in Arabic and Islam*, 14 (1992), 115–52.
Shoufani, E., *Al-Riddah and the Muslim Conquest of Arabia*, Toronto 1972.
Stroumsa, G. G., 'Seal of the Prophets: The Nature of a Manichaen Metaphor', *Jerusalem Studies in Arabic and Islam*, 7 (1986), 61–74.
Sulaym b. Qays al-Hilālī, *Kitāb al-Saqīfa*, Dār al-Kutub al-Islāmiyya, n.d.
Al-Ṭabarī, *Jāmi' al-bayān*, ed. Maḥmūd Muḥammad Shākir and Aḥmad Muḥammad Shākir, Cairo 1373–88/1955–69.
Jāmi' al-bayān fī tafsīr al-Qur'ān, Cairo [1321/1903] (this edition will be quoted unless otherwise stated), 30 parts in 11 vols.
Ta'rīkh al-rusul wa l-mulūk, ed. M. J. de Goeje et al., Leiden 1879–1901 (quoted as Ṭabarī), 3 vols.
Al-Thaqafī, Abū Isḥāq Ibrāhīm, *al-Ghārāt*, ed. Jalāl al-Dīn al-Muḥaddith, Tehran 1395/[1975].
Tyan, E., *Institutions du droit public Musulman*, Paris 1954–56, 2 vols.
Veccia-Vaglieri, L., 'Il conflitto 'Alī–Mu'āwiya e la secessione Khārigita riesaminati

alla luce di fonti ibaḍite', *Annali Istituto Orientale di Napoli*, NS 4 (1952), 1–94.
Von Kremer, A., *Geschichte der herrschenden Ideen im Islam*, Leipzig 1886.
Al-Wāqidī, *Kitāb al-Maghāzī*, ed. M. Jones, London 1966.
Watt, W. M., *Islamic Political Thought*, Edinburgh 1968.
Muḥammad at Mecca, Oxford 1953.
Muhammad: Prophet and Statesman, Oxford 1961.
Wellhausen, J., *Das arabische Reich und sein Sturz*, Berlin 1902.
Muhammed in Medina: Das ist Vakidis Kitab alMaghazi in verkürzter deutscher Wiedergabe, Berlin 1882.
Die religiös-politischen Oppositionsparteien im alten Islam, Berlin 1901.
Skizzen und Vorarbeiten, VI, Berlin 1889.
Wensinck, A. J., *Concordance et indices de la tradition musulmane*, Leiden 1936–88.
Muḥammad and the Jews of Medina, trans. W. Behn, Freiburg 1975.
Yaḥyā b. Ādam, *al-Kharāj*, ed. T. W. Juynboll, *Le Livre de l'impôt foncier de Yaḥyā Ibn Ādam*, Leiden 1895.
Al-Ya'qūbī, *Ta'rīkh*, ed. M. T. Houtsma, Leiden 1883, 2 vols.
Yāqūt, *Mu'jam al-buldān*, ed. F. Wüstenfeld, Leipzig 1866–73, 6 vols.
Al-Zamakhsharī, *Rabī' al-abrār*, ed. Salīm al-Nu'aymī, Baghdad 1976, 4 vols.
Al-Zubayr b. Bakkār, *al-Akhbār al-Muwaffaqiyyāt*, ed. Sāmī Makkī al-'Ānī, Baghdad 1972.
Jamharat nasab Quraysh wa-akhbārihā, I, ed. Maḥmūd Muḥammad Shākir, Cairo 1381/1961.
Al-Zubayrī, Muṣ'ab, *Kitāb Nasab Quraysh*, ed. E. Lévi-Provençal, Cairo 1953.

Index